Derrida Vis-à-vis Lacan

John D. Caputo, ***series editor***

Perspectives in
Continental
Philosophy

ANDREA HURST

Derrida Vis-à-vis Lacan

Interweaving Deconstruction and Psychoanalysis

FORDHAM UNIVERSITY PRESS
New York ▪ 2008

Library of Congress Cataloging-in-Publication Data
Hurst, Andrea (Andrea Margaret)
Derrida vis-à-vis Lacan : interweaving deconstruction and psychanalysis / Andrea Hurst. — 1st ed.
p. cm.
Includes bibliographical references (p.) and index.
ISBN 978-0-8232-2874-4 (cloth : alk. paper) —
ISBN 978-0-8232-2875-1 (pbk. alk. paper)
1. Derrida, Jacques. 2. Lacan, Jacques, 1901–1981. 3. Psychoanalysis. 4. Deconstruction. I. Title.
B2430.D484H87 2008
150.19′52—dc22 2008004258

Printed in the United States of America
10 09 08 5 4 3 2 1
First edition

To Bert
The wind in my sails

Contents

Acknowledgments

This study grew out of an exchange of ideas with Bert Olivier, who was wrestling with Lacanian psychoanalytic theory while I was similarly engaged with Derrida's quasi-transcendental thinking. It was he who first suggested to me that there were moments in Lacan's writing that readily agreed with the logic of Derrida's thinking and that a deeper study of an accord between them held promise. There were, of course, many moments when I cursed him for ever having tempted me along this tortuous path, and perhaps many more when he cursed himself for having exchanged the patient ear of his understanding interlocutor, lover, and hiking partner for the unsympathetic, self-involved, and distant creature facing the computer screen. Nevertheless, through the inevitable ups and downs, he has been, as always, the relentlessly persistent, if restless—being of romantic temperament—wind in my sails. It is with my deepest thanks that I have dedicated this text to Bert, without whom there would be for me the paralyzing bliss of a calm life.

There are more people than it is possible to mention who deserve my thanks and appreciation, but first and foremost I am greatly honored to have had John Caputo, Joan Copjec, and Thomas Busch as constant companions, although they may not always have been consciously aware of their extensive spectral travels to distant African shores. I am particularly grateful for the gift from both Jack Caputo and Joan Copjec of a fair, balanced, and open-minded hearing. As lovers of Derrida and Lacan respectively they represent the antagonistic discourses that I have tried to bring into conversation, yet both have reaffirmed in their practice the quintessential philosophical attitude inscribed in Aristotle's insistence that his love for philosophy supersedes his love for Plato.

I would like to express my gratitude to the intellectual community at Villanova University, and particularly the philosophy department, for extending the gift of learning across international borders. Here I would specially like to thank Farhang Erfani, not only for some illuminating discussions concerning politics but also for his hospitality and continuing friendship. Finally, a special word of acknowledgment and thanks to my family and friends who have had to put up with egregious neglect for far too long.

Derrida Vis-à-vis Lacan

Introduction
"For the Love of Lacan"

And it is with this event, this justly deserved and spectacular homage to Lacan, that I was happy to be asked to associate myself. Not only but also because, in our time—and I mean the time of culture and especially Parisian culture—I find a political significance in this homage. I consider it an act of cultural resistance to pay homage publicly to a difficult form of thought, discourse, or writing, one which does not submit easily to normalization by the media, by academics, or by publishers, one which rebels against the restoration currently underway, against the philosophical or theoretical neo-conformism in general (let us not even mention literature) that flattens and levels everything around us, in an attempt to make one forget what the Lacan era was, along with the future and the promise of his thought, thereby erasing the *name* of Lacan.

As you know, there are countless ways to do this, sometimes very paradoxical ways; in his lifetime, Lacan underwent the experience dubbed "excommunication." Some of those who claim to draw on Lacan's name, and not just his legacy, can be not the least active or the least effective in this operation. Here, once again, the logic of the "service rendered" is highly tricky, and censorship, suturing, and defense of orthodoxy do not in the least exclude—quite the contrary—a façade of cultural eclecticism. Whether one is talking about philosophy, psychoanalysis, or theory in general, what the flat-footed restoration underway attempts to recover, disavow, or censor is the fact that nothing of that which managed to transform the space of thought in the last decades would have been possible

> without some coming to terms *with* Lacan, without the Lacanian provocation, however one receives it or discusses it—and, I will add, without some coming to terms *with* Lacan in his coming to terms *with* the philosophers.[1]

Derrida, it would seem, loves Lacan. It is, he insists, "for the love of Lacan" that he emphasizes the important political obligation to embrace a difficult thinking that rebels against normalization. Lacan in turn is not entirely averse to being loved by Derrideans. Concerning a certain deconstructive reading, he is quoted as saying, "I can say, in a way, if it is a question of reading, that I have never been read so well—with so much love."[2] Naturally enough, Derrida's love is not unconditional: "As always, Lacan left me the greatest freedom of interpretation, and as always I would have taken it even if he had not left it to me, as it will have pleased me."[3] One must, of course, read Lacan's texts with deconstructive vigilance, and, at least on the face of it, this is what Derrida aims to do. In turn, Lacanian psychoanalysis in principle must encourage inventive interpretation and independent thinking among its readers. Lacan, reflecting upon the "veritable aporia" of the Freudian doctrine, again on the face of it, does not expect unconditional love. To the contrary, he insists:

> All of us share an experience based upon a technique, a system of concepts to which we remain faithful, partly because this system was developed by the man who opened up to us all the ways to that experience, and partly because it bears the living mark of the different stages of its elaboration. That is to say, contrary to the dogmatism that is sometimes imputed to us, we know that this system remains open both as a whole and in several of its articulations.[4]

Seemingly tied together by mutual respect and resistance, it is fair to expect a Derridean/Lacanian philosophical legacy that reflects a dynamic interchange of ideas. Yet, for a complex set of reasons, there is relatively little productive interchange between deconstruction and Lacanian psychoanalysis. If Derrida and Lacan are named together with mantric regularity under the general banner of "poststructuralism," more detailed work on the shape of an accord between their discourses is relatively scarce. One is more commonly confronted with mutual ignorance or resentment between Derrideans and Lacanians, interchanges characterized by clear misconstructions of either Derrida's thinking or Lacan's, or both. In consequence, the interface between deconstruction and psychoanalysis is at risk of becoming a limiting border rather than a permeable space of generative cross-fertilization.

The misconstruction of Derrida's thinking that trumps them all, as John Caputo points out, is the argument that he has destroyed his own grounds for protest about being misunderstood, since his "anything goes" postmodernism undermines the very idea that there can be such a thing as misunderstanding.[5] There are two versions of this misconstruction. The first is derived from a catchphrase that Derrida, and those who love him, have good reason to regret sorely, namely, "*il n'y a pas de hors-texte*" ("there is no outside-text").[6] Many take this phrase as confirmation of Derrida's apparently uninhibited celebration of an utterly nominalist, relativist freeplay of differences, supposedly based on the premise that there is nothing "out there" beyond the text, which dooms us to the infinite play of texts upon texts upon texts, all of indifferently equivalent nonvalue and endlessly referring to nothing but themselves. Derrida persistently and explicitly rejects this misreading, which is the contemporary equivalent of Hegel's mistaken characterization of Kant's "transcendental turn" as a subjective idealism, and it may be subjected to the same kind of rejoinder; namely, that transcendental constitution does not create existence, but interprets or synthesizes what is given, thereby constituting a phenomenal world.[7] Derrida's phrase "there is no outside-text" makes the equivalent claim. "Something" must occur before there can be interpretation (i.e., texts), but there are no uninterpreted objects for us because it is precisely through the process of interpretation that they are first constituted as elements that belong to a phenomenal reality. In his words:

> I believe always in the necessity of being attentive first of all to this phenomenon of language, naming, and dating, to this repetition compulsion (at once rhetorical, magical, and poetic). To what this compulsion signifies, translates, or betrays. Not in order to isolate ourselves in language, as people in too much of a rush would like us to believe, but on the contrary, in order to try to understand what is going on precisely *beyond* language and what is pushing us to repeat endlessly and without knowing what we are talking about, precisely there where language and the concept come up against their limits.[8]

The second misconception of Derrida's thinking derives from the phrase "interpretation of interpretation." He is often correctly cited as describing two interpretations of interpretation, one that remains nostalgic for the kind of totalizing system of synthetic rules that Kant envisaged, and one that affirms the freeplay of interpretative differences.[9] He explicitly insists, in accordance with what he later calls the "plural logic of the aporia" (I will return shortly to this axial notion), that it is never a matter of choosing between them. Nevertheless, time and again he is taken to have made precisely a choice (for the side of unregulated play) that he expressly interdicts. Claims that Derridean thinking represents a cynical version of "anything goes" postmodernism, based on such arguments, could only be the consequence of not having read his texts with sufficient care.[10] By now this kind of misconception should have given way to more balanced treatments of his thinking. Its persistence, nevertheless, can probably be attributed to the fact that it suits enthusiasts, who desire his endorsement for various "anything goes" stratagems, as much as detractors, both of whom read his texts highly selectively, taking snippets here and there to support one-sided agendas.

Even though the majority of Derrida's texts reveal a sustained engagement with psychoanalysis, his readings on topics other than language and the "purloined letter" draw little explicit attention from many Lacanian theorists, and citations more often than not take the form of typical misconstructions. For example, in a collection thematizing Lacan's theory of discourse, there is but a single reference to Derrida, which refers to Jacques-Alain Miller's claim that in contrast to intellectuals such as Derrida, Lacan "saw patients": that is, he put his theories to work in the world outside the esoteric self-referential circle of the academic text.[11] More importantly, when reference is made to Derrida, it is often to his early work on the sign, which is reduced to an endorsement of freeplay—a misreading that precludes serious engagement with his later writings on ethical issues in the broadest sense of the term, which are in constant dialogue with psychoanalysis.

Kaja Silverman's approach to Derrida's work provides a clear but by no means unique example of this reduction. In *The Subject of Semiotics* she focuses on his commitment to "the endless commutability of the signified"[12] together with the "principle of deferral," which is taken to mean simply that "signification occurs along a chain in which one term displaces another before being itself displaced."[13] These commitments are brought together under the notion of "freeplay."[14] While Silverman's observations are not inaccurate, and Derrida does indeed insist on this aneconomic interpretation of *différance* (naming it "*différance* as spacing"), she gives no voice at all, at least not in Derrida's name, to its economic counterpart, namely "*différance* as temporization."[15] I shall address this complexity in chapter 3; suffice it to note here that her one-sided starting point assures a reductive interpretation of other Derridean notions. For example, her remark in *The Acoustic Mirror* that Derrida has "appropriated from sexual difference" a signifier [namely "invagination"], with which he has attempted to erase the opposition between 'inner' and 'outer,'" can only sound strange to Derridean ears.[16]

Silverman is not isolated in this respect. Even Joan Copjec, from whom, as will become apparent over the course of this study, I have learned the most concerning the Lacanian version of the "plural logic of the aporia," assumes that the Lacanian equivalent, which she names the "paradoxical logic of the whole," is the distinguishing factor that presses Lacan's thinking beyond Derrida's.[17] Her assessment here is consonant with Slavoj Žižek's, as reflected for example in his essay "The Real of Sexual Difference."[18] Žižek's writing might be exceptional in the sense that it does indeed engage directly with Derrida's later work, but his treatment of it, as I hope to show in chapter 2, is marred by a one-sided reduction of *différance* to its aneconomic moment.

On the other hand, it is Derrida himself who gives his readers apparent license to pass over Lacan's texts in silence. Judging by Derrida's explanation in the 1971 interview "Positions" of the almost total absence of references to Lacan in his work up to that point, the reasons are complex, having to do with personal antagonisms, striking differences in intellectual temperament, and, least of all (in my view), clear theoretical differences.[19] First, Derrida accuses Lacan of an aggressive response to his own work that takes the form of "kettle logic," or the accumulation of incompatible assertions. In his words: "1. Devaluation and rejection: 'it is worthless' or 'I do not agree.' 2. Valuation and reappropriation: 'moreover it is mine and I have always said so.'"[20] The justice of the accusation is questionable, and despite the avowedly "minor importance" Derrida attaches to it, there is no doubt that it contributes to the antagonistic tone of subsequent interchanges.[21] In this odd game of getting even, as Barbara Johnson puts it, "the priority of aggression is doubled by the aggressiveness of priority."[22]

More seriously, Derrida charges Lacan with a cavalier, facile, and obfuscating use of metaphysically loaded terms such as "'being,' 'authentic,' 'full,' 'true,'" without subjecting this rhetoric to the necessary philosophical rigor. The interview is characterized throughout by a compulsively repetitive refrain to this effect, to wit: "despite many elliptical and rhapsodic variations, since then I have never encountered any rigorous questioning"; "but in the absence of any theoretical and systematic explanation"; "to resolve such problems in a phrase seems to me rather slight"; "a light-handed reference"; "but without any specific investigation." He sums up the charge as follows: "In relation to the theoretical difficulties that interested me, I read this style, above all, as an art of evasion. The vivacity of ellipsis too often seemed to me to serve as an avoidance or an envelopment of diverse problems."[23]

Moreover, Derrida argues that Lacan's supposedly casual rhetoric leaves him naïvely trapped within the so-called metaphysics of presence. While he might wax lyrical about loving Lacan in *Resistances of Psychoanalysis*, he does not shift his critical stance in this later text. Instead, he speaks here of the ironic chiasmus between himself as a deconstructive "philosopher" and Lacan as a philosophizing psychoanalyst, which makes Lacan's discourse, in his words, "too much at home with the philosophers."[24] Backed by Derrida's damning criticism, it is unfortunate but unsurprising that many Derrideans on this account tend to avoid even opening Lacan's texts. Despite the fact that psychoanalysis haunts Derrida's own texts, it does not fare well in the commentaries on Derrida's work. Caputo's *Deconstruction in a Nutshell*, for example, seems to cover everything but psychoanalysis, and Bennington's "Derridabase" offers suggestive but extremely cursory remarks concerning Derrida's encounters with psychoanalysis. This is all the more surprising since it deals with the quintessentially psychoanalytical theme of singular subjectivity.[25]

Many Derrideans, moreover, uncritically trusting Derrida's assessment, make the fundamental mistake of assuming from the start that Lacan's discourse is characterized by an essentialism that belongs within the ambit of the metaphysics of presence. Derrida argues that in the thinking of *différance*, one "puts into question the authority of presence, or of its simple symmetrical opposite, absence or lack. Thus one questions the limit which has always constrained us . . . to formulate the meaning of Being in general as presence or absence, in the categories of being or beingness (*ousia*)."[26] By contrast, he charges Lacan with the hypostatization of "lack," or, that is, the formulation of the meaning of being in general as absence, which implies that his discourse does not move beyond the categories of being. Lacan denies this charge emphatically, arguing a similar point: the thinking of the Real, he insists, "does not lend itself to ontology . . . it is neither being, nor non-being, but the unrealized."[27]Again, in response to the argument of *The Title of the Letter*, whose authors remain subject to precisely this prejudice, Lacan insists to the contrary that "it cannot be ambiguous that I oppose to the concept of being—as it is sustained in the philosophical tradition . . . the notion that we are duped by jouissance."[28] In fact, Lacan grumbles, "it is as if it were precisely upon reaching the impasse to which my discourse is designed to lead them that they considered their work done, declaring themselves—or rather declaring me, which amounts to the same thing given their conclusions—confounded."[29]

Nevertheless, many thinkers continue blithely to ignore Lacanian protests and typically misconstrue Lacan's claims, taking them as evidence of a closet essentialism. Caputo offers a clear description of this prejudice in his exposition of Drucilla Cornell's treatment of Lacan's claim that "Woman does not exist."[30] Cornell, he reports, expresses disappointment in Lacan for undermining the revolutionary implications of this statement by insisting, as Caputo puts it, "that woman is essentially the truth of castration, or of the hole, essentially the place of the lack." Moreover, by contrast, a Derridean approach is supposed to provide the corrective for Lacan's phallocentric essentialism:

> Derrida turns Lacan's statement around into a statement of non-essentialism. Woman does not exist if existence is given the sense of fixed identity and permanent presence. She does not exist, not out of lack or defect but excess, for the feminine disrupts the proper place, including and especially the proper place to which she is assigned by Lacan as lack.[31]

According to Copjec, then, the interpretative mistake many keep making is to take what Lacan calls the "hard kernel of the real" to be "some essence or quasi-transcendental *a priori* that manages to escape the contingent processes of history."[32] This is, again, the mistake Judith Butler makes, for example, in her reading of Lacan's account of sexual difference, where she takes "the Real of sexual difference" to imply an *a priori* gender dimorphism in Lacanian discourse, conditioned by normative heterosexuality, which, as usual, defines woman as the negative of man.[33] Again, Lacanians deny this charge of covert phallocentrism: an admission such as Colette Soler's, for example, that Lacan indeed "affirms the 'phallocentrism' of the unconscious," must be placed within the context of his wholesale revaluation of values (for example, in *Seminar XX*), where such an affirmation can only function as a critique of the one-sided "phallic logic" that characterizes the "Symbolic Order."[34]

Derrida may be right that Lacan does not always explicitly offer rigorous philosophical explanations for the terms he uses, and readers regularly preface their works with caveats concerning Lacan's style. Dylan Evans, for example, remarks that Lacan's psychoanalytic language "has often been accused of being infuriatingly obscure and sometimes of constituting a totally incomprehensible 'psychotic' system."[35] But as many commentators have demonstrated, this by no means justifies the charge of philosophical facileness. I disagree without qualification with Derrida's characterization of Lacanian discourse as so different from his own "in its mode of elocution, its site, its aims, its presuppositions" that reference to it "would only result in the accumulation of fog in a field already not lacking in it."[36]

In fact, quite to the contrary, one faces a curious mirroring symmetry here. On the one hand, in contrast to the "utter nominalism" attributed to Derrida (on the basis of a fundamentally one-sided misconstrual of *différance*), Lacan is supposed to offer a far more sophisticated, complex, paradoxical style of thinking. On the other hand, in contrast to Lacan's apparent "closet essentialism" (a characterization derived from a fundamental misconception of the Lacanian Real), Derrida is supposed to offer a far more sophisticated, complex, paradoxical style of thinking. The obvious move, I should think, is to step back from the mutual antagonism that has built up around these thinkers and compare what the Lacanians say about Lacan with what the Derrideans say about Derrida. One finds that this comparison yields the interesting result of a rather precise match: the style of thinking underpinning Lacanian psychoanalytic theory precisely matches the "plural logic of the aporia" by which Derrida describes his own quasi-transcendental thinking. In other words, as I hope to show here, it is easy enough to detect a deep theoretical accord between them, the explication of which would help clarify the field within which both operate.

The field in question is that opened up by Kant's critique of "ontology" and his consequent "transcendental turn," according to which human cognitive powers are implicated in the constitution of phenomenal reality. One might say that the overall task of this study is to demonstrate that both Derrida and Lacan carefully insist not only upon Kant's "transcendental turn" but also on a second paradigm shift (reflected in Lacan's thinking of the "impossible Real" and Derrida's equivalent thinking of *différance*) whereby transcendental thinking, which concerns itself with the conditions that make what is given in experience possible, becomes "quasi-transcendental."[37] Quasi-transcendental thinking, as the nickname suggests, does not step beyond the transcendental paradigm but remains parasitic upon it even as it ruins it, by adding that economic conditions of possibility are simultaneously the very aneconomic conditions that also make the given, strictly speaking, impossible. As the logic of such aporetic (im)possibility, then, quasi-transcendental thinking names a qualified, relatively ruined form of transcendental thinking from which there is no escape: there is no restituting return from the paradoxical state of being to an ancient beginning, and no remedy in a projected ideal.

Derrida has proposed various keys for gaining access to quasi-transcendental thinking besides the now notorious term "deconstruction." In his words, a thinking of the nonfinite number of quasi-concepts announced in the movement of deconstruction is certainly "called for by a thinking of writing," as demonstrated in much of his earlier work.[38] However, he maintains that this deconstructive movement is "better thematized and formalized . . . in its relation to the *double bind*, to the *stricture of the double band* and, especially, of a *remaining* that is *not* and that does not stem from ontology any more than it lends itself to dialectical sublation."[39] In *Aporias,* therefore, Derrida prefers to formalize the "logic" that explains the persistence of such quasi-concepts in terms of the strictures imposed by three different forms of aporia: namely, the economic aporia of "closure" or "totality," the aneconomic aporia of "openness" or "infinity," and, finally, the aporia of paradox. This aporia describes the aporia of the aporias, or, that is, the double bind or dilemma that arises because the first two aporias are joined together as a paradox, since, as just mentioned, economic conditions of possibility (the conditions of systematic closure), while necessary, are ruined by the equally necessary aneconomic moment intrinsic to them. Derrida also names this aporia "the impossible."[40] Consequently, under the obligation to negotiate the ruin of the transcendental paradigm (as neither fully in it nor properly outside), his readers must expect to find themselves tied up, along with him, in the complex "plural logic of the aporia" that has imposed itself on his thinking with what he calls a "*formalizable regularity.*"[41]

This kind of thinking does not aim to contradict the age-old tradition of formal logic, and it by no means denies its necessity and force. Nevertheless, Derrida exploits its resources for nontraditional purposes, that is, *not* for the sake of reducing, clarifying, or simplifying philosophically interesting issues but, on the contrary, to insist upon their irreducible complexities. Without claiming expertise in the language game of formal logic, it seems clear enough to me that Derrida's articulation of life's inevitable antagonisms takes the argumentative form of dilemma, paradox, or *aporia*, rather than that of the strict contrary or contradictory oppositions within which either/or choices still make sense.

William Angus Sinclair formalizes a dilemma as follows: "*If p, then q, and if not-p then r* [where both *q* and *r*, one should add, are equally unsatisfactory]; *But either p or not-p*; *(Either q or r.)*" Hence the double bind of having to choose between equally unsatisfactory alternatives.[42] This is a slightly more elaborate form of what Simon Blackburn calls the simplest form of a dilemma, which is an argument of the form "If *p* then *q* [namely a particular unsatisfactory outcome], if *not-p* then *q* [that is, precisely the same unsatisfactory outcome], so in any event *q*."[43] Clearly, here, either/or choices make no sense, for the alternatives, inclusively, either remain equally unsatisfactory or in the end amount to precisely the same unsatisfactory outcome. Derrida insists, however, that this difficulty (that is, the impossibility of a choice ever being completely satisfactory) does not obviate the necessity for actively going ahead and negotiating such choices.

Lacan similarly became increasingly concerned with developing a theoretical discourse of rupture and inconsistency, and according to Lee, he assiduously studied paradox: set theory, logical puzzles, classic Greek paradoxes, "the paradoxical Möbius surfaces of topology," and Borromean knots.[44] He also demonstrates a correlative enjoyment of the mind-twisting grammatical constructions available to the play of language. For example, as Paul Verhaeghe notes, if "corporeal contingency" is inscribed in the phrase "to not stop being written," Lacan writes "necessity" as "it doesn't stop being written" and "impossibility" as "it doesn't stop not being written."[45] These figures and enjoyments already indicate that his interests lie in the direction of paradox.

Pressing this point further, one may argue that the so-called fundamental concepts of Lacanian psychoanalysis are articulated according to a complex, paradoxical relationality that precisely matches the "plural logic of the aporia." I do not at this point wish to enter into the full complexity of Lacanian discourse; suffice it to mention here that Lacan's formulation of the Real as "rupture" introduces the double trouble that Copjec names the "problem of the All" and characterizes as an opposition between paranoiac universalism and hysterical nominalism, which matches Derrida's distinction between the economic and aneconomic aporias.[46]

Notably, Lacan names the logic of their articulation the "vel of alienation" and, with a touch of black humor, offers as an example "the mugger's choice": your money or your life.[47] This turns out to be no choice at all, for, as Copjec notes: "Once the choice is offered, you're done for—no matter which alternative you take."[48] The Hegelian lose/lose proposed here, then, is that in choosing one the other is lost; yet, because they are interdependent, this is also thereby to lose the original choice (for life is the necessary condition for having money, and, these days, money is the necessary condition for having a life). Lacan defines the task of psychoanalysis as that of leading analysands to the point where they may make the move beyond the lose/lose situation of the mugger's choice. Notably then, as Copjec demonstrates, Lacan (like Derrida, one should note) refuses the limitations of a choice between the aporias of paranoiac universalism and hysterical nominalism and prefers a third stance, which invokes the win/win formulation of "the revolutionary's choice: freedom or death."[49]

Counter to the commonsensical claim, namely, that the freedom that costs a life is not freedom, the revolutionary's choice issues from the insistence that life without freedom is not life.[50] Here, to choose to fight for freedom, to the point of risking all for its sake, is to retain the eternal freedom of a Ché Guevara. On the other hand, to choose death rather than forsake one's freedom similarly leaves intact forever the freedom of a Socrates. But what is the meaning of this freedom in Lacanian psychoanalysis? It names, first, freedom *from* the economic and aneconomic aporias of ideological automatism and paralyzing transgression for its own sake. Correlatively, this is a freedom *for* decisive action. When it comes down to it, then, this "freedom for," as the only possible freedom, is the paradoxical "freedom" offered by a refusal to submit to the constrictions of the either/or choice given by a binary determination of options and the willingness in consequence to brave the double bind of the aporia of aporias, or, that is, all of the ethical, political, or, as broadly speaking as possible, conceptual paradoxes and dilemmas that can neither be overcome nor evaded but must be worked through interminably.

As I hope to show in the investigations to follow, both Derrida and Lacan in their singular ways devise "the same" inventive, paradoxical "logic" by means of which one may grasp and put into practice the revolutionary's choice. In this sense, for both thinkers, all binary determinations (regulated by the "mugger's choice") must make way for a third style of thinking supported by another "logic" that exceeds the binary. Accordingly, the logic reflected in the Lacanian response to the "vel of alienation," formalized as "the revolutionary's choice," can be generalized as a heuristic that allows one to gather together what Lacan says in relation to diverse themes in a way that gives his ideas a formalizable coherence yet remains subtle and complex enough not to flatten them into a system. This enables one to show, as one example among many, that his theory of the transcendental relation is not a product of unmitigated structuralism, as some might insist, but of, in Bruce Fink's felicitous phrase, a "Gödelian structuralism" in which "every system is decompleted by the alterity or heterogeneity it contains within itself."[51] (One should not miss the striking resonance here with Derrida's formulation of the aporia of the aporias: that is, the double bind that arises as a consequence of the fact that the aneconomic moment intrinsic to all economic conditions of possibility ruins any hope for their perfection.)

The ultimate aim of this study is to counter the adversarial trend according to which (ironically) symmetrically opposed misconstructions on both sides convert the Lacan/Derrida encounter into a "mugger's choice." By contrast, at the risk of a repetition compulsion, I repeat my hope that in the end I will have demonstrated that the "plural logic of the aporia" offers a means to break through the impasse of mutual Derridean/Lacanian antagonism and a key to a more productive interchange between deconstruction and Lacanian psychoanalysis. The significance of such an accord is tied to the importance for dealing with practical issues in everyday life, claimed for both by Derrideans and Lacanians alike, and to the dangers of not taking either seriously. Against those "blasé souls" who claim to have gone beyond psychoanalysis, Copjec insists that the revolutionary insights of psychoanalysis, which remains "the mother tongue of our modernity," lie ahead of us rather than behind.[52] In a similar vein, Caputo takes up "Derrida's deconstructive critique of hermeneutics," not to get beyond the hermeneutics but to liberate its revolutionary tendencies against "the metaphysical desire to make things safe," which, ironically, "has become consummately dangerous." He argues, then, that a radicalized hermeneutics enables us to face with less innocence "the fix we are in."[53]

However, stylistically speaking, each discourse is frustratingly and unnecessarily difficult and tends toward a jargonistic hermeticism that restricts it to circulation among a small group of dedicated initiates, placing a not inconsequential obstacle in the way of greater cross-fertilization. It is hardly surprising that both are widely misinterpreted by followers and adversaries alike. As Lee notes, Lacan's discourse is loaded with "multireferential and multilingual wordplay . . . neologisms, portmanteau words, and more or less spectacular puns." Moreover, he adds, Lacan's "discourses on that which ruptures discourse quite precisely exhibit and even enact the very rupture in question."[54] Inspired by surrealism, Lacan's texts often function as montages that represent paradoxes in the visually oriented manner (so to speak) characteristic of Freud's primary process. Bruce Fink, too, remarks that Lacan's "texts and lectures seem designed to introduce us to the very kind of work analysis itself requires, sifting through layers of meaning, deciphering the text as though it were a long series of slips of the tongue."[55] All of this makes for certain stylistic grotesqueries, and, to be sure, it requires concentrated labor to make sense of it.[56] I have sympathy for Derrida's insistence that the labor in his case would hardly have been worth the effort and that he had far more rewarding, creative, and urgent things to do philosophically than grind through Lacanian *arcana*.[57]

But Derrida himself, ironically, similarly tends to exploit the multiple resources of language (logical, semantic, poetic, etc.), often mimicking the text he is dealing with and condensing (that is, encrypting) into his opening sentences or paragraphs text of plutonium density, which he will subsequently unravel in minute detail. Moreover, in working through Derrida's deconstructive readings, it takes sustained concentration to avoid mistakenly attributing to Derrida himself the claims that he is trying to elucidate (and in the process deconstruct, by pressing each to the logical extreme at which it becomes illogical). Reading Derrida, then, demands almost inhuman patience, since his essays reward only those willing to submit to the painstakingly slow movement of the deconstruction, and they persistently trap the impatient into hasty (mis)judgments. In both cases, then, I agree with Bruce Fink that "the excitement of seeing such an active and creative mind at work is often overshadowed by the difficulty involved in isolating an identifiable thesis."[58]

My approach here aims to be explicatory, then, in the sense that I propose to interpret the relevant texts as carefully as they will allow. The difference between the work of clarification I aim to do here in the name of interpretation, and what Derrida does in the name of the same concept, will amount to the difference between what he has called the "first" reading of a text, which is a respectful countersignature that says "I hear you," and the second, disrespectful, inventive, countersignature that "plays"—or, more carefully, that plays thinkers off against themselves, bringing out the surprise that was always already there. Although I shall avoid complicating an already difficult field by engaging in such "play," my aim for clarity is not intended to make things easier in the bad sense. Instead, in striving to make the complexities clearer and more accessible, I hope to open up a way into Lacanian and Derridean discourses that avoids the abyssal superficiality of mutual antagonism that has so far characterized most of their encounters. The text to follow is divided into four parts, each of which is introduced by a summary of its overall aims and arguments.

PART 1

From Transcendentals to Quasi-Transcendentals

It would certainly pay dividends to examine, along with Husserl and other thinkers who have inventively appropriated Kantian insights, what nevertheless remains unsatisfying about Kant's transcendental philosophy. One could, with Derrida, also consider what goes against itself in Husserlian phenomenology to engender such proliferation in its name, since it is the impossibility of Husserl's enterprise that first impels Derrida toward the "ontological" shift, reflected in what he nicknames *différance*, whose correlative is the "plural logic of the aporia."[1] However, I have here elected to follow another path from transcendental to quasi-transcendental thinking, namely via psychoanalytic theory. While it is, without doubt, only one of many possible readings, the assumption that Derridean and Lacanian discourses may be linked through their mutual interest in Freud's writings, which one may in turn hold partially responsible for the shift from transcendental to quasi-transcendental thinking, has the advantage of proposing a shared historical context (the relative "ruin" of the transcendental tradition) within which Derridean and Lacanian discourses may be brought into dialogue.

Assuming that the general field from out of which the "plural logic of the aporia" emerges is that opened up by Kant's "transcendental turn," I shall begin by sketching out briefly a certain trajectory in the transcendental tradition that links Kant, Husserl, Heidegger, and Nietzsche in a movement of thought that is not historically linear but proceeds in terms of an increasing sense of "ruin." In chapter 1, then, I begin by laying out the earliest account of transcendental constitution as it appears in Kant, indicating subsequently in what ways Husserl's phenomenological style departs from Kant's preoccupations. I then turn to Heidegger's critique of Husserl, and, finally, to the challenge Nietzsche's remarks concerning the nature of language poses for Heidegger, which may also be understood in terms of the conflict between essentialism and nominalism.

I shall not pretend to be fair to either Heidegger or Nietzsche here. By focusing on snippets of what in both cases is ultimately a highly complex, self-subverting oeuvre I do end up drawing caricatures of both. In Heidegger's self-critical later writings, for example, the moment of *aletheia* that closes up the economic circulation I describe here is given the more paradoxical form of an articulation between *Ereignis* and *Enteignis*, where he argues that *Enteignis*, "forgetting," or stabilizing the oscillating play of *Ereignis*, is a necessary structural feature of the events of being as appearance (understood as worldviews, programs, or paradigms, for example) and that philosophy's troubles begin with the forgetting of this forgetting.[2] Similarly, Alan Shrift, upon whom I rely for a helpful exposition of Nietzsche's series of metaphorical translations between experiential spheres,[3] points out that one must not expect to find "that there is a uniformity to Nietzsche's corpus" or a nonevolving consistency in his views.[4]

My aim here, however, is not primarily to offer a just exposition of Heidegger or Nietzsche but to use certain insights in each to help me pose a contrast between the economic and aneconomic moments that stand together in unresolved conflict in Freud's writings. In other words, I sketch this trajectory of inventive appropriation primarily in order to address the question of Freud's place in it, for it remains uncertain whether his thinking is closer to the economic spirit of *aletheia*, which characterizes the motif of "circular return" in Heidegger's early work in *Being and Time*, or to the aneconomic spirit represented by the Nietzschean account of the work of metaphorical transfer in the cognitive process, which is directed by the movement of the "will to power."

To support the contention that Freud's psychoanalytic theories cannot easily be "placed" at all since there are internal tensions that pull his thinking in conflicting directions, it is necessary to outline Freud's views in some detail, if only to counter the ubiquitous reduction of another highly complex, self-subverting oeuvre to the mind-numbing absurdities of pop psychology. Nevertheless, to reduce Freud's oeuvre to a few summary pages, as I do in chapter 2, is itself necessarily a simplification that risks violating a complexity attributable not only to the magnitude and novelty of his subject matter (an integrated account of all psychical functioning from the instinctual to the ethical) but also to the fact that his texts are not presented as the final "writing up" of a theoretical foundation produced by intellectual labor already undertaken. They are, rather, the provisional documentation of theoretical insights that remain open to modification in the light of new evidence.[5] Yet, moving in the direction of Kuhnian paradigmatic shifts, his various models of the psyche or conceptions of the unconscious, for example, are successive rearticulations that do not progress toward greater adequacy of evidence.[6] They may overlap to some extent, but the later articulations do not supersede and replace the earlier ones, since the terms cannot be matched precisely as progressive modifications and each model or conception retains its advantages and disadvantages. Freud, therefore, never got down to an eidetic structure, or essence, of the psyche.

Such complexity, together with the exegetical and conceptual difficulties posed by many unresolved enigmas make it impossible to do justice here to Freud's account of the transcendental relation, and I will lay out only just enough to offer a basis for my treatment of Derrida's deconstructive readings as well as for understanding the interpretative and theoretical controversies that have motivated certain important Lacanian revisions. Here, then, I offer a reconstruction of Freud's theory of the transcendental relation, tying it to a genetic account of subjective development, which does not address his theories concerning the pathological but follows the path of so-called normal cognitive and libidinal development from infancy to adulthood. An outline of this development should at least make it clear that Freud, like few others, doggedly braved the immense complexities involved in the question of the human psyche, and as the Derridean and Lacanian appropriations of his texts demonstrate, the philosophical insight gained along the way makes it well worth the effort of tracing a path through the labyrinth of "blindness and insight" that is his legacy to his readers.

Freud's thinking, as much as Heidegger's and Nietzsche's, forms an important precursor for the quasi-transcendental thinking that emerges in the hands of Derrida (and equally Lacan, as I hope to show later). I should mention here that I begin with Derrida not only because, aside from its performance in every text, he has written extensively about the "plural logic of the aporia," but also on the contingent grounds of a greater familiarity with Derrida's work. From this basis, I make the move toward the less familiar territory of Lacanian psychoanalysis. This strategy certainly risks the hermeneutic problem of imposing the terms of the familiar upon the unfamiliar, but no interpretation can claim innocence in this respect. In mitigation, I hope to demonstrate that Derrida's formulation of the "plural logic of the aporia" can be "read into" Lacan's texts without excessive distortion because it is already there to be found behind the lexical differences.

In chapter 3, I offer a more detailed account of Derrida's quasi-transcendental thinking. One of the main purposes of this account is to undo the ties of the interpretative straitjacket that binds his thinking into an aneconomic freeplay of differences, which sees "deconstruction" as merely the hysterical dismantling of any construction. A further purpose is to lay a basis for grasping his deconstructive readings of Freud. While I acknowledge the injustice of fingering only particular thinkers, I begin by criticizing Richard Rorty's early misreadings, which provide excellent material for an attempt to counter the one-sidedness of readings that make of Derrida's philosophical strategy a freeplay relativism. I, rather guiltily, for I love him otherwise, place Žižek in Rorty's company.

To counter such misreadings, I offer an account of *différance* in accordance with the "plural logic of the aporia," aligning "*différance* as temporization" with the economic aporia and "*différance* as spacing" with the aneconomic aporia. Finally, I address the question of their "interweaving," by asking whether a Derridean account of this connection would be unambiguously antinomial or dialectical. These alternative "logics" of articulation are addressed briefly to show that Derrida's thinking does not "fall from the sky" but remains in critical dialogue with other options in the transcendental tradition. Derrida, however, following Heidegger here, uncovers a third "logic" of interweaving, not quite consonant with either of these, which acknowledges that the conjunction between the economic and aneconomic aporias is irremediably paradoxical. This "logic," to which one could assign the nickname "quasi-transcendental," although it goes by many other nicknames too, my preference being the "plural logic of the aporia," is therefore what Derrida calls "iterable," that is, a "form" that can be repeated but also cannot avoid being different each time. I conclude this chapter with a discussion of Derrida's analysis of "the gift" as an exemplary case of how quasi-transcendental thinking highlights the aporias involved in an apparently simple act or a supposedly self-evidently meaningful social practice. I hope to have demonstrated by the end that whatever one chooses to do with Derrida, as enthusiast or detractor, it is important at least to avoid starting out with the oversimplifications already abundantly in circulation.

1

The "Ruin" of the Transcendental Tradition

Introductory Remarks: Transcendental Constitution

The word "ontology," derived from the Greek word for "being," is often reduced to a name for the branch of metaphysics that concerns itself with characterizing what exists via, as Simon Blackburn puts it, "*a priori* arguments that the world must contain certain things of one kind or another: simple things, unextended things, eternal substances, necessary beings, and so on" that "often depend on some version of the principle of sufficient reason."[1] After Kant, however, the thinking of being can no longer simply characterize "what exists" as if one could determine what things would be like regardless of whether there are humans around to experience them.[2] Kant saw that the path so far traveled had brought metaphysics to such a state of vacillation that any way forward had become impossible.[3] Reason's very nature, characterized by what he called the "principle of unconditioned unity,"[4] combined with a fundamental commitment to some form of representational relation between perceiving humans and an independently determined external world, had engendered a "two-fold, self-conflicting interest,"[5] which trapped reason in metaphysical antinomies that, he argues, old-style metaphysicians could neither pass beyond nor turn away from. Reason has a two-fold interest in moving from universal to particular in determinative judgment and from particular to universal in reflective judgment. Ideally, for him, these movements should be reversible, but they led instead to opposing conclusions about the nature of the world-whole, the self, and God. Pure

Reason's "peculiar fate" was its inability to live up to its most fundamental principle, namely complete, systematic unity.

He argues that one can avoid the gridlock of reason's antinomies and preserve Reason's "principle of unconditioned unity" only on a constitutive, rather than representational, account of the relation between "thought" and "thing" (henceforth, the transcendental relation). In this case, subjective processes are recognized as unavoidably implicated in the constitution of the "external objective world," thus converting it from a supposedly independently determined thing-in-itself to "phenomenal reality."[6] On Kant's account of the transcendental relation, then, one is obliged to take into account three rather than two terms: "phenomenal reality" as the constituted effect, and, working back to its transcendental conditions, the embrace between two irreducible poles: "the transcendental subject," described as an interpreting or synthesizing subject already equipped with certain sensory and cognitive powers, and an "*object* = *X*," described as an existing materiality not created by us, to which we respond via receptive sensory systems. After Kant, "thought" (or that aspect of it we can call synthetic, cognitive processing) is implicated in the shaping of spatiotemporal things (now viewed as phenomena) in response to the force field of our sensory reception, which, in turn, is occasioned by an otherwise unknowable hyletic substratum.

Put differently, phenomenal reality is the effect of transcendental constitution, involving a relation between a perceiving subject and a perceived materiality, neither of which is visible as such in the phenomenal effect. Accordingly, philosophical thinking proceeds by transcendental questioning: on the basis of what does appear phenomenally, one proceeds by asking after its antecedent conditions of possibility. In so doing, one aims to determine, lay out, or explicate the tacit conditional structures of transcendental constitution (the synthetic process, or "intentional life") by virtue of which subjects let objects be.[7]

For Kant, transcendental constitution involves a combination of the a priori syntheses of productive imagination and the a posteriori syntheses of meaning-giving cognition. Although there are also important differences (for example, concerning where to draw the dividing line between unconscious and conscious processing), one finds certain parallels in Husserl's passive and active genesis, Heidegger's prethematic and thematic hermeneutics (understanding and interpretation), Nietzsche's distinction between "our spiritual *fatum*" and concept formation, and Freud's primary and secondary processes.[8] Although not strictly in accordance with Freud's more technical terms, I shall here use the terms "unconscious" and "conscious" as roughly synonymous with "implicit" and "explicit."

In view of these later developments, Kant's important distinction between a priori and a posteriori synthesis warrants the slight digression needed here for an elaboration. He accepts that human infants enter the world prematurely, not only because they are physically underdeveloped but also because there is no pregiven phenomenal reality, and a sense of both "self" and "world" has to be learned.[9] This is clearly not because there is nothing around them nor because healthy infants lack the intrinsic cognitive potential necessary to constitute objects. Rather, he argues famously, the a priori power of synthetic processing, which enables us to constitute an ever more complex field of experience, is only actualized in response to sensory encounters. In the total absence of sensation, any a priori given cognitive faculties would lie dormant and there would be no phenomena. (I should add here that, as emphasized in his well-known "cinnabar" example, if the hyletic substratum that occasions sensation occurs as an utterly irregular chaos, no subject would be capable of constituting a coherent objective reality.) In other words, he accepts that phenomenal reality is built up through repetition and surprise in the play of sensations, by means of which infants learn to constitute abiding habitualities and, on the basis of these, associations and expectations.

By the same token, if we did not already intrinsically possess the power of recognition (for example, of sameness and difference) and anticipation, even given our full sensory capacity, no such learning at all could take place. I should qualify the meaning of intrinsic here. While granting that subjective cognitive faculties are contingently given and remain corruptible, what remains incontrovertible for him, however, is the universal form these powers must take if an individual is to participate in a "nondefective" transcendental relation, whose constituted effect is the apparently coherent experiential reality we all supposedly share. The presuppositions inscribed here will come into question in the work of other thinkers.

For Kant, the a priori powers of recognition and anticipation, together with intuition, constitute the power of "productive imagination." This faculty describes the power to bring a mass of sensations together (or synthesize them) by organizing them according to an articulated system of a priori concepts to form a spatiotemporal manifold of objects. When sensory events occur, this synthetic process is a matter of making multiple basic judgments, which he believes one can describe theoretically as fundamental questions of quantity, quality, relation, and modality: for example, is it enduring, instantaneous, fleeting, continuous, discrete, regular, irregular, necessary, contingent, universal, particular, singular?[10]

Through experiential learning, then, based on the interaction between sensation and productive imagination, infants gradually acquire a phenomenal reality (or, in Husserl's terms, a transcendental "monad"), which may be described as a continuously experienced phenomenal field capable of being apprehended at a glance. Importantly, although we have to learn to synthesize (that is, to make the kind of basic judgment just listed, or to bring our sensations under these fundamental concepts), this synthetic process, starting almost from birth and increasing in complexity as we mature, is implicit and generally unconscious. Once developed, synthetic operations for the most part work automatically to constitute the world that I now continuously "have" around me (I do not have to reconstitute the objective manifold anew each time I open my eyes). The a priori conceptualization that is the work of "productive imagination" goes on all the time and is presupposed by other mental processes.[11]

For Kant, as indeed for Husserl, the kind of world that would be given by "productive imagination" alone (or passive genesis), is imaginable as a neutral manifold of objects stripped of all meanings and affects. Husserl makes this point clearly:

> The ready-made object that confronts us in life as an existent mere physical thing (when we disregard all the "spiritual" or "cultural" characteristics that make it knowable as, for example, a hammer, a table, an aesthetic creation) is given, with the originality of the "it itself," in the synthesis of a passive experience. As such a thing, it is given beforehand to "spiritual" activities, which begin with active grasping.[12]

In other words, for both thinkers, the spatiotemporal manifold given perceptually in productive imagination or passive genesis is also subsequently given meaning and affective charges through active explication. Here, Husserl's "active genesis" is the equivalent of what Kant names a posteriori, or empirical, conceptualization, which enables one to say, for example, that this "this" is a cat. The kind of a posteriori judgments he has in mind here would answer such questions as: What color is it? How does it feel to the touch? Can I eat it? Is it alive?

Husserl adds that in the work of "active genesis," or explication, one projects intentions (or anticipatory expectations concerning "parts and features" of things) on the basis of present experience. These expectations are either confirmed (made evident) and retained as acquisitions or disconfirmed and discarded. Moreover, for Husserl, active genesis is "productively constitutive or generative." One can, for example, actively generate endless kinds of numbers or sentences. However, both thinkers hold that the conscious, meaning-giving processes of active genesis can only produce new objects on the basis of the ready-made objective world generated by productive imagination or passive genesis. As Husserl puts it, "the physical thing given beforehand in passive intuition continues to appear in a unitary intuition; and no matter how much the thing may be modified therein by the activity of explication, of grasping parts and features, it continues to be given beforehand during and in this activity."[13] Accordingly, in order to determine the tacit conditional structures of transcendental constitution, it is the a priori conditions of productive imagination or passive genesis that are given priority. Notably, it is as a consequence of their analysis that both Kant and Husserl find it necessary to posit the transcendental subject as the seat of unified temporality.

The philosophical interventions of many more thinkers than the few I shall touch upon here have brought about a second paradigmatic shift that subjects transcendental philosophy to the "ruinous" articulation that necessitates the prefix "quasi." This shift, engendered by various inventive appropriations within the transcendental tradition, is not a matter of rejecting the form of the "transcendental relation" articulated by Kant, but of reinventing, ultimately, all of its terms. In its later quasi-transcendental articulation, Kant's noumenal *object* = *X* becomes "event," "trauma," *différance*, or the Lacanian Real. His unified "transcendental subject" becomes the split subject, whose most complex articulation takes the form of Lacan's Gödelian structuralism. Finally, the coherent, systematically ordered phenomenal reality he envisaged becomes the product of desire rather than a description of the actually experienced state of affairs, which is now best described as "flux" or "becoming" (noting that the opposite of "being" is not "becoming" but "chaos"). The shift that makes the antecedent conditions of experience quasi-transcendental rather than transcendental, then, reflects the "truth" that the state of affairs we call "phenomenal reality" is an irremediably paradoxical articulation of "being" and "chaos." Of course, to do justice to this immense topic would take a book in its own right, and what I outline here is just a brief indication of the shift from Kant's systematic philosophy to hermeneutics in Husserl and the challenges posed to this by Heidegger and Nietzsche.

Kant's Quest for Metaphysical Security

Kant thought he could establish the grounds for certain knowledge concerning phenomena by specifying a rationally guaranteed order on both occulted sides of the transcendental relation. On the subject side of this relation, as noted, he argues that the fundamental spatiotemporal shape of the phenomenal world can be known with certainty, since this shape is given to it by our own a priori given cognitive powers. Transcendental analysis of these powers, moreover, yields the insight that constituting phenomenal objects via productive imagination involves the application in judgment of twelve a priori categories, all schematized as time determinations, to as yet undetermined sense data, so that objective reality appears in synthesized form as a three-dimensional spatiotemporal manifold. To specify the rules according to which productive imagination works to constitute this manifold, therefore, is also to lay out and delimit the scope of a priori synthetic knowledge. Thus the form of any object that is experienced at all can be described with absolute certainty in terms of the unified, complete set of constitutive predicates that make a spatiotemporal manifold or objective field possible in the first place. For Kant, then, the spatiotemporal form of the phenomenal world is universally shared among rational beings across immeasurable empirical diversity.

Turning to the other side of the transcendental relation, Kant insisted that one could only render empirical knowledge of phenomenal reality absolutely certain by presupposing a harmony between the hyletic substratum (which gives it its immeasurably diverse empirical "content," so to speak) and the subjective faculties according to which we interpret it. We must minimally be capable of showing that the noumenal *object* = *X* lends itself to spatiotemporal appropriation and that it must remain a unity, or a constant, over the various ways in which it can be taken.[14] He acknowledges, however, that from the point of view of theoretical understanding there is nothing to explain or guarantee the regular repetition of forces in the hyletic substratum necessary for actual objective experience. Requiring just such an explanation and guarantee (for him, the inability to explain everything amounts to the inability to explain anything), Kant, to cut a very long story short, ultimately echoes Descartes' turn to God, although here God supports an edifice that combines theoretical understanding and moral necessity in the notion of natural teleology.[15] The necessary convergence of the true, the good, and the beautiful (in God's infinity) becomes the ultimate guarantee of the unity of form and content, of universal and particular, and of the reversibility of determinative and reflective judgment. In sum, for the sake of rendering phenomenal reality "scientifically" certain and rationally grounded on both sides of the transcendental relation, Kant imports an illegitimate *deus ex machina* into his thinking.

Hermeneutics and Husserl's Intervention

Even Husserl drops Kant's quest for such metaphysical security, arguing that the constitution of phenomena does not depend on there being an *object* = *X*, conceived of as fully present in principle in the perspective-free vision of a divine "eye," which underlies and holds together the finite spatiotemporal perspectives of human subjects. Instead, the future continuation of the world can at best be inductively projected on the basis of past experience. This, notably, leaves open the possibility that what humans or other beings do risks the future course of the world in unexpected, unpredictable ways. As Caputo puts it, describing Husserl's thesis of the "annihilability of the world":

> Husserl understood as well as anyone that we have to do with contingent unities of meaning, with constituted products, that nothing has dropped from the sky. For Husserl, everything rises slowly from below, is formed and reformed, and remains subject always to discreditation, to what he called, in an uncanny experiment, the possibility of the destruction of the world. The one "thing" which alone resists this destruction is no thing at all but the pure flux of internal time.[16]

This reference to time introduces Husserl's important intervention on the subject side of the transcendental relation. In Kant's terms, transcendental analysis of the synthetic faculty yields the a priori rules according to which productive imagination operates. In Husserl's equivalent terms, phenomenological analysis of passive and active genesis ultimately yields "the eidetic laws governing a passive forming of perpetually new syntheses." For both thinkers this yield describes the structure of unified temporality, but they conceive of it very differently. Kant, as noted, understood temporality as a closed system of twelve logical categories. Husserl, by contrast, offers an existential understanding of intentional life constituted, in his words, as "an infinite nexus of synthetically congruous performances—at levels, all of which fit the universal persisting form, *temporality*."[17] In short, all of a subject's multiform intentional streams are held together and organized as streaming off in two directions from the now-point of immediate perception: toward the past (from retention through memory to history) and toward the future (from protention, through anticipation or expectation, to hope).

Thus, as Caputo sums it up: "Consciousness builds up and constitutes, makes up the object by making up for what is missing at any given moment—and this by a retention (repetition) which is compounded with protention in such a way as to bring the flow of *Erlebnisse* to a contingent rest."[18] Here, then, Husserl offers a hermeneutic theory of constitution that recognizes that the only absolute is subjective consciousness, described in terms of time as an ordered flow (rather than as a logical system of cognitive rules), consisting of the present point and its horizon of protentions and retentions.[19]

What Husserl challenges, then, is not Kant's "transcendental turn" but his interpretation of synthetic constitution. For the sake of epistemological certainty, Kant not only makes of the event beyond the phenomenal appropriation a "thing-in-itself," which must be postulated as sublimely present and guaranteed to be regular even if it is inaccessible as such, but he also presupposes that the rules for synthetic cognition can be understood as a unified set of robust transcendental conditions. A significant shift beyond Kant, then, as reflected in Husserl's insistence upon the necessity of making one's way through the flow of experience without metaphysical guarantees, may be described as a shift in the transcendental theory of constitution from metaphysics to hermeneutics.[20]

One might wish to break off at this point, before Husserl subverts his hermeneutic side and "falls into complicity with Platonism."[21] Yet, as Caputo notes, while one must emphasize Husserl's hermeneutic side to correct exaggerated misreadings in the other direction, "this is not to say that Husserl did not close off with one hand what he opened up with another, that he did not do his best to bury his revolutionary side under the most traditional metaphysics of subjectivity and transcendental reflection."[22] Caputo explains that Husserl's reactionary gesture turns on a misconception of science as an activity that concerns itself with pure, neutral description unhampered by ontological presuppositions.[23] Science, for him, as the activity of making fully evident the essential structure of a thing's pure "quiddity," refines away all that is supposedly unnecessary to its essence (via *epoche* and imaginative variation), including its existential status (that is, whether the thing in question exists, ever has existed, or ever will exist).[24]

But this emphasis on the activity of pure description supposedly unhampered by ontological presuppositions depends on, as Heidegger points out, a certain self-deception, for it is not as if Husserl's commitment to ontological neutrality escapes being an ontological presupposition. Taking "the Being of consciousness to be such that it *can* neutralize itself or purify itself of worldly contamination," Caputo adds, Husserl was in fact "inspired by a Cartesian ontology which supposes the separability of reflective consciousness from concrete first-order experience which is embodied in language, historical tradition, and culture."[25] Husserl then, on one hand, argues that consciousness or intentional life may in principle, or fundamentally, be described in terms of time as an ordered flow. Yet, on the other hand, he inconsistently "clings to the ideal that the reflective ego enjoys a mode of intentional life—free from potential, implicit, horizonal, historical, and predelineatory factors—which he otherwise insists belongs to the make-up of intentional life at large."[26]

Thus, as Caputo points out, Husserl's residual Cartesian commitment affects the initial hermeneutic projections on the basis of which he undertakes his phenomenological analyses. He projects the subject too narrowly as a being who first of all looks-at, or passively perceives, generating a primary objective manifold characterized as neutral, which is only subsequently given meaning and affective charge in active genesis. This mistakenly implies that one can disengage from the constituted effects of active genesis at will and return to the neutral manifold by adopting a philosophical attitude. In this case, Caputo notes, "Husserl in effect asks us to believe in two selves, one situated in the world and the other, its transcendental double, as Foucault calls it, capable of reflecting on that situation, taking hold of it and laying it out . . . in a way that makes consciousness transparent, exposing all the preconditions under which it labors."[27]

Husserl's conservatism shows itself, moreover, in his attempt to exclude signification (the work of signs) from the inner core of transcendental life in order to preserve its absolute self-presence.[28] Like Kant, Husserl presupposes the primacy of thought over language, considering language to be merely a more or less (in his case less) convenient vehicle for its expression. Husserl accepts that the articulation of "sense" in the interior monologue is carried out in a language, but for him the fact that this same articulation can happen in any language demonstrates that the medium of "sense," the inner "voice" of cognitive articulation, transcends any natural language. He grants that in conversing one must resort to material signs (spoken signifiers) that express the logically intended sense (signified). If natural languages were ideal for this purpose, there would be perfectly univocal correlations between expressive signs and the sense expressed by them (and perfect translatability between languages).

For Husserl, this is regrettably not the case, and the equivocality of material signs often obstructs communication. However, he thought such obstacles could in principle be overcome. The final aim of conversation, then, is to reach (via spoken or expressive signs) the point of perfect communion between interlocutors, where such signs are no longer necessary and language, having served its purpose of communication, quietly drops out of the picture. Again, he grants that the preservation of intellectual acquisitions is secured only through indicative signs, especially writing, since they outlast the living. Husserl's ideal writing is phonetic: at best a copy of spoken language. But if speech threatens the communication of "sense," so much greater is this threat with writing, since the written word is often encountered without the clarifying interactive process of conversation.[29]

We have it from multiple sources, however, that signifying activity is not simply the (somewhat unreliable) representation of cognition but a prior condition for cognition. Husserl might have criticized contemporaries for beginning not with the primordially given (synthesized perceptual experience) but with second-level theoretical constructs (atomistic sense impressions or metaphysical systems). But his own starting point similarly fails to meet this demand, since the primordially given is the symbolically infused space and time of action in the lifeworld and not his own second-level theoretical construction, namely, the supposedly "ready-made" objective manifold that is neutrally synthesized in passive genesis.

Heidegger and the Economic Motif of "Circular Return"

Heidegger insists on a return to Husserl's hermeneutic side, arguing that his understanding of scientific consciousness is deflected by a misconception of science as the quest for scientific absolutes (stable, eternal, atemporal essences or eidetic structures), in the name of which he is forced to propose a mode of consciousness that can be extracted from the existential flux. Heidegger insists instead that the notion of perception as a "pure," neutral looking-at is an impossible idealization, for we are first and foremost beings whose existential cares and interests affect and direct the initial perception that constitutes the manifold.[30] He argues, therefore, that the manifold of intentional objects is not primordially a series of neutral spaces but a surrounding environment saturated with existential significance and affective charges. Instead of characterizing the primary act of synthetic constitution as a neutral, cognitive, passive genesis, he argues that we build up an implicit, holistic grasp of ourselves and our surrounding environment through the concernful interactivity by which we deal with events. Notably, Heidegger's generic term for the beings that we are is *Dasein*. For him, humankind is the exemplary *Dasein*, indeed, the only one we know of, and the one he takes as his model.[31] One may say that *Dasein*'s constitution of the world through concernful dealing-with (which is never purely cognitive but, just as originally, emotional and charged with significance) remains unconscious in the sense that it involves the implicit, intuitive, prethematic, prereflective grasp of a surrounding environment. His correlative version of Husserl's "active genesis" takes the form of hermeneutic explication, which becomes a matter not of adding sense and affective charge to a "ready-made" manifold but of explicating, bringing to light, or uncovering what is already implicitly grasped. Accordingly, he insists that constitution must be understood in terms of what he calls the structural unity of "care": that is, the unity of "thrownness," "projection," and "falling."

"Thrownness" and "Projection"

By "thrownness," Heidegger means to say that all phenomena emerge in the midst of a preexisting heritage, and it is only within this context that they may be given the shape of something new or anomalous. Accordingly, *Dasein* is primordially "delivered over" to a preexisting actuality, already pregnant with significance, to which it is bound to respond.[32] He regards actuality as Janus-faced.[33] It represents the factical situation that always already encompasses and "looms ahead" of *Dasein* as the condition of the possibility of its future projects. In other words, actuality is both the source and limitation of *Dasein*'s potential. In the "hard" sense, one is born with certain physical and psychical endowments, or gifts, that make individuals "what they are," beyond which they cannot stretch and within whose limitations only future projects may be actualized. In a softer sense, one is born into a preexisting world whose codes of significance and modes of being again offer an initial endowment, to which *Dasein*'s projected future is always a response.

For Heidegger, the preexisting world into which *Dasein* is "thrown" is inherently resistant to novelty and strives to stand fast against relentless forces of dissolution and change (of re-forming, revolution, or evolution) by subjecting all things in existence to an inertial tug or drag toward conservation, repetition of the same, self-preserving habits, and so on. This inertial drag (which Freud appositely names the death drive, *Thanatos*, in its conservative guise) is an entirely necessary existential force; without some degree of repetition, there would be nothing there to undergo change. In other terms, the "weight of the world" tends to slow down the pace of change enough for things to take shape and take hold, but it would slow to a stop were it not the case that all existing things are equally engaged in a battle against such inertial forces.

Resisting their backward drag, existing things are also projected toward a future: growth and development, increase rather than decrease, complexity rather than simplicity, potentiality (what can be) rather than actuality (what already is). *Dasein*, as "primarily Being-possible," is characterized by the power to grasp the significance of its situation. As a being that "'knows' *what* it is capable of," *Dasein* possesses a sense of its own orientation toward a purpose; a sense that there is something "for-the-sake-of-which" it acts.[34] It consequently has the power to wrest freedom for the future from the weight of a past heritage, not indeed by escaping from it entirely but through inventive appropriation of the potentialities inscribed within that heritage. The idea of projection, then, inscribes the resolute affirmation of *Dasein*'s power of choice not over what happens but over its appropriation. Thus there is a constant dynamic tension between thrownness and projection, which may be understood in existential, hermeneutic, and discursive terms.

Dynamic Tensions: Existential, Hermeneutic, and Discursive

Existential projection, as Caputo puts it, is a "forceful setting free"[35] (a matter of forming and reforming, of giving life), whereas existential thrownness is a matter of keeping shape, preserving, and resisting change. The forces of projection constantly press a thing past the boundaries of what actually is toward what it *can* be. But *Dasein*'s possibility, in Heidegger's words, "as an *existentiale*, does not signify a free-floating potentiality-for-Being in the sense of a 'liberty of indifference' (*libertas indifferentiae*). In every case *Dasein* . . . has already got itself into definite possibilities."[36] In other words, seeking to conserve what is already in place, resistant actuality forces projections to remain "realistic." *Dasein* that is free for possibility, then, must recognize necessary limitations in any actual situation, as the base from out of which a projection of something new can be made. However, free *Dasein* is simultaneously required to recognize provisional limitations, so as to avoid being imprisoned by them.

For Heidegger, to be authentically free *Dasein* means to *be the play* between these two forces and to find the courage to maintain this tension, that is, to keep actuality open for possibility, without flight into the impossible (the madness, fantasy, illusion of wholly unrealistic projections) and without "falling" into unthinking, inflexible, sedimented habits. The tension between these two dynamic existential forces, one may add, involves a constant feedback loop: where novelty disrupts a system, the system must accommodate and domesticate it or break apart; both accommodations and break-ups cause shifts in relations whose effects are to produce more novelties that must be accommodated on pain of destruction. Hence the incessant flux of the world, which in turn demands never-ending hermeneutic explication.

A parallel tension occurs in theoretical activity (Husserl's active genesis), between the hermeneutic forces of understanding (*Verstehen*) and interpretation (*Auslegung*).[37] Heidegger famously remarks that *Dasein* may be described essentially as the being for whom its own being is an issue.[38] In other words, healthy humans do not remain innocently or passively caught up in their existential context, but experience it originally in terms of an implicit, prethematic, prereflective, prepredicative horizon of understanding derived from the necessity of dealing with everyday events. In short, we already possess an intuitive or unconscious sense of how things stand: who we are, what a thing is, and how to act accordingly.[39]

Given this horizon of understanding, our attempts to theorize (that is, to project an explicit, predicative, thematic, reflective grasp of something) are never free from presuppositions.[40] That is, interpretations aim to make conscious or explicit the implicit presuppositions formed from our concernful dealing with items and situations in the "everyday." In Heidegger's words: "when something within-the-world is encountered as such, the thing in question already has an involvement which is disclosed in our understanding of the world, and this involvement is one which gets laid out by the interpretation."[41] Again, maintaining the play between two forces: while interpretation works to shake up sedimented presuppositions by uncovering them and subjecting them to reflective questioning, in the same sense that thrownness aims to keep existential projections "realistic," hermeneutic presuppositions aim to keep interpretations honest.

A similarly parallel tension exists in the sphere of discourse. Unlike Kant and Husserl, Heidegger does not presuppose the primacy of thought over signification. In other words, for Heidegger, "prethematic" does not mean "prelinguistic"; signifying activity goes all the way down, so to speak. In his words: "*Discourse is existentially equiprimordial with state-of-mind and understanding.* The intelligibility of something has always been articulated, even before there is any appropriative interpretation of it. Discourse is the Articulation of intelligibility. Therefore it underlies both interpretation and assertion."[42]

Heidegger, in other words, makes a division within signifying activity, between two forms of articulation or discourse. Claiming that "talking is the way in which we articulate 'significantly' the intelligibility of Being-in-the-world," Heidegger describes an expressive use of language that is the correlative of prethematic understanding.[43] Expressive discourse may be understood as a matter of "speech-acts" ("as assenting or refusing, as demanding or warning, as pronouncing, consulting, or interceding," etc.), to which also belong the possibilities of "*hearing*" and "*keeping silent.*" Here, one engages in talk in which something is said, without what is said necessarily becoming the theme (or content) for an assertion in which one gives something "a definite character."

Heidegger describes expressive discourse as having a broad, context-related significance that exceeds the words spoken. The words "no, not that one," for example, in the context of a workshop, may signify that a particular hammer is considered to be too heavy for the task at hand.[44] The words also signify being with another who is directed to procure the appropriate tool. Further, the intonation of the words signifies much about the nature of the directive, the relation between the parties involved, and the mood of the speaker. Accordingly, Heidegger suggests that the success of expressive discourse depends upon a mutual attunement, which allows even the briefest of gestures ("without wasting words"), as well as silence, to have significance.[45]

By contrast, when what is primordially understood is converted into something about which we speak, we shift to the mode of thematic assertion. He defines assertion as "a pointing-out which gives something a definite character and which communicates."[46] Assertion, then, is characterized by apophansis (pointing out), predication (giving the subject a definite, if partial and reductive, character by asserting a predicate of it), and communication (passing along the expression of an entity in its absence in "further retelling" or hearsay).[47]

The tension between the modes of expression and assertion may be articulated as follows. Expressive discourse might be rich in context-specific evocative significance, but it remains local, insular, singular, and idiosyncratic. In assertion, for Heidegger "the predicate which we are to assign . . . and make stand out, gets loosened, so to speak, from its unexpressed inclusion in the entity itself."[48] In being thus highlighted and thereby made open to general examination, assertions are capable of shaking up expressive discourse. Yet at the same time they run the risk of falsification, for assertion "veils" the complexity of expressive discourse by singling out limited predicates to give an entity a definite character.[49] In other words, no longer taken "environmentally" or contextually, the significance of the entity, while universal and shareable, is dimmed down and flattened out. In Heidegger's words: "By looking at the world theoretically, we have already dimmed it down to the uniformity of what is purely present-at-hand."[50] In sum, if the mode of assertion draws expressive discourse out of itself, expressive discourse remains resistant to the attenuating effect of the assertions it necessarily exceeds, and it therefore poses a permanent and necessary challenge to their hegemony.

"Falling"

For Heidegger, "falling" occurs when something breaks down in the tensional relationships just described. It is not being among everyday actualities themselves that constitutes fallenness. Rather, falling is the all too human attitude toward these otherwise innocently ordinary superficialities of the "everyday," in which *Dasein* allows itself to become caught up and dissipated in them, using its busyness among them as an excuse to avoid committing itself to the sometimes bitter struggle to see a project through. Consequently, in fleeing from the demanding call of conscience and sinking back into the comfortable inertia of everydayness, *Dasein* loses itself to a lifeless repetition of its given heritage, to a perpetual present without future prospects.

The hermeneutic tension is similarly broken in the tendency to rest content with a heritage of presuppositions that are taken over as unquestionable truths. Philosophers, for example, have developed systems of knowledge based on an interpretation of "Being" as essentially eternal substance, which has seldom been questioned in relation to experience. In fact, given that being is experienced as more of a flux than anything—more of a verb than a noun—one cannot maintain the argument that Being is essentially eternal substance except by elaborate artifice. To insist on the artifice nevertheless converts intelligence into pattern recognition or puzzle solving, operating in the domain of illusion rather than genuine wisdom, and philosophy, thereby, is converted into what Heidegger calls "idle talk."[51]

To fall into idle talk, finally, is to break the discursive tension. Again, assertions are innocent enough with regard to the mode of falling, but they lend themselves to idle talk, which consists in the thoughtless taking up of assertions and communication of information about entities in their absence, in "further retelling" or hearsay, "without previously making the thing one's own."[52] Discourse, here, becomes caught up in the proliferation of empty catchphrases that everybody uses without question and without knowing what they are really saying. This, in turn, allows assertions expressly to be taken out of context and placed in the service of interests other than the quest for *aletheia*, for example, a desire for power and mastery.

Falling is interrupted by a disturbance of the peace. The challenge may derive from the anxiety that announces a brush with the possibility of death, from confronting the abyss of value (in Nietzsche's terms), or from a trauma (in Freud's terms). Something happens, in other words, that challenges the viability of depressed nihilism, vacuous boredom, cynical weariness, or ideological comfort and forces one to see that there are questions still to be asked, projects to be revitalized, and truths to be retrieved.

Aletheia *and "Circular Return"*

At this point, one may invoke Heidegger's circular notion of *aletheia*, uncovering, or "retrieval," which marks the moment when a projection has returned from a fallen state to its primordial truth. *Aletheia* depends upon Heidegger's claim that "in the circle is hidden a positive possibility of the most primordial kind of knowing."[53] On his account, in the silent call of conscience, *Dasein* knows itself, and this self-knowledge stands as the measure of what it explicitly claims as a vocation. Moreover, within the implicit horizon of understanding, *Dasein* knows how things stand in its world, and this understanding provides the measure against which all explicit interpretations, which try to bring it to light, hold sway or falter. Finally, expression marks, as Heidegger puts it, the "co-understanding" prior to "what is said-in-the-talk," on the *basis* of which one may judge "whether the way in which it is said is appropriate to what the discourse is about thematically."[54]

However, we only genuinely capture this implicit knowledge in our explicit projects, interpretations, and assertions, when we resist the tendency to let them fall. That is, in Heidegger's words, "when, in our interpretation, we have understood that our first, last, and constant task is never to allow fore-having, fore-sight, and fore-conception to be presented to us by fancies and popular conceptions, but rather to make the scientific theme secure by working out these fore-structures in terms of the things themselves."[55] As Caputo explains: "Hermeneutics is able to 'retrieve' the primordial only insofar as it dismantles the overlaid accretions and derivative understandings of the world, of Dasein—and of Being."[56] However, to undo, or de-construct, the damages and distortions associated with falling is by no means to do away with presuppositions altogether but to replace them with better projections that are drawn not from idle talk or hearsay but from the things themselves. But how can we tell whether a new projection has the power to "elucidate these things, illuminate and disclose them, set them free"?[57] Heidegger's answer, Caputo notes, is that "only by being worked out in detail can the projection of existence prove its worth."[58] The question remains, he adds, of how to tell when the "working out," the explication, has finally secured the interpretation. For Heidegger, Caputo argues, "everything turns on the fact that we already 'understand' who we are. . . . Everything turns on our ability to say that *this* . . . is the account which brings to words what we have all along understood but have been unable to say because of . . . prejudices."[59] In other words, having found the appropriate fore-structures—drawn from the things themselves and not forced upon them to serve interests other than that of *aletheia*—and having worked them out in detail, recasting them where necessary, we should be able to recognize ourselves, the event, situation, or thing in the interpretation.

There is, therefore, a kind of "essentialism" in Heidegger's stance: in the absence of the interpretations that bring the primordial events to light, they remain in truth just what they always were before any interpretative efforts. Admittedly, the moment of *aletheia* represents a movement of both uncovering and covering-over, but for the Heidegger of *Being and Time*, the risk of covering-over occurs not as intrinsic to the moment of *aletheia* (as will certainly be the case in later texts) but subsequent to any uncovering, as the risk of falling: first, when one tries to hold onto the moment of truth for too long in a world characterized by flux, which therefore demands its persistent rearticulation, and second, in the inevitable emptying out or deterioration when one tries to communicate it to others.

Interestingly, Heidegger and Nietzsche similarly rely upon the notion that what is implicit or unconscious is the domain of "truth." The movement of *aletheia* depends on the view that there is an essentially true state of affairs that is always already genuinely (if implicitly) grasped; it is this genuine grasp that is presupposed in the notion of a recognizing response that confirms the revelatory power of an interpretation. For Nietzsche, by contrast, the unconscious "truth" lies in "the great stupidity [that] we are . . . our spiritual *fatum* . . . what is *unteachable* very 'deep down.' "[60] Importantly, however, this "spiritual *fatum*" simply cannot be imagined, spoken, or conceived. As soon as one attempts a translation into images, words, or concepts, falsification inevitably occurs. In other words, conscious processing intervenes absolutely between the unconscious singularity that I am and any synthesizing interpretation, leaving no hope of any "return" from interpretation to understanding in a revelatory match. The unconscious remains the domain of "truth," but the notion of truth has been rearticulated. It indicates the truth of the secret or the secret of truth: the truth that there is no Truth.[61] Nietzsche's thinking, therefore, represents the most extreme point of "ruin" for transcendental thinking, for what is there to stop the Nietzsche in us from insisting that the contingent points of *aletheia*, at which we attempt to capture this essential "untruth" via images, words, or concepts, constitute illusions produced by the "pathos of truth," which is an effect of the will to power?

Nietzsche: The "Will to Power"

Nietzsche's style of thinking is derived from the insight that all values are context bound and therefore inherently indeterminate and shifting (the same thing can, for example, be good in one context and evil in another).

In contemporary terms, this insight is codified in the oft quoted Saussurean dictum that "there are no present terms, only relations of difference."[62] That is, a term's significance or value cannot be determined in isolation from a complex network of other terms that condition it. For Nietzsche then, the unforgivable philosophical error derives from the so-called dream of purity inaugurated by Plato, in whose wake traditional philosophers dream of establishing fundamental concepts, the value or character of which could be determined unconditionally, whereas in fact, he insists "everything unconditional belongs in pathology."[63]

Moreover, he continues, because any value is, by contrast, contextually determined through the contaminating traces of other values, one cannot establish a philosophically grounded system for organizing things according to clearly antithetical values between which straightforward either/or choices would be structurally possible. Nevertheless, he complains, just such crude oppositional thinking predominates in intellectual life precisely where one should acknowledge "only degrees and many subtleties of gradation"[64] or "degrees of apparentness and, as it were, lighter and darker shadows and shades of appearance—different 'values' to use the language of painters."[65] Yet again, in his words:

> When one is young, one venerates and despises without that art of nuances which constitutes the best gain of life, and it is only fair that one has to pay dearly for having assaulted men and things in this manner with Yes and No. Everything is arranged so that the worst of tastes, the taste for the unconditional, should be cruelly fooled and abused until a man learns to put a little art into his feelings.[66]

Further, even though it may cause "distress and aversion in a still hale and hearty conscience," Nietzsche insists not only upon "a doctrine of the reciprocal dependence of the 'good' and the 'wicked' drives," but more radically still, and at the risk of seasickness, "a doctrine of the derivation of all good impulses from wicked ones."[67] But he presses those thinkers with the stomach for it to journey along with him, for treasures await the adventurer. With the proposition that so-called evil and its derivatives (falsity, aggressivity, lust, etc.) lie at the origin of what is ordinarily valued as "good" (truth, stability, order, beauty, system, etc.), one reaches the bottom line of Nietzsche's "logic of contamination," from which emerges his formulation of the "will to power." This is succinctly expressed in his claim that "life is *essentially* appropriation, injury, overpowering of what is alien and weaker; suppression, hardness, imposition of one's own forms, incorporation and at least, at its mildest, exploitation."[68]

An extreme sense of "ruin" concerning transcendental constitution is indicated here by the shift in tone where Nietzsche speaks of "appropriation." If, for Kant, constitution is a matter of rational appropriation of the *object* = *X*, which requires an external guarantee, for Husserl and Heidegger it becomes a matter of hermeneutic appropriation of the event, whose only guarantee is inductively derived from experience. For Nietzsche, however, life as "*essentially* appropriation" becomes the inventive destruction of what is. New forms, he argues, emerge from the destruction, dissolution, or incorporation (in a word, "contamination") of something already existing. What is inventive breaks with or "traumatizes" the conventional, reconfiguring it in a way that passes beyond the point of no return. In this case, appropriation remains without the *aletheic* guarantee of primordial experience, for all life is essentially a series of such inventive destructions, and nothing previously invented can stand as a guarantee for the new. A form's only "guarantee" is its power to prevail for the present in aggressive competition with myriad threatening forces.[69]

Heidegger retains a circular conception of *aletheia* whereby the "new" is a revivification of the primordial, or a retrieval of an original/originary richness from a state of decline or fallenness. For Nietzsche, by contrast, the flux of the world is more violently linear, if only in the sense that it presses toward incessant change rather than teleological progress. I am assuming here that it is unnecessary to get carried away by the seeming contradiction contained in Nietzsche's perplexing notion of "eternal recurrence." While, no doubt, the sense of this notion remains a contentious issue, I shall take up Bert Olivier's suggestion that one may most plausibly understand this notion in ethical, rather than cosmological, terms. In agreement with Karsten Harries and Alexander Nehamas, Olivier argues that the eternal recurrence is primarily an ethical notion insofar as it exhorts individuals to live in such a way that they would be able to will the eternal repetition of their lives down to every last detail or decision. Notably, for Nietzsche, to live according to this ethic would be the only way to overcome the spirit of revenge, or resentment, which is the source of bitter regrets.[70]

To return to Nietzsche's ontological concerns, a form's power to prevail, he insists, always already entails a gesture of "forgetting": to consolidate and stabilize a new form one necessarily "forgets" or represses the very condition that underpins all origination, namely the possibility of contamination. Thus, for him, any products, inventions, or instituted systems (conceptual, ethical, epistemological, or ontological) can only be erected insofar as one "forgets" the untruth of contamination. Any erection, then, comes into being on the basis of a lie, a fake stability, or, if you like, the necessary originating myth of its own form. Paradoxically, while "system" as such, or order, is traditionally associated with "justice" (the convergence of the good, the true, and the beautiful), Nietzsche contends that any system is unavoidably established by means of an originary "injustice" (by that which is false and therefore, traditionally speaking, also evil and ugly).

Once a form, he adds, is erected by "forgetting" its originary "evil" (its contamination and aggressivity) and consolidating its stabilizing fiction, it has to commandeer recognition from others to be sustained. Durability here is directly proportional to the power to seduce or conquer all others. Such universalization, however, has two unfortunate consequences. First, he argues, to gain a purchase on the minds of the majority the singular "untruths" of innovative ideas must be "thinned down, shrouded, sweetened, blunted, falsified." The more universally a new form is shared, the more it is falsified or emptied of the "untruth" by which it was engendered, until only a superficial façade covers over the vacuity that is left.[71] Second, the more ensconced in conventionality a new form becomes, the more its originator becomes enamored of the façade, falling prey to the self-deluded belief that the invented myth is indeed the Truth and forgetting that it was ever necessary to establish it by "forgetting" an originary injustice. Thus the invention becomes resistant to the very kind of "evil" that engendered it, to the point of condemning any other similar injustices within its system.

The dynamic of the will to power, in short, describes the structure of ideological conditioning. Importantly, this is not an indictment of productive "life" as the expression of the will to power, but an account of what happens. Nietzsche's objections are directed elsewhere: toward philosophy's willful blindness to this necessary dynamic of originary injustice, its concealment, the concealing of this concealment, and, therefore, its tendency to succumb to the will to power or to allow itself to devolve into ideology, epitomized, for him, by the fundamental metaphysical "*faith in opposite values.*"[72]

The Implication of Language in Thinking

According to Nietzsche, then, all theoretical activity is structured by the "will to power," which is also, as Derrida notes, a matter of what he sees as "castratism."[73] Moreover, Nietzsche argues that all such activity, up until his own efforts, has repeatedly suffered its self-poisoning, since it does not acknowledge the "will to power" or "castration effect" that describes its operation and for this reason becomes trapped by it. The path of cognitive decline occurs via four stages, between which it is possible to intercalate the three-stage metaphorical transfer that characterizes Nietzsche's account of the role language plays in cognition. Thus, drawing from an exposition by Alan Shrift, one may outline the following schema.[74]

The first stage of cognitive activity, belonging to the sphere of physiology or sensory events, may be marked by the following claim: "I am the untruth."[75] Between this stage and the next, a metaphorical transfer occurs whereby nerve stimuli are translated into images. Here, what is essentially unimaginable is given shape or form (e.g., spatiotemporal) via what one could think of as the equivalent of productive imagination. In other words, for the purpose of constructing an image of an event, the event is forcefully stabilized. In Nietzsche's words: "The impression is petrified for this purpose."[76] In this transfer, then, individuals are castrated or cut off from their own singular untruths.

Marked by the claim "I have the Truth," the second stage of cognitive activity, or image-thinking, is named the sphere of intellect. Between this stage and the next, a second metaphorical transfer occurs whereby images are imitated or indicated by sounds. By means of this conversion into sounds (that is, signs or words), images are abstracted. In other words, what is essentially unspeakable is given linguistic form, placing the original event at an even further remove from the cognitive form by which "it is captured and stamped."[77] Thus, as Nietzsche notes, "words are the seducers of philosophers: they struggle in the nets of language."[78]

Marked by the claim "I give the Truth," the third stage of cognitive activity, namely linguistic activity, is labeled the sphere of acoustics-linguistics. Between this stage and the next, a third metaphorical transfer occurs whereby sounds or words give rise to concepts, which are even further removed from the originary untruth. What is essentially inconceivable (because it is uniquely singular) is given conceptual form, that is, universalized and rendered shareable. In Nietzsche's words, "it is killed, skinned, mummified, and preserved as a concept."[79] Thus, finally, marked by the claim "I master the Truth," the fourth and final stage of cognitive activity, or conceptualization, is named the sphere of abstraction.

In sum, in the process of discovering, forming, sharing, and universalizing "the truth," we inevitably end up achieving quite the opposite effect: that of arriving at greater and greater falsity. According to Nietzsche, then, to say in the first place that "I have the Truth" is always the beginning of self-delusion, for the process of inevitable fictionalizing is the true state of affairs. What poisons this process, as already noted, is the refusal to accept this untruth, motivated by the traditional philosophical quest for Truth in the form of absolute certainty, which, in turn, is driven by the desire for absolute mastery.

In other words, honesty demands our thoroughgoing suspicion of any claims to have finalized the Truth. But such suspicion cannot be admitted by traditional philosophy since it operates on the basis of an either/or choice between absolute Truth and utter skepticism (if you can't explain everything, you can't explain anything). Instead of allowing the thought of ineradicable suspicion to take hold, traditional philosophers are motivated by what Nietzsche calls the "pathos of truth."[80] As if describing the moment of *aletheia*, he notes that this pathos or feeling of truth is experienced in rare "moments of sudden illumination." These are, he adds,

> moments in which the person stretches out his commanding arm as if to create a universe, draws up light from within himself and shines forth. At such a moment he is pierced by a certainty which fills him with happiness, the certainty that that which exalted him and carried him into the farthest regions . . . should not be allowed to remain withheld from all posterity.[81]

Instead of seeing in the flash of insight something singular and momentary, what offends philosophers deeply, Nietzsche insists, "is the thought that an instant of supreme universal perfection should vanish like a gleam of light, as it were, without posterity and heirs."[82] Thus, he continues, a philosopher affected by the "pathos of truth," implicitly disdaining both the singular and the momentary, dreams of shaping "culture," which is thought of as a great unifying chain linking eternal truths to one another. However, as he notes, this dream has to impose itself on a resistant reality: "Terrible cultural struggle is kindled by the demand that that which is great shall be eternal. For everything else that lives exclaims 'No!'" On his account, it is hardly greatness that prevails among humans. Rather, "suffocating, choking, darkening, and deceiving," it is the small-mindedness of human culture that "billows around what is great and blocks the road which it must travel toward immortality." As already noted, he argues that to make sense of and share a moment of illumination that is, "to organize it into a secure, static, systematic body of beliefs"—is automatically to kill it off.[83] Moreover, when traditional philosophers develop a paranoid defense of their systems against any possible challenge, they succumb to the power of an all too human small-mindedness, and having thus been castrated, they aim to castrate those who listen to their words.

One should not think that Nietzsche, for this reason, dreams of returning to the unspeakable, unconscious, silence of being-the-untruth. He is mercilessly critical of those among the "addicts of fame" who desire to claim their immortality independently of a public and in total disregard of time. Here again, the worst afflicted are the philosophers who presume to rise above the cultural morass, for they teach but a single lesson: disdain for the merely mortal "span of being." In his words, "it is the nature of philosophical reflection to disregard the present and momentary. He possesses the truth: let the wheel of time roll where it will, it will never be able to escape from the truth."[84] For Nietzsche, such disdain for the present is exemplified by "the wise Heraclitus." One may give thanks for history, he notes sarcastically, for "unless he has been instructed to the contrary by history, no one will be able to imagine such regal self-esteem, such boundless conviction that one is the sole fortunate wooer of truth."

Heraclitus, however, remains in the unreachable confines of his own solipsistic universe, whose loneliness is like being "in the wildest mountain wasteland, while growing numb from the cold." "Such a being," he adds, "might seem more comprehensible in a remote shrine, among images of the gods and amidst cold, sublime architecture."[85] Nietzsche grants that one might admire his striving for singular self-knowledge, but this gesture is thoroughly undermined when he presents his insights "as immortal wisdom, eternally worthy of interpretation in the sense in which the prophetic speeches of the sibyl are immortal. It is sufficient for the most distant generations."[86] Yet what precisely is this immortal wisdom? It is precisely nothing but the injunction to think for yourself: "may they interpret it only as the sayings of an oracle—as Heraclitus, as the Delphic god himself 'neither speaks nor conceals.'" Thus, as Nietzsche exclaims: "Truth! Rapturous illusion of a god! . . . And what was the Heraclitean 'truth'! And where has it gone! A vanished dream which has been erased from mankind's countenance by other dreams! It was hardly the first!"[87]

Nietzsche, however, goes on to argue that humanity would despair if we knew the true state of affairs: "the truth that . . . [we all are] eternally condemned to untruth." Clinging, therefore, to the "belief in attainable truth," do we not, he asks, "actually live *by means of* a continual process of deception?"[88] His answer is, of course, affirmative, but he adds that such deception (or one might say fictionalization) should not be taken as a tragic error to be mourned over, but as the chance for inventive action. Instead of trying to arrest the destructive flux of the world or cover it up with the fiction of Truth, one should learn to affirm and celebrate it, because it is precisely due to this flux that life becomes by no means the destruction of value as such but precisely the promotion of value in the subtle art of inventing, resisting, transvaluing, and reinventing all determinate values. "Art," Nietzsche concludes, "is more powerful than knowledge, because *it* desires life, whereas knowledge attains as its final goal only—annihilation."[89]

Essentialism and Nominalism

I have set up the above contrast between Heidegger and Nietzsche mainly to identify and characterize the two economic and aneconomic styles of thinking that stand together uneasily in Freud's writings. Before I turn to the question of Freud's place in the trajectory of inventive appropriation just outlined, I should emphasize that there is no choosing between "Heidegger" and "Nietzsche," for I have taken them to represent opposing aporias, which may be formalized as a tension between "essentialism" and "nominalism."

From a purely essentialist or economic point of view, what exists as the Real (as enduringly present for all time, or endlessly repeatable as the same) is a universal essence of some sort (conceived variously from "thing" to eidetic or existential structures) rather than any particular instance of it. In this case, only its conceptual articulation or hermeneutic construal is open to error or decay, and in many cases its name, or the nominal unity that describes it, functions merely as a convenient, arbitrary labeling service for this construal. When an event occurs, the obvious question is "what happened"? From this point of view, one takes the responsibility for making an interpretative stand, or for specifying what happened. Or, again, assuming that this event is that of my singular being, I take responsibility for projecting "who I am" and commit to becoming it. But since a projection can only become what it is by erasing (repressing) all of the aneconomic figures of unpredictability, chance, anomaly, irreconcilability, and conflict, in making a stand one converts the complex, undecidable, or singular event into a present "thing," and in so doing loses it due to the inevitable oversimplifications that sustain all ideologies.

On the other hand, nominalism, or these days "particularism," as Copjec puts it, involves the claim that "*there are only particular persons and things*, despite the fact that culture continually builds and unbuilds—while mistaking them for givens—series of arbitrary and alterable universals, whether these be nations, institutions, identities or moral laws. Universals are seen by nominalists simply as illusions to be deconstructed and dispersed."[90] From a purely nominalist or aneconomic point of view, then, what exists as the Real is the particular instance, which is considered a unique and unrepeatable event. In this case, we impose a certain repeatability and therefore "thing-quality," or durability, on such unique events by means of hermeneutic constructions, or, that is, by imposing nominal unities. Here, what has any kind of durability at all is no essence but the imposed nominal unity, whose repeatability is a matter of habit, convention, and pragmatism. Erase the nominal unity and no "thing" remains, only unique events. Facing an event, one is accordingly tempted to abdicate all responsibility for making a stand, on the grounds that nobody can ever legitimately say what happened, or who they are, since the abyss of metaphorical transfer separates interpreter and event. Any attempt to "make sense" of something (that is, convert an event into concepts that may be grasped) is not seen as interpretation at all but pure fictionalization. In other words, one does not ever really "read" (interpret) a situation; rather, one always "writes" (invents) it. In this refusal of recognition, however, the event is again lost, but this time to pure absence or nondefinition.

Instead of choosing between essentialism and nominalism, both of which are aporetic taken alone, Derrida and Lacan insist on the necessity of negotiating the contaminated and treacherous path of an antiessentialism that must therefore risk becoming a form of nominalism, a quasi-nominalism that does not fall prey to the excesses of pure nominalism. Or, vice versa, both tread the path of an anti-nominalism that risks becoming a quasi-essentialism. One may borrow from psychoanalytic theory one of the most accessible among very many figures offered for grasping this alternative: "trauma." I assume here that the term "trauma" denotes an event that both cannot and must be assimilated into the everyday economy of sense. Notably, "trauma" does not necessarily denote only "negative" events of pain and suffering. Love, joy, and unexpected success, for example, can be equally traumatic.

The figure of trauma offers a negotiated position between essentialism and nominalism in the following way. A traumatic event in principle so exceeds an individual's or group's framework of ordinary experience that it cannot be accommodated within this framework. The imperative, nevertheless, to accommodate this "unspeakable" event calls the wounded to the task of hermeneutic construal, of "speaking," or of gathering together a nominal unity, which aims to make sense of events, even if this means stretching one's experiential framework. Such necessary fabrication of sense is a matter of converting events into things in the world, thus bringing phenomena into being for the first time. This is the sense in which the nominal unity, and not the trauma "itself," is the thing in the world.[91] This implies, however, that the very revealing flash of *aletheia* is always already contaminated by its own undoing. In the moment of *aletheia*, the interpretation may be authenticated on the basis of experience, but it is simultaneously rendered inauthentic because there is always already a bit of Nietzschean fabrication in every appropriation of the event.

But this, in turn, represents only a quasi-nominalism, for something that cannot be assimilated remains after and beyond every possible construal. Since, in principle, the traumatic event exceeds the constituted world of the affected person or group and cannot therefore be fully assimilated, it remains as a surplus that challenges any nominal unity, repeating itself as a rent in the fabric of this world, which calls constantly for further hermeneutic work. Even after the operations of interpreting, speaking, or constituting have brought the event into being, it is this unspeakable "remaining behind" that keeps calling again and again for a repetition of the operation by which it is brought into being. In other words, even if all such construals were to be erased, one is not left with nothing. Rather, something persists in the event of which these are construals, yet it is impossible ever to define it precisely and it remains more or less resistant to different hermeneutic construals. The nominal unity, then, cannot replace the trauma, which remains independently of it as "something" that has happened, and it is this remaining that allows us to speak here of a quasi-essentialism.

The subversion of any radical suspicion concerning truth would be found in the Heideggerian insight that discourse does genuinely appropriate the event in some way. There is a measure (if not a positive measure of authenticating essence, then at least the negative measure of resistance) according to which some interpretations may be called more appropriate than others. The Real resists some appropriations more than others. For example, while one cannot say of the traumatic event marked by the nominal unity "9/11" precisely what it is, there is sufficient resistance in the event itself to ensure that I will make little headway if I construe it as a propaganda drive engineered by the Chinese government to showcase the insanity of in-fighting among Western religions in order to sell more copies of the *Tao Te Ching*. If one cannot make a case for truth as responsible appropriation, then one is simply lost in the funhouse of solipsistic inventive fantasy. But why invent (a text, for example) at all if it is intrinsically impossible to communicate across the abyss of metaphorical transfer? Nietzsche might answer that one writes not to convey meanings, ideas, notions, or opinions, but to stimulate thinking, but he also acknowledges that one must make room for a recognizing response, a public, for writing to be stimulating at all—and this brings one back to the inevitable necessity of a certain moment of *aletheia*.

Concluding Remarks: Freud

To return to the question of Freud, both Derrida and Lacan have found that his thinking is neither entirely economic in spirit nor entirely aneconomic. In fact, as I hope to show in subsequent chapters, Derrida, who, like Lacan, reads Freud with the greatest of care and attention, emphasizing the aporias that unsettle all of his "fundamental concepts," brings to light a thoroughgoing tension between radically aneconomic and conservatively economic motifs in his theoretical enterprise, neither of which can be explained away to arrive at the "true" Freud (who does not exist). Similarly, Lacan explicitly focuses on those enigmatic formulations in Freud's text that resist an economic reading and presses what is paradoxical, incoherent, and difficult, for the sake of constructing a revised psychoanalytic theory that saves it from recuperative domestication by "ego-psychology." Notably, Lacan does not presume to "return" to the "true" Freud either. In fact, his revision presupposes a deconstructive reading, even if it does not go by this particular nickname.

Such a reading shows that in Freud's writing every concept is divided between its economic articulation and the aneconomic moment that unsettles it. On top of this, these two moments are both irreconcilable and ineradicable, and Freud cannot do without either in his theorizing. However, since he does not have the heuristic of the "plural logic of the aporia" at his disposal, he tends to vacillate between them, leaving a legacy of inconsistencies, tensions, and contradictions. Derrida and Lacan, for example, both see Freud in his conservative moments resorting, first, to the naïve realism characterized by the notion of the re-found object, and second to the economics of *aletheia*, both of which submit his thinking to the metaphysics of presence. But in his radical moments, by contrast, he reinforces a critique of presence, since his notion of "trauma" belongs together with the notion of "event" or many other such nicknames, all of which aim to indicate the paradoxical fact that something repeats, not because it is there, but rather because it is ineffable. In this case, he insists that if we were honest enough in our "reality-testing," we would have to acknowledge an essentially incoherent world that we make coherent as an effect of the desire for security. It is left to Lacan, who "returns to Freud" with precisely this heuristic in hand, to take up all of Freud's "fundamental concepts" and subject them to a "spectral analysis" that takes the paradoxical complexity of an articulation between economic and aneconomic moments into account. But I am getting way ahead of myself, and it is to Freud that I now turn.

2

Freud and the Transcendental Relation

Introductory Remarks: Psychopathology and the Unconscious

> If we throw a crystal to the floor, it breaks; but not into haphazard pieces. It comes apart along its lines of cleavage into fragments whose boundaries, though they were invisible, were predetermined by the crystal's structure. Mental patients are split and broken structures of the same kind . . . and can reveal a number of things to us that would otherwise be inaccessible to us.[1]

In his daily practice, Freud saw an extraordinary contamination: fantasy mixed with reality, discrepancies, conflicts, excessive certainties and uncertainties, symptomatic gaps, slips, blindness, resistances, denials, self-deceptions, and so on, making it impossible to draw a distinct line between delusion and truth or, for that matter, between pathological and nonpathological states.[2] Unsurprisingly, he concludes that the certainty we feel concerning the autonomy, unity, and integrity of our own ego, or subjectivity, is deceptive.[3] Not only is the ego "continued inwards, without any sharp delimitation, into an unconscious mental entity which we designate as the id and for which it serves as a kind of façade," but it is subject to a further differentiation in the form of an internal superego to which we may attribute, among other things, delusions of observation that seem alien to the subject.[4] Further, concerning all unconscious mental activity (which extends beyond the id to parts of the ego's own activity—for example, unconscious repression—and parts of superego activity too), Freud notes, "we have the same relation to it as we have to a psychical process in another person, except that it is in fact our own."[5] I should immediately add that Freud's notion of the unconscious undergoes a complex series of rearticulations (moving from an early conception of it as a repository to a later conception of it as a matter of active processing), which I shall not detail here, suffice it to insist only that on its basis he contests the presupposition that we are endowed from the start with a unified cognitive faculty.[6]

Moreover, although we tend to assume a clear demarcation between ourselves and the outside world, he finds this boundary to be unstable, uncertain, or inaccurately drawn. In his words: "There are cases in which parts of a person's own body, even portions of his own mental life—his perceptions, thoughts, and feelings—appear alien to him and as not belonging to his ego; there are other cases in which he ascribes to the external world things that clearly originate in his own ego and that ought to be acknowledged by it."[7]

Freud's therapeutic experience leads him, like Nietzsche, to reject a philosophical tendency to presuppose in principle a fundamental coherence in intentional life. He projects from the start a phenomenal reality in which psychopathology, extending from extreme disorders to the minor neuroses of everyday life, remains ineradicable. He finds himself obliged, therefore, to ask the transcendental question concerning the a priori conditions that underpin the persistence, despite the best of human efforts, of errance and anomaly in the genesis of a phenomenal reality. Notably, however, he does not go so far as to deny the necessity and force of coherent experience. Rather, he insists on the theoretical obligation to account for not only the coherent world constituted through productive imagination or internal time, but also the persistence of its moments of errance or anomaly.

In his attempt to fulfill this obligation, he proposes a split in synthetic processing on the subjective side of the transcendental relation, but not, with Husserl, between a primary, passive genesis, neutral in affect and meaning, and a subsequent or secondary active meaning-giving genesis. Rather, with Heidegger, he takes the genesis of a phenomenal reality to be actively, albeit unconsciously, infused with meaning and affect from the start. The split he proposes, then, occurs between primary, primitive, archaic, atemporal, alogical, ahistorical, associative, hallucinatory, and therefore idiosyncratic or singular processing (beholden to the demands of the pleasure principle) and secondary, temporal, logical, successive, coherent, ordered, linguistic processing (guided by the reality principle). As Freud sees it, it is through secondary processing in intentional life that we indeed build up, much as Husserl suggests, a robust phenomenal reality (although it would no longer be a perfectly coherent system if we were honest in our reality testing).

In subjective development, secondary processing takes over from primary processing, subjects it to repressive measures, and tends to predominate in most adult subjects. But primary processing never falls into disuse. Instead, it operates unconsciously alongside secondary processing, often under the pressure of conflicting aims. This insistence on an ineradicable internal conflict counters what for Freud is an unwarranted prejudice in Husserlian phenomenology, which turns out to be less the privilege of pure consciousness over some notion of the unconscious as a "container of contents" than unjustified assumptions concerning the unity, neutrality, and rationality of our synthetic powers.[8]

Pleasure and the Drives

Freud, as noted above, sharply diverges from Husserl's view that we are originally perceivers and that "looking at" and later "reflecting upon" are privileged noetic modes that make of transcendental constitution a unified seeing-as, which is in principle neutral (or neutralizable) and shareable because it is rationally organized.[9] Noting that sensations are caused by both endogenous stimuli from internal organs and exogenous stimuli from the environment and that such stimuli are experienced by infants purely in terms of the pleasure-unpleasure series, Freud insists that pleasure (and, in a more complex articulation, sex and death) is not added to objects later but is the primary determinant of mental activity.[10] For us, the quest for a neutral sensory-perceptual grasp of the object inscribed in the question "what is it" is submitted to the primacy of erotic concern, motivated, Freud emphasizes, not first by a desire for truth, but by a drive for the kind of pleasure whose *telos* is, paradoxically, death.[11]

His introduction of the death drive in "Beyond the Pleasure Principle" allows him to posit two kinds of drives, which express the opposing tendencies between which life is suspended and to which he gives the names *Eros* and *Thanatos*.[12] These drives not only oppose each other, but each is internally aporetic. In the form of Eros (the preserver of life), self-preservative libido (which Freud calls "narcissistic") aims to "keep the peace," to isolate the organism in a self-protective enclosure that would maintain its simplicity, constancy, or equilibrium, whereas the outwardly directed sexual drives, the "disturbers of the peace," keep traumatizing this enclosure and breaking it open to the "other," or the "outside." As he puts it: "Eros, by bringing about a more and more far-reaching combination of the particles into which living substance is dispersed, aims at complicating life and at the same time, of course, preserving it," whereas Thanatos (the death drive), is less conspicuous and harder to point to: "in the end we came to recognize sadism as its representative. Its task is to lead organic life back into the inanimate state."[13] The death drive, in short, involves both an inertial resistance to a change of state, which serves self-preservation, but also an entropic moment of destructiveness or dissolution, which lies at the basis of aggressivity.

Freud insists that Eros and Thanatos form an alloy. First, both are characterized by the conservative aim to restore "a state of things that was disturbed by the emergence of life."[14] The sexual drives aim for a boundary-shattering excitement that, in fact, increases tension in the organism. But they do this for the sake of jouissance or ultimate satisfaction, and it is not for nothing that orgasm is dubbed, paradoxically, "little death." Moreover, he acknowledges not only an intrinsic aggressivity or sadistic element in Eros but also a vacillation in Thanatos, which can either direct its destructive tendency toward the outside (in a gesture that looks a lot like self-preservation) or inward, causing the individual to become self-destructive. Given his admission that "the distinction between the two classes of instincts does not seem sufficiently assured,"[15] one might suggest, with Lacan, that all drives are death drives.[16] Perhaps it is as well to remind oneself here that Freud is grappling with two thoroughly paradoxical notions, without the help of the plural logic of the aporia that both Derrida and Lacan will subsequently make so much of. Ironically, in complexifying central notions, this logic also clarifies much in psychoanalytic theory.

The Precipitation of Subjective Agency (Id, Ego, and Superego)

For Freud, then, newborn infants enter the world as a "fragmentary and fragmenting" play of erotic and thanatic drives.[17] From much of what he writes, one may justly assume that he views the ego (accepting with Husserl that it is a unity formally characterized by internal time) not as apodictically pregiven but as a developmental precipitate that is, moreover, only part of a conflictually articulated subjectivity.[18] Briefly outlined, he argues that subjective agency develops in our efforts to master the drives, first in the form of the "id," which later diversifies not only under pragmatic pressures stemming from the external world but primarily due to the threat of castration, which precipitates the development of an "ideal ego."[19] The ideal ego represents the individual's narcissistic love of itself as a unified whole "distinct from" but not separate from its discrete experiences. Freud names such incipient self-love "infantile" or "primary" narcissism and associates it with a childhood megalomania in which the actual ego and the ideal ego are unrealistically experienced as coinciding. Healthy individuals, he argues, undergo a further psychical diversification as a result of life's hard knocks, which detaches the ideal ego from the ego. In this case, the ideal ego becomes a model not of what the ego actually is, but of what it ought to be (a superego or projected ideal unity).

I should note immediately that this broad framework is beset with interpretative difficulties, including the head-spinning discrepancy concerning Freud's notion of the ego as a whole, tied to his concept of ego-libido. He infers from certain disorders (such as sexual fixations on different parts of the body) that libido is grafted onto all bodily organs.[20] The trouble, however, is that he does not call this overall libidinal energy "organism-libido" or some such term, but "ego-libido." This implies that there always was "ego" to go with "libido." As if to confirm this position, he describes ego-libido as "narcissistic." The conjunction of "ego-libido" and narcissism implies, contrary to the developmental account just outlined, that there is an originary ego or egoism, and that the term "primary narcissism" should be associated not with the formation of an ideal ego but with a primordial, "oceanic" state of wholeness, thought of as an encompassing "Allness" (All is me and I am All), in relation to which the ego as a precipitated unity is merely a shrunken residue. The formation of an ideal ego, then, becomes a secondary or nostalgic narcissism. In confirmation of this, one may cite the Freud of *Civilization and Its Discontents*, where he refers to an original "oceanic state," described as an erotic, inclusive sense of "Allness," which he again names "ego." But, as Strachey points out, in Freud's *New Introductory Lectures*, a parenthetical reference suggests that he identifies "id" rather than "ego" in its undifferentiated primitive state with "the whole person."[21]

The discrepancy amounts to proposing on the one hand that we enter the world in a fragmentary state, from out of which a unity called "ego" is later gathered, and on the other hand that we enter the world in a state of oceanic wholeness, which is later reduced to fragments, namely id, ego, and superego. The same discrepancy appears when Freud tries to locate the libido. According to Strachey, once he had developed the notion of "id," he insisted that the id was "the great reservoir of libido" from out of which ego develops.[22] But he subsequently appears to contradict this view by locating the libido in the ego, which supports the contention that the ego is original.[23]

Perhaps such vacillation between describing the wholeness of the ego as a developmental precipitate (an achievable unity) or an encompassing Allness that is lost is an effect of his attempt to do the impossible, that is, to take account of different conceptions of the whole within the bounds of an either/or logic that mandates a choice between them. However, in both cases the conception of the whole is impossible (because it involves an aporia), and it is philosophically more viable to "begin" with the paradox of their articulation, as Lacan does, using the figure of the "lamella."[24] However, once the claim is made for the paradoxical status of the origin, all of Freud's central notions become shifty. Granting that Lacan's radical revisions, which exploit such discrepancies, are called for, I shall nevertheless defer further discussion of them and follow a more traditional line of interpretation here, which chooses the first, more predominant account of the ego as a developmental precipitate.

The Development of Synthetic Processing

According to a traditionally favored reading of Freud's genetic account of the transcendental relation, from out of a fragmenting play of partial drives, infants strive "to create a pure pleasure-ego," which entails both repeating pleasures and expelling pains.[25] In infancy, all subjective sensations are simply judged in terms of the pleasure-unpleasure series and are either accepted by the infant psyche as satisfying and "good" or rejected. For Freud, primordial infant judgment begins with oral satisfactions:

> Expressed in the language of the oldest—the oral—instinctual impulses, the judgment is: "I should like to eat this," or "I should like to spit it out"; and, put more generally: "I should like to take this into myself and to keep that out." . . . The original pleasure-ego wants to introject into itself everything that is good and to eject from itself everything that is bad. What is bad, what is alien to the ego and what is external are, to begin with, identical.[26]

Somatic needs provide an inextinguishable (or only temporarily and intermittently extinguishable) source of tension (for example, hunger), which increases in severity to the extent that the needs go unsatisfied. Self-preservative somatic instincts aim to extinguish (or discharge) such painful tension, or, that is, they aim for a state of complete satisfaction. Such somatic satisfactions are, however, dependent on sources external to the individual. In infancy, they are bound up with an infant's first relation to another person, the primary caregiver or *Nebenmensch*.[27] Because of this, immediate protective discharge of tension (satisfaction) using internal resources alone ("abreaction" or reflex action, such as screaming) is ineffective.[28] This dependence on external sources of satisfaction and the intrinsic inadequacy or unreliability of the source acts as a trigger for cognitive development.

Importantly, Freud adds that sexual life operates alongside somatic instincts from the beginning. In his words, "sexual activity attaches itself to functions serving the purpose of self-preservation and does not become independent of them until later."[29] Indeed, he notes: "Sucking at the mother's breast is the starting point of the whole sexual life, the unmatched prototype of every later sexual satisfaction."[30] During suckling, oral stimulation accompanies the somatic satisfaction and engenders a residual wish to repeat the pleasure, even when hunger is not urgent. This residual wish for pleasure describes the libidinal component that is grafted on to the somatic function, but libido can become independent, in the form of autoerotic gratification or self-stimulation (for example, thumb sucking). The impulse for libidinal gratification associated with the oral zone forms one component of the sex drive, which appears long before the infant is capable of constituting the discernible, robust objects that are subsequently attached to it.[31]

Certain experiences soon enough demonstrate the inadequacy of an infant's primitive mode of judgment and the importance of knowing whether a source of satisfaction actually exists in the external world as something one may get hold of if necessary. The weaning process (or its equivalent) is the first of these. Cognition is not associated with the intermittent appearance and withdrawal of the breast before weaning. There is a sense of immediacy here, whereby an infant simply registers a level of uncomfortable tension and responds with automatic distress signals, which disappear upon the necessary satisfaction.

Weaning acts as the trigger for psychical development whereby both somatic instincts and sexual drives diversify. In both cases, however, the process of diversification is complex and troubled. In relation to the somatic drives (which are tied to what Lacan calls the "return of need"), the weaning process forces infants into cognitive processing whereby they gradually learn to distinguish clearly between subjective and nonsubjective. In other words, genesis of a relatively robust objective world is initiated by a first precipitous trauma caused by the infant's emerging awareness of something amiss in what was, from the infant's point of view, the closed circuit of need and satisfaction in its seamless interconnection with the *Nebenmensch*. As a consequence of the weaning process or its equivalents, for Freud, the child becomes aware that the *Nebenmensch*, the single source of all possible satisfaction, also seems to instigate its perpetual loss in, for example, her always uncomfortably too abrupt withdrawal of the nourishing breast. According to Freud, this realization generates extreme anxiety: "You will realize how real a situation of danger is indicated by this anxiety. If a mother is absent or has withdrawn her love from her child, it is no longer sure of the satisfaction of its needs and is perhaps exposed to the most distressing feelings of tension."[32]

Simultaneously, weaning is associated with a traumatic experience of lost libidinal satisfaction and, because of the drive to reconstitute a pleasure-ego, a strong demand for its restitution, through what Freud calls a "secondary function" whereby the satisfaction must be "produced" by specific (or intentional) action of some kind. Screaming itself as a primary function will not satisfy hunger, but, developed as a specific action, it might generate the appropriate response in the *Nebenmensch*. Further, the infant soon experiences the difference between the autoerotic oral satisfaction that can be produced at will and the satisfying breast that is withdrawn periodically and only reappears (unreliably) in response to specific actions.[33] Subjective agency develops as the seat of increasingly sophisticated "specific action," which nevertheless serves the same fundamental purpose, namely, "to create a pure pleasure-ego."

Before I elaborate on Freud's complex account of the cognitive processing and subjective diversification necessary for specific action, it should be noted that the drives simultaneously undergo an equally complex diversification. Through experiences of intermittent satisfactions and frustrations, infants soon enough discover that the pleasure requirement is not easily met. As Freud puts it: "The boundaries of this primitive pleasure-ego cannot escape rectification through experience."[34] Suckling never was a pure pleasure, and during the weaning process, it becomes increasingly frustrating and anxiety provoking, as incomprehensible prohibitions engender in the infant aggressive hatreds and fears, directed toward the withdrawing breast, which now compete with the earlier libidinal loves and pleasures. Eventually unable to tolerate the extreme tension associated with breast feeding, the infant represses the breast as a sexual object. In other words, the infant psyche withdraws libidinal cathexis from the breast, shifts its sexual interest to other bodily zones, and prohibits a libidinal return to the breast, thus beginning a lengthy process of libidinal diversification.

The agent responsible for this "primary repression" is the newly emerging ego. From the point of view of this emerging ego, the danger associated with the libidinal urge is precisely its close association with the now abandoned source of somatic satisfaction and its tendency, therefore, to resurrect heavily charged hostile associations that would instigate a fresh release of dangerous unpleasure. While the repression itself generates unpleasure associated with libidinal frustration, the prohibition of discharge prevails as a "primary defense" against an urge that has become unbearably ambivalent. The necessary repression of the suckling impulse at what Freud calls the "oral" stage of psychosexual development leaves a trace, an unconscious "fixation" or charge of ambivalent energy around oral activity, which never leaves us. In other words, such "primary repression" constitutes the unconscious as a residual desire for pleasure, which persistently presses for the interdicted release. Subject to constant repressive pressure, however, it is detached from the breast and deflected onto substitute satisfactions (thumb sucking, kissing, smoking, etc.).

Emphasizing the force of weaning as a trigger for cognitive development and the concomitant emergence and strengthening of the ego function, Freud suggests that the most passively accepted source of somatic and libidinal satisfaction is lost through weaning "just at the time, perhaps, when the child is able to form a total idea of the person to whom the organ that is giving him satisfaction belongs."[35] In other words, the traumatic loss that occurs when the infant becomes aware of a rupture in the closed circuit of the mother-child dyad is simultaneous with (and necessary for) its power to constitute the mother as an other (an object) and, accordingly, itself as an active power or agent. Notably, the anal phase that succeeds the oral as the dominant center of constellation for the drives characterizes a far more self-centered, self-sufficient, and active infant.

The obvious motivation for learning to distinguish between endogenous and exogenous stimuli (that is, for constituting the transcendental relation) is self-preservation, for without this distinction it would be impossible to procure satisfactions from the external world independently. Such independence requires the power to convert drives into representations of objects (desires) that promise the appropriate satisfaction. This, in turn, requires a sophisticated synthesizing or processing system, which can bring memory traces together in order to constitute memory "images" (sensory images) of satisfying objects and project a course of specific action to obtain them. Moreover, the infant psyche must learn how to negotiate the unavoidable dissonance between inner and outer experience. As Wollheim notes, "many drives go unsatisfied by the world, and the world is not as man's drives would have it be."[36] It must therefore learn to assess these projections and the proposed course of action in terms of "reality-value" (and, later, ethical or social acceptability).

Freud explains the advance from the simple judgment of good or bad to the judgment of existence as follows: "All presentations," he argues, all mental images or intentional objects, "originate from perceptions and are repetitions of them." Freud here assumes that in the immediate encounter with a thing, the very existence of a presentation is the guarantee of the reality of what is presented. In other words, the presentation has as its immediate correlative something really existing in the world.[37] Further, the psyche has the capacity for memory, understood as retention. Freud speculated that strong enough sensations flowing in from both endogenous and exogenous sources must be impressed upon the *mnemic* system as an accumulation of discrete fragments or traces that are retained as acquisitions.

In addition, because the psyche has the capacity for memory, we can, as he puts it, "bring before the mind once more something that has once been perceived, by reproducing it as a presentation without the external object having still to be there." Freud envisages the mechanism of such intentional projection as a matter of articulating discrete memory traces. In the process, we develop a highly complex network of neural connections that are initially elastic enough to be modified by additional experience or educated by a repetition that batters them into shape and reinforces them.

Reinforced linkages are called "facilitated" because once forged through habituation, they remain as permanent modifications of the system and so allow for easier processing and discharge in similar situations. However, such links, while relatively stable if they have become habitual, are never carved in stone. Notably, Lacan has criticized the translation of *Bahnung* as "facilitation" because the term does not evoke the important sense of "articulation" or joining.[38] Taking his point, one should bear in mind that for Freud the overall task of the processing system is projective synthesis (conjoining discrete memory fragments or traces to form a mental presentation). Synthesis moves from "wishes" to projected mental representatives of the objects wished for and representations of the bodily movements necessary to seize them. However, projections are not always (or even often) faithful repetitions of past experiences but might be modified by omissions or distortions or newly generated by connecting memory fragments associatively to put together a fabricated object. Such projections may or may not meet the ultimate test of perceptual reality, in which they are confirmed or disconfirmed by experience. At this point, comparison with Husserl's theory of intentionality certainly suggests itself.

Freud, however, argues that humans are endowed with a potentially dangerous split between a primary process that is infantile and archaic in evolutionary terms and a secondary process that develops later in the path of individual maturation and is, moreover, a more recently evolved faculty. Importantly, for Freud both primary and secondary systems have their own characteristic modes of operation and remain irreducible to one another. The secondary system is not based on the primary system. Rather, it has the task of modification and control in relation to the primary system, which remains in operation alongside the newer mode and interferes with it constantly. It is in this persistent conflict between systems that Freud detects one of the weaknesses that makes our mental life so vulnerable and so accounts for the precarious state of phenomenal reality.[39]

The "Id" and Primary Processing

The "id," mandated by the drives to secure their discharge at all costs, is the synthesizing agent responsible for primary processing, which predominates in infancy where the drives hold sway. Primary processing, however, can reemerge in adults, where the "imperious" sexual or aggressive drives, which do not accept frustration gracefully, are "dammed up" by interdiction of their direct expression or by external obstacles.[40] These persist as powerful wishes that heighten psychical tension and press for discharge. Endeavoring to secure their discharge immediately, the id makes use of the multiple connectivity of every trace in the "overconnected" network of the *mnemic* system in two main ways.

First, as Freud argues, while neurons tend toward habitual paths of discharge, each is nevertheless capable of multiple side connections, allowing impulses to be discharged in disguised or deflected form. Even though memory traces are permanent, the use to which the processing system puts them is entirely flexible and revisable. On the one hand, therefore, primary processing fends off excessive libidinal tensions by allowing the system to find alternative paths for their immediate discharge if habitual patterns for some reason fail (practical obstacles, overload, ethical interdiction, etc.).[41] This accounts for the notable plasticity of sexual impulses, or the sexualization of a diverse array of things.

On the other hand, primary processing represents, paradoxically, a potentially lethal "safety mechanism," for if suitable outlets cannot be forged for high libidinal tensions, the id brings the uncomfortable tensions to expression in hallucinations: that is, in projected images synthesized from sensory traces associated with high satisfaction and invested with the strength and vivacity of present perceptions. As Wollheim puts it: "When the individual wishes . . . sufficiently strongly, he typically cannot distinguish between the representation he makes to himself of the object of his wish and that object itself."[42] Discharge occurs (and, depending on the external circumstances, some degree of satisfaction will be achieved). But satisfaction from hallucinations, while immediate, is usually ultimately inadequate and can be dangerously pathological (particularly in adults).

According to Freud, then, pathology is often explicable as a regression to primary processing, which operates entirely under the sway of the pleasure principle and without concern, therefore, for pragmatic judgments of reality, efficacy, and safety. As Freud puts it: "In this connection it is easy to observe a certain indifference as to the path along which the discharge takes place, so long as it takes place somehow."[43] The id is also indifferent to ethical judgments or, for that matter, logical judgments of consistency or contradiction.[44] But primary processing also manifests in everyday phenomena such as dreams, slips, and physical symptoms.[45] In fact, Freud argues that the most reliable evidence for its (notably prelinguistic)[46] *modus operandi* comes from the study of dreams. In his words: "We there discovered that the processes in the unconscious systems were fundamentally different from those in the preconscious (or conscious) systems. In the unconscious, cathexes can easily be completely transferred, displaced, and condensed."[47] Further, Freud claims that "in the id there is an exception to the philosophical theorem that space and time are necessary forms of our mental acts."[48] As he explains:

> There is nothing in the id that corresponds to the idea of time; there is no recognition of the passage of time, and . . . no alteration in its mental processes is produced by the passage of time. Wishful impulses which have never passed beyond the id, but impressions, too, which have been sunk into the id by repression, are virtually immortal; after the passage of decades they behave as though they had just occurred.[49]

By contrast—and this introduces Freud's notion of the ego-function and secondary processing—Freud argues in another text that "our abstract idea of time seems to be wholly derived from the method of working of the system *Pcpt-Cs.*, and to correspond to a perception on its own part of that method of working."[50]

The "Ego" and Secondary Processing

To safeguard itself, the psychic apparatus must take on a more complex mode of operation, which projects not merely the sensory experience of the satisfying object but also the ordered connection of actions and circumstances that must be repeated to secure it. It is the task of the newly emerging ego, then, to intersperse between drive and action the delay of practical "thinking" or "reality testing," which is still motivated by the aim of gaining satisfaction but requires a postponement of pleasure for the sake of a more robust sense of the external world.

Naming the ego "that portion of the id which was modified by the proximity and influence of the external world, which is adapted for the reception of stimuli and as a protective shield against stimuli,"[51] Freud argues that it has a dual purpose. Facing inward, it "develops from perceiving the instincts to controlling them," by inhibiting the strong flows of libidinal energy that precipitate hallucinations—fortunately—for the id cannot foresee the dangers of its blind efforts to satisfy the drives.[52] As Freud notes:

> The ego must on the whole carry out the id's intentions, it fulfils its task by finding out the circumstances in which those intentions can best be achieved. The ego's relation to the id might be compared with that of a rider to his horse. The horse supplies the locomotive energy, while the rider has the privilege of deciding on the goal and of guiding the powerful animal's movement. But only too often there arises between the ego and the id the not precisely ideal situation of the rider being obliged to guide the horse along the path by which it itself wants to go.[53]

To address this task, the ego, facing outward, must construct an accurate "picture" of the external world, against which, in a process he calls "reality testing," it can pass judgment on projected psychical presentations, distinguishing between representations derived from reality and the representatives of the drives.[54] In contrast to the id's indifference with regard to objects, then, the ego is characteristically "more particular about the choice of both an object and of a path of discharge."[55] The ego, as Freud puts it, must be capable of allotting to the object of the drive (the projected desire that stands as a psychical representative of the drive) its "proper place in a considerable assemblage, by its being taken up into a coherent context."[56] Implicitly, then, the hallucinatory primary process, driven by the pleasure principle, disturbs our sense of reality only if the ego is not strong enough to control it.

Importantly, "reality testing," for Freud, is seemingly based on a clear distinction between what is "unreal" (a merely subjective presentation whose source is internal) and what is "real," which is "also there *outside*."[57] Freud describes it as a form of judgment in which it is a matter of discovering "whether something which is in the ego as a presentation can be re-discovered in perception (reality) as well." In other words, as he notes, "it is evident that a precondition for the setting up of reality testing is that objects shall have been lost which once brought real satisfaction." Again: "The first and immediate aim, therefore, of reality-testing is, not to *find* an object in real perception which corresponds to the one presented, but to *refind* such an object, to convince oneself that it is still there."[58]

In contrast with the primary process, which works by atemporal free association, the secondary process, for Freud, works according to modes of ordered causality (that is, according to the unified temporality that Husserl envisaged) and the rational association of ideas. Linking time and thought, Freud characterizes the ego, in contrast to the id, in terms of an intrinsic tendency toward unity.[59] However, primary processing does not disappear upon the development of secondary processing and, as Wollheim notes, there are areas of life over which the writ of the reality principle never runs.[60] In short, Freud acknowledges that rational association is but one type in a much broader range of associative "logics" (visual puns, homophonies, morphological similarities, etc.), all of which have a sense, albeit not the sense of logical connections. Admittedly, there is plenty of evidence that Freud privileges the rational association of the secondary process, notably in the claim that in healthy adults the reality principle dethrones the pleasure principle.[61]

However, the ego is not entirely identifiable with a neutral transcendental synthesis. In addition to its function of consciously directing attention to external and internal stimuli in reality testing, it also has an unconscious function, namely to resist (ignore, suppress, filter, divert, interdict) the conscious expression of repressed materials. One might suggest that the ego as a conscious psychical function or synthetic operator gradually develops its power under pragmatic pressures, whereas its unconscious function, including an emergent self-awareness (or its sense of itself as a whole) develops in relation to its libidinal attachments, and it is this unconscious function, as Lacan argues, that pulls the carpet from under the feet of what has so far appeared to conform to a naïve realism.

Lacan, indeed, will eventually subject Freud's entire analysis of "reality" to revision, for Freud has already, perhaps without explicitly acknowledging it, offered the means to see something beyond the claim that primary processing tends to trip the subject up by interfering with the coherence supposedly offered by honest reality testing. Based on an alternative understanding of reality as essentially in flux, Lacan shows that the pleasure principle tends toward hallucinating a stabilizing fiction. Honest reality testing of such fictions would not yield absolute repeatability but at best "iterability," which means in consequence that an absolutely secure reality is re-found only at the cost of repressive measures. This account, incidentally, promises to explain why an otherwise thorough and perspicacious thinker like Husserl "tends systematically to repress" what is radically subversive in his thinking, allowing himself the comfort of self-deception, rather than exposing his security-desiring self to the anxiety of open and honest confrontation with the implications of his own thinking.[62]

The Question of Language

Concerning the problem of the microarticulation between word and thought, Freud argues that our capacity to have and use ideas, to make sense, or to think about something is an essentially complex phenomenon consisting in the articulation of two combinations of auditory, visual, kinaesthetic, and other *mnemic* residues to form mental presentations, one of which, based on primary processing, is open ended (the thing-presentation), while the other, based on secondary processing, is closed and rational (the word-presentation).[63] According to Wollheim,

> Freud now asserted, first, that thing-presentations cannot become conscious until they have become linked with residues from perceptions of words, and, secondly, that the word presentations belong to the pre-conscious, not to the unconscious—indeed they are one of the prime agents in giving that stability and cohesiveness to our mental life which characteristically differentiates the secondary from the primary process.[64]

In other words, reflecting the Nietzschean movement of metaphorical transfer between spheres, for Freud, a thing-presentation first becomes preconscious through becoming connected with the word-presentations corresponding to it.[65] Recalling that consciousness, for Freud, is a form of perception, he adds that "once the links have been formed, the idea will thereby have attracted to itself sufficient sensory quality to become the object of an internal perception." Thus, it is through the "translating" interposition of word-presentations that "internal thought processes are made into perceptions."[66]

Like Nietzsche, then, Freud challenges Husserl's requirement that language remain essentially uninvolved in conscious thinking, which relegates it to the secondary role of communication and preservation. One can see in this association between "thing presentations" (signifieds) and "word presentations" (signifiers) the precursor to Saussure's insistence that "ready-made ideas" do not exist in consciousness before words and that language, therefore, is merely a self-contained system of material marks that represents or doubles a purely cognitively constituted phenomenal world.[67] Saussure grants that at whatever level it operates, signification is always the association of two terms, namely the indicative or signifying term, the signifier (the mark, sound, signal, symbol, or word) and the indicated or signified term (the thing, referent, concept, idea, meaning, sense). However, on his account of the signifying process, he insists upon the inescapable unity of signifier and signified in the sign. There is never a sign in the absence of this unity. In his words: "I call the combination of a concept [signified] and a sound-image [signifier] a *sign*, but in current usage the term generally designates only a sound-image, a word, for example (*arbor*, etc.). One tends to forget that *arbor* is called a sign only because it carries the concept 'tree,' with the result that the idea of the sensory part [the signifier] implies the idea of the whole."[68]

Accordingly, this association of terms cannot simply be a matter of supplying a material marker for a preexisting meaning. Rather, the meaning is constituted in the act of association. Based on further Saussurean insights, however, both Derrida and Lacan challenge in turn Freud's conception of language. There is nevertheless something radically innovative in his insistence that language is not a subsequently appropriated, ideally transparent, and univocal vehicle for the mere transmission of thought, but that it is implicated directly and originally in mental processing.

Libidinal Vicissitudes

As experience fills the mnemic system with traces and the ego's power for secondary processing slowly gains the upper hand over the primary processing in the id, the drives simultaneously undergo a process of differentiation. Libido remains dominated by the id in the anal and phallic phases that follow the oral, and, under the influence of the unmodified pleasure principle, infants form new erotic attachments and autoerotic satisfactions, which again, due to necessary repression, leave residual "fixation" points. Here, then, the play of partial drives produce in an infant, as Copjec puts it, "a dispersed body and polymorphous and perverse pleasures."[69] Constituted in terms of autoerotic attachments to parts of the infant's own body—mouth, anus, genitals, and other openings onto the external world through which the drives circulate—the ego's sense of itself as a whole is not robust.[70]

In an erotic attachment Freud names the Oedipus complex, the first person to become a love object is the *Nebenmensch* (the primary caregiver and protector, who is predominantly the mother).[71] This first love-relation, however, is doomed to dissolution, but not primarily because of the immoderate character of infantile demands for nourishment and love, the impossibility of fulfilling childish sexual wishes, and the ambivalence of a child's attachment to the parents. All this, Freud argues, is insufficient to dissolve the Oedipus complex, and what does the trick in the end is the castration complex: the castration threat in boys and its equivalent in girls, namely that "girls hold their mother responsible for their lack of a penis and do not forgive her for their being thus put at a disadvantage."[72]

According to Freud, the threat need not be explicit. Rather, it is an experienced fear of castration, equivalent to a feared loss of love, "which is evidently a later prolongation of the infant's anxiety if it finds its mother absent."[73] Under the pressure of this threat, a child is forced to abandon its Oedipus complex, so renouncing the intense libidinal investment (or object cathexis) it has placed in its parents.[74] The castration threat, then, constitutes the first great parental betrayal, and it initiates the lengthy "metamorphosis of the parental relationship into the superego."[75] Two dramatic, correlative changes occur: first, an ideal ego is formed through identification and second, the ideal is libidinally cathected through sublimation, whose consequence is narcissism.

On the basis of the argument that "if one has lost an object or has been obliged to give it up, one often compensates oneself by identifying oneself with it and by setting it up once more in one's ego," Freud claims that when the *Nebenmensch* withdraws as a love-object and becomes a threatening figure, the ego, in a self-protective and compensatory gesture, identifies itself with the lost love and forms itself on the model of the lost *Nebenmensch*.[76] He defines "identification" as "the assimilation of one ego to another one, as a result of which the first ego behaves like the second in certain respects, imitates it and in a sense takes it up into itself."[77] In contrast to object choice, then, which retains some distance between ego and the object it would like to have, identification imitates or assimilates the object that the ego wants to be like and, for this reason, alters the ego.[78]

Thus altered, the ego presents itself to the id in a *bid* (notably, for success is not guaranteed) to get the id to love the simulacrum (the ideal ego) in place of the *Nebenmensch*. Importantly, Freud notes that the construction of an ideal ego should not be "confused with the sublimation of an instinct."[79] In his understanding, such "sublimation" would be the equivalent of some success in the ego's bid. Success here means that the child's libido is detached from the dispersed body parts that serve as attachment points to the *Nebenmensch*, and the quota of libido released thereby is internalized and concentrated upon the newly formed ideal ego. The consequence of this libidinal displacement is the condition of "narcissism," which involves a sense of the ego as a whole, or self-awareness. Notably, "narcissism" denotes not love for the ego as an object, but as a whole, which Freud tends to think of as a unity neither separate from, nor identical to, the sum total of my experiences. Further, Freud argues, "we are bound to suppose that a unity comparable to the ego cannot exist in the individual from the start; the ego has to be developed. The auto-erotic instincts, however, are there from the very first; so there must be something added to auto-erotism—a new psychical action—in order to bring about narcissism."[80]

He does not name this new psychical action here, but, given that narcissism is described as the consequence of the internalization of the quota of libido released from object-cathexes and concentrated on the ego, it evidently enough refers to "sublimation." This is confirmed later in the text, where sublimation is described as the transformation of sexual object-libido into narcissistic libido.[81] Further, he argues that childhood megalomania points the way to an account of this action of sublimation, for such megalomania comes into being at the expense of object-libido.[82] Since excess libidinal energy, liberated by its withdrawal from the external object (by the frustration or prohibition of sexual interest in the mother), must go somewhere, it is redirected back into the ego-libido and initially stored up in the ego.[83] Freud refers to such sublimated libido as "desexualized."[84]

Henceforth, the ego never relinquishes control over the deflected, "desexualized" quota of libido. To this extent, for the rest of its life, the ego becomes the "great reservoir from which libidinal cathexes are sent out to objects and into which they are once more withdrawn, just as an amoeba behaves with its pseudopodia." To tie this development back to the earlier discussion of secondary processing, Freud notes:

> If this displaceable energy is desexualized libido, it may also be described as *sublimated* energy; for it would still retain the main purpose of Eros—that of uniting and binding—in so far as it helps towards establishing the unity, or tendency to unity, which is particularly characteristic of the ego. If thought-processes in the wider sense are to be included among these displacements, then the activity of thinking is also supplied from the sublimation of erotic motive forces.[85]

Having taken up the deflected libido, the now self-aware ego initially invests all of it in self-love (megalomania). Narcissistic libido is at first entirely invested in a magnificent, all-powerful, superhuman, ideal ego modeled on the parents, which a child identifies with its actual ego. But the gesture soon becomes ambivalent because the child experiences "real-world" limitations, whereas the ideal ego remains fixed in the unconscious, and a gap gradually opens up between the ideal ego and the ego.[86] First, as Freud notes, when the child renounces its Oedipus complex and forms the ideal ego, the parental figures are "quite magnificent," but they subsequently lose much of this initial grandeur. The ego certainly also identifies with these diminished parental figures, but, he argues, these later identifications only affect the ego and not the ideal ego, "which has been determined by the earliest parental imagos."[87] Moreover, the child also experiences its own actual limitations, which, again, affect the ego but not the ideal ego.

However, as Freud notes, humans are incapable of giving up a libidinal satisfaction once enjoyed. We prove to be unwilling to give up on the "narcissistic perfection" of childhood. Thus, as adults, "disturbed by the admonitions of others" and our own emerging power of self-criticism, to the point that we can "no longer retain that perfection," we seek to "recover it in the new form of an ego ideal." Thus we now project a substitute ideal for the lost narcissism (wholeness, perfection) of childhood, in which each was her/his own ideal.[88] Experience, then, is the source of the further development whereby the ego diversifies, forming within itself "the new form of an ego ideal," namely an idealized super-ego. Freud sums up and condenses the lineaments of this new development in a later passage: "The development of the ego consists in a departure from primary narcissism and gives rise to a vigorous attempt to recover that state. This departure is brought about by means of the displacement of libido on to an ego ideal imposed from without; and satisfaction is brought about from fulfilling this ideal."[89]

To elaborate: The ideal ego is now raised above the actual ego to form a "superego," and reflects not what I imagine I am but what I believe I should be. In this sense, "the new form of an ego ideal," the superego, is imposed from without. Further, Freud argues that the superego operates as the vehicle of cultural reproduction over the generations, for "a child's super-ego is in fact constructed on the model not of its parents but of its parents' super-ego."[90] Notably, then, cultural reproduction, for Freud, is not a secondary acquisition but is inscribed in the psyche as part of its constitution. In his words: "Mankind never lives entirely in the present.

The past, the tradition of the race and of the people, lives on in the ideologies of the super-ego, and yields only slowly to the influences of the present and to new changes; and so long as it [the past] operates through the super-ego it plays a powerful part in human life, independently of economic conditions."[91]

A libidinal shift occurs when the narcissism of childhood megalomania, which loves the actual ego as identical to the ideal ego, is displaced onto this new form of the ideal ego, which makes of it an acknowledged ideal to be sought after.[92] (I prefer the term superego for this new form, simply because it avoids the incessant irritation of dyslexic confusion with the ideal ego and the ego-ideal.) Narcissistic or internally directed libido, then, shifts from megalomania (I love what I am, what I was) to hero worship (I love what I'd like to be).[93] Love of this superego goes hand in hand with negative criticism directed toward the ego.[94] Such criticism is negative, rather than a matter of realistic self-appraisal, because the superego represents an idealization the ego can never match.[95] According to Freud, the ego strives to recover its state of primary narcissism, where ego and ideal ego are matched, and satisfaction (self-esteem) derives in part from its degree of success in this direction.

As a child's critical faculty matures, this overvaluation of the ego that underpins both megalomania and self-criticism is, in the best of all possible worlds, gradually rectified. Some form of compromise between the two, in realistic self-appraisal, may be attributed to the dampening-down effect of an increased capacity for reality testing. However, Freud finds the primary mitigating force in the resurgence of sexual libido at puberty. Hitherto predominantly dispersed over partial drives and autoerotic satisfactions, the sex drive, under the pressure of a new aim, reproduction, gathers together under a dominant genital organization and directs itself "altruistically" toward a potential life partner.[96] Accordingly, besides the narcissistic choice of love-object, marking internally directed libido, or ego-libido, an "anaclitic" choice reemerges, marking externally directed libido or object-libido. Notably, as Bruce Fink points out, these remarks have inspired generations of analysts to assume that successfully reaching the genital stage represents a departure from the narcissism and selfishness of oral and anal relations in the name of a harmonious state "in which one takes one's sexual partner as a subject, not an object, as a Kantian end-in-himself or herself, not as a means to an end." By contrast with autoerotic satisfactions, it is in genital relations, which supposedly reflect a harmony between the sexes, that one becomes "truly altruistic, that is, capable of doing things for another person without any thought of the advantages it may bring to oneself."[97]

To return to Freud, ego-libido and object-libido are interchangeable by inverse proportion: it is necessary to withdraw libidinal energy from the one to give more to the other.[98] The choice for one or the other is differently motivated. Ego-libido provides independent satisfaction (via sublimation) that is reliable but rarely sufficient. Its extreme, in almost total internalization of libido, marks a reversion to infantile narcissism and megalomania that shows up in certain disorders.[99] Object-libido provides high satisfaction, but since it is derived from an external source, it is unreliable.

With the reemergence of object-libido at puberty, Freud can now argue that the ego as self-aware remains at a reflective distance from the superego and can take on the role of distributing libido in inverse proportion between narcissistic edification and the outward path of the sex drive. Sublimation becomes a matter of removing libido from these newfound sexual objects and turning it inward onto the superego, allowing the subject to take nonsexual, narcissistic pleasure in ensuring that the ego matches the superego. Sexual love for objects, tied to "crude" body-pleasures, is supposedly converted by sublimation into self-regard or self-esteem, which is the consequence of taking a more refined pleasure in edification such that the subject may become an exemplary representative of a particular culture or group, and, in this capacity, an ethical being.

With the resurgence of object-libido, then, comes a fresh wave of "repression" or censorship, which "proceeds from the self-respect of the ego."[100] Even if the desired object and the projected means to achieve it are practically viable, what now intrudes is the culturally acquired question, arising with the formation of the superego, of their social and ethical acceptability. The repressed libidinal impulses that arise from fixation points in the erotogenic zones, and their derivatives, persist in the id unchanged and continually press for satisfaction. From the point of view of the developed and differentiated ego, the expression of these impulses arouses unpleasurable feelings. Not only do they come to be seen as perverse, but they also conjure up one of the infantile situations of extreme danger (helplessness in early immaturity, loss of love, fear of castration).[101]

They therefore provoke repressive opposition from the ego, whose aim is always to eradicate unpleasure.[102] According to Freud, the ego succeeds in this task if it is strong and has drawn the instinctual impulse concerned into its organization. In this case, the "perverse" impulse may be totally destroyed and the libido permanently diverted along other paths (as occurs in the normally resolved Oedipus complex). In nonpathological development, these urges find paths to discharge through derivatives. "If these derivatives have become sufficiently far removed from the repressed representative, whether owing to the adoption of distortions or by reason of the number of intermediate links inserted, they have free access to the conscious."[103]

In the case of repression, however, the ego is conflicted: it is unable to resist the pressure of interdicted libidinal urges but cannot tolerate the pain that floods in upon their satisfaction. To deal with this conflict, it severs ideas from their affect and subjects ideas to repression.[104] Affect, then, is inhibited, attached to another idea, or transformed into anxiety. Several responses to such anxiety are possible, which Freud associates with varying degrees of pathology. An anxiety attack can be fully generated and the ego withdraws entirely from the objectionable excitation.[105] Blocked libido may regress to one of the earlier libidinal fixation points, preserved in the id, combining forces to form symptoms (via primary processing). In what Freud names the "return of the repressed," which marks the failure of repression, this complex of forces is taken up into the ego in various ways (as reaction-formations, as the intensification of certain dispositions, as a permanent alteration of the ego), and if it is excessively strong, all manner of compulsions and pathologies can gravitate around it (such as the myriad eating disorders that persist despite all we know via nutritional science).[106]

For Freud, finally, the sex drive becomes the source of resistance to cultural edification, and sexual liberation provides the antidote to the excessive repressions and oppressions demanded by the process of "civilization." This argument, however, binds humanity into an impossible choice between the mutually exclusive demands of sex and civilization, or, in equivalent terms, between pathological urges and the will, or again, between happiness and ethics. Hence, Freud's notorious pessimism concerning the endemic discontent associated with civilization.

Concluding Remarks

I think it is fair to say, in conclusion, that Freud presents multiple enigmas on both sides of the transcendental relation. On the side of the subject, his most radical innovation is to insist that nothing comes to consciousness in the absence of language. However, on the one hand, he divides preconscious and unconscious processing on the basis of a difference in mode of articulation between the nonrational, open-ended, image-based primary process responsible for "thing-presentations" and the closed, unified, rationally ordered, language-based secondary process responsible for "word-presentations." On the other hand, Lacan and Derrida find plenty of evidence in Freud's texts, particularly *The Interpretation of Dreams*, to show that words can be as much "things" as images and have irrational "affinities" that allow them to enter into associative relations of condensation and displacement, characteristic for Freud of the primary process, just as easily as images. In fact, Lacan argues, condensation and displacement are synonymous with metonymy and metaphor.

In short, having made a distinction between unconscious and preconscious processing, Freud also blurs it in a way that subsumes both thing and word presentations under the broader banner of signification in general.[107] This blurring has two important reciprocal implications. First, if signifying practice is the broader category to which language belongs as one example of associative processing, it can no longer be characterized as a closed system. Second, for Lacan, this implies that what is called "the unconscious," namely primary processing, is "structured like a language."

Instead of making a distinction between unconscious and conscious processing, then, Lacan prefers Saussure's distinction between two fundamental principles of association.[108] The principle of arbitrariness dominates the intrasign, paradigmatic associations among and between signifiers and signifieds. A concept can be linked to any succession of sounds, as demonstrated by the multiplicity of associated signifiers in different languages. This associative link, then, has no rational basis, for there is no reason for preferring one such succession to another. The principle of linearity dominates the intersign, syntagmatic associations. The signifying elements (for example, letters, words, phrases, and sentences in a written text) are presented in linear succession; "they form a chain" whereby signs take on and change significance as a result of "different oppositions to what precedes and what follows."[109] Importantly, then, meaningful terms arise and are maintained as the effect of an articulated (joined) network of differential interrelationships. Here, meaning becomes a function of arbitrary paradigmatic associations between signifiers and signifieds, combined with the place a sign occupies relative to others in a chain. Moreover, whatever the forces of change are, whether they are "phonetic changes undergone by the signifier, or perhaps changes in meaning which affect the signified concept," and whether they occur "in isolation or in combination, they always result in a *shift in the relationship between the signified and the signifier*." It is this shift in relationship that constitutes an altered signification.[110] To say, in sum, that meaning is constituted diacritically is to say that it is constituted by the relations of difference that operate both at the paradigmatic, metaphoric, vertical level of the "code" (of that which stands in the place of another) as well as at the syntagmatic, material, horizontal level of "articulation" or joining.

According to Lacan, one could argue that all synthetic processing is in principle accessible to analytic unraveling and interpretation, albeit with some effort, since synthetic articulations are not always logical or rational but associative, metaphorical, or metonymic. What is properly unconscious and therefore entirely inaccessible to interpretation or analysis makes itself felt not in any synthesizing or interpretative processes but in what Freud calls "*die Not des Lebens,*" which should be read not as life's needs but as something "infinitely stronger": "something that *wishes.*"[111] When one turns to the question of what causes such wishing in the first place, one uncovers questions, enigmas, and aporias on the material side of the transcendental relation, associated with Freud's treatment of the notion of the "real" and repetition. On the one hand, Freud goes no further than Husserl's inductive assumption of repeatability, without guarantee of absolute repetition. On the other, he proposes a theory of the Real as trauma, which is intrinsically incompatible with any form of the metaphysics of presence.

Taking up and elaborating on Freud's account of "trauma," Lacan launches not only a critique of all consciousness philosophy derived from the *Cogito* but also of the ego psychology that is compatible with it. Ego psychologists take to heart one of Freud's conceptions of the analytic task: namely that the therapeutic intention of psychoanalysis "is, indeed, to strengthen the ego, to make it more independent of the super-ego, to widen its field of perception and enlarge its organization, so that it can appropriate fresh portions of the id. Where id was, there ego shall be. It is a work of culture—not unlike the draining of the Zuider Zee."[112]

On the supposition that knowing "the truth" frees us from its unconscious effects, the aim of ego psychology is to cut through symptomatic disguises and the protective defenses and resistances that hold them in place, in order to help analysands recognize the supposedly true traumatic events that lie behind them and interpret the vicissitudes of such traumas in their narratives. What Lacan objects to in this approach is a marked philosophical naïveté concerning truth and reality, in opposition to which he aims to save what is radically enigmatic in Freud's formulation of trauma. His aim is to rescue psychoanalytic theory from domestication by an ego psychology that Freud sometimes endorses but that undoes his most valuable insights in its subjection to the "metaphysics of presence." Lacan demonstrates instead that instabilities in Freud's theory of constitution already render impossible such a theory of "proper," recollective, analytical reflection. For Freud has already made such a theory enigmatic by an autodeconstructing double that acknowledges the abyssal nature of analysis, which does not get down to a "hard kernel of truth" (the true "reality" behind the symptomatic disguises) but the "hard kernel of the real," which paradoxically remains a traumatic tear, or "navel," or "a swarming void" around which the fabrication of "sense," or the constitution of "phenomenal reality," ceaselessly turns. But here, Freud acknowledges that analysis may function not to strengthen the ego but to aid the subject's self-invention.

One of the ways in which quasi-transcendental thinking emerges, then, is in the recognition that Freud's thinking, poised on the threshold between the metaphysics of presence and its "ruin," but without the Derridean or Lacanian means to negotiate it (via the "plural logic of the aporia"), renders every fundamental "concept" enigmatic by drawing together incompatible economic and aneconomic formulations. As I shall explicate more fully in the further course of this study, despite all of the acknowledged innovative genius of Freud's account of the transcendental relation, it is in Lacan's revision that a move to quasi-transcendental thinking in psychoanalytic theory becomes explicit. In general terms, although there is not nothing on the material side of the transcendental relation, Freud inadvertently shows that there is no determinable ground for insisting upon its repeatability. Again, on the grounds of the generalized theory of signification, which Lacan draws from Freud's practice, it can be demonstrated that there are no stabilizing grounds on the subjective side of the relation either, because signification cannot ever become a closed system. Ultimately, the transcendental relation is characterized by open-endedness on both sides.

As an effect of such open-endedness, everything constituted is made possible by our capacity to wrest it out of its open-endedness and artificially stabilize it. But because it has been artificially constituted, its very possibility is always under threat, making anything essential, absolute, final, perfect, or incorruptible strictly impossible. When something is made possible, it is also strictly speaking made impossible. Lacan, as I will discuss in chapter 7, turns to what he calls the *tuché* for an understanding of what causes the aporetic trouble in the transcendental relation, whereby the desire for pleasure causes us to economize in the *automaton* rather than face the truth.

Derrida calls this same "cause" of all the trouble "*différance*." But this is where Derrida's own troubles start, because *différance* has been so thoroughly misconstrued as a figure of "freeplay." In what follows, I aim to demonstrate instead that Derrida's texts are never a matter of freeplay but are, in one way or another, the performance of the inescapable *aporias* engendered by the necessity of operating within a philosophical discourse that speaks of the conditioned and its conditions while faced with the impossibility of these conditions ever being "proper." He insists that there are good reasons for acknowledging and working with this necessary "impropriety" within transcendental discourse, and, therefore, for why his work must be thought of neither as transcendental thinking nor as being entirely in opposition to it, but as answering to the demands of a "logic" that is somewhere (that is, nowhere) in-between, which is marked by prefixing the transcendental with the "quasi" that ruins it. To support the argument that the "plural logic of the aporia" that (dis)orders all of Derrida's writings (including those on the Freudian text) can help make sense of Lacan's "return" to Freud—which is not a return but inventive repetition—it is first necessary to counter the still widespread prejudice that reduces Derrida's quasi-transcendental thinking to only one of its sides, namely, a freeplay of differences. It is to this task that I shall now turn.

3

Derrida: *Différance* and the "Plural Logic of the Aporia"

Introductory Remarks: Questions of Interpretation

If Derrida's name is almost synonymous with mad misunderstandings, perhaps one has to grant that his texts are frustrating to read at the best of times. Take, for example, his insistence that to ask the question "what is *différance*?" is already to have misunderstood what he means by this nickname, since the question implies that *différance* can be made present, that it has an essence or existence of some kind, or that it can be some thing, form, state, or power, which can be given a "proper" name (a name that can be capitalized and capitalized on).[1] But, on his account, *différance* simply is not, and any attempt to think it has to remain negative: *différance* is not a word, not a concept, not a present being of any kind, does not have a proper name. Yet, this negativity does not mean, he insists, that *différance* can be thought of as the diametric opposite of presence; that is, it cannot be thought of in terms of absence.[2] Faced with this apparent obscurity and vacillation, one might understandably snap the book shut in frustration and turn instead to one of the numerous commentaries. But this is where the risks multiply exponentially.[3] Besides astonishingly diverse and perverse misrepresentations of Derrida's thinking, many sympathetic commentaries generate their own difficulties. In writing "about" Derrida's texts, some interpreters apparently feel compelled to match the facility with which Derrida exploits the resources of language or to repeat the Derridean gestures they aim to elucidate, making for texts almost as opaque as those upon which they remain parasitic. Readers of these readers soon enough find themselves lost again in the dense thickets of wordplay, caveat, and qualification.

I agree with Rorty that attempts at "what Bennington calls 'Derridean' readings of Derrida" tend to be "tiresome and unprofitable."[4] By contrast, Rorty's writing is erudite and superbly readable: a delicious mix of irreverence toward stuffy academia and seeming good sense. Yet, precisely because of their linguistic clarity, his influential early readings have aided and abetted the persisting misconception that Derrida's thinking is anti-philosophy and views itself instead as "just the self-consciousness of the play of a certain kind of writing."[5] Despite his avowed "twenty-odd" years of reading Derrida,[6] his interpretations, until about the close of last century, have remained perversely resistant to Derrida's argumentation,[7] shifting from early attempts to yoke it to the anti-Kantian side of a contrastive duality that opposes neo-Kantian analytical philosophy to Hegelian dialecticism[8] to an approbatory acknowledgment that Derrida himself, on his bad days, might not want to escape altogether from "the dusty fly bottle" of transcendental philosophy.[9]

Rorty's Double Vision

I should acknowledge the injustice of fingering an outdated, twentieth-century "Rorty," which I risk nevertheless, because his persistent attempt to reduce Derrida's thinking to one side of a contradictory opposition between "philosophical" foundationalism and antifoundational "textuality" serves conveniently as a foil for an account of Derrida's quasi-transcendental thinking, which, by contrast, articulates these terms according to the "plural logic of the aporia."[10] Moreover, if Rorty's early interpretations are not mad enough to be laughed off, their one-sidedness makes them imprecise enough to skew the pitch, and, given their mantric repetition in diverse contexts, they are influential enough to matter.

According to Rorty's two-fold framework, "philosophy" stands for the belief that reason enables humanity to establish once and for all the basic conditions for founding the perfect system (social organization, political dispensation, system of justice, educational institution, etc.), granted that such perfection, attainable only over generations, is held out as a regulative ideal and a measure for human progress. By contrast, "textuality" denotes an intellectual freeplay engendered by the recognition that no term whatsoever has an immutable, essential nature and everything is constituted diacritically (by differential relations). Moreover, since no basic principle can be fixed as the ultimate regulator of these diacritical relations, they cannot be organized into a closed stable structure or system (architectonic, hierarchy, or teleology).

There is certainly common ground between Rorty and Derrida insofar as both promote ways of thinking that threaten foundationalist philosophy. Yet, as I hope to show, Derrida resists Rorty's consequent brand of pragmatic postmodernism whereby the ruin of foundationalism necessarily entails giving up "philosophy" altogether in the name of "textuality" or an out-and-out nominalism.[11]

Derrida's thinking is more complex than either foundationalism or nominalism thus understood, since it resists the limitations imposed by the either/or logic that still binds and blinds Rorty's intellectual moves.[12] He refuses to deny the necessity of living with the idea and the logic of foundational thinking. But he also shows that, just as necessarily, every foundation established will always already have been ruined, without delay, from the instant of its institution, without this being reason enough to give up on it. For Derrida, then, foundationalism is linked to antifoundationalism not through contradiction but aporia, in response to which an either/or choice is inappropriate.[13]

In this case, Derrida's thinking does not properly fit on either side of the slash that, for Rorty, clearly separates "philosophy" from the unregulated play of an essentially antifoundationalist "literature." Preferring the "antifoundationalist" side of his oppositional schema, he criticizes Derrida relentlessly for selling it short and in so doing coming "perilously close" to a regrettable, retrogressive nostalgia for "the tradition of onto-theology."[14] Dismissing persistently quasi-transcendental motifs in Derrida's texts ("we nominalists have no use for a refurbished version of Kant's 'transcendental logic'"),[15] his only recourse is to split Derrida in two.[16] He denounces a bad, backsliding, early Derrida who tries to account for what he does with language by resorting to a quasi-philosophical term like "trace," and he celebrates a good, later, antifoundationalist Derrida who saves himself from such pseudofoundationalism via *différance.*

Rorty supports this division with a snippet in which he sees Derrida rebuking himself for the covert foundationalism attached to "trace":[17]

> For us, differance remains a metaphysical name; and all the names that it receives from our language are still, so far as they are names, metaphysical . . .
>
> Older than Being itself, our language has no name for such a difference. But we "already know" that if it is unnamable this is not simply provisional; it is not because our language has still not found

or received this *name*, or because we would have to look for it in another language, outside the finite system of our language. It is because there is no *name* for this—not even essence or Being—not even the name "differance," which is not a name, which is not a pure nominal unity, and continually breaks up in a chain of different substitutions . . .

There will be no unique name, not even the name of Being. It must be conceived without *nostalgia*; that is, it must be conceived outside the myth of the purely maternal or paternal language belonging to the lost fatherland of thought. On the contrary we must *affirm* it—in the sense that Nietzsche brings affirmation into play—with a certain laughter and with a certain dance.[18]

It is quite clear from this citation that Derrida's remarks concerning the lack of a "proper" name or "pure nominal unity" for what *différance* improperly names certainly poses a challenge to philosophy's so-called dream of presence. However, these remarks can hardly be taken to make the opposite claim for antiphilosophy. Derrida's persistently reiterated protest should be taken seriously: "on the subject, in the name, or from the point of view of . . . [philosophy *in general*] I have never spoken, no more than of antiphilosophy, as a consequence, which has always seemed to me the thing least deserving of interest in the world."[19] If philosophy has tended to place some version of pure, simple, unified Being at the origin, Derrida replaces Being not with a pure disseminative drift but with the complexity, impropriety, or better, "impossibility," of paradox that *différance* improperly names. His aim in this essay is to write about quasi-transcendental constitution as the aporetic interweaving of incompatible but equally necessary economic and aneconomic aporias. These aporias are indicated in the nickname *différance* by (1) the aneconomic, disseminative drift of "*différance* as spacing"; and (2) the regulated, economic difference and deferral of "*différance* as temporization." I shall address both in more detail shortly.[20] The question Derrida poses here is not one of choice but of articulation: "*Différance* as temporization, *différance* as spacing. How are they to be joined?"[21]

Clearly *différance* is not a "unique name" for the aporia of the economic and aneconomic aporias. Rather, as already mentioned, there are countless nicknames for this "plural logic of the aporia," which can be reiterated in a chain of context-bound, not precisely synonymous, substitutes, to which "trace" belongs as much as any other.[22] It is due to such iterability ("which, like *itara*, from which the word derives, says both the repetition of the same and alteration")[23] that Derrida claims for his deconstructive analyses a clearly articulated logical "form," but, paradoxically, denies this form the status of a proper name and compels it to keep taking on various context-specific nicknames—such as "deconstruction," "archi-writing," "the plural logic of aporia," "quasi-transcendental interweaving"—all of which "inscribe *différance* within themselves."[24] In short, allowing that the singularity of a context makes a difference, which prevents any fixed method of analysis, one may nevertheless conclude that a formalizable logic repeats its play in every Derridean text. But if "trace" and *différance* substitute for one another (albeit always a little imperfectly), they do not submit to Rorty's sharp division and cannot be used to argue that Derrida (on his good days) abolishes transcendental philosophy altogether (still residual in the word "trace") in favor of the unregulated "textuality" supposedly designated by *différance.*

It pays to revisit Derrida's text to see what was cut in Rorty's snipping. Notably, he quietly ignores the very next sentence, where Derrida invokes the Heideggerian *hope* that comes after the laughter and dance in which the play of *différance* is affirmed without nostalgia; that is, he invokes the "other side of nostalgia," which reinscribes philosophy's traditional "quest for the proper word and the unique name" and insists that the question of the "proper" name "enters into the affirmation put into play by *différance.*"[25] The sense of this addition, which turns on what one makes of the phrase "enters into," remains studiously undecidable. It certainly does suggest that Nietzschean affirmation writes off any quest for the proper name, but it simultaneously suggests that such a quest enters into the picture and must be taken into account. Rorty, in his carefully selective reading, has decided the undecidable, and in so doing simply misses the complexity of Derrida's quasi-transcendental argument.

As if in confirmation of this blindness, he insists that good pragmatists "cannot understand why Derrida wants to sound *transcendental.*"[26] He argues that one can simply convert the unnecessarily complicated "transcendental-sounding" jargon of "conditions of possibility or impossibility" into the clearer terms of his formula for the coimplication of binary opposites.[27] That is: "you cannot use the word 'A' without being able to use the word 'B,' and vice versa, even though nothing can be both an A and an B." Moreover, he argues, if his own formula still sounds a bit transcendental, it is only in the "uninteresting" sense that a contrastive duality is always more basic than either of its terms, and even makes them possible.[28] For Rorty, then, this formula expresses no more than Saussure's diacritical claim that positive terms are second-order effects of more primary differential relations.[29] Finally, he insists, this admittedly improved philosophy of language has no conceivable relevance for political and ethical deliberation. In his words: "A theory of meaning seems as irrelevant here as a theory of *a priori* knowledge—*différance* as irrelevant as *Grund*; Saussure and Derrida as irrelevant as Kant and Hegel."

It is only by sleight of hand, however, that Rorty's formula reduces what is quasi-transcendental in Derrida's thinking to a trivial fact about meaning production. To show this, one might simply try out substitutions that would already take the coimplication of binaries beyond the domain of word usage: for example, you cannot practice "justice" without being able to practice "law," and vice versa, even though nothing can be both "just" and "forced by law."[30] But if Derrida's quasi-transcendental thinking can be "converted into" the terms of Rorty's formula, it is not reducible to it. "For," as Caputo puts it, "justice and the law are not supposed to be opposites but to interweave: laws ought to be just, otherwise they are monsters; and justice requires the force of law, otherwise it is a wimp."[31] Instead, Derrida's thinking complicates matters by showing that both "A" and "B" are equally impossible, but in different senses, because they harbor opposite aporias; further, their coimplication means that one side of the opposition not only haunts but also ruins the other, and in so doing, because they are interdependent, ruins itself. (The application of law ruins the notion of justice, but in the ruin of justice, law is destroyed, because there is no law without justice. Justice requires the suspension of law, but in the suspension of law, there is no justice, because there cannot be justice without law.) These formulations, then, unavoidably tie us up in the aporias of paradoxes, for certain phenomena indeed cannot be characterized in incompatible ways simultaneously, as Rorty suggests, but they nevertheless *must* be so characterized, for otherwise the phenomenon is lost. In other words, to make the either/or choice between incompatible characterizations (e.g., justice is the application of law, or justice is the suspension of law) is always to have lost the phenomenon ("justice itself"). The phenomenon as such (that which answers to the question, "what *is* justice, gift, democracy, ethics, etc.?") remains irremediably impossible, without this being reason enough to give up on it.

Quasi-transcendental conditions, Derrida adds, "can only take a negative *form* (without X there would not be Y)": without the application of law there will not be justice; equally, without the suspension of law there will not be justice. He rejects the positive alternative outright: justice occurs in the application of law; justice occurs in the suspension of law, or in broader terms, "on this condition there will surely have been event, decision, responsibility, ethics, or politics." In his words: "One can be certain only of this negative form. As soon as it is converted into a positive certainty, one can be sure that one is beginning to be deceived, indeed beginning to deceive the other."

To sum up so far, Rorty's readings are persistently skewed by the compulsive repetition of a violent interpretative strategy that reduces Derrida's complex position to the two-fold terms of his oppositional framework (philosophical foundationalism versus antifoundational textuality) and mandates a choice between them. This strategy is a driving force behind many attempts to assert the impotence of Derridean thinking when it comes to addressing practical (juridical, political, ethical, economic) issues. Accurately citing Derrida's persistent reminder that our only access to an event is through the artifice of linguistic or protolinguistic interpretation, and taking note of his deliberate recourse to linguistic techniques that highlight the irreducible gap between an event and the language used to describe it, critics of a certain kind typically leap to the conclusion that Derrida privileges a "textuality" that remains too narcissistically self-involved or playfully ironic to be politically or ethically relevant.

But there is nothing clear at all about the argumentative leaps necessary to draw this conclusion, not least because the same initial observation concerning Derrida's insistence upon an irreducible gap between the event and the language used to describe it can support precisely the opposite (but equally problematic) conclusion. Here, critics of a newer kind, such as Žižek, do not charge Derrida with textual narcissism but with making the opposing error of a misanthropic denigration of all that lies within the domain of the human "text" (legal systems, political measures, institutional structures), for the sake of preserving the absolute purity of a sublimely inaccessible, or absolutely absent, referent—Justice itself, for example. Again, if for exactly opposite reasons, he is charged with an essential inability to gain any purchase on reality and, therefore, with practical irrelevance.

While this double, contradictory accusation might at first seem perplexing, one may make sense of it, on reflection, as opposite sides of the same coin. The underlying charge that sustains both accusations is that Derrida sharply divides "text" from "referent," supposedly allowing the domain of the text to take on a life of its own while leaving the referent untouched. Depending on the use one wants to make of deconstruction as a foil for another argument, one can now accuse him of either celebrating or denigrating textuality and, accordingly, of either disregarding the referent altogether or striving to preserve its essential purity.

Žižek and "Derrida's Operation"

Žižek's more contemporary charge commands attention because it deals with the concerns of the so-called later Derrida. He is also one of the exceptional few whose critical remarks do not rely entirely on hearsay but are backed by complex and subtle argumentation that addresses the underlying logical structure of Derridean thinking. Most importantly, however, in his essay "The Real of Sexual Difference," he explicitly stresses the total incompatibility between Lacanian discourse and deconstruction in its "post-secular" guise, which he describes in terms of a "Derridean appropriation of Levinas."[32] Clearly, in the spirit of this study, which aims to demonstrate an accord between these discourses, I must raise and try to justify an objection here.

It is telling that Žižek's claim is supported by the insistence that an adequate understanding of the Lacanian Real would dispel any illusion of compatibility between "the Levinasian Other" (read, "post-secular" deconstruction) and "the Lacanian Thing." I agree with Žižek that attempts to link the Levinasian Other and the Lacanian Thing are misguided. What I would question instead is the precision with which he establishes the link between "post-secular" deconstruction (if there is such a thing) and the Levinasian Other. Correspondingly, it is certainly true that the misconstruction he names "Derrida's operation" is incompatible with the Lacanian logic he later outlines through the figures of "spectral analysis" and the Borromean knot. But, as I hope to demonstrate, to rectify his imprecise account of Derrida's appropriation of Levinas would be to bring Derrida into accord with Lacan rather than Levinas. In short, Žižek offers a brilliantly illuminating account of the structural logic underpinning Lacanian discourse, but in his construal and critique of "Derrida's operation," he does not treat the Derridean with equal justice. Moreover, because he mostly reports Derridean claims perfectly accurately, it is easy to be taken in by his argument and difficult to establish just why it nevertheless strikes one as misconstrued. Ultimately, the trouble lies in his neglect of the "plural logic of the aporia." Under the misnomer of "Derrida's operation," Žižek persistently hammers Derrida's claims into an imposed Levinasian structure, to which they in principle have never submitted. One is tempted here to echo in reverse Lacan's complaint: "It is as if it were precisely upon reaching the impasse to which my discourse is designed to lead them that they considered their work done, declaring themselves—or rather declaring me, which amounts to the same thing given their conclusions—confounded."[33]

Žižek's Critique of "Post-Secular Deconstruction"

The sophisticated argument by means of which Žižek declares Derrida confounded begins with the claim that "post-secular deconstruction" does not imply a return to any metaphysics of presence or onto-theology that requires the notion of a fully present, supreme being for its support. Rather, it takes shape as an appropriation of Levinas whereby the deconstruction of presence is supposed to "clear the slate for a new, undeconstructible form of spirituality, for the relationship to an unconditional Otherness that precedes ontology."[34] The shape of this Levinasian relationship, then, would consist of a "primordial passivity, sentiency, of responding, of being infinitely indebted to and responsible for the call of an Otherness that never acquires positive features but always remains withdrawn, the trace of its own absence."[35] In Žižek's assessment, one here encounters the same religious matrix as ever; the only difference between garden-variety onto-theology and the Derridean/Levinasian position being that a positive figure of God is replaced by its exact opposite: the Wholly Other, a hypostatized Absolute Absence, or the forever-to-come.[36] Importantly, inscribed in this observation is the claim that postsecular thinking retains the religious insistence upon an abyssal divide between the transcendent Other and the earthly sphere of immanence, which keeps each side absolutely uncontaminated. There can be no overlap between the two, no chance that the gap might collapse, not even a little, not even for an instant. Finally, Žižek notes, all of this means that the relationship between human subjects and the Other would not be characterized by active hermeneutic mediation or appropriation.

This postsecular configuration, he continues, repeats itself in what he thinks of as Derrida's fake "'fidelity' to the spirit of Marxism." On his account, Derrida insists on the necessity of respecting (saving or reasserting) the purity of the Absolute Other (the messianic promise, essential core, authentic spirit of the Marxist tradition) by renouncing any particular, contingent, determinate, and historical analyses, strategies, and measures involving "actual people in their actual circumstances." In his words, "reasserting the authentic spirit of the Marxist tradition means to leave behind its letter (Marx's particular analyses and proposed revolutionary measures, which are irreducibly tainted by the tradition of ontology) in order to save from the ashes the authentic messianic promise of emancipatory liberation."[37] Crucially, then, he adds, "the point is not simply that Marx's particular formulation and proposed measures are to be left behind and replaced by other, more adequate formulations and measures but rather that the messianic promise is betrayed by *any* particular formulation, by *any* translation into determinate economico-political measures."[38] The conclusion that he draws concerning "the underlying premise of Derrida's 'radicalization' of Marx" is this: since no "determinate economico-political measures," no matter how radical, may escape this form of betrayal, Derrida's discourse engenders the exact opposite of radicalization, namely, "the renunciation of any actual radical political measures" in the name of a radical, primordial passivity in face of the infinite debt.[39]

According to Žižek, this pseudoradical, Levinasian position is supposed to provide the Derridean alternative to the twin troubles that arise when the gap between "textual" reality (the immanent, interpreted, appropriated, phenomenal structures of experience) and the ineffable Other is collapsed. Derrideans, he remarks, see that collapsing this gap always involves a short-circuiting whose consequence would be either of twin troubles (aporias), standing in binary opposition.[40] On the one hand, if this gap is allowed to collapse in a way that privileges phenomenal reality (human law) and reduces all transcendent otherness out of the picture, one is left with no option but to promote Rorty's kind of unprincipled pragmatism. Here, one might add, having agreed to institute a shared regulatory economy (a legal system, for example, that aims to be just, fair, ordered, and good), community members may work to improve its efficiency and streamline its operation by eradicating its faults: moments of unfairness, singularities, loopholes, quirks, inefficiencies, and disorders. Fairly obviously, the consequence of complete success here would be a static system that quickly loses its application in a quintessentially dynamic and messy ethical and political reality. Instead of the hoped-for justice, one ends up with a rigid system of prescriptions imposed from on high by the calculating *automaton*s we tend to label by means of two highly ironic terms, namely, "civil" and "servant," who do not dare or care to think beyond the rules. Ironically, then, when law prevails over Justice, the law itself becomes totalitarian; in its stasis, it assumes transcendent status over a dynamic phenomenal reality.

On the other hand, the gap can collapse in a different way, whereby phenomenal reality is reduced out of the picture and the Other is privileged in an anarchic moment of singular totalitarianism. In the case under discussion, an idealized "Justice itself" prevails over law. Here, as Žižek notes, the problematic of totalitarianism in political and ethical life is understood in terms of "a short-circuit between messianic Otherness and a determinate political agent."[41] Žižek explains this short circuit in terms of "sublimation" (notably, in its Freudian sense, which is closely allied to idealization). "In sublimation," he explains, "something—an object that is part of our ordinary reality—is elevated into the unconditional object that the subject values more than life itself."[42] One may understand this in two correlative senses. By believing that her particular decision actualizes Justice itself, a determinate political agent assumes a transcendent or

God-like status. Correlatively, the messianic Other (whether we name this "Democracy," "Justice," or "Ethics") relinquishes its futural status as the forever-to-come and pretends to be fully actualized in a decision, act, or system whose principle is elevated to supreme status. Here, notably, individuals might legitimately assume the autonomous right to apply personally held supreme principles at their own discretion. But all others must be accorded the same right. Without a means of collective arbitration, then, one ends up facing out-and-out power struggles whose only principle will be a lack of principle. In other words, the consequence of successful totalitarianism would have to be unprincipled pragmatism.

Such circularities suggest that one here faces two different kinds of aporia, neither of which can be chosen without some form of violation. On Žižek's account, the "lesson of deconstruction" is therefore this: never collapse the gap between phenomenal reality and the messianic Other, since this leads to an impossible situation of opposing aporias. Yet, since, as already argued, the otherness of the messianic Other is preserved only by disallowing any worldly contamination and remains "the impossible itself," Derrida's thinking supposedly traps itself between two equally untenable positions: two forms of impossibility. More broadly speaking, the supposed "lesson of deconstruction" is this: since everything is impossible, we may justly abdicate in face of the pragmatic demand for determinate decisions concerning actual practical measures in the name of Levinasian passivity. Consequently, Derrida merely plays around without any hope for better social configurations, more just laws, and so on, leaving himself no option but to doom his discourse to practical irrelevance.

A Derridean Response

I cannot pretend to do justice to Derrida's complex and multiple adjudication of the tension between phenomenology and Levinasian ethics in drawing upon his essay "Violence and Metaphysics" to explain why Žižek's interpretation of Derrida's appropriation of Levinas is misconceived. But at least one can say unequivocally that there cannot be a Derridean who would not immediately point out that when Derrida painstakingly lays out the disagreement between Husserl and Levinas concerning the question of the Wholly Other he hardly comes up on the side of Levinas.[43] In fact, ironically, much of Žižek's critique of what he takes to be "Derrida's operation" finds a precise echo in Derrida's critique of Levinas. First, Derrida criticizes Levinas precisely because he orders his thinking around a fundamental dichotomy or binary opposition between the centripetal, philosophical Greek spirit, which tends inward toward "closure" (totality, sameness, immanence, history, philosophy, and war), and the infinite openness of the centrifugal, eschatological, implicitly "Hebraic" spirit (infinity, otherness, transcendence, ethics, and peace).[44] Further, he criticizes Levinas for insisting on an abyssal gap between these poles, assuming an either/or choice between supposed opposites, and renouncing violent, phenomenological "totalization" for the pure nonviolence that he associates with an appeal to a prior infinity, and which he calls pure Ethics.

Accordingly, Derrida's basic strategy is to show that Levinas' insistence on the purity of the Wholly Other remains inconsistent, since his discourse in fact requires the phenomenology he rejects.[45] This qualification is, in fact, announced in the opening pages of the essay. Having noted Levinas' early, still tentative and inconsistent, reticence concerning the "imperialism of *theoria*" in Husserl's phenomenology and pointing to the paradox involved in maintaining "a philosophical discourse against light," he remarks that "thirty years later, when the charges against theoretism and (Husserlian) phenomenology became the essential motifs in the break with tradition, the nudity of the face of the other—this epiphany of a certain non-light before which all violence is to be quieted and disarmed—will still have to be exposed to a certain enlightenment."[46]

Derrida goes on to point out, for example, that Levinas rejects Husserl's account of the constitution of the alter ego (which accounts for the other as ego through the symmetry of analogical apperception) because it compromises the alterity of the Wholly Other by reducing the other person to another one just like me.[47] Yet Levinas also insists that the other manifests as the power of "saying." But it is impossible to explain how "the power to say" becomes a mark of the other *ego* (the Wholly Other as opposed to the relative otherness of that which does not speak: animals or objects) without a relational theory of empathy. How can I tell that *this* other, in contrast with other others, has "the power of saying" and is therefore Wholly Other, except by "seeing" that she/he is a being who (like me and unlike other others) is distinguished by the power to speak? In short, Levinas himself does not sustain a commitment to the Wholly Other without contradiction, for he cannot get around the fact that one has to be the same (another person) in order to be the Wholly Other. In Derrida's words, "the other is absolutely other only if he is an ego, that is, in a certain way, if he is the same as I. Inversely, the other as *res* is simultaneously less other (not absolutely other) and less 'the same' than I."[48]

Further, Derrida argues, again contra Levinas, that we have no access to any pure, passive spirit of nonviolence but, at best, must choose the least possible violence, which is to choose neither totality (symbolic network, text) nor infinity (Thing), but to negotiate between these paralyzing extremes.[49] This negotiation, he argues, is better achieved by Husserl than by Levinas. For Levinas, the alterity of the Wholly Other is respected only by abandoning active hermeneutic appropriation altogether. Phenomenology, by contrast, can tolerate the inescapable violence of active appropriation, since it accepts that inadequation (the impossibility of perfect evidence) marks a kind of "immanent transcendence." Phenomenology, in his view, both accommodates an indefinite potential for phenomenality (for being "seen" in the broad sense of this term, associated with showing, illumination, and evidence) on the part of any other and respects its alterity (its darkness and its secrets), since no other can ever be given with perfect adequacy.

Broadly speaking, then, Derrida objects to the extremity of Levinas' rejection of the "Greek logos" (whose element is the phenomenon of Being) and his attempt to liberate "the immediate, but buried nudity of experience itself . . . from the Greek domination of the Same and the One (other names for the light of Being and of the phenomenon) as if from oppression itself," on the grounds that this is done (inconsistently, as it turns out, for naming is a philosophical gesture) for the sake of something he is willing to *name* the "non-Greek."[50] In short, if Derrida appropriates anything from Levinas, it is precisely not his religious matrix, which entails a sharp division between phenomenal reality and the Absolute Other—for not even Levinas can sustain the notion of the Wholly Other itself.

Nevertheless, he does believe that there is something to be gained from Levinas' extremity, given the power with which it highlights the structural violation of otherness built into traditional philosophy (including phenomenology), since such violation is incessantly necessary every time we wish to speak, act, create, define, differentiate, and so on. Notably, if Derrida draws upon phenomenology to critique Levinas, he also, in a reverse move, derives from Levinas the means to critique what remains of a traditional metaphysics of presence in phenomenology. Against Husserlian phenomenology, then, he launches a renegotiated and adapted version of the Wholly Other, which points not to any transcendent ideal standing in opposition to the sphere of immanence but to the unpredictability inscribed within every immanent horizon of experience.

To elaborate, Derrida explicitly insists upon the impossibility of choosing between the so-called spheres of immanence and transcendence, since neither by itself presents a viable option, and he prefers "incoherence" as the most rational alternative. As he puts it: "We will not choose between the opening and the totality. Therefore we will be incoherent, but without systematically resigning ourselves to incoherence."[51] It is probably unnecessary to underline the oddity of Žižek's claim that Derrida (of all people) insists on a sharp divide that preserves the absolute purity of messianic Otherness, given his relentless and consistent insistence on the ineradicable necessity of incoherence, impurity, and contamination (let us risk the word "collapse" here), clearly exemplified, for example, in the figure of the "pharmakon" (poison and cure simultaneously) and no less clearly in the plural logic of the aporia, which is also the logic of contamination.

As I see it, Derrida's recourse to "incoherence" is analogous to what Žižek understands by the Lacanian Real. To explain this contention, one may yet again take recourse to the problematic of Justice and law. For Derrida, "incoherence" is a way of saying that the dream of Justice, joined to the impossibility of its full actualization in the practice of law, indicates the moment of errance internal to legal practice. Such incoherence renders it (mercifully) incapable of completing itself—of establishing its final destination as either human law (unprincipled pragmatism) or the divine law (totalitarianism)—and therefore keeps it permanently open to traumatic shattering and reconfiguration. I will not resist the temptation at this point to remark that the aporetic complexity inscribed in articulating the dream of Justice with the impossibility of its full actualization is the traumatic Real of law.

In more general terms, one could say that the "impossible itself" (for which *différance* and undecidability are nicknames) refers to the double movement whereby all phenomena are constituted by means of an articulation that joins (as a paradox) the dream of actualizing the All (the desire for infinity, best understood in terms of Freud's paradoxical death drive) with the impossibility of its full actualization. Notably, the absolute All, the object of the death drive, is itself an incoherent notion. It may be understood in terms of the difference between two internally aporetic senses of the infinite, which highlight its inconceivable nature either way: namely, an "all-at-once" infinite (which names the impossibility of grasping a totality that has no bounds) and a successive infinite (which names the impossibility involved in trying to grasp the absolute "all" of an endless succession). It is because of this incoherence at the "origin" that the dream of actualizing the All takes the opposing (but equally aporetic) economic and aneconomic forms between which Derrida refuses to choose. Instead, he insists that one must learn to live with the incoherence represented by the paradox of "immanent transcendence" marked by the figure of the undecidable. That is, because all phenomena are constituted by this double economic/aneconomic exigency, they remain unresolved: one can never bind all possible threads into an absolutely systematic network according to the exigencies of the "all-at-once" infinite, but we are not for that reason left in a fray of loose ends. For Derrida, then, the irreducible disjunction in the conjunction between the dream of Justice (for example) and its actualization in law is not at all due to a sharply oppositional ontological dualism (which argues for the impossibility of any appropriation) but emerges instead, with Husserl, as an indication of a necessary, internal errance in appropriation. Consequently, it is when one, by the force of illusion, suppresses errance and pretends that the nature of human experience is decidable one way or the other that one faces inevitable economic and aneconomic aporias. In other words, coherence is achievable only if one can (*per impossible*) justify the choice for an economic or aneconomic absolute, that is, ultimately, for either originary cosmos or chaos. One might, by contrast, find the "lesson of deconstruction" condensed in the paradoxical injunction "give economy its chance": allow economy a chance to happen; allow the aneconomic chance to happen to an economy.

Symptomatic Contaminations

When one reads Derrida "himself" (against the misappropriations), his thinking clearly does not fit the mould of Levinasian postsecularism. Interestingly, in an effort to think away some of these anomalies, Žižek inadvertently opens up avenues that lead toward an accord between Derrida and Lacan. He grants, for example, that the Derridean account of the democracy "to come" is not a positively determined ideal whose future actualization requires us to tolerate present restrictions and sufferings as its preconditions. He also accurately formulates the Derridean alternative. In his words, "in contrast to such strategic economy of the proper dose of (un)freedom, 'democracy to come' refers to the unforeseeable emergencies/outbursts of ethical responsibility, when I am suddenly confronted with an urgency to answer the call, to intervene in a situation that I experience as intolerably unjust."[52]

Interestingly, this formulation of the Derridean alternative contains a hint that "the impossible" (the democracy to come) does not refer to an absolutely absent Other but to the traumatic eruption of errance (a here-and-now experience of intolerable injustice) possible in any current political situation (even if it is already named democratic). It is the shock encounter with errance that opens politics to the chance happening of democracy, that is, an actual, albeit imperfect, democratic event, where, in response to the emergency of intolerable injustice, we are called—

obliged—to take responsibility, as best we can, for determinate democratic practice. In other words, in such "outbursts of ethical responsibility" there is a momentary, traumatic overlap (a genuine collapse of the gap) between messianic Otherness and determinate political agents that is *not* the kind of totalitarian short-circuit described above.

Žižek, however, offers this hint of an alternative reading really only in order to dismiss it, since he immediately insists (without saying why) that Derrida *nonetheless* "retains the irreducible *opposition* between . . . a spectral experience of the messianic call of justice and its 'ontologization,' its transposition into a set of positive legal and political measures."[53] Thus, he adds, if the messianic call for justice is called Ethics, then totalitarianism is inevitable when Ethics becomes politics.[54] Yet he again touches upon a way in which this gap may be collapsed *without* pure totalitarianism, by acknowledging that the ethical *is* undecidability and that the ethical domain proper is *différance*, while the political involves the risk of making decisions. Here, Derrideans might argue that one cannot grant this definition of the ethical and still hold onto an abyssal divide between the ethical and the political, since *différance* and undecidability (ethics) are not somehow opposed to the phenomenal realm but indicate the internal play of paradox that makes all appropriation (politics) necessarily self-subverting and therefore only totalitarian by artifice or delusion. To say that ethics is the internal *différance* that traumatizes the political is another way to say that the political cannot escape traumatization since the very conditions that make any political phenomenon possible also render its pure form impossible.

Žižek grants the elegance of this way of thinking, but nonetheless dismisses its efficacy as a theory of ethical action: "it is to be opposed to the act in the Lacanian sense, in which the distance between the ethical and the political collapses."[55] But why? "Consider the case of Antigone," he suggests, as if providing an argument for his dismissal. Yet the ensuing discussion is not a considered argument for why Derrida's quasi-transcendental thinking, or, in other words, the plural logic of the aporia, remains unacceptable as a means to understand Antigone's act. It is merely a restatement of the erroneous claim that Derrida insists on the absolute impossibility of such a collapse.

Here he points out that from "the standpoint of the ethics of *Sittlichkeit*, of the mores that regulate the intersubjective collective of the polis," Antigone's insistence on her singular power to answer the call of justice itself "is effectively 'mad,' disruptive, evil."[56] A Derridean account, he argues, has no option but to call Antigone's act totalitarian, since she allows herself to be invaded by, and remains blindly faithful to, the singular call of the Divine, which nobody else can understand. Since she insists upon an "unconditional fidelity to" that which lies beyond human law, she is, in effect, assuming the right to play God, and would therefore take the form of a "proto-totalitarian figure."[57] He notes here that misreadings of Lacan's interpretation of Antigone's act similarly argue that she condemns herself by losing the proper distance from the Thing. On the other hand, refusing to make any exception to the letter of human law, Creon, in Žižek's words, "acts like a pragmatic state politician, mercilessly crushing any activity that would destabilize the smooth functioning of the state and civil peace."[58] Again, for Žižek, against the short-circuiting involved in both Creon's strategy and Antigone's act, the "lesson of deconstruction" repeats itself: the gap between the Thing and the determinable object must remain irreducible.

In short, despite the anomalies noted above, Žižek evidently remains convinced that Derrida misses the contaminating complexity indicated by the mutual contamination of immanence and transcendence. Interestingly, however, Derrida himself finds a "structural complication of the political" even in Levinas, which he interprets in terms of a paradoxical "enclave of transcendence."[59] He argues that the border between the ethical and the political becomes uncertain when Levinas acknowledges that the outside of the State—"peace, hospitality, paternity, infinite fecundity, etc."—has a framework within it. In fact, he notes: "The border between the ethical and the political here loses for good the indivisible simplicity of a limit. No matter what Levinas might have said, the determinability of this limit was never pure, and it never will be. It would be possible to follow the inclusion of excess, or this transcendence in immanence, through subsequent texts."[60]

Derrida interprets the inclusion of excess here as an originary transgression that "brings about a disjunction in the immanence to self." It is not much of a stretch to interpret Derrida's phrase "the other's decision in me" in terms of this paradoxical notion of immanent transcendence.[61] What can be thought of as "the other's decision in me" has nothing to do with cultural or linguistic determinism, that is, with heteronomy. It is not that "I" am spoken by the Other in the form of the Symbolic Order. Nor does it imply the opposite form of absolute sovereignty; it is not a matter of the Thing in me that decides. It does not imply, for example, the blind insistence of an Antigone on her sovereign right to do just what she decides, whatever it is. Rather, playing on the homophonic associations of "scission and division" in the word "de-cision," "the other's decision in me" refers to the undecidability (or *différance*) that stands as the quasi-transcendental condition for the simultaneous possibility and impossibility of genuine decisions.

Derrida insists, in the first place, that without undecidability there would be no call for ethical, juridical, and political decisions. Without undecidability, there would only be the economic delusion of perfect rational calculability where the law is merely applied under the illusion that we know enough to do this, or the abdication of responsibility on the basis of the aneconomic illusion that we cannot know anything. It is precisely because things are ultimately undecidable—because nothing is absolutely possible or impossible, because individuals can neither know for sure nor claim absolute ignorance—that we are obliged to go through the singularizing ordeal or trauma of undecidability, of having to make decisions and take responsibility for them without the comfort of certainty. Thus a decision, if it is to live up to its concept, must always in principle be capable of precipitating a new configuration of rules, from which there is no return. This is not to say that every decision must precipitate something new; just that decision making in principle requires a primary openness to change, even if one ultimately elects to reinstitute the existing rules.

However, the injunction to risk making determinate proposals, fabrications, institutions, constructions, or interpretations (texts) must suspend undecidability in order to reinvent the rule, as Žižek puts it, "out of a singular situation where this intervention has to obey pragmatic/strategic considerations and is never at the level of decision itself."[62] For Derrida, actual proposals are never at the level of "decision itself" because they of necessity decide the undecidable. In other words, by necessarily operating as if this can be done, actual decisions automatically violate or suspend the very condition of undecidability that makes a decision possible in the first place. Notably, for Derrida, this double bind, which cannot be resolved, by no means leads to the renunciation of all actual proposals. Rather, its recognition is simply a warning concerning any naïve belief in the infallibility of proposed or instituted measures.

Allowing for its due complexity, I am certain that "Derrida's operation" would give the lie to Žižek's implicit contention that it does not offer adequate means to grasp the complexity of the Lacanian proposition that "the (ethical) act proper" is neither a matter of obeying rationally constructed moral codes nor a passive and abject "response to the unfathomable Other's call" but occurs rather in the suspension of otherness in both of its forms (Symbolic Order and Thing).[63] When the Symbolic Order is suspended, Antigone momentarily becomes the Thing, thereby also suspending its secret. In other words, both forms of the other become contaminated. In Žižek's words:

> What gives Antigone such unshakable, uncompromising fortitude to persist in her decision is precisely the direct identification of her particular/determinate decision with the Other's (Thing's) injunction/call . . . for a brief, passing moment of decision, she *is* the Thing directly, thus excluding herself from the community regulated by the intermediate agency of symbolic regulations.[64]

Spectral Analysis and the Plural Logic of the Aporia

When Žižek undertakes to explain what he means by the ethical act, it is very difficult to see how it differs from what Derrida has in mind with the plural logic of the aporia. In some ways, the elaboration of this argument does not belong here, for it presupposes much of what still needs to be laid out concerning both Lacanian and Derridean discourses. Rather than interrupting the argumentative flow by deferring its discussion, however, one may treat what follows as setting the tone for what I wish to argue in more detail in the rest of the text. To explain the Lacanian proposition concerning the status of Antigone's act as paradoxically both actual and absolute (or unconditional), Žižek requests a shift in mindset, from any kind of dualistic thinking to the structural threesome that may be represented graphically by the figure of a "Borromean knot."[65] Such a knot is often, but not exclusively, represented by three interlinked rings of the kind most commonly associated with Venn diagrams. The linkage here is such that three structures are interdependent in such a way that each one holds the other two both together and apart in a tensional relationship. Breaking one, therefore, destroys the axis between the other two, causing them to collapse into one another.

Further, to understand the logical structure underpinning Antigone's act, one must first submit "the topic of the other" to "a kind of a spectral analysis," which divides it into three kinds.[66] Here, Žižek names the Imaginary other, which names other people like me, or, that is, my neighbor as my mirror image; the Symbolic "big Other," which refers to the impersonal set of rules that coordinate our intersubjective coexistence; and the other as Real, which indicates "the impossible Thing," the traumatic kernel of unfathomable or radical, monstrous otherness in each of us. Žižek names it the "inhuman partner," and describes it as "the Other with whom no symmetrical dialogue, mediated by the symbolic Order, is possible . . . the neighbor (*Nebenmensch*) as the Thing means that, beneath the neighbor as my semblable, my mirror image, there always lurks the unfathomable abyss of radical Otherness, a monstrous Thing that cannot be 'gentrified.'"[67]

Notably, like Derrida, Žižek implicitly claims that the term "other" cannot be made to cohere since its gathers together incompatible senses, none of which can be reduced out of the picture nor privileged in any form of hierarchical ordering. Instead, Žižek argues that the various senses of the term "other" form a Borromean knot, whereby the linkage between them is such that "no axis between two terms can subsist without the third one." He goes on to address what would happen in each case if one of these terms were to be suspended. Significantly, the consequence of suspending one term, which engenders the collapse of the other two, is precisely the kind of aporetic predicament that Derrida consistently insists upon. I hope, then, that the more formal exposition of the "plural logic of the aporia" to follow in the next section, and its elaboration in the rest of this study, will demonstrate just why, beyond their lexical and stylistic differences, Lacan and Derrida say precisely the same thing concerning so many issues.

To begin with, Žižek addresses what would happen if the "big Other" (the Symbolic Order) is suspended. He argues, first, that the domestication of the monstrous Thing (its "socialization," if you like), which usually produces a "normal fellow human," requires a third, mediating agency to which both self and other are willing to submit. Notably, the word "normal" here condenses his reference to the one like me, the other person as a mirror image that I can identify with at the level of the Imaginary Order. In his words:

> In order to render our coexistence with the Thing minimally bearable, the symbolic order qua Third, the pacifying mediator, has to intervene: the "gentrification" of the homely [ugly] Other Thing into a "normal fellow human" cannot occur through our direct interaction but presupposes the third agency to which we both submit—there is no intersubjectivity . . . without the impersonal symbolic Order.[68]

Accordingly, to suspend the functioning of the Symbolic Order (the "big Other"), as Antigone did, is to risk a situation in which "the friendly neighbor coincides with the monstrous Thing" whom nobody can understand. In the terms of Derrida's plural logic of the aporia, one can articulate the resulting aporia as follows: this suspension of the Symbolic Order is the necessary condition for the very life of a social system. Why? It enables such a system to resist its own tendency toward economic inertia and opens it to the life-giving advent of aneconomic otherness (chance, anomaly, etc.). Without such suspension, then, *rigor mortis* sets in and one risks the aporia of inertial stasis or paralysis. Yet it simultaneously breaks the cultural bond. In this moment of suspension, nobody can communicate, necessarily leaving an individual as alone as Antigone was to face the singularizing trauma of the ethical act (genuinely decisive action). In this case, one risks not inertial stasis but the entropic dissolution or fragmentation of community, which amounts to another kind of paralysis.

Žižek next addresses what would happen if neighborliness is suspended, arguing that "if there is no neighbor to whom I can relate as a human partner, the symbolic Order itself turns into the monstrous thing that directly parasitizes upon me." Here, the Derridean aporia may be described in terms of the following example. The suspension of neighborliness is the necessary condition for fair labor practice in an institution such as a university. There must, of course, be administrative structures and measures in any institution, for instance, to prevent nepotism. In the absence of such structures, the institution risks falling prey to entropic dissolution. Yet the suspension of neighborliness means that there is no call upon me for an empathetic response, and in this case, ethical action is reduced to mere calculation based on a cold-hearted system of specific duties and obligations. The consequent destruction of a tradition of collegiality opens a university to the tyrannical dictatorship of impersonal administration and risks the inertial paralysis summed up in the phrase "rules are rules."

Finally, Žižek addresses what would happen if the traumatic Thing is suspended. In his words: "if there is no Thing to underpin our everyday, symbolically regulated exchange with others, we find ourselves in a 'flat,' aseptic, Habermasian universe in which subjects are deprived of their hubris of excessive passion, reduced to lifeless pawns in the regulated game of communication."[69] Again the Derridean aporia emerges in the following: one must suspend aneconomic insecurity as the necessary condition for securing our law-bound institutions or face entropic paralysis. Yet if the "savage soul" is destroyed, humanity is indeed rescued from multiple insecurities (associated with all excess: secrets, passions, mysteries, etc.), but paradoxically this security is simultaneously threatening, for the tyranny of absolutely clear, systematic regulation, of inertial paralysis, is consummately dangerous.

On the basis of this spectral analysis, Žižek argues that the ethical act in the Lacanian sense, the moment of decision, is made possible in the first scenario, when the Symbolic Order is suspended and the actual Antigone becomes the Thing. In this moment of collapse, she herself becomes singular, unfathomable, inimitable. To repeat Žižek's words: "for a brief, passing moment of decision, she is the Thing directly." Thus she is the one for whom there is no mirroring neighbor, and she excludes herself from the network of rules that constitutes communal life, becoming the traumatic cause of her own framework of value. I do not see Derridean discourse engendering contrary claims concerning what it means for someone like Antigone to become the Thing in the temporary moment of decision. As Caputo, for example, notes: "The only thing that can be called 'just' is a singular action in a singular situation, and this only for the while that it lasts, in the instant of decision. The warm glow of justice never settles over the law, the rule, the universal, the 'maxim' that can be drawn from this singular 'event,' or still less over the person deciding, who can never say, 'I am just.'"[70]

Notably, both emphasize that the moment of decision is fleeting; for were this not the case, no intersubjective life would be possible at all. To reestablish intersubjective life subsequent to the moment of decision, the "Antigones" of the world and all those around them must confront such a singular, traumatic reconfiguration of value, and in some way or another come to terms with it; that is, make sense of it, domesticate and codify it, and therefore face again the aporia of inertia that the moment of decision originally served to disrupt.[71] Thus, the human condition remains an irresolvable predicament, since it is suspended between the aporias of either inertia or entropy. Recognizing the human condition as a predicament recalls philosophy to questioning vigilance in face of what Nietzsche, long before Levinas, exposed as its centripetal tendency toward ideological closure, and it keeps it open toward the unforeseeable to come. In other words, the logic of the predicament serves as a reminder that philosophy, and *mutatis mutandi* law, ethics, politics, psychoanalysis and all other institutional practices, are paradoxically required to resist death by risking their very lifeblood. For the sake of philosophy, the question of philosophy—that is, philosophy's question of its very possibility—must forever remain a question; a question to be answered, certainly, but without final answer.[72] Likewise, no institutional practices can afford to close off the question of their very possibility: for in refusing to risk their foundations, which is indeed genuinely the risk of paralyzing entropic destruction, these practices submit themselves to the equal risk of inertial destruction, which is just another word for death.

In conclusion, to acknowledge the human condition as an aporetic predicament, which emphasizes irreducible undecidability, is hardly to doom us to indecisiveness and therefore practical impotence, apathy, and abdication. Indeed, Derrida insists on the precise opposite. For him, the incoherence within law, marked by Justice, or the undecidability within politics, marked by Ethics, has never been an excuse for staying out of juridicopolitical battles but is rather precisely the reason for entering into them.[73] Right from where we find ourselves now, he insists, we remain under a constant obligation to negotiate the relation between the calculable and the incalculable, without the kind of rigid rule that cannot be reinvented. This requirement indicates a double movement. First, there is an unlimited responsibility for constant learning: reading; interpreting; interrogating what justice is, has been, and can be: its origin, grounds, and limits. It is essential to make decisions, on the basis of particular analyses, involving actual people in actual circumstances, which respond to the letter of the law, with determinate economicopolitical proposals, revolutionary or otherwise.

But this "responsibility" must be tempered by a structurally necessary anxious moment: for, inevitably, the justice called possible or determinate will always already be contaminated by the injustice that haunts this possibility. This recognition, in turn, will not let anyone rest content, since the "idea of justice," which understands justice as "impossible" in the sense that it is always "to come," will always call, unsatisfied, from beyond its determination. This "idea of justice" opens up the space in which law may be recast or transformed, for it acknowledges that there is no justice (only law) unless some event is possible, which exceeds "knowledge" (calculation, rules, programs, anticipations). This has amounted to a very brief preliminary sketch of how one may begin to read Derrida and Lacan together. What follows is a formalization of the above attempts to rescue the quasi-transcendental complexity of Derrida's thinking from the influential misreadings just addressed, both of which, in their own ways, reduce deconstruction to its aneconomic moment. To do this, I shall in a sense return to the beginning; to one of Derrida's early seminal texts, "*Différance.*"

Différance *and the "Plural Logic of the Aporia"*

In "*Différance*," Derrida's introduction of his well-known neologism takes as its point of departure a semantic analysis that, while "simple and approximate," was intended to lead readers "to within sight of what is at stake."[74] Here he links *différance* to Latin rather than Greek roots, since, alongside its obvious sense, "to differ," the Latin root has an additional motif, not found in the Greek, which he equally wishes to exploit, namely "to defer." In light of the typical oversimplifying misinterpretation just described, it is important to emphasize here that *différance* is always the articulation of "difference" and "deferral" but that both notions, in turn, harbor incompatible economic and aneconomic senses. On this basis, Derrida goes on to argue that there are always two "economies" of *différance*: as temporization, it names the productive work of economic difference and deferral (a "restricted economy"); as spacing, it names the disseminative play or drift of aneconomic difference and deferral (a "general economy").[75] Derrida later replaces these terms with the more accurate economic/aneconomic distinction that I give preference to here.[76]

Unfortunately, "the problematic of the sign and of writing" with which he merely began his essay has proved to be something of a straitjacket, for it tempts many readers to view *différance* as pertaining solely to language and texts rather than standing as a nickname for his theory of constitution. It is to escape the strictures of the reception that binds his thinking to a theory of language that, as mentioned earlier, he proposes the "plural logic of the aporia" as a better mode of access to the double bind that *différance* improperly names. *Différance*, in short, is one way of saying that all phenomena are constituted by equally imperative economic and aneconomic aporias, between which, as I shall repeat compulsively, it is never a question of choosing but of articulation. If the constitution of phenomena happens as *différance*, then, in his words: "It would be necessary to recognize both the typical or recurring form [economic] and the inexhaustible singularization [aneconomic]—without which there will never be any event, decision, responsibility, ethics, or politics."[77]

Différance ***as Temporization and the Economic Aporia***

Saussure's diacritical model of signification supports both economic and aneconomic *différance*, for Saussure notes a rather paradoxical situation in which the fundamental principle of arbitrariness in the signifier/signified association is the condition of both the immutability and the mutability of the sign. He argues that the relative immutability of the signifier/signified relation is not only due to a pragmatic, inertial conservatism. Rather, signification resists change in principle, again not because of some natural or rational bond between signifier and signified but precisely because of the arbitrariness of their association. On the basis of such arbitrariness, Saussure came to his famous conclusion that terms are constituted within a complex network of differential relations. But the terms within this network are determined not only by coterminous associative relations but also by linear relations of antecedence and anticipation.

It is this equally fundamental principle of linearity that restricts the freeplay of coterminous associations without arresting the movement by which meanings shift. This is the case both syntagmatically (for example, in the linear chain that forms a sentence, words prefigure what follows and confer sense on what has gone before) and paradigmatically, in the sense that a term cannot but retain traces of its heritage and engender expectations. What a term has meant historically, then, co-constitutes its present sense vis-à-vis this heritage, as, for example, the same as ever, an alteration of some kind, or a radical break. Whatever the case, such traces already co-constitute the sense of a present term, and for Saussure, this effect of convention ensures that signification remains in principle resistant to change.

In its economic guise, then, constitutive activity strives to incorporate and systematize every component in a calculable network of differential interrelations.[78] Here, nothing ought to be wasted; there should be neither incomprehensible excess nor unrecoverable loss. In other words, the risk that a term faces in the play of relational differences is merely the risk of losing a particular position or identity but not the loss of identity or meaning *as such*. The negation, repression, or deferral of a term, or its fall from privilege in a hierarchy, therefore, remains meaningful insofar as it is accommodated within the economy as an investment in the service of a better arrangement. Here, there is nothing but meaning: even what is still to come can be made to make sense as a future that is always already anticipated.

Further, consciously invoking Freud's "reality principle," which, while still serving pleasure, requires its suspension or deferral as a protective mechanism for the sake of achieving "proper" gratification at a more appropriate moment,[79] Derrida describes "*différance* as temporization" as an "economic detour" whereby something is deferred, made negative or "other," repressed and held in reserve, in order to *work toward* "proper" presence in the future. "Deferral" in its economic sense, then, consists of two moments. Derrida describes the first as "the effort of life to protect itself by *deferring* the dangerous investment" or, again, "the action of putting off until later, of taking into account, of taking account of time and of the forces of an operation that implies an economical calculation, a detour, a delay, a relay, a reserve, a representation."[80] Importantly, then, it is "*différance* as spacing" (marked in the proliferation of differences) that is here deferred. In alternative terms, the "All" is deferred for the sake of the present. The second moment consists of the concomitantly produced teleological hope for its future restitution, marked by a movement that "always aims at coming back to the pleasure or the presence that have been deferred by (conscious or unconscious) calculation."[81]

Contrary to those accounts that understand *différance* only in terms of "dispersion," "*différance* as temporization," in Derrida's words, "conserves the stakes, remains in control of the play, limiting it and elaborating it by giving it form and meaning . . . this economy of life restricts itself to conservation, to circulation and self-reproduction as the reproduction of meaning."[82] Again, economic *différance* designates "a constitutive, productive and originary causality, the process of scission and division which would produce or constitute different things or differences."[83]

This economic account of *différance* accords with Derrida's economic account of the relation between structure and play,[84] whereby "structure" is said to come before and condition, regulate, or limit the relational play of elements in a system. Notably, "structure" here has always designated a centered system in which each element acquires value relative to a fixed point of reference that regulates the elements in play without itself becoming part of the play. A centered structure, then, designates an actual or projected systematic totality, whether this closure is thought of as architectonic (a transcendental principle regulates the play of elements), genetic (the system, even if open ended, has an *arche* or beginning that dominates and directs what comes after), or teleological (what closes the system is projected as a goal that directs activity toward its achievement). Its fixed point of reference, determined independently of the other elements in a system, is named the "transcendental signified," which in its full (albeit impossible) power designates the philosophical dream of finding the basic metaphysical principle that could regulate all elements in all systems in all contexts.[85] To awaken from this "dream of absolute presence"[86] is to have accepted the impossibility of any absolute in any domain (be it absolute justice, scientific truth, unimpeachable principles or rules, a completed philosophical system, true beauty, pure goodness, etc.) and to have given up on the dream of projecting any program for the perfection of knowledge (such as Leibniz's "universal characteristics") or for the totalization of political, ethical, religious, and social systems.[87]

Having awakened from this dream, the term "transcendental" is still used, but now to describe the conditions that make specific systems or economies possible, where otherwise diverse elements can be related to one another because of the value conferred upon them by their relation to elected transcendental "constants."[88] Lacan's term for such elected transcendental constants is the "*point de capiton*," which Žižek describes as the ultimately fake "quasi-transcendental master signifier that guarantees the consistency of the big Other."[89] This economic relativity, which accords with economic *différance*, suggests that there is a way of making relatively responsible knowledge claims: one may calculate, evaluate, order, and regulate terms insofar as each can acquire comparative value through its relation to an elected standard, and thereby to other terms, within the enclosed bounds of a specified system.

Economic *différance* also accords with the notion *problema* ("that which one poses or throws in front of oneself"), which for Derrida has a double signification. It signifies "projection" ("the projection of a project, of a task to accomplish") and "protection": "the protection created by a substitute, a prosthesis that we put forth in order to represent, replace, shelter, or dissimulate ourselves, or so as to hide something unavowable—like a shield . . . behind which one guards oneself *in secret* or *in shelter* in case of danger."[90] In posing a problem, one implicitly accepts that a solution *is* possible. The problem can be worked out in the near or distant future, given the right circumstances, instruments, formulas, etc. Therefore, in posing a problem at all, one has substituted for the flux of events or meanings a prosthetic device of manageable proportions. For example, in this protective gesture the call for justice becomes the "problem" of applying appropriate laws in a given situation. But any legal system acts as "a prosthesis that we put forth in order to represent, replace, shelter, or dissimulate" justice, so as to hide the fact that justice, which must do justice to the singular too, is never quite finally done in the application of law.

As this example suggests, without ever denying their necessity, Derrida insists that constituted systems will never be adequate to the "inexhaustible singularization" of that which they aim to systematize. Every time the singular is reduced to the economic articulation it exceeds, as Derrida puts it, "error, recklessness, the unthought, and irresponsibility are given the so very presentable face of good conscience."[91] Economic *différance*, therefore, involves a certain kind of aporia: the economic constitution of any closed or regulated system, in any domain, necessarily goes hand in hand with the suppression of the "aneconomic," or that which in relation to a system remains errant, dis-ordered, resistant, aleatory, unexpected, or nonsensical. Any kind of constitution or institution, therefore, cannot avoid the violence of exclusion. This aporia of limiting borders, allowing no free passage in or out, describes the dangerous logic of all ideologies: that of closure, stasis, security, protection, unity, gathering, nationalism. Here, the nonpassage of the aporia, Derrida insists, "resembles an impermeability; it would stem from the opaque existence of an uncrossable border: a door that does not open or that only opens according to an unlocatable condition, according to the inaccessible secret of some shibboleth. Such is the case for all closed borders (exemplarily during war)."[92]

Différance ***as Spacing and the Aneconomic Aporia***

To avoid the tendency toward terror inherent in economic *différance*, a theory of constitution must also do justice to the singular, by refusing to reduce it to what it must exceed, by suspending all borders and limits to accommodate the unthought excess. Thus, and this constitutes the enigma of *différance*, Derrida argues that it is simultaneously necessary to allow for the unproductive, aneconomic terms of what he calls "*différance* as spacing," which is placed alongside "*différance* as temporization," since it commands equal (but not greater) necessity. I shall address the question of their articulation below.

Difference in its aneconomic sense, whether this is "a question of dissimilar otherness [differents] or of allergic and polemical otherness [differends],"[93] again takes its cue from the arbitrary nature of the signifier/signified connection. Although the principle of linearity favors a certain historical continuity, it does not necessarily interdict abrupt and wholesale changes in the signifier/signified associations. For Saussure, as a second consequence of the arbitrary nature of the sign, "language is radically powerless to defend itself against the forces which from one moment to the next are shifting the relationship between the signified and the signifier."[94] In the referential models of language he sought to supplant, arbitrariness attaches itself to the relation between name and referent, which means a shift in signifier should be of no great import, for the meaning would remain intact no matter what signifier is used. But in a diacritical model, a shift in signifier changes the signified too, since the meaning is constituted in their relationship. In this case, there is no guarantee that the signified will remain intact from one context to the next.

Taken in its aneconomic sense, then, the Saussurean dictum that there are no positive terms, only relations of difference, marks an "endless proliferation of differences" marking the impossibility of final definition, since the number of defining differences to consider has no natural, nonselectively imposed limit. Accordingly, because no imposed limit has the ultimate power to curb a restless, playful, disseminative drift in which differences (and, therefore, terms) proliferate relentlessly in an unregulated, entropic, play without gain, "deferral" takes on its opposing sense as the deferral of meaning.[95]

Aneconomic *différance* designates a situation in which something singular and inconsistent has taken the place occupied by the constant, shareable, transcendental standard described above. In this case, what confers relative value may be the singular judging subject, for example, or a unique group that is contingently determined by a specific, historical, cultural, social, and linguistic background. Here, there are as many measures of value as there are subjective positions from which relative values are conferred. There is also no basis for choice among these positions, for every preference is itself merely a similarly subjective evaluation. Further, nothing in this subject prevents contingent, often capricious, changes of mind. This implies not only that nothing has an absolute (intrinsic, essential) value but also that no system of relativity, no relational structure or context, no transcendental *telos* or *arche* can be constituted that would plausibly, for the most part, be valid from multiple different standpoints and could, therefore, confer relatively stable, shareable values on the relevant elements. According to Derrida, then, the aneconomic imperative of *différance* requires a shift from the notion of centered structures to that of "discourse," by which he means "a system in which the central signified, the original or transcendental signified, is never absolutely present outside a system of differences."

In other words, if the center is caught up in the play of differences, we are bound to conclude that "play" comes before and conditions "structure." Yet a diacritical relationality unregulated by the presence of a transcendental signified inevitably "extends the domain and the play of signification infinitely," making it impossible to see how one could constitute enduringly present "things" at all, or, that is, institute scientific, legal, political, economic, ethical, or religious systems. In an aneconomic sense, then, a different kind of aporia arises. Here, as Derrida puts it, "the nonpassage, the impasse or aporia, stems from the fact that there is no limit. There is not yet or there is no longer a border to cross, no opposition between two sides: the limit is too porous, permeable, and indeterminate."[96]

Here, then, it is not merely that one cannot find the solution to a problem. Rather, as Derrida notes, it is "because one could no longer find even a problem that would constitute itself and that one would keep in front of oneself, as a presentable object or project, as a protective representative or a prosthetic substitute." Unlike posing a problem, which depends on this, the *aporia* here strips us of any recourse to generalities, to shareable standards, formulas, values, and so on. Facing this *aporia*, we are in Derrida's words "singularly exposed in our absolute and absolutely naked uniqueness, that is to say, disarmed, delivered to the other, incapable of even sheltering ourselves behind what could still protect the interiority of a secret."

The Aporia of the Aporias: Paradoxical Articulation

Economic *différance* operates in the domain of the possible, in the sense not only of what is already apparent but also of what can be imagined or teleologically projected. In other words, the possible is that which *can* become a problem or the object of a project. It is that for the sake of which one develops a program of research or activity. On the other hand, without disputing the necessity of drawing the encircling border that encloses "the possible" within any economy, structure, or research program, Derrida notes that one simultaneously co-constitutes what remains unspeakable or inconceivable within it. For example, all legal systems represent "the possible," the "element of calculation," in any juridical discourse, in relation to which Justice itself remains incorrigibly elusive, "an experience of the impossible." In Derrida's words: "Every time that something comes to pass or turns out well, every time that we placidly apply a good rule to a particular case, to a correctly subsumed example, according to a determinant judgment, we can be sure that law (*droit*) may find itself accounted for, but certainly not justice. Law (*droit*) is not justice."[97]

While opposing and negating one another, economic and aneconomic imperatives command equal force. Concerning justice, to continue the example, the task (the impossibility) we face is of reconciling "the act of justice that must always concern singularity, individuals, irreplaceable groups and lives, the other or myself *as* other, in a unique situation, with rule, norm, value or the imperative of justice which necessarily have a general form."[98] It is therefore the question of conjunction that finally imposes itself. Mimicking the pattern of questioning that opens "The Force of Law," one may ask whether the logic of their interconnection in Derrida's thinking is economic.[99] Does it "insure, permit, authorize the possibility of" meaning in general? Does it enable "a discourse of consequence" on meaning, that is, an economic account of the conditions of its possibility? "Yes, certain people would reply; no, replies the other party." On the other hand, isn't this logic aneconomic? May one legitimately insist that it does not permit any making of sense, any sensible discourse on meaning in general, but instead threatens sense because it ruins its very condition of possibility? "Yes, certain people would reply; no, replies the other party." Derrida's own response, as mentioned repeatedly, is to challenge this style of questioning: "I can offer no response, at least no reassuring response, to any questions put in this way ('either/or,' 'yes or no'), to either party or to either party's expectations formalized in this way."

The aporetic logic that makes it necessary to avoid a choice between economic and aneconomic *différance* does not fall from the sky but emerges in dialogue with other options in the transcendental tradition. Derrida finds his thinking persistently haunted by what could, up to a certain point, be called antinomial antagonisms between equal economic and aneconomic imperatives, or, if you like, between law and justice, ethical systems and responsibility, institution and invention, truth and fiction, present and gift, philosophy and literature, and so on indefinitely.[100] Yet, in the end, he denies the interchangeability of "antinomy" and aporia, insisting instead on "aporia rather than antinomy" to describe the impasse he regularly faces in the course of his own thinking. The difference is this: the impasse in metaphysics reflected in the antinomies of Kant's *First Critique* is closer to Derrida's articulation of the concept *problema*. Kant was convinced that these antinomial conflicts were resolvable, since they were the consequence of faulty logic operating in tandem with a faulty ontology, which had led old-style metaphysicians into the trap of illegitimately attributing excessive powers to speculative (or theoretical) reason.[101] In his view, therefore, one could cut a passage through this metaphysical impasse by virtue of an alternative, more correct, transcendental way of thinking.

Derrida grants Kant's "transcendental turn," but in the shift to quasi-transcendental thinking, he still finds himself tied up in aporetic predicaments, since inescapable paradoxes persist after one has circumvented, via the "transcendental turn," the logical and ontological errors Kant detected. In short, unlike Kant's antinomial conflicts, which are resolvable not indeed through either/or logic but through an alternative philosophical path, the antagonisms that haunt Derrida's thinking remain irresolvable and present instead "an interminable experience" that is not simply antinomial but incorrigibly aporetic.

If such antagonisms, for Derrida, are not linked as resolvable antinomies, just as little can they be linked and resolved through the dialectical synthesis proposed by Hegel, which rejects Kant's "transcendental turn" outright.[102] Hegel credits Kant with an all-pervading philosophical principle of synthesis, but he criticizes him particularly for his resolution of the antinomies via the transcendental turn, with its correlative "scandal to philosophy," which, unhappily according to Hegel, constitutes human consciousness as structurally lacking and doomed merely to desire what it is constitutionally unable to achieve, namely a speculative grasp of the unconditioned. In his view, the gap left in reason by Kant's "transcendental turn," improperly mediated by an unsatisfactory teleological bridge, blocks the true dialectical mediation of one with all in the encompassing unity of absolute knowledge. Instead, he insists that a true synthesis, as opposed to an architectonic (where mutually opposing domains remain inescapably separate and require a bridging device), requires the work of dialectical negation.

Following Rudolphe Gasché, one can find in the figure of the *symploke* (interweaving, synthesis) an indication of what Hegel, after Plato, understood by the dialectical interweaving of opposites through the work of negation.[103] For Plato, the desired interwoven unity of a soul or community is achievable precisely because opposites negate each other, which means that they can be linked dialectically, or in active harmony, whereby one moderates the other. Plato's true statesman acts as a sovereign weaver (that is, as a philosopher), who constitutes the city-state by plaiting together warring opposites in souls and communities. Such a statesman has to know just the blend of clashing virtues that would, for example, make for courage rather than arrogant recklessness or weak cautiousness.

Implicitly, Hegel takes the *symploke* to be the figure par excellence of the philosophical enterprise, although he gives it a teleological aspect.[104] For him, the interweaving of mutually negating opposites, for the sake of constituting an ultimately unified, harmoniously mediated whole, is the very principle governing world history: an originally absolutely internal, self-contained "Spirit" undergoes an originary alienation whereby it is externalized as the dark matter of the world. The teleological movement of world history is directed, through an intricate and elaborate series of dialectical linkages, toward the circular return of Sprit to Spirit through the detour of matter. The dialectical struggle to achieve this telos occurs as the cyclical repetition of "diremption" (the splitting of a unity into opposing but interdependent terms) and "*aufhebung*"; that is, the mutual negation of opposing terms, which turns out to be self-negation, for the terms are interdependent, leading to the collapse from whose ashes will arise a "higher" unity that immediately generates a new "diremption." I suppose the point, for Hegel, of this Ulyssean journey to the outer limits and back again is that through it Spirit will have gained self-awareness. Instead of just being the unity of all with all, it will now know itself as this unity.

Yet, as Derrida has argued, it is only by repressing contingent and capricious interconnections or, that is, relations that are not "proper" dialectical oppositions, that Hegel can privilege dialectical mediation as a viable principle for interweaving elements into a unified whole.[105] Derrida, in contrast, is not willing to effect this reduction, although he is equally unwilling to give philosophical interweaving up entirely to the unregulated play of such connections. In his view, the philosophical task becomes one of interweaving the kind of economic interconnections that fall within the scope of the *symploke* with unpredictable or nonsystematic linkages. However, in answer to the teleological movement of Hegel's dialectical interweaving, he insists that system and nonsystem, while indeed facing one another as reciprocally negating opposites, nevertheless constitute two necessities that do not mediate one another in a progressive movement toward the elevated condition of a higher synthesis.

Both Kant and Hegel, still working in the blinding light of the Principle of Reason, found an asymmetric, incomplete architectonic or system intolerable. In the wake of the later Heidegger's appraisal, however, there is good reason to suspect this "principle of all principles."[106] Heidegger argues that faith in the Principle of Reason has directed the movement of Western philosophy toward extreme impoverishment, whereby the truth of being (which is its restlessness, or its tendency to withdraw from presence) is progressively suppressed for the sake of static or abiding configurations of present beings. Indeed, many traditional philosophers (including Kant, Hegel, and Husserl), dreamed of finally arresting philosophical thinking, leaving all others to come only the amusements of teaching, applying, and elaborating their systems, without grounds to challenge its foundational first principles. Heidegger, in contrast, aims to recover a future for thinking from the prospect of a preprogrammed repetition of the same, by questioning the very coherence and therefore legitimacy of the Principle of Reason.

He notes that this principle seems self-evident to modern minds. The insistence that "nothing is without reason" suggests a natural dissatisfaction until reason has reached the "unconditioned" in a regressive quest for conditions. But pressed harder, this "self-evidence" becomes enigmatic. The principle that requires an adequate reason for everything must by that token offer an adequate reason for itself. But this, Heidegger points out, is precisely what cannot be done; one cannot offer an adequate explanation for why there must be the principle of reason itself. If we apply the principle of reason to itself, then, we are cast into the obscurity of an abyss, where the foundation of all foundations itself lacks a foundation. In other words, the principle of reason, when turned upon itself, becomes, paradoxically, a little irrational. Moreover, if this enigma *is* its truth, then, for Heidegger, what we call "the truth" is conceivable not as self-evidence or systematic clarification but as enigma or paradox.

It is abundantly clear that Derrida takes to heart Heidegger's insistence upon truth as paradox and that it forms the basis of his refusal to choose between economic and aneconomic *différance*.[107] Remaining for the present within the domain of signification, Derrida points to a paradox or incoherence that unsettles (without being able to dismiss) the revision of the concept "sign" on which Saussure's diacritical model of language is based. Instead of "sign" designating the material mark that represents a predetermined referent, Saussure shows "sign" to be the concept that always already unifies mark and referent, or, in his revision, signifier and signified, such that one implies the other, just as one side of a sheet of paper implies the other. As mentioned earlier, this unity, along with the arbitrary nature of the connections between all signifiers and signifieds, means that it is impossible to prevent a certain slippage not just between mark and referent (which does not matter) but in the signified concept itself (since any shift in the signifier is automatically a shift in the signified).

By extension, no concept is in principle immune to such slippage. But, Derrida argues, this is precisely what cannot happen. In his words, "as soon as one seeks to demonstrate in this way that there is no transcendental or privileged signified and that the domain or play of signification henceforth has no limit, one must reject even the concept and word 'sign' itself—which is precisely what cannot be done."[108] That is, if we hope to defend the idea that Saussure's diacritical model of language unsettles the so-called metaphysics of presence, the concept "sign," which lies at its basis as the condition of the possibility of such sliding, cannot itself slide. Instead, one requires "sign" to have the fixed sense "sign-of," which indicates the unity of signifier and signified as well as the arbitrary nature of their connection. A fixed signification, then, is paradoxically the very condition of the possibility of unregulated diacritical relationality. A wholly unregulated, anchorless freeplay of differences is self-annulling, since the "play of differences" itself implies and requires the very constitution and preservation of different terms that it simultaneously threatens. But to constitute and preserve present terms, then, it becomes necessary to put *différance* as *spacing* out of play, to suspend it in favor of *différance* as *temporization*, by subjecting the play of differences to calculated economic or structural decisions about where to draw the lines and on what basis. There is, then, an incoherence or double bind at the heart of the aneconomic concept of "play": for there to be a play of differences at all, rather than formless chaos, such play must first be put out of play. But "play" that is made possible only on the basis of economy or structure (a center, standard, constant, or transcendental condition) cannot be "play" in any strict sense of the term.

From this circularity one cannot but conclude that there is something incoherent at the heart of aneconomic *différance*, and one might consider rejecting it altogether in favor of its counterpart. Yet as Derrida has argued, the concept of the "center," which lies at the basis of economic *différance* (system, structure, problem, possibility) equally engenders a paradox, for if it is the fixed "center" (or selected constant) that makes the play of permutations possible at all, it is also the notion "center" that, as Derrida puts it, "closes off the play which it opens up and makes possible."[109] By regulating the play of elements without itself playing, the center is included within a relational system as regulator and remains external to it as an independently determined point of stability outside of it. As Derrida puts it: "The concept of centered structure is in fact the concept of a play based on a fundamental ground, a play constituted on the basis of a fundamental immobility and a reassuring certitude, which is itself beyond the reach of play."[110] However, as Derrida notes, the economic conception of the center as a point of presence determined independently of the relations of difference within a system is disrupted by the unsettling recognition that it has a history (demonstrated by the substitution of one center for another).[111] In sum, just as Heidegger finds an incoherence at the very heart of the Principle of Reason, namely that the ground of all grounds cannot itself be grounded, so there is an incoherence that unsettles economic *différance*, for the fixity that is required to come before and condition a differential play of permutations both must and cannot avoid playing.

By listening for the enigma that sounds in the Principle of Reason, Heidegger suggests, we come to the awareness that there is always a double movement going on. On the one hand, there is the active articulation or configuration of the being of beings, associated with research, where, in accordance with the Principle of Reason, one tirelessly seeks the fundamental reasons for what is given. On the other hand, there is a passive, receptive movement of give and take, whereby ever restless being gives what it gives (like the rose), and those who are surprised by the gift receive it without the power of knowing its "why" or anticipating its "when." In this case, the recipient steps back from the question "why?" resting content with appreciative contemplation. Following in Heidegger's wake, Derrida articulates the logic of just such a double movement, which interconnects the economic attitude that promotes active, research-oriented questioning with an aneconomic attitude that celebrates what comes our way by chance or takes us by surprise.

For Derrida, what is finally at stake in the "plural logic of the aporia" is the experience of what happens when, in trying to determine certain notions as practical concepts, we find ourselves facing a kind of paralysis (for example, the double bind, dilemma, the undecidable, or the performative contradiction). He describes this third type of aporia, associated with the figure of the impossible, as the impasse of paradox. Derrida does not strive to overcome such incoherence but insists upon its inevitability.[112] As he puts it, when dealing "with names (event, decision, responsibility, ethics, politics—Europe) of 'things' that can only exceed (and *must* exceed) the order of theoretical determination" or, that is, "the order of the *present* or of *presentation*," we find that such names gather together under a "single" notion equally necessary but mutually ruinous senses.[113] Since such notions are "ruined" by an irremediable internal dilemma regarding their very definition, they cannot, in principle, cohere or be unified. Moreover, this plural logic "appears to be paradoxical enough so that the partitioning [*partage*] among multiple figures of aporia does not oppose figures to each other, but instead installs the haunting of the one in the other."[114] In other words, one is not here dealing with straight contradictions but economic and aneconomic senses that are bound together in a knot such that loosening one side tightens the other, in a movement Derrida calls "stricture."[115] This "plural logic of the aporia," according to Derrida is at work in "all the figures called undecidable that imposed themselves under the names of *pharmakon*, supplement, hymen, differance, and a great number of others, which carried with them predicates that are contradictory or incompatible between themselves, in their very *between*, in their interlacing, their chiasmatic invagination, their *sumploke*, or their *Geflecht*."[116]

The Analogy of the Gift

Derrida demonstrates this vertiginously circular "plural logic of the aporia" in relation to something ostensibly simple and concrete, namely the giving of a gift.[117] Ordinarily speaking, as Derrida points out, it seems to go without saying that in giving a gift: (1) some "one" (some recognizable unity, be it a person or group) (2) gives some identifiable "thing" (which could be material or symbolic) (3) to some "one other" (singular or collective).[118] These basic transcendental conditions of there being a gift, he notes, seem innocuous enough, even tautological. Yet if one looks at them more closely, these conditions of possibility give rise to a paradox, for they are simultaneously the very conditions that make the gift impossible. The same conditions that produce the gift simultaneously produce its ruin. In his words:

> For this is the impossible that seems to give itself to be thought here: These conditions of possibility of the gift (that some "one" gives some "thing" to some "one other") designate simultaneously the conditions of the impossibility of the gift. And already we could translate this into other terms: these conditions of possibility define or produce the annulment, the annihilation, the destruction of the gift."[119]

Derrida argues as follows:[120] For there to have been a gift, strictly speaking, the giving of something to someone cannot be taken up in any way into a circular economy of reciprocity or exchange. Yet, by simply recognizing the gift for what it is, one seems to destroy it as such, since this recognition binds the giving into just such an economy. In recognizing and keeping a gift, the recipient becomes caught up in a circle of debt, gratitude, and reciprocation, where she feels obliged somehow to repay the giver, even with a simple word of thanks, either now or sometime in the future. And even if she refuses the gift, it still remains that she has perceived or recognized the meaning of the giving and offered this acknowledgment in return. Thus, instead of simply gaining by receiving something, the recipient finds herself equally a debtor. But even before such acknowledgment or recognition turns the recipient into a debtor, it is enough for it to be annulled as a gift that the gift be perceived, intended, or recognized as such by the giver, since the giver, as soon as the intention to give is made clear, begins to repay herself with approving recognition. In this case, instead of simply giving (and incurring the loss), the giver becomes just as much the receiver.[121]

In view of this, one might want to suggest that if there is to be the giving of the gift, instead of the mere exchange of presents, it would only occur in a way that escapes the circular economy of exchange. This giving, then, would have to be a sharing without return, where the receiver does not owe anything (not even recognition), and the giver is not in a position to expect or desire restitution. For there to have been a gift (a giving that entirely escapes the economy of grateful or self-congratulatory recognition), neither the recipient nor the giver must be able to recognize the "thing" given or the giving for what it is. By extension, then, for a gift to be possible, there cannot, strictly speaking, be a recognized recipient or a recognized giver either. In other words, the giving of a gift can only happen if everything about the event is hidden or withdrawn. But this means that the gift as such cannot ever appear; it can never be present as a phenomenon. One could say that in this case, the gift could never be converted into a mere present.

We are, in sum, caught up in a double bind. For there to be the giving of a genuine gift (a gift that lives up to its definition, the gift as gift, the gift itself, which exceeds its recognition as a present), the giving cannot be caught up in any economy. It must, instead, remain utterly aneconomic. Yet, if the giving of a gift must remain aneconomic, then, paradoxically, the only way a gift can *be* a gift is if it were *not present* as a present: for the gift to be what it "truly" is, it cannot be. In both cases, then, of economy and of the aneconomic, there is no gift. In other words, Derrida's analysis of the gift takes the form of a dilemma. If the gift has to be recognizable in order to be a gift, then the gift is impossible, for the recognition destroys it by converting it into a present. On the other hand, if the gift has to be unrecognizable in order to be a gift, then the gift is again impossible, for in the lack of recognition there is no gift.

The gift, therefore, is impossible. In face of this impossible, however, Derrida by no means allows one simply to throw up one's hands in frustration or give in to paralyzed inactivity. Giving still happens all the time. Derrida's point is simply that as soon as it is recognized as such, or made present, the giving is ruined by the gift. Further, he insists that one must still give recognizable gifts, but without naïveté. One must give, but in the knowledge that the gift is ruined by the giving. For Derrida,

> it is a matter—desire beyond desire—of responding faithfully but also as rigorously as possible both to the injunction or the order of the *gift* ("give" ["*donne*"]) as well as to the injunction or the order of meaning (presence, science, knowledge): *Know* still what giving *wants to say, know how to give*, know what you intend to give, know how the gift annuls itself, commit yourself [*engage-toi*] even if commitment is the destruction of the gift by the gift, give economy its chance.[122]

Thinking in terms of Derrida's theory of constitution, one may say analogously that the aneconomic aspect of *différance* submits to "the injunction . . . of the *gift*" while its economic aspect respects "the injunction . . . of meaning" or, that is, the *present*. Derrida insists that one ought to be serious about economy: one should not abdicate the responsibility for economizing, taking decisions, drawing boundaries, and actively inventing economic or relational systems, in the name of aneconomic freeplay, since this, in any event, remains impossible. But even if, as he remarks, economy cannot abide laughter, the aneconomic will nevertheless not fail to show itself in the "return of the repressed," in the symptomatic laughter that rings out whenever one takes an economy too seriously.[123] One must constitute recognizable phenomena, but without naïveté, in full awareness that they are already relatively ruined in the violence of the constitutive process. If one must economize on the play of the world, such economic "putting out of play" can only ever be a temporary suspension, for one is also acted upon by the aneconomic play of differences, which always resists and interrupts the work, sways an economy off course. The play of the world, which goes on relentlessly, without why, and regardless of our decisions, will inevitably ruin anything dreamed of as possible: chance events unspeakable and unpredictable within the economy make an absolute institution impossible and compel one time and again to reinvent its bounds and project its aims anew—which is a good thing. Thus, the aneconomic movement of *différance* still happens all the time as the "virus" in any system, but as soon as it is recognized as such, or made present, the rebellious power of aneconomic *différance* is ruined in the recognition.

We are, then, again trapped in an aporia whereby on both economic and aneconomic accounts of *différance*, the happening of *différance* as such, and what it gives are lost. Like the gift, both *différance* and what it gives are, strictly speaking, impossible. In the interweaving of active constitution and the passion of "going through" the ordeal of the impossible, which ruins all that is constituted, Derrida acknowledges the necessity and inevitability of the "plural logic of the aporia" and insists on the value of learning to live with it.

Concluding Remarks: Deconstructive Reading

By uncovering the aporias that inevitably arise whenever we try to convert ethical, political, aesthetic, and theoretical issues into problems, Derrida gives those who come after him a "logic" to work with, which offers a suitably complex and sophisticated way of "making sense" of the incorrigible persistence of interpretative differences across the spectrum of human practices. But at the same time, his gift does not take the responsibility for thinking and decision making out of another's hands, for the logic he offers can never be reduced to the mere application of a predetermined method. Instead, it is precisely the aporias, which announce the impossibility of Justice, Ethics, Meaning, and so on (conceived in terms of a preprogrammed set of a priori rules), that make a genuine experience of justice, ethics, or meaning possible; for it is the lack inherent to thought-numbing rules that calls one to engage seriously in the never-ending, difficult, but liberating task of thinking and rethinking what makes for an *ethos*, what responsibility enjoins, what the text desires.

Concerning the question of reading, Derrida describes two styles of deconstructive reading. The more historical (or more anamnesic) style proceeds through close readings of texts. If one reads a text that claims to have uncovered the ultimate foundations of anything or the systematic interconnection of everything (philosophy's favorite themes), one can be sure to find gaps, logical leaps, and moments of ambiguity or vagueness, which function as symptoms of the fact that the impossibility of ultimate foundations or final systemizations has had to be dissimulated. The other, more demonstrative and apparently ahistorical style concentrates on demonstrating logicoformal paradoxes in the formation, institution, or making present of concepts, ideas, or systems (such as law and justice, ethics and obligation, economy and gift, and so on). Derrida's reading of Freud's texts, to which I shall now turn, employs both strategies. Notably, this places his careful and detailed deconstructive reading of Freudian psychoanalysis in marked and curious contrast with his sparse and unjustly dismissive treatment of Lacan's texts.

PART 2

Derrida Reading Freud: The Paradoxes of Archivization

> Freud advanced only by suspending, without any possibility of stopping, all the theses at which his successors or heirs, his readers in general, would have liked to see him stop.[1]

While, no doubt, countless other pathways may be broken through the thickets of Derrida's encounter with Freud, my reading here is organized around the theses that Derrida risks in *Archive Fever*, but it will, in turn, draw from the material of other essays where relevant. For Derrida, the theme of archivization is intimate to psychoanalysis because it ties itself directly to the acts, processes, and places of memory both as individual psyche and as documentation. Addressing the Freudian legacy in these terms, he risks "*three plus one*" theses (or prostheses) "on the subject of Freud's theses" toward the end of *Archive Fever*.[2] Three of these theses, he remarks, "have to do with the concept of the archive." But, as he aims to show, "what is the concept of the archive?" is the wrong question here. To approach the theme more obliquely, he begins not at the archive "itself" but with the name *arkhē* that it shelters. This word, he notes, "brings together two principles: one of commencement, but also a nomological principle of commandment."[3]

One may wish, as a start, to order Derrida's theses along the lines of these two principles. The first two theses, which address psychoanalysis in its "*theoretical exposition*,"[4] refer to, as Derrida puts it, "the *arkhē* in the *physical, historical or ontological* sense, which is to say to the originary, the first, the principal, the primitive, in short to the commencement."[5] The first addresses psychoanalysis as a sustained and sophisticated study of memory (*mneme*) and faces precisely the question of its origin in the psychical apparatus. The second addresses psychoanalysis as a theory of the archival process and concerns itself with the role of the death drive and related notions (such as repetition) in the processes of transcendental constitution, and, grafted onto this, those of "deconstitution" in analysis (*anamnesis*). The third thesis is directed toward archivization as documentation (*hypomneme*). It therefore has more directly to do with psychoanalysis as an institution and gathers together related questions that concern "the archivization of psychoanalysis itself, of its 'life,' if you will, of its '*acts*,' of its private and public procedures."[6] Unlike the first two theses, then, at least apparently, this thesis refers to "the *arkhē* in the *nomological* sense, to the *arkhē* of the *commandment*."[7]

But there is one other, deconstructive, thesis, having to do with "the concept of concept,"[8] which disrupts the neat order of division just articulated. According to this thesis, the word *arkhē*, sheltered in and remembered by the word archive, is already fractured by a multiple fission that makes it impossible to gather up a unified concept of the origin. For example, Derrida notes, even before the word marks the split between the "physical, historical, or ontological principle" of an occasioning "event" and the "nomological principle" of its constitutive and protective recording, the very notion of the *arkhē* as an occasioning "event" is already split between nature and history: that is, between *physis* as gift (implying the chance of surprise or unexpected events) and "*thesis, tekhne, nomos, etc.*," in the form of the constituting recognition that is caught up in the ec-stases of time, of past and future, memory and anticipation, and, therefore, the authority of history (convention, prior knowledge, and tradition). The principle of commencement is already contaminated by what is at work in the principle of commandment. This difficulty at the origin, announced in the word *arkhē*, accordingly, is the ruin of any attempt to conceptualize the archive, which is traditionally supposed to come after the originally present "event" as its record. "Archival violence" is, therefore, in Derrida's words,

> the first figure of an archive, because *every* archive . . . is at once *institutive* and *conservative*. Revolutionary and traditional. An *economic* archive in this double sense: it keeps, it puts in reserve, it saves, but in an unnatural fashion, that is to say in making the law (*nomos*) or in making people respect the law. A moment ago we called it nomological. It has the force of law, of a law which is the

law of the house (*oikos*), of the house as place, domicile, family, lineage, or institution.[9]

In other words, what one may call for short "the archontic principle" (the principle of commandment) is the condition of the possibility of the archive. But, because it is "unnatural," that is, an imposition of "law" or artifice upon physis (event), this very condition, while necessary, simultaneously makes the archive strictly impossible. This aporetic vacillation means that, as Derrida notes: "Nothing is less reliable, nothing is less clear today than the word 'archive.'" Again: "Nothing is thus more troubled and more troubling today than the concept archived in the word 'archive.'"[10]

Further, Derrida implicates Freud at the core of this trouble. He argues, on the one hand, that an aneconomic archive fever is the direct consequence of much that Freud wrote. If nothing is less clear than the word and the concept "archive," then, in Derrida's words: "What is more probable, on the other hand, and more clear, is that psychoanalysis is not without responsibility in this trouble." Again:

> In naming psychoanalysis here, one refers already, in any case, to the archive which is classified, at least provisionally, under the name of "psychoanalysis," of "Freud," and of a few others. In other words, if we no longer know very well what we are saying when we say "archive," "Freud" is undoubtedly not without responsibility. But the name of Freud, the name of the Freuds . . . itself becomes plural, thus problematic.[11]

In many ways, what Freud writes implicitly or explicitly challenges what Derrida calls the "logocentric closure" of traditional Western metaphysics, for the syntax and labor of Freudian discourse slips apart from and is not reducible to the concepts, all of which, despite themselves, retain residual metaphysical commitments. Or, put in another way, Derrida also argues that Freud's insights, his intuitions, exceed both his concepts and his discourse or, that is, certain performatives in the construction of his texts.[12] In short, part of the Freudian legacy, according to Derrida, is to have undermined the very possibility of forming coherent concepts and thus to have ensured that every word and every concept, beginning with the word *arkhē* and including all those that make up the corpus of psychoanalysis as a science, are inherently divided against themselves.

"Concerning the archive," Derrida notes, "Freud never managed to form anything that deserves to be called a concept. Neither have we, by the way."[13] To the word "concept," which would be too rigorous, he opposes the word "notion," by which he aims to indicate "the open imprecision" or "relative indetermination" of a series of impressions insistently associated with a word "through the unstable feeling of a shifting figure, or of an in-finite or indefinite process." He insists that this imprecision does not indicate a theoretical feebleness destined to be rectified by further clarification. On the contrary, he argues, "I consider it to be the possibility and the very future of the concept, to be the very concept of the future." In other words, "there are essential reasons for which a concept in the process of being formed always remains inadequate relative to what it ought to be, divided, disjointed between two forces."

Yet, on the other hand, Freud also betrays the radically aneconomic tendencies in much of his writing. In the construction of his theoretical texts, in his conceptualization of psychoanalytic practice, or in his concern for his own legacy, he repeats certain metaphysical gestures that he has already subverted. His insights, then, are also threatened by the fact that his discourse does not shake entirely free of certain metaphysical residues. There are, therefore, incessant and unresolved conflicts and slippages in Freud's texts. In Derrida's words, "the principle of the internal division of the Freudian gesture, and thus of the Freudian concept of the archive, is that at the moment when psychoanalysis formalizes the conditions of archive fever and of the archive itself, it repeats the very thing it resists."[14]

Accordingly, he argues, "Freud's discourse on the archive, and here is the thesis of the theses, seems thus to be divided. As does his concept of the archive. It takes two contradictory forms. That is why we say . . . *archive fever*."[15] In sum, his fourth, deconstructive "thesis of these theses," dis-organizes the first three, spreading them across economic/aneconomic tensions according to the circular logic of paradox.[16] In his words: "One should be able to find traces of this contradiction in all Freud's works."[17]

Derrida's three theses on Freud are bound together by a common thread, namely the divisive specter of death at the heart of life. The first concerns the paradoxically decentering centrality of death (*hypomnema*) at the core of the so-called living psyche. Derrida argues that Freud outlines a theory of the psyche in which the traditional figures of death (repetition, writing) are found to be crucially intrinsic to psychical life, making it irreducible to *mneme* (living memory) or *anamnesis* (the act of recollection—rememoration).

One assumes naïvely that the archive "begins" with the force of impression, that the beginning or commencement is a past present, "at once *institutive* and *conservative*." Pressures imprint on substrates, making "for the first time" recognizable marks—traces inscribed in the psyche, circumcisions traced on the skin, footprints left in ash—leaving lasting impressions, records, which condition the archivization to come and to which one may dream of returning, via the archive (here reduced to a mere *hypomnesic* supplement), at which point the archive becomes redundant. But it merely raises a difficulty to note that the archive "begins" with the force of impression. At what point precisely does the pressure of the impressing force become an imprint left behind? What if the "space" that supposedly clearly separates the "original" from the archival trace that indicates it turns out to be an im-possible khôra? What if the *différance* that must be in order to make an impression or copy possible also, without remedy, makes it impossible? What if the print (the trace, copy, citation, or interpretative recognition) "is the first figure of the archive"?[18] And what if Freud both recognized and refused this? For, in the end, Derrida argues, despite all the difficulties associated with establishing where the so-called living psyche ends and the supposedly "dead" archive begins, Freud does ultimately resort to this distinction. In chapter 4, I amplify this thesis by reading it together with an earlier text, "Freud and the Scene of Writing," where Derrida considers three of Freud's metaphorical models of the psyche, demonstrating that each successive model shifts closer to the thinking of *différance*, yet metaphysical residues still remain.

Derrida's second thesis, addressed in chapter 5, has to do with the reinterpretation of Freud's concepts in terms of the death drive as the "nonoriginary" motivating force behind psychical (synthetic) processing. Derrida argues that the quasi-conceptuality of the death drive, which coordinates the divergent thematics of conservation, return, aggression, destruction, and dissolution, entangles the psychoanalytic theory of constitution in the double bind of economic and aneconomic aporias, so opening it to the multiple risks (but also the chances) of fiction, fabrication, prosthesis, and delusion, which are brought together (in *Archive Fever*) in the quasi-figure of the specter. Yet simultaneously, Freud resists his own radical insights, since the enlightenment figure in him does not, apparently, always want to speak with phantoms.[19] He does not always believe in the fundamentality of fabrication but sometimes resorts in the final analysis to "the originary effectivity of a base of immediate perception."[20] Paradoxically, he does not always believe in belief but sometimes believes in knowledge, truth, and reality. I have grafted onto this thesis the related dilemma concerning the de-constitution or analysis of the psyche imposed by the isomorphism of analysis and the death drive (or repetition compulsion). The second part of chapter 5 addresses similar aporetic entanglements associated with Freud's conception of the task of psychoanalysis.

Chapter 6 addresses Derrida's third thesis, which concerns the double bind of return and destruction (killing and repeating the "name of the father"), which dis-organizes all of the notions that are essential to establish a living tradition: "institution," "interpretation," "invention," "convention." According to Derrida, Freud's genius, here, is to have uncovered the stifling economic structure of what I shall call for short the "archontic circle." Freud shows that the rebellion of a group against a strongly authoritarian tyrant leaves the group in a power vacuum where, due to a powerful residual need for authority, ambivalent forces of pride, guilt, and fear predominate. This intolerable ambivalence, if left unresolved, leads the group to impose upon themselves the very restrictions they have just thrown off. The prohibitions once imposed on them by the tyrant are now internalized and self-imposed. Moreover, he tacitly uncovers a way out of it via the aneconomic feminine Oedipus complex. But Freud of all people, after all he has demonstrated concerning the circular trap of authority, remains within the archontic circle, not only in his insistent patriarchy but also in his attempts to institutionalize psychoanalysis. This in turn opens up the question of the status of any reader or interpreter of Freud.

Here, then, apart from demonstrating that Derrida reads the tension in Freud in terms of an aneconomic moment and an economic recapitulation that resists it, I also hope to give the necessary background reading to come to grips with Lacan's revision. One should bear in mind that Derrida clearly does not highlight these traces of contradiction (in the weak sense) for the sake of forming better psychoanalytic concepts or to demonstrate how to escape the aneconomic and economic demands placed upon readers of Freud. The point is to show that psychoanalysis, if perhaps without Freud's explicit blessing, demonstrates that concept formation as such, while always necessary, is nevertheless aporetic: violent, paradoxical, contradictory, in a word, impossible. And this applies to Freud's own concepts too. When pressed to their logical conclusions, they too reveal their aporias in the form of paradoxical or contradictory theoretical requirements or in the form of performative contradictions. In other words, as Derrida insists, "the contradiction in the Freudian corpus, is not negative, it modulates and conditions the very formation of the concept of the archive and of the concept in general—right where they bear the contradiction."[21]

4

The Im-Possibility of the Psyche

Introductory Remarks: Derrida's First Thesis in Outline

Addressing Freud's theoretical exposition of the psychical apparatus, Derrida proposes on the one hand that Freud's theorization in both content and structure moves increasingly toward a radically aneconomic "archi-writing," or *différance*, so subverting the dominant Cartesian commitment that shapes conceptions of the psyche in Western philosophies.[1] This commitment may be understood in terms of the relation between *mneme*, *anamnesis*, and *hypomnema*.[2] *Mneme*, "living memory," designates a place of storage "in the flesh." Lacking intrinsic agency, it belongs with a constellation of concepts related to nature (passivity, materiality, extension, blind force). The power of *anamnesis* (the revivification of memories through conscious recall), therefore, is attributed to a conscious agency external to *mneme* and essentially different from it. *Anamnesis* belongs with a constellation of concepts related to spirit, the spoken word, and other traditional figures of "life" (activity, intentionality, spontaneity). Ostensibly, subjective awareness, as "simple, conscious, present perception of the thing itself,"[3] is first on the scene, registering impressions and experiences, which are only then laid down in memory and stored for future reactivation. Finally, the "psyche proper," divided between *mneme* and *anamnesis*, may be extended artificially by various recording and archiving machines; it may be supplemented by *hypomnesic* devices, or external prostheses, condensed in the figure of writing, a traditional figure of death.

Derrida argues that Freud, in contrast, made it possible to think of the psyche as an active process of inscription or encryption (archivization, "psychic spacing," or synthetic processing) that, in his words, "cannot be reduced to memory: neither to memory as conscious reserve, nor to memory as rememoration, as act of recalling. The psychic archive comes neither under *Mneme* nor under *Anamnesis*."[4] As he demonstrates, the implications of this are incalculable, for Freud here risks the traditional borders between the figures of life and death, whose order of priority is figured in the privilege accorded to the first term in dichotomies such as internal/external, originary/secondary, mind/machine. Indeed, he argues, Freud's "incessant and increasingly radical invocation of the principle of difference"[5] pushes his thinking past the "metaphysics of presence," beyond either positivism or phenomenology, toward a rethinking of the psychical apparatus along the lines of what can be offered for thought under the nickname *différance*.

On the other hand, Derrida also calls attention to discrepancies due to residual metaphysical commitments that belie Freud's radical insights. These, paradoxically, confirm the very reduction of psyche to *mneme* and *anamnesis* that the "other side" of Freud's thinking has already subverted. Although it should, his modeling of the psychic apparatus does not ultimately divert him from the classical metaphysical gesture of sharply separating technical archiving devices (such as writing in the ordinary sense) from the psychical archive, or, as Derrida puts it, "holding the technical prosthesis to be a secondary and accessory exteriority" and maintaining "a primacy of live memory and of anamnesis in their originary temporalization."[6] In other words, he sees the living psyche as prior to and constituted independently of the "dead" prosthesis, or the technological apparatus that merely records events. Derrida shows that Freud as a result faces insurmountable difficulties associated with establishing where the so-called living psyche ends and the supposedly "dead" archive begins. Consequently, if his theoretical exposition of the psychical apparatus ought to forbid this, "psychoanalysis, in its archive fever, always attempts to return to the live origin of that which the archive loses while keeping it in a multiplicity of places."[7] Freud still dreams of a psychoanalytic "archaeology"—of returning, via the archive, to the proper origin of an original impression, at which point the archive is in effect effaced, transparent, redundant. Here, then, after theorizing memory (in its aneconomic sense of active synthetic processing) as the irreducible essence of the psyche,[8] Freud paradoxically reduces the archive to a mere supplement, a secondary, dead, and external "ladder," there only to throw away once the analytic goal has been reached and the original impression comes "alive" and "speaks by itself."[9]

Derrida lays the basis for this two-part thesis in an earlier essay, "Freud and the Scene of Writing," in which he studies Freud's theoretical modeling of the psyche from the *Project for a Scientific Psychology* (1895), through *The Interpretation of Dreams* (1900), to the "Note Upon the 'Mystic Writing Pad'" (1925).[10] Following the paths of two serial metaphors, "text and machine,"[11] which describe respectively the contents/functioning of the psychical apparatus and its structure, Derrida notices a "strange progression" in each series whereby "from a system of traces functioning according to a model which Freud would have preferred to be a natural one, and from which writing is entirely absent, we proceed toward a configuration of traces which can no longer be represented except by the structure and functioning of writing."[12]

However, the movement toward "writing" is not parallel. If Freud describes the content and function of the psychical apparatus in terms primarily associated with writing, he describes its structure in topographical or spatial terms. It is only by analogy with the "Mystic Pad" that the apparatus finally becomes, in Derrida's words, "a writing machine of marvelous complexity into which the whole of the psychical apparatus will be projected."[13] Here, "long disjointed and out of phase, the two series of metaphors will then be united."[14]

Why should the vicissitudes of Freud's metaphorical investments matter? Derrida has persistently argued that metaphors are hardly innocent; while they enable and direct thinking, they also constrain and limit it. This is amply demonstrated in Freud's writings. His mechanical metaphors for the psychical apparatus persistently belie the radical insights produced by the textual metaphors that describe psychical content. Moreover, Derrida in the end troubles the very sense of "metaphor" here, by setting into play the tension between its sense as representation and its more literal sense as resemblance. Drawing out the implications of Freud's metaphorical investments, Derrida emphasizes the ambivalence of Freud's legacy born of a tension between his courageous theoretical openness and a residual Cartesian commitment.

In the exposition to follow, I shall take the path Derrida traces from *mneme* through *anamnesis* to *hypomnesis* in "Freud and the Scene of Writing." Before I begin, however, I should make a few observations. First, I cannot avoid passing over many complex byways in this multilayered essay, which, in the name of a justice I am not equal to here, call for more intricate studies. Second, Derrida's assessment presupposes some familiarity with Freud's texts. Without this background, his already complex arguments become dishearteningly opaque. At various points, therefore, I have tried to lay out the essentials of the Freudian models under discussion. Finally, in light of today's textbook neurophysiology, which reveals inaccuracies in his neurological speculations, Freud would have been obliged to make significant modifications to his models. Freud, for example, thought that the transmission of impulses through the neural network resembled the movement of an electrical current, whereas it is now understood in terms of chemical propagation.[15] However, as Derrida notes, physiological inaccuracies notwithstanding, it remains philosophically interesting to study the presuppositions, metaphorical figures, and theoretical exigencies that govern Freud's efforts to model the psychical apparatus.[16]

The *Project*: Freud's "Psyche" is Irreducible to *Mneme*

A Reconstruction of Freud's Model

Freud's problem in the *Project* is to explain how the psychical apparatus can be "permanently altered by single occurrences" (a requirement for memory) and simultaneously perpetually "virgin," as required by conscious perception.[17] Rejecting hypotheses that attribute this difference to intrinsic material differences in the neural substrate, he proposes instead that developmental and structural factors affect the permeability of neurons and consequently the relative amounts of excitation they can resist, retain, or discharge.

For Freud, then, nervous tissue forms a single system, whose functioning is divided into primary and secondary levels.[18] The reflex arc, obeying the principle of inertia, describes the primary function; neural excitation from sensory stimuli immediately discharges itself fully in motor activity. In contrast, the secondary function involves the effort (work, labor) of securing discharge for endogenous stimuli through independent, "specific" (rather than reflex) actions.[19] Because the secondary function necessitates a delay between stimulus and action, he hypothesized that the nervous system must abandon the principle of inertia for that of constancy. It must accumulate and retain a constant, basic, optimum level of "cathexis" (neural excitation or energy) to meet the demands of specific actions. Since neurons receive excitation through dendrites and discharge it through axons, their structure, he thought, accords well with the requirements of both primary and secondary functions, for the accumulation of excitation in the neurons required by the secondary function could be explained in terms of "contact-barriers" (synapses) between interconnecting neurons, which can be understood as "gateways" that resist incoming excitation and outgoing discharge.[20]

Freud, therefore, thought he could resolve the apparent paradox (that the passage of excitation must both permanently alter the neurons and leave them uninfluenced) by positing two classes of neurons.[21] The first class consists of relatively "permeable" neurons, serving perception, which allow excitation "to pass through as though they had no contact-barriers and which, accordingly, after each passage of excitation are in the same state as before." The second class consists of relatively "impermeable" neurons, where resistance in the "contact-barriers" makes the passage of excitation difficult or partial. This partial passage explains how these neurons "may, after each excitation, be in a different state from before." It makes sense, then, that these neurons would be "the vehicles of memory and so probably of psychical processes in general."[22] These are, moreover, arranged in three neural systems: (ψ designates permeable or perceptual neurons, (ψ designates impermeable or psychical/mnemic neurons (given that permeability and impermeability are never absolute), and (ω designates consciousness. I have named these systems throughout as "the perceptual system," "the *psychomnemic* system," and "consciousness."

Freud goes on to argue that the neurons constituting "the perceptual system," due to their permeability, are not affected by the magnitude of the excitation passing through them, but respond to its quality (olfactory, tactile, visual, etc.). Further, the neurons that constitute the *psychomnemic* system, in direct contrast with the permeable neurons, are affected only by the magnitude of the excitation passing through them, not by its quality (memories, he insists, are essentially devoid of sensory quality). His model therefore demands an explanation of the effect of repetition on our mnemic capacities in terms of pure quantities of force. We know that solving a complex equation, for example, may be difficult the first time. But, solving the same equation again, even a few months later, is much easier, and solving it a third time the very next day is the least difficult of all. Further, solving a similar equation on first encounter is easier than solving the very first one. Solving an equation that is not similar but is nevertheless still an equation is easier on first encounter than solving the very first one. But these computational efforts will not make it easier to learn to ride a bicycle.

As noted in the first chapter, diverse stimuli affect the *psychomnemic* system from various sources. Contact barriers, Freud speculated (incorrectly), allow for energy storage, which, in turn, offers some degree of resistance to excitation (tonic cathexis). If impulses from external sensations and endogenous stimuli are to register here, they must be strong enough to overcome such resistance or, that is, break down contact barriers, and, so to speak, fill up the *psychomnemic* neurons with "freely mobile cathectic energy," which is associated with heightened tension. In accordance with the pleasure principle, heightened tension in the system is registered as "unpleasure" and its "binding" or conversion into tonic cathexis—the process by which memory traces are forged and retained—which brings relief registered as pleasure, becomes a priority. This "binding" occurs as an outward passage that again breaks through barriers, tracing an associative pathway through the system toward discharge. His incorrect physical speculations aside, Freud correctly understood that the *psychomnemic* system registered and retained discrete traces, or sensory fragments, and that discharge is a matter of forging links between trace-retaining neurons (contemporary neurophysiology estimates a figure of ten thousand or more connections per neuron).[23] In other words, to form perceived "memories," these traces require synthetic processing, literally re-membering or articulation, to form the projections that will eventually be presented to consciousness.

Proposed as a theory of *Bahnung* (facilitative breaching) in the *psychomnemic* system,[24] Freud argues that the force of this effraction alters the contact barriers in its wake, leaving them "more capable of conduction, less impermeable." A scar or trace, then, remains as a permanent neural pathway, an acquisition that, in turn, facilitates the passage of similar stimuli but still resists different or novel stimuli. Memory, then, on his account, as an active system of synthetic processing, would be "one of the powers which determine and direct" the outward pathways of excitations.[25] Different pathways are traced in three possible ways. First, large quantities of excitation under particular circumstances tend to batter the related series of connected neurons into further permeability, thereby reinforcing those pathways and not others.[26] Second, excitation does not occur as a uniform flow through a neuron but may selectively trace alternative pathways through any of its multiple contact barriers. Differences in facilitated pathways through the interconnected network of neurons, then, can be attributed to varying levels of resistance at the synapses, for Freud adds that the simultaneous cathexis of adjacent neurons affects the contact barriers between them and may reinforce or compete with paths offered by other contact barriers.[27] Leaving aside for now the difficulty of seeing why one or another pathway "should be preferred" on any purely quantitative account of facilitation, it is notable that memory can only operate insofar as there are differences between facilitations. Already in the *Project*, then, as Derrida puts it, "quantity becomes *psyche* and *Mneme* through differences rather than through plenitudes."[28]

Finally, consciousness, Freud argues, is a matter of pure quality to the exclusion of quantity (besides a minimum tonic cathexis). In his words:

"Consciousness gives us what are called *qualities*—sensations which are *different* in a great multiplicity of ways and whose *difference* is distinguished according to its relations with the external world. Within this difference there are series, similarities and so on, but there are in fact no quantities in it."[29] Clearly, the seat of consciousness is not to be found in the *psychomnemic* system, since the process exclusive to this system, "reproducing or remembering . . . is *without quality*."[30] Consciousness is something not inherent in, but added to, the processes in the *psychomnemic* system.[31] Freud considers placing the seat of consciousness in the perceptual system. However, while this accords with the fact that qualities are linked with sense perception, he rejects the idea that consciousness is reducible to perception, which is a primary function operating according to the reflex arc, and favors "seating consciousness in the *upper* storeys of the nervous system."[32]

If the only alternative, then, is to posit a third neural system, we immediately meet with a difficulty.[33] Given that the permeability of the neurons is the result of constant "battering" by excitations of high magnitude, Freud argues that the almost total exclusion of quantity in the consciousness system would leave the neurons constituting consciousness highly impermeable. However, he continues, this is contradicted by the mutability of conscious content, the transitory nature of attention, and "the easy linking of qualities simultaneously perceived," which is compatible only with complete permeability of the neurons and "total restoration of their former state." Here we face "complete facilitation, which does not arise from quantity." There must, therefore, he speculates, be more to the passage of excitation than the transference of quantity; it must have another characteristic, namely periodicity (frequency). Further, the contact barriers must resist the transference of quantity but not periodicity. Thus, we can say that the neurons of consciousness do not respond to quantities of excitation but appropriate the *period* of the excitation. In his words: "This state of being affected by period while filled with a minimum . . . [cathexis] is the fundamental basis of consciousness."

Freud's model undergoes various modifications as he tries to accommodate these specifications to his fundamental quantity/quality division. What emerges finally is the following:[34] In the perceptual system, which by nature involves consciousness, the neural paths from sensory organs directly to consciousness do not conduct quantity at all, but they encode differences (qualities) by matching them precisely to different periods (frequencies) of neuronal motion.[35] This transmission of quality (encoded as periodicity) is not durable; it leaves no traces behind and cannot be reproduced in the absence of the actual stimulus. The paths from internal sources, by nature unconscious (e.g., instincts), do not directly affect consciousness but first pass through the *psychomnemic* system, which conducts only differences in quantity (there is neuronal motion here, but it remains constant and therefore monotonous in character, that is, without quality).

The two-way transmission between consciousness and the *psychomnemic* system presents difficulties. First, Freud places the neurons of consciousness between the perceptual and *psychomnemic* systems, so that the perceptual system transfers its quality to consciousness, which, in turn (somehow), "transfers neither quality nor quantity" to the *psychomnemic* system "but merely excites this system—that is, indicates the pathways to be taken by free energy." Second, while certain *psychomnemic* processes themselves remain unconscious, they do "subsequently acquire a secondary, artificial consciousness through being linked with processes of discharge and perception (speech-association)." However, his explanation, namely that deviations from the monotonous psychical period that is specific for the *psychomnemic* neurons come to consciousness as qualities, presents clear difficulties in relation to his initial division of these systems along the lines of a quantity/quality opposition. Freud remained eternally dissatisfied with his attempt to map the structure of psychical functioning onto a neural substrate and soon gave it up, conceding that the science of neurophysiology was, at the time, not up to the demand.[36]

Derrida's Response

Broadly speaking, Derrida's response to the model outlined in the *Project* turns on the difficulties for Freud that arise from the irreducible mutual implication of the notions "facilitation," "repetition," and "periodicity." If Freud aims to reserve facilitation (linked to quantity) for the *psychomnemic* system and exclude time (periodicity) from it, and conversely, to reserve quality for the perceptual system and exclude facilitation from it, then introducing a third system to explain consciousness produces entanglements that sabotage these aims. His model runs into difficulties because it depends on a conceptual division between quantity and quality that, due to the entanglement of the three notions just listed, cannot be made decisively.

Derrida notes that it is already tricky to explain facilitation in terms of pure quantities of force if, as he puts it, "trace as memory is not a pure breaching that might be reappropriated at any time as simple presence; it is rather the ungraspable and invisible difference between breaches," for how is a path selected, all forces being equal?[37] Implicitly, then, if the power within the *psychomnemic* system to determine pathways of discharge for endogenous excitation (in dreams, for example) does not reach "the transparency of meaning," it nevertheless involves the delay of selective activity that cannot entirely be reduced to the opposite of meaning, namely the opaque mechanics of natural forces.

Further, difficulties arise concerning the role played by repetition in reinforcing facilitations. Repetition of the same stimulus should not contribute to the further weakening of contact barriers that leads to increased permeability, for, as he notes, frequency (periodicity) supposedly "adds no quantity of present force, no *intensity*." Yet repetition does have the power of breaching (the more often a stimulus is repeated, the clearer and more permanent the memory trace), and Freud acknowledges that the frequency of repetition supplements the magnitude of an impression. But, Derrida argues, what supplements its breaching force, then, is not pure quantity but a measure of an "absolutely heterogeneous" type (periodicity, the diastem that separates discrete repetitions). In short, Freud cannot explain the breaching power of repetition in the *psychomnemic* system without recourse to the very measure of quality that he has already excluded from it. Derrida concludes that "neither the difference between full quantities, nor the interval between repetitions of the identical, nor breaching itself, may be thought of in terms of the opposition between quantity and quality. Memory cannot be derived from this opposition."[38]

These difficulties are merely compounded when Freud, adumbrating what comes out explicitly in "Beyond the Pleasure Principle," explains facilitation not only in terms of the movement of differential forces but in terms of deferral, or, in Derrida's words, as "the effort of life to protect itself by *deferring* a dangerous cathexis, that is, by constituting a reserve."[39] Freud explains that the *psychomnemic* system is breached repeatedly due to the exigent stresses and pains of everyday living. Although it aims to avoid the burden of excess excitation, by immediate discharge through existing facilitations, it is regularly compelled to deal with the "overflow" by deferral, that is, by deferring excesses through the detours of side-cathexes, in the process enlarging the system's capacity. This excess, therefore, is the very condition of its growth and development (that is, its life). In its development, it manages the excessive cathexis from traumatic breaches (which, in extreme terms, would mean death) by incorporating them, that is, by repeating or copying them as new facilitations. Thus, when resistances are again overwhelmed, threatening excitations (from surprise or pain, for example) may again be deferred along the defensive detours of newly formed paths in an effort to attenuate the threat of overload and facilitate the most expedient discharge.

Here, one might assume that facilitation is the process by which repetition happens to an initial perceptual impression in the stand-off between two opposing present forces: external stimulus and *psychomnemic* resistance. A facilitation would represent the track of "footprints" left behind by an initial perceptual impression, marking out a path in the *psychomnemic* system for future use. Facilitation, in short, would be the secondary repetition of an initial impression.

However, if Freud's theory of facilitation is pressed, Derrida argues, difficulties arise that unsettle this priority of perceptual presence over archival repetition.[40] Facilitation, as Freud insists, presupposes an initial resistance in the *psychomnemic* system. But, even without posing the problem of where the initial resistance originates, "of phylogenesis and of hereditary breaches," it is already impossible to establish whether it is originally the repetitive forces of perceptual impressions that produce the differential resistances in the *psychomnemic* system or whether it is originally the resistances that pre-date and enable the repetition. In other words, do perceptual impressions shape processing or does processing shape the perceptual impressions? According to Derrida: "It is the very idea of a *first time* which becomes enigmatic."

Already, then, facing this enigma of a *first time*, one must be wary of formulating facilitation in terms of the deferral of an already constituted perceptual experience. In Derrida's words: "To defer . . . cannot mean to retard a present possibility, to postpone an act, to put off a perception already now possible." Again, "there is no life present *at first* which would *then* come to protect, postpone, or reserve itself in *différance*." Rather, Freud's conception of facilitation already tends toward the argument that presence requires facilitation (deferral) as a support; in other words, a conscious perceptual experience is the constituted product of synthetic processing. Already, then, a note has crept into Freud's account that poses a challenge to the traditional priority of life in the form of presence. In Derrida's words: "Is it not already death at the origin of a life which can defend itself against death only through an *economy* of death, through deferment, repetition, reserve?" In other words, to suggest that the presence of life depends on the traditional figures of death for its own protection, that life occurs as *différance* (differentiation and deferral), is as much as to suggest that "life *is* death" and that "repetition and . . . [the death drive] are native and congenital to that which they transgress."

To sum up, because he insists upon a quality/quantity division despite its difficulties, one may suspect that Freud's thinking is guided by a metaphysical prejudice that still hopes to divide mental life along the lines of spirit and nature. At the very least, however, what was begun in the *Project* leads inexorably to the conclusion that there is more to memory than *mneme*, the opacity of merely natural forces. It suggests that memory is not a mere receptacle but an active *spacing*, a process of difference and deferral, which exceeds the neat structure of separable systems by which Freud first tries to contain it. Derrida argues, however, that Freud cannot explain facilitation in the *psychomnemic* system, nor indeed consciousness (insofar as it is a matter of pure periodicity), without recourse to something like difference and deferral, and that this common recourse to *différance* unsettles (without destroying) the borders between systems and, therefore, between conscious/unconscious, mind/body, inside/outside, life/death, with, of course, "formidable" implications for metaphysics. Freud, in fact, very soon begins to rethink the "entire system of the *Project*."[41]

The "Interpretation of Dreams": Freud's "Psyche" Is Irreducible to *Anamnesis*

Freud's reconception of memory as a stratified system of at least three powers of registration and transcription in his *Interpretation of Dreams* continues a transition "from the neurological to the psychical"[42] begun in a letter to Fliess.[43] "If I could give a complete account of the psychological characteristics of perception and of the three registrations," Freud announces in this letter, "I should have described a new psychology." Briefly, he argues that the first essentially unconscious registrations of sensory stimuli in the *psychomnemic* system, "arranged according to associations by simultaneity," are subsequently retranscribed by the different unconscious and preconscious powers of primary and secondary processing, according to relations described more fully in *The Interpretation of Dreams* as condensation, displacement, considerations of representability, and censorship. The novelty of this conception, he insists, lies in "the thesis that memory is present not once but several times over, that it is laid down in various species of indications." Importantly, each of these synthesizing powers can subject "the material present in the form of memory-traces . . . to a *re-arrangement* in accordance with fresh circumstances—to a *re-transcription*." The work of the *psychomnemic* system, in other words, here becomes decidedly more than a process of registration. It becomes explicitly a matter of encoding and of translation between "a number of agencies arranged in a series one behind the other."[44]

Freud's more complex account of the *psychomnemic* system is developed in *The Interpretation of Dreams*, where, taking his cue from "the dream-work" (the processes by which dreams are constructed, or "written"), he supports his "method" of dream interpretation with a description of psychical functioning as labor. Notably, this elaboration gains in significance in light of his claim that "*the interpretation of dreams is the royal road to a knowledge of the unconscious activities of the mind.*"[45] Again: "The study of dreams may be considered the most trustworthy method of investigating deep mental processes."[46] Here, concerning content in the *psychomnemic* system, Derrida notes, "trace will become *gramme*" (an element in a system of writing).[47] Further, if dreams play themselves out in a "scene of writing," this is not, he insists, "a writing which simply transcribes, a stony echo of muted words, but a lithography before words: metaphonetic, nonlinguistic, alogical." Concerning psychical function, therefore, "the region of breaching" will explicitly become "a ciphered spacing." However, he argues, Freud attempts to map this content and functioning onto a conception of "*the psychic apparatus in its structure*" that lags behind his conception of "*the psychic text in its fabric.*"[48] This, he shows, paradoxically re-binds Freud's thinking to a metaphysics he has already subverted.

The Dream-Work

According to Freud, dreams cannot be reduced to illusions formed from impressions made indistinct by sleep.[49] Because these impressions "are sometimes subjected in dreams to the most peculiar and far-fetched interpretations," he argues, there must be other, predominantly mental, factors that determine what memory images are activated in dreams. He therefore rejects attempts to explain dreams in purely "positivistic" terms, in favor of the popular belief that dreams are the result of significant mental work, and that their meanings, while cryptic, can be interpreted.[50] But he is not uncritical of this popular tradition.[51] He rejects a "symbolical" method of interpretation, which, as Derrida puts it, "treats dream content as an indivisible and unarticulated whole, for which a second, possibly prophetic whole may be substituted."[52] He prefers the "decoding" method found in dream books, "since it treats dreams as a kind of cryptography." Here, discrete elements (signs) can be translated independently into other signs having a known meaning, and significance arises from the associative links between such elements. But he rejects the idea that the translation of one element into another can always occur according to the permanent code proffered by this or that "dream-dictionary." Also, as Derrida notes, popular methods of interpretation exhibit "an excessive preoccupation with *content*, and an insufficient concern for relations, locations, processes and differences."[53] For Freud, in contrast, the manifest content of the dream has far less importance than the latent network of dream thoughts, uncovered in its analysis, that form its associative context.

The dream thoughts and the dream content, Freud notes, are like two versions of the same subject presented in "different modes of expression," and the "dream-work" describes the "character and syntactic laws" of the processes by which dream thoughts are translated into dream content.[54] First, he insists, "dreams are brief, meager and laconic in comparison with the range and wealth of dream-thoughts." Since only a few elements from the dream thoughts appear as dream content, any element is chosen for the extent to which it can be overdetermined, that is, loaded with "multiple meanings," which allude to "a whole series of other figures." As he later adds, such "condensation" operates mainly by constructing "collective and composite figures."[55] Imagine for example, the figure of a satyr whose face incorporates a husband's mouth and a father's eyes. Through condensation, Freud argues, the dream thought may be reduced to a minute, single detail that marks its essence.[56] In "dream-displacement," by contrast, the essence of the dream thought may not appear in the dream at all.[57] Displacement works both to reduce the intensity of certain elements and to create new values from elements that carry low psychical value. In consequence, "a *transference and displacement of psychical intensities* occurs in the process of dream-formation." Displacement, a major player in dream-work, brings about the differences between dream content and dream thoughts and the distortion of unconscious dream wishes.

Besides condensation and displacement, Freud names two further determinants of the dream content. First, if in the dream-work, a "colourless and abstract expression in the dream-thought" is "exchanged for a pictorial and concrete one,"[58] then considerations of how to represent dream thoughts in images undoubtedly influence the choice of elements that constitute the dream content. Since the dream-work does not have the immediate means to represent logical relations ("if," "because," "just as," "although," "either-or," etc.), it tends to represent subject matter rather than connections.[59] Also, among the subsidiary thoughts associated with the essential dream thoughts, the choice will fall to those most easily represented visually. But, he argues, exploiting the graphic and phonic materiality of words, "the dream-work does not shrink from the effort of recasting unadaptable thoughts into a new verbal form—even into a less than usual one—provided that the process facilitates representation."[60]

Finally, elements in dreams only appear subject to secondary revision or censorship.[61] For Freud, criticism within a dream (e.g., the critical remark "this is only a dream") is evidence that an agency beyond that responsible for primary processing may contribute to the dream content. In his words, "the censoring agency, whose influence we have so far only recognized in limitations and omissions in the dream-content, is also responsible for interpolations and additions in it." Such secondary revision is aimed at making a dream coherent, although it does not often or wholly succeed. Those dreams that exhibit the most coherence are, for him, "dreams which might be said to have been already interpreted once, before being submitted to waking interpretation."

That which finally appears in consciousness as the dream is above all discontinuous. Consciousness skips from node to node along a chain of associations, whose intermediate links are recognizable only upon reflection and with varying degrees of difficulty, for there are unconscious diversions in the chain of associations (due to the four factors just outlined), which substitute disguised references to unconscious wishes for fairly obvious associations. By this means, the fulfillment of an unconscious wish is hallucinated in a dream without that wish first becoming conscious. Dreams, Freud warns, are "*not made with the intention of being understood.*" Nevertheless, concerning the art of dream interpretation, which involves a "restoration of the connections which the dream-work has destroyed,"[62] he insists that dreams "present no greater difficulties to their translators than do the ancient hieroglyphic scripts to those who seek to read them."[63]

First Reading: Economics of Anamnesis *(Translation and Interpretation)*

The dream-work supports the idea that the scene through which dreams regress (old facilitations) is a "scene of writing" in the broad sense of encryption, encoding, and substitution. In Derrida's words: "Freud doubtless conceives of the dream as a displacement similar to an original form of writing which puts words on stage without becoming subservient to them; and he is thinking here, no doubt, of a model of writing irreducible to speech which would include, like hieroglyphics, pictographic, ideogrammatic and phonetic elements."[64] But this does not necessarily spell a radical departure from the "metaphysics of presence," for even if Freud acknowledges that in the production of a dream the displacements of an "originary writing" precede its reduction to logical coherence and discourse, it is still the verbal and logical that prevail at both the origin (the dream thought) and the telos (the dream interpretation). In their logical structure, Freud argues, dream thoughts are no different from waking thoughts.[65] Their distinctiveness lies only in the fact that they have been repressed for some reason (e.g., their perceived moral unacceptability or upsetting affective charge) beyond the reach of intentional conscious recall. The dream-work—the "character and syntactic laws" of which have emerged in the course of "comparing the original and the translation"—becomes a process of transcription that converts abstract latent thoughts into pictographic manifest content.[66] From this it would seem that a verbally articulated meaning is already there and that the dream-work merely translates it (through identifiable means) from a verbal to a pictographic mode of expression. At first brush, therefore, there appears to be nothing in the dream-work that in principle belies the reversibility by which the analytical work of dream interpretation (*anamnesis*) translates dream content back into the dream thoughts that underpin it. In short, if the displacements of an originary writing merely amount to a codified process of transcription or translation, *anamnesis* can still prevail, in principle, as a telos.

Second Reading: The Impossibility of Translation

However, on the other hand, and here is the most radical form of the Freudian break with tradition: Freud insists that there is no preexisting code governing how the dream elements might "properly" or meaningfully be related. There is no code to govern the substitutions according to which associations, condensations, displacements, representations, and omissions are made by the *psychomnemic* system in the construction of a dream. Rather, as Derrida puts it, "in its operations, lexicon, and syntax a purely idiomatic residue is irreducible and is made to bear the burden of interpretation in the communication between unconsciousnesses. The dreamer invents his own grammar."[67] Because of this idiomatic residue, a single image or figure in a dream bears multiple meanings that are, certainly, different for different people but also at variance in the same person. Meaning, in short, is overdetermined by idiomatic residues that resist complete interpretation. At best, Freud acknowledges, a responsible interpretation can emerge from the context of a dream's associative interconnections.

Extended to psychical operation in general, Derrida argues, this suggests that the way traced through facilitations by unconscious processes (such as repression) is idiosyncratic and inventive.[68] In other words, unconscious experience in which facilitations are constituted, prior to the dream, produces its own signifiers. In his words, it "does not create them in their materiality, of course, but produces their status-as-meaningful (*signifiance*)." But since a signifier presupposes its link to an intersubjectively confirmed signified, "they are no longer, properly speaking, signifiers." However, given that "a system of translation is possible only if a permanent code allows a substitution or transformation of signifiers while retaining the same signified," this means that "the possibility of translation, if it is far from being eliminated . . . is nevertheless in principle limited." And yet, as Derrida notes, this does not prevent Freud from persistently translating. One must not forget that "Freud never stopped proposing codes, rules of great generality." This discrepancy is a symptom of residual metaphysical commitments on Freud's part, but, as Derrida's reading suggests, these should not blind one to the extent to which Freud's thinking has moved toward the thinking of *différance*.

While Freud does not resist the temptation to venture a discussion of typical dream elements, he nevertheless stipulates essential limitations.[69] The most important of these for Derrida concerns the transition by which unconscious thoughts become conscious via the preconscious.[70] Whether speaking of the dream-work or other psychical processes, he argues, the danger of describing this transition as mere translation is that it "presupposes a text which would be already there, immobile . . . whose signified content might be harmlessly transported into the milieu of a different language, that of the preconscious or the conscious." But in the last chapter of *The Interpretation of Dreams*, he notes, Freud insists that this transition is not transcriptive in the sense that it generates a second conscious thought alongside the original unconscious one. Implicitly, in his words,

> the conscious text is thus not a transcription, because there is no text *present elsewhere* as an unconscious one to be transposed or transported. . . . There is no unconscious truth to be rediscovered by virtue of having been written elsewhere. There is no text written and present elsewhere which would then be subjected, without being changed in the process, to an operation and a temporalization which would be external to it. . . . The unconscious text is already a weave of pure traces.

In other words, the unconscious text would consist of unarticulated wishes, urges, desires, intuitions, notions (these terms are too definite) that are only made concrete, that is, "produced" as definite, conscious events, through psychical work as hallucination and, later, verbal articulation. In this case, the transition from memory to consciousness, as Derrida puts it, "is not a derivative or repetitive writing, it occurs in an original manner and, in its very secondariness, is originary and irreducible."[71] It is a very short step from here to the paradox of the supplement. Before the "supplementary" repetition (the "yes" of confirmation, the delays and detours of retranscription via the agencies of the *psychomnemic* system, the condensations, displacements, considerations of representability, and censorship), the present is not "there"; the happening of an "event" is only the call for the confirming "supplement," the footnote or postscript that is both unnecessary and necessary for its completion. But this means that the delay, the repetition, is both extraneous and essential to make the present experience what it is and to keep making it what it is. This "is," then, becomes unstable, indefinitely vulnerable to the power of reconstitution or reinvention inscribed in the delay.

Precisely here, Derrida insists, one must not shrink from Freud's insight by reading his texts through the metaphor of writing in its conventional sense. He must be read, on the contrary, "in terms of the labor of the writing which circulated like psychical energy between the unconscious and the conscious." One could call such labor a matter of "transcendental" constitution, were it not that the transcendental tradition still remains caught up in the "metaphysics of presence." That is, "transcendental" writing would necessarily be intersubjectively coded and, therefore, the same for everyone. But there is something irreducibly idiosyncratic about psychical writing, which Freud wants to respect too. Here, Derrida concludes: "That the present in general is not primal but, rather, reconstituted, that it is not the absolute, wholly living form which constitutes experience, that there is no purity of the living present—such is the theme, formidable for metaphysics, which Freud, in a conceptual scheme unequal to the thing itself, would have us pursue."[72]

Clearly, on this second reading it would be impossible to submit the *psychomnemic* system to the authority and power of *anamnesis*. If the involuntary thought activity that takes place in *images* were reducible to, or governed by, the power of *anamnesis*, which is a function of the conscious system where voluntary thought activity takes place in *concepts*,[73] then the possibility of proper decoding in *anamnesis* must presuppose proper psychical encoding of the original. Proper encoding, which comes first, would be precisely reversible in the form of proper decoding, which would trace its way back to the original, the true state of affairs, with nothing lost along the way. In this case, perfect translation between psychical agencies would have to be entirely possible. But since in the dreamwork we are dealing with a process of inventive substitution and disguise, this is not the case. As Derrida sums it up, in the sense that "the figurative content of the dream is . . . a signifying chain in scenic form . . . it summarizes a discourse, it is the *economy of speech*. . . . But the reciprocal economic transformation, the total assimilation into discourse, is, in principle, impossible or limited."[74]

Freud's Economic Recapitulation to Metaphysics

It is interesting to see what happens when Freud tries to tie "the labor of the writing which circulated like psychical energy between the unconscious and the conscious" to a model of the psychical structure. Concerning the relation between energy and place, Freud, as indicated above, has already made problematic the idea that translation is the transcription of an original text, which "would separate force [act] and extension [content], maintaining the simple exteriority of the translated and the translating,"[75] which would imply that meaning is there in its place and the agencies of transcription move it along through the psychical systems intact. On the contrary, "energy cannot be reduced; it does not limit meaning, but rather produces it." This is the sense in which one can say force (energetics, agencies) and meaning are inseparable.

And yet, Derrida argues that Freud's considerations of structure, which take the metaphorical form of an optical machine,[76] will imply precisely the opposite conclusions to the ones just outlined. In short, "Freud, who still insists on *representing* the psychical apparatus in an artificial model, has not yet discovered a mechanical model adequate to the graphematic conceptual scheme he is already using to describe the psychical text."[77]

Briefly, conscious perception, analogous to the aperture of a telescope, which allows a restricted number of light rays into the device, occurs in the perceptual system that in itself "retains no trace of what has happened." Freud's three different "registrations" of perception within the *psychomnemic* system are viewed as analogous to the various lenses of the machine, which focus light rays into an image and cast this image onto a surface. The first registration of the perceptions "is quite incapable of consciousness and arranged according to associations by simultaneity." The second registration of the perceptions occurs as the productive, inventive, synthetic work and tracing attributed to a kind of unconscious "psychic writing." The third transcription involves its discursive reconstitution (or interpretation) in the verbal system of the preconscious. Finally, consciousness acts like the viewfinder that enables one to "see" the image.

Derrida argues, however, that this metaphor presents the danger of reducing "energy" (the spacing of difference and deferral) to a naïve understanding of space and time or, that is, "system."[78] The optical model leads one to think of the psychical text as somehow already "there," significance intact, ready to be translated into consciousness via the agencies of the *psychomnemic* system. An optical device suggests that one achieves an internal copy or translation of what is outside, via a series of "transcendental" or enabling lenses arranged successively in a localized, spatial order.

These lenses may well also distort or disguise the image in the process, but, since the nature and extent of the distortion can be measured, interpretation can circumvent or overcome its effects.

On the other hand, granted that "a certain spatiality, inseparable from the very idea of system, is irreducible," Derrida argues that "its nature is all the more enigmatic in that we can no longer consider it as the homogeneous and serene milieu of dynamic and economic processes."[79] For Freud also insists that psychical entities (such as dream thoughts) are "virtual." In his words, "ideas, thoughts and psychical structures in general must never be regarded as localized in organic elements of the nervous system but rather, as one might say *between* them," in the virtual spaces of resistances and facilitations. Again: "Everything that can be an object of our internal perception is virtual, like the image produced in a telescope by the passage of light-rays."[80] The psychical text, in short, is never always already there but is produced or invented in the interstices between the agent forces. One may read Freud's metaphorics of delay as *Nachträglichkeit* in support of this conclusion. Here, the traumatic memory of a "primal scene" is preserved in the unconscious, but it has no significance. It is only under certain circumstances, that is, after a delay (in this case, after the physical and psychical maturation of puberty), that the primal scene becomes what it "is," granted that there is in principle no limit to such *nachträglich* constitution. In other words, it is the active force of the energies/agencies at work in the *psychomnemic* system that produces, after the fact, the significance of this trace. The work of the *psychomnemic* system, then, cannot be understood in terms of the topography of various discrete systems, which act differently on material traces always already there in their full significance.

Admittedly, Freud argues that these agencies are not necessarily organized spatially, but temporally.[81] However, Derrida notes that this specification changes little about the difficulties already raised, for this argument makes the supposed "timelessness" of the unconscious enigmatic. Freud has argued that the unconscious is timeless, but this would have to be the case only insofar as he identifies time with "phonetic time." In a way that already makes "time" problematic as a measure for differentiating unconscious and conscious systems, "phonetic time" would designate the abstract, logical sequence of preconscious and conscious processes. Here one present now-point follows another in irreversible succession, which would tend to repress all but a dominant, progressive line of connection. Presumably, then, the unconscious processes are "timeless" because they work like hieroglyphics, in terms of connections that do not follow on from one another in a progressive line. But according to Derrida, this spacing out of meaning is not a matter of timelessness. Here, he argues, there is synopsis, not stasis, not timelessness.[82] But then again, this synoptic temporality of the unconscious processes does not, in turn, accord with the "phonetic time" of the optical machine just described. In short, whether Freud views the unconscious processes as timeless or in terms of a temporality different from that of linear succession, his model, understood in terms of phonetic time, conflicts with its subject.

These conflicts, then, represent the dangers of trying to understand energy within the naïve metaphorics of space and time inherent to the spatiotemporal system of an optical machine. Derrida argues that it becomes necessary, without abandoning the concepts of space, time, and system altogether, to rethink the topology of Freud's nontranscriptive (inventive, or productive) writing. It might make more sense to see the psychic apparatus itself as a writing machine, but one may in the end have to rethink the machine metaphor.

To sum up so far: Freud's conjectures concerning facilitation in the *Project* oblige him to attribute some kind of agency to the unconscious system. However, this obligation, with its aneconomic implications, remains incompatible with the quality/quantity distinction of an artificial model by which he still appears to reduce "psyche" to *mneme*. Further, what Freud calls dream-work in *The Interpretation of Dreams* not only confirms that unconscious primary processing within the *psychomnemic* system has an agency independent of and prior to conscious intentionality, but that both are productive and inventive. Thus, far from being reducible to the conscious power of *anamnesis* (proper translation), unconscious processes can indeed pose a threat to it. Yet, as Derrida notes, Freud's optical model runs counter to these insights. So far, then, "the concept of inscription still remains simply the graphic *element* of an apparatus which is not itself a writing machine. . . . We might think that the machine itself is subject to another principle of organization, another destination than writing."[83] Indeed, Freud's structural metaphors have persistently tied his thinking back to a conceptual scheme ordered by Cartesian metaphysics. When the structural metaphor, in the form of the "Mystic Writing Pad," finally becomes a writing machine, it might seem that Freud has all in place for thinking the psyche entirely in terms of *différance*.

The "Note Upon the 'Mystic Writing Pad'": Freud's "Psyche" and *Hypomnesis*

According to Derrida, Freud's account of the Mystic Pad as a model draws the analogy between the psychical apparatus and writing at three progressively more complex levels, beginning with the stratified layers of the writing surface, then with the order of contact between the various layers, and, finally, with the temporality of its operation.[84] Before he outlines these analogies, however, Derrida cites a passage from Freud's "Note" and makes a preliminary observation that sets the scene for his deconstructive reading of these pages. Here, slightly abbreviated, is the passage cited:

> If I distrust my memory . . . I am able to supplement and guarantee its working by making a note in writing. In that case, the surface upon which this trace is preserved . . . is as it were a materialized portion of my mnemic apparatus, the rest of which I carry about with me invisible. I only have to bear in mind the place where this "memory" has been deposited and I can then "reproduce" it at any time I like, with the certainty that it will have remained unaltered and so have escaped the possible distortions to which it might have been subjected in my actual memory.[85]

If, Derrida observes, Freud, like Plato, appears to take for granted the metaphor of writing as *hypomnesic* ("writing . . . as an external, auxiliary technique of psychical memory which is not memory itself"), he simultaneously, if implicitly, subverts this assumption, for, unlike Plato, he sees what is written upon a surface as a materialized portion of a person's mnemic apparatus.[86] The difference turns on a distinction between two senses of the term "metaphor," which in turn generates incompatible readings of Freud's text.[87] The first, didactic or rhetorical, sense of "metaphor" is linked to representation in the modern sense, which implies an abstract link between two self-enclosed present entities, whereby something of one order can stand for something of an entirely different order. The use of a metaphor in this sense, then, allows one to link psyche and the note made in writing (the archiving device) while nevertheless opposing them on the basis of a life/death distinction. Here the presupposition underlying Freud's modeling process is that writing as *hypomnesic* might represent or double memory, but, as a mere device, it is, after all, of a different order to living "memory itself."

The second sense of metaphor, taken more literally, is linked to the premodern notion of "resemblance." A relation of resemblance suggests a connection between things of the same order, where something in the one is repeated in the other. What grounds the relation of resemblance at issue here is what Derrida calls the "solid metaphor," that is, "metaphor" in its literal sense as the actual transference of memory from the enclosure of individual minds to the written documents of an archive, or, in Derrida's words, "the 'unnatural,' historical production of a *supplementary* machine, *added to* the psychical organization in order to supplement its finitude." If one takes Freud at his word that a person's *mnemic* apparatus can literally be materialized (in part or as a whole), then, Derrida argues, the production of this literal transfer from mind to machine via technologies of writing is of an entirely different order to "metaphor" thought of in terms of representation. Resemblance, in contrast, therefore, would imply, as Derrida puts it, that "a certain Being-in-the-world of the psyche did not happen to memory from without, any more than death surprises life. It founds memory." But if this is the case, Derrida argues, then the kind of materialization possible (from slate and sheet to e-mail) should, reciprocally, have a bearing on the nature of the psyche. Here, already, he notes, questions arise concerning the status of this "*hypomnesic supplement.*"

Although Derrida thinks it should have, Freud's interest does not turn in this direction but remains focused on demonstrating the superiority of the Mystic Pad, due to its stratification, as an analogy for the entire psychical apparatus.[88] (Briefly, no other surface satisfies the double requirement of virginity and permanence. If it satisfies the former, e.g., slate, it excludes the latter, and vice versa, e.g., paper.) Nevertheless, Derrida notes, by the end of his increasingly complex analogy between the "Mystic Pad" and the psychical apparatus, the figures of life and death are so interwoven that Freud really ought to have reconsidered the status of the *hypomnesic* supplement. The device he has in mind consists of a wax tablet covered by a sheet of wax paper protected by a celluloid overlay. For Freud, the celluloid overlay and the wax paper that it shields are analogous to the two layers of the perceptual/conscious system, which consists of "an external protective shield against stimuli whose task it is to diminish the strength of excitations coming in, and of a surface behind it which receives the stimuli."[89]

Freud goes on to compare the wax slab with the unconscious system behind the perceptual/conscious system. The pressure of an implement applied to the outer celluloid layer affects the wax tablet through the celluloid and the wax paper. This pressure on the wax causes a reverse reaction whereby it sticks to the wax layer, producing a mark. Importantly, the writing will not appear on the wax paper (in consciousness) unless the wax slab (the unconscious) has already been affected by the pressure of the implement, and has, in the reverse reaction of synthetic processing, as it were, affected the wax paper. Perception, then, is a reconstitution on the basis of stimuli that have always already passed through the detours or delays of the essentially unconscious facilitations traced out in advance by psychic writing. "Writing," the traditional figure of death, as

Derrida notes, "supplements perception before perception even appears to itself."[90]

Further, if the double-layered covering sheet is lifted off the wax slab, then the writing vanishes from the wax paper and does not reappear on it. Here, in Freud's words: "The surface of the Mystic Pad is clear of writing and once more capable of receiving impressions. But it is easy to discover that the permanent trace of what was written is retained upon the wax slab itself and is legible in suitable lights" (e.g., in the light of psychoanalysis). Until this point in the description, Derrida argues, it has only been a matter of the space of writing.[91] But the movement by which writing becomes visible and is erased is inherent to the very structure of the Mystic Pad. In his words: "The becoming-visible which alternates with the disappearance of what is written would be the flickering-up . . . and passing away . . . of consciousness in the process of perception."[92] Here, then, there is also "a *time of writing*": the Mystic Pad includes in its structure permanence, succession, and simultaneity. In fact, he argues, Freud's "discontinuist conception of time" ("writing as the interruption and restoration of contact between the various depths of psychical levels") reflects "the remarkably heterogeneous temporal fabric of psychical work itself."

With this third and, for Derrida, most interesting analogy, the model lends itself to the thinking of *différance*, for it reduces away neither time nor the multiplicity of sensitive layers, neither deferral nor difference (which are *par excellence*, notably, figures of death). Here, Derrida writes: "We find neither the continuity of a line nor the homogeneity of a volume; only the differentiated duration and depth of a stage, and its spacing."[93] Moreover, Freud's metaphor does not describe the structure of an object but the structure of an operation. For "the machine does not run by itself." It takes two hands to operate it: one that writes, while the other periodically erases this writing. Again, Derrida notes the irreducibility of *différance* in this description, from which we might conclude not only that "pure perception does not exist: we are written only as we write," but also that the simplicity of the classical subject is a myth.[94] In his words: "A two-handed machine, a multiplicity of agencies or origins—is this not the original relation to the other and the original temporality of writing, its 'primary' complication: an originary spacing, deferring, and erasure of the simple origin, and polemics on the very threshold of what we persist in calling perception?"[95]

In proposing that subject and psyche are integrated as a complex of relations within a single order, or, that is to say, within the singular ordering/disordering of *différance*, however, Derrida acknowledges that he has taken Freud further than the latter would be willing to go. Freud does not read all of this into the qualification "the machine does not run by itself."[96] Instead, having presented a theory in which the traditional figures of death are found to be crucially intrinsic to psychical life, Freud insists, ironically, that the Mystic Pad, for all its "marvellous complexity," does not resemble the psyche because the psyche, which is after all alive, is capable of spontaneity. As separate from the machine as life is from death, it is uniquely the living psyche that "runs by itself." For Freud, then, this qualification merely points to the limitations that make of his metaphor a relation of representation rather than resemblance.

This implies that the spontaneous, living psyche is already present before its representation and merely waits for science to find a suitable metaphor. Freud's repeated attempts to represent the psychical apparatus and its contents in a scientific model are motivated by the ostensible possibility of progress toward the ultimate, mature model, which would double the psychical apparatus in a representation. In the end, despite the greatly improved representative value of his final metaphor, Freud never finds a model perfectly adequate for its purpose. But the imperfection of the model, he insists, is not accidental but necessary, for the living psyche is, after all, essentially unlike any of the machines we can propose as its double. One of the assumptions underpinning his modeling process itself is a clear division between *mneme* and *hypomnema*. But this means that Freud's attitude toward the limitations of his mechanical models betrays the residue of an entirely conventional metaphysical distinction between life and death, *mneme* and *hypomnema*, that he has already undermined, at least intuitively, at the level of content, for the necessity of "being alive" in order to genuinely be psyche is precisely what Freud has enabled philosophy to bring into question.

Derrida argues, therefore, that Freud, in light of "all he had thought about the unity of life and death,"[97] should have examined the status of the materialized supplement (the writing surface), which is necessary to the alleged spontaneity of memory. If the spontaneity of memory is defined as its power to reproduce a memory intentionally at any time, in the knowledge that it will not have been distorted, then it makes little sense to insist that the supplementary archiving machine and the living psyche are of entirely different orders (linked only through representation), on the basis that the machine, unlike the psyche, is a pure absence of spontaneity (it "does not run by itself"). For, first, the guarantee of spontaneity is said to lie in the supplement (the materialized portion, the *hypomnesic* archive), and second, the necessity of this guarantee bears witness to the finitude of actual memory, since it demonstrates that "actual memory" can by no means be perfectly spontaneous. Rather, the so-called spontaneity of actual memory is "differentiated in itself, thwarted by a censorship or repression which, moreover, could not act on a perfectly spontaneous memory."[98]

If the relation of resemblance implied by Freud's claim that the *hypomnemic* supplement is a materialization of the psychical apparatus implies a certain externalization of the psyche, one might also foresee a certain internalization of the archiving machine. If the resemblance between the archiving machine and the psyche lies in the operation of psychical writing as spacing and timing (*différance*), it becomes impossible to establish a unique domain for psychical writing on the basis of oppositions such as spontaneous/mechanical, inside/outside, and living/dead. What is there, then, to prevent one from imagining that the archiving machine, reciprocally, is essentially psychical? It is precisely Freud, according to Derrida, who gives us to think the enigmatic difficulty of any sharp division between an inside and an outside.[99] Is there, for example, a unique place where psyche happens? Is psyche strictly an internal matter of living flesh, or can a psychical substrate also exist on the outside, for example in electronic media? In rejecting the necessity of a neurological substrate for the psyche, Freud has opened up the possibility of thinking that psyche/archive may be inscribed in the virtual space of a language or cultural tradition, for example. On the other hand, if the archive is always already implicated in the "original" impression, then what is supposedly "outside" the living psyche, all the "prostheses of living memory" (the so-called dead material collected in libraries, available on the Internet or in other media, inscribed in languages, cultures, traditions) may be thought of as an essential constitutive element of the psyche itself, and, in this sense, the *hypomnesic* prosthesis is always already on the inside. Hence the question Derrida poses in *Archive Fever*: "But where does the outside commence? This question is the question of the archive. There are undoubtedly no others."[100]

Moreover, to interpolate the related issue of technological change addressed in *Archive Fever*, Derrida notes that Freud makes it possible to ask whether changes in archival technoscience have any bearing upon the shape of the psychical apparatus. In his words: "Is the psychic apparatus *better represented* or is it *affected differently* by all the technical mechanisms for archivization and for reproduction, for prostheses of so-called live memory?"[101] Freud, Derrida argues, has given us the means to see that the archive is not merely the secondary recording and keeping of a past history whose events would have occurred just as they were whether or not there had been observers to record and conserve them. Instead, "the technical structure of the *archiving* archive also determines the structure of the *archivable* content even in its very coming into existence and in its relationship to the future. This archivization produces as much as it records the event."[102] It follows that a change in the technological means of producing the archive would coincide with a change not only in the production of "content" or events but also in the very structure of what we call "the psyche." This is supported, for example, by Leonard Shlain, who argues that the advent of widespread alphabet literacy radically changed the general disposition of the psychical apparatus.[103] Topographical brain specialization underpins the argument that the predominance of brain activity in a certain area, particularly if it is regularly repeated, would amount to training, development, and reinforcement of neural paths in that area. Once developed, we have a tendency to rely on these paths, or modes of processing, at the cost of others. Shlain argues that learning to write (in the ordinary sense of the term), because it amounts to a powerful and regular training program for the brain's left hemisphere, shifts the brain's disposition toward the modes of processing characteristic of this hemisphere. As a consequence of alphabet literacy, the brain's disposition, having first relied on modes of processing characterized by Freud's primary process, shifts dramatically in favor of the secondary process.

Derrida poses a related question: do the archival machines of today, of which Freud could hardly have dreamed, change anything essential in his discourse?[104] Derrida invites one to consider the difference between traditional letter writing and e-mail correspondence, which far more readily embraces a possibility (the radical destruction of the archive) that Freudian psychoanalysis opens up but also resists.[105] Letters between notable scientists (for example, those collected and immortalized texts of the Freud-Fliess correspondence) are carefully worded documents, written with an eye to their future preservation in an archive. E-mail correspondence, by contrast, is predominantly written to be deleted, quickly, carelessly, and in abbreviation. As easily produced as eradicated, it circulates in an ephemeral electronic medium that, globally everywhere, universally open in principle, has no proper place and no archon.[106] E-mail, then, more readily than traditional correspondence by letter, incorporates the notion of archivization as process rather than place. Derrida might arguably have been overimpressed by the ephemerality of this medium, but the point of the example remains valid: if technological upheavals can engender changes in the disposition of the psychical apparatus, then it becomes impossible for science still to envisage the psyche as a stable apparatus with essential, universal characteristics, already and inherently possessed by individuals, which can be represented in a model. As Derrida puts it:

"it would be a question no longer of simple continuous progress in representation, in the *representative* value of the model," but rather of "an entirely different logic," which emphasizes the irreducibility of the "figures of death" in an account of the psychical apparatus and which sees in "writing," in its broadest sense, "the stage of history and the play of the world."[107]

The impossibility of the archive "properly speaking" points toward other texts by Derrida, where all the associated difficulties that make Freud's conception of the psychical apparatus enigmatic are condensed and repeated in questions concerning the very possibility of an analysis of the psyche. In Derrida's words: "That which, in Freud's discourse, opens itself to the theme of writing results in psychoanalysis being not simply psychology—nor simply psychoanalysis."[108] In the chapter to follow, I shall take up the aporetic troubles that point to something "beyond" analysis in Freudian psychoanalysis, which is already both augured and resisted in the Freudian text.

5

The Death Drive and the Im-Possibility of Psychoanalysis

Introductory Remarks: The Aporetic Complexity of the Death Drive

In Beyond the Pleasure Principle, Freud introduces the death drive at the most fundamental level in psychoanalytic theory and subsequently redescribes central notions in its terms. Again, Derrida finds in this notion a reiteration of the quasi-transcendental complexities already described, for any final determination of the death drive is suspended by our inability to demarcate its attributes clearly and on this basis establish orders of preference among them. In trying to conceptualize the death drive, one remains caught between the economic motifs of archivization, namely those of proper repetition associated with conservation and return and the equally necessary aneconomic motifs of anarchiving violence, of improper repetition associated with aggression, destruction, and dissolution. In other words, incompatible economic and aneconomic motifs belong irreducibly to the notion of the death drive, making it inescapably aporetic. In consequence, if one can say that the death drive is the fundamental transcendental principle governing the proper constitution of the archive (psyche), it also makes such proper constitution impossible, for one must also acknowledge that the death drive is not a principle. As Derrida notes, "it even threatens every principality, every archontic primacy, every archival desire. It is what we will call, later on, *le mal d'archive*, 'archive fever.'"[1] In short, a fundamental but inescapable incoherence in the definition of the death drive tempts Derrida to suggest that beyond the pleasure principle lies a disruptive drive, beyond "principality" itself, for as a quasi-transcendental condition, the death drive both must and cannot function as a fundamental principle in any traditional sense.[2]

In what follows, the aporetic complexity underscored by the introduction of the death drive is addressed from two points of view. First, unraveling a thread from the material condensed in the second of the theses that Derrida risks in *Archive Fever*, I shall briefly outline the archiving/anarchiving entanglement by which the psyche is constituted insofar as it is recast in the terms of the death drive.[3] Second, I have grafted onto this discussion of Derrida's thesis a related argument concerning the "de-constitution" of the psyche, found in the first part of his essay "Resistances," which, again viewed through the prism of the death drive, highlights the complexity associated with conceptualizing "psychoanalysis" as a therapeutic practice, this time stemming from the aporias associated with the notion "analysis."[4] Here, Derrida argues that an attempt to explicate two crucial psychotherapeutic notions, namely "analysis" and "resistance," yields a curious isomorphism whereby both notions, like the death drive, incorporate irreducible but incompatible moments of return and destruction. These conceptual entanglements pose difficulties for the very possibility of psychoanalysis as a therapeutic practice.

I should reiterate that, for Derrida, rereading Freud in a way that highlights certain possible/impossible complexities can be nothing but a good thing, for this vacillation between what can be actualized and what forever remains out of reach in psychoanalysis is the source of its critical distance from its own death drive and, therefore, of its life as an institution, discipline, and tradition. Moreover, as I hope to demonstrate in part 3, it is precisely in the general terms of this paradoxical im-possibility that one can best approach Lacan's appropriation of Freud, for there is a demonstrable accord between what Derrida and Lacan theorize here under the nicknames of "event" and the Real, respectively. This accord, as already noted, can be established by associating both with the Freudian notion of "trauma." For Derrida's arguments in *Archive Fever* and "Resistances" and Lacan's arguments in "Tuché and Automaton," which I shall address in detail in chapter 7, to be anything other than opaque, Freud's conception of the death drive and its associated notions ("trauma" and "repetition compulsion") require elaboration. For this reason, and because "Beyond the Pleasure Principle," where the death drive is first introduced, is, as Derrida notes, "not just any book by Freud and . . . not just any book by Freud for Lacan," I have prefaced my discussion of these arguments with a fairly lengthy summary of it.[5]

"Beyond the Pleasure Principle": Introducing the Death Drive

In this essay, as its title suggests, Freud revises his hypothesis that the pleasure principle is fundamental in psychical regulation and argues ultimately that a more fundamental death drive may override it. According to the pleasure principle, "unpleasure" arises from a heightening of excitation, whose discharge brings relief and concomitantly produces pleasure. Failing complete discharge, the psyche strives to keep excitation low and constant.[6]

While the pleasure principle dictates activity that avoids pain and promotes pleasure at all costs, its full sway is checked by certain necessary frustrations.[7] First, in negotiating the physical and social world, it is inefficient and dangerous and is soon checked in mental life by a "reality principle," under the dictates of which the psyche temporarily endures pain while it finds safer, more calculated, reasoned, or differentiated paths to pleasure. But powerful instinctual forces constantly threaten such imposed constraints, often "to the detriment of the organism as a whole." Freud, therefore, predicts enduring psychical conflicts due to the reality-determined frustration of pleasure-seeking libidinal instincts. Second, he argues, community life requires the painful frustration of instinctual life in order to rescue the psyche from opposite extremes: selflessness as libidinal self-sacrifice or selfishness as narcissistic sacrifice of others. Since neither extreme is conducive to harmonious communal life, they are usually accompanied by painful emotions of resentment or guilt if they find occasional outlets. Nevertheless, in these cases, Freud argues, the psychical economy, guided by the pleasure principle and the reality principle that checks it without disputing its supremacy, usually secures an ultimate pleasure gain.

However, most of the unpleasure we experience stems from external sources, either in direct perceptions of pain or indirectly in painful anticipations of danger. Freud argues that a common psychical reaction to externally imposed pain, namely the compulsive repetition of painful experiences, may point to something beyond the pleasure principle. But he is not about to give the game away at the start. Instead, he outlines four cases where this reaction *might* challenge the primacy of the pleasure principle. But in each case he initially presses the explanatory power of the pleasure principle as far as it will extend.

Freud first describes the case of "traumatic neurosis."[8] Here, after experiencing an unexpected shock, victims compulsively, and at the cost of their general health, replay its events in fantasy or dreams, renewing the terror each time as if fixated there. The condition is associated primarily with fright, with its emphasis on surprise rather than anxiety (which prepares one for dangers, known or unknown) or fear (which requires a definite, already known, object). It is certainly difficult, he admits, to explain this condition in terms of the pleasure principle, according to which all dreams function to deflect any repressed and therefore pressing unconscious motives that might disturb sleep, thus releasing psychical tension by offering hallucinatory fulfillment of the disturbing wishes.[9] It would only be consistent with the pleasure principle if victims dreamed of a healthy past or future respite instead of becoming victim to a persistent renewal of pain and terror. He proposes some avenues for investigation (not all dreams are wish fulfillments; this condition upsets all mental functions, including dreams; the ego tends towards masochism) but concludes that the condition remains at best underinvestigated.

His second case derives from his grandson's initially puzzling habit of repeatedly flinging his toys into the far reaches of his surroundings, accompanied by an expression decipherable as the German word *fort* (meaning "gone").[10] He notes that the child sometimes (although not regularly) included a second act in this drama of disappearance, namely the joyful *da* ("there") of reappearance. According to Freud's interpretation, the boy's repetitive game of "being gone" is a dramatization through which he "compensated himself" for his mother's upsetting departures from the house. Notably, he argues, this game enabled the child to resist an instinctive urge to protest his mother's absence. In other words, this "renunciation of instinctual satisfaction," which indicates the capacity for repression, compensatory sublimation, and delayed gratification, marks the inaugural moment of a "great cultural achievement." But his primary interest in the example relates to the problem of how the game accords with the pleasure principle. This would be unproblematic if the child played the entire *fort-da* game most frequently, for the painful first act would be a prelude to the evidently greater pleasure of the second. But the first act alone is much more frequently replayed, and the game primarily involves not the avoidance of pain but its repetition, which suggests that it might be motivated by something beyond the impulse for pleasure.

Freud considers two candidates: power and revenge. To master the event, the child may have needed to repeat it in play, despite its painful nature, at the same time reversing the power relations so that he becomes the active perpetrator rather than the passive victim of a painful separation. Moreover, by throwing away objects that represent the mother, exacting revenge by proxy, he could then release otherwise suppressed hostile feelings toward her. But one may argue that these repetitions, while painful, still serve the pleasure principle, for the associated unpleasure would be offset by the greater, albeit different, pleasure of activity, mastery, and revenge. It is unnecessary, then, to postulate something beyond the pleasure principle to supply a motive for children's play. Citing dramatic tragedy as another example of how the repetitive enactment of painful situations can be experienced as enjoyable, Freud concludes that "even under the dominance of the pleasure principle, there are ways and means enough of making what is in itself unpleasurable into a subject to be recollected and worked over in the mind." By itself, the play impulse does not necessitate the postulate of independent tendencies more primitive than the pleasure principle.

Freud's third case is drawn from "the transference phenomena of neurotics."[11] Initially, he believed, the psychoanalytic task was to discover the unconscious material veiled by the analysand's discourse, draw together its various elements in an interpretation, and present it at the appropriate moment. However, since this careful presentation of the analyst's reconstruction did not always have the intended therapeutic effect, there was evidently more to do, namely, elicit confirmation of this interpretation from analysands by helping them find and acknowledge the evidence for it in memory. The emphasis shifts to unmasking resistances to such recollection (for it is unacceptable material that is repressed in the first place) and teaching analysands to overcome and abandon these resistances. Again, it became apparent that even this could not always achieve the psychoanalytic aim of bringing the unconscious into full view. If the essential details of the repressed material are especially resistant to recollection, analysands remain unconvinced that an analyst's reconstruction is accurate. Here, instead of remembering repressed material as belonging to the past, Freud notes, analysands unwittingly and compulsively repeat it as current experience in the relationship with the analyst, that is, in "the sphere of the transference." The analyst's task here is to engender awareness in the analysand that what is reexperienced in the sphere of the transference is only the reflection of a forgotten past. As a rule, Freud notes, analysands cannot be spared this painful phase of treatment.

But does this neurotic "compulsion to repeat" accord with the pleasure principle?[12] First, according to Freud, resistance during treatment does not arise directly from repressed material in the unconscious, for the psyche, persistently seeking an outlet for it, aims precisely to force it into consciousness or to discharge it through action. Such resistance, rather, arises from the system that originally carried out the repression: the ego.[13] The repetition compulsion describes a means by which repressed material presses for an outlet under the constraints imposed by the ego. Without doubt, he argues, the ego's resistance to treatment obeys the pleasure principle, since its aim is to avoid any unpleasure generated by the release of repressed material. Psychotherapy, in contrast, appeals to the reality principle, encouraging the temporary endurance of pain for the sake of long-term relief. What about the repetition compulsion? Like the ego, the agency of this compulsion resists the economic compromise of enduring unpleasure in one system for the sake of satisfaction in another. Unlike the ego, however, it does not act in the name of pleasure. Instead, Freud notes, analysands repeat all manner of distressing experiences and emotions usually from early childhood (loss of love, failure, disappointment, jealousy), reviving them "with the greatest ingenuity" in the sphere of the transference. Here, he argues, "we come now to a new and remarkable fact": analysands compulsively but often unwittingly revive past experiences that can never have been satisfying. Moreover, no doubt these would cause less current unpleasure if their repetition took the form of memories or dreams instead of fresh experiences. Yet, in these cases, the psyche does not learn from past pains but repeats distressing experiences compulsively, regardless of the pain. Here, Freud admits, the pleasure principle loses its efficacy as an explanatory principle.

He cites a final case that he regards as equally difficult to explain in terms of the pleasure principle. In everyday life, he observes, people are affected by precisely the kind of repetition compulsion evidenced in the transference phenomena of neurotics[14] (for example, those whose friendships or love affairs repeatedly take the same disastrous course, or those who abandon unhappy encounters with authority figures, restrictive ideologies, or religious cults only to replicate them in new contexts). Here, one gets the impression, he remarks, that some people are "pursued by a malignant fate or possessed by some 'daemonic' power" dedicated to their continued misery.

To sum up so far, in pressing the explanatory power of the pleasure principle, Freud is most successful in the domain of play, but in the other cases enough is left unexplained to justify a new postulate: that of a repetition compulsion in psychic life "more primitive, more elementary, more instinctual than the pleasure principle" and capable of overriding it.[15] Notably, then, he does not infer that there is something beyond the pleasure principle from his grandson's *fort-da* game. Nevertheless, once the primacy of this compulsion has been established on grounds of the transference phenomena and their replication in everyday life, he is inclined retrospectively to see it at work in certain play activities as well as in the hitherto unexplained "traumatic neurosis," although he adds that it rarely operates in isolation from other motives.

Freud's proposed scientific explanation of this compulsion is tied to his theory of the psychical apparatus,[16] which I shall not repeat; suffice it to note his emphasis on defense.[17] "*Protection against* stimuli," he argues, "is an almost more important function for the living organism than *reception of* stimuli." In relation to outer stimuli, pain triggers the defense mechanisms of a protective shield that safeguards the organism from overstimulation. In relation to inner excitations, the psyche tends to treat those associated with excessive pain as if they were acting from without, so as to apply against them the defenses of the protective shield.[18] Taking a step beyond the pleasure principle, he describes as "traumatic" any external excitation strong enough to break through the otherwise efficacious protective shield, producing a wholesale disturbance in the organism's energy balance.[19] In face of this flood of stimuli, the pleasure principle becomes ineffectual. Instead, another task presents itself: that of mastering this excess by binding excitation in order to discharge it. To achieve this, he claims, "cathectic energy is summoned from all sides to provide sufficiently high cathexes of energy in the environs of the breach. An 'anticathexis' on a grand scale is set up, for whose benefit all the other psychical systems are impoverished, so that the remaining psychical functions are extensively paralysed or reduced." From this, Freud adds, we can infer that an already cathected system (one that is alert, focused, trained, educated, or ready for action) readily takes up additional excitation and converts it into "quiescent cathexis," or, that is, binds it psychically. Moreover, presumably up to a point, he argues that "the higher the system's own quiescent cathexis, the greater . . . its binding force." Conversely, therefore, a system that is dormant, idle, unobservant, ignorant, uneducated, or unprepared for action will be more violently affected by a breach in the protective shield.

With these speculations in hand, Freud can now suggest that traumatic neurosis occurs in the event of a trauma, when, in addition, the affected systems were unprepared for it, that is, when they were not hypercathected as they would have been in, for example, a state of anxiety.[20] Moreover, he adds, this condition suggests for the first time an exception to the hypothesis that all dreams are wish fulfillments.[21] The dreams of those suffering from traumatic neuroses are tied instead to another task, which must be accomplished before the pleasure principle comes into play. These dreams help to master or bind excessive excitation retrospectively, by developing the anxiety whose absence led to the traumatic neurosis. Thus, Freud concludes: "If there is a 'beyond the pleasure principle,' it is only consistent to grant that there was also a time before the purpose of dreams was the fulfilment of wishes."

Turning from external to internal sources of excitation, Freud first reminds his readers that the main internal sources of excitation are the instincts.[22] Since the excitations arising from the instincts "have the unconscious systems as their point of impact," they obey the primary process, which is identified not with "bound" or quiescent excitation but with the freely mobile type that presses for discharge. It would be the task of "the higher strata of the mental apparatus" to bind excitation arising from instincts to appropriate facilitations. Since failure here would provoke traumatic economic disturbances, he again concludes that the task of mastering or binding excitations from internal sources would take precedence over the pleasure and reality principles.

The repetition compulsion, Freud claims, is instinctual in character. Unbound, it would manifest blindly, independently, and sometimes in disregard of both the pleasure economy and the tempering influence of the reality-oriented higher strata (e.g., the rational faculties). But in saying this, he consciously invokes opposing senses of the word "instinctual." Children's play, for example, is characterized by an instinct for, and delight in, repetition. But one could say that the enjoyment of reexperiencing identical pleasures over and over serves the purpose of education (training and mastery). The instinctive repetition here, which does not contradict the pleasure principle, accords with a traditional view that instincts press living organisms toward change and development. Yet when the repetition compulsion acts in opposition to the pleasure principle, as in the transference phenomena, then calling it instinctual would immediately place into question this traditional understanding of the instincts, for it would suggest, as Freud puts it, "*that an instinct is an urge inherent in organic life to restore an earlier state of things* which the living entity has been obliged to abandon under the pressure of external disturbing forces . . . or, to put it another way, the expression of the inertia inherent in organic life."[23]

Freud adduces biological evidence from heredity and embryology in favor of this view that the instinctual is "an expression of the *conservative* nature of living substance."[24] But he also raises a plausible objection to this claim, namely that one could think in terms of both "conservative instincts which impel towards repetition" and progressive instincts directed toward "the production of new forms." Deferring an immediate pronouncement on this objection, he invites readers "to pursue to its logical conclusion" the hypothesis "that all the organic instincts are conservative, are acquired historically and tend towards the restoration of an earlier state of things."[25] Here, to avoid confusion, one must remain alert to the hypothetical nature of this train of thought. The structure of his argument is as follows: The hypothesis that *all* organic instincts are conservative in the inertial sense is contradicted on various grounds. Nevertheless, one cannot for this reason justly deny the postulate of death instincts altogether.

It would follow from the above hypothesis, Freud argues, that the elementary living entity must resist change from the start and would constantly repeat the same course of life in the absence of external disturbances. Alluding to his theory of facilitation, he adds, development would be imposed upon a reluctant organism by irresistible environmental forces, whose traces must be managed (stored up for further repetition). Conservative instincts, therefore, may seem to promote change and progress. But, he argues, it would run contrary to their conservative nature to aim at a state never yet attained. They are instead "seeking to reach an ancient goal" along circuitous paths, both old and new. Thus, paradoxically, he concludes: "If we are to take it as a truth that knows no exception that everything living dies for internal reasons—becomes inorganic once again—then we shall be compelled to say that '*the aim of all life is death*.'"[26]

An equally paradoxical conclusion is reached "if we firmly maintain the exclusively conservative nature of instincts" (that is, the tendency to return to an inorganic state) against the opposing hypothesis of inherent self-preservative instincts (here understood as the instinct that presses us to maintain life at all costs).[27] One could try to overcome this opposition by arguing that the life-preserving instincts function only in the hope of securing a natural death for the organism. Paradoxically, however, as Freud notes, one would then have to say that "the living organism struggles most energetically against events (dangers, in fact) which might help it to attain its life's aim rapidly—by a kind of short-circuit." Thus to begin with, for Freud, the hypothesis that the nature of the instincts is exclusively conservative lacks support because it generates paradoxes.

Moreover, it is also contradicted when it comes to sexuality.[28] Here, Freud suggests that the germ cells (sperm and ova), as "elementary organisms that survive the whole individual," might plausibly offer an exception to the rule that all living organisms die. These cells, he argues, repeatedly separate from the composite organism (the body), which independently pursues its path to an inorganic state, and under favorable conditions begin anew "the performance to which they owe their existence." In this way, they gain for themselves a kind of potential immortality, although, as he notes, "that may mean no more than a lengthening of the road to death." Further, there are sexual instincts that guard the destinies of the germ cells (that shelter them and bring them into contact with other germ cells). Freud grants that one may indeed call the performance of these cells "conservative" in a variety of senses. For example, their conservatism may be indicated in the fact that they "bring back earlier states of living substance," "are peculiarly resistant to external influences," and "preserve life itself for a comparatively long period." However, he argues, such "conservatism" does not stretch to include the inertial sense that strives to return all living organisms to an inorganic state. On the whole, he counters, the activity of these cells is instead essentially life-preserving, since it embodies an impulse toward combination and development. For Freud, the sexual instincts "are the true life instincts." But this again opposes the hypothesis that "all the organic instincts are conservative" in that they lead to death.

Although Freud does not support the claim that *all* instincts are inherently death instincts, this is not to deny altogether the postulate of a basic or primordial death instinct. To achieve certainty that there is no such thing as a death instinct, he argues, one would have to make the case that natural death first came into being with multicellular organisms, where there can be a distinction between the mortal soma and the immortal germ-plasm.[29] In unicellular organisms, the body and the reproductive cell are still one and the same. Thus if unicellular organisms were immortal, this would give the lie to the idea that all living organisms have an inherent death instinct—the instinct to return to the inorganic state. But, as he demonstrates at some length, the question of immortality versus natural death in unicellular organisms is far from decided. He concludes that "our expectation that biology would flatly contradict the recognition of death instincts has not been fulfilled. We are at liberty to continue concerning ourselves with their possibility if we have other reasons for doing so."[30] Moreover, he adds, speculation among biologists that two contrary processes ("one constructive or assimilatory and the other destructive or dissimilatory") are constantly at work in living substance adds support to the hypothesis of an inherent opposition between life and death instincts.

Invoking Schopenhauer ("For him, death is the 'true result and to that extent the purpose of life,' while the sexual instinct is the embodiment of the will to live"),[31] Freud in the end prefers the proposition that the development of the organism, which he understands in terms of change as opposed to progress,[32] is a response to environmental forces that are negotiated in terms of an inherent opposition between two groups of instincts (the erotic and the thanatic). As he puts it earlier in the essay: "It is as though the life of the organism moved with a vacillating rhythm. One group of instincts rushes forward so as to reach the final aim of life as swiftly as possible; but when a particular stage in the advance has been reached, the other group jerks back to a certain point to make a fresh start."[33]

Having posited this instinctual life/death opposition, Freud's final task is to integrate it with current psychoanalytic libido theory.[34] He is required to show that libido manifests as an opposition of instincts at its inception. Tracing out the developmental vicissitudes of his libido theory, he first demonstrates in what sense these new speculations substantiate this theory as it stands, which ties libido to Eros (sexuality and reproduction, union, and narcissism). As he sums up in a later note, "we came to know what the sexual instincts were from their relation to the sexes and to the reproductive function. . . . With the hypothesis of narcissistic libido and the extension of the concept of libido to the individual cells, the sexual instinct was transformed for us into Eros, which seeks to force together and hold together the portions of living substance."[35]

Briefly, if the sexual instincts are viewed as that part of Eros directed outward toward objects, narcissism describes that part of libido that is directed inward toward the ego in self-love. Narcissism embodies the desire to see in all otherness merely a reflection of the ego, that is, to incorporate all otherness in the sphere of the self. This self-preservative instinct must, therefore, also be understood as libidinal. Second, Freud suggests that psychoanalytical libido theory might be applicable at a cellular level in multicellular organisms, given the tendency of cells to join together in vital associations, whereby cells take one another as libidinal objects, partly neutralizing the effects of the death instincts, which allows the community to survive even if individuals must die. In this case, "the libido of our sexual instincts would coincide with the Eros of the poets and philosophers which holds all living things together."[36]

So far, Freud notes, psychoanalysis has only given credence to *Eros* and neglected *Thanatos*.[37] However, this could be remedied by demonstrating that a death instinct is intrinsic to libido (a condition for its function).[38] Since psychoanalysis has already characterized "object-love itself" by a polarity between affection and aggressiveness, one could demonstrate that libido contains the death instinct if this polarity was shown to be derived from the opposition between the life and death instincts. Thus, granted that psychoanalysis already acknowledges a sadistic side to the sexual instinct, it remains to be seen how one may derive "the sadistic instinct, whose aim it is to injure the object . . . from Eros, the preserver of life." Here, Freud argues, the destructive side of *Eros* manifests in the instinctual craving for power over the object of libidinal investment. Initially, erotic mastery over an object is expressed as the power to destroy it. Later, serving the reproductive function, this destructive instinct becomes a sadistic tendency to injure the sexual object, overpowering it "to the extent necessary for carrying out the sexual act." Freud concludes that this "original sadism," serving erotic purposes, points "the way for the libidinal components of the sexual instinct, and that these follow after it to the object."[39] In short, a certain destruction of the other as "other" is the condition for erotic union. Moreover, adumbrating the theme of *Civilization and Its Discontents*, Freud suggests that this primary sadism might go hand in hand with its reversal in a primary masochism ("the turning around of the instinct upon the subject's own ego" in self-sacrifice, sacrifice of my own instinctual narcissism, for the sake of erotic union).[40]

We have already seen in what sense mastery of forces in the external environment (including other people) as well as internal forces (self-mastery via repression of the instincts) is associated with the primary motivation of the pleasure principle.[41] Moreover, the "Nirvana principle" that it serves (that is "the dominating tendency of mental life, and perhaps of nervous life in general . . . to reduce, to keep constant or to remove internal tension due to stimuli") is "one of our strongest reasons for believing in the existence of death instincts." Yet, the "proper" confirmation of their existence would arise from our power to demonstrate that the repetition compulsion is intrinsic to the life instincts. It is difficult, however, to ascribe to the sexual instincts the characteristic of a compulsion to repeat. (They are, indeed, extremely rich in the phenomena of repetition, but not, it seems, in the inertial sense ascribed to the death drive.) To achieve this, Freud insists, we would have to trace the origin of the instinct for sex to the need to restore an earlier state of things. But natural science cannot help here, for it has next to nothing to tell us about the origin of sexuality, that is, how and why reproduction in certain organisms became a union of sexually differentiated germ cells instead of multiplication by cell division.

Leaving biological science to its darkness, then, Freud turns to literature, specifically to "the theory which Plato put into the mouth of Aristophanes in the *Symposium*," which "traces the origin of an instinct to *a need to restore an earlier state of things*."[42] One might, he suggests, "follow the hint given us by the poet-philosopher" and venture a hypothesis: perhaps the condition of coming to life is the fragmentation of a substance whose particles (retaining their chemical affinity) subsequently strive to reunite. This desire to return to an earlier state (this death instinct "brought into being by the coming to life of inorganic substance")[43] would be the basis of the sexual instincts. Requiring protection in this endeavor from "an environment charged with dangerous stimuli," these fragments would have evolved a protective layer (a body), thereby achieving a multicellular condition. But the instinct for reuniting would be retained in the germ cells.

Here, Freud breaks off his speculative train of thought with a few words of critical reflection. At this point, he insists, conviction concerning these hypotheses is not yet at issue. "It is surely possible to throw oneself into a line of thought and to follow it wherever it leads out of simple scientific curiosity, or, if the reader prefers, as an *advocatus diaboli*, who is not on that account himself sold to the devil."[44] He describes his thought process as one of translating observations into theory, which is inevitably open to sources of error, for example, from overestimation of the significance of certain observations or from deep-seated prejudices. But, he adds, "it is impossible to pursue an idea of this kind except by repeatedly combining factual material with what is purely speculative and thus diverging widely from empirical observation." The wider the speculation, the more untrustworthy the final result, and the degree of its uncertainty is initially undecidable. In short, despite the acknowledged provisional status of his theory, Freud's caution here is in the name of "proper" scientific practice, where, for example, falsification operates in the name of a future truth. Further, while acknowledging that psychological, physiological, or chemical terms belong to the figurative language of their own language games, he does not question the possibility of translation between them. Indeed, he believes that the possibility of translating the psychological into the privileged figures of natural science would remedy the deficiencies in his description. Although he grants that some of these are exacerbated by the prevailing obscurities in the science of biology, the relation of priority holds nevertheless: clarity in biology could either support or "blow away the whole of our artificial structure of hypotheses."[45]

Freud's final remarks sum up what has been gained from these speculations.[46] In his words: "If it is really the case that seeking to restore an earlier state of things is such a universal characteristic of instincts, we need not be surprised that so many processes take place in mental life independently of the pleasure principle . . . but it does not follow that any of them are necessarily opposed to it." The relation between the instinctual processes of repetition and the pleasure principle, he concludes, could be stated as follows: the predominant function of the mental apparatus "is to bind the instinctual impulses which impinge on it, to replace the primary process prevailing in them by the secondary process and convert their freely mobile cathectic energy into mainly quiescent (tonic) cathexis." This process must occur regardless of any increase in unpleasure. But the pleasure principle is not hereby rejected. To the contrary, Freud argues, such binding occurs as a condition for the pleasure principle: "the binding is a preparatory act which introduces and assures the dominance of the pleasure principle." Reciprocally, the pleasure principle "is a tendency operating in the service of a function whose business it is to free the mental apparatus entirely from excitation or to keep it as low as possible" and is thus "concerned with the most universal endeavour of all living substance—namely to return to the quiescence of the inorganic world."

The Constitution of the Psyche: Derrida's Second Thesis

Derrida argues, as noted, that Freud's "death drive" is spread across two irreducible and incompatible motifs (of conservation/return and of aggression/destruction), which makes it inescapably aporetic. Accordingly, if the difficulties enumerated in the previous chapter concerning repetition at the origin already trouble the coherence of the notion "facilitation" as the condition of the possibility of the psyche (or the archive), this trouble is repeated when Freud recasts the constitution of the psyche in terms of the death drive. In the second thesis of *Archive Fever*, Derrida argues that, on the one hand, Freud admits the aporetic complexity of the death drive.[47] In his words: "All the texts in the family and of the period of 'Beyond the Pleasure Principle' explain in the end why there is archivization and why anarchiving destruction belongs to the process of archivization and produces the very thing it reduces, on occasion to ashes, and beyond."

To put such aporetic complexity in telegraphic form (I shall elaborate below): without the economic prospect of proper repetition (formulated in terms of the death drive as conservation), there can be no psyche/archive as a record of original events to which a proper return is possible. But because what happens "originally" is in principle traumatic, such an "event" lacks sense and cannot be properly repeated and recorded in the archive. Therefore, as soon as there is archivization (under the pressure of the death drive to return to a pretraumatic state), it is certain that the "event" only appears in the guise of an economizing, appropriating fabrication. Just as originally and necessarily, then, the death drive always already incorporates a moment of aneconomic, anarchiving destruction, for the moment of archiving appropriation in which phenomena are constituted is automatically an interpretative violation of the intrinsically impossible "event itself," or what Lacan calls the Real. The "original experience" that one returns to via the archive is never a proper copy of the traumatic "event itself," but the first decisively formative fabrication.

Additionally, since, as Freud has demonstrated, the fabrication is inevitably singular or idiosyncratic, the "archive itself" can no longer be understood as merely the proper repetition of intersubjectively shared experiences.

Importantly, then, when Freud suggests that part of the psychoanalytic task is to return via *anamnesis* to the "kernel of truth" in a delusion, such "truth" is not to be understood as a "past present," that is, a true copy in memory of some past perceptual evidence. Rather, the "kernel of truth" here refers to the originary, decisive fabrication, which, drawing into service existing memory scraps or traces, shapes the course of an inventive appropriation of the event. This appropriation might have little correlation, or none at all, with what is perceptually given. In "Constructions in Analysis," Freud graphically illustrates this point via a favorite metaphor that links the psyche to an archeological site. The analyst, as archaeologist, he explains, is required to "construct" an analysand's narrative by putting together a story (or complex interpretative construction) from fragmentary scraps of leftover material made available by direct or indirect means (e.g., parapraxes). Similarly, in his view, in first constructing a phenomenal reality (seen as an attempt to effect a "cure" for the traumatic Real), an individual follows precisely the same constructive process in order to "make sense" of something that has happened. A pathological construction of reality, or a delusion, named because it persists despite clear contrary experiences, gains its power of persuasion from the hallucinatory vivacity of certain memory scraps that have been used in its construction (but might well derive from much earlier experiences). To treat a dysfunctional delusion, then, is to help the analysand reconstruct a better narrative, perhaps by a retrospective reordering of the same fragments, perhaps with the aid of alternatives.[48]

Thus, acknowledging the quasi-conceptuality of the death drive, Freud irrevocably "ruins" the traditional aneconomic/economic distinctions between fabrication and truth, belief and knowledge, literature and science, inside and outside. Here, he implicitly acknowledges the im-possible, impure "spectral space"[49] between so-called original and copy (which is the milieu of the quasi-transcendental) that Derrida has nicknamed *différance* or *khôra* and therefore opens psychoanalysis to the multiple risks, but also the chances, of the prosthesis (fiction, fabrication, and delusion).[50]

Yet despite all this, Derrida argues, "as classical metaphysician and as positivist *Aufklärer*," there is a residue in Freud's writing that does not altogether respect the "logic of repetition" (that is, iterability) and, therefore, the quasi-conceptuality of the death drive, which he otherwise takes into account. He does not consistently believe in belief (the fundamentality of fabrication) but sometimes believes in knowledge, as if the belief in knowledge were not itself the hallucinatory projection of a paranoiac wish. Freud, then, against the grain of his radical insights, still sometimes dreams of presence; he dreams that a return to the indestructible grain of truth in the delusion corresponds not with a return to the decisive fabrication but with, as Derrida puts it, "a return to reality, here to the originary effectivity of a base of immediate perception." Notably, this argument echoes and elaborates on Lacan's similar observation that Freud's conception of the real is intrinsically troubled by an internal vacillation between perceptual repetition, tied to reality testing, and fabrication, tied to pleasure.[51]

The Death Drive as Condition of the Possibility of the Archive

In "Beyond the Pleasure Principle," according to Derrida, Freud shows that the conservative death drive is precisely what allows psychical life to take hold in the first place, thus making the archive possible in the most obvious sense of repetition. For Freud, biologically speaking, any living organism's continued existence depends primarily on its enclosure within a "membrane" or "barrier" of some kind, which forms a protective shield between itself and the external environment. Precisely this separation between an inside and an outside is the condition of the possibility of an archival medium vulnerable to impressions made by occasioning forces. Of course, complete enclosure as a consequence of impenetrable resistance to the imposition of external forces would be self-defeating, which is why the tendency toward protective closure can be thought of as a death drive. However, this separation between an inside and an outside is simultaneously the condition that makes receptivity possible, whereby an "imprint" is conserved as a modification of the archival medium that has at least a certain durability.

In conformity with the biological principle that protection from external stimuli supersedes reception, Freud insists that the first psychical task is to form a defensive shield against overstimulation from external events.[52] For Freud, then, our defensive/receptive perceptual system is the psychical equivalent of the membranous barrier that surrounds unicellular organisms and maintains their integrity. The "first" moment of the archive, then, is the resistance to the outside that constitutes a protected "inside." Derrida names this "first" moment an "originary finitude," whose correlative is a sense of "expropriation," or loss of an outside. Notably, "originary finitude" here is the Derridean equivalent of Lacan's notion of "lack."

Lacan's name for Freud's "defensive shield" is libido, represented by the figure of the "lamella," which replaces the traditional myth of origin as a body without organs.[53] The lamella again functions as a protective/receptive "border," which ensures that the organism is neither open to the outside nor closed off from it and, therefore, protects the organism from overstimulation (or "lack of lack") and from lack of stimulation. As neither inside nor outside the organism, it functions as the "original division" that "separates" life (the pleasure economy) from death ("proper" or full jouissance). As the *khôral* "region" of the not-yet, it is the Lacanian equivalent of what Derrida will speak of as "originary dissemination" (more on this in chapter 8).

The sense of expropriation correlating to "lack" is, as Lacan also makes clear, misplaced, for "the outside" was never actually held as a property to be taken away. The sense of "expropriation," accordingly, marks what Lacan describes as the supposed "loss" of what is only retrospectively constructed as a primary experience of being "the All." The death drive toward full reappropriation of the "outside," then, is necessarily frustrated, for satisfaction here would be a matter, impossibly, of eradicating the protective barrier that both enables the inside to resist the "outside" and opens the one up to the other.[54]

Along with Lacan, Derrida finds that the resistance named by this receptive/defensive barrier (*khôra* in Derridean nomenclature, "lamella" in Lacanian) may only be grasped in terms of its multiple paradoxes, which makes it the troubling quasi-condition of the possibility and impossibility of repetition. The "protective shield," for example, names a receptivity whereby the very condition of repetition (namely, the resistance that allows a durable impression, imprint, or "copy" to form in the archival medium) is simultaneously its "ruin," for the nature of the medium allows only "selected bits of the real" to gain a purchase.[55] Just as light is refracted differently when it passes through different substances, so the archival medium "receiving" the imprint presses back, so to speak, and in so doing, codetermines the very nature of the imprint. This is why, to put it bluntly, individuals experience "the same" events differently.

In its conservative sense, moreover, this resistance both offers the chance for repetition (life) to "take hold," and poses the threat of stasis or death. In the everyday life of the psyche, as Freud explains, outside forces persistently breach its protective shield, upset psychical equilibrium, heighten tension, and threaten its integrity. Under the constant, self-protective, thanatic pressure to contain the threat of traumatic overload, eradicate excess tension, and return the organism to its pretraumatic state, the psyche, as noted, takes both unconscious and conscious measures to master traumatic incursions. It may bind them into the existing web of facilitations (interpretations) or adapt and extend the web by establishing new passages for the expression of excess energy.[56] Further, it conserves new facilitations as expedient, preprepared outlets for future use. Freud describes such conservatism as "a kind of compulsion to repeat which, when a regulation has been laid down once and for all, decides when, where and how a thing shall be done, so that in every similar circumstance one is spared hesitation and indecision."[57] Facilitations, therefore, are new memory traces made in response to the violation of an organism's innate, conservative death drive, or its tendency to resist the new. Thus, ironically, the defensive pressure of the death drive, in spite of its being a fundamental inertial drive to return to an earlier state, promotes the development of the psyche as an archival web of facilitations. It is in this sense that the death drive, associated with repetition in the economic sense of conservation, makes the psyche (or archive) possible.

The defensive conditions that enable psychical development, by conserving (repeating) facilitations, may also impede it, for the death drive promotes what Freud calls "psychical inertia," namely, a strong investment in existing orders, even if they are dysfunctional dis-orders, and the psyche can become a pathological straitjacket. As Freud notes, "the nature and trend of the ideas already united in the ego" determines whether the psyche will recognize and accept a new idea or reject or censor it.[58] In ambivalent cases where the psyche recognizes an idea as intolerable, it defends itself against the idea by forcing it out of consciousness and conscious recall. But, he insists, the psychical trace of it "must be there." Thus, for example, he envisages the archival structure of the neuroses (here hysteria) as a circle segmented (as one would cut a cake) into themes, each of which contains a series of chronologically ordered memories. These are overlaid by a second series of divisions, depicted as concentric circles, representing layers of resistance to conscious recall. The memory traces in each theme, then, are also arranged from the more accessible in the outer layers toward the more deeply concealed. At the core lies the interdicted unconscious wish.[59]

This nucleus, Freud argues, may become pathogenic "precisely as a result of its expulsion and repression." While the ego, having originally forced it "into hiding," persistently opposes its return to memory, the excitation it generates nevertheless requires expression, under the pressure of the death drive. The psyche, therefore, finds disguised ways to express the material contained in this nucleus, by following a twisted and ramified path of associative links through the web of traces that surround it. Accordingly, it undergoes a process of "conversion" whereby the idea becomes ostensibly unimportant, and its associated affect is transferred onto a substitute.[60] Freud cites many cases in which violent but unacceptable desires are dissociated from the ego (disavowed to the point of being forgotten) and strong affective energies are converted into manifest discursive or physical symptoms. Such conversion, for him, never occurs arbitrarily but follows an articulated, if complex, pattern of links that connect seemingly disconnected memories.[61]

In short, one of the effects of the conservative death drive is the guarantee that nothing once traced through the psyche is ever permanently lost.[62] Thus, Freud insists that a "kernel of truth" may be found in any delusion, which directs the fabrication, however bizarre the connections between any number of reinscriptions on its path to discharge. In this case, it would in principle always be possible for an analyst to pick up the thread of these links, returning from node to node toward the center, dissolving resistances encountered along the way, and thus clearing new paths for appropriate discharge once the "kernel of truth" is brought to light.

The Death Drive as Ruin of the Archive

But—and here is the autodeconstructing vacillation that undoes any proper conception of the archive—Freud remains justly ambivalent concerning the status of this "kernel of truth." So far in this discussion there has been little to prevent one from assuming that he thinks of it as the replica in the archive of an original, actual trauma and that facilitations in the first instance reflect actual material forces, experiences, or things "out there" in the external world, although the ego may sometimes disavow these and disguise them after the fact. It would seem, therefore, that the death drive, insofar as it combines the motifs of conservation and return, makes the psyche possible as a proper archive. Here, the psyche becomes the place where impressions take hold and are kept (repeated) and organized as facilitations in a complex network whose ordering is not arbitrary, even if it is sometimes alogical (associative and idiosyncratic) and dependent upon the character—the maturity, experience, flexibility, and scope—of the individual.

In turn, there is little so far to prevent one from dreaming, along with the ego psychologists, of refinding traumas of the past in psychoanalytic hermeneutics. Freud is not entirely immune to this dream of proper remembrance or genuine *Anamnesis* that would return, via the archival records, to the trace that left "the first" impression and can be revivified as a true past present. In this respect, Derrida likens him to the archaeologist Hanold, one of the principal characters in Jensen's novel *Gradiva*, who goes to Pompeii in search of a trace. Hanold dreams, in Derrida's words, "of reliving the singular pressure or impression which Gradiva's step [*pas*], the step itself, the step of Gradiva herself, that very day, at that time, on that date, in what was inimitable about it, must have left in the ashes. He dreams of this irreplaceable place, the very ash, where the singular imprint, like a signature, barely distinguishes itself from the impression."[63] I cannot here unravel the complex ironies attached to this citation; suffice it to note that Gradiva is a fantasy figure in the imagination of a literary character, Hanold, who, in turn, is the product of Jensen's imagination. Moreover, the novelist whom one meets here is himself a product of the archive, that is, of my reading of Derrida's reading of Freud's reading. This performance of an archival *mise en abyme* suggests that fabrication remains inescapable, even for the kind of Freudians who dream of the end of analysis in, as Derrida puts it, a moment of "pure auto-affection," before the distinction between "the active and the passive," the "touching and the touched," "where, suddenly indiscernible from the impression of its imprint, Gradiva's footstep speaks by itself!"[64]

The point of this performance, then, is to show that this would be to seek what Freud has already found to be impossible, namely, the moment of truth as yet uncontaminated by the processes of archivization, for the detour between occasioning force and its archiving recognition is not nothing. As Freud demonstrates as early as his *Project for a Scientific Psychology*, a so-called originary impression is produced in consciousness only after it has already traced its way through psychical facilitations. This quest for the past present therefore goes against the grain of his awareness that the archive is no passive record of a "kernel of truth," preexisting the archive and determinable independently of it, but a process of fabrication that co-constitutes the "first" perceptual experience. In other words, for Freud in his aneconomic moments, the "kernel of truth" is the decisively formative fabrication. As a general "principle," then, the recognized phenomenon never copies the event, which withdraws in this very recognition and therefore potentially retains the power of surprise. Freud shows, in short, that humans live in the milieu of more or less dysfunctional constructions of reality.

This gap between the interpretative prosthesis and the "event" is precisely what gives the death drive its chance in its aneconomic guise of inventive destruction and poses the danger of destructive invention. The aneconomic, anarchiving motif of the death drive is always already implicated in archivization, which automatically entails an aggressive violation of the other (the traumatic, the event, the Real) in the name of appropriating, interpreting, sense. This reductive gesture by which an archive is constituted and preserved means, paradoxically, that a certain "originary forgetting," which may be called the forgetting of trauma (event, Real), is the guardian of memory. Such "originary forgetting" cannot be subsumed under Freud's notions of repression and foreclosure. If the psyche configures experiential reality as a web of habitually employed prosthetic interpretations, what is repressed has already figured as something meaningful within this network, but it has been disavowed by the ego as unbearable, and interdicted. Earlier than this, the psyche may foreclose upon or reject an interpretation found to be impossible to integrate into the fabric of its other interpretations. Here, the interpretation is not archived as a concealed memory trace. Rather, it leaves its mark by affecting the very weave of the web, so preventing in advance similar interpretations from being produced as conscious phenomena. Repression and foreclosure, one could say, become disorders insofar as they represent the idiosyncratic rejection of phenomena that have already been adequately "reality tested" through intersubjective confirmation. However, pressed by the thanatic drive toward reduction and simplification, interpretation, which aims to make of "what happens" a present, archivable phenomenon, hides the complexities of "contamination" (paradoxes, fissures, anomalies, difficulties, and undecidabilities) behind prosthetic substitutes. Intersubjective confirmation and reality testing themselves are therefore homogeneous with the withdrawal of the Real in a necessary "originary forgetting" of contamination.

The psyche, resistant to change, strives to master threatening external forces to suit its own purposes (to return to a lower state of tension), at almost any cost. As Freud puts it: "The psychical apparatus is intolerant of unpleasure; it has to fend it off at all costs, and if the perception of reality entails unpleasure, that perception—that is, the truth—must be sacrificed."[65] Indeed, describing the everyday psychical processes of inventive destruction, Freud insists that "each one of us behaves in some one respect like a paranoic, corrects some aspect of the world which is unbearable to him by the construction of a wish and introduces this delusion into reality."[66] "Every single phantasy is the fulfilment of a wish, a correction of unsatisfying reality."[67]

According to Derrida, if fictionalization (whether conservative and limiting or inventive) is an integral part of the interpretative processes that constitute reality, then it is Freud (among others) who has damaged the "proper" concept of the archive (as a noninventive reserve of recorded memory traces). Freud acknowledges, it would seem, that facilitations/

interpretations are both enabling and dysfunctional (reductive, distorting, fabricated), more or less noticeably in particular contexts. Facilitation, in other words, is less about reflecting some primordially and independently true state of affairs than the pragmatics of functional fabrication. To the extent that one gets by well enough on a delusion, it is not generally taken as an indication of mental illness. For example, Freud thinks of religion as an attempt to "procure a certainty of happiness and a protection against suffering through a delusional remoulding of reality."[68] In his view, "by forcibly fixing them in a state of psychical infantilism and by drawing them into a mass-delusion, religion succeeds in sparing many people an individual neurosis. But hardly anything more."[69] Nevertheless, he does not recommend the mass psychoanalytic treatment of all the world's religious.

Thus, to sum up so far, not even Freud escapes what psychoanalysis teaches: that the archival prosthesis shelters, memorializes, covers over the "event" in order to protect it, save it from oblivion, keep it intact, but in this very sheltering, it simply keeps it secret by putting something else in its place. The archive hides as much as it reveals. It is not only that the thing burns up in the grasping, but, more radically, there will always "be" that for which one does not even know to look. Speaking of Freud's legacy, Derrida notes: "We will always wonder what, in this *mal d'archive*, he may have burned." But more than this:

> We will always wonder, sharing with compassion in this archive fever, what may have burned of his secret passions, of his correspondence, or of his "life." Burned without him, without remains and without knowledge. With no possible response, be it spectral or not, short of or beyond a suppression, on the other edge of repression, originary or secondary, without a name, without the least symptom, and without even an ash.[70]

But before anybody gets ready to abdicate all responsibility for historical "truth" or accuracy, Derrida warns against an entirely aneconomic view of the archive and archivization. These fissions, instead, leave us in a state not of subjective idealism but of archive fever, a double bind or irresolvable *aporia* where strictly speaking a purely economic account of the archive and the process of archivization is impossible, yet we cannot do without it. One cannot abandon the economic thinking of the archive (archivization at bottom records truths) to its aneconomic aspect (all is fabrication), since in this case the archive as such would be equally impossible. Then there would be no history, but a collection of stories no different in value. If one cannot maintain grounds for arguing that certain versions and revisions of events, and not others, constitute an abuse of the archives, then all writings and rewritings of history would be equally (in)valid, and one could say with equal force, for example, that the Holocaust or Rwanda, the Gulf War, or "9/11" did and did not happen, or one could confuse the abusive rewriting of history with a different kind of rewriting that includes what was left out of an archive for political or ideological reasons.

Psychoanalysis and the Death Drive

If the constitution of the psyche remains tied up in aporias, one may wonder how this reflects upon psychoanalytic practice, as deconstitution or analysis of the psyche for therapeutic ends. Derrida finds a double anagogic/philolytic motif inscribed in the word "analysis." In his words:

> There is, *on the one hand*, what could be called the *archeological* or *anagogical* motif, which is marked in the movement of *ana* (recurrent return toward the principal, the most originary, the simplest, the elementary, or the detail that cannot be broken down); and, *on the other hand*, a motif that could be nicknamed *lytic*, *lytological*, or *philolytic*, marked in the *lysis* (breaking down, untying, unknotting, deliverance, solution, dissolution or absolution, and, by the same token, final completion).[71]

Described in terms of this double motif, psychoanalysis, which, as a therapy, aims to equip an analysand to master in retrospect the psychical overload caused by an unassimilated trauma, hopes to return through the detours of dysfunction to its repressed source, untying improper bindings along the way and cutting through resistant symptomatic knots. Having confronted the subject with the "trauma" anew, its further task is to rehabilitate misdirected, entropic, or destructive energies by encouraging the proper binding of excitation, or, that is, obtaining for it the appropriately directed release that would allow the psyche to regain its balance.[72]

Questioning the coherence of these anagogic/philolytic motifs, however, Derrida focuses on the phrase "resistance to analysis." "Resistance" is intrinsic to "analysis" as a notion. It is that point at which analysis stops, either temporarily or permanently, depending on the type of resistance. Freud, Derrida notes, recognizes various types of "resistance to analysis," proceeding from the ego, id, and superego, all of which require different psychotherapeutic strategies.[73] But if these strategies depend on the type of resistance faced, things would get complicated were it to turn out that the various kinds of "resistance" cannot be unified into the regulated polysemy of a concept but remain incompatible moments brought together in a notion, for the unity or "proper" sense (if there is such a thing) of psychoanalysis is intrinsically bound up with how the ultimate resistance that ends an analysis is conceived.

Derrida's investigation into the possibility of psychoanalysis, from the point of view of a conceptual analysis of "analysis" and "resistance," occupies the first part of his essay entitled "Resistances." Unsurprisingly, he argues that resistance indeed defies unification into a concept and instead condenses an entangled meshwork of multiple *and* conflicting threads that can neither be separated out nor harmoniously coordinated. In short, the notion "resistance" functions as a quasi-transcendental condition of analysis. He ties his investigation to a retrospective note of three sentences appended to Freud's analysis of his dream of "Irma's injection." The note consists of a confession and two remarks "whose juxtaposition and heterogeneity would deserve interminable analysis."[74] It reads as follows: "I had a feeling that the interpretation of this part of the dream was not carried far enough to make it possible to follow the whole of its concealed meaning. If I had pursued my comparison between the three women, it would have taken me far afield.—There is at least one spot in every dream at which it is unplumbable—a navel, as it were, that is its point of contact with the unknown."[75] Reading this note as an instance of Freud's own "kettle logic,"[76] Derrida claims that these sentences imply incompatible senses of resistance. This suggests a framework for tracing out three scenes in which the corresponding descriptions of psychotherapy also are found to be incompatible. Scene one: what ends analysis is the original unconscious wish, and, accordingly, the philolytic and anagogic motifs in psychotherapy work together under the auspices of the "principle of reason." Scene two: what ends analysis, rather, is a provisional resistance to analysis, in relation to which psychotherapy becomes a political, polemical, and erotic play of forces, but still governed by the "principle of reason." Scene three: what ends analysis is a knot in the psychic weave that cannot be untied. Here psychotherapy works in the dark, without rule, as therapeutic synthesis.

Thus, depending on how the limit to analysis is understood, there is either an economic account of psychoanalysis "properly speaking" (scenes one and two) or an aneconomic account of psychoanalysis as (paradoxically) synthetic (scene three). But, Derrida asks, and this introduces his deconstructive hypothesis, can one make sense of resistance and psychoanalysis in terms of an either/or choice: as either homogeneous to sense (making psychoanalysis entirely possible) or heterogeneous to sense (making psychoanalysis entirely impossible)? In short, are these two positions related by the logic of contradiction? Clearly not. Rather, as it turns out, resistance is homogeneous with the space of analytic work, and this entangles psychoanalysis in the circular logic of paradox or aporia. What follows is an elaboration of this argument.

Resistance in Analysis/Analysis as Economic

Freud's retrospective confession that the analysis of a certain dream fragment had not gone far enough and his suspicion that a concealed *meaning* exceeded (limited, resisted) the analysis reveals an attitude akin to that described as his dream of presence. Briefly, his self-criticism here displays no doubt that what is concealed at present has a sense. Moreover, it is only contingently concealed: as a provisional excess or hidden meaning, it implies that certain knots impossible to untie during an analysis may be appropriated to sense in retrospect. It is, therefore, in principle possible progressively to uncover the hidden meaning completely, given the analyst's energy, patience, skill, knowledge, and/or motivation to take the analysis as far as it will go.[77]

In this case, then, resistances to analysis are understood as contingent but potentially meaningful obstacles to the progress of an analysis toward the final resistance: the "grain of truth" or unconscious wish that is not amenable to further breaking down. Further, because the resistances to analysis all remain intelligible, and therefore analyzable, up to the final resistance, analysis "properly speaking" works in accordance with the "principle of reason." Analysis in psychotherapy, therefore, would first of all be a hermeneutic unveiling in the most traditional sense.[78] It would involve the philolytic task of untying knots, dividing and separating out tangled threads, systematizing, putting things in their proper place and order, making sense, giving meaning, which, in turn, implies the task of dissolving or overcoming barriers to analysis and therefore incorporates the "anagogic" move to get to the bottom of things or to return to what is most originary.[79] On this account, then, in the recovery of a fully meaningful, original idea or wish that resists further analysis, psychoanalysis has a limit, an end, but for this reason, it has no limitation; in *anamnesis*, it can in principle reach the truth that is its end. In this case, importantly, resistances are not viewed as intrinsic to what is under analysis (a dream, a psyche) but stand as a function and indictment of the analyst's hermeneutic powers.[80]

Psychotherapy took shape initially, Derrida notes, when Freud tacitly acknowledged that his patients had some justification for resenting his technique of "surgically" eradicating painful reminiscences by interdicting them through hypnotic suggestion. His felt obligation to pursue the therapeutic goal without resorting to hypnosis coincided with the basic theoretical shift from out of which psychotherapy took shape.[81] Here, instead of hoping to eradicate symptoms by supporting the processes of repression and, in effect, adding strength to the ego's defenses against painful memories, Freud found that, to the contrary, a more durable relief from symptoms was achieved by breaking down the resistances that prevented an analysand from consciously acknowledging painful memories and working through their implications. The analysand's reluctance to air these recollections, and the effort required to uncover them, suggested to him that the ego, the force that had first interdicted them, remained invested in defending itself from them. Nevertheless, he found that he could often overcome the analysand's reluctance to face certain recollections with the help of a simple technique: a hand on the forehead combined with the injunction to speak.[82] The psychoanalytic task for Freud became a matter of, as Derrida puts it, "transforming the patient, the resister, into a 'collaborator' (that is Freud's word) to whom one supplies explanations and in whom one arouses an investigator's objective interest in himself."[83]

For Freud, the persistence of defenses, whose aim was to prevent the conscious recall of distressing ideas, suggests that such ideas, while apparently forgotten, remain inscribed in the psyche. Further, he insists that it will always be possible in principle to pick up the logical thread of linked archival traces engendered by the "original" idea, dissolve the knots of resistance, and return to the core, at which point the original impression speaks by itself—purified of the archive. A complete analysis, here, confronts the analysand finally with the original pathogenic idea and a map of the resistances employed to avoid its exposure.[84]

However, as Freud puts it, "it was my view at that time (though I have since recognized it as a wrong one) that my task was fulfilled when I had informed a patient of the hidden meaning of his symptoms."[85] This admission, Derrida notes, brings into view, "the question of whether psychoanalysis—whether the idea of analysis which gives it its name—finds suitable lodging in the history of reason."[86] For the faith in reason, he continues, which allows one to envisage resistances as protecting hidden *meanings*, seems remarkable since Freud is about to take a step that "will be in truth a leap." Derrida here refers to what is implied in the two remarks of Freud's note, both of which unsettle the above conception of the psychoanalytic task as purely analytical. Moreover, as Derrida shows,

Freud produces a rupture between these remarks, making the second more radically unsettling than the first.

Resistance to Analysis/Analysis as Polemic and Erotic

There is a curious discrepancy between the progressive register of Freud's confession and his first remark, in which he insists that pursuing a comparison between certain women in his dream analysis would lead him not down to a kernel of truth but "far afield." Why? Derrida asks: "How can he know that he would go astray where he confesses or claims to confess that he didn't go see, not far enough?"[87] Finding no good reason ("He does not say, not really"), Derrida adds: "Right here, at this point, it would not be impossible to speak of resistance to analysis."

Having laid out a map of an analysand's pathology, Freud discovered soon enough in his practice that the analysand may refuse to acknowledge the interpretation, without rendering good reasons. (Notably, in the above example, Freud, in the position of analysand, resists his own analysis, for he refuses to pursue a particular line of thought, without rendering sufficient reason.) Here, however, resistance is no longer viewed as an obstacle to the progress of hermeneutic reason, experienced only from the position of the analyst. Rather, in this case, the analyst has reached a solution, *the* solution supposedly, but the analysand refuses to accept it.[88] For Freud, as mentioned above, the sources of such resistances are various, the deepest and most intractable of which is the repetition compulsion.[89]

Accordingly, beyond the domain of pure hermeneutics, where it was merely a matter of informing analysands of the hidden meaning of their symptoms, acknowledging the force of this new kind of resistance meant that Freud's conception of psychoanalytic strategy had to extend to the "not nonviolent" task of actively engendering an affective transformation in the analysand. Here, analysts are obliged not only to uncover and present solutions but also to assume responsibility for whether analysands accept them.[90] Thus, it becomes equally necessary to overcome the variously layered resistances to these solutions by uncovering or identifying their underlying sources and overcoming the affective barriers these represent.

Freud, however, acknowledges that resistances can be nonrational, which means that the struggle against them has to mobilize forces other than those of rational enlightenment. It is never for Freud merely a matter of offering, as Derrida puts it, "a theoretical explanation of the origin and the elements of a defense system." Rather, resistance must not only be "comprehended and communicated in its *intelligibility*, but transformed, transposed, transfigured."[91] In other words, to persuade analysands to accept interpretations, analysts are required to capitalize on the emotional dynamics of a "*poleros*," that is, the polemics and erotics of resistance, power, and authority (for example in the sphere of the transference). As Derrida puts it: "It is thus not a matter of simply and in total neutrality substituting an unveiled truth for what resists it, but rather of leading the patient to awareness . . . by actively and energetically using counter-resistances, other antagonistic forces, through an effective intervention in a field of forces."[92]

Thus, as he notes, if Freud initially insisted that the analyst was responsible for the analytic solution but not the analysand's resistances,[93] he here changes his mind about the task of analysis. In the context of his frustration with Irma for her resistance to treatment, Freud dreams of her, but substitutes her for a friend. Musing over this swap, he suggests:

> Perhaps I should have *liked* to exchange her: either I felt more sympathetic towards her friend or had a higher opinion of her intelligence. For Irma seemed to me foolish because she had not accepted my solution. . . . Her friend would have been wiser, that is to say she would have yielded sooner [by implication to my advice, to my demand—or to my advances]. She would then have *opened her mouth properly*, and have told me . . . more than Irma.[94]

This, according to Derrida, exemplifies a law: "The one that in general commands one to interpret as resistance to analysis, to the solution, to the resolution . . . the reservation of anyone who does not accept *your* solution."[95] Freud, he adds, says as much himself: "*I reproached Irma for not having accepted my solution; I said: 'If you still get pains, it's your own fault.'*"[96]

To the objection that "the objective truth . . . or analytic neutrality, removes the passions of resistance . . . from this *poleros*,"[97] Derrida counters that Freud himself has already undermined any possibility of "objective truth" and "analytic neutrality." Nevertheless, he notes, if the work of analysis is a struggle between intellectual forces and emotive forces of resistance, such a battle between psychical powers is still here understood as having meaning: "Resistance must be interpreted; it has just as much meaning as what it opposes."[98] This strategic capitalization on the dynamics of the *poleros* still allows that resistances, albeit not always rational, make sense and can be analyzed. Analysis, then, is still possible as the uncovering of meaning, including the meaning of the nonrational resistances. Once analysts understand the meaning of these, they may gain in polemical or persuasive power, for now such resistances can be dealt with (e.g., shown up for their irrationality) within the framework of the supposedly more true, rational, everyday reality represented by the analyst. Here, the anagogic/philolytic task of analysis remains in the order of meaning. The primary step of analysis remains a hermeneutic return to the origin by analysts who apparently know analysands better than they know themselves. But it now includes the progressive analysis (uncovering and dissolution) of resistances as analysts attempt to draw analysands along an *anamnesic* path, through their resistances, to the truth of the matter and the "proper" solution to their problems. Freud does not here grant, Derrida concludes, that

> a resistance might be, in this context, something other than a resistance to his solution, to his analysis, or, beyond this context and in general, that a resistance might be something other than a resistance full of meaning. Even if it is definitive, resistance belongs, along with what it resists, to the order of sense, of a sense whose secret is only the hidden secret, the dissimulated meaning, the veiled truth: to be interpreted, analyzed, made explicit, explained.[99]

Resistance as Absolute/Analysis as Synthesis

Freud's second remark adumbrates his famous proposition later in the text concerning the navel of the dream.[100] Having suggested that the meaning of a dream, only provisionally held at bay by resistances, continues to promise itself to progressive approximation, he then paradoxically names the navel of the dream as an absolute limit to this progress:

> There is often a passage . . . in even the most thoroughly interpreted dream which has to be . . . left obscure; this is because we become aware during the work of interpretation that at that point there is a tangle . . . of dream-thoughts which cannot be unraveled . . . and which moreover adds nothing to our knowledge of the content of the dream. This is the dream's navel. . . . It is at some point where this meshwork . . . is particularly close that the dream-wish grows up, like a mushroom out of its mycelium.[101]

Here as Derrida notes, we are no longer treading the ground of provisional limits to analysis. This proposition, in his words,

> concerns rather a night, an absolute unknown that is originarily, congenitally bound or tied (but also in itself unbound because absolute) to the essence and to the birth of the dream, attached to the place from which it departs and of which it keeps the birthmark: the

umbilicus, the omphalic place is the place of a *tie*, a knot-scar that keeps the memory of a cut and even of a severed thread at birth.[102]

Inscribed in this, according to Derrida, is another "unconditionally posed law": "*every* dream, *always*, carries within it at least one place . . . that situates it as . . . impenetrable, unfathomable, unanalyzable, like a navel. . . . And Freud adds . . . that through this place it is knotted, attached, connected, or suspended . . . with the unknown."[103]

Here, as Derrida notes, this birthplace of the dream-wish, the very origin which terminates the process of "unbinding" knots and overcoming resistances, remains an obscure knot absolutely tied up, "in short an unanalyzable synthesis"[104] of threads. But this means that what finally resists analysis is not the dream wish in the form of an intelligible phenomenon or "transcendental signified" at the bottom of it all. Rather, the ultimate resistance to analysis, it would seem, takes the form of an irreducibly nonsimple knot of multiple entanglements that still appeals to analysis even as it challenges it.[105] In other words, Freud's remark here implies another, an entirely other, conception of resistance to analysis.

The thought that in every dream there is no ultimate, intelligible, presentable point of resistance that stops its analysis must in turn trouble any conception of dream analysis "properly speaking." This trouble, however, is not limited to the analysis of dreams. One should bear in mind Freud's insistence that the analysis of dreams is the "royal road" to the workings of unconscious processes in the psyche, and that the dream wish is intimately tied to the pathogenic idea targeted by psychotherapy. Because of this linkage, one may legitimately argue that Freud's remark also tacitly troubles the notion of analysis in psychotherapy, which has been described so far in terms of the anagogic/philolytic process of hermeneutic uncovering and polemical overcoming.

Up to this point, under the assumption that a pathogenic idea is present but provisionally kept out of consciousness by resistances, Freud insisted that, having uncovered what is really at stake in the analysand's situation, and having overcome all resistances to this solution, moving from the weaker to the most resistant, namely the repetition compulsion, the pathogenic idea will be exposed in its naked truth and acknowledged for what it really is. Having granted it credence, the analysand would now be free to address the problem of reintegrating it properly into the rationally organized framework of everyday experience. The governing assumption so far has been that the forces of resistance, down to the last, can be understood as standing decisively in opposition to those forces (like the psychoanalytic) that seek expression for the original pathogenic idea.

But Freud's insistence that at the navel, the birthplace, the very origin, of every dream (and by implication every unconscious process) lies an impenetrable tangle gives pause for thought, for it hints at as yet unacknowledged complexities or difficulties in the notion of resistance, which is, in turn, supposed to determine the concept "analysis" upon which, again, psychotherapeutic strategy rests. What is at stake in the definition of analysis if the ultimate resistance to analysis turns out not to be what analysis has always sought as its end, namely, the fully present analytic element that cannot be broken down any further, but an impenetrable tangle? On a certain account of resistance, one could say analysis is unlimited (or absolutely possible, in the sense that it can in principle reach its telos) because it has a limit. But on a different account of resistance, one would have to grant that analysis is limited; an absolute, or complete, analysis becomes impossible precisely because it has no limitation. The end of an analysis, in this sense, must remain arbitrary, for more analysis is in principle always possible.

All of this suggests that one should look more carefully at what Freud's insistence upon this navel might imply concerning the place of resistance in psychotherapy. How sound is the assumption that resistance, as a defense that covers the very nucleus that psychotherapy aims to uncover and express, is simply a force that opposes the direction and telos of psychoanalysis? Freud names five kinds of resistance. But, Derrida notes, "the multiplicity of resistances does not necessarily threaten the concept of resistance."[106] It would be easy enough to think of the concept of resistance as a genus with several species, and understand it according to a regulated polysemy. "Its unity of meaning and place, as well as its validity would even be confirmed by this diffraction: it itself, the same, is what one would find again throughout."[107] But, he asks, how does one determine this "it itself, the same?" In determining the nature of resistance, it makes sense to take as a paradigm the most resistant resistance: namely, the repetition compulsion.[108]

One may describe the repetition compulsion as an extreme (and therefore pathological) version of the everyday psychical processes of "inventive destruction." In everyday cases, facing a traumatic event, the psyche undergoes a process of learning, in which it redesigns the fabric of its psychic life in an effort to cope. In the event of a traumatic shock of such novelty or magnitude that it remains impossible to assimilate through habitual psychical economies, a kind of "system overload" occurs whereby excitation remains to some degree unbound. Here, the death drive compels the psyche to master the overload by reinstating its pretraumatic equilibrium. But, equipped with ingrained patterns of appropriation that are entirely unequal to a monstrous event, it lacks the power necessary to grant it a place in reality, which is the first step toward the adaptation required in order to cope with it. Instead, in a pathological response, the psyche attempts to regain equilibrium by avoiding the issue altogether and repressing the unacceptable situation.

Repression works in various ways. A victim of abusive incest, for example, may repress the intolerable monstrosity of an "evil" parent by constructing a "reality" in which this kind of violation can be conceived of as a gain, by inventing a masochistic, guilty self who requires punishment. But she thereby dooms herself to laborious efforts to combat the many unsettling symptoms of something amiss in her constructed world, for she now requires constant confirmation of the construction that keeps her reality intact. Such a victim, then, tends obsessively to seek out situations in which the abuse is repeated.[109] Further repressed material improperly bound in this way continues to produce tension that presses for discharge at all costs. Under the pressure of the death drive, it must resurface. But, since it remains subject to the ego's refusal under the pressure of the pleasure principle, the psyche settles for an economic compromise in which, as mentioned earlier, this material resurfaces via the detour of disguises. In other words, as a consequence of this unsatisfactory compromise, repressed material persistently and compulsively reappears in obsessions, dreams, parapraxes, neuroses, projections, paranoias, and other symptoms. This tends to exact a price, for the death drive, prior to any intelligible pleasure calculus, serves constancy blindly, instinctively, without reason, and potentially at the cost of all—family, friendship, health, pleasure, philosophy, and so on, and, importantly, therefore, of emotional, social, professional, and intellectual development. Thus, driven either to assimilate or reject change but lacking the necessary competence to do either, the psyche remains in suspension. Unable to return properly to a previous state or decisively move on to something new, it becomes fixated on, or seemingly doomed to repeat, its ultimately unsatisfactory efforts to master the traumatic breach.

Psychotherapy works on the assumption, however, that dysfunctional constructions, once invented, can in principle be reinvented. Even so, the repetition compulsion, as resistance to change (any change, even change for "the good") represents the most intractable resistance to psychoanalytic reinvention, for the earlier constructions become obstacles that stand in the way of revision. The psyche clings to them, due to their dubious success in keeping the psychic world intact, where it seems to the one who suffers that the only alternative is to fall apart or break down.

This, however, is where the trouble starts and notions become entangled, for Derrida finds that the repetition compulsion both opposes and mirrors the direction and telos of psychotherapy. In other words, the repetition compulsion is quasi-transcendental: as "the most resistant resistance," it both gives and unsettles the meaning of resistance, and this, he claims, "disorganizes the very principle, the constitutive idea of psychoanalysis as analysis of resistances."[110] In his words: "The paradox that interests me here is that this repetition compulsion, as hyperbolic paradigm of the series, as absolute resistance, risks destroying the meaning of the series to which it is supposed to assure meaning (this is an effect of formal logic . . .), but still more ironically, it defines no doubt a resistance that *has no meaning*—and that, moreover, is not a resistance."[111]

First, the repetition compulsion, he argues, has no meaning in the sense that it is not, like the others, a resistance that makes economic sense. Instead of being a cover that disguises an already constituted nucleus, the repetition compulsion is implicated in the very constitution of the nucleus. Further, the repetition compulsion as the consequence of an impossible situation, an aporia, represents the site of a compromise (a navel) that gives birth to a highly idiosyncratic fabrication that does not make sense. When psychoanalysis, therefore, returns to the so-called origin, the last line of defense, the most resistant resistance, it finds "at bottom" not a kernel of truth but a synthesis of strands, a tangle or navel, in which the repetition compulsion is always already implicated. From the start the most resistant resistance and the pathogenic idea are already bound up with one another in a knot that is impossible to untangle.

Further, the repetition compulsion, as Derrida puts it, "resists analysis in the form of nonresistance, for the primary reason that it is *itself of an analytic structure or vocation*."[112] In "Beyond the Pleasure Principle," Freud argues that repressed material in the unconscious should not resist psychoanalytic treatment, for both have an aim in common (namely its expression). Resistance, rather, arises from the ego. The repetition compulsion, then, is the attempt to master psychical overload by finding substitute expression for material that is repressed under the pressure of constraints imposed by the ego. The repetition compulsion is, therefore, not a resistance, strictly speaking. Yet it nevertheless poses the most recalcitrant barrier (resistance) to psychotherapy, precisely because it serves a similar aim, namely, to regain psychical equilibrium, and to some extent it achieves this restitution via substitutes that, although inadequate, it is unwilling to give up. This ultimate resistance that is supposed to put a stop to analysis as philolytic/anagogic mirrors the structure of analysis. Analysis, therefore, finds its end and its limit not in the originary "grain of truth" that cannot be analyzed further, but in more analysis. It is, paradoxically, infinite analyzability that resists and limits analysis. As Derrida notes: "This compulsion combines the two essential motifs of all *analysis*, the regressive or archeotropic movement and the movement of dissolution that urges towards destruction, that loves to destroy by dissociating—which is why a moment ago I called it *philolytic*."[113]

Not only does the repetition compulsion "destroy" the original trauma by dissociating it from what is finally expressed in consciousness, but the fabricated reality becomes increasingly entangled if the ego, over time, is obliged to elaborate the defense to explain away incongruities. Thus, as already noted, Freud saw that what links the trauma to its expression in a symptom is a chain of idiosyncratic interpretations and associations (transcriptions that are not translations). This is the sense in which, as Derrida puts it, "the link can be interruption itself" rather than a smooth logical chain. To compound the entanglement, facing the repetition compulsion, psychotherapy begins to defy its analytic (intellectual, hermeneutic, economic) character. Facing the singularity of this knot, having turned the analysand into an analytical collaborator, having pushed back all other resistances to analysis, psychoanalytic strategy itself becomes singular, reliant on an affective factor, namely, the personal influence of the analyst. In Freud's words:

> We must endeavour, after we have discovered the motives for its defence, to deprive them of their value *or even to replace them by more powerful ones*. This no doubt is where it ceases to be possible to state psychotherapeutic activity in formulas. One works to the best of one's power, as an elucidator (where ignorance has given rise to fear), as a teacher, as the representative of a freer or superior view of the world, as a father confessor who gives absolution, as it were, by a continuance of his sympathy and respect after the confession has been made.[114]

Here, aligning psychoanalysis with teaching and religion, the psychoanalytic task is redefined. The analyst intervenes in the activity of the repetition compulsion, *no longer* to dissolve it by theoretical explanation, nor even to overcome it through active counterresistance techniques, but to reconfigure its shape, by "re-binding" or reconfiguring the threads of its invention of value. But what psychoanalysis has enabled one to see is not only that fabrications legitimate themselves on pragmatic grounds ("it works for me") but also that it is only on those pragmatic grounds, rather than the grounds of an alternative true reality, that psychotherapy can offer a challenge to the analysand. One respects the "reality" of the analysand and assesses its merits not in terms of some ideal of true reality in the everyday but in terms of its internal costs and benefits.

Paradoxically, then, facing what at bottom has no rational meaning, the task of analysis is reformulated in a way that repeats precisely the reconstructive character of its most difficult adversary. It becomes nonanalytic, synthetic: taken up, that is, in the fabrication of adaptive facilitations, in the construction of new narratives or new disguises for the unanalyzable event—the event that cannot be dissolved, the scar that cannot fade. In short, psychotherapy as analysis, a process or practice that directs itself toward an end, mirrors, speculates on, that which most strongly resists this process, namely, the repetition compulsion as a synthetic construction and revision that cannot be concluded. In Derrida's words: "Some would be tempted to infer from this that psychoanalysis is homogeneous to it and that psychoanalytic theory, treatment, and institution represent the death drive or the repetition compulsion *at work*."[115]

One faces in the end the *mise en abyme* of a double mirroring, for "psychoanalysis" and "resistance" become inextricably entangled with one another, since they prove to be isomorphic. On the one hand, the quintessential resistance to analysis, which should give sense to all the others, namely the repetition compulsion, turns out to repeat the very structure of analysis. Instead of putting a stop to analysis, then, the repetition compulsion is itself analytical in structure, making for an abyssal aneconomy of infinite analyzability. On the other hand, psychoanalysis, as synthetic, turns out to repeat the repetition compulsion. This puts psychoanalysis in a spin: if psychotherapy mirrors the aim and the activity of the repetition compulsion, since the repetition compulsion resists psychoanalysis, this entangles us in the impossible (aporetic) thought that psychoanalysis itself, *as the death drive*, poses the greatest resistance to analysis.

This, of course, Derrida notes, would not necessarily be cause for complaint. What is successful in psychotherapy depends on the insistence that, in principle, one must always be able to revise fabrications through careful intervention. It therefore demonstrates, on the one hand, the irreducibility not of the repetition compulsion but of repetition as iterability, as repeating-differently. On the other hand, one is obliged to ask for whom, or according to what definition of "mental illness," the analysand's interpretations are called fabrications, and, moreover, who decides, and in the name of what, which are the better constructions? In other words, psychoanalytic intervention, insofar as the analyst assumes the place of authority, teacher, or father-confessor, is equally in danger of being taken in by its own repetition compulsion, namely that commanded by a certain disciplinary or institutional status-quo. There is, then, no simple answer to the question of whether psychotherapy overcomes the repetition compulsion or is overcome by it.

Concluding Remarks

To sum up, then, Derrida sees psychoanalytic strategy shift, according to the kind of resistance it faces, from the hermeneutic task of "comprehension and communication," through the effective *polemic* and *erotic* task of active engagement, and finally, "beyond all these discursive and intellectual situations" to the affective factor of personal influence, in a reconstructive synthesis where there are no more general rules to follow.[116] But in this case, he argues, psychoanalysis exceeds the concept of analysis that traditionally dominates philosophy, logic, and science, which, he claims, "could not intervene, at least as such, in an effective and affective fashion, in a *decisive* fashion to remove resistance of any sort." These effective, affective, personal, and synthetic factors in psychoanalysis tempt one to think that it simply inaugurates another concept of analysis, which would, in turn, dismiss the possibility of there being a single scientific tradition.

However, Derrida remarks, "things are surely not so simple."[117] First, Freud did not invent a new concept, but without choice, if he wished to be understood, had to submit to the inherited legacy of the two motifs that constitute every notion of analysis. Second, in his attempt to inaugurate a science, "he had to justify his discourse and his institution before the tribunal of traditional analysis, before its norms and its law." These remarks suggest, on the one hand, that "analysis" in psychoanalysis overlaps with the traditional concept of analysis, in the sense that it must submit to its tradition.

Yet, on the other hand, Derrida insists, this imbrication of psychoanalysis and the tradition of analysis equally places this tradition into question, particularly since psychoanalysis, "in the form of its philosophical or scientific knowledge," has developed "as a practical analysis of the cultural, political, and social resistances represented by hegemonic discourses."[118] Here, he argues, if psychoanalysis belongs (with philosophy, logic, and science) to a single tradition of analysis, it would have been defined as a unified concept. But the unity of psychoanalysis in turn depends on a similarly unified concept of resistance. Yet, in his view, "this was never the case." Thus: "If it is true that the concept of *resistance to analysis* cannot unify itself, for nonaccidental or noncontingent reasons, then the concept of analysis and of psychoanalytic analysis, the very concept of *psychoanalysis* will have known the same fate." Instead, psychoanalysis is divided between two motifs. As Derrida puts it: "on the one side, an Enlightenment progressivism, which hopes for an analysis that will continue to gain ground on initial obscurity to the degree that it removes resistances and liberates, unbinds, emancipates, as does every analysis, and, on the other side, a sort of fatalism or pessimism of desire that reckons with a portion of darkness and situates the unanalyzable as its very resource."[119] Accordingly, if psychoanalysis and the tradition of analysis overlap, then it brings out into the open what has always been repressed in order for there to be a tradition: namely, that analysis as a concept is incoherent and that, therefore, a single tradition of analysis is constituted only on the basis of repression, as is any hegemonic discourse.

Psychoanalysis can neither reject nor embrace either economic analysis, which values objectivity, neutrality, and truth, or aneconomic synthesis, which embraces a Nietzschean motif of self-invention. How, then, are these extremes to be related? It would be an error, of course, to assume that the economic and the aneconomic in psychoanalysis form proper opposites between which one can make an either/or choice.[120] For Derrida, instead, these sides are caught up in an aporetic vacillation, which, unable to come to rest, reflects the incoherence of the notion "psychoanalysis." This is not, one must add immediately, intended as criticism. As he insists: "The inability to gather oneself, to identify with oneself, to unify oneself, all of this is perhaps tragedy itself, but it is also (the) chance." Again: "To say that psychoanalysis does not have *the* concept of what it itself is in its auto-identification, because it cannot give itself a concept of resistance, is certainly not to describe a paralysis of psychoanalysis, at least not a banal and negative paralysis. . . . It gives movement, it gives one to think and to move."[121]

6

Institutional Psychoanalysis and the Paradoxes of Archivization

> We know that in the mass of mankind there is a powerful need for an authority who can be admired, before whom one bows down, by whom one is ruled and perhaps even ill-treated. We have learnt from the psychology of individual men what the origin is of this need of the masses. It is a longing for the father felt by everyone from his childhood onwards. . . . The decisiveness of thought, the strength of will, the energy of action are part of the picture of a father—but above all the autonomy and independence of the great man, his divine unconcern which may grow into ruthlessness. One must admire him, one may trust him, but one cannot avoid being afraid of him too.[1]

Introductory Remarks: Derrida's Third Thesis in Outline

With unsurpassable subtlety, Freud "analyzed, that is also to say, deconstructed," what Derrida calls "the archontic principle of the archive," which, he notes, concerns the "nomological *arkhē* of the law, of institution, of domiciliation, of filiation."[2] This principle describes the movement by which the authority that presided over the archive is repeated across generations. As (arguably) the paternal and patriarchic principle, it presupposes that the authority vested in the father is directed toward its repetition in the sons. Freud uncovers the paradox whereby not even the strongest rebellion (parricide) circumvents the circular return of this same authority. At best, the archontic principle of the archive dictates that parricide will merely amount to the pseudodemocratic "takeover of the archive by the brothers." This archontic circle, then, names the principle of the movement that traps "father" and "son" in a stifling circle of neurotic repetition.

However, as a self-inventive theoretical pioneer, Freud himself subverts this archontic principle. He did not merely draw out the unknown in the existing archive—what was, until then, secret in it—but insisted upon something radically heterogeneous to it, so highlighting the character of the archive as itself an invention.[3] One could, therefore, legitimately expect from him not only some indication of a way out of the archontic circle of patriarchy in the recognition of an excess that threatens every archive but also extreme sensitivity to the dangers of getting caught in its trap himself, through his institutionalization of psychoanalysis.

Yet, in practice, Derrida argues, Freud remained patriarchal: "He declared, notably in *The Rat Man*, that the patriarchal right (*Vaterrecht*) marked the civilizing progress of reason." Moreover, he was overly concerned with constituting psychoanalysis as a discipline, with assuring his legacy by remaining the archon, the patriarch, who had always already configured what could be said by his children in his name. In Derrida's words, "in life as in his works, in his theoretical theses as in the compulsion of his institutionalizing strategy, Freud repeated the patriarchal logic." He remained under the spell of the archontic principle, "to the point" Derrida notes, "that certain people can wonder if, decades after his death, his sons, so many brothers, can yet speak in their own name. Or if his daughter ever came to life."

To adumbrate the theme of part 3, Derrida's remark here tacitly raises the related questions of Lacan's "return to Freud" and of women. Does Lacan's "return" automatically trap him in the archontic circle to the point that he cannot speak in his own name? Or, if he claims to speak in his own name, is he still practicing psychoanalysis? In more general terms, can there be a reinvention of Freudian psychoanalysis that is still psychoanalysis? Derrida's arguments in various contexts unequivocally affirm that there can, indeed must, be inventive appropriation of any institution. Moreover, as addressed at length in the previous chapters, it is precisely Freud, in his aneconomic moments, who gives him the means to make this argument. Derrida, then, in demonstrating that psychoanalysis always already inscribes its own aneconomic subversion beyond its more traditionally accepted economic description, offers just such an inventive appropriation of it. Curiously, however, he does not grant Lacan the equivalent reinventive power, presumably because he does not see in Lacan's arguments the "plural logic of the aporia." Here I have to disagree with him. Instead, it is more likely that Lacan similarly reinvents psychoanalysis, drawing Freud's thinking past its residual metaphysical and patriarchal commitments into the domain of the aporia. Simultaneously,

Lacan's reinvention of psychoanalysis is a matter of bringing the feminine to life: sadly, not Freud's daughter, however, who, in Lacan's view, remains a faithful servant of the conservative in Freud.

Freud's Insight into the Structure of the Archontic Circle

Freud's Myth of Parricide in Totem and Taboo

Since Derrida's thesis explicitly refers to Freud's articulation of the archontic circle in *Totem and Taboo,* it will be necessary to open this and a companion work, *Moses and Monotheism.* But here one encounters a richly spun web of highly contentious speculations concerning an original parricide, stretching across diverse fields of enquiry, the proper critique of which would require expertise beyond the scope and focus of this chapter. However, even if Freud's historical/anthropological speculations are all questionable as hypotheses concerning actual events in prehistory, they nevertheless reveal a good deal about the circular structure of archontic authority. On the whole, then, it seems justifiable to sidestep the myriad difficulties concerning Freud's historical and sociopsychological speculations by leaving aside the issue of "material truth" and by treating his speculative hypothesis of an original parricide as a mythical construction that offers a certain "psychical truth" concerning the structure of the specific kind of authority relation inscribed in the "archontic circle."

Based on Darwin's proposal, Freud speculates that the earliest humans must have lived together in hordes, that is, small groups of women and small children presided over by "a violent and jealous father who keeps all the females for himself and drives away his sons as they grow up."[4] Presumably, those who survived this cruel eviction would eventually snatch a female or two from some other horde and begin their own. However, Freud notes, this original state has never been observed, and the most archaic social form observable today replaces the dominant patriarch with bands of males who enjoy equal rights subject to the dictates of a totemic system within which the fundamental taboos are prohibitions against injuring the totem and incest.[5]

Freud insists that the more democratic form of organization that characterizes the totem clan must have developed from out of the primal horde. His question is: "along what lines?"[6] An account of such a transition, he argues, would have to explain why the new "social contract" went hand in hand with the intense emotional ambivalence and irrational excesses of totemism, which he sees as the precursor to current forms of religious practice. It would also have to explain the mystery of the incest taboo. The necessity of a prohibition implies that there are no reliable natural barriers against the temptation to practice incest. In fact, our first choice of a love object is often incestuous. Moreover, such a taboo could not have been supported at its origin, as it might be today, by modern genetics or by experience of the detrimental effects of inbreeding (such "decadence," were it clearly established, would in any case have taken generations to manifest). Also, mythology teaches that incest is allowed to the gods, and ancient history teaches that incestuous sister-marriage was required of certain rulers. Thus Freud concludes incest "was a privilege forbidden to the common herd" and its taboo was a matter of power rather than science.[7]

Psychoanalytical experience, Freud argues, particularly concerning the Oedipus complex and obsessional neurosis, enables one to bring together under a single explanatory construction the otherwise mystifying ideas and practices at the origin of civilization, including the social contract, the fundamental taboos that prohibit injury to the totem and incest (thereby promoting exogamy), and the paradoxical "totem-feast," vestiges of which remain in certain contemporary religions.[8] The young males in the horde, he speculates, must have experienced the contradictory feelings at work in "the ambivalent father-complexes" of contemporary children and neurotics. Although no doubt they loved their formidable father as an admired model, they must also have hated him for the harsh embargo he placed on their aspirations toward power and sex and sorely envied his privileged access to the women. If their hatred becomes overpowering, the love and awe are repressed and they find themselves denying that the father has any good qualities. Conceivably, then, the ousted brothers finally banded together and, so united, gained the courage and strength to do what each individual youth desired but could not have done alone, namely kill and devour their father, so identifying themselves with him and gaining for each a portion of his power.[9]

But how could such a murder be the inaugurating moment of civilization? Having disposed of the father, Freud notes, one would expect the brothers to turn upon one another in a bitter struggle for succession. No doubt this did occur, but it could not have been the predominant or final outcome of the parricide, for in this case, one tyrant would simply have replaced another without generating any impetus toward what Freud sees as "the next social stage, at which numbers of males live together in a peaceable community."[10] To account for the prevalence of democracy among men in human societies, Freud offers the following psychological explanation: "After they got rid of him, had satisfied their hatred and had put into effect their wish to identify themselves with him, the affection which had all this time been pushed under was bound to make itself felt." Moreover, he notes, more cynically: "This fresh emotional attitude must also have been assisted by the fact that the deed cannot have given complete satisfaction to those who did it. From one point of view it had been done in vain. Not one of the sons had in fact been able to put his original wish—of taking his father's place—into effect."[11]

As an expression of remorse, then, the brothers hoped to bring about a symbolic reconciliation with the murdered tyrant by replacing him with a substitute or "totem," which epitomized the good father. A totem is defined as a sacred thing, endowed with awe-inspiring powers, and treated with the greatest veneration and self-sacrifice. According to Freud, appropriate animals were the natural first candidates to represent the lost father, but over time totems became more various, successively taking on part-animal/part-human forms, all-human forms, the spiritual forms of gods and demons, and abstract forms such as names.[12] Totemism, he continues, is a covenant between the brothers and their father-substitute, "in which he promised them everything that a childish imagination may expect from a father—protection, care and indulgence—while on their side, they undertook to respect his life, that is to say, not to repeat the deed which had brought destruction on their real father."[13]

The brothers thus amplify the goodness and the power of the totem, which will protect them as long as they obediently measure up to its demands. Thus, totemism contains an element of self-justification: "If our father had treated us in the way the totem does, we should never have felt tempted to kill him."[14] Having become totem worshippers, the brothers impose on themselves myriad taboos that prevent any hint of injury to the totem and confirm their obedience.[15] Taboos, however, are not ordinary prohibitions with a clear, pragmatic basis (such as a prohibition against swimming in waters where there are known dangers). Instead, they are excessive prohibitions, often taking the form of arbitrary, seemingly irrational, unusually severe restrictions on physical mobility and pleasure. They appear to be loaded with the demand for expiation or atonement and inflict physical suffering or punishment seemingly in advance of any actual transgression or offense against the totem. In other words, these taboos reflect a self-punishing renunciation of the fruits of their crime in an effort to allay the guilt associated with the original murder. Herein lies the emotional motive for instituting the incest taboo, by which the brothers renounce the very women they desired and for access to whom they had murdered the father. This sense that the women truly belong to the powerful, or, anticipating the Oedipus complex, that the mother truly belongs to the father, explains psychologically why the incest taboo is a matter of power rather than science.

This renunciation might have been supported by pragmatic concerns. Sexual desire, as Freud explains, is divisive; it turns all men into rivals. Although the brothers needed one another to overpower their father, each would have harbored a wish to take his father's place as sole despot concerning women. Struggles of all against all probably took place, to the detriment of the group. To preserve the unified brotherhood that was their strength and power, therefore, Freud concluded that "the brothers had no alternative" except "to institute the law against incest."[16]

So far, Freud has gathered together in a single explanatory framework the "indispensable constituents" of totemism, which are, in his words: "the worship of the totem, which includes a prohibition against injuring or killing it, exogamy—that is, renunciation of the passionately desired mothers and sisters in the horde—the granting of equal rights to all the members of the fraternal alliance—that is, restricting the inclination to violent rivalry among them."[17] Notably, however, the fundamental taboos of totemism reflect precisely the will of the murdered father. In Freud's words, "what had up to then been prevented by his actual existence was thenceforward prohibited by the sons themselves."[18] Ironically, then, in this "deferred obedience" of totemism, the specter of the dead father returns as powerful as ever. Moreover, the actual tyrant is merely replaced by another master, a sacred object whose seemingly absolute and self-evident authority engenders the very emotional ambivalence that led to the original murder. As Freud notes, the very word "sacred" has attached to it the ambivalence of "consecrated" and "detestable."[19] Thus, he notes, "we find that the ambivalence implicit in the father complex persists in totemism and in religions generally."[20] In this way a vicious and stifling circle is closed. Whether it is hatred for the father or love for the father-substitute, the sons are caught in the trap of their unresolved emotional ambivalence toward the authority figure, where to loosen the knot of hatred on one side is to tighten the knot of love on the other.

As a repressive defense against this ambivalence and the imperfection it implies both in their worship and in the totem's power, love and awe for it are amplified further. The worshippers exist entirely under the shadow of a defense system that works to preserve the immense goodness of the totem. Even in the face of the most miserable misfortune, they find a way to exculpate the totem, just as original sin exculpates God. Driven by the guilty belief that they deserve such misfortune as punishment for the inadequacy of their worship, they impose on themselves even more severe taboos. As Freud puts it, describing the relation between the ancient Jews and their god, "driven by the need to satisfy this sense of guilt" (which will be insatiable as long as there is misfortune), they impose taboos that "grow ever stricter, more meticulous and even more trivial."[21] In this way, Freud grants that great moralistic heights (or extremes) are reached, but this rectitude, he insists, as originating not from desire for the good but from "the sense of guilt felt on account of a suppressed hostility to God," displays the irrational excesses characteristic of "obsessional neurotic reaction-formations."

Moreover, although any hint of injury to the totem is prohibited, as Freud cannily points out, the prohibition is only necessary because at some level it is recognized that the worshippers desire precisely such injury. Their awe and respect is never free of the tinge of fear, suspicion, envy, and hatred. If the totem persistently withdraws its promise of protection and bounty, the worshipper may repeat the murder, or wish to.[22] In recognizing this parricidal desire, one also implicitly recognizes the imperfection of the totem. Totemism, then, not only expresses remorse and offers the hope of atonement and self-justification, but paradoxically it also serves as a reminder that the group ultimately has power over the totem. According to Freud, satisfaction concerning the triumph of the group over the father underpins the ritualized "totem-feast," described as a festival at which the totem clan as a group kill and devour the totem (an act that is taboo to individuals). This festival, during which the restrictions of "deferred obedience" are lifted, Freud argues, "would thus be a repetition and a commemoration of this memorable and criminal deed, which was the beginning of so many things—of social organization, of moral restrictions and of religion."[23]

If Freud acknowledges that totemism as a religiosocial institution is no longer an explicit form of life in modern societies, vestiges nevertheless remain, in pathologies, in all religions, and in (as Derrida points out) the archontic principle of the archive. If totemism, in Freud's words, "arose from a filial sense of guilt, in an attempt to allay that feeling and to appease the father by deferred obedience to him," then, he insists, "all [religions] have the same end in view and are reactions to the same great event with which civilization began and which, since it occurred, has not allowed mankind a moment's rest."[24]

To sum up, Freud's parricide myth of *Totem and Taboo* offers a psychological account of how an ideology perpetuates itself. In outline, he shows that the rebellion of a group against a strongly authoritarian tyrant leaves the group in a power vacuum where, due to a powerful residual need for authority, ambivalent forces of fear, guilt, and pride predominate. This intolerable ambivalence, if left unresolved, leads the group to impose upon themselves the very restrictions they have just thrown off. The prohibitions once imposed on them by the tyrant are now internalized and self-imposed. Freud's genius, then, is to have seen this paradoxical circularity of the archontic principle. If, due to an overwhelming need for authority, the overcoming of tyranny results in totemism, the irony is that the greatest resistance to the father merely strengthens the tyrannical hold of his power over his sons. Notably, an economic relation to traditional institutions, which has often been privileged as the only genuine relation, takes the form of an archontic circle. This economic relation presupposes that an inventor is inspired with the truth and is compelled to pass it on to those to come, who, in turn, must maintain its purity against dissipating forces. Freud, then, offers a psychological account of why this economic archontic circle has such a compulsive power to hold "father" and "son" in its grip. He shows that power is perpetuated because an ideology, placed above the individual players as a "totem," invents/defines the players (whether father or son), repeats itself through them, and prevents them from inventing themselves.

Following Freud's indications, it is clear that to some extent, his classical articulation of the Oedipus complex, which he names "the central experience" of the formative years in early childhood, describes a movement at the individual level parallel to the archontic circle reflected in the parricide myth.[25] However, Freud views the archontic circle as the neurotic consequence of an inability to resolve the emotional ambivalence generated by the oedipal desires, and he measures health in terms of a successful resolution of this ambivalence.[26] Given that he calls the archontic circle neurotic, the ultimate point of his efforts must be to show that it is also necessary to overcome the desperate need for a master, which motivates us to replace the father with a totem, in spite of the unhappiness this necessarily causes us. Consequently, one would expect a healthy outcome to correspond with the ability to step beyond the archontic circle. Presumably, totemism is overcome (if ever) with the realization that no sacred object or being can live up to the demands placed upon it. However, since the so-called healthy resolution of the Oedipus complex is itself troubled by internal tensions, it remains to be seen whether Freud's "classical" articulation of the Oedipus complex is sufficient to his ultimate requirement, for taking a step beyond the archontic circle implies subverting the desire for absolute power.

Freud's Classical Articulation of the Oedipus Complex

> As if Sophocles was saying to him: "You are struggling in vain against your responsibility and are protesting in vain of what you

have done in opposition to these criminal intentions. You are guilty, for you have not been able to destroy them; they still persist in you unconsciously. And there is psychological truth in this. Even if a man has repressed his evil impulses into the unconscious and would like to tell himself afterwards that he is not responsible for them, he is nevertheless bound to be aware of this responsibility as a sense of guilt whose basis is unknown to him."[27]

According to Freud, the Oedipus complex, whose nature can be deduced from the name he gave it, namely an erotic attachment to the mother and a desire to kill the father, is "a situation which every child is destined to pass through and which follows inevitably from the factor of the prolonged period during which a child is cared for by other people."[28] A number of years of "pre-Oedipal" psychosexual organization and development precede the conflicts that characterize this complex, which occurs at a stage where sexual differences are being noticed and integrated by a child. For him, the Oedipus complex, as the first expression of sexual difference, occurs differently for boys and girls.

Freud's initial formulation of the Oedipus complex in terms of sexual difference presents endless difficulties. One either stalls on these or acknowledges that there is nevertheless something to be gained from studying it. I tend to agree with Roy Schafer that it is precisely its adaptability that gives Freud's Oedipus complex its power. As he puts it, "for *us* [psychoanalysts] the most adaptable, trustworthy, inclusive, supportable, and helpful storyline of them all [is] the Oedipus complex in all its complexity and with all its surprises."[29] But to enter into this complexity (beginning with Freud's own suggestions concerning a positive and negative version for each sex) would be to step beyond the scope of this chapter. As a starting point, I shall outline Freud's "classic" statement of the Oedipus complex, taken from his *An Outline of Psycho-Analysis*, which was written near the end of his life as a gathering together of his ideas. Notably, however, it is already possible to find in this statement the loose thread Lacan will take up in his revisions, and one will find in Lacan's revisions a guiding thread through the labyrinth of sexual difference. I will take up Lacan's arguments in detail in the chapters to follow.

The Masculine Oedipus Complex

On the one hand, Freud argues, a boy's awakening genital sexuality is directed toward his mother as a desire to possess her physically. On the other hand, while admired as a model of enviable physical strength and authority, the boy's father now becomes a rival and an obstacle to his attempts at seduction. Powerful fantasies of destroying the father and taking his place are supported by the father's periodic absences. In Freud's words, "his satisfaction when his father disappears and his disappointment when he emerges again are deeply felt experiences."[30] Eventually constrained to curb her child's sexual attentions, the mother places a prohibition on masturbation, whose effect is only to modify the means by which he satisfies himself. Forced into greater severity, therefore, she threatens castration, and, moreover, assigns to the boy's father the task of carrying it out. Freud concedes that this castration threat can be imagined; it is put together from hints, prohibitions, and early sexual hypotheses.[31] The threat, real or fantasized, gathers credibility and force when the boy notices that some humans (sisters) really do lack penises, and its consequences are, Freud insists, "multifarious and incalculable."[32]

The castration threat, as noted, represents the first great parental betrayal whereby the boy's parents are lost to him as libidinal objects. As Freud puts it: "If the satisfaction of love in the field of the Oedipus complex is to cost the child his penis, a conflict is bound to arise between his narcissistic interest in that part of his body and the libidinal cathexis of his parental objects. In this conflict the first of these forces normally triumphs: the child's ego turns away from the Oedipus complex."[33] Freud acknowledges that circumstances dictate the impact of the castration threat on a boy's "budding sexual life," but generally speaking, faced with the danger of losing his penis, the boy's masculinity wilts; to save his precious organ he takes measures to avert the dangerous rivalry with his father. He renounces his mother, represses all desire to seduce her, gives up masturbation, and becomes passive toward his father, who therefore becomes no longer a rival but a fearsome threat.

I have already addressed at some length the installation of the superego via the formation of an ideal ego through identification with the lost libidinal objects (the parents). Here, according to Freud, the admired father, now lost to fear, is introjected into the ego, where it forms the nucleus of the superego, which takes over the authority of the father and perpetuates his prohibition against mother-incest. In this way, for Freud, the libidinal trends belonging to the Oedipus complex are desexualized and sublimated, or, that is, inhibited in their aim and changed into impulses of affection. But the boy's fantasy life is magnified and, simultaneously, unconscious fears and hatreds directed towards his father intensify.[34] Further, despite his conscious renunciation of his mother, he remains dependent on her love, for the threat of betrayal (of being handed over to the father for castration) looms large. As a general rule, unable to master these oedipal conflicts, he finally represses them. "The Oedipus complex is abandoned, repressed, and, in most normal cases, entirely destroyed, and a severe super-ego is set up as its heir."[35] Alternatively, these repressed conflicts remain "preserved in the unconscious," ready to resurface as symptoms when triggered by related stresses.[36]

Sex-related conflicts tend to resurface at puberty, when the boy is confronted with a new developmental task, namely that of detaching his libidinal wishes from the parent figures and directing them toward "a real outside love object." In relation to his parents, he is required to effect a reconciliation where oppositional relations have persisted and free himself from residual subservience. Moreover, Freud insists, he is required to "tame and restrict" his sexual instinct and "subject it to an individual will which is identical with the bidding of society."[37] As compensation for his libidinal renunciations, a share in his father's authority is promised to his future, which he is free to exercise at will (for example, over the woman he selects as a mother substitute).

There are certain parallels between the structure of the parricide myth and that of the Oedipus complex as described so far. The boy's incestuous and aggressive oedipal desires are the equivalent of the hypothesized original parricide in *Totem and Taboo*.[38] The fear of castration, which forces the boy to repress his oedipal desires and to install a superego modeled on his father, matches the brother's fear and remorse, reflected in their efforts to repress or forget their deed by substituting a totem father for the lost father and submitting to what would have been their father's desire by instituting various taboos. The ambivalence of the boy's subsequent unconscious fantasies mirrors the brother's emotional ambivalence toward the totem in the form of self-punishing guilt, but also in the satisfaction over the killing as reflected in the totem feast. The divergence occurs, at least apparently, when Freud announces that the ambivalent emotions of the Oedipus complex must be resolved if the boy is to become a healthy adult. Such resolution indeed parallels what is reflected in the incest taboo (namely, the promotion of exogamy) and in the social contract (as a brotherhood among men), for it includes the obligation to find an outside love object and to subject an overpowering libido to the bidding of the group. But it also includes the task of reconciliation with and detachment from the parent figures and the superego that represents their authority. Remarkably, Freud notes, these universal tasks are seldom "dealt with in an ideal manner."[39] He adds: "By neurotics, however, no solution at all is arrived at: the son remains all his life bowed beneath his father's authority and he is unable to transfer his libido to an outside sexual object."

In his attempt to resolve his Oedipus complex, a boy will find a place somewhere on an unbroken continuum between debilitating obsessional neurosis and healthy independence.[40] Briefly, those who suffer from obsessional neuroses are terrorized by violent impulses they disavow as alien and objectionable and against which they compulsively carry out various protective "prohibitions, renunciations and restrictions."[41] Facing these internal terrors, sufferers become overconscientious and "more than ordinarily correct" in their behavior.[42] Accordingly, Freud notes, "these impulses never—literally never—force their way through to performance. . . . What the patient actually carries out—his so called obsessional actions—are very harmless and certainly trivial things, for the most part repetitions or ceremonial elaborations of the activities of ordinary life."[43]

Nevertheless, such obsessional actions place excessively severe restrictions on objects, words, or actions, which require compulsive rituals of expiation and purification if the prohibition is even inadvertently transgressed.[44] While sufferers are quite capable of self-censure on account of the irrational and debilitating nature of these actions, they cannot help themselves, and they remain caught up in "extremely tedious and almost insoluble tasks." Moreover, given this discrepancy, their mental life remains ambivalent. Obsessions impose themselves with dogmatic persistence, while niggling intellectual doubts ensure that sufferers experience "an ever-increasing degree of indecision, loss of energy and restrictions of freedom."

In cases of obsessional neurosis, Freud explains, a sufferer has failed to detach his libido from its oedipal objects.[45] Had his ego condoned this fixation, his sex life, Freud insists, would have remained infantile and therefore perverse, but no neurosis would have developed. The self-imposed taboos and rituals of an obsessional neurotic, however, are symptoms that help bind the extreme anxiety caused by the ego's reactions against its infantile libidinal fixations.[46] These taboos, in other words, although displaced onto other objects or into seemingly irrational, unconnected rituals, are ultimately found to be prohibitions on killing the father or on incest with the mother or sisters. To explain why obsessional actions seem to have the contrary purpose of preventing rather than substituting for satisfaction, Freud reminds one that to prohibit something implies a desire for it and a dread of that desire. Symptoms are therefore, in his words, "the products of a compromise and arise from the mutual interference between two opposing currents; they represent not only the repressed but also the repressing force which had a share in their origin."[47] Again, as Freud notes, "most of the urges of sexual life are not of a purely erotic nature but have arisen from alloys of the erotic instinct with portions of the destructive instinct."[48] As noted above, obsessional symptoms are commonly provoked by excessive sadistic impulses, and the symptoms, he argues, "serve predominantly as a *defence* against these wishes or give expression to the struggle between satisfaction and defence." But a sadistic impulse can be satisfied "safely" by directing it against the self, turning sufferers into consummate "self-tormentors."[49]

Notably, Freud suggests that a good alternative for the name "obsessional neurosis" would be "taboo-sickness."[50] In other words, he places the outcome of the parricide myth (in totemism, which is the precursor to religion and exemplar of the archontic circle) on the side of obsessional neurosis. In his words: "I have never doubted that religious phenomena are only to be understood on the pattern of the individual neurotic symptoms familiar to us—as the return of the long since forgotten, important events in the primaeval history of the human family—and that they have to thank precisely this origin for their compulsive character."[51]

But if an obsessional neurosis (whether individual or writ large in totemism) stems from an inability to detach oneself from one's oedipal objects and a consequent inability to escape the trap of the archontic circle, by implication, the successful resolution of the Oedipus complex, which achieves independence from the father's authority and the mother's sexual power, should break it open. However, independence from parental power is not identical to a critique of its source, namely patriarchal convention. Rather, the boy's oedipalization is encouraged by the promise of a share in the power of the brotherhood, which will free him from the personal power of his father. With the pseudodemocracy of the brotherhood (that is to say, patriarchal convention) behind him, he can do what he cannot do alone, namely assess, criticize, and stand up to the father as an equal. But he pays a price: to be recognized as a member of this totem clan, each brother has to renounce his singularity. The promised respite for the son vis-à-vis the father, namely the pseudodemocratic vice grip of patriarchal convention, turns out to be equally restrictive, for it is just "the takeover of the archive by the brothers," not a critique of it. The aporia of masculine oedipalization, then, is that both neurosis (remaining subjugated to the will and power of the father) and health (remaining subjugated to the patriarchal convention inscribed in the law of the brotherhood) represent a betrayal of singularity.

This, in turn, troubles the very idea of psychoanalytic therapy, which claims its greatest successes in relation to the neuroses.[52] Success in the psychoanalytic treatment of neurosis, which is supposed to help one finally resolve one's Oedipus complex, could be measured in terms of the dissolution of symptoms, but this may turn out to promote independence merely as detachment vis-à-vis the parents and acceptance into the brotherhood. But success in treatment could also be measured by the extent to which the subject has developed enough power (not merely rational prowess) to distance the ego from the superego, assess the merits of its commands, and act with critical judgment.[53] Here, one assumes that successful psychoanalysis helps engender in an individual the power to go beyond masculine "health": to achieve instead the power to refuse power, to assess the merits of the archons, institutions, ideologies, or discourses that constitute his lifeworld, and in this way to step out of the archontic circle.

Despite his pessimism regarding the "mass of mankind" and indications to the contrary in his mantric repetition of patriarchal prejudices concerning women, Freud undeniably opens up a gap here in the archontic circle. In other words, one might, and should, be suspicious of his masculine Oedipus complex. It has its surprises, however, for Freud implies here that such critical power is not derived from "strengthening" the ego against the scattering effects of the sex drive (or object-libido) by a "gathering together" aimed at shoring up its unity, integrity, and rationality, as if it is required to stand fast against an adversary. Rather, the subject's critical power is a function of its recognition of its own singularity and flexibility, which goes hand in hand with the enabling power of inventive self-sublimation and ethical decisiveness.

If one suspects, therefore, that Freud has already begun to show more than he intended regarding a possible critique of patriarchy, this suspicion is confirmed in reflection upon the feminine version of the Oedipus complex. Reading Freud somewhat against himself, one may propose, with Lacan, that he here demonstrates what he saw without seeing: namely, that if an archontic ideology needs a binary against which to define its source of power, as does patriarchy, this will be the source of its undoing. Moreover, in unwittingly demonstrating the structure of its undoing in the feminine Oedipus complex, Freud, against his overt convictions, confirms that patriarchy is not necessary or normative, but historical.

The Feminine Oedipus Complex

Since the parricide myth mirrors the Oedipus complex only in its masculine articulation, one is led to assume that the construction of the social contract and the development of cultural institutions such as law, morality, and religion may be attributed entirely to the masculine psyche. Notably, the parricide myth outlined in *Totem and Taboo* has almost nothing to say about feminine agency. Women figure in it only as objects of incestuous desire and as passive subjects of and to taboos (that are specially designed to control masculine desires). For Freud, the two fundamental taboos of totemism created by the brothers out of their filial sense of guilt correspond only to the two repressed wishes of the masculine Oedipus complex: to kill the father and to seduce the mother.[54] One gets the impression that, having already constructed the Oedipus complex in masculine terms, Freud simply tried to inscribe a girl's oedipal experience in it, as its negative or as its symmetrical (binary) opposite.

In outline, for Freud, the infant girl equally desires the mother and vainly attempts to seduce her, but has as rivals not only the father but also the brothers for her exclusive attention.[55] However, she finds herself to be intrinsically underendowed in relation to these rivals. In Freud's words: "A female child has, of course, no need to fear the loss of a penis; she must, however, react to the fact of not having received one."[56] This claim can in fact be translated into less comical terms: Without ever having noticed a boy's genitals, it would have taken precious little for a Victorian girl to recognize that she lacked preference vis-à-vis her brothers. Forced to react to this inferior status, she would naturally have envied them their privilege and desired that favor for herself.

Initially, Freud insists, she simply attempts to mimic the boys in all respects. Concerning masturbation, however, in his words, "it often happens that she fails to obtain sufficient satisfaction and extends her judgment of inferiority from her stunted penis to her whole self. As a rule she soon gives up masturbating, since she has no wish to be reminded of the superiority of her brother or playmate, and turns away from sexuality altogether."[57] However, unconsciously she remains unappeasably envious of the boys, to the extent that, Freud insists, "her whole development may be said to take place under the colours of envy for the penis." She does not need to be forced to abandon the mother, for her penis envy is sufficient motivation: she "cannot forgive her mother for having sent her into the world so insufficiently equipped," and her resentment motivates her to find a substitute. The father is the obvious candidate, for unlike the mother, he appears capable of giving her what she lacks. According to Freud, this substitution takes shape in her unconscious as "a wish to have his penis at her disposal, but it culminates in another wish—to have a baby from him as a gift."[58] In other words, she soon realizes that her route to power will have to lie in renouncing "she" who is powerless and in seducing "he" who has it potentially to give. She, therefore, enters into competitive rivalry with her mother for the father's affections.

Again, when these unconscious conflicts resurface, she is confronted with the same task of detachment and reconciliation and the same promise of health, if this is successful, or risk of neurosis, if it is not. However, on Freud's account, the consequences of the Oedipus complex are asymmetrical for men and women. It is a lack, rather than the threat of a loss, that forces females into their Oedipus complex, which occurs as unconscious aggression toward the mother and a desire to seduce the father. In the formation of an ideal ego, she identifies herself with the being whose place she covets, but there is no compensation in this identification with an inferior being for whom her residual disgust remains irremediable and apparently irrelevant. In Freud's words: "It does little harm to a woman if she remains in her feminine Oedipus attitude. She will in that case choose her husband for his paternal characteristics and be ready to recognize his authority."[59] Her bleak destiny in a patriarchal order, then, masquerading as health, becomes one of self-hatred and dependence. On the other hand, what is described by Freud as her "neurosis" (her inability to transfer her father-love to a husband and her refusal to reconcile with her mother) can be translated as her "hysterical" refusal to accept the authority of a lesser god (convention) and resign herself to her inferiority.

It is hardly surprising that this version of the Oedipus complex has met with outright resistance, and one is tempted to laugh the whole thing out of court. But there is nevertheless something important to be gained from this articulation, namely that by default it shows that in relation to women, something in the archontic circle breaks open, leaving a gap for the critique of patriarchy. In "health," that is, in resignation to her inferiority, a girl remains equally trapped by patriarchy. But in neurosis, she refuses to be submissive and remains attached to what she views as the potential source of her own power. Here, then, the archontic circle cannot close. In the feminine version of the Oedipus complex, neurosis is a position of critique that cannot be reappropriated by patriarchy. It is hardly surprising that a woman may resist the cure and choose rather to challenge an order that defines her health in terms of her inferiority and dependence.

To sum up, reflection upon Freud's articulation of the Oedipus complex yields the following ironies: In its most conservative masculine version, "health" names the perpetuation of patriarchal convention whereby an individual renounces his singularity in the name of the group. Here, the singular authority of the father is simply replaced by the "superego," which represents the internalization of patriarchal convention. However, and this marks the opening of a gap, a preferred position beyond such "health" is indicated, whereby the singular asserts its power of critique vis-à-vis the superego. This gap is opened wider in the feminine version of the Oedipus complex, for, as it turns out, feminine "health" is here defined in terms of her acceptance of an inferior status and submission to a husband's authority. What is, conversely, called "neurosis," namely the refusal to submit to a patriarchal order, may just be the equivalent in feminine terms of the preferred position that takes a man "beyond health."

So far, I have tried to amplify the first part of Derrida's thesis by reconstructing Freud's account of the neurotic archontic circle in *Totem and Taboo* and by showing that to some extent, through the gaps, wittingly and unwittingly, opened up in his articulation of the Oedipus complex, he indicated a way out of it. However, the tension between these openings provided by his theoretical statements and his own continued patriarchy and archontic commitments in practice leaves one troubled by questions concerning the movement of the archontic circle in Freudian psychoanalysis.

The second part of Derrida's thesis, then, concerns the tension whereby Freud remains under the spell of the very archontic principle he has so insightfully brought to light and decisively subverted, for the archontic circle springs its trap only if one takes for granted the seemingly obvious relationship of priority between the "inventive signature" and the "interpretative countersignature" (or, one might add, between the notion of a purely active, giving-out that constitutes writing a text, and the supposedly passive, receiving-in that characterizes reading it). Yet he remained curiously bound by the precisely equivalent binary associated with the terms of his parricide myth, father and son, master and disciple. Certainly, one does not break out of the circle, as Freud demonstrated, by murdering the father. Rather, as Derrida confirms in both "Psyche," which stresses the "paradoxical predicaments" in which the concept "invention" remains tied up, and "Ulysses,"[60] which focuses on the related aporetics of interpretation, the archontic circle is internally ruined precisely because the interpreter as much as the inventor invents the invention, or, in other terms, in the "event of signature"[61] the double, interpretative "yes" co-constitutes the "singular," inventive "yes."[62] To relate it to the "inventor of psychoanalysis," the relations between Freud as "inventive son" and as "father-inventor," and between inventive-inventor and his "interpreters," are reciprocal, aporetic, entangled, contaminated. The mutual threats posed to each other by the "double yes" of repetition and the singularity of the inventive "yes" are double sided, related in one direction to the past archive and in the other to the archive to come. This binds Freud to an inescapably ambivalent relation both to the past archive and to the archive to come.

Conversely, one may argue, the archontic circle is perpetuated insofar as one does not recognize this intrinsic mutual contamination of "father" and "son." Because Freud did not recognize this contamination, his position is divided incompatibly between what is aneconomic about the inventiveness by which he instituted psychoanalysis and what is economic about its institutionalization. Moreover, insofar as the murderous sons, as readers of the father-inventor, do not themselves recognize this contamination, psychoanalysis becomes an ideology, and they remain caught in the circular trap of the archontic circle. By contrast, in making this kind of argument, Derrida sees himself as a paradoxically "inventive interpreter" of Freud who is, therefore, not entirely bound into the archontic circle. Anticipating the theme of part 3, it seems to me that Lacan's notorious "return to Freud" places him in precisely the same relation.

Invention/Convention: Derrida's Analysis of Freud's Economic Recapitulation

Freud was the inventor of psychoanalysis. But what does this mean if the concept "invention," as Derrida points out, is periodically reinvented and has shifted in determination from "inventive discovery" to "productive discovery"?[63] Reflecting its more primordial, aneconomic sense, one is tempted to think that there will be no invention unless there is an unpredictable, inspired or lucky stroke of genius, a revealing flash in which something original-originary occurs as a singular transgression that shakes off the debris of past convention.[64] Moreover, as Derrida notes, the uniqueness or novelty of invention requires that this first time is also a last time: "archaeology and eschatology acknowledge each other here in the irony of the *one and only* instant."[65] On this understanding of invention, psychoanalysis as the genius of Freud's singular inventiveness would unavoidably strike the past archive as a traumatic disruption, a rewriting that changes everything, without any possibility of return, for it will have made of the tradition a lie or at least showed it up for the invented fiction it "really" was. In many respects, Freud made precisely this impression on the past archive. Classic examples are his propositions concerning the psychical apparatus as divided and internally conflicted, unconscious motivating forces in behavior, the aetiology of the neuroses in childhood sexuality, and the tie between religion and neurosis.

But, as Derrida warns, along the lines of quintessentially Freudian argument treated at length in the previous chapter, "things are not so simple." This purely aneconomic determination of "invention" is impossible, for it indicates "a misunderstanding . . . of the real constraints on invention."[66] Here, one must pose a question concerning temporality: Can

Freud's invention of psychoanalysis have occurred in an atemporal, original-originary flash of inspiration, in a momentous reconfiguration (at the moment that he renounced hypnosis) that configures the shape of all that is to come? Alternatively, to occur at all must it have extended over time?[67] The answer, for Derrida, is undecidable. If "invention" is to remain true to its concept, one must indeed think of inventive novelty in terms of an aneconomic instant. Yet, simultaneously, the concept cannot but bear traces of temporal relativity. Concerning the temporal mode of the past, the "event" of invention only makes sense against possibilities already instituted. As Derrida insists, "invention" has never meant creation *ex nihilo* but rather the uncovering for the first time of something always already possible but previously unrecognized and calling out for inventive recognition.[68] In other words, the inventive positing of something, the "inventive yes," already occurs in response to (and concomitantly as a threat to) another call (of the archive past, or beyond this, of being, a god, justice, gift, thing, Real . . .) anterior to its instituting or inventive performance.[69]

As always already a response, then, an invention is given its status as "original" or "transgressive" only if it is, in Derrida's words, "protected by a system of *conventions* that will ensure for it at the same time its recording in a common history, its belonging to a culture: to a heritage, a lineage, a pedagogical tradition, a discipline, a chain of generations."[70] But this means that "invention" can never have been the inaugurating event of something entirely novel. As Derrida notes, any "inventor" faces the paradox of always already having had to "sign-away" the originality of an invention, of having to presuppose the numerous conventions implied in making something at all and in making it public ("a contract, consensus, promise, commitment, institution, law, legality, legitimation").[71] Consequently, as much as Freud's inventiveness threatens the past archive, so, to the extent that the father as archon can control the archive, dictate its contents, and keep control over its effects, the impression made on Freud by the ideological power of the past archive poses threats to Freud's inventiveness, not least of which is the threatened imposition of the archontic circle. Freud faced a double threat in "the name of the father." In relation to his actual father, he persistently resisted paternal attempts to draw him back into the religious fold of the totem clan. In relation to the brotherhood, the traumatic novelty of his propositions concerning the psyche, sexuality, and religion is strikingly juxtaposed with his unreflective, patriarchal conventionality concerning women.

So far, I have addressed only one side of the story, for "invention" has a relation not only to the temporal moment of the past but also to the future. As mentioned, "invention" has gradually been reinvented, so that the notion today refers predominantly to "productive" rather than "inventive" discovery. In this shift, "invention" turns away from the past and faces the future: it is thought of less readily as the uncovering of hidden "content" and more readily as, in Derrida's words, "the productive discovery of an apparatus that we can call technical in the broad sense, technoscientific or techno poetic."[72] That is, "invention" becomes the invention of machines, methods, or theoretical structures and systems specially designed to help us perceive what is missing in our knowledge, invent the means to find it, and eliminate controversy. Here, in its economic articulation, inventions "program" the production of more inventions.

A shift in perspective from considering Freud as an inventive son vis-à-vis the archontic fathers to viewing him as the father-inventor of psychoanalysis whose aim was to codify his ideas into a scientific institution mirrors this shift from the aneconomic sense of invention to the economic. Here, then, the discovery of psychoanalytic truths would be programmable through its already invented artifacts, the logicodiscursive mechanisms, theoretical structures, and methods authored and authorized by Freud (such as the Oedipus complex), which are designed to ensure the repeatability of its truths.[73] As Derrida notes, invention would be subject to "powerful movements of authoritarian prescription and anticipation."[74] The obvious danger is encapsulated in Leibniz's claim for his "universal characteristics," namely that it "saves the mind and the imagination, the use of which must above all be controlled."[75]

In trying to predict and control what comes to us as invention, would we not have lost the sense of inventiveness altogether? As Derrida asks, can we still call a programmed invention an invention?[76] Rather, it would seem, even as he was himself "inventive," to the extent that Freud refused to recognize his dependence on his interpreters—his contamination by them—he became a force determined to suffocate inventiveness. Here, the father-inventor tried to secure the immortality of his invention, positing it only to repeat itself in his "sons" as his legacy. As father-inventor, Freud would assume the kind of mastery that constitutes his interpreters as submissively obedient disciples or murderous dissidents, placing them all permanently under the shadow of a debt they can neither escape nor pay off. He of all people should have been sensitive to the paradox that the father's very demand for immortalization as repetition of the same in the sons brings upon him, in consequence, the fatal effects of their emotional ambivalence.

To clarify this argument, Derrida does not here reduce Freud's scientific enterprise to its economic moment. He is, however, justifiably suspicious of the authoritarian streak in Freud that does not want to relinquish his control over psychoanalysis. Such authoritarianism risks the radical grain in Freud's writings for the sake of constructing "programmable truths," which goes against the grain of his own inventive scientific practice, which drew from investigations constantly under way in his everyday psychoanalytic work. Since generalization is intrinsic to the definition of science, one might say that he based his science on what his one-to-one relations with singular analysands indicated about more general psychical structures and relations. The urge towards "programming" takes over when one refuses to allow these structures to mutate in the hands of other analysts. In the course of his own investigations, Freud allowed his theoretical structures to mutate on the basis of what he learned from his practical encounters. But to the extent that he does not grant his "followers" the same inventiveness, he succumbs to the urge toward "programming."

What remains unacknowledged in any hierarchical master-disciple relation is that the inventive gesture only ever begins as a promise. It is never a matter of positing something complete or even something potentially complete that merely requires patient actualization. Rather, inventive positing is at best an intention to be the beginning of something. As a gesture, it is internally structured as a kind of "telephonic spacing": as inherently calling for, or desiring, the repeated responsive affirmation from an understanding interpreter at the other end of the line, who ought to put the seal on the identity and integrity of the invention.[77] In other words, to become what it is, Derrida insists, invention "will also need the signature or the countersignature of the other, let's say here that of the son who is not the invention of the father . . . as if the son's countersignature bore the legitimating authority."[78] In the unforeseeable time-to-come, then, the power of recognition may or may not constitute the event as an invention (as the inauguration of a possibility that will remain at the disposal of everyone). Moreover, even if the interpreter responds with an affirmation, the interpretation is, in principle, never adequate to its constitutive task, making it impossible to terminate the call.

Clearly, therefore, both Freud as singular father-inventor and the legacy of institutionalized Freudian psychoanalysis are vulnerable to the lack of repetition. Freud as singular inventor is vulnerable to parricide in the name of psychoanalysis as an ideology (as the great source of truth that defines both father and sons and supersedes even Freud). In this case, in the assumption that she or he, even better than Freud, knows what psychoanalysis truly is, even the most "inventive" psychoanalyst remains trapped within the archontic circle. What this son loves in the father is the projection of his own desire for omniscience, omnipotence, and immortality, that is, his own desire to identify with the power-giving ideology, which is to be the father (which does not necessarily coincide with the father's desire for the son). What the son hates in the father does not stem from his harshness so much as the son's, which regrets the father's tendency to fall short of the demands of the ideology (which is itself often a constituted effect of the son's projection). Thus regarding the singular father-inventor with admiring, affectionate awe but also with frustration, the interpreter does not return to Freud as an orthodox mimic of his word but to what is profoundly true in his words, the kernel of truth Freud may not have explicitly recognized or remained faithful to. Here, the son's loyalty lies with the ideology of psychoanalysis, not with Freud, and in this sense, Freud is murdered. But psychoanalysis becomes, in his place, the "mystical" authority, the totem.

As already an institution, Freud's invention is threatened less by the nonresponse of schizophrenia (in which the lack of temporal continuity erases memory and history) than by the possibility of violent misrecognition. But psychoanalysis is also, on the contrary, vulnerable to overconscientious repetition. The inventiveness of Freud's invention is threatened by the very precision of the repetition in orthodox Freudianism. For if the interpretation repeats the invention mechanically or compulsively, the inventive stroke is converted from being a "decision" after which everything changes shape into merely the first of a programmable, predictable series of expected acts. In this way, it is delivered a "death threat" (the threat of stasis, sterility, or paralysis).

To sum up so far, because invention (in both senses) and interpretation contaminate one another and cannot be separated out into coherent concepts, Freud's relations as inventive-son and father-inventor tie him up in a double bind. Paradoxically, his invention of psychoanalysis must claim uniqueness "even if," in Derrida's words, "the uniqueness has to be repeatable," since an invention never takes place without convention or recognition. If, as Freud has so clearly demonstrated, "invention *begins* by being susceptible to repetition, exploitation, reinscription," it can be neither the ephemeral insignificance of a one and only chance instant nor entertain its own destruction as the predictable effect of a conventional past and the advent of a programmable future. Invention, in either sense, is impossible. Again, for the invention of psychoanalysis to come to life at all, it has to be repeated or affirmed in a recognizing response. But perfect repetition places it under the threat of living-death. Repetition, therefore, both necessarily constitutes and threatens to destroy it. By the same token, for there to be living, recognizing repetition at all, there must first have been an invention. But its priority, in which is inscribed its power for institutionalization (the power to form a "history of effects" or tradition, as opposed to being forgotten or passed over), threatens to suffocate the ones who come second under the weight of debt. The invention, therefore, both necessarily constitutes and threatens to destroy the interpretation.

Concluding Remarks

If one cannot resolve these double binds, how then does one respond to the invention of psychoanalysis? According to Derrida, a negotiation of psychoanalysis requires one to hear within the Freudian call for response a tone of laughter that always haunts the disempowering laugh of omnipotence and mastery.[79] This is the affirmative laugh of "the gift," which does not cut down the power of commentary in advance but instead cuts itself open, gives itself out as a provocation, and dares the surprise in another reading (which as a "reading" would still be, and yet is not, a repetition of the same). Such negotiation also requires the interpreter to take advantage of the opening conferred by this gift, to embrace the paradox of having to repeat the "first yes" differently. As a reader, one must simultaneously respectfully recognize the "first yes" and disrespectfully suspend it in order to reinvent it, or to make anew the decision concerning a responsible response: that is, a response that is still a recognition (and not a violation beyond the point of no return) but that is, at the same time, not faithful to the point of death. In other words, just like the invention, the responsible response has to be both the affirmation that confers a certain "conventional" legitimacy and determinacy upon what is already there and an inventive stroke of genius in its own right. In short, in response to Freud's invention, one must, in turn, become an inventive interpreter.

Does one move "beyond psychoanalysis" by treating Freud's inventiveness as a gift rather than by accepting his invention as the imposition of a science whose truth must be preserved and refined? Derrida's answer, characteristically, is a refusal to answer, precisely because Freudian psychoanalysis troubles itself by this very question. If Freud, on the one hand, consistently tried to codify his ideas into a science, on the other hand, psychoanalytic notions, without Freud consistently and explicitly recognizing this, already, from the start, resist themselves, or autodeconstruct, implicitly opening psychoanalysis to this step beyond it. Consequently, one could argue, insofar as it aims to be a science, those who acknowledge its autodeconstructive element step beyond it. But insofar as psychoanalysis autodeconstructs, it has already inscribed this unsettling moment of radical destruction within it. In acknowledging such autodeconstruction, one does not step beyond psychoanalysis but instead brings to the surface what is already unconsciously inscribed in it.

To adumbrate the further development of this study, one may ask what is at stake in the question concerning Lacan's notorious "return to Freud." The foregoing discussion indicates three alternatives. The least plausible is that Lacan's "return to Freud" should be taken literally, thereby placing him among the neurotic sons who are unable to resolve their oedipal attachment to Father-Freud and simply repeat his desire in obsessive orthodoxy. As he notes: "You all know that on occasion I know how to take liberties with Freud's texts and affirm my distance."[80] It is also implausible, given the strong motif of ideology critique in his writings, that Lacan's affirmation of his distance from the letter of Freud's texts places him among the murderous brothers who would negate Freud's singularity as self-inventor in the name of psychoanalysis as an ideology. The third and most plausible suggestion, then, is that his "return to Freud" is ironic, since he has moved beyond "health" to the power of critique. Importantly, in turn, the question of Lacan's "return to Freud," it seems, turns on whether he acknowledges the autodeconstructive moment in psychoanalysis or whether his critique aims to replace Freudian psychoanalysis with a new master discourse, in this way ensuring that he remains, for all his inventiveness, caught up in the metaphysics of presence. If Derrida places his money on the latter, mine, as I hope to show in the remaining chapters, is on the former.

PART 3

Interweaving

Having outlined the genesis and structure of Derrida's articulation of the "plural logic of the aporia"[1] and having demonstrated how this logic informs his reading of certain Freudian texts, I hope to have shifted the terrain of any Derrida/Lacan encounter beyond a prejudicial reading that sees *différance* as an endorsement of a merely textual "freeplay" (the aneconomic aporia). In part 3, I begin to shift my attention to the other side of the coin, so to speak. At this point, my broad aim is to gather further support for the claim that beyond the prejudicial readings on both sides, Lacanian psychoanalysis can be read most productively by viewing deconstruction not in adversarial terms but as another resource for decoding Lacan's theoretical formulations, for his infamous "return to Freud" already inscribes the complication that Derrida underscores in his reading of Freud, namely, the necessity and the impossibility of returning to either a positive doctrine or an entangled knot, neither of which is exactly "there." Lacan's launchpad is certainly always Freud's text, but he "returns" to the ineradicable paradoxes, aporias, or dilemmas that rupture every Freudian concept, and his constant observation is that Freud left behind a legion of enigmas.[2] Moreover, one cannot argue that Lacan revisits these texts to resolve the enigmas and establish finally the kind of fundamental scientific concepts that bear faithful repetition. To the contrary, Lacanian psychoanalysis is an inventive appropriation that, in much the same spirit as Derrida's deconstructive reading, uncovers the autodeconstructing tensions in Freud's text as a warrant for his radicalizations.

Here, I hope to show how one may counter Derrida's misreading of Lacanian discourse by sketching out three broad areas of interweaving: concerning the Real, sexual difference, and feminine sexuality. In chapter 7, I aim to demonstrate that there is a clear isomorphism between Derrida's formulations of *différance* and Lacan's formulations of the Real. In fact, the Lacanian Real functions as a nickname for *différance* (both understood in their proper complexity, of course). This isomorphism again shifts the terrain, but this time beyond Derrida's prejudicial reading that leaves "Lacan" in bed with the metaphysicians of presence.[3]

By addressing the Lacanian Real first, I diverge from the approach to commentary reflected in Sheridan's "Translator's Note" at the beginning of Lacan's *Écrits*: "Of these three terms, the 'imaginary' was the first to appear. . . . The notion of the 'symbolic' came to the forefront in the Rome Report. . . . The 'real' emerges as a third term."[4] In my estimation, Lacan's conception of the traumatic Real is intrinsic to his radical reinvention of psychoanalysis and remains the most important notion for interpreting his texts. In fact, I shall go so far as to claim that this notion forms the "punctuation mark" that retroactively gives the "truth" to his theoretical endeavor.[5] However, like Derrida's *différance*, it confers a strange kind of "truth" on his discourse, namely, the "truth" that "truth" is not a matter of "Truth" ordinarily conceived, but the intrinsic inevitability of paradox.[6]

Lacan's conception of the Real, according to Sheridan, "began, naturally enough, by presenting, in relation to symbolic substitutions and imaginary variations, a function of constancy: 'the real is that which always returns to the same place.'"[7] This statement by no means implies that Lacan promotes some version of naïve realism. Instead, the Real is another word for Freud's "trauma," and, as already explained, the happening of a trauma constantly remains, or repeats, in the sense that it can be neither ignored nor resolved through assimilation. If Lacan returns to Freud's "realistic" conception of the Real, whose status is guaranteed by the repetition of the external object, it is to question this formulation via the means Freud himself provides for grasping "reality" as an economic fabrication that weaves the threads of an "imaginary" narrative around the ineradicable trauma. Lacan calls such "reality" the "automaton." By contrast, to return to Sheridan, the Lacanian Real becomes "that before which the imaginary faltered, that over which the symbolic stumbles, that which is refractory, resistant. Hence the formula: 'the real is the impossible.'"[8]

I shall approach Lacan's notion of the Real as trauma (repetition and resistance) by reading the section of seminar 11 entitled "Tuché and Automaton,"[9] which is a characteristically dense account of the paradoxes involved in Freud's notion of the "real." In the terms of the "plural logic of the aporia," Lacan's distinction between *automaton* and *tuché* turns on the contrast between "reality" (the economic aporia) and the "impossible Real" (which is already an articulation of paradox). Notably, Lacan here bypasses the aneconomic aporia by dismissing out of hand the idea that psychoanalysis is a subjective idealism. Further, Lacan's text represents a choice for the paradoxical, the *tuché*, as that which indicates the truth of the Real. Notably, Lacan here gives a theoretical account of why inventive repetition (in Kierkegaard's sense of repeating forward) is the only possible repetition.[10] This alone is an indication that he understands his "return" to Freud (that is, his repetition of Freud) in terms of the same paradoxical notion of repetition that Derrida nicknames "iterability."

Finally, the Lacanian Real, according to Sheridan, "begins to appear regularly, as an adjective, to describe that which is lacking in the symbolic order, the ineliminable residue of all articulation, the foreclosed element, which may be approached, but never grasped: the umbilical cord of the symbolic."[11] As Lee puts it, Lacan identifies the Real as "that which prevents one from saying the whole truth about it. Saying the whole truth is impossible not simply because words ultimately fail to reflect the multifaceted character of the real, but because the very fact of language has so ruptured the real that there is no whole to be described."[12] It is on the basis of this notion of "rupture" that Lacan introduces the aporetic trouble that Copjec formulates in terms of the "problem of the All" and addresses in terms of the "vel of alienation" that articulates universalism and particularism, or, one could say, economic and aneconomic *différance*.[13] Notably, then, it is through the figure of the Real as trauma that one may gather together its incompatible senses (as repetition, resistance, and rupture) in a way that does not make utter nonsense of the notion but shows how the logical structure of the Lacanian discourse accords with "the plural logic of the aporia."

By the same token, a Lacanian account of sexual difference exemplifies the logic of *différance*, and it is again with a view to challenging misreadings on both sides and showing in what sense Derrida's analytical work can stand as a resource for grappling with Lacan's notoriously abstruse formulations that I have offered a detailed treatment of the Derridean conception of sexual difference that emerges from his deconstructive reading, in "*Geschlecht*," of Heidegger's thinking on the subject. Chapter 8, broadly speaking, addresses a trouble that both Lacan and Derrida persistently grapple with: that of understanding difference in terms of binary oppositions. For many, sexual difference would seem to be the quintessential binary opposition, but there are, traditionally, two opposed views concerning what to make of it. Some thinkers argue that this binary is a fundamental, undeconstructible bottom line that one cannot get beyond. The opposing view is that this binary opposition is as deconstructible as any other and should give way to an unregulated proliferation of differences. The former is assumed to be the Lacanian position (but not, of course, by Lacanians); the second is supposed to be the Derridean (but, again, not by Derrideans). There is, in other words, mutual misrecognition on both sides of this equation.

Contrary to the aforementioned reading, it seems clear enough that Lacan's infamous claim concerning the sexual relation—namely, that it does not exist—offers a deconstruction of any conception of sexual difference as binary.[14] (Notably, I here intend "deconstruction" in the Derridean sense, rather than the sense given to this term by many misreadings.) Many expositions testify to this interpretation. Fink, for example, argues that Lacan's claim is an attempt to subvert the dream of a harmony of opposites whose lineage can be traced back as far as Aristophanes' speech in Plato's *Symposium* (if not further), where he describes the symmetrical splitting asunder of originally spherical beings, and accounts for the origin of love in the desire to make good the loss in an emotional and physical bond with the missing complement (the other half).[15] Such subversion is implicit in Lacan's claim that "Love is impotent, though mutual, because it is not aware that it is but the desire to be One, which leads us to the impossibility of establishing the relationship between 'them-two.'"[16] Evans confirms this view, arguing that among the many points condensed in Lacan's aphorism is the claim that "there is no reciprocity or symmetry between the male and female positions because the symbolic order is fundamentally asymmetrical."[17] On Žižek's account, which I shall address in more detail in due course, the binary conception of sexual difference (or, that is, "the imposition of a balanced symbolic structure") is an attempt to heal the wound of sexual difference taken as the "antagonistic gap" that divides asymmetrical, noncomplementary forms of jouissance.[18]

There was never any doubt that Derrida deconstructs binary oppositions. There should not be any doubt, moreover, that Derrida never undertakes a deconstruction in the name of a simple "postmodern" proliferation of differences, but rather in the name of an asymmetrical relation (indeed, an "antagonistic gap") between different kinds of difference. By working through "Geschlecht," then, I aim to show that Derrida deconstructs the binary articulation of sexual difference in the name of understanding sexual difference as another nickname for *différance*, for which the traumatic Real, as mentioned, is a nickname, as indeed are other names taken up from Žižek's essay, "The Real of Sexual Difference" (such as the terms "antagonistic gap," "empty signifier," and "zero institution").[19]

Following on from this treatment of sexual difference, which sees it in terms of an asymmetrical relation between noncomplementary kinds of jouissance, I turn, in chapter 9, to the question of why both Derrida and Lacan persist in labeling these kinds of jouissance "feminine" and "masculine," when both explicitly argue that these are by no means biological categories but structurally or logically "ordered" libidinal styles, both of which can be adopted by biological women and men. As Fink puts it: "It should be recalled that sexuation is not biological sex: what Lacan calls masculine structure and feminine structure do not have to do with one's biological organs but rather with the kind of jouissance that one is able to obtain."[20] Here, I agree with Fink that there is no necessity attached to the masculine and feminine designations, one could just as well, for example, name these libidinal styles paranoid and hysterical, economic and aneconomic, and so on.[21] As I hope to demonstrate, however, in addressing Derrida's deconstructive reading of Nietzsche on the question of woman and truth (in *Spurs*), there are nevertheless good political reasons, given the still ubiquitous dominance of patriarchy, to retain these sex-specific designations. Notably, Derrida's reading of Nietzsche allows a conception of feminine sexuality to emerge that is quite consonant with what is to be found on this topic in Lacanian discourse.[22] Lacan's isomorphic treatment of feminine sexuality will be addressed in greater detail in part 4, where I shall argue that Lacan's theorization of the transcendental relation, based on these asymmetrical libidinal styles, again accords with the "plural logic of the aporia."

7

The Lacanian Real

> One is led to the idea of a traumatic event, an event that cannot be an object of positivist historical study because it never takes place in the way historical situations do, but rather defines the place in which these situations come to inscribe themselves, a rupture that constitutes the never present origins of a race [for example]. Why "never present"? Because it is a structural impossibility to be present at one's own origin—except in the experience of the uncanny. This is as good a definition of the uncanny as one will find: the experience of encountering one's own origins. Freud theorized that such an encounter was felt by the ego as a threat that initiated a preparedness for action or flight. The flight that ensues need not, however, be considered as merely reactive; the act for which the encounter prepares us can also be one of invention.[1]

Introductory Remarks

The first move of Lacan's treatment of the paradoxical Real in "Tuché and Automaton"[2] is to defend psychoanalysis against the charge of subjective idealism.[3] Psychoanalysis, he notes, is often enough reproached for reducing experience to illusion or for promoting "some such aphorism as *life is a dream*," but nothing could be further from the truth. As he insists: "No praxis is more orientated towards that which, at the heart of experience, is the kernel of the real than psycho-analysis."[4] In countering the charge of subjective idealism, however, Lacan by no means resorts to the opposing doctrine of naïve realism. To the contrary, he threatens this stance too, because the "kernel of the real" turns out to be a thoroughly paradoxical notion. Accordingly, posing the question, "where do we meet this real?" he answers: in an essential encounter with what eludes us.[5] Lacan introduces a term borrowed from Aristotle, "the *tuché*," to name this encounter, which may be described alternatively as the traumatic cause of the repetition compulsion or simply as the Real. The *tuché* is here contrasted with "the *automaton*," which designates the fabric of phenomenal reality that we humans tend to weave around the Real.

The Real as Trauma: A Reading of "Tuché and Automaton"

The Automaton

Lacan describes "the *automaton*" as "the return, the coming-back, the insistence of the signs, by which we see ourselves governed by the pleasure principle."[6] Again, he calls it "the subjectifying homeostasis that orientates the whole functioning defined by the pleasure principle."[7] These definitions presuppose his thoroughgoing revision of the relationship that Freud envisaged between the pleasure and reality principles in psychical functioning, a clear, concise account of which appears in his earlier "Ethics" seminar.[8] Here, Lacan finds that Freud's conception of the "real" is intrinsically troubled.

On the one hand, it stems from a naïve realism that finds the guarantee of phenomenal reality in the repetition of external objects (objects refound via reality testing). Early in his theoretical endeavor, Lacan expresses surprise that so perspicacious a thinker as Freud should misrecognize the working of the very unconscious he so powerfully uncovered. In his words:

> The theoretical difficulties encountered by Freud seem to me in fact to derive from the mirage of objectification, inherited from classical psychology, constituted by the idea of the *perception/consciousness* system, in which Freud seems suddenly to fail to recognize the existence of everything that the ego neglects, scotomizes, misconstrues in the sensations that make it react to reality, everything that it ignores, exhausts, and binds in the significations that it receives from language: a surprising *méconnaissance* on the part of the man who succeeded by the power of his dialectic in forcing back the limits of the unconscious.[9]

On the other hand, Freud does insist that pleasure plays an originally determining role in the constitution of phenomenal reality and he holds the pleasure principle responsible for our tendency to construct it as a comfortable, economic fabrication, rather than submit to a brutally honest account of actual experience. This vacillation, as already noted in chapter 5, is the consequence of necessary trouble in the "original" relation of "repetition" between what happens and its presentation to consciousness.

However, if the pleasure principle does not relinquish control over the perceptual process, Freud believed he had saved "reality testing" from desire because it belongs to the secondary process, which is supposedly sharply divided from the primary process. Once this division becomes untenable, as Lacan has argued, then one has to accept that desire bears upon word presentations as much as on thing presentations, and therefore on one's judgment concerning the reality status of any intentional object. In other words, the "reality testing" of the secondary process never was a safeguard against the deceptions of the primary process (not even for Freud).[10]

Thus, if the primary process tends toward an "identity of perception" (I believe that what I imagine is identical to what is real), Lacan extends the argument to insist that the secondary process tends toward "an identity of thought" (I believe that what I think is identical to what is real). How so? If reality testing gradually leads to "anastomosis" (the cross-connection of ideas and perceptions that allows for something like Husserl's adequacy of evidence), one also tends to move beyond "the testing of the surrounding system of different objects present at that moment of its experience" toward anticipated pleasure or projections. But, instead of always sticking to testing such projections against experience for viability and adequacy, one tends to allow them a certain degree of autonomy. Here, incidentally, Lacan tacitly poses a challenge to Freud's respect for any postulation that resulted in an increase in generality and to his heuristic principle: "A gain in meaning is a perfectly justifiable ground for going beyond the limits of direct experience."[11]

In this process of projection, coherence and delusion often become fused. Persistent and consistent reality testing would oblige one to admit that all coherent systems (ideologies, institutions, etc.) are further away from what is Real than their proponents desire them to be, for honest reality testing would demonstrate that the Real is split, ambivalent, and paradoxical. Coherence is in fact fabricated as a defense, because we desire and require it, and our desire for coherence colors perception. As Lacan puts it: "something sifts, sieves, in such a way that reality is only perceived by man, in his natural spontaneous state at least, as radically selected. Man deals with selected bits of reality."[12] Tacitly invoking Kant's warning concerning the Ideas of Reason, Lacan argues: "One might say that the backcloth of experience consists in the construction of a certain system of *Wunsch* [desire] or of *Erwartung* [expectation] of pleasure, defined as anticipated pleasure, and which tends for this reason to realize itself autonomously in its own sphere, theoretically without expecting anything from the outside. It moves directly toward a fulfillment highly antithetical to whatever triggers it."[13] In other words, if thinking is triggered by the inexplicable, in the form of a singular event, the pleasure principle (rather than reality testing) ensures that its fulfillment is the production of an ideal system in which everything is explained, integrated, unified, stabilized, and systematized. In this case, one "domesticates" the singular (the flux, the complex, the paradoxical), expelling ideas that are "incompatible" with a comfortably synthesized worldview, so that it is no longer traumatic. That is, the event as understood is never what it "really is," but is something antithetical to this, namely merely a circumscribed part of a system of facilitations—a stable, habitual acquisition that is Imaginary rather than Real. Knowledge, therefore, is directed first toward achieving my pleasure; desire gets in the way of truth (which is uncertainty). While humans do seek truth, supposedly, we tend to accept as "true" only what conforms to our economic pleasure requirements.

In conclusion, the *automaton* (the system of signifying relations) marks off the two extremes, the origin and the *telos*, of the metaphysics of presence. It envisages the present original as the cause of repetition, or the anticipated structured whole of an ultimately closed system that guarantees repetition of the same in anticipation. Notably, Lacan does not here suggest that we can escape this tendency to produce systems. Nevertheless, it is important to be aware that these are "held together" in a "prosthetic" Imaginary Order, according to which we assume that there must have been a beginning on the basis of the experienced present, or that there be a whole on the basis of the partial objects we experience. In the absence of such awareness, the prosthesis tends to become a restricting armor.

The Tuché

According to Lacan, as Freud discovers that the function of fantasy is to construct an acceptable "reality," he becomes preoccupied with the question "what *is* the first encounter, the real, that lies behind the phantasy?"[14] But since Freud has already construed this originary encounter as a traumatic event, Lacan argues that his analytic drive to uncover an actual, historical occurrence as cause of the repetition compulsion is the quest, to the point of anguish, for the impossible. Here, then, Freud offers yet another incompatible articulation of "the real," this time in terms of the *tuché*, the encounter with the Real, "which always lies behind the automaton," as a traumatic event and cause of the "repetition compulsion," which, as Lacan will argue, repeats precisely because the repetition named by "reality testing" is not possible.

In the analytic situation, a repetition compulsion is suspected when repeated hitches or obstacles to analysis seem to occur in an analysand's narrative "*as if by chance*," that is, as if it is a matter of surprising coincidence rather than implicit engineering. Yet, as Lacan notes, analysts rightly remain suspicious of the apparent contingency of such events in the analysand's narrative and tend to view them as unconsciously caused. The *tuché* certainly designates this unconscious causality by which, in response to a traumatic event, subjects repeatedly reengineer order in their lives. But in the cases of disordered order dealt with in psychoanalytic treatment, the reengineering is overtly paranoiac in character; every new occurrence is bent into the shape of the disordered order, and the subject unconsciously obstructs or resists analysis in order to keep an invented structure in rigid paralysis, for the alternative, it seems, is to fall to pieces. As John Forrester describes it: "The salient feature of the paranoiac universe is that it has no place for a future, no room for manoeuvre, leaving only the option for apocalypse as marking the difference between now and what is to come."[15]

If psychoanalysis aims to undo "the Laplacean determinations the patient constructs for him or herself,"[16] Lacan argues that the efficacy of conventional or institutional Freudian psychoanalysis is blocked by a misconception of the *tuché* that assimilates it to the *automaton*, for, following Freud's desire to uncover the impossible Real, but ignoring this very ambiguity, analysts have mistakenly identified the repetition compulsion with the transference. In other words, Lacan argues, the repetition compulsion is accurately seen to be the "real cause" of what occurs in the transference, but what is repeated compulsively is taken by such analysts to be simply a reproduction in the space of the analytic relation of the original historical traumatic encounter with the Real. Here, then, the relation to the Real in the transference is expressed in terms of the *automaton*: such analysts presuppose that since one cannot apprehend what was never there in the first place, there must have been something present to apprehend, an original event, a first encounter, the positively present "real thing" that lies behind the fantasy. It is, supposedly, this determinable event in narrative history that the analysand repeats or acts out (in disguise) in the transference. In this case, the analyst presupposes that it is in principle possible, working by analogy or substitution, to uncover the original trauma as the key to the analysand's disorder and lead the analysand to reproduce the trauma in memory as precisely what it is.

In so conceptualizing the Real that causes the repetition compulsion, Lacan argues, the "true nature of repetition" is veiled. As he notes, this construal of the repetition compulsion as merely "the return of the signs, or reproduction, or the modulation by the act of a sort of acted-out remembering" in the transference simply covers over the enigmas of "repetition" and of "trauma."[17] In hoping to uncover the original traumatic encounter with the Real, Freud and some of his followers desired too much, for on Freud's own account, this encounter with the Real that is the cause of the repetition compulsion is essentially a "missed encounter." According to Lacan, the trauma "determining all that follows, and imposing on it an apparently accidental origin," is in principle impossible to assimilate into the analytic experience.

Lacan grants that if repetition supports or guarantees something's status as real, then the repetition compulsion suggests that something traumatic really happened. The required reality, which absolves psychoanalysis of the charge of subjective idealism, corresponds to encounters (events), which are radical points in the Real that cannot be effaced, forgotten, or assimilated.[18] Derrida confirms this insight: "'To mark a date in history' presupposes that 'something' comes or happens for the first and last time [that is, something singular], 'something' that we do not yet really know how to identify, determine, recognize or analyze but that should remain from here on . . . unforgettable, an ineffaceable event."[19]

The paradox of these ineffaceable radical points in the Real is that, precisely because they are "traumatic events," they both must and cannot be assimilated. There is a necessity and an impossibility of appropriation in a trauma that, Derrida insists, "*at once opens itself up to and resists experience.*"[20] Similarly, as Lacan puts it, "the trauma is conceived as having necessarily been marked by the subjectifying homeostasis that orientates the whole functioning defined by the pleasure principle." I take "marked by" here to mean that the trauma can only be recognized as such, and must be dealt with, in the realm of the *automaton*: the economic negotiation between pleasure principle and reality principle. Yet the traumatic Real, which causes the repetition compulsion, cannot by definition ever have been a fully present event (explainable in terms of the mechanical causality of the *automaton*). Thus, Lacan notes, psychoanalytic experience raises a problem, for the trauma persists, and at the center of the primary processes, "reappears, in effect, frequently unveiled."[21] A dream, for example, "the bearer of the subject's desire," may "produce that which makes the trauma emerge repeatedly—if not its very face, at least the screen that shows us that it is still there behind."

In other words, when such an event is made to comply with the demands of "the subjectifying homeostasis," an unassimilated and unresolved excess necessarily remains, keeping the event permanently in suspense, in abeyance or delayed—awaiting attention. In French, this is translated as *souffrance*—which also means the pain of heightened tension.[22] Again, one finds confirmation in Derrida's words:

> The experience of an event, the mode according to which it affects us, calls for a movement of appropriation (comprehension, recognition, identification, description, determination, interpretation on the basis of a horizon of anticipation, knowledge, naming, and so on), although this movement of appropriation is irreducible and ineluctable, there is no event worthy of its name except insofar as this appropriation *falters* at some border or frontier. A frontier, however, with neither front nor confrontation, one that incomprehension does not run into head on since it does not take the form of a solid front: it escapes, remains evasive, open, undecided, indeterminable. Whence the unappropriability, the unforeseeability, absolute surprise, incomprehension, the risk of misunderstanding, unanticipatable novelty, pure singularity, the absence of horizon.[23]

In short, the psyche covers over this abyssal remainder with a screen of economizing, fabricating representatives (*objet petit a*, for Lacan). These objects *a* take shape as the consequence of repressions, disguises, dissociations, fragmentations, deflections, intellectualizations, reductions, displacements, and discussions, which work both to cover over, and point to, the fact that the traumatic event cannot be assimilated.

Moreover, it is precisely because the trauma is preserved as impossible to assimilate that we find ourselves repeatedly attempting such assimilation. In Derrida's words:

> "Something" took place, we have the feeling of not having seen it coming, and certain consequences undeniably follow upon the "thing." But this very thing, the place and meaning of this "event," remains ineffable . . . out of range for a language that admits its powerlessness and so is reduced to pronouncing mechanically a date, repeating it endlessly, as a kind of ritual incantation, a conjuring poem, a journalistic litany or rhetorical refrain that admits to not knowing what it's talking about. We do not in fact know what we are saying or naming in this way: September 11, *le* 11 *Septembre*,

September 11 . . . we repeat this, *we must* repeat it, and it is all the more necessary to repeat it insofar as we do not really know what is being named in this way, as if to exorcise two times at one go: on the one hand, to conjure away, as if by magic, the "thing" itself, the fear or the terror it inspires (for repetition always protects by neutralizing, deadening, distancing a traumatism . . .), and, on the other hand, to deny as close as possible to this act of language and this enunciation, our powerlessness to name in an appropriate fashion, to characterize, to think the thing in question, to get beyond the mere deictic of the date.[24]

Paradoxically, the event as trauma causes the repetition compulsion that screens precisely the impossibility of its repetition. In other words, the repetition is compulsive because there can never be a proper repetition of the event, which, having happened, without being there, can never be re-found. One cannot get over, past, beyond the trauma precisely because it cannot be repeated. We repeat not in order to master the trauma but precisely because we cannot in principle achieve such mastery. But notably, for Derrida as for Lacan, we repeat as much for protection as for the sake of inventive sublimation.

Lacan concludes: "the reality system, however far it is developed, leaves an essential part of what belongs to the real a prisoner in the toils of the pleasure principle."[25] In other words, *Zwang*, compulsion (that is, the death drive and its impossible aim of jouissance) governs the very diversions of the primary process. Recall that the primary process operates in the gap between perception (for example, of sounds) and consciousness (a sound that has meaning for me), by which perceptual events are converted into an interpreted, meaningful, articulated phenomenal reality.[26]

For Lacan, one may apprehend this state of primary processing, directed by the death drive, by way of an example, namely, the experience of dreaming "under the effect of" perceptual events just before one awakens. He describes a situation in which an impatient knocking became manifest in his own dream as something other than a knocking at the door. On awakening, he notes, it is only by detaching from his dream representation (the scenario presented to consciousness through the dream) and re-constituting the event of the knocking as a perceptual representation that he becomes aware of it as a knocking at the door that bears with it knowledge "that I am there, at what time I went to sleep, and why I went to sleep."[27] In other words, the dream representation associated with the knocking is not at all the same as the perceptual representation of "the same" event.

Turning to the questions of what "really" wakes us up from such a dream and what we "really" awaken to, it seems obvious that it was the knocking in the real world that caused the dreamer to wake up. One could say that one wakes up from a dream (a hallucination) to reality. But, of course, things are more complex than this: there is, for Lacan, far more at issue in the notion of the Real. As he hints: "Perhaps we shall see better what is at issue, by apprehending what is there that motivates the emergence of the represented reality," here defined as "the phenomenon, distance, the gap itself that constitutes awakening."[28] Lacan, notably, has subtly reversed the above formulation: it is also possible to say that one awakens from the Real manifest in the dream to the fantasy (a hallucination) of a coherently articulated phenomenal reality. In this case, Lacan argues that the true cause of my awakening is not the perceptual event incorporated into the dream (the knocking) but a different kind of encounter, namely an essentially missed encounter with the Real, which is tied to the knocking associatively.

To explain this claim further, Lacan discusses a famous example from Freud's *Traumdeutung*: "the unfortunate father who went to rest in the room next to the one in which his dead child lay—leaving the child in the care, we are told, of another old man." The old man, "unable to maintain his vigil," nods off, a candle falls, and the bedclothes around the body of the dead child catch alight. At the same time, the father dreams "that the child is near his bed . . . takes him by the arm and whispers to him reproachfully . . . Father, can't you see . . . that I am burning?" The father is then "awoken by something."[29]

Problematizing two of Freud's hypotheses, namely, that dreams are wish fulfillments and that they function to prolong sleep, he argues that indications in Freud's texts allow us to produce the question: "*What is it that wakes the sleeper*? Is it not, *in* the dream, another reality?" For, as he argues, the father does not persuade himself in the dream that his child is still alive. Rather, "the terrible vision of the dead son taking the father by the arm designates a beyond that makes itself heard in the dream." One wonders, Lacan remarks, if there is more of the Real in the vision than in the perceptual "reality of what is happening in the room next door"?[30]

In other words, in a dream one connects perceptions together in a way that refers to and threatens to expose (unveil) another "reality"—the Real that is associated with a traumatic event. As concerns the dreaming father, perhaps this Real is represented by the traumatic desire for immortality and consequent self-recrimination that are tied to the fear of unnatural causes (a sense of the uncanny, of the devil, in the event of a child predeceasing the parent) and the sense that the child would have survived had he been a proper father, an immortal believer, a match for the fever. Whatever it is, Lacan argues, he awakens in order to avoid having to confront the traumatic Real, attached like a cotton thread to the accusation in the sentence "*Father, can't you see I'm burning*?" To escape the abyssal encounter with the Real, the father awakens—to another reality. Thus, Lacan asks: "Is not the dream essentially, one might say, an act of homage to the missed reality—the reality that can no longer produce itself except by repeating itself endlessly, in some never attained awakening?"[31] In a remark echoed in the earlier citation from Derrida's "Autoimmunity" ("pronouncing mechanically a date, repeating it endlessly, as a kind of ritual incantation, a conjuring poem, a journalistic litany or rhetorical refrain that admits to not knowing what it's talking about"), Lacan adds that "it is only in the dream that this truly unique encounter can occur. Only a rite, an endlessly repeated act, can commemorate this not very memorable encounter—for no one can say what the death of a child is."[32]

The awakening that re-situates us in a constituted phenomenal reality, Lacan argues, offers evidence that we are not dreaming: "the awakening shows us the waking state of the subject's consciousness in the representation of what has happened—the unfortunate accident in reality, against which one can do no more than take steps!" In other words, the waking state of the subject's consciousness puts together or represents what actually happened according to the causality of the *automaton*, which one could just as well name "internal time consciousness." But how does one understand what is put together or represented in the dream, in "the terrible vision of the dead son taking the father by the arm" and in the voice that is heard to ask, "*Father can't you see I'm burning*?" As Lacan remarks: "This sentence is itself a fire-brand—of itself it brings fire where it falls—and one cannot see what is burning, for the flames blind us to the fact that the fire bears . . . on the real."[33] Again, note the echo where Derrida speaks of Freud's legacy in terms of an "archive fever." As already cited (in chapter 5), Derrida wonders what may have burned secretly, "without remains and without knowledge. With no possible response, be it spectral or not, short of or beyond a suppression, on the other edge of repression, originary or secondary, without a name, without the least symptom, and without even an ash."[34]

In more prosaic terms, the dream imagery (as the counterpart of conscious representation according to the causality of the *automaton*), puts together "what happened" (as "event," "trauma," "knot," "navel," or the Real) according to the causality of the *tuché*, as the cause of the repetition compulsion. What the unconscious puts together as a veil that covers/

uncovers an unspeakable, inconceivable happening, a missed encounter, is "essentially determined" by the *Vorstellungsrepräsentanz* (object *a*). Object *a* (the representative of a "representation") can be understood as that which gives "shape" to that toward which the death drive drives: namely, a hoped for immortality, which is itself already an aporetic, retrospectively constituted representation of the All as totality, infinity, or paradoxically open ended.[35] Object *a*, then, marks no worldly object but the loss of itself that the subject first experiences upon facing the dread of its necessary constitution as a lacking being whose paradoxical, possible/impossible task is to refind itself (its immortality). Immortality, then, as that toward which the drive drives, directs the unconscious synthesis by which individuals project into consciousness a representative (object *a*), invested with the supposed power to restore their immortality, and to which they return compulsively in an inventive repetition that can only ever be an "iteration." The generalized statement of insatiable desire, in other words, is that "I" should have been immortal.

Lacan concludes his analysis of the dream with the remark that "awakening works in two directions." If awakening re-situates us in a constituted phenomenal reality and offers evidence that we are not dreaming, it also carries out the task of separating us from and covering over the traumatic Real: in this case, it offers evidence that we are fantasizing. In this discussion, then, he points to the ambiguous status of phenomenal reality as escape, as delusional fantasy of coherence and interpretability.[36] Moreover, he adds, one would have to search for the Real beyond the dream imagery, "in what the dream had enveloped, hidden from us, behind the lack of representation of which there is only one representative." In other words, behind the dream imagery (which is nonrepresentational in the sense that it does not represent actual reality but stands as the projection of a desire for immortality), there lies the object *a*, representative of the drive and cause of desire. This desire for an "impossible" immortality ("impossible," in the sense of ineradicably aporetic), he claims, "is the real that governs our activities more than any other and it is psychoanalysis that designates it for us."

According to Lacan, then, one may find in the *tuché* (the kind of causality bound up with the Real, which suggests that the true motivation for our actions has to do with an unconscious desire for immortality) Freud's solution to the problem that Kierkegaard centers on repetition.[37] Freud's "solution" is an explanation of why self-constitution is, in its psychoanalytically preferred sense, a matter of Kierkegaard's new category of "repetition" (the kind that paradoxically re-finds the immortal self by reproducing it "forward," so to speak). The idea that self-constitution is always a matter of "repetition" (of re-finding the self) goes down to Freud's understanding of the origin of the self as essentially split from itself (its own immortality) due to the paradoxical *khôral* space/gap constituted by the "lamella." Notably, for Lacan (to adumbrate what is to come in later chapters), the kind of healthy analysand that psychoanalysis ultimately aims to engender is a subject who is capable of genuinely ethical action, which is inscribed in the paradox of repetition imposed by the phrase "become who you are."[38] Unlike a paranoid or hysterical subject, whose desired immortality is represented as the delusion of totality or infinity respectively, such a subject dreams of immortality in the form of a paradoxical open-endedness. But if this is the case, it is less that Kierkegaard poses a problem for which Freud offers a solution than of providing through psychoanalytic theory an enriching "translation" of Kierkegaard's solution.

Lacan's remarks here not only presuppose familiarity with Kierkegaard's *Repetition*, to which they respond, but they are also too condensed for the progression of an argument to be much more than conjecture.[39] Nevertheless, one may advisedly take the hint and turn to Kierkegaard's "essay in experimental psychology" for help. Naming him the "most acute of the questioners of the soul" before Freud, Lacan initiates his discussion by expressing admiration for the way in which Kierkegaard's essay "abolishes the mirages of love" by showing that "I" am the true object of my desire, or, in other words, that desire is essentially narcissistic.[40] Notably, in Lacanian discourse, "primordial narcissism" names the desire for immortality.[41] What Lacan has in mind here is the first point of crisis in a complex love affair narrated by Constantine (one of Kierkegaard's many pseudonyms).

Constantine tells of a young man who, having already provoked his interest due to both the promise of "a profound nature which possessed more than one register" and the seductive immaturity and pliability of youth, commands his serious attention when he announces that he has fallen in love.[42] As Constantine recounts: "He told me that he had already been in love for some time but had concealed it from me, now he had attained the goal of his desire, had declared his love and found it reciprocated." Again: "The young man of whom I speak was deeply and sincerely and beautifully and humbly in love. For a long while I have not been so delighted by anything as by looking at him. For it is often a dreary thing to be an observer."[43]

Yet, as Constantine astutely observes, the fact that the event of falling in love is traumatic for the young man is already manifest in his mood of unappeasable melancholic longing when apart from the beloved, as if she were already lost and he stood at the end of the relationship instead of at the beginning.[44] This mood, for him, prefigures an "awakening" to the truth that, he intimates, is inevitable for a thinking person: namely, that on "attaining the goal of his desire" he will find it to be spurious, for the loved worldly object merely represents a desire directed toward something more profoundly lost at birth: one's own immortal self. A profound loss of self, Constantine reflects, is inevitable from the moment of birth. Yet, he insists, there must be a living spirit in me that refuses this death and opens out to the future, to the chance of repetition by which I regain myself. In his words: "It must be true that one's life is over at the first instant, but there must be vitality enough to kill this death and transform it into life."[45] Constantine, however, mistakenly believes that the chance for repetition is intentionally made through strength of will, perseverance, and rational action. In his estimation, the young man's soul is too soft for this hardship. (Ultimately Kierkegaard argues that one is given the chance for such repetition, when all is lost, by virtue of the absurd—as a gift from God.)

The predicted "awakening" soon occurs and the young man admits to Constantine that "the young girl was not his love, she was the occasion of awakening the primitive poetic talent within him and making him a poet."[46] He recognizes "that he no longer had need of the rung of the ladder on which he had climbed" and that "in reality her existence or nonexistence was in a certain sense of no importance to him."[47] Paradoxically, the love that is directed toward her has revealed and blocked, awakened and diverted, his true narcissistic desire to regain himself. As his muse she is the "visible semblance" of his immortal poetic soul. As his beloved she threatens to divert his desire and imprison it in the mundane mortality of marriage, procreation, and domestic routine. (In the terms of the prevailing courtship conventions, Kierkegaard's poet has no honorable option but to marry the woman to whom he had declared his undying love.)

However, this leaves him in a double bind, for he can no more admit this to the girl than continue with the relationship.

> To construct a real relationship out of this misunderstanding was impossible for him, it would have meant to make her the victim of an eternal deception. To explain to her the mistake by letting her know that she was only the visible semblance, whereas his

thought, his soul, was seeking something else which he transferred figuratively to her—would mortify her so deeply that his pride revolted against it.[48]

Unwilling to be guilty of her unhappiness, then, he strives to keep up the pretence of loving her. But he knows that in committing his love to the worldly object, to the mere semblance, he destroys his chance to become what he is. Thus, simultaneously, "he cursed existence, his love and the darling girl" who was the obstacle that both revealed and barred his chance for repetition.[49]

One conclusion to be drawn from Kierkegaard's account is that love for any worldly object is always a deflection of desire. For Lacan, this would not necessarily amount to the criticism that worldly love imprisons the soul in inadequacy (as it might appear to be from Kierkegaard's account). On the contrary, as I shall show in chapter 11, which deals with ethical action, he insists upon the importance of this structure of deflection for the revised notion of sublimation (love sublimates the object) that plays a crucial part in ethical action. Yet, to return to the task of decoding, he observes that Kierkegaard's account does demonstrate how one may become a prisoner of love. Love's exultation of the other spuriously makes of it the source of all possible satisfactions. In so doing (unlike the poet, who was aware of his double bind), one unwittingly demands from the other a fullness of satisfaction that it cannot give, namely, what Lacan calls "narcissistic satisfaction." By loving her, I place a demand on her to complete me, or, that is, extinguish my desire. It is a false demand because in truth the other is not my missing complement; I am. The loved other is merely the façade that reveals and conceals this.

For Kierkegaard, the repetition through which the "true" self is re-found occurs when one is given the chance to rise above the deflecting desire for worldly others and to assume the true object of desire, namely, the self. In other words, repetition occurs when you are given the chance to "become who you are," or, in Lacan's terms, to "assume your desire." Clearly, when speaking of such repetition, both Kierkegaard and Freud are dealing with a form of repetition that is beyond the re-found object of everyday pragmatics. In Lacan's words, "Freud is not dealing with any repetition residing in the natural, no return of need, any more than is Kierkegaard. The return of need is directed towards consumption placed at the service of appetite. Repetition demands the new."[50]

This is an allusion to Kierkegaard's articulation of "the dialectic of repetition." Notably, Kierkegaard distinguishes his conception of repetition from a traditionally philosophical, recollective nostalgia that bows out of time from the beginning. As Caputo puts it: "For the Greeks eternity always already has been; it is a presence which we always already possess but with which we have lost contact. Eternity is a lost actuality. Thus the point of philosophical speculation is to ease oneself out of time, as one would back out of a dead end, to steal back into eternity."[51] In contrast, Kierkegaard insists, repetition leaps forward within time from what has been; each repetition is a renewal of what has been, without which, what has been will not have been. In his words: "The dialectic of repetition is easy; for what is repeated has been, otherwise it could not be repeated, but precisely the fact that it has been gives to repetition the character of novelty."[52]

But, as Lacan goes on to note, one must be careful not to misunderstand such "novelty" in terms of the power of variation. The demand for something new in one's activities, that is, novelty as variation, is not the same as the novelty intrinsic to repetition. In fact, concerning repetition, we are rather talking about the paradoxical novelty implied in the demand for the same again, for the very necessity of this demand shows up the true secret of repetition—"namely, the most radical diversity constituted by repetition in itself."[53] Referring to Freud's observation that children cannot "have their *pleasurable* experiences repeated often enough, and they are inexorable in their insistence that the repetition shall be an identical one,"[54] Lacan notes that children here are implicitly aware of the diversity intrinsic to repetition that threatens it:

> It can be seen in the child, in his first movement, at the moment when he is formed as a human being, manifesting himself as an insistence that the story should always be the same, that its recounted realization should be ritualized, that is to say, textually the same. This requirement of a distinct consistency in the details of its telling signifies that the realization of the signifier will never be able to be careful enough in its memorization to succeed in designating the primacy of the significance as such.[55]

This citation contains a tacit reference to what is revealed through Constantine's actions and reflections, namely that the requirement for constancy "in the telling" (in the Symbolic Order) tacitly acknowledges the impossibility of repetition in the Real yet insists upon its possibility as engineered from above in the ostensibly transcendent Symbolic Order. To resolve the internal conflicts of the tormented young poet, Constantine hatches a game plan, which promises to manipulate events according to a precisely engineered strategy, such that the poet, by acting the part of a faithless philanderer, escapes his love relationship in a way that preserves his poetic nature and the lady's honor.[56] This release, as Constantine notes, would carry the small cost to the poet of his own public reputation, but where it really counts, in his own eyes, he will have acted honorably. The young man, however, loses the nerve for this eminently rational scheme, balks at submitting to an unjust public charge of guilt, and simply absconds. In Constantine's estimation: "His soul lacked the elasticity of irony. He has not the strength to take irony's vow of silence, nor the power to keep it. . . . Only he who really is able to love is a man, and only he who is able to give his love whatsoever expression it may be is an artist."[57] But it is in contrast to Constantine's paranoiac "artistry" that the young poet is to discover the new category of repetition.

The poet's lack of nerve for engineering events such that he could be free for repetition unsettles Constantine enough that he undertakes a (parodic) experimental journey to see if repetition is indeed possible. He finds only the inexorability of flux, and he even returns home unexpectedly to face the terrorizing chaos of unauthorized spring cleaning. He is set to wondering whether one should rather be swept along in the stream of life as unconcerned by its events as a child in a pram. But he has not the nerve for such faith in the world, and his ultimate solution to its flux is a deathly imposition of constancy (in psychoanalytic terms, a repetition compulsion):

> A monotonous and uniform order was restored in my whole household economy. . . . For though I had convinced myself that no such thing as repetition exists, yet it is a sure truth that by firmness of purpose and by dulling one's talent for observation one can attain a uniformity which has a far more anesthetizing effect than the most capricious diversions, and which with time becomes stronger and stronger, like a formula of incantation.[58]

For Constantine, then, freedom for repetition is understood as achieved by the autonomous power of conscious will, reflection, thought, and signifying practices. It is articulated in terms of the power to extricate the self from the worldly flux of conflicts and paradoxes, maintain an ironic, reflective distance from pathological being, and control its manifestations by imposing on it a self-made order. To avoid the problem of stasis, one may institute, via the "rotation method" (the rational synthesis of repetition and variation), a controlled variation, a regulated movement. What Kierkegaard calls "repetition as shrewdness" treats worldly objects (people, passions, objects, situations) as game pieces to be manipulated in order to serve one's will, to fit into an order of one's own making. Yet,

Constantine reflects, "is it not true that the older one gets, the more deceptive life proves to be, that the shrewder one becomes and the more ways one learns to help oneself, the worse scrapes one gets into."[59] "Repetition as shrewdness" founders on self-contradiction: "by dulling one's talent for observation," one leaves phenomenal reality behind and achieves only the freedom of fantasy, which is no freedom at all. In psychoanalytic terms, the strongest repetition compulsion is no guarantee against the "return of the repressed."

To sum up so far, in relation to self-constitution, repetition refers to the task of forging an identity anew each time. But it is not a matter of producing this or that identity for myself and varying it when it suits the situation. As Lacan puts it: "To develop it [novelty] by varying the significations is therefore, it would seem, to elude it [novelty in the sense of repeating forward]."[60] Rather it is a matter of forging an identity that can persevere in time through constant renewal as the same. In Kierkegaard's words: "In the individual, then, repetition appears as a task for freedom, in which the question becomes that of saving one's personality from being volatized and, so to speak, a pawn to events."[61] Yet if the self is to be saved from being volatized by events, it does not suffice, as Kierkegaard argues through the figure of Constantine, to think of the self as in control of events. In other words, what one may glimpse again here is the function of the *tuché*—as a condition of possibility/impossibility, a causality—of a different order that underpins the paradoxical injunction to "become who you are."

Kierkegaard's new category of repetition becomes apparent in the contrast between Constantine and the young poet. As Kierkegaard insists, it is left to the young poet to move beyond Constantine (the quintessential contemplative reflector and aesthete) and in so doing discover the new category of repetition. Kierkegaard will make Constantine "step aside for the young man, who with his religious primitiveness is to discover repetition."[62] So what we see finally in *Repetition* is the transformation of the young man.

After he disappears, through letters to Constantine (with no return address), we find out that for him everything is lost—his love, his muse, the poetry—and he remains paralyzed and in torment. He has lost everything that he already is, or has been, or has already counted as his identity. The implication is that freedom to repeat yourself, the ability to become who you are, does not depend on what the other is to you or on what the other does intentionally. Nor does it depend on your own intentional acts. It will depend, as we shall see, on a gift. All that was left to the poet was the persevering insistence that he was not guilty. "What really attracted him to Job, however, was the fact that he was in the right. On this point now everything turns. Fate has played him a trick in letting him become guilty. If this is the way it stands, he can never more recapture himself."[63] Then he reads a notice in the paper of her marriage to another man. This is the unexpected thunderstorm that releases him for poetry and returns him to himself. The chance for freedom, paradoxically, is found to be not a matter of the imposition of will but a gift from God. Freedom to become who you are is, paradoxically, given to you as a gift—as a thunderstorm that you cannot predict and cannot make happen. Then I "receive myself again, and precisely in such a way that I must feel doubly the significance of it." In this case he "transfigures repetition as his own consciousness raised to the second power."[64] "Now freedom breaks forth in its highest form, in which it is defined in relation to itself."

In his revision of Freud's interpretation of his grandson's famous game of "*fort-da*," Lacan argues that it illustrates the origin of the structure of self-loss that underlies the repetition involved in the phrase "become who you are" or "assume your desire." As mentioned earlier, although Freud raises the question of whether the repetition of painful experiences challenges the primacy of the pleasure principle, he ultimately comes to the conclusion that one can read the game as conforming to the demands of the pleasure principle. For Freud, the cotton reel, among other possibilities, could be said to represent the absent mother. In this case, the child replays in a game the traumatic moment of her departure, gaining mastery over it by making her absence intentional: I have thrown you away. But this interpretation remains entirely in the domain of "the return of need" (the satisfaction of the need for mastery over objects and events).

Lacan thinks there is more to it than this. The child does not cry, nor does he look at the door. In relation to the grandson's game, Lacan argues, against Freud, that the game does indeed represent something that exceeds the pleasure principle: the game replays a traumatic event—a splitting in the subject and the inauguration of a death drive or repetition compulsion. The child repeats not in order to master the event but precisely because mastery is impossible. The cotton reel for him represents not the mother but the object cause of desire, which is the part of the subject that splits off from it forever upon the loss of the mother. It represents, in other words, the imaginary missing complement that is attached to the subject by the thread of desire—the desire for restitution—the desire to bring it back, to put ourselves back together. But each time the child retrieves the cotton reel, it becomes again only a cotton reel and not the sought after restitution that would complete the self, so the game is repeated endlessly.[65]

Ultimately, Lacan, like Kierkegaard, argues for the *tuché* as the "real" cause of the "true" self. These remain in scare quotes because the real cause of the self (the *tuché*) turns out to be no-thing—not nothing, but an inarticulable, traumatic event (the gift of God, in Kierkegaard's idiom)—and the "true" self turns out to be the lacking being or split subject, whose ethical task is (as Kierkegaard suggests) to "become who she is" in the recognition and assumption of her desire. If Lacanian psychoanalysis adds a caveat, it will be that such a task, as his version of the *fort-da* game indicates, is finally impossible (which, as Derrida would add, is no reason for abdicating).

To sum up, the contrast between *automaton* and *tuché*, as the contrast between two types of causality, is also viewed by Lacan in terms of the difference between law and cause.[66] The cause (unlike the law) is never present in the field of consciousness that it affects. But that does not mean that it is absent/nothing. Just as justice is never present in the field of law, for example, trauma is never present in the field of repetition. Phenomenal reality, constituted in and by what is law governed in our use of language, belongs to the economic domain of the possible. Here, the death of a child is only real insofar as I can account for it phenomenally: he had a fever, he died at four o'clock, and so on. The Real by contrast "appears" as failures, ruptures, and inconsistencies caused by the *tuché*. Here, the death of a child is only "real" insofar as it cannot be represented, for as soon as I economize it in phenomenal terms, it loses its status as "real" to fictional constructions. This, however, is not to say that the death of a child is absolutely unrepresentable. It is represented negatively as that which lies behind and hollows out all the attempts at representation.[67] In other words, while "impossible" and only negatively inscribed in the *automaton* as that which goes wrong, this Real is not nothing. In the aftermath of the fall of subjective idealism, then, one cannot resort to naïve realism but must instead insist that there is "not nothing."[68]

Although a discussion of Lacan's account of the impossible Real in "Tuché and Automaton" is already enough to demonstrate an accord between Lacan's notion of the Real and Derrida's thinking of *différance*, I shall graft onto this account another way of addressing the Real: through Copjec's account of Lacan's remarks concerning the lesson to be learned from set theory. Addressing what she calls "the problem of the All," this graft serves to demonstrate how Lacan addresses the aneconomic and economic aporias of nominalism and universalism and the "vel of alienation" according to which they are articulated.

The Real and Inventive Sublimation: The Lesson of Set Theory

Turning to the question of what is real, another consideration arises, hinted at in the last paragraph of "Tuché and Automaton," namely the problem of universals and particulars. In relation to this issue, according to Copjec, Lacan argues that there is something important to be learned from what set theory had to absorb when faced with Bertrand Russell's "notorious demonstration of our inability to move automatically from a particular concept to the existence of a numerable set, an all or whole."[69] Perhaps unaware of just what he would set in motion, Russell "proposed a concept (or predicate or condition) from which it was impossible to form a set. That concept was 'a set that does not include itself.' "[70] This is a perfectly ordinary concept that describes a perfectly common kind of set. For example, the set of all cats does not include itself, because it is a set, not a cat. The set of all things that are not cats would include itself. But one cannot form a set from the concept "sets that do not include themselves." Assuming that "Set A" aims to be the set of all sets that do not include themselves, the difficulty is this: If "Set A" includes itself, it cannot conform to its own definition and must not, therefore, include itself. But if "Set A" does not include itself, then it must include itself. This perfectly ordinary condition, then, is paradoxical, and the set that it conditions consequently becomes self-undermining, or autodeconstructing. Concerning what to make of this difficulty associated with the formation of sets (or wholes or universals), which is in fact the problem of how to understand the Real, there are certain (hopefully by now quite familiar) aneconomic, economic, and aporetic options. Notably, the following discussion represents a way of recasting the aporetic articulation of nominalism and essentialism addressed in chapter 1.

Nominalism and the Aneconomic Aporia

On the one hand, Copjec argues, Russell's demonstration could be taken in support of the nominalist claim that only particulars exist and that thought gets tangled up in paradoxes because it tries to introduce "universals" (categories, sets, or classes) that have no real existence. That is, it might be taken to demonstrate the impotence of abstract thinking, which "continually builds and unbuilds—while mistaking them for givens—series of arbitrary and alterable universals."[71] In different terms, one might use the paradoxes of set theory as support for the proposition that thought is never adequate to being because being consists only of predicates, and what thought thinks, namely an underlying more general "thing" behind the predicates that would support them and bind them together, does not exist.[72] Thus, for example, there is no "humankind as such" but only particular, unique, singular humans. Likewise, there is no "bare life" whose absolute sanctity remains incontrovertible but only particular individual lives. Any such universals or wholes, then, can be seen as subjectively constituted and vulnerable to collapse when it is seen that absolutely nothing underpins them.

Implicitly, here, if it were possible to strip away (or erase) all determinations of being, all predicates or particular concepts, nothing at all would be left. The idea of such erasure, in Copjec's words, "is intended precisely to foreground historical contingency, to demonstrate that the accretion of particular features by this or that subject, that the cumulate deposits of ego identifications, are the result of historical circumstances that could have been otherwise and that these particular features are therefore inessential. They could easily be stripped away, effaced, by subsequent or alternative circumstances."[73]

In this case, however, thought seems impotent: it cannot think the All of being because the All of being is an infinite number of particulars (atoms) that cannot be gathered together in a unity. Here, thought faces the impasse of an aporia. The condition that makes an All possible, namely that nothing be excluded from it, is precisely the condition that simultaneously makes it impossible, for the imperative not to exclude anything makes it impossible to think everything since, as Copjec puts it, "no all can form where inclusion knows no limit."[74]

Universalism and the Economic Aporia

On the other hand, Copjec argues, Russell's demonstration of the paradox in set theory might be taken in support of the essentialist claim that only universal structures exist and that thought gets tangled up in paradoxes because it tries to accord existence to particular, contingent, nominal unities (empirical concepts) that have no real existence. In other words, Russell's demonstration might be taken as a reminder of thought's impotence, exemplified in the assertion that being-as-such transcends every particular attempt to impose an appropriation on it.[75] This economic stance, in contrast to aneconomic nominalism, confirms the existence or ultimate presence of "being as such" or the "thing itself" (for example "humankind" as such), while granting that no predicate will be sufficiently large to grasp it properly.

On this account, the idea of erasure is understood differently. As Copjec puts it: "From politics to aesthetics, the negative gesture that helped define modernism—erasure—was able to wipe the slate clean, all the way down to the material support itself, pure, pristine, and generalizable: humanity itself; Being as such; a neutral, Cartesian grid."[76] In this case, as she notes, erasure does not erase all, leaving nothing at all, but would make one exception. In her words:

> Despite its self-presentation, erasure encounters its *limit* when it reaches the empty page or blank slate, not evidence that the process has been finally accomplished. As long as this empty support—an uninflected, neutral humanity; Being as One, as uniform—remains behind, we can be sure that something has survived untouched by the processes of historical contingency. The notion of a universal humanity stands outside and domesticates history, making the latter the agent of merely minor variations on its already decided script.[77]

Again, thought is assumed to be impotent; it cannot think the all of being because the all of being, while unitary, transcends any particular concept of it.[78] According to the logic of exclusion, thinking and being are separated in a way that puts being out of reach and makes of it a lost origin or a future ideal to strive for. In this case, the condition that makes an All (a whole) possible, namely the exclusion that constructs an ultimate limit (a *telos*, center, or ground), is precisely the condition that simultaneously makes it impossible, for any exclusion or limit simultaneously constitutes both an accredited inside and a prohibited outside, which means that in the moment it is constituted as a whole it is also constituted as something that lacks what is outside and is, therefore, not-All.

Inventive Sublimation

In each of the above cases it is assumed that thought is in some way impotent. We cannot think the All of being, in the first case because it amounts to an infinity of atoms that cannot be counted, and in the second, because it represents a totality that transcends any concept. In other words, in both cases "thought" and "being" (defined as pure absence or as pure presence) are viewed as external to one another. Notably, these two kinds of inability to say everything, or two kinds of dissatisfaction with the world, are not only both internally aporetic but are paradoxically related, or joined through Lacan's "vel of alienation." For the sake of historicity, nominalism denies what universalism desires, namely something "there" that resists erasure, but this denial is self-undermining, for utter abyssal groundlessness is just as inimical to historicity. On the other hand, for the sake of the repetition necessary for a "history of effects," universalism insists on precisely what nominalism denies. However, to name a preexisting totality as a guarantee of repetition is similarly inimical to the very notion of historicity. As always, it cannot be a matter of choosing between these opposing options. Following Lacan, Copjec prefers an alternative approach based on the argument that trauma both resists erasure *and* is the condition of history.

Lacan argues that the "hard kernel of the real" is, as Copjec puts it, "the indivisible and invincible remainder of the process of erasure," but what he has in mind here, as should have become clear through the previous discussion, is the Real as trauma. Here, the metaphor of a "hard kernel" is to be taken in the sense of it being the most resistant resistance—that which cannot be erased or subtracted away, that which always remains as a residue that cannot be circumvented precisely because what remains is paradoxically neither an absence nor a presence but an unassimilable "trauma," a "swarming void," an entangled "knot," or a "navel." For example, Copjec argues that when Freud, considering his own Jewish identity, tries a process of erasure by which he might have been expected to arrive at the clean slate of a neutral identity, "he discovers that something resists his efforts at erasure, something refuses to be wiped away—his Jewishness."[79] The event of "being Jewish," can be substituted with "being woman" or "being black," with "Rwanda" or "9/11," or with endless other "original/originary" events. What survives erasure survives not because it is some set of positive features but precisely because it is traumatic.[80]

Moreover, as Copjec notes: "It is precisely because it cannot be negated that we say it eternally returns or repeats."[81] Thus, to turn in a circle, the most resistant resistance, the "hard kernel" that puts a stop to analysis is also a seed, as disseminative as *différance*, as productive of new life. By virtue of a paradox by which the death drive, at its heart, produces the seeds of new life, it is the Real as trauma, the "event," which "guarantees that nothing escapes history."[82] Trauma is the condition of history because it sets the movement of "iterability" in motion.

On Lacan's account, Copjec adds, Russell's paradox exposes not confusions in the domain of impotent thought, placed in an external relation to being, but the power of thought in its constitutive relation to being. To think is not to introduce a split between "being" and a power external to "being" that reflects upon entities. Rather, thinking and being are mutually implicated, such that to think is to introduce an internal splitting that detotalizes being. By insisting upon such detotalization, Lacan does not deny the existence of universals. Rather, he insists that universals (Jewish, woman, black, Rwanda, sexual difference) are Real. These "universals," moreover, form an internal limit to thought: they have on the one hand a synthesizing function that universalizes by causing thought to revolve ceaselessly around "them" and not some other event. Remaining impossible they persistently draw thought into the attempt to appropriate, grasp, or make sense of them—to discuss, reason, argue, come to agreement, confirm, conform, etc.

A responsible appropriation of an event or thing, whether as a scientific, aesthetic, poetic, or any other phenomenon, may indeed grasp "what it is." But, on the other hand, the internal limit formed by the Real also has a detotalizing function, since it subtracts itself from thought. That is, it can never be assimilated to this or that thought, for the very grasp compounds its being such that it becomes what it is plus what is made of it. Its very appropriation by thought constitutes the particular phenomenon at a particular moment and in a particular context, and, paradoxically, increases it in a detotalizing gesture that has no knowable limits. Thought, in Derridean terms, gives both the present and compounds it by making of the present a gift. One might say that the phenomenon is "iterated" rather than repeated, and because this movement is limitless the object of reflection is sublimated.[83] Such detotalization only "happens" as a "parasitic" by-product or residue, when there is thought. The Real, then, also ruptures the Symbolic such that it is impossible for language to function literally. The failure of the signifier to specify precisely what it wants to say opens the space in the Symbolic for grasping that "what happens" exceeds sense—but not as a beyond posited before language, but as its product. Thought, then, is both separated from the Real and tied to it in an endless circulation. The concept becomes a veil that both reveals and conceals, captures and loses, the traumatic originary event, making it both repeatable and unrepeatable. This paradoxical iterability is what makes trauma the guarantee of historicity.[84]

These formulations of the Lacanian Real come so close to the formulations already offered of *différance* that one could without injustice argue for an accord between the two notions. In the chapter to follow, which addresses sexual difference as a nickname for *différance* and for the Lacanian Real, I hope to press this accord further, in so doing adding further, more detailed support for my contention that one may counter Derrida's prejudicial misreading of Lacanian discourse by demonstrating their interweaving.

8

Sexual Difference

Introductory Remarks: Mutual Misrecognition

In "Choreographies," Derrida formulates the question of sexual difference as follows: "Must one think 'difference' 'before' sexual difference or taking off 'from' it?"[1] This question immediately lends itself to two equally misconstrued answers, related to how one determines both "sexual difference" and "difference." On the one hand, Lacanians make the claim that one must think difference as taking off from sexual difference. However, this claim presupposes an understanding of "sexual difference" as Real (traumatic) and by no means, therefore, subject to a formal binary determination. As Žižek puts it: "if sexual difference may be said to be 'formal,' it is certainly a strange form—a form whose main result is precisely that it undermines every universal form which attempts to capture it. . . . Far from constraining the variety of sexual arrangements in advance, the Real of sexual difference is the traumatic cause which sets their contingent proliferation in motion."[2] If one does not recognize this complexity, it becomes easy to mistake the Lacanian claim concerning the priority of "sexual difference" over "difference" for an argument that all concrete variations of sexual life are "constrained" by an implicit, pseudo-transcendental, normative condition of binary sexual difference, or what Judith Butler calls "ideal gender dimorphism."[3] It is in consequence of this mistake, Žižek argues, that Butler imposes on Lacan the view that social life is "based in fictive and idealized kinship positions that presume the heterosexual family as constituting the defining social bond for all humans."[4] In other words, granted that because of their diversity "sexed bodies do not fit squarely within ideal gender dimorphism," sexual difference in Lacanian discourse is nevertheless said to serve as an ideal (a measure by which one may separate normal from perverted sexuality) that reality can never match.[5] The basic fault in Butler's account, then, according to Žižek, lies in an interpretation that attributes to Lacan a binary determination of "sexual difference" that he demonstrably does not adopt.[6]

On the other hand, on Žižek's reading, Derrida patently argues that one must think "difference" before "sexual difference," reading "difference" here as a neutral "freeplay" of sexual arrangements that is inevitably betrayed by determinate sexual difference. Žižek reads this as the illegitimate hypostatization of absolute difference, which is covertly the hypostatization of sameness. In his words,

> philosophers as different as Alain Badiou and Fredric Jameson have pointed out, regarding today's multiculturalist celebration of the diversity of lifestyles, how this thriving of differences relies on an underlying One, that is, on the radical obliteration of Difference, of the antagonistic gap. The same goes for the standard postmodern critique of sexual difference as a "binary opposition" to be deconstructed: "there are not only two sexes, but a multitude of sexes and sexual identities." In all of these cases, the moment we introduce "thriving multitude," what we effectively assert is the exact opposite: underlying all-pervasive Sameness.[7]

Žižek has good grounds for his objection to what he calls "the standard postmodern critique of sexual difference as a 'binary opposition' to be deconstructed." However, the path through Derrida's reading of Heidegger in "Geschlecht" conclusively demonstrates (thus, hopefully, justifying its tortuousness) that this standard postmodern critique does not suffice as a characterization of "Derrida's operation." Žižek, here, attributes to Derrida a determination of "difference" (as freeplay) that he demonstrably does not adopt. Rather, for Derrida, "difference" connotes the *différance* that one may say, mimicking Žižek, is the "traumatic cause" that sets in motion the contingent proliferation of different sexual arrangements. In short, what I hope to have demonstrated by the end of this chapter is that both Derrida and Lacan deconstruct the presupposition that there is primordially a determinate characterization of sexual difference (e.g., binary), for the sake of uncovering a more primordial kind of difference, allied with the traumatic Real, for which "sexual difference" and *différance* are synonymous nicknames.

This means, briefly, that sexual difference is never actually *present*, since it has no intrinsic character, sense, or meaning. But because it occurs, it is therefore not *not-present*, and for this reason, it repeats as that which cannot be erased. It occurs, then, as that which both calls for interpretation and resists (eludes, exceeds) all interpretations, so rupturing the order of interpretation that the call for reinterpretation never ceases.

Žižek sums it up neatly: "far from serving as an implicit symbolic norm that reality can never match, sexual difference as real/impossible means precisely that there is no such norm: sexual difference is that 'bed rock of impossibility' on account of which every 'formalization' of sexual difference fails."[8] Again, "we should be as precise as possible here with regard to the relationship between trauma as real and the domain of socio-symbolic historical practices: the Real is neither presocial nor a social effect. Rather, the point is that the Social itself is *constituted* by the exclusion of some traumatic Real. What is 'outside the Social' is not some positive *a priori* symbolic form/norm but merely its negative founding gesture itself."[9] Again, "sexual difference is not a firm set of 'static' symbolic oppositions and inclusions/exclusions (heterosexual multiplicity that regulates homosexuality and other 'perversions' to some secondary role) but the name of a deadlock, a trauma, an open question—something that *resists* every attempt at its symbolization. Every translation of sexual difference into a set of symbolic opposition(s) is doomed to fail, and it is this very 'impossibility' that opens up the terrain of the hegemonic struggle for what 'sexual difference' will mean."[10] Again, "the claim that the Real is inherent to the symbolic is strictly equivalent to the claim that 'there is no big Other': the Lacanian Real is that traumatic 'bone in the throat' that contaminates every ideality of the symbolic, rendering it contingent and inconsistent."[11]

Well, yes, yes exactly! One need only replace "sexual difference as real/impossible" in the first citation and in the others, "some traumatic Real," "a deadlock, a trauma, an open question," "the Lacanian Real," with *différance* (understood in its complexity, of course) or any number of its other nicknames, in order to have Žižek affirming precisely the Derridean conception of sexual difference that emerges from Derrida's reading of Heidegger's thinking on the topic proposed in his essay "Geschlecht."[12]

Derrida Reading Heidegger on *Geschlecht*: Outline

In "Geschlecht," Derrida argues that despite (or because of) a remarkable silence on the topic of sexual difference, that aspect of Heidegger's thinking named by "the ontological difference" opens a way for rethinking the question of fundamentals concerning sexuality. He demonstrates that the form of the question concerning sexual difference that opens this chapter is, as always, misleading, because the complex answer given by an interrogation of Heidegger's silence—which has to do with the sense in which "the ontological difference" marks the difference between two irreducibly (quasi-transcendentally) interrelated kinds of "sexual difference"—does not obey the either/or logic it presupposes. Notably, Derrida's primary aim in this avowedly preparatory text is to render the complexity and difficulty of Heidegger's thinking concerning sexuality so that he can commence a nonfacile critique of it, which will follow the slow, painstaking rhythm of a lengthy seminar.[13] Despite the introductory character of this reading, however, the direction that his critique will take is indicated adequately enough for my purpose in this chapter, which is to show that the position on sexual difference that emerges from his critique of Heidegger is compatible in structure with Lacan's treatment of this subject, despite the lexical or metaphorical diversity of their respective discourses.

Derrida anchors his reading to three points of troubling silence in Heidegger's text, or, that is, three points of "reduction," in each of which there turns out to be more at issue than first meets the eye. While it is somewhat violent and reductive on my part to do so, since Derrida's text retains a complex interconnectedness that exceeds this heuristic, I have accordingly isolated three main thematic moments in his argument, which follows a course of increasing problematization and difficulty. In outline (I elaborate below), his reading first predominantly thematizes the sense of "neutralization" in Heidegger's thinking. The outcome of this initial analysis is a demonstration that, for Heidegger, the operation of "neutralization" does not desexualize *Dasein*. Rather, neutralization of binary sexual difference at the ontic level reveals, as *Dasein*'s "naked trait," a "sexuality" defined as originary positivity.

Neutralization, accordingly, also makes explicit what is meant by "the ontological difference" thought of (in terms whose resonance with presence and positivity will soon be problematized) as the difference between beings and Being. Before moving on to address Derrida's analysis of the two related difficulties consequent upon Heidegger's conception of "originary positivity," I have taken the liberty of injecting Lacan's correlative articulation of "primordial" (originary) narcissism. A Lacanian spectral analysis of narcissism offers clarifying and enriching terms for articulating the "bare self-relation," or *Dasein*'s "naked trait," arrived at through neutralization, which adumbrates what Derrida will ultimately get to in his deconstruction of Heidegger's reduction of negativity.

In the second moment of his argument in "Geschlecht," Derrida demonstrates that it would be a mistake to think that Heidegger reads "originary positivity" as a matter of pure presence. Rather, taking up Heidegger's treatment of *Dasein*'s *ipseity* (the ontic and ontological meanings of being-a-self), he shows that there is what he calls an originary "disseminality" in *Dasein*, a "multiplication" that stands as the condition of the possibility of "multiplicity" at the ontic level. There are many points of connection here with Lacanian discourse, but I have given particular attention to the match between Heidegger's ontological difference (now read as the difference between two kinds of difference) and Žižek's account of the "zero-institution," where something like Heidegger's ontological difference operates in the Lacanian discourse on sexual difference. I add the qualification "something like" because I think that the Lacanian discourse is in sympathy with the Derridean critique and modification that emerges from Derrida's reading of Heidegger here. While the terms may be slightly different, Derrida makes the same point as Žižek (namely, that "sexual difference" signals difference as such, prior to signaling any determinate differences), for it becomes clear enough that "originary disseminality" can be read as a synonym for "originary sexuality."

The final section of Derrida's essay represents his deconstructive moment of critique. If he affirms Heidegger's stance to the extent that he resists determining positivity as pure presence, favoring instead a notion of "originary disseminality," he nevertheless resists Heidegger's simultaneous attempt to eradicate negativity from both ontic and ontological levels. By doing so, Derrida argues, Heidegger excludes a conception of aneconomic (hysterical) *Dasein*, which he in fact requires for an account of corruption. This engenders an irreconcilable tension that can only be negotiated by means of a logic other than that of *aletheia* or economic circular return. One may conclude by suggesting that the "other logic" hinted at here takes the form of the plural logic of the aporia, which aims to "formalize" the traumatic condition of an originary relation of paradox between economic (paranoid) and aneconomic (hysterical) *Dasein*. While I have separated the following exposition into three parts, I have nevertheless tried as far as possible not to stray from the order of Derrida's argument. I hope that a certain amount of repetition will be compensated for by the fact that this makes for easier reference to Derrida's text.

Neutralization and Narcissism

First Moment: Neutralization

To begin with, Derrida notes that "Heidegger apparently said nothing about sexuality by name in those places where the best educated and endowed 'modernity' would have fully expected it."[14] In the existential analytic of *Dasein* in *Being and Time*,[15] for example, it is true that one would be hard put to find even "the beginning of a discourse on desire and sexuality," and the same must be said of the deeper-level analyses of the sense of being.[16] Now, if "sexuality" does not appear to be, as Derrida puts it, the "guiding thread" for analyzing the existential and more fundamental ontological structures of *Dasein*, then the matter of Heidegger's silence seems settled. Heidegger allows himself to pass over sexual difference in silence simply because he construes it as a secondary, determinate, ontic predicate, which may properly be abandoned to the life sciences, whereas, by contrast, his own thinking is directed toward the more fundamentally ontological question of the meaning and truth of a *Dasein* prior to all ontic predicates, which would therefore be sexually neutral (that is, a *Dasein* "that would not be sexed").[17]

Trusting "Heidegger's manifest silence," one might find a number of grounds for objection, including, for example, the feminist point that a supposedly sexually neutral (nonsexual or desexualized) *Dasein* always ends up being covertly masculine.[18] But how prudent is it, Derrida asks, to trust Heidegger's silence? This cautionary note is sounded not in anticipation of finding some covert new Heideggerian text that would disturb the fact of this silence. Rather, readily admitting this fact, Derrida insists on the necessity of interrogating the places of silence in Heidegger's extant text. Chances are, he wagers, that Heidegger has in fact said quite a lot in the places where sex is not-said.[19]

In Derrida's assessment, the matter of *Dasein*'s sexuality in fact remains profoundly unsettled and must have been so even for Heidegger, since he apparently immediately felt compelled to explain himself in a course given in 1928 in Marburg, where the title of *Dasein* ("its sense as well as its name"), acquired by decree in *Being and Time*, is "more patiently qualified, explained, evaluated."[20] However, as Derrida points out, the nature of this elaboration is nothing if not curious. He underlines two statements whose juxtaposition attracts attention.[21] Here are the statements in question, as cited by him:

> For the being which constitutes the theme of this analytic, the title "man" (*Mensch*) has not been chosen, but the neutral title "*das Dasein.*"[22]

> That neutrality means *also* [my emphasis—J.D.] that *Dasein* is neither of the two sexes [*keines von beiden Geschlechtern ist*].[23]

Heidegger first of all determines *Dasein* as "neutral," in the sense that, as Derrida explains, having subtracted "every anthropological, ethical or metaphysical predetermination," its primary, "naked trait" is a bare self-relation, or self-awareness. According to Derrida:

> This relation to self is not a relation to an ego or to an individual, of course. Thus *Dasein* designates the being that "in a determined sense," is not "indifferent" to its own essence, or to whom its own Being is not indifferent. Neutrality, therefore, is first of all the neutralization of everything but the naked trait of this relation to self, of this interest for its own Being (in the widest sense of the word "interest"). The latter implies an interest or a precomprehensive opening up to the sense of Being and for the questions thus ordained.[24]

I have cited Derrida at some length here because this observation concerning *Dasein*'s "naked trait" immediately brings to mind the psychoanalytic notion of primary narcissism, and it is (*inter alia*) this link that supports the thesis of a match between Derridean and Lacanian discourses on sexual difference. In fact, to show that Lacanian discourse offers an illuminating elaboration of what Derrida calls "the naked trait of this relation to self" and describes in terms of *Dasein*'s primordial "interest for its own being," I shall take the liberty of interjecting a Lacanian "spectral analysis of narcissism" at the close of my exposition of the first moment of Derrida's reading. Moreover, I am convinced that the complexity of the Lacanian analysis here is ultimately confirmed by Derrida in "Geschlecht" at the point of his deconstructive critique of Heidegger in the third moment of his argument.

To return for now to the Marburg statements, what is remarkable enough in Heidegger's words to elicit Derrida's attention has to do with the second statement, whereby neutrality is explicitly made a matter of *sexual* neutrality.[25] There are, as the grammatical place of the "also" in this statement suggests, many traits besides the sexual (e.g., race, age, nationality) that Heidegger could have listed as "examples of determinations to be left out of the analytic of *Dasein.*" Why, then, does he not only begin with sexuality but never get to any other examples?[26] If, in other words, one would be justified in thinking that he attaches some privilege to sexuality, how is this privilege to be understood? Of course, one could simply say that it makes a certain grammatical common sense for sexuality to come to mind first in the terminological transition from "*Mensch*, indeed *Mann*, to *Dasein*," for one is here electing the neutral over and above the masculine.[27] But there is more to it than this, for as Derrida notes, "neutrality" also inscribes the notion of binarity: "If *Dasein* is neutral, and if it is not man (*Mensch*), the *first* consequence to draw from this is that it does not submit to that binary partition one most spontaneously thinks of in such a case, to wit 'sexual difference.' If 'being-there' does not mean 'man' (*Mensch*), *a fortiori* it designates neither 'man' nor 'woman.' "[28]

In this case, Heidegger's prioritization of sexuality as the first trait to be neutralized might simply reflect the view that *Dasein* insofar as it is first "concretized" is concretized in terms of binary sexual difference: man/woman.[29] "Heidegger doesn't doubt that there are two."[30] Here, Derrida gently begins to shift the terrain: if *Dasein* does not submit to a binary determination of sexual difference, then sexuality (as a binary opposition) is again placed firmly in the ontic domain. Having correctly seen that Heidegger's insistence on the asexuality of the ontological structures of *Dasein* has to do with the insight that the "discriminative belonging to one or another sex" inscribes a negativity (understood in the Hegelian sense of mutual negation associated with dialectical opposites), it still seems plausible at this point (although Derrida will soon show why this is misguided) to argue that the Heideggerian discourse, defining sexuality as *fundamentally* a binary opposition, disallows sexuality at the fundamental ontological level in favor of a "neutral" (read, nonsexual) *Dasein*.[31]

To uncover what is amiss in this argument, Derrida begins by noting that the asexuality of *Dasein* as neither "man" nor "woman" is so nearly common sense that it hardly seems to justify the privileged attention Heidegger accords it here. After all, he had nothing to say of it in *Being and Time*, and, in fact, once he has made the point that "*Dasein* is reducible neither to human-being, nor to the ego, nor to consciousness, nor to the unconscious, nor to the subject, nor to the individual, nor even to an *animal rationale*," it is difficult not to think that the question of sexual difference is so obviously secondary to those of the sense of being and of the ontological difference "that even its dismissal did not deserve privileged treatment."[32]

Yet, as we have seen, precisely the opposite happens: having proposed the neutrality of *Dasein,* Heidegger's attention is first focused on emphasizing its sexual neutrality or asexuality. Shouldn't this precautionary overemphasis, Derrida asks, raise our suspicion that reducing sexuality to the ontic realm, for Heidegger, is not a matter of course, for there is more at stake here than first meets the eye? For Derrida, the answer is affirmative: if binary sexual difference clearly does not belong to the ontological structures of *Dasein,* yet Heidegger apparently takes a little too much trouble to reduce sexuality to the ontic level, then "the difficulties are going to begin to accumulate."

It is true, he argues, that in common parlance the terms "neutrality" and "asexuality" imply a certain negativity: besides the negativity of the "neither/nor" (neither male nor female), there is also the stronger negativity of the "not" (not sexual). Yet, if one reads Heidegger's text seriously, one comes to see that such negativity "manifestly runs counter to what Heidegger . . . wishes to mark out" in his use of these terms. In fact, albeit counterintuitively, it is by means of these negativities that one "must be able to read what Heidegger does not hesitate to call a 'positivity' (*Positivität*), a richness, and even, in a heavily charged code, a power (*Mächtigkeit*)." In other words, where sexuality is "neutralized" by Heidegger, it will indeed have been a matter of negating binary sexual difference at the ontological level and reducing it to the ontic level (as is commonly suspected). However, *Dasein*'s "sexuality" as such is not thereby negated. What is annulled, instead, through neutralization, is only its binary (dual) determination, and this, in turn, has the effect of liberating a "positivity" in *Dasein*. This pre-dual sexuality, which, notably, is not thereby rendered "unitary, homogeneous or undifferentiated," becomes "the positive and powerful source of every sexuality."[33]

At this point, Derrida outlines in schematic form the movement of the argument he will elaborate in the course of the essay. First, sexual difference as binary does not constitute a positivity that neutralization would annul. Rather, it is precisely sexual difference determined as binary that leads to negativity. This means, he adds, that "neutralization" has a double and contradictory sense: it "is *at once* the effect of this negativity and the effacement to which thought must subject it to allow an original positivity to become manifest."[34] On the one hand, one may take Derrida's claim that neutralization is the effect of the negativity for which binary sexual difference is responsible, to be an allusion to the feminist point, derived from Hegel, that binary sexual difference is self-annulling, for, paradoxically, the determination of sexual difference as a binary opposition surreptitiously erases sexual difference in favor of masculine privilege, disguised as a neutral subject.[35] He elaborates this argument in "Choreographies," where he remarks that "when sexual difference is determined by *opposition* in the dialectical sense . . . one appears to set off 'the war between the sexes'; but one precipitates the end with victory going to the masculine sex."[36] One can link together, he notes, "sexual difference thus determined (one out of two), negativity, and a certain 'impotence.' "[37] In Lacanian terms, this impotence is named by the lose/lose of the "mugger's choice."

However, on the other hand, Derrida continues, one must account for the loss, or impotence, which occurs with the division into two sexes, or, that is, for the fact that the binary does not exhaust the notion of sexuality. In other words, to argue that binary sexual difference is basic would mean that *Dasein* itself lacks in a double sense. It lacks internally because it is a priori divided by an either/or, which, moreover, covers all that is possible. Thus, it also lacks an excess or outside, for such a choice between mutually contradictory opposites assumes a closed totality. In this case, it is impossible to account for more than two sexual styles. The fact that there are more than two sexual styles, then, would then have to be explained away as perversions or accounted for by a different logic. To support a different logic, one requires the notion of an "originary positivity" (or in the later Derridean and Lacanian modifications respectively, "originary dissemination" or "a-sexual libido"), which is prior to (or in excess of) the binary division of masculine and feminine libido.

Heidegger accounts for what exceeds the binary opposition by means of another sense of "neutralization," associated with the "ontological difference." Briefly, his conception of the "ontological difference" names the difference between beings, taken in noun form, as concretized, embodied or phenomenal, and the be-ing, taken in verb form, that underlies them. It also inscribes the necessity that what is named by the term be-ing is "forgotten" (suspended) in the constitution of beings. The very fact that there are phenomenal beings, then, is a sign of the suspension of be-ing; or, in other words, such determinate phenomena bear the trace of this suspension and consequently remain congenitally not-All or lacking (to import useful terms from Lacanian discourse).[38]

Accordingly, "neutralization" becomes the effacement to which thought must subject the not-All, or negativity, brought about by a binary determination of sexual difference, in order to recover originary positivity and power.[39] Derrida adds that it is not, therefore, as if there is either binary sexual difference or asexual neutrality, the two standing opposed. Rather, they are on the same side in the sense that asexual neutrality becomes the condition/power whose erasure/effacement/forgetting first makes the sexual binary possible. Thus asexual *Dasein* both calls for and exceeds phenomenal beings divided by the either/or of sexual difference. Derrida emphasizes that the order of implication here is important: originary positivity, at the ontological level, is the condition of the possibility of ontic difference rather than *vice versa*. This is important because it allows one to question the necessity of determining sexual difference as dual. If sexuality can be understood as not-yet sealed by a two at some point, can it be understood as no-longer sealed by a two? One should tread carefully here, for Derrida indeed argues that it is necessary to start thinking of an ontological sexuality that is no longer two, but not, as is often thought, through the thematics of unregulated dispersal, but via the "plural logic of the aporia."

When Heidegger goes on to develop the motifs of "neutrality, positivity, originary power, the originary itself," Derrida continues, he does so without direct reference to sexual difference.[40] Perhaps his aim is to preempt the kind of easy misunderstanding that would persist in interpreting *Geschlecht* one-sidedly only in terms of the ontic system of binary sexual difference. Nevertheless, Derrida insists on two important points. First, he notes that Heidegger's elaboration of the notion of neutralization prepares the ground for the more complex and nuanced understanding of the relations between binary sexual difference and sexuality (*Geschlecht* and *Geschlechtlichkeit*) that he aims to draw out of Heidegger's text in an examination of "dissemination" and related notions. In other words, here he makes the argument that Heidegger's conception of the "ontological difference" names not only the difference between beings and be-ing but also the difference between two kinds of difference. In this case, it is the kind of difference named by the term be-ing (*Dasein* in its ontological temporalization) that is "forgotten" (suspended) in the constitution of the determinate systems of differences or ontic manifold to which beings belong. Correspondingly, then, Heidegger treats sexuality in terms of two kinds of difference: as a kind of "originary dissemination" that underlies determinate (here, binary) sexual difference. The fact that these two forms of difference are not contradictory opposites subject to an either/or logic but are on the same side, subject rather to a quasi-transcendental logic of implication, makes it equally impossible to reduce sexuality to the ontic level and to posit it as an ontological category. Second, he emphasizes Heidegger's insistence that "neutralization" has a sense that should not be understood as negative but as the means to return to " 'the power of origin' which bears within itself the internal possibility of humanity in its concrete factuality." The problematics associated with negativity will be thematized explicitly in the final stage of his argument.

Derrida concludes this first stage of his analysis with the remark that for Heidegger, "*Dasein* only exists in its factual concretion, to be sure, but this very existence has its originary source [*Urquell*] and its internal possibility in *Dasein* as neutral."[41] The analytic of *Dasein*, then, should not be confused with a discourse on sexuality that remains at the level of factual concretion. As Derrida puts it, "a discourse on sexuality of this order (wisdom, knowledge, metaphysics, philosophy of life or of existence) falls short of every requirement of an analytic of *Dasein* in its very neutrality." He then poses an interesting question: "Has a discourse on sexuality ever come forward that did not belong to any of these registers?"[42] Heidegger, albeit implicitly, came close to fashioning such a discourse. But it seems to me that his thinking requires the Derridean modification to come in order for the answer to be affirmative. Moreover, as a Lacanian "spectral analysis" of narcissism should go some way to showing, the Lacanian discourse is an obvious candidate for an affirmative answer.

A Lacanian "Spectral Analysis" of "Narcissism"

It is easy enough to associate *Dasein*'s primordial "interest for its own being" with the psychoanalytic notion of narcissism and, through its determination as self-love, with libido. *Dasein*'s "naked trait," translated into psychoanalytic terms, would be narcissistic libido. But, as Derrida notes, "this relation to self is not a relation to an ego." This statement is clearly incompatible with the traditional Freudian notion of narcissistic libido, and to make the match one must take account of the Lacanian revision, whereby narcissism is submitted to a similar kind of "spectral analysis" as that to which Žižek submits the notion of the Other in "The Real of Sexual Difference" (as discussed in chapter 3).

For Freud, as previously noted, narcissism in the subject first emerges in tandem with the construction of an ideal ego, defined as love for the ego as a whole. The construction of a loved ideal ego occurs through the process of sublimation, here defined as the deflection of libido from the external *Nebenmensch* toward its internalized reflection, resulting in a primary narcissism expressed as childhood megalomania. In Lacanian terms, however, such ego-love, which is associated with the metaphor of the mirror image, is not the most primordial kind of narcissism. Instead, childhood megalomania belongs to the Imaginary Order. Freud goes on to develop the notion of narcissism along with the shift from ideal ego to superego. In this shift, narcissism is rearticulated: it no longer characterizes my love for what I think I am but for my conception of what I ought to be. Narcissism, then, is here associated with a rearticulation of sublimation that takes it as a process of idealization and relates it inversely to altruism. This dimension of narcissism (or superego-love), in Lacanian terms, belongs to the Symbolic Order.

If Freud calls childhood megalomania a "primary" form of narcissism in relation to superego-love and implies thereby that the self-relation begins as self-awareness, Lacan argues, to the contrary, that there is another, even more primary narcissism at the unconscious level of the traumatic Real, for which the term "soul-love" (borrowed from *Seminar XX*) is a sufficiently appropriate name.[43] It is this dimension of "primordial" narcissism that brings Lacan's account in line with *Dasein*'s "naked trait." Generally speaking, soul-love may be understood as a synonym for libido (defined, in its widest sense, as the expression of drive as such), which is the correlative of lack (or the originary finitude to which belongs a sense of expropriation).[44] For Lacan, further, there is no drive other than the death drive, that is, the drive toward a complete satisfaction that perpetually is not-yet. Soul-love, or primordial narcissism, names the love I experience for the retrospectively constructed illusion of my own being as One, or as "the All." My so construed "ownmost" being, toward which the death drive drives, is (and intrinsically remains) in excess of what I am.

One could also call soul-love my love for my own sublimity. As Lacan puts it: "Analysis demonstrates that love, in its essence, is narcissistic . . . it is but the desire to be One."[45] Notably, then, "sublimation" becomes something other than deflection of libido from its investment in sexual relations with others, to the narcissistic interest in self-improvement (measured in terms of the superego ideal). Instead, one may subject "primordial narcissism" (soul-love) to its own further spectral analysis, which reveals (always retroactively or *nachträglich*) that it is determined in terms that match any of three libidinal styles. For Lacan (like Heidegger, on Derrida's reading), primordial narcissism may be also be named "a-sexual libido." A-sexual libido, as Fink is quick to point out, does not mean desexualized libido (this would be a contradiction in terms).[46] Fink remarks upon a possible, and useful, distinction between the terms "a-sexual" and "asexual," which is elaborated by Paul Verhaeghe through a distinction between phallic sexuality and "the other jouissance."[47] "A-sexual" here does not mean "asexual" (not sexual or sexually neutral) but implies a sexuality (a libidinal interest, "the other jouissance") that is "not-phallic, hence, not signified by the symbolic" (or, one could say, a libidinal interest that is not yet subject to symbolic determinations, which predominantly take the idealized form of neat binary oppositions). Suzanne Barnard agrees that such a-sexual libido is the "nonsymbolized libido that both masculine and feminine subjects lose with the advent of sexual being." She describes such libido as "libido not yet marked by castration or the cut of sexual difference."[48] We are always already "sexed beings" in the sense that we are beings with libidinal interest, or, that is, beings defined in terms of our original separation from, and therefore primordial interest in, jouissance.

Primordial sexedness does not suggest that sexuality is necessarily originally divided into masculine and feminine. It implies only a generalized, nondual, libidinal interest in the restoration of the self as the All it supposedly once was, via a hypothesized path of return to the originary or an anticipated restitution of the All in the future. In other terms, primordial narcissism names the libidinal interest in the "other jouissance" or that which, beyond phallic sexual pleasure, lies in the impossible domain of totality, infinity, or paradox, before it is retroactively (*nachträglich*) cast in terms of any determinate division between masculine and feminine. In Lacan's words: "As for being . . . a being that would be posited as absolute, it is never anything but the fracture, break, or interruption of the formulation 'sexed being,' insofar as sexed being is involved [*intéressé*] in jouissance."[49] For Lacan, then, "a-sexual libido" names the soul's death drive: its all-consuming interest in restoring its "ownmost" sublimity, believed to be more primordial than, and prior to, its "ontic" determination as this or that being. Primordial narcissism, accordingly, is libido directed toward a supposedly "primordial" past that was, in fact, never present, since it represents either of two retrospectively constructed illusions of "wholeness" (totality or infinity) or the "true," traumatic state of paradox.

Thus, when "the sublime in me" (the All toward which the drive drives) is understood as an ideal, soul-love is retroactively determined according to two possible illusions: that of the All as a totality and that of the All as an infinity. When "the sublime in me" is recognized as the traumatic kernel of the Real, soul-love is retroactively determined according to the All as *différance* or the paradoxical "truth" that is no longer Truth. It is only when subjects develop the tendency to rely upon characteristic libidinal styles that one can retroactively determine the character of their "primordial narcissism." In those who tend to experience boundaries as marking out the domain of security, beyond which they become anxious to the point of breakdown, one may detect an economic, paranoid libidinal style, derived from the retroactively constituted illusion that the All of their desire (that is, the past that was never present) was the closed circle of an all-encompassing unity. By contrast, in those who tend to experience boundaries as restrictive limitations to be resisted at all costs, even blindly, simply because they are there, one may detect an aneconomic, hysterical libidinal style, derived from the retroactively constituted illusion that the All toward which they strive was the infinite flow of an oceanic Nirvana. In those who are able to experience boundaries as "permeable" (everything simultaneously has its natural and imposed limits and remains potentially open to chance events), one may detect the paradoxical libidinal style, derived from the power to face the truth that the All toward which they strive remains a traumatic kernel. Self-knowledge is retroactive: on the basis of what is given in experience, one may say that the All must have been accorded the value of totality (economic interpretation), infinity (aneconomic interpretation), or its paradoxical modification.

On the basis of such a "spectral analysis" it becomes much clearer how Lacanian discourse can accord with the "plural logic of the aporia," which, as I hope to show, Derrida introduces into Heidegger's thinking on sexual difference by way of critique. To my mind, the proposition of correlating a Heideggerian/Derridean discourse on sexuality (granting the Derridean modification still to be addressed) with an equivalent Lacanian discourse has begun to look substantially more plausible than it might have done at the start of this explication. The plausibility of this connection increases as one progresses further along the path of Derrida's reading. To trace out how this is so one must return patiently to "Geschlecht" and to Heidegger's qualification of *Dasein*'s "originary positivity," which makes of it, in fact, an "originary disseminality."

Dissemination and the "Zero Institution"

Second Moment: Dissemination

Introducing a new stage in his argument, Derrida turns to a second place of silence in Heidegger's text, this time in *Vom Wesen des Grundes*, where Heidegger further develops the argument concerning "neutralization" as the reduction of *Dasein* to the bare self-relation. As Derrida puts it, "it is a matter of determining the ipseity of *Dasein*, its *Selbstheit* or being-a-self."[50] What Heidegger has in mind in this text is "an ipseity *starting from which* certain differences become manifest, for example, those between "egoism" and "altruism," or "between 'being-I' and 'being-you' (*Ichsein/Dusein*)." Neutral with respect to these determinations, *Dasein* is neutral, Heidegger adds, "with all the more reason with regard to 'sexuality.'" Here, again, Derrida notes, where sexuality is named to be silenced, the logic of the a fortiori operation imposes itself: neutrality is insisted upon, and *with all the more reason* with regard to binary sexual difference. Again, he asks, "why insist? Where is the risk of misunderstanding? Unless the matter is not at all obvious, and there is still a risk of mixing up once more the question of sexual difference with that of Being and the ontological difference."[51]

This a fortiori operation, as Derrida notes, implies presuppositions concerning sexuality similar to those outlined in relation to the Marburg statements. First, sexuality is assumed to be merely "the assured predicate of whatever is made possible by or beginning with ipseity." Second, Heidegger implies that sexuality does not belong to the neutral power of asexuality, which characterizes the structure of an ipseity that is not as yet determined as "human being, me or you, conscious or unconscious subject, man or woman." In short, one again might mistakenly assume that Heidegger clearly reduces sexuality to the ontic level and insists that one must above all "protect the analytic of *Dasein* from the risks of anthropology, of psychoanalysis, even of biology" (i.e., from discourses that might insist on the fundamentality of binary sexuality). Again, on Derrida's reading,

> if Heidegger insists and underlines ("with all the more reason"), it is because a suspicion has not yet been banished: What if "sexuality" already marked the most originary *Selbstheit*? If it were an ontological structure of ipseity? If the Da of *Dasein* were already "sexual"? What if sexual difference were already marked in the opening up to the question of the sense of Being and to the ontological difference? And what if neutralization, which does not happen all by itself were a violent operation?[52]

One should note that Derrida's text works rather like a palimpsest. In these questions, he opens the way to the new analysis that will thematize the link between "originary sexuality" and "dissemination." He also repeats the concerns of the previous analysis of "neutrality" and hints at the concerns of the analysis of "negativity" to come. In relation to the current analysis, his question concerns whether here again (as in the previous analysis) "there still may be a door open for other words, or another usage and another reading of the word "*Geschlecht*," if not the word 'sexuality.'" Tellingly, if one thinks of the Lacanian discourse of the "other sexuality" elaborated in *Seminar XX*, he adds: "Perhaps another 'sex,' or rather another '*Geschlecht*,' will come to be inscribed within ipseity."[53]

Here, the "other words" with which one may speak of the predual positivity and power returned to via neutralization in the previous analysis all belong to "the very subtle differentiation of a certain lexicon," which will bring with it translation problems that cannot be thought of as "secondary or accidental." In Derrida's words: "The lexical hive brings together (or swarms) the series 'dissociation,' 'distraction,' 'dissemination,' 'division,' 'dispersion.'" Like "neutrality," dissemination draws together opposing senses. The "dis" of this lexicon, already the figure of partitioning, also signals a partition within itself, for "dis" often has "a negative sense, yet sometimes also a neutral or nonnegative sense."[54]

To begin this new analysis, Derrida lays out in advance what is at issue. Most importantly, at this point, he aims to show that the positivity to which one returns via neutralization indicates something other than "pure presence." Further, the analysis here remains parallel to the previous one in which Derrida finds that for Heidegger, a predual, asexual positivity at the ontological level is the condition of the possibility of sexual difference at the ontic level. Here, according to Derrida, "*Dasein* in general hides, shelters in itself the internal possibility of a factual dispersion or dissemination . . . in its own body . . . and 'thereby in sexuality.' "[55] The order of implication remains crucial: "the dispersing multiplicity is not due to sexual difference; rather, the flesh draws *Dasein* into the dispersion and *in due course* into sexuality." Finally, "the dispersing multiplicity" at the ontological level should not be understood in the negative sense of a fall or accident. Here again, "it is not a *neither-nor*, but rather what is properly concrete in the origin, the 'not yet' of factual dissemination, of dissociation, of being-dissociated."[56]

Derrida points out that the words prefixed by *dis-* or *zer-* do indeed have a negative resonance that is difficult to eradicate. He will return to this difficulty, but for now, something else is at issue here: namely, another meaning of multiplicity, a "multiplication" that is "recognizable in the isolation and factual singularity of *Dasein*," which is neither a simple multiplicity or diversity nor "a grand original being whose simplicity was suddenly dispersed," but an originary manifold. For Heidegger, "it is rather a matter of elucidating the internal possibility of that multiplication for which *Dasein*'s own body represents an organizing factor."[57] In other words, for Heidegger it is a matter of elucidating the way in which being embodied is the place in which past, present, and future are gathered together. To put this in other terms, the being of *Dasein* in general is already characterized by an originary dissemination (temporal dispersion or disseminality) that is the condition of the possibility of dispersion (scattering, diffusion, dissipation, distraction) at the ontic level.

According to Derrida, Heidegger uses the word *Streuung* once for such "disseminality," and thereafter, the word is always *Zerstreuung*. In an adumbration of his critique of Heidegger's thinking, he notes that using the latter term,

> would add . . . a mark of determination and negation, had not Heidegger warned us just a moment before against the value of negativity. Yet, even if not totally legitimate, it is hard to avoid a certain contamination by negativity [or, that is, an aneconomic moment] indeed by ethico-religious associations that would link that dispersion to a fall or to a corruption of the pure originary possibility (*Streuung*), which appears thus to be affected by a supplementary turn. It will indeed be necessary to elucidate also the possibility or fatality of that contamination. We will return to this later.[58]

Returning to his exposition and interpretation of Heidegger's text, Derrida offers some examples of what Heidegger might mean by an originary dispersion or disseminality. Pointing out that we never primarily look at an isolated object but at a manifold of co-appearing beings, Heidegger argues that appearance is a manifold for us not because there is beforehand a plurality of objects: "actually it is the converse that takes place."[59] In other words, this multiplicity is made possible because, according to the Heideggerian version of Kant's productive imagination, *Dasein* is dispersed over the temporal modes of intuition, memory, and anticipation. It is also the case, Derrida argues, that *Dasein*'s relation to itself is so dispersed, in the sense that *Dasein* occurs as a temporal spacing, which, prior to the determination of measured time or space as *extensio*, "comes to extend or stretch out being-there, the *there* of Being, *between* birth and death."[60] *Dasein* is the suspension "between," the "intervallic tension" that gives birth and death their meaning. As Derrida puts it: "The link thus enter-tained, inter-twined . . . held or drawn in, over or through the distance between . . . birth and death, maintains itself *by* dispersion, dissociation, unbinding."

"The 'transcendental dispersion' (as Heidegger still names it) thus belongs to the essence of *Dasein* in its neutrality."[61] Stated in reverse, "transcendental dispersion" or originary dissemination is the condition of the possibility "of every dissociation and parceling out into factual existence." Further, "transcendental dispersion" itself is a matter of "thrownness," which, notably, becomes the precursor to *différance* and Lacan's traumatic Real. In Derrida's words: "There is no dissemination that does not suppose such a 'throw.' . . . Thrown 'before' all the modes of throwing that will later determine it: project, subject, object, abject, trajectory, dejection; throw that *Dasein* cannot make its own in a project, in the sense of *throwing itself* like a subject master of the throw."[62]

"The ontological difference," in sum, does not name the difference between beings and Being in any positive determination but in fact marks a fundamental distinction between different kinds of difference: (1) the specific, contingent systems of differences (often binary) that characterize beings at the ontic level and are derived from analyses offered by the various sciences of the "already present"; and (2) the temporal differentiation or dispersal of Being, at the underlying ontological level, or, that is, the fact that Being is essentially not-one but differentiated and dispersed over the three ec-stases of time and must therefore be taken not as the ultimate noun nor as a "thing" (here, the ultimate already present) but as a verb that in principle exceeds all determination. This temporal differentiation allows Heidegger to construe be-ing as the originary power of making-present. Heidegger's conception of be-ing, then, carries with it connotations of potency and creative force reminiscent of Nietzsche's "will to power."

Bearing in mind that "the disseminal throw of being-there" includes the fact that *Dasein* is always already *Mitsein* (being-with), it is "at this point," Derrida argues, "that the theme of sexual difference can reappear." As always, Heidegger specifies an order of implication: for him, you cannot explain being-with (the disseminal throw) starting from a being originally divided by sexual difference (or, that is, belonging to a genre), or as a consequence of "any generic organization or from the community of living beings as such."[63] In contrast to this, Heidegger insists that belonging to a genre, and the union of genres (sexual union or "love"), presupposes "the dissemination of *Dasein* as such, and thereby *Mitsein*." Yet again, the order of presupposition matters, for it shows that Heidegger's aim is by no means "to distance sexuality from every originary structure."[64] Rather, as Derrida points out, "neutralization, negativity, dispersion [and] distraction . . . are, if we follow Heidegger, indispensable motifs for posing the question of sexuality."[65] Moreover, this is so even though sexuality is not named in *Being and Time*, where these motifs are treated in a complex, differentiated fashion.

Žižek and the "Zero-Institution"

To conclude this section, I turn to Žižek's account of the way in which something like Heidegger's ontological difference, or, that is, the difference between two kinds of difference, operates in the Lacanian discourse on sexual difference.[66] Again, this account adumbrates what Derrida will get to by the end of "Geschlecht," namely that originary dissemination, for which another name might just as well be originary sexuality, or "lamella," cannot be understood in purely economic terms but must be understood as traumatic.

In answer to the question of how to understand sexual difference as "the name of a deadlock, a trauma, an open question," Žižek draws "an analogy to Claude Lévi-Strauss' notion of the 'zero-institution.'" Analyzing one of the Great Lakes tribes, Lévi-Strauss discovered that an individual's understanding of the ground plan of their village was determined by his or her attachment to one or the other of the two subgroups that divided the tribe. As Žižek explains it: "Both groups perceive the village as a circle. For one subgroup, however, there is within this circle another circle of central houses, so that we have two concentric circles, while for the other subgroup, the circle is split into two by a clear dividing line."[67] Žižek names the first subgroup, in which the village is seen as disposed symmetrically around the central temple, "conservative-corporatist," and the second, for obvious reasons, "revolutionary-antagonistic."[68] According to Žižek, Lévi-Strauss goes on to argue that "the very splitting into the two 'relative' perceptions implies a hidden reference to a constant."[69] This constant, Žižek adds, is not something objectively present "but rather a traumatic kernel, a fundamental antagonism the inhabitants of the village were unable to symbolize, account for, 'internalize,' or come to terms with: an imbalance in social relations that prevented the community from stabilizing in a harmonious whole."[70] Interestingly, then, as Žižek reminds one, "the 'real' here is not the actual arrangement [of houses in the village] but the traumatic core of the social antagonism that distorts the tribe members' view of the actual antagonism. The real is thus the disavowed *x* on account of which our vision of reality is anamorphically distorted."[71]

According to Žižek, "Lévi-Strauss makes a further crucial point here: since the two subgroups nonetheless form one and the same tribe, living in the same village, this identity has to be symbolically inscribed somehow." Such identity, is made possible

> through what Lévi-Strauss ingeniously calls the "zero-institution,"—a kind of institutional counterpart to "mana," the empty signifier with no determinate meaning, since it signifies only the presence of meaning as such, in opposition to its absence. This zero-institution has no positive, determinate function—its only function is the purely negative one of signaling the presence and actuality of social institution as such in opposition to its absence, that is, in opposition to presocial chaos.[72]

Like "the modern notion of the nation" (or, for that matter, the "we" of community echoed in the word "*Geschlecht*"), Žižek notes: "it is the reference to such a zero-institution that enables all members of the tribe to experience themselves as members of the same tribe."[73] "Is it necessary," he asks, "to add that things are exactly the same with respect to sexual difference?" As he elaborates: "What if sexual difference is ultimately a kind of zero-institution of the social split of humankind, the naturalized, minimal zero-difference, a split that, prior to signaling any determinate social difference, signals this difference as such? The struggle for hegemony would then, once again, be the struggle for how this zero-difference is overdetermined by other particular social differences."[74]

Third Moment: Heidegger's Reduction of the Negative

In the final part of his reading, Derrida explicitly takes up the theme of negativity that has already persistently haunted it. For Heidegger, he points out, neutralization is related to the notion of "privative interpretation," or subtraction, by way of which fundamental a priori structures are uncovered. According to Heidegger, for example, the mode of being of the living requires a privative interpretation, "since life is neither pure *Vorhandensein* nor a *Dasein*."[75] It is accessible only by a negative operation of subtraction: subtract away all, until what remains is nothing but life, which is neither this nor that. Yet, as Derrida notes, this whole analytic organization is problematic. In his words: "Heidegger never elaborated that ontology of life, but one can imagine all the difficulties it would have run into, since the 'neither . . . nor' that conditions it excludes or overflows the basic structural (categorial or existential) concepts of the whole existential analytic."[76] In other words, what Heidegger posits here is the notion of "some thing" (something along the lines of Lacan's traumatic Real) that can only be approached, like God, through the secular equivalent of a negative theology. Yet, at the same time, his thinking is organized around the attempt to subject "positive forms of knowledge to regional ontologies, and these to a fundamental ontology, which itself at that time was preliminarily opened up by the existential analytic of *Dasein*."[77] In short, Derrida detects a tension in Heidegger's thinking between negative and positive moments, or, that is, between a side that points in the direction of *différance* and a side that retains the character of any traditional metaphysics of presence.

Further, Derrida argues that precisely the same tension between negativity and positivity has asserted itself so far in what he has drawn out of Heidegger's text concerning sexuality and sexual difference. Heidegger's "way of privation" or neutralization involves the negation or subtraction of everything inessential until one is left with nothing but the bare or naked trait, which is neither this nor that. Notably, this is another way of saying that, through neutralization or subtraction, one arrives at a traumatic kernel. Thus, while one can never capture the naked trait in a positive determination, it is, nevertheless, not negative: it is instead an originary positivity, even if it is moreover not a unity but an originary dissemination.

"Why," Derrida asks, "do negative determinations impose themselves so often within this ontological characteristic"? "Not at all by 'chance,'" he insists. Why must one proceed by way of privation or subtraction? Heidegger, like Nietzsche, acknowledges the necessary forgetting of be-ing in order for beings to appear. The underlying be-ing as "presencing" (as a verb) must be "forgotten" or repressed for beings, understood as entities occurring in time (or what is present at an ontic level), to be at all. All beings, then, no matter what kind, are only constituted on the basis of forgetting be-ing; be-ing is necessarily occluded in beings. Further, for

Heidegger, again like Nietzsche, phenomena are "emptied out" (dissembled, disfigured, displaced, or covered-over) in the necessary "evil" of their communication across borders and generations. The negative effects of merely passing ideas along and taking them over without thinking must in turn be annulled and "the originality of the phenomena" recovered by negative statements whose true sense is supposedly "positive." But, as Derrida points out: "The negativity of the 'characteristic' [neither this nor that] is therefore not any more fortuitous than the necessity of alterations or dissemblances which it attempts in some manner methodically to correct"—that is, these dissemblances cannot be avoided, "like contingent faults, any more than one can reduce inauthenticity to a fault or a sin into which one should not have fallen."[78]

In other words, negativity is essential for Heidegger at both ontological and ontic levels. Curiously, however, Heidegger very seldom uses negativity to qualify the very thing that requires correction through subtraction or neutralization: as Derrida notes, "inauthenticity, displacement, and covering-over, are not of the order of negativity (the order of the false or of evil, of error, or of sin)." By the same token, he notes that "no negative signification is ontologically attached to the 'neuter' in general, particularly not to this transcendental dispersion . . . of *Dasein.*"[79] Supposedly, then, for Heidegger, without attaching a negative value to either one of these registers, one must only take note of the hierarchical order that characterizes their relation.

At this point, Derrida cautions that it becomes difficult for Heidegger to sustain this "reduction" of negativity. First: "In certain contexts, dispersion marks the most general structure of *Dasein.*" Then again: "yet elsewhere, dispersion and distraction . . . characterize the inauthentic ipseity of *Dasein*, that of *Man-selbst*, of that *One* which has been 'distinguished' from the authentic and proper . . . ipseity."[80] Moreover, pointing for instance to his analysis of Heidegger's attempts to situate Trakl (in *Geschlecht II*), he argues that Heidegger cannot avoid speaking of the "decomposition and the de-essentialization . . . that is to say also a certain corruption, of the figure of man."[81] Derrida's remarks concerning these difficulties serve the purpose of opening up a space for a conception of negativity and corruption (aneconomy) that is not reduced away to the economic positivities. This again adumbrates and hints at the direction of his ultimate critique of Heidegger.

Concluding Remarks: The Derridean Modification

To sum up, what one gains from Heidegger in answer to the question posed at the outset is a complex account of two different kinds of difference between which it is always a question of the "order of implications that Heidegger wants to preserve."[82] Does this answer enable us to construct a discourse on sexuality beyond the Hegelian motif of negation that depends on sexual difference as two? In answer to this, for Derrida, the first thing that Heidegger demonstrates is that sexuality is not a predicate but gains its sense from the general structures of *Dasein*. Indeed: "What would a 'sexual' discourse or a discourse 'on-sexuality' be that did not evoke farness . . . the inside and the outside, dispersion and proximity, the here and the there, birth and death, the between-birth-and-death, being-with and discourse?"[83] Second, Heidegger's insistence upon a specific order of implications

> opens up thinking to a sexual difference that would not yet be sexual duality, difference as dual. As we have already observed, what the course neutralized was less sexuality itself than the "generic" mark of sexual difference, belonging to one of two sexes. Hence, in leading back to dispersion and multiplication . . . may one not begin to think a sexual difference (without negativity, let us clarify) not sealed by a two? Not yet sealed or no longer sealed?[84]

Derrida acknowledges that there is no thinking of *différance* without accepting Heidegger's conception of the ontological difference: that is, the division between two kinds of difference, which may also be read as the division between "originary disseminality" and any determinate division at the ontic level. His persistently Nietzschean disagreement with Heidegger concerns Heidegger's tendency to tie both originary disseminality and factical dissemination up in the logic of an economic circle (via a reduction of negativity that one may also name the movement of *aletheia*). For Derrida, this move simply does not leave him the theoretical room at any level that he nevertheless requires for an account of corruption, or, as Derrida might put it, an aneconomic or "entropic" waste.

Even Plato (in the *Timaeus*) noticed a question of errance in human life or in the phenomenal world that cannot be explained away and must therefore be accounted for. Nothing is ever quite perfect, complete, economical, efficient, or predictable. Inevitably, of necessity, there is a "bastard cause," a chance event, that creeps in to surprise or upset the best possible economies. For Derrida, this opening to chance events, to the aleatory, is a relief, a good thing, for economy at its most efficient involves a profoundly dangerous aporia. This is not to say that one must refuse economy its chance—for aneconomy at its extreme is an equally dangerous aporia.

I should immediately add that Derrida does not follow Nietzsche all the way (at least as Nietzsche is often understood). It is not that the economic circle of *aletheia* is entirely erased in his thinking; it is just persistently and equally originally undermined by an ineradicable, aneconomic moment. In other words, the "originary" is not just dispersed over three ec-stases of time and tied together in an economic circle. There is always also an aneconomic moment of dispersion, or shattering, a kind of entropic dissipation or disassociation that opens up the space for the aleatory. Derrida, in short, replaces both Heidegger's circular economy and Nietzsche's aneconomic fictionalization with the aporetic oscillation between the two that he names *différance* and characterizes in terms of the "plural logic of the aporia." For Derrida, then, at the ontological level, *différance* occurs as both economic temporalization ("paranoid" deferral for the sake of a proper return) and aneconomic spacing (a "hysterical" obsession with the impossibility of any proper return). The aporia of the aporias reflects the impossibility of reducing away either of these two impossibilities and the necessity of negotiating their mutual contamination.

In the end, then, if Derrida dreams of a proliferation of sexualities (the binary and everything in-between), it is only because, like Lacan, he insists on a more fundamental traumatic *différance* (disseminality) whose repression stands as the condition of the possibility for such diversity. I shall close my reading of "Geschlecht" by citing the following remark, in which one cannot but hear the Lacanian echoes: "The withdrawal . . . of the dyad leads towards the other sexual difference."[85] One may formalize a way of thinking otherwise about "the other sexual difference" by means of three "styles" associated with the "plural logic of the aporia." In the chapter to follow, which acts as a precursor to the Lacanian equivalent that will be explicated in more detail in part 4, I shall take up Derrida's description (in *Spurs*) of the three "women" that both characterize and horrify Nietzsche.

9

Feminine Sexuality

Introductory Remarks: Patriarchy

Derrida's remark that the "withdrawal . . . of the dyad leads towards the other sexual difference" condenses his criticism of the binary determination of sexual difference not in the name of a hysterical proliferation of differences (which amounts to a covert promotion of sameness) but in the name of a *differance* that is the equivalent of Lacan's notion of the traumatic Real.[1] In what follows, I aim to establish the basis for linking this difference between two kinds of difference (binary difference and *differance*) to the Lacanian account of feminine sexuality, dealt with in part 4, by arguing that for Derrida too "the dyad" (or binary difference) to be withdrawn is an effect of what one could call a "masculine libidinal operation," whereas "the other sexual difference" is an effect of a "feminine libidinal operation." One might immediately suspect this sex-specific labeling, but, as I shall try to explain before turning to Derrida's reading of Nietzsche in *Spurs*, both Derrida and Lacan have good, subversive reasons for retaining this nomenclature.

For both thinkers, these libidinal operations must be understood as "structural" or noncontingent "universals." Insofar as these universals are Real, they are essentially not-yet either feminine or masculine. Instead, their contingently given, manifest character or meaning (for example, as specifically feminine or masculine operations) is an effect of the unconscious Symbolic Order (the "big Other") that underpins contemporary social life. Speaking in general terms, Lacan's Symbolic Order names the unspoken rules that tacitly govern any language game or discourse. As Žižek points out, these unspoken rules are, for example, responsible for all the "stereotypes and obligatory scenes" from whose invidious comfort one may find a degree of relief in non-Hollywood movies.[2] Such tacit rules tend to remain implicit, subtle, and unremarkable until something goes wrong, does not work out, or seems amiss. Indeed, their very existence (if not their precise character) is always clearer to "outsiders," particularly to those who, having transgressed them without knowing it, stand mystified by the behavior of associates.

The economic logic of the dyad, of binary thinking, may be explained as precisely an attempt to tie the unspoken rules of a discourse into a secure and determinate system by binding them all to a central *point de capiton* or "quilting point" (a desired "master signifier that guarantees the consistency of the big Other") and subsequently to defend its hegemony against both external forces and internal corruption.[3] According to Lacan, the "Phallus" is a generic term that covers all of the particular, contingent determinations of this quilting point. In Lacan's words, "it is the signifier intended to designate as a whole the effects of the signified, in that the signifier conditions them by its presence as a signifier."[4] It therefore has many nicknames—"center," "transcendental signified," "master signifier," to which we may now add "empty signifier" and "zero institution." In other words, it is a generic term for that which would give unity, consistency, sense, or truth to a discourse were it only achievable or accessible, which it is not.

Yet it is unconsciously accepted, as noted with Žižek in the previous chapter, that the rules of a discourse form a coherent or meaningful system, knotted together at a quilting point, even though nobody knows precisely how to determine it, and inevitably, when put to the test, the consequence is irresolvable conflict over what it really means.[5] "Phallic logic," accordingly, names the operation by which we attempt to secure the discourse by giving specific content to the empty signifier. Again, there are plenty of nicknames for this operation: one may call it, for example, the economic aporia, a paranoid libidinal style, a dream of totality, or "the logic of the Law and its constitutive exclusion." Importantly, as Žižek notes, Lacan emphasizes that the "quilting points" specified in phallic logic are contingently determined impositions, each of which is, as much as any other, only a relatively adequate appropriation of the Real and therefore in some sense a fabrication, fake, or necessary fiction, "an empty signifier without a signified," adopted for the sake of consistency and efficiency.[6] If this is so, each determinate quilting point essentially remains an enigma. In Žižek's words: "suffice it to recall how a community functions: the master signifier that guarantees the community's consistency is a signifier whose signified is an enigma for the members themselves—nobody really knows what it means, but each of them somehow presupposes that others know it, that it has to mean 'the real thing,' and so they use it all the time."[7]

As a consequence of this inability to put a finger on the precise character of the knot that ties together the rules of a discourse, one faces the dialectical trouble Lacan names the mugger's choice. Those who do insist on defining precisely what "the knot" is entangle themselves in the economic aporia, described in Lacanian terms as the aporia of "the Law and its constitutive exception." Paradoxically, as Žižek explains it, "every universal series involves the exclusion of an exception (all men have inalienable rights, with the exception of madmen, criminals, primitives, the uneducated, children, etc.)."[8] In an effort to avoid the aporia of "the Law and its constitutive exception," one might simply refuse to determine "the knot." Yet in the absence of any universal condition or predicate, for the series or set, all members of the set become exceptions. In this case, one becomes entangled in the aneconomic aporia; since each member of the set is unique, all generalizations are rejected as violations, making it utterly impossible to claim there are more or less suitable or responsible appropriations of the Real. This mugger's choice has already been encountered in chapter 7, articulated by Copjec as the problem of the All. Notably, as Žižek points out, "Lacan's point, of course, is that psychoanalysis should enable the subject to *break* with this safe reliance on the enigmatic master signifier," without, one should add, falling into hysterical nihilism.

Addressed more specifically in terms of sexual difference, phallic logic represents the effort to make sense of what in "truth" remains only a structural, antagonistic gap between libidinal styles marked by the empty signifier "sexual difference," by grouping certain traits under the banner of masculinity and insisting that the opposing traits are feminine.[9] The fact that "sexual difference" remains an empty signifier is supported by a lengthy history of shifting and conflicting interpretations tied to biological predispositions, genitalia, testosterone levels, reproductive function, prehistoric division of labor, religion, patriarchal power relations, various feminisms, and so on.

Patriarchy is by no means the only example of phallic logic, but it is, as Žižek puts it, the most efficient. According to patriarchal dictates, the "quilting point" is defined as the true law of masculine superiority, while the constitutive exception is, accordingly, feminine weakness. It is no secret, then, that in the condition of patriarchy, marked by "the logic of the

Law and its constitutive exception," the testosterone-induced traits that do indeed predominate in actual, biological men are taken to constitute an exclusive constellation of predicates that delimit the set of "real" men. According to this process of reductive definition, then, the set of "real" men excludes "real" woman as its binary opposite. As an effect of such binary thinking, all "real" women, accordingly, do not possess the specified masculine traits. Patriarchy relies on a clear-cut binary order, in whose name the insistent "grey areas" of ordinary factical existence become signs of freakish anomaly and corruption to be strongly resisted and ultimately eradicated in the "brave new world" of future binary purity. As the logic of clear-cut binary oppositions and hierarchical privilege, phallic logic also privileges itself above other logics (for example, the contaminated logic of paradox) as the path to a true account of the worldly state of affairs.

It is in the overlap between these two domains of privilege in a patriarchy that the link is forged between masculinity and phallic logic. I should again emphasize that this link is entirely contingent: "Masculinity," as contingently defined in a patriarchy, is contingently tied to phallic logic, which, again contingently, privileges the values of security, totality, system, order, reason, hierarchy, economy, universality, and so on, as the order of truth. Finally, subjects contingently born into a patriarchy enter a circle of reinforcement whereby actual biological men are encouraged to adopt phallic logic, since it offers them unearned supportive affirmation, whereas actual biological women are (as Freud noticed) better candidates for hysterical rebellion, since they are automatically excluded from the domain of privilege and are therefore more likely to remain skeptical concerning the truth value of phallic logic. In other words, one is more likely to be reflective, resentful, hostile, and critical toward a superego that devalues what one is not through choice but by birth.

Nevertheless, there is no necessity involved here, for noncontingent reasons. Despite a massive, global effort to establish and maintain its hegemony, this quilting point of masculine privilege (or, that is, the binary that establishes this privilege on the basis of the feminine exception) necessarily remains an enigmatic empty signifier. In consequence, as Žižek notes, the symbolic Law (paternal Name) is just one (the most efficient or established) in the series of imposed, relatively fictional systematizations, none of which ever reflect the "truth" of sexual difference, since the truth of sexual difference is that the term "in itself" has no precise meaning but remains traumatic.

Yet, and here is the double bind, one cannot do without meaning. While all such relatively fictional systematizations of sexual difference are not, of course, natural or true, they nevertheless have powerful and important actual effects in the world, and the actual or effective political struggles concerning sexual difference take place in this arena of fabricated meaning. Moreover, once established, meanings remain inertial. The difficulty concerning patriarchy, then, does not concern the claim that the meaning of sexual difference is fabricated. Phallic logic is always necessary in order to avoid the other extreme of hysterical dissolution. Thus, even if, as Nietzsche was quick to point out, many feminisms equally represent examples of phallic logic, and, as much as patriarchy, run the risk of paranoiac protectiveness (that is, ironically, they risk becoming masculine), one should not give up on them in favor of the kind of proliferation of difference that gives way to sameness. This, as noted earlier, due to the inertial dominance of patriarchy, inevitably turns out to favor masculinity in any case.

Feminism, then, cannot oppose patriarchal fabrication with either the hysterical shattering of all acts of fabrication or so-called feminist truth. Instead, its best option is to offer a more salutary fabrication. This, however, presupposes the prior work of shaking patriarchal subjects out of their lethargic tendency to forget that all meaning-giving is a matter of fabrication rather than truth and out of their paranoid attempts to assert the absolute dominance of what remains merely an imposition of value (even if patriarchy is no longer always inscribed in formal law and the situation is undoubtedly more fluid for some; conventional practices and values are tardy in catching up with the law). One way of proceeding is to untie the illegitimate associations, reductions, privileges, and evaluations underpinning the mutually reinforcing connection between phallic logic and patriarchy. Such deconstructive activity, as feminists such as Lacan and Derrida have demonstrated, arrives at the traumatic condition of the enigmatic Phallus, thereby opening patriarchal discourse up to something beyond the phallic dyad (or, that is, patriarchy's masculine/feminine binary). In other words, they aim to uncover another sexuality, which takes shape as a libidinal style that exceeds the binary altogether. If, in a condition of patriarchy, the phallic dyad is called masculine, this other sexuality could just as well be called feminine, but in this case it would not be a femininity defined in relation to the masculine as its binary opposite.

It is for political reasons, in sum, that both Derrida and Lacan consciously disrupt the inertial, patriarchal interpretations of sexual difference, not simply by reversing the binary (for example, retaining a traditionally masculine conception of the ethical domain and simply turning it over to the feminine), but rather by revaluing traditional values, including ethics, castration, truth, system, reason, and so on, according to another logic, a "feminine operation" that exceeds the mugger's choice between binaries.

In the chapters to follow, I shall lay out Lacan's account of the transcendental relation as an articulation, isomorphic with the plural logic of the aporia, of (1) the binary division, imposed by phallic logic, between masculine paranoia and feminine hysteria; and (2) the "other" feminine sexuality that exceeds it through embracing the logic of paradox. First, however, I propose to show in more detail that Derrida's thinking concerning feminine sexuality accords with Lacan's, by addressing Derrida's reading (in *Spurs*) of a rather unlikely figure: Nietzsche. Like Lacan, Derrida takes the risk of supposing that "woman" is the figure of paradox, that is, *différance*. He imposes this reading on Nietzsche with an ever so gentle inventive twist of interpretation whose "butterfly effect" yields a dramatic revaluation of values.

Derrida Reading Nietzsche: "Supposing Truth Is a Woman—What Then?"

> The power of moral prejudices has penetrated deeply into the most spiritual world, which would seem to be the coldest and most devoid of presuppositions, and has obviously operated in an injurious, inhibiting, blinding, and distorting manner. A proper physio-psychology has to contend with unconscious resistance in the heart of the investigator, it has "the heart" against it.[10]

In a philosophical milieu that could not abide contamination, Nietzsche's unconventional style of thinking, as noted in chapter 1, announced itself rebelliously as the midwife of a new breed of philosopher, whose time is still to come. The philosophical tradition, to recall his view, under the pressure of its "will to power," is subject to a dynamic of self-poisoning whose outcome is the dogmatist's fake "Truth," or, that is, any ideology driven by an imaginary power to determine fixed, universal values for supposedly oppositional terms (whole/part, self/other, good/evil, etc.), and on this basis lay fundamental grounds for science, morality, aesthetics, and so on. Nietzsche, by contrast, insists upon the necessity of overcoming this "will to power" and liberating thinking by recognizing and negotiating a complex logic of contamination that eschews any simplistic division of the world according to antithetical values (or, that is, resists a traditional faith in binary thinking). In short, his analysis of the inevitable dynamic of self-poisoning associated with "the will to power" and consequent insistence upon an overcoming that resists its ideological outcome through recognizing the "truth as untruth" inscribed in the "logic of contamination" demonstrates his understanding of "truth" as a complex, paradoxical notion.

If the aim of Nietzsche's "logic of contamination" is to free philosophical thinking from its conservative tendency toward restrictive categorization in terms of binary values, one might justifiably anticipate a complex and subtly nuanced analysis of reciprocal contamination concerning the concepts "truth" and "woman" in response to the question posed in the first words of the preface to *Beyond Good and Evil*: "Supposing truth is a woman—what then?" If truth is a woman, Nietzsche answers, then her lovers (the dogmatic philosophers) have been exceedingly clumsy in their efforts to win her, and, indeed, none has succeeded nor will succeed, since philosophical methods are inappropriately designed nets for this butterfly. In short, just as traditional men are characterized by their inability to understand "what woman wants," so traditional philosophy is constructed so as to ensure that philosophers will never understand the nature of the prize they seek, namely, Truth.

As this answer indicates, on Nietzsche's account the notion "truth" juxtaposes two versions of a paradoxical truth as untruth: (1) the philosopher's Truth, which is in actual fact an untruth born of a misunderstanding that imagines there is some Truth that can be discovered, captured, and pinned by the right method; and (2) the "un-truth" of the actual state of affairs, namely, a state of contamination (gradations, nuances, paradoxes, or aporias), which dogmatic philosophy is not designed to capture. To accept this un-truth is to recognize that ultimate Truth is a fantasy projected into the past or future to serve a dogmatic desire for metaphysical closure. In different senses, then, the notion "truth" is found to be contaminated at the core by its opposite, namely, "untruth."

On the basis of these two versions of the truth as untruth, Nietzsche may have drawn two radically different kinds of analogy between truth and women: one confirming sedimented, ideological values associated with "woman" and the other paving the way for their salutary ruin. This is precisely the proposition Derrida examines in addressing Nietzsche's rhetorical use of "woman" as an analogy for "truth" in *Spurs*. Without doubt, as Derrida acknowledges, there is a plurality of "women" in Nietzsche's texts: "There is no such thing as a woman, as a truth in itself of women in itself [i.e., 'woman does not exist']. That much, at least, Nietzsche has said. Not to mention the manifold topology of woman in his work, its horde of mothers, daughters, sisters, old maids, wives, governesses, prostitutes, virgins, grandmothers, big and little girls."[11] However, it is clear enough that the predominant, explicit move in *Beyond Good and*

Evil is to draw a single analogy between "truth" and "woman," which aims to condemn the philosopher's Truth by calling it feminized. This move, ironically, is a consequence of the very kind of ideological conditioning (here patriarchal) that his "free-thinking" resists in principle. Yet, even if Nietzsche became a little seasick when thinking of "women," Derrida insists that his logic of contamination is implicitly, perhaps unconsciously, already at work in his writings concerning "woman"—if one reads a little inventively.

Reading Nietzsche inventively, then, Derrida argues that in such notions as "woman" a plurality of senses is gathered into a matrix of interrelations, which form not a unified system or ordered plurality but multiple aporias and paradoxes. Granting a margin of errance, entropic loss without reserve, or nonmastery as the "essential limit" of any effort at codification—without this being reason enough to "choose sides with the heterogeneous or the parody (which would only reduce them once again)"—he risks proposing just such a matrix for reading Nietzsche's propositions concerning women.[12] In his words, "rather than examine here the large number of propositions which treat of the woman, it is instead their principle, which might be resumed in a finite number of typical and matrical propositions, that I shall attempt to formalize."[13] His main line of argument is that Nietzsche typically makes at least three kinds of aporetic proposition relating "truth" and "woman": the first links the traditional philosopher to the "castrated woman" he reviled; the second, the "masked artist" to the "castrating woman" he dreaded; and the third, the "free thinker" to the "affirming woman" he loved.[14] Derrida begins strategically by addressing the third proposition first, reading Nietzsche with a deliberately subversive twist that finds implicit in his text resources to undermine more obvious interpretations according to which Nietzsche condemns philosophy by calling it feminized. I shall deviate from the order of his argument here by first examining the analogy between "truth" and "woman" that Nietzsche explicitly draws in *Beyond Good and Evil.*

Truth and the "Castrated Woman" Nietzsche Reviled

Nietzsche's opening question is intended clearly enough as a provocation directed at the tradition of systematic philosophy proceeding from the inventive Platonic inauguration, the sting of which is supposed to inhere in the analogy between the philosopher's Truth and castrated/castrating "woman." Notably, for him, the philosopher's Truth was not always a "woman" but became feminine at a historical juncture, namely, when

Plato made philosophy a matter of objectivity and intersubjectivity. The present philosophical tradition, then, is the span of decadent feminization between an illustrious inaugural moment of free thinking—marked by the paraphrase of original/originary singularity, namely, "I Plato, am the truth"—and the promise of a future in which the courage for such singular "un-truth" has been restored to "man."[15] Nietzsche hopes that the future philosopher will have the courage to insist that "'My judgment is my judgment': no one else is easily entitled to it."[16]

His logic of contamination tempts one to assume that he must have understood such "un-truth" to be an interminably negotiable interplay between the singular insight named "my judgment" and its intersubjective confirmation, or, in Derrida's terms, the play of signature and countersignature, where "signature" stands proxy for "my" traumatizing power of invention and "countersignature" stands for the curtailing, binding, and conservative force of convention (as a necessary condition for the repeatability and communicability of an invention).[17] Yet, contrary to the promise of his logic, Nietzsche's disdain for "the other" is such that he finds it fitting to condemn the feminized philosopher's Truth further by calling it "intersubjective." In his words: "One must shed the bad taste of wanting to agree with many. 'Good' is no longer good when one's neighbor mouths it. And how should there be a 'common good'! The term contradicts itself: whatever can be common always has little value."[18] Again, "around every profound spirit a mask is growing continually, owing to the constantly false, namely *shallow*, interpretation of every word, every step, every sign of life he gives."[19] This inauspicious evaluation of the communal combines with a similarly unfavorable evaluation of "woman" as the despicable figure of castration in the rhetoric by which he condemns the fake Truth of the dogmatists and promotes instead the singular, masculine "un-truth" that belongs to the past and future.

For Nietzsche, ironically enough, what "castrates" Plato is the obscene fantasy of monumental penile hypertrophy. The feminizing castration effect occurs because Plato does not view philosophizing as a matter of singular self-fashioning through subjectively won insight but dreams of the ultimate philosophical Erection, or, psychoanalytically speaking, dreams of giving content to the Phallus, making it stand for a universal, ultimate, objective Truth that lasts an eternity.[20] But in this case, as Derrida puts it, "once this inaugural moment has given way to the second age, here where the becoming-female of the idea is the presence or presentation of truth, Plato can no more say 'I am truth.' For here the philosopher is no longer the truth. Severed from himself, he has been severed from truth."[21] Due to this "castration effect," he adds, "the idea withdraws, becomes transcendent, inaccessible, seductive. It beckons from afar. . . . Its veils float in the distance. The dream of death begins. It is woman."[22]

So begins, for Nietzsche, the "ancient, eternal story" of philosophy's will to power.[23] A philosophical idea emerges, in his words, as "an assumption, a hunch, indeed a kind of 'inspiration'—most often a desire of the heart that has been filtered and made abstract."[24] Yet it is mistaken for a Truth, not invented but discovered through cool, disinterested reason. Moreover, its universalization derives not from a will to truth but from an unconscious power lust. In his words: "I do not believe that a 'drive to knowledge' is the father of philosophy; but rather that another drive has, here as elsewhere, employed understanding (and misunderstanding) as a mere instrument."[25] Moreover, each such singular drive, he notes, "would like only too well to represent just *itself* as the ultimate purpose of existence and the legitimate *master* of all the other drives. For every drive wants to be master—and it attempts to philosophize in *that spirit*."[26] This power lust, again speaking psychoanalytically, in turn becomes a "death drive" toward the absolute stasis of eternal validity.

The castration effect is not limited to the singular individual who invented an idea and dreamed of its eternalization. Rather, universal Ideas act at a distance from everyone, and as noted, Nietzsche insists that the more universally they are confirmed, the less substantial they become. This "distance effect" of castration renders an Idea more beautiful or enchanting, perhaps, but all the more spectral. Thus cut off from a singularizing desire, the philosophical Idea in its maturity is rendered as passionless as a woman, as superficial, vacuous, and decadent. On Nietzsche's testimony in *Beyond Good and Evil*, behind the spectral veils of dissimulating finery, "woman" bustles with petty trivia: she is false, irrational, erratic, unfaithful, weak minded, superstitious, sentimental, animalistic, resistant to culture, swayed by emotional excess and fecund sexual urges, weak, soft, unfaithful, inconsistent, wily, cunning, sexually promiscuous, licentious, incontinent, decadent, claustrophobic, violent, unpredictable, vicious, nihilistic, frivolous, whimsical, heteronymous, swayed by love, particularistic, atavistic, uneducable, wild, and utterly incapable of free thinking.[27]

Worst of all, for Nietzsche, philosophy's adherents become as skeptical as aged women. In his words: "I am afraid that old women are more skeptical in their most secret heart of hearts than any man: they consider the superficiality of existence its essence, and all virtue and profundity is to them merely a veil over this 'truth,' a very welcome veil over a pudendum—in other words, a matter of decency and shame, and no more than that."[28] If philosophers, by analogy, have ever lifted the veils to see the abyssal flux that threatens the beautiful Idea, then, like women, they cannot act resolutely upon this "un-truth" but veil the lack with their magnificent imaginary erections. Nietzsche raises an eyebrow at how little is considered sufficient support for "such sublime and unconditional philosopher's edifices as the dogmatists have built so far."[29] Effete metaphysicians, then, knowing that their erections are soft inside, nevertheless go through the motions, lacking both passion and the imagination to will anything innovative. Skepticism, for Nietzsche, represents a "paralysis of the will": timidly abdicating all responsibility, skeptics "no longer know independence of decisions and the intrepid sense of pleasure in willing."[30]

Artistry and the "Castrating Woman" Nietzsche Dreaded

Taking the analogy with women further (for the beauty of a system or elegance of an argument is highly seductive), Nietzsche adds that woman castrates because she is castrated. As Derrida puts it: "In fact, what is emblazoned in the '*it becomes female* . . .' might be shown to be a 'she castrates (herself).' Castrated, she castrates and plays at her castration in the parenthetical epoch. She feigns her castration—which is at once suffered and inflicted."[31] This castration effect, in other words, works as follows: She is utterly skeptical about Truth. On Nietzsche's account, woman "does not *want* truth."[32] In fact, in answer to the question "what is truth to woman?" he claims, "from the beginning, nothing has been more alien, repugnant, and hostile to woman than truth—her great art is the lie, her highest concern is mere appearance and beauty." If "woman," as Derrida notes, is not the least interested in truth and does not believe in it, she is nevertheless canny enough to see that "man" needs Truth.[33] As Nietzsche continues: "Let us men confess it: we honor and love precisely *this* art and *this* instinct in woman—we who have a hard time and for our relief like to associate with beings under whose hands, eyes, and tender follies our seriousness, our gravity and profundity almost appear to us like folly." It is in her interest to fake the Truth. She uses her seductive arts of dissimulating adornment to confound the credulous men into believing in the illusion of their power to win her, to pin her down, and in so doing she secures her power over them (as Nietzsche warns, "she surely wants to inspire fear of herself"). By analogy, then, traditional philosophers, while skeptical in the innermost recesses of their hearts, still deceive, beguile, and seduce others with cunning promises of elevation and delight, so mastering their desires and cutting them off from the freedom of their own inventive powers.

But in a reverse action, "woman" also "castrates" herself. She is unequalled, Nietzsche claims, in the art of "seducing one's neighbor to a good opinion and afterwards believing piously in this opinion."[34] Analogously, philosophers, having mistakenly, if inevitably, configured the world to suit themselves, force this invention on themselves and others for so long that they can no longer remember the invented status of their own Ideas, and, coming in this way to believe in them, they succumb to ideological tyranny. In criticism of the Stoics, for example, Nietzsche argues: "For all your love of truth, you have forced yourselves so long, so persistently, so rigidly-hypnotically to see nature the wrong way, namely Stoically, that you are no longer able to see her differently."[35] In its feminized form, then, philosophy can only gauge its effect of truth through intersubjective confirmation, but the success with which it deceives others beguiles its adherents into self-deception. Like "women," philosophers become enchanted by the beauty of the disguise and aggressively paranoid about preserving the deception, growing poisonous in their aim to eradicate in others the very kind of inventive life that engendered their own power.[36] As Derrida sums it up, she castrates in order to master the master from a distance. In his words: "From afar she would master the master and with the same blow (in fact 'the same thing') that produced his desire, kill him."[37] Her artistry, therefore, aiming to deceive, manipulate, stunt, and control, lacks innovative power and stagnates. It becomes a stultifying power of death that is hostile to life, and since "life itself is *will to power*," her desire poisons the will to power.[38] Analogously, then, for Nietzsche, philosophy castrates philosophers. His words here could be taken for any contemporary account of the power within a discourse to "speak" a subject.

> That individual philosophical concepts are not anything capricious or autonomously evolving, but grow up in connection and relationship with each other; that however suddenly and arbitrarily they seem to appear in the history of thought, they nevertheless belong just as much to a system as all the members of the fauna of a continent—is betrayed in the end also by the fact that the most diverse philosophers keep filling in a definite fundamental scheme of possible philosophies. Under an invisible spell, they always revolve once more in the same orbit; however independent of each other they may feel themselves with their critical or systematic wills, something within them leads them, something impels them in a definite order, one after the other—to wit, the innate systematic structure and relationship of their concepts. Their thinking is, in fact, far less a discovery than a recognition, a remembering, a return and a homecoming

to a remote, primordial, and inclusive household of the soul, out of which those concepts grew originally: philosophizing is to this extent a kind of atavism of the highest order.[39]

Nietzsche clearly despises all ideological conditioning as an effect of the supposedly feminine system of castration. Beware, he warns, of suffering for the sake of truth: "it makes you headstrong against objections and red rags; it stupefies, animalizes, and brutalizes when in the struggle with danger, slander, suspicion, expulsion and even worse consequences of hostility, you have to pose as protectors of truth upon earth."[40] His injunction to the free-thinkers of the future, therefore, is to overcome the poisonous feminine will to power, or to keep one's distance from "woman." His new philosophers will be severe men who have no time to waste on the cunning feminine falsity of philosophical "untruth," no wish to be pleasured or amused by her. In his words:

> They will be *harder* (and perhaps not always only against themselves) than humane people might wish; they will not dally with "Truth" to be "pleased" or "elevated" or "inspired" by her. On the contrary, they will have little faith that *truth* of all things should be accompanied by such amusements for our feelings. They will smile, these severe spirits, if somebody should say in front of them: "This thought elevates me; how could it fail to be true?" Or: "This work delights me; how could it fail to be beautiful?" . . . Perhaps they do not merely have a smile but feel a genuine nausea over everything that is enthusiastic, idealistic, feminine, hermaphroditic in this vein.[41]

Accordingly, Nietzsche claims that free thinking occurs beyond the castrated and castrating dream of establishing universal laws grounded by objectively determined philosophical systems or principles, which merely organize existing conventional values into neat binary categories (e.g., of good or evil). But he dismisses as nihilistic the option of keeping an absolute or pure distance from "women," that is, of mere rebellious destruction in response to ideological forms, which invents nothing to replace the devastation of value. Indeed he insists, "the same means in the fight against a craving—castration, extirpation—is instinctively chosen by those who are too weak-willed, to degenerate, to be able to impose moderation on themselves."[42] (Notably, if invention must take place, there is no getting outside of the will to power. I will return to this.)

Instead, Nietzsche's free thinking becomes a matter of deliberate self-legislation. The notion of autonomy is hardly new, but he insists that autonomy conventionally understood has always still been a heteronomy, the dictatorship of all-powerful reason. Proposing that "independent" thinking obeyed the rigors of reason rather than blindly accepting traditional forms, philosophy assumed that what was discovered through reason shorn not only of prejudice and habit but also of dis-orders such as paradox and aporia could in principle command universal agreement. Nietzsche, however, insists that the true state of affairs belongs within the domain of aporia, paradox, dilemma, contamination, which conventional reason cannot abide. For him, to face the "truth" is to "recognize untruth as a condition of life," which means putting all conventional values at risk by facing the abyss that replaces them. "A philosophy that risks this," he adds, "would by that token alone place itself beyond good and evil."[43]

To sum up so far, under the rubric of "castration," Nietzsche equates the becoming-ideology of a philosophy under the pressure of the will to power with its feminization. Rejecting outright destruction of all value as nihilistic, he heralds and commends a self-affirmative, inventive free-thinking as the condition for overcoming the feminization of philosophy and, moreover, for opening the way for genuinely ethical action. Such free-thinking, which empowers thinkers, on the one hand, to keep their distance from feminized philosophy, and on the other, to face and overcome nihilism, is placed squarely within the ostensibly hard, masculine domain of brutal honesty about the "truth" as untruth. Yet, pressed by a firmer commitment to Nietzsche's "logic of contamination," Derrida recognizes that the free-thinking he heralds demands equal attention to the alternative supposition that it is the free-thinker's "truth as untruth," rather than the elusive object of the philosophers' desire, that is analogous to "woman."

Free Thinking and the "Affirming Woman" Nietzsche Loved

Reading Nietzsche against the grain, Derrida aims to show that a small inventive twist in interpretative reading enables one to derive an opposing evaluation of the feminine from Nietzsche's analogy between "truth" and "woman." Aiming, as mentioned, to bring forth the most unconventional reading first, before the weight of convention crushes it out, he elicits from a scrap of *The Gay Science* what can only be the thinnest of whispers: a barely audible spectral sound that hovers above the word "distance."[44] But let us play along with Derrida here and allow him to summon this ghost for us, for it represents a significant element of his matrix. In the fragment Derrida cites here, Nietzsche imagines the effect of women on men to be like the sudden appearance, to a man standing amidst the crashing breakers of a stormy sea, of a great ship in the distance, which passes "like an immense butterfly over the dark sea." As Nietzsche puts it:

> as if born out of nothing, there appears before the gate of this hellish labyrinth, only a few fathoms away—a large sailboat, gliding along as silently as a ghost. Oh, what ghostly beauty! How magically it touches me! Has all the calm and taciturnity of the world embarked on it? Does my happiness itself sit in this quiet place? . . .
>
> It seems as if the noise here had led me into fantasies. All great noise leads us to move happiness into some quiet distance. When a man stands in the midst of his own noise, in the midst of his own surf of plans and projects, then he is apt also to see quiet, magical beings gliding past him and to long for their happiness and seclusion: *women*. He almost thinks that his better self dwells there among the women, and that in these quiet regions even the loudest surf turns into deathly quiet, and life itself into a dream about life.

If the "almost" is not enough to break the enchantment, Nietzsche, in explicit confirmation of the analogy first drawn, issues this warning: "Yet! Yet! Noble enthusiast, even on the most beautiful sailboat there is a lot of noise, and unfortunately much small and petty noise. The magic and the most powerful effect of woman, is, in philosophical language, action at a distance, *actio in distans*; but this requires first of all and above all—*distance.*"

I have already outlined in what sense for Nietzsche this "action at a distance" inscribes the entire system of castration in which philosophy has been trapped since Plato. Yet for Derrida, in the phrase "action at a distance" there is enough of a symptomatic slip to suggest, *contra* the conscious Nietzsche, that "woman" is the quintessential figure of the free thinker he heralds as the philosopher of the future. Derrida, in other words, here deliberately takes up an association between woman and "truth as untruth" in the second sense outlined above, instead of the more obvious association between woman and the philosopher's Truth. Taking up Nietzsche's injunction to keep one's distance from "the feminine operation," as well as his insistence that the feminine operation is an "effect at a distance," Derrida makes the subtle shift whose "butterfly effect" is a radical transvaluation of the values of sexual difference. To begin with, he plays along with Nietzsche. In his words: "A woman seduces from a distance. In fact, distance is the very element of her power. Yet one must beware to keep one's own distance from her beguiling song of enchantment. A distance from distance must be maintained."[45]

The injunction to maintain "a distance from distance," then, is the injunction to "keep one's distance from the feminine operation (from the *actio in distans*)," or, that is, to become reflectively aware of it. Such reflection upon the feminine operation, Derrida notes (and here is the shift), does not amount to approaching it. Rather, tacitly invoking the myth of the veil of Isis, he insists, one approaches the feminine operation "at the risk of death itself."[46] Why? It might be because "woman" is not some determinable thing comparable to other things, waiting there at a distance, to be approached, inspected, dissected, and pinned down, or ignored and left behind. "Perhaps," as he puts it, "woman—a non-identity, a non-figure, a simulacrum—is distance's very chasm, the out-distancing of distance, the interval's cadence, distance itself, if we could still say such a thing, distance *itself*."[47]

In other words, to put it bluntly, Derrida does not interpret the phrase "a woman seduces from a distance" to imply, as Nietzsche would have it, that a "woman" is only beautiful and enchanting at a distance, for when you approach her (or, that is, if you are brutally honest) there is nothing but a superficial façade veiling an ugly decadence. Rather, Derrida takes it to imply that "woman" is another name for the operation of *différance*. On the one hand, its operation as "spacing" acknowledges Nietzsche's truth as untruth, or, that is, the unstable, open-ended state of contamination or uncontrollable proliferation of differences that characterizes the actual state of affairs. On the other hand, the operation of *différance* as "temporalization" acknowledges that, for anything at all to take shape, one must violently put the play of differences out of play for a while, that is, restrict or defer the play or place it in reserve. To know that *différance* as temporalization violates *différance* as spacing and vice versa is to know that what takes shape via the operation of *différance* as temporalization could never be an eternal essence (an unconditionally present term) but must always be a necessary but temporary fiction, a making-sense or an invention that does not forever escape the undermining forces of *différance* as spacing. Thus, on Derrida's reading, one can take the "effect at a distance" that names the feminine operation to mean that:

> There is no such thing as the essence of woman because woman averts, she is averted of herself. Out of the depths, endless and unfathomable, she engulfs and distorts all vestige of essentiality, of identity, of property. And the philosophical discourse, blinded, founders on these shoals and is hurled down these depthless depths to its ruin. There is no such thing as the truth of woman, but it is because of that abyssal divergence of the truth, because that untruth is "truth." Woman is but one name for a that untruth of truth.[48]

Derrida implicitly challenges one to reread all of the statements in which Nietzsche insists upon drawing an analogy between truth and "woman," or "the veiled movement of feminine modesty," or upon the "complicity (rather than the unity) between woman, life, seduction, modesty," in a way that strengthens the proposition that "woman" is the name for the salutary un-truth that characterizes the actual state of affairs. Take for example the following statement: "But perhaps this is the greatest charm of life: it puts a golden-embroidered veil of lovely potentialities over itself, promising, resisting, modest, mocking, sympathetic, seductive. Yes, life is a woman!"[49] This statement could imply, as Derrida suggests, that "woman" as un-truth is one of the nicknames for a *différance* that remains distant, inaccessible, abyssal, and both seduces and mocks "the credulous and dogmatic philosopher" who understands "nothing of truth, nor anything of woman" if he "*believes* in truth just as he believes in woman."[50] Moreover, she is implicitly wiser than he is, for, in Derrida's words, "if woman *is* truth, *she* at least knows that there is no truth, that truth has no place here and that no one has a place for truth. And she is woman precisely because she herself does not believe in truth itself, because she does not believe in what she is, in what she is believed to be, in what she thus is not."[51]

In a similar vein, Derrida takes Nietzsche's answer to the question that opens *Beyond Good and Evil* to suggest the following: If truth is a woman, it remains in excess of what it seems at face value, and any philosopher who tries to capture "truth" makes of it a lie. As Nietzsche admits soon after: "What is certain is that she has not allowed herself to be won—and today every kind of dogmatism is left standing dispirited and discouraged. *If* it is left standing at all!" It is self-affirming "woman" who actively limits the tyrannical dream of philosophy. In Derrida's words: "Woman (truth) will not be pinned down. That which will not be pinned down by truth is, in truth—*feminine.*"[52] The feminine is a power of self-affirmation that shakes off all ideology (including patriarchy)—that is, she does not react against it but is unaffected by its power; instead she affirms her own power. Woman, or the feminine, in this case is the quintessential figure of Nietzsche's new free thinker, who understands the truth that there is no truth without skepticism or passive nihilism but with cheerful inventive affirmation.

Concluding Remarks: The Feminine as the Site of Transgression

What! In all honesty, it takes some Derridean subtlety and ingenuity to sustain this subversive gesture that makes Nietzsche let slip an alternative valuation of the feminine "effect at a distance" by equating it with the self-affirmative, Dionysiac power of inventive renewal he endorses as the proper response to the abyss of truth as un-truth. Nevertheless, if Nietzsche did not have the stomach for the entire journey, it is important that Derrida, as one of the new thinkers he heralds, is of stronger constitution and is willing to risk supposing that truth as un-truth is a woman. From this transvaluation in the domain of sexual difference, it follows that dogmatic philosophy, demanding, as Derrida puts it, "truth, science, and objectivity in all their castrated delusions of virility"—not to speak of faith, continence, consistency, sublimation as sexual abstinence, universality, predictability, coldness, obedience to reason as system, law, and order, duty, progress, educability, and *Bildung*—must be understood as a matter of blind masculine narcissism rather than feminine deception.[53] In short, if Derrida accepts the complex logic of Nietzsche's new style of thinking, he resists the metaphorical configuration that characterizes his rhetoric, insisting instead that the becoming-ideology of philosophy (the entire dynamic of castrated and castrating) is not a process of feminization but of masculinization.

Ironically, to sum up, for all his perspicacity, Nietzsche did not foresee that the proverbial "untimely" character of his thinking would undergo a strange turnaround that renders it out of step not only with its own time but also with "ours." He is *par excellence* the thinker beyond the "castration effect" of conventionally determined values and binary oppositions, and his free-thinking is formally characterized by the permanent suspicion of all ideologies, which has become a powerful strand in the contemporary mindset. His own logic of contamination implies, of course, that he should have been the first to recognize patriarchy as a phallocentric ideology. Yet his rhetorical use of the epithet "feminization" to condemn the becoming-ideology of philosophy relies for its effect on assuming the most stereotypical and conventional values for the concept "woman," pregiven by this ideology of all ideologies that cuts across all discourses. It is therefore a stronger commitment to his style of thinking, on the part of the new thinkers he heralds, that uncovers an outdated, even quaint, patriarchal conventionality that dooms his pronouncements concerning sexual difference (buttressed by a stereotypical binary opposition between the communal and the singular) to a less romantic kind of untimeliness.

The performative contradiction here seems obvious; in the very gesture by which he condemns the philosopher's Truth as ideological and exhorts thinkers to move beyond conventionally given values and oppositions toward the complex style of deliberate free-thinking he heralded, Nietzsche reveals that he remains unreflectively subject to precisely the kind of conventional, ideological, heteronymous, and oppositional thinking he so strenuously resists in principle. Notably, acknowledging that the notion "woman" is characterized in his texts by a diverse plurality exacerbates the performative contradiction, for it strengthens the case that Nietzsche (of all thinkers!) had the least reason to allow himself recourse in *Beyond Good and Evil*, of all texts, to a rhetorical construct that criticizes traditional philosophy by calling it "feminized." The obvious move here might be to retain the valuable critique of ideology made possible by his insight into the dynamic of the will to power as well as his logic of contamination while jettisoning the self-undermining, phallocentric rhetoric that constructs sexual difference in the terms handed down by patriarchy. However, as I hope to have demonstrated through the foregoing exposition of Derrida's reading, retaining these terms and pressing them to the point of their undoing has certain advantages.

Nietzsche's unconscious recourse to commonly held stereotypes in turn puts into question the very possibility and value of absolute singularity, or, that is, "truth as declamation": truth as the *speaking* of passion (desire), presupposed in the very possibility of saying "I, Plato, am the truth." Nietzsche, as noted in chapter 1, argues that it is impossible to put the un-truth that "I am" into words. Yet, in a claim that is antagonistic to this insight, he insists that his own views concerning women are singular rather than a matter of "learning." While he grants that learning, like nourishment, changes us, he insists that deep down lies an unteachable kernel from which "speaks an unchangeable 'this is I,'" described as "the great stupidity we are" or as a "spiritual *fatum*" that remains "*unteachable* very 'deep down.'"[54] Nietzsche (astonishingly, given his arguments for the impossibility of *speaking* passion) thinks that this preamble will more readily permit him to "*state a few truths* [my emphasis] about 'woman as such'—assuming that it is now known from the outset how very much these are after all only—*my* truths."

It is precisely his logic of contamination that should have warned Nietzsche against claiming as his own "truths" the commonly held stereotypes he repeated concerning sexual difference. Moreover, this places into question his claim that the "masculine" un-truth inheres solely in the singular, inventive power of each rugged individual who must walk his own lonely path to insight, shaking off as degradation any confirmation and evaluation by what Ibsen called the "compact majority." He might have reminded himself of what he already knew concerning the insidious, unconscious nature of ideological conditioning, for he remains perfectly aware that the free-thinking required by a genuinely ethical stance (which he understood in terms of a singular responsibility for independent decision making) is less a matter of having the strength to stand up for and act upon individual convictions than of, above all, having the courage to question them, and not just intermittently (when things go wrong).[55] More radically, it is a matter of keeping such convictions permanently in question, since no thinkers can ever quite be "honest enough in their work."[56] In other words, no individual no matter how perspicacious is capable of the absolute self-transparency required to master finally the undertow toward conventionality and habit inscribed in the will to power, precisely because it operates to a large extent unconsciously, which means that its effects only become visible in retrospect, when something has gone wrong with it. Nietzsche knew all of this, but he did not live up to his insight, allowing himself the greatest indulgence (in his own terms, the greatest weakness of spirit) when it came to "the other" in general, and particularly women.

Turning to Nietzsche's new thinkers, whose style turns out to be feminine, one should immediately note that "the feminine"[57] as the site of transgression in a patriarchy, derived from the recognition of un-truth as the actual state of affairs, is not a matter of embracing anticastration as the precise opposite of castration but a movement beyond the binary altogether.[58] "Woman," in Derrida's words,

> no more believes in castration's exact opposite, anti-castration, than she does in castration itself. Much too clever for that (and we ourselves—who we?—might learn from her, or in any case from her operation) she knows that such a reversal would only deprive her of the powers of simulation, that in truth a reversal of that kind would, in the end, only amount to the same thing and force her just as surely as ever into the same old apparatus. She knows that she would only find herself trapped once again in a phallocentrism.

Interestingly, Derrida's prejudicial reading of Lacanian discourse surfaces briefly here. In his words: "perhaps at this point one ought to interrogate—and 'unboss'—the metaphorical full-blown sail of truth as declamation, of the castration and phallocentrism, for example, in Lacan's discourse." In the single stroke of one sentence, Derrida aims to align everything that calls for deconstruction in Nietzsche with what he sees as Lacan's poisonous "will to power." The term "unboss" (*décapitonner*) alludes to Lacan's *point de capiton*, generically named by the Phallus, which Derrida apparently takes to reflect a phallocentric logic and a poisonous will to power that calls for deconstructive decapitation. His implicit challenge here turns on the "puffed up" affectation that he detects (and detests) in the figure of "truth as declamation" in Lacan's discourse. That is, underpinned by the claim that "I, Lacan, am the truth," he sees Lacan inaugurating the movement of the castration effect in psychoanalytic discourse, which is further exacerbated by Lacan's castrating claim to a position of mastery in relation to his students and readers. Unlike self-affirming "woman," then, Lacan (in Derrida's eyes) remains trapped within a paranoid masculine will to power.

Admittedly, it might seem a stretch to suggest, to the contrary, that Lacanian psychoanalysis (like deconstruction) offers the theoretical means to take up Nietzsche's logic of contamination while liberating oneself from the prejudices concerning *inter alia* "woman" and "the other" that undermine it. Yet if Derrida can trace a path through and beyond Nietzschean prejudice, not by rejecting outright his definition of "the feminine" in terms of "lack" or "castration" but by insisting that Nietzsche's logic of contamination supports a transvaluation of these values, there is no reason to suggest that Lacan could not have made a similar move in his reinterpretation of Freudian psychoanalysis. Freud, after all, is hardly more notorious than Nietzsche for defining women negatively, in terms of her lack of masculine accoutrements, and no more pessimistic in his assessment of the "compact majority."

In fact, the logic of Lacanian psychoanalysis operates precisely in terms of a transvaluation of values rather than the mere reversal of binaries, since it proposes a division in the feminine site of transgression, whereby transgression takes shape in two ways, namely the hysterically nihilistic will to pure destruction of all value that Nietzsche dismissed as another kind of feminine weakness but also the self-affirmative domain of ethical action Nietzsche typically reserves for masculinity. For Lacan, then, as for Derrida, the moment of self-affirmative inventiveness that characterizes free-thinking rightly belongs to femininity in a patriarchy, for it presupposes an initial willingness to transgress any established order of value and to face the prospect of nihilism. Against the current of the Derridean prejudice, then, in the following chapters, I aim to show that from Lacan's earliest writings, the "plural logic of the aporia" is at work in his psychoanalytic articulation of the transcendental relation, which, in fact, cannot do without it. If anything, this logic only becomes more explicit and its formulation more complex as his work progresses.

PART 4

Lacan and the "Plural Logic of the Aporia"

Lacan's complex theoretical edifice, like Freud's, is developed from a heady mix of clinical observation, theoretical speculation, and his appropriation of a vast array of literary and philosophical texts. Moreover, as Fink notes, his notions are "shaped and reshaped in the course of his career," necessitating a choice between presenting them developmentally or structurally. Some, he remarks, will no doubt find a structural account "overly static and closed, one of the many fascinations of his work lying precisely in its constant transformations, self-corrections, and reversals of perspective."[1] Like Fink, however, I have elected nevertheless to provide a synchronic "cut of Lacanian theory," for this approach is better suited to the purpose of demonstrating that the "plural logic of the aporia" functions as a generalizable, useful heuristic for interpreting what Lacan has to say about the transcendental relation, the ethics of psychoanalysis, and intersubjective power relations in the *Seminar on the Purloined Letter*.

As with my treatment of Derrida's texts, I offer no pretense of a comprehensive survey of Lacan's daunting textual labyrinth, believing this to be as intrinsically impossible as reading the "whole" of Joyce. In any case, Lacan's surrealist strategy of composition allows one some license to build up an account of "Lacanian" psychoanalysis from fragments, and my exposition involves less a progression of ideas than a layering, each lamination adding detail and tone to the same interpretative skeleton, which I have derived from Derrida's "plural logic of the aporia." I shall engage directly with some of Lacan's texts, but much of my account of the Lacanian version of the "plural logic of the aporia" can be seen as a sustained engagement with Copjec's Lacan, as set out in *Imagine There's No Woman*.

In chapter 10, I address Lacan's complex articulation of "the transcendental relation." Lacan offers an overwhelming variety of schemas, models, formulas, mathemes, and diagrams, which cover greater or smaller aspects of this relation. These may be helpful to those of a certain intellectual temperament but alienating to others. Favoring more concrete metaphorics over mathematical symbolization, I have taken the articulated imagoes that appear in his early essays as an orienting armature to explain the "Gödelian structure" of the transcendental relation. These also serve to emphasize that other humans are the primary and most significant "objects" or "others" implicated in the constitution of the subject in the transcendental relation. The "other," which takes the three generalized forms of *Nebenmensch*, alter egos, and speaking others, is not a neutral, inert object. It is not merely touched, but it touches back with a shaping power of its own, teaching infants, through an encouraging or prohibiting circulation of desire, a certain version of reality. In Lacan's early essays, these generalized or "structural" forms of the other are associated with three "imagoes" that take their names from traditional family figures, and the transcendental relation is described as an articulated armature of three subject-object complexes associated with the maternal, fraternal, and paternal imagoes.[2]

One does not have to retain these traditional names, and Lacan would be the first to agree that various actual individuals of different sexual orientations may fill the roles of *Nebenmensch*, alter ego, or speaking other. Following Copjec, I have tended to substitute the "*Nebenmensch*-complex" for the "maternal-imago," but I have retained the "fraternal-complex" on the assumption that fraternity these days can be pressed beyond the connotations of brotherhood. I have also retained the "paternal-complex" as a reminder of the patriarchal residues still inscribed in the Symbolic Order. Names aside, I shall follow Lee in holding that the family complexes of Lacan's early writings offer a metaphorical organization that, while certainly subject to refinement, elaboration, and modification in the lengthy course of his investigations, remains a productive and orientating heuristic for understanding the complexities of his account of the transcendental relation.[3]

By using these structural metaphors, Lacan is at pains to point out that subjective development is not shaped by instincts but by complex imaginary constructs that inaugurate drives.[4] In other words, what shapes subjectivity are basic, impersonal structural complexes that remain constant no matter how they are concretized. Moreover, individuals respond to the demands of these complexes without necessarily being consciously aware of them: an infant has yet to develop the means for critical self-reflection, but in adults the force of unconscious habituation is difficult to resist because the inertial death drive works to resist novelty and change. Finally, although the imagoes do appear at successive junctures in human development, they are not developmental stages that are passed through.[5] Instead, each complex may be viewed as a lamination that successively adds complexity and depth to Lacan's notion of the subject. Accordingly, I shall treat these complexes separately, showing in turn how each may be read according to the three moments of the "plural logic of the aporia." Before entering the dense thickets, however, it may be helpful to construct an aerial map, so to speak, of their articulation.

A Lacanian account of the transcendental relation, according to Copjec, begins from the claim that "the Other does not exist and that the subject is constituted from an originary lack."[6] This is not an argument for the absence of either but for the aporetic structure of each. In fact, Lacan conceives of a multiple *and* "castrated" (split) other, in relation to which a similarly multiple and castrated subject is constituted. Subject first of all to a "spectral analysis" of "the other" in terms of the Real, Imaginary, and Symbolic orders (for which the Borromean knot stands as a graphic figure),[7] Lacan theorizes subjectivity as an articulation of three subject-other complexes. First, within the *Nebenmensch*-complex (in the register of the Real), the "lacking/desiring-I" is constituted in its relation to the primordial other defined as the object of the drive.[8] Second, within the fraternal hall of mirrors (in the register of the Imaginary), the constitution of the subject as ego, or *moi*, occurs in relation to the other as alter ego (the mirror image, siblings, the Oedipal parents, and other significant others). Third, the constitution of the subject as active, speaking *je* (in opposition to the described or "spoken" *moi*) occurs in relation to the impersonal, generalized "other" of discourse or culture (inscribed in language), in the register of the Symbolic. (This would be the paternal-complex in a patriarchy.)

These three complexes, which already make for a plural subject, are not gathered together as a unified and ordered plurality. Instead their articulation remains aporetic, for they are mutually incompatible and antagonistic. But the aporetic entanglement does not end here, for there is a further complexity: in all three complexes the other is not only multiple but "castrated," or, that is, split by an aporetic or antagonistic "disseminality" and structurally unable, therefore, to form a whole. Yet we are libidinally driven (by means of the death drive) precisely to attempt a reconstruction of the other as the lost primordial whole, to which a return is in principle possible. Attempts to grasp the other as that toward which the drive drives are, in turn, split across an aporetic multiplicity; that is, the other is reconstructed as a closed totality, an open infinity, or a paradoxical open-endedness (whereby the other is sublimated or compounded by my very attempt to grasp it). All three conceptions, as Derrida has shown, are "impossible" (traumatic) because they harbor different kinds of aporias. This division in the other is matched on the subject side of the transcendental relation by a split along the lines of incompatible libidinal responses to the primary castration of the other, divided in terms of sexual difference.

For Lacan, importantly, sexual difference is not in the first instance a biological (binary) or gender (differential) distinction.[9] Instead, it describes three structurally incompatible ways of organizing the sexual drives that are elicited in response to the aporetic impossibility of the desired object/other (which is ultimately the narcissistic desire for immortality). While he calls these incompatible libidinal styles of organization "masculine" and "feminine," he argues that biological men or women may organize their libidinal drives under the banner of either and can accordingly be unconsciously dominated by, or consciously give preference to, any libidinal style.[10] It is important to note, then, that when he speaks of "masculine" or "feminine" sexuality, he does not intend any essentialist argument concerning the sexual nature of biological men or women. Rather, "masculine sexuality" names the structure of a paranoiac organization of the libidinal drives well suited to ideological interpellation (whose binary counterpart is a "feminine" hysterical organization). By contrast, the other "feminine" sexuality names a transgressive organization of the libidinal drives ill-suited to ideological interpellation. It is worth repeating that ideological interpellation and the two forms of transgression just described are, for Lacan, universal structures, which are only named, respectively, "masculine" and "feminine" in a patriarchal culture.

To return to the task of mapping the transcendental relation, it is important to emphasize here that, for Lacan, the paranoid and hysterical libidinal styles represent impossible extremes, and a fixation to one or the other means that the death drive, in either one of its opposing moments of (paranoiac) return and (hysterical) destruction, has gained the upper hand. Accordingly, one may derive from the Lacanian text an oppositional relation in each of the three above-mentioned subject-other complexes between masculine paranoia and feminine hysteria whose logic of articulation is, once again, the "vel of alienation." As a consequence of its lose/lose logic, to reiterate, Lacan shares Derrida's conviction that there is no choosing for either side of this kind of opposition and that it is possible, indeed important, to develop the third option that escapes the lethal pitfalls of either. One finds, therefore, not only an economic and aneconomic subject-object relation in each complex but also a third, paradoxical libidinal style, which Lacan prefers (as does Derrida), for it is in this "feminine" modification that Lacan finds room for the ethically able subject aimed at in psychoanalytic treatment.

In some respects, this three-way structure may seem to be an imposition, for Lacan's intellectual strategy is not always precisely aligned with the "plural logic of the aporia" and he as often as not contrasts a masculine economic style with the third, paradoxical style, which he calls feminine, allowing the aneconomic position, which is also feminine but in its more lethal aspect, to slip into the wings.[11] But even when he shifts directly from a rejection of the masculine/conservative death drive to the feminine libidinal style associated with the acknowledgment of paradox, he is emphatic that this shift should not lose itself to the extreme of atomistic dissolution and dispersal (which reflects the other side of the death drive). I have therefore made space for an aneconomic, feminine death drive for the sake of a clearer view of the basis upon which he rejects the opposing extremes named by masculine paranoia and feminine hysteria and works toward an articulation of the nonlethal feminine style. In accordance with the "plural logic of the aporia," in sum, each of the three self-other complexes that for Lacan constitute the transcendental relation are in turn subject to a traumatic split between economic, aneconomic, and paradoxical aporias.

In chapter 10, I read the *Nebenmensch*-complex according to this proposed schema in a fair amount of detail, because it prepares the way for Lacan's radicalizing reinterpretation of Freud's understanding of both fraternal and paternal relations. I do not address the fraternal and paternal complexes in as much detail, but I briefly sketch out a reading of each along the lines of the "plural logic of the aporia," leaving it to the laminating effect of the following chapters, which deal broadly speaking with ethics and power, to add some of the texture and tone.

Notably, across all three libidinal styles, the subject's entry into the Symbolic Order (thematized in terms of the paternal complex) is understood in terms of active appropriation of, as Fink puts it, "making 'one's own' something that was formerly alien."[12] In this case, according to Fink, a complete reversal occurs vis-à-vis the Other's desire, for the individual assumes responsibility for "what had previously been experienced as an external, extraneous cause, a foreign roll of the dice at the beginning of one's universe: destiny." In other words, the *je* is required to "become the subject of his or her own fate. Not 'it happened to me,' but 'I saw,' I heard,' 'I acted.' "[13] "Hence the gist of Lacan's multiple translations of Freud's '*Wo Es war, soll Ich werden*': where the Other pulls the strings (acting as my cause), I must come into being as my own cause."[14]

In chapter 11, I shall elaborate on the theme of action and its implications for Lacan's psychoanalytic account of ethical action. In outline, I shall show that the masculine *je*, formed via a rejection of castration, dominated by the death drive as return, and bound by the stereotypes of an existing order, operates from a position of ideological paranoia, whereby his lot is the fixated action of an obedient functionary of the externally imposed law. In contrast, the feminine *je*, formed via wholesale acceptance of castration, dominated by the death drive as dissolution, and bound to smash up existing stereotypes, operates from a position of hysterical transgression, whereby her lot is the paralysis of pure destruction. Beyond these two libidinal styles, related in terms of the vel of alienation (which articulates castration and anticastration), Lacan derives a third style, namely one of inventive sublimation. This style, which invokes the aporia of a paradoxical interweaving of inventive and destructive action, is the key to Lacan's account of ethical action, and, notably, to his resolution of the antinomy Freud faced between sex and civilization. This account of ethical action lays the basis for the final chapter of this study, which explains Lacan's claim that the task of psychoanalytic intervention is ethical.

If psychoanalysis aims to engender an ethically able subject, it presupposes the desirability of feminine sublimation as one of the intrinsic possibilities of the transcendental relation. But this is not to suggest that realizing the capacity for such sublimation is automatic; rather, it must be achieved. If Lacan criticizes psychoanalysis for setting itself up to produce ideologically adapted rather than ethically able subjects, he also chastises psychoanalysts for forgetting the fundamental tool of the trade, namely language: psychoanalysis is not for nothing dubbed "the talking cure." His emphasis on the interventionist value of speaking underscores a second feature of the subject's entry into the Symbolic Order, namely that, again across all three libidinal styles, the formation of the *je* is a matter of learning to speak. As Lee notes, "psychoanalysis situates the development of the Oedipus complex at precisely the period in which children are most effectively acquiring the language of their parents (beginning from about the age of two-and-a-half years). For Lacan, successful negotiation of oedipal conflicts is quite literally a matter of learning to speak properly."[15]

Precisely what this means and how it is tied to questions of ethics and power will be addressed in chapter 12, with the help of Lacan's *Seminar on the Purloined Letter*. I shall merely note here that for Lacan, again read in accordance with the "plural logic of the aporia," speech on the one hand may be what he calls "empty," that is, unaware of the unconscious conditions (rules of the game) that determine its character. Such "empty" speech manifests as fixated on either the rule of law or the law of exception. On the other hand, in what he calls "full" speech, the individual gains analytical insight into the logic named by the vel of alienation and in so doing occupies an anomalous or paradoxical position between the rule and its "outside," which is precisely the displacement from which one must risk decisive action.

To read Lacan's *Seminar on the Purloined Letter* in terms of the "plural logic of the aporia" poses a direct challenge to Derrida's reading of this text, which sees in it only confirmation that Lacan is too at home with a traditional philosophy caught up in the metaphysics of presence. To conclude this study, then, I shall address the specifics of Derrida's unjust reading of this seminar, detailed in "Le Facteur de la Vérité," from out of which his protocols for reading Lacan emerge. With the help of Barbara Johnson's seminal essay "The Frame of Reference," I shall assess the possibility of nevertheless finding something of value to be gained from what is unquestionably a one-sided misrecognition of Lacan's theoretical strategy.[16]

If it is easy enough for me to outline a viable form of theoretical accord between Derrida and Lacan based on the "plural logic of the aporia," it is highly unlikely that Derrida would have missed this. I agree with Barbara Johnson that he is too astute a reader not to have framed Lacan on purpose. Moreover, if one returns to the scene of the rift between them—Derrida's reading of Lacan's *Seminar on the Purloined Letter*—it is easy to see where (in order to build up the case that eight tightly interwoven motifs in this seminar place Lacan squarely within the metaphysics of presence) Derrida reduces only to its economic moment everything that for Lacan has the paradoxical ambiguity given to it by the third moment of the "plural logic of the aporia." In other words, Derrida decides the undecidable in Lacan, which is highly ironic, since this is exactly the mistake many make when reading Derrida (although they tend to decide the undecidable in the other direction).

Barbara Johnson insists that Derrida does this intentionally as a kind of lesson in rhetoric. But if this is so, he never comes clean later on about the setup. However, whatever Derrida's motivations concerning Lacan may be, the lesson in rhetoric remains a valuable demonstration of how easy it is to miss the point in confronting the "plural logic of the aporia." To decide the undecidable one way or the other will be to misread both Derrida and Lacan.

10

The Transcendental Relation in Lacanian Psychoanalysis

Introductory Remarks: Immortality

In *Civilization and Its Discontents,* Freud attributes the persistent human dream of a mythical beginning, where all was encompassed in the circle of self-sufficiency, to the unconscious mnemic trace in all of us of the primordial mother-child dyad (or its equivalents), which is to the infant an original, albeit never actually experienced, "oceanic" plenum.[1] As Copjec notes, one might immediately think of the "body without organs" depicted in Plato's *Timaeus* as an early example of such a dream.[2] However, she argues, given Freud's insistence that the body through which infants are attached to the *Nebenmensch* (and later the wider world) is not just pragmatically functional but infused from top to toe with an erotic charge, psychoanalysis conceives of this mythical state in terms of libidinal fullness, or immortal jouissance, rather than mere biological self-sufficiency.[3]

Challenging Freud's insistence on the eventual dominance of the reality principle, which raises pragmatic concerns of physical need above erotic interests, Lacan replaces the Timaean-type myth with his own "myth of the lamella," which underscores the primacy of libidinal interests over the "return of need."[4] As noted in chapter 5, the figure of the "lamella" (thin membrane) refers to the protective/receptive outer membrane that, as Freud argues in "Beyond the Pleasure Principle," characterizes all living organisms.[5] On the one hand, the lamella figures as a protective layer that encloses the living organism and separates it from an infinite environmental beyond. But simultaneously, on the other hand, it opens the organism up, for the membrane exists as a multiplicity of libidinally charged "mouths" that attach the organism, through the drives, to the environment around it. In other words, the lamella represents a strange border that both separates the limited being from the unlimited All and attaches it to this "outside." In equivalent terms, it represents a split that allows for a relation between the mortal living subject (presided over by pleasure) and the "immortality lost" (lost jouissance) that is, ironically, the consequence of life itself. In Lacan's words: "The relation to the Other is precisely that which, for us, brings out what is represented by the lamella . . . the relation between the living subject and that which he loses by having to pass, for his reproduction, through the sexual cycle."[6]

Condensed in this citation is a reference to Freud's treatment of mortality as "immortality lost" in "Beyond the Pleasure Principle." Lacan draws out subtly conflicting conceptions of mortality in this essay, which in turn have a bearing upon our understanding of the primary human libidinal interest in immortalization, or of our death drive toward the restitution of "lost" immortality.[7] He notes the irony that Freud situates mortality "at the advent of the living being, that is to say, at sexed reproduction," which is also, on one interpretation, our only means of immortalization.[8] Here, one could argue, Freud makes the fairly commonsensical observation that because human reproduction occurs via sex rather than, say, cloning or spontaneous cell division, human being is "originally" split between Eros and Thanatos. The germ cells, under the sway of Eros, are pulled toward a return to the beginning in a bond that renews life. These then, are split off from other somatic processes, which, subject to Thanatos, strive for the abolition of all tensions and are pulled in the direction of inertial protectiveness and entropic dissolution, or, that is, death.[9] In other words, if individual bodies remain merely mortal, we may nevertheless seek immortalization through genetic replication. This reflects a fairly common traditional notion that "he" reproduces "himself" through his children.

Lacan, however, presses Freud's observation further, suggesting that what the organism loses via sexed reproduction is any prospect at all of individual immortality, defined as the endless replication of precisely the same being. As he puts it: "the living being, by being subject to sex, has fallen under the blow of individual death."[10] In other words, the consequence of sexual reproduction is not immortalization through genetic replication but, to the contrary, a guarantee that every individual is entirely unique, that is, mortal. Accordingly, Lacan takes this to imply that our mortality is not reducible to the mere death of our bodies (which, in turn, promotes the idea that immortality belongs to the species as the ideal whole that endures beyond any individual).[11] Rather, mortality may be defined as the singularity of our very living being.[12] Here, Lacan has drawn from Freud's text a subtle shift in nuance concerning our conception of mortality (from the death of the individual body to the singularity of the individual life), which engenders a paradox. If "mortality" denotes the unique singularity of an individual life, then it coincides, paradoxically, with the definition of individual immortality, for this singular life is an event in the temporal fabric that cannot be erased, repeated, or replaced. It is this plural conception of the relation between mortality and immortality that may be elaborated into a Lacanian account of the *Nebenmensch*-complex. Notably, in the first place it is this conception of a relation, and therefore an intrinsic separation, between the mortal self and its "other," which is signified by the cut of castration. But, as noted earlier, the castration metaphor includes the further complexity that the separated "other," which now becomes that toward which the drive drives, is itself subject to an intrinsic splitting, and this, in turn, engenders a complexity in the drives.

The *Nebenmensch*-Complex

The *Nebenmensch* or "maternal imago" stands as a metaphor for the primordial castrated Other of the drive, in the register of the Real, named by various synonymous substitutes such as jouissance, immortality, or the All. As castrated, the *Nebenmench* is intrinsically split between three senses: first, "*das Ding*" (object *a*, writ large, as the delusional "A"), which is divided between two senses that form a binary opposition (totality and infinity); and second, the sublimated object *a*, the paradoxical part that functions as a whole. It is due to the intrinsic divisibility of the *Nebenmensch* as co-constitutive "Other" that, in turn, the constitution of the subject as lacking and desiring has different senses.

Accordingly, in outline, on an economic account of this complex, the *Nebenmensch* as *das Ding* is understood, in the first of its two senses, as a single totality. The associated libidinal style of the driven subject, characterized by paranoia, manifests as a masculine death drive toward totality, or the restitution of jouissance or immortality understood as a return to the unity of *das Ding*. Because such totalization is impossible, the consequence of this libidinal style is endemic dissatisfaction or, at its opposite extreme, the paralysis of paranoiac inflexibility. By direct contrast, on an aneconomic account of this complex, the *Nebenmensch* as *das Ding* is understood, in the second of its two senses, as an infinite concatenation of parts. The associated libidinal style of the driven subject, characterized by hysteria, manifests as a feminine death drive toward the dissolution of all bonds (since all bonds are automatically excluding) for the sake of recovering a state of infinite inclusiveness. Again, the consequence of this style is either endemic dissatisfaction or the paralysis of hysterical destructiveness. On a paradoxical reading of this complex, the Other of the drive is interpreted not in the idealized form of *das Ding* (as totality or infinity) but as the sublimated object *a*, the part that functions as a whole. The associated libidinal style is one of feminine inventive sublimation, whereby the death drive circles around the object *a* in what one could think of as an open-ended invention of satisfactions (that is, satisfaction endlessly compounded by satisfaction).

The Primary Castration of the Other and the Lacking-I

To elaborate, one may begin with the question of why such intrinsically mortal beings experience a primary libidinal interest in immortalization or, as Copjec puts it, "a longing for a pleasure remembered yet never actually experienced."[13] Directed by his radical reconception of the Real as a splitting of being, Lacan ties his answer to another nickname: "castration." The first traumatic (and multiple) splitting in being, or the primary cut of castration, he argues, occurs not between child and *Nebenmensch* as the force that motivates the dissolution of the Oedipus complex but at a much earlier point in the development of the transcendental relation. In other words, he places the first traumatic cut, which breaks the spell of the mythical plenum and forces the infant into a relation with immortality, at the point of weaning or its equivalents, when an infant first faces what Copjec calls a "structural disturbance" in its dyadic fusion with the *Nebenmensch*.[14] Lacan offers a complex interpretation of primary castration, reflecting the correlative sides of the lamella. On the one hand, the castration that separates the infant from the breast during weaning represents the subject's recognition of its own mortality, while on the other hand, the correlative castration that separates the mother from the breast and the breast from itself represents different senses of the subject's recognition of its loss of immortality. Notably, the maternal metaphorics are derived from the legitimate assumption that the mother and the *Nebenmensch* still predominantly coincide.

Addressing the subject side of the lamella, the first cut of castration reflects the infant's traumatic realization, as a consequence of weaning, that the source of jouissance is in fact on the "outside" of the ego. This first awareness of lack, which ruptures the closed circuit of the mother-child dyad, occurs in an infant's recognition of an ambivalent split in the mother: she is the source of all possible satisfaction but she also instigates its loss in, for example, her always too precipitous withdrawal of the breast. Since pleasure is identified with the life of the ego in an infant psyche, this unexpected and unsanctioned splitting away of the primary source of pleasure (the *Nebenmensch*) is experienced as a profound loss of self/being that carries with it the fear of death, which must be circumvented at all costs.[15] In other words, the lacking-desiring "I," who now requires a synthetic (cognitive) process to re-find this pure pleasure in relation to "the outside," is constituted simultaneously with the death drive, which aims for the restitution of jouissance.

The death drive, however, is intrinsically aim inhibited; that is, it is blocked by an object that represents this aim, or, in other terms, it is blocked by desire, which Lacan defines as "interpretation itself."[16] The notion of the aim-inhibited drive, then, which expresses itself in a desire for something, introduces the axiomatic term of the *Nebenmensch*-complex, namely, *Vorstellungsrepräsentanz* ("ideational representative"), that is, object of the drive. Depending on how it is read, this term is designated as "A" or "a" in the Lacanian algebra (I will return to this important difference). Notably, however it is conceived, this "object of the drive," which interests psychoanalysis, should not be confused with everyday physical objects (located in the domain of needs and satisfactions), for this "neglects the symbolic dimension of desire."[17] Recall that for Freud, all that an infant has experienced is sedimented in the mnemic system as a collection of discrete traces, loosely tied together in an overconnected network of potential associative links. Cognitive processing is a matter of gathering up, synthesizing, or articulating such traces for the sake of projecting an intentional "object," or, better, since the synthetic process is not disinterested or neutral but driven by the urgent compulsion to restore jouissance, what is presented to consciousness is the wished-for jouissance projected in the form of a representative: a desired object that stands in for, or is a simulacrum of, the lost jouissance. The "ideational representative," then, functions as the object-cause of the drive. As Fink sums it up, Lacan theorizes "the object [of the drive] as *cause* of desire, not as something which could somehow *satisfy* desire."[18]

Given that the "ideational representative" is projected into consciousness in the hope that it will be re-found in experience via reality testing, three terms come into play: the jouissance to come; the projection of the "ideational representative" (or object of the drive) that stands as the representative or simulacrum of jouissance and both causes and blocks the drive; and the *Vorstellungen*, the ideas derived from perceptual experience by virtue of which the jouissance to come ideally should be refound in the world.[19] However, the restitution of jouissance (or immortalization), which implies that any discrepancy between the object of the drive and the perceptual object must be eradicated, remains impossible. The object of the drive cannot ever be re-found "on the outside," in the world of perceptual objects, or matched with something neutrally observed and exactly repeatable, for it never was a neutrally synthesized and rationally reality-tested intentional object, but as the internally constituted psychical representative of jouissance, it stands in for an ineffable, unspeakable pleasure.[20] Projected as a mental representative of that which will restore jouissance, the object aimed at by the drive incorporates an uncountable surplus that cannot finally be articulated or actualized.

To sum up, even if the subject grasps that there has been a loss of jouissance, it cannot grasp precisely what has been lost, and this means that any form of the ideational representative, whose aim is to do exactly this, will be aporetic in some sense. Nevertheless, importantly, Lacan emphasizes the necessity of an "ideational representative," which hallucinates what will restore jouissance "in the form of a system of references." For in its absence, "a world of perception cannot be organized in a valid way, cannot be constituted in a human way."[21] In other words, Lacan does not here uncover our dependence on an aporetic "fundamental hallucination" for the sake of eradicating it. Rather, he aims to explain its structure. As I shall explain in more detail below, the difference in how the cut of castration on the object side of the transcendental relation is conceived underpins his derivation of different versions of the "ideational representative." This complexity in turn generates different nuances of interpretation in a constellation of associated terms (the lacking I, the death drive, the object of the drive, sublimation, and narcissism), which characterize three prototypical mortal-immortal relations. I shall describe these prototypical relations respectively as economic, aneconomic, and paradoxical readings of the *Nebenmensch*-complex.[22]

The Masculine Death Drive: An Economic Reading

An economic reading of the *Nebenmensch*-complex takes its cue from Freud's juxtaposition of the traumatic castration associated with weaning (which, as discussed, separates the infant from the breast, representing the subject's recognition of its mortality) and the cut of castration that appears on the object side of the lamella (representing the subject's recognition of its loss of immortality). The "castration" of the Other, here, stands for a primary split that, from the infant's point of view, severs the mother from the breast. As Freud puts it, the *Nebenmensch* is split into "two components, of which one makes an impression by its constant structure and stays together as a *thing* [*als Ding*], while the other can be *understood* by the activity of memory—that is, can be traced back to information from [the subject's] own body."[23] Translated, these metaphorics reflect the subject's emerging notion of the *Nebenmensch* as a whole related in some sense to the collection of *mnemic* sediments or discrete memory traces that constitute the partial objects of an infant's actual experience of her/him (breast, voice, gaze, etc.).

Freud's juxtaposition of whole and part leads one fairly naturally to the proposition that the cut of castration separates the immortal totality of the *Nebenmensch* as a whole from the mortal, limited, lacking, and partial aspects that are actually experienced, that is, submitted to judgment. As an excess that eludes judgment, the *Nebenmensch* as a whole "drops off into a void" that cannot be grasped or for which there are no signifiers. She thereby becomes ambivalent, that is, both satisfying as a collection of familiar phenomenal experiences and threatening as an "alien thing." In Copjec's words: "The *Ding*-component is this alien, untranslatable part of the *Nebenmensch*, which is thus forever lost to the subject and constitutes, as Lacan puts it, 'a first outside.'"[24]

On an economic reading of the *Nebenmensch*-complex, then, the lost jouissance is projected into consciousness as a lost totality. In Lacanian nomenclature, the "ideational representative" is a projection of the other as *das Ding* ("A"). This projection manifests in any desire for secure, grounded, universal orders in which, Lacan notes, one may recognize various "nostalgias of humanity: the metaphysical mirage of universal harmony, the mystical abyss of affective fusion, the social utopia of a totalitarian guardianship, and every outburst of the obsession with a paradise lost before birth or of the most obscure aspiration toward death."[25] Here, restitution of jouissance would amount to "a perfect assimilation of the totality of being."

This basic mistaken assumption of an originally present albeit "lost" totality, which underpins any metaphysics of presence, covers over a crucial enigma Lacan formulates as follows: "*Das Ding* has, in effect, to be identified with the *Wieder zu finden*, the impulse to find again that for Freud establishes the orientation of the human subject to the object," but the kind of repetition required for securing the reality of *das Ding* is impossible because jouissance was never originally there to be lost.[26] Consequently, because what desire stands for is unspeakable, the demands of any system, which manifest as "desire spoken," remain forever inadequate; that is, they never fully express or capture desire precisely because desire is an interpretation that stands in for the impossible. Honest reality testing must demonstrate that any projection of *das Ding* as an originally present totality cannot be re-found. Instead, it remains larger than life, surpassing each phenomenal experience, and even all such experiences put together. The desired jouissance, therefore, is never experienced.

On this account, one quite easily but mistakenly, as Copjec points out, slips into a Kantian analogy: "the *Ding*-component of the *Nebenmensch* is to the *Vorstellung*-component as the noumenal Thing-in-itself is to the idea we have of it, its phenomenal appearance."[27] Further, she continues, this suggests that psychoanalysis endorses "the philosophical separation between thinking and being: as we gain access to language and thus thought, we lose our access to that being which is the maternal Thing." In other words, inherent perceptual or linguistic limitations lie behind our failure to represent fully "the being of the Thing," which nevertheless lies behind every necessarily failed attempt to "say" it.

The assumption that the "Thing-in-itself," while inaccessible, remains present behind its phenomenal appearance goes hand in hand with the idea that the death drive is blocked by an idealization: beyond worldly perception and inaccessible in it or through it, the sublime object of the drive remains an unreachable ideal. In this case, the restitution of jouissance is converted into a promise of restitution in the ideal future, which no present worldly state can match. Individuals, therefore, face the prospect of a congenital dissatisfaction with everything temporal or worldly.

Yet since the pleasure-drive tends to intervene in reality testing, promoting the fabrication of paranoiac defenses against such ineradicable lack, those caught up in a libidinal style that interprets jouissance as a lost totality to be re-found are predisposed toward finding in reality only what confirms certain "larger-than-life" projections that privilege imagined coherent totalities. They accordingly tend quietly to ignore actual perceptual evidence to the contrary, which points to flux and incoherence.[28] To the extent that the belief prevails that jouissance has indeed been refound, an individual becomes fixated upon a delusion created under the pressure of the death drive. Such tendency toward paranoia, whereby the promise of totality becomes a fatal attraction, characterizes what I shall henceforth refer to as the masculine death drive.

Feminine Suspicion

Lacan's radicalization of Freud, Copjec remarks, "constitutes a refusal to be seduced by" the Kantian analogy, on the grounds that it derives from a misconception concerning the primary cut of castration; namely, that it separates out the merely partial objects of experience from a supposed totality that underlies them.[29] Becoming wise to the implicit "metaphysics of presence" in the masculine delusion entails the recognition that what is unforgettably lost in the cut of castration never was conceivable as an originally present "Thing." In other words, the interpretation of lost jouissance as a bounded totality (a past perfect present) is a retrospectively constructed illusion. When Lacan, as a suspicious woman, insists, instead, that he sets out "from the fact that there is something that establishes a fracture, a bi-partition, a splitting of . . . being," he has in mind a redefinition of "castration" as an original/originary splitting that occurs not between phenomenal being and its noumenal beyond, but within being.[30]

On this account, the cut of castration behind the structural disturbance associated with weaning marks not the infant's dawning awareness of the mother as a noumenal whole to whom the breast belongs as a phenomenal part but rather the recognition that the breast is not-All and that there is in addition to it an uncountable series of other partial objects around which the drives can turn. Lacan's insistence that the cut of castration fragments the *Nebenmensch* into partial objects ("a") radically reconfigures its function in relation to the drives. Freud indeed argues that an infant is originally subject to a play of fragmentary and fragmenting partial drives, or component instincts, which constitute a dispersed body and polymorphously perverse pleasures.[31] However, supporting the economic, masculine death drive, sustained by the Kantian analogy, he argues that the drives follow a developmental path toward unification. Thus, precipitated by the castration threat, they are ultimately bundled together under the genital organization that serves the aim of reproduction. An economic account of the *Nebenmensch*-complex differs from Freud's account only insofar as the precarious unification of the drives to form the masculine death drive, aimed at a maternal whole (or its substitutes), depends not on the castration threat but on an earlier, retrospectively constituted illusion of the primordially lost Other, according to which it "must have been" some version of the "Thing-in-itself" reflected in the Kantian analogy.

The Kantian analogy, however, is only seductive if one ignores the "drift" or partialization of the drives and assumes that there is simply libido as such, or one unified libidinal drive aiming to recover the "lost"

Thing that will complete its circuit. According to Lacan's redefinition, as Copjec notes, "castration" takes on a different function: "It appears now to participate in the formation of the partial drives rather than . . . to intervene belatedly after they are formed, to bundle them.[32] Moreover, denying a "relation of production between one of the partial drives and the next," Lacan argues that drives remain irremediably partial.[33] In Copjec's terms, object "a" is an "inherent obstacle" that "simultaneously *brakes* the drive and *breaks it up*."

One must not, however, on account of his critique of the economic, masculine death drive, assume that Lacan swings to the equal but opposite misinterpretation of "castration" that underpins its aneconomic, feminine counterpart. In brief, to constitute object *a* as an infinite concatenation of parts (that is, as the direct binary opposite of "A" as *Das Ding*) is, ironically, to reinscribe the drives in the sphere of the delusional "A"; this time, however, the Other as "All" is understood in opposite terms as an infinite oceanic flow rather than a totalized "Thing-in-itself."

The Feminine Death Drive: An Aneconomic Reading

On an aneconomic account of the *Nebenmensch*-complex, the cut of castration that splits the other of the drive into the little objects of partial drives is misconceived as the fragmentation of the *Nebenmensch* into a plurality of discrete parts. Here again, the *Nebenmensch* "drops off into a void," but in a different sense, for "she" is no longer projected as an originally present totality whose loss indicates that the whole exceeds all representation by thought. Rather, she is projected as the illusion of infinite inclusivity. The *Nebenmensch*, interpreted as the concatenation of all possible, atomistically conceived fragments, may still be thought of as a profoundly lost plenum, which must be recovered at all costs. The "ideational representative" of the drive (its aim) is still presented to consciousness as the wished-for jouissance, projected as a drive toward something Other remembered but never experienced. But the Other is now understood as an unbounded, nonobjective, oceanic "Allness," a dissolving fusion of all with all that cannot become a unified totality. The loss of jouissance is still here conceivable as a consequence of human limitations or mortality. I lack because no matter how extensive the inclusion of partial objects, the gathering itself always forms a totality too small to match the boundless All. Jouissance is therefore forever beyond experience. Moreover, no defining borders of a totality can be legitimate if jouissance is understood as the inclusion of all parts in a boundless infinity that remains perpetually defined as $n+1$. If the feminine death drive is still intrinsically aim inhibited, that is, necessarily blocked by an object, all such objects of the drive (the interpretations that represent a desire for something) are not viewed as protective defenses against the threatening, annihilating aspect of jouissance but as restrictive, limiting, illusory obstacles that inhibit the prospect of achieving oceanic bliss.

The drive to refind jouissance is formed, therefore, not as the desire for a representative intentional "object" that stands in for the lost jouissance but as the desire to smash up, shatter, undo, disavow all such objects as alienating fakes. If the restitution of jouissance means that any discrepancy between the object of the drive and the perceptual object must be eradicated, the subject perpetually and impossibly aims to refind jouissance as a state before and beyond worldly objects through the dissolution of all limiting borders and objective totalities. The aneconomic libidinal style, then, highlights the other side of the paradoxical death drive: not its inertial drive toward binding all up into a unity of all with all, but its entropic drive toward the unbinding dissolution of all tensional bonds for the sake of a boundless, flaccid, fluidity and flux.

The drive to refind jouissance, then, is still associated with a congenital dissatisfaction with the worldly, for the lost jouissance is projected as an infinite collection of parts, which the worldly cannot stretch to encompass: there will always be one more part to include, one more step, one more conquest. Dominated by the feminine death drive, the subject finds in worldly objects limitation rather than pleasure. To the extent that this form of the death drive prevails, the subject becomes fixated on utter destruction or rebellion, taking pleasure only in boundary shattering and self-destruction. This aneconomic account of the *Nebenmensch*-complex underlies the stance taken by certain "postmodern" thinkers who celebrate the fragmentation of the object, which goes hand in hand with the self-shattering desire to reinstate a polymorphous perversity of the fragmentary and fragmenting drives that, laudably enough, aims to detach sex from the ideology that commits it to mere reproduction, but in the process obliterates the subject. Lacan certainly rejects the economic, masculine death drive and in so doing turns to another libidinal style, but he equally warns against this diametrically opposed, aneconomic position for which, notably, I have retained the label "feminine," to mark the phallic logic of binary opposition for the sake of showing more clearly how Lacan subverts it. In Lacanian discourse, then, feminine libido, as that which exceeds the binary altogether, involves another sexuality or libidinal style because it embraces the paradox of object "a." To grasp this nuance, one must return once more to the beginning, to the notion of "castration."

Feminine Sublimation: Aporia of Paradox

Lacan's definition of "castration" calls for a more careful interpretation than that underpinning the aneconomic account just imposed. When he writes of the splitting of being, it not only refers to the initial state of partialization (partial objects and drives) but also to the splitting of the partial object from itself. Extending the primary metaphor of the *Nebenmensch*-complex, "castration" does not merely cut the mother from the breast and nor does it simply fragment the mother; rather, "castration" cuts the breast from itself, making of the breast a partial object that does not coincide with itself (object "a").

This nuance is based on the observation that an infant's relation to the breast is always already inherently double. To repeat Freud's argument, the difference that makes something an object not only of perception but of the drives as well can be understood in terms of the libidinal graft associated with all organs. While the breast, for example, is the source of nutritive satisfactions, it is simultaneously the object of a libidinal attachment that gives it an immeasurable surplus value. The mouth, accordingly, is divided between somatic satisfactions and libidinal satisfactions. Thus, in Lacan's words: "Even when you stuff the mouth—the mouth that opens in the register of the drive—it is not the food that satisfies it, it is, as one says, the pleasure of the mouth."[34]

But this is not to suggest that there is no actual object to support the libidinal drive. It is not the food that satisfies the libidinal drive but, as Copjec emphasizes, the breast. The breast, then, is both a perceptual object and an object of the drive (object "a"), which endows it with an ineffable surplus value, or a "thing quality" (assuming Heidegger's sense of "thing"). In short, when the subject projects an object as an object of the drive (when it loves something), the object acquires a surplus value by this very act, and in the process it is elevated to the status of a Thing.[35]

This surplus value makes of it more than a mere fragment. One may grasp the difference as one between a part that belongs to a whole and one that (paradoxically) functions as a whole.[36] Copjec explains the difference via an example from filmmaking: a close-up shot does not function as simply a closer view of a bit of the whole. Rather, the close-up focuses on that element, included in the scene without belonging to it, which is symptomatic of the unencompassable whole. Focusing on it, one finds that the scene has become infinitely more than what it had been at face value. In another example, it is only upon noticing the small splash in the ocean in Breughel's "Fall of Icarus" that the idyllic and restful country landscape takes on an unencompassable dimension. Žižek expresses this logic by insisting that the symptom frames the frame.[37] In becoming elevated to an object "a," ordinary objects become nonidentical to themselves. The object becomes in my experience what it is perceptually plus the libidinal interest that increases it in a way that remains unspeakable, and for this reason, the subject's attraction to the loved thing is continually compounded by its own desire. There is, therefore, an "otherness" intrinsic to every partial object of the drive, an "alien" residue or supplement, constituted by the subject's libidinal interest.

The misunderstanding of castration equal but opposite to the retrospective illusion of the masculine death drive, then, is to view the *Nebenmensch* as merely partialized into a collection of fragments of indifferently equal value. Instead, Lacan argues that certain perceptual objects acquire an internal excess because they are the object not only of pragmatic interests but also of the libidinal drive. As Copjec notes, if one could think of object "a" as a delegate of the excess named by *das Ding*, it would have to be a delegate that betrays the mandator, for there are only delegates, with nothing behind them.[38]

Object "a" still functions as an "inherent obstacle" to the drive that divides it into partial drives and prevents it from reaching its aim, namely jouissance. However, in this case, the lacking-I lacks jouissance not because jouissance is constitutionally out of reach (either because it is outside my finite limitations or because an infinite gathering of finite parts is impossible). Rather, jouissance is impossible in a different sense, for it is paradoxically both always available in the present and always excessive because it is self-generative, leaving desire forever unfinished. In alternative terms that invoke the notion of "the event," if the restitution of jouissance means that any discrepancy between the object of the drive and the perceptual object must be eradicated, it still remains impossible to refind jouissance, not because it exceeds the subject's phenomenal grasp absolutely but because this grasp keeps adding to it, in this way constantly reinventing the same object anew. In this case, the subject's desiring "grasp" is not a protection from jouissance but a flexible opening out to the excess within the partial object in an act of inventive sublimation that contrasts with the fixated attempts to tie it up or undo all ties that characterize the destructive dialectic of idealization or negation. As Copjec sums it up: "Rather than pursuing the Nothing of annihilating dissatisfaction, the now partial drives content themselves with these small nothings, these objects that satisfy them."[39]

The Fraternal-Complex: Narcissism, Self-Sublimation, and Aggressivity

In outline, Lacan demonstrates that the castrated other of the fraternal-complex, implicated in the constitution of the subject as *moi*, takes shape as an alter ego, that is, an alien and alienating double represented by the mirror image, which is divided between its interpretation as prosthesis, armor, and, one may suggest, an "iterating double." On an economic account of this complex, which extends the masculine libidinal style developed in the *Nebenmensch*-complex, the other as alienating double of the self is interpreted as a prosthetic ideal to strive for. The narcissistic pleasure derived from the assumed power to constitute the *moi* as one with the ideal accounts for infantile megalomania. The correlate of such masculine narcissism is an aggressivity that manifests as jealousy. On an aneconomic account of this complex, extending the feminine libidinal style, the other as alienating double of the self is interpreted as a restrictive armor one is compelled to resist by self-shattering in the name of matching the *moi* with the infinite-All. The correlate of such feminine narcissism is an aggressivity that manifests as envy. On a paradoxical reading of this complex, the mirror image as "iterating double" indicates the paradox of a self that does not coincide with itself and calls the subject toward a forward repetition captured in the formulation "become who you are." Such inventive self-sublimation is not without its correlative aggressivity, understood in terms of the necessary violence associated with inventive decision making.

The Mirror Stage and Aggressivity

Following upon the *Nebenmensch*-complex, Lacan describes a child's recognition of itself in the mirror as the prototypical event of identification, in which the *moi* is formed in relation to the Other as alter ego. It is, as he puts it, "a first captation by the image in which the first stage of the dialectic of identifications can be discerned."[40] The "dialectic of identifications" here refers to the succession of other possible reflective alter egos after the mirror image (*Nebenmensch*, siblings, parents, friends, other concrete others) in the hall of mirrors we call "fraternity." More importantly, as the term "captation" (captivation and capture) suggests, this dialectic refers to the ambivalence of the identification process, intrinsic to which are the correlates "narcissism" and "aggressivity."

Freud's notion of "narcissism," as the metaphorics of reflection suggest, denotes the ego's love for itself projected as a "whole," or ideal ego, which is an introjected version of the lost *Nebenmensch*. If the castration threat, moreover, can no longer be adduced as the immediate cause of narcissism, Lacan is obliged to propose an alternative cause.[41] His candidate is "sublimation." Notably, I have already referred to this notion, taking for granted the Lacanian redefinition that makes of it the elevation of the object of the drive rather than the deflection of the sex drive. I shall return to it in more detail in the following discussion of the paternal-complex. At this point, it suffices to note that in the displacement that occurs at "the mirror stage," whereby the infant takes its own mirror image as a substitute for the *Nebenmensch*, it is the ego itself, reflected in the mirror as a whole form, which becomes the object of the drive. Lacan aptly calls sublimation "an identificatory reshaping of the subject,"[42] and it takes on its character as self-sublimation, again in contrast to self-idealization or self-negation, depending on which of the three versions of the whole is adopted as the model (a bounded unity, an oceanic fluidity, or an open-ended, self-renewing "Thing"). In turn, the aggressivity intrinsic to the *moi* takes on different nuances in relation to these different articulations of narcissism.

The axial notions of the fraternal-complex, namely "narcissism," self-sublimation," and "aggressivity," build upon the complex articulation just elaborated as three versions of the *Nebenmensch*-complex, and it is accordingly possible to derive a similar series of readings in relation to the constitution of the *moi*. Although Lacan's essays "The Mirror Stage" and "Aggressivity" are early works in which all of these complexities are not fully explicit, they nevertheless form a useful basis for understanding this series, which bears gracefully enough the elaboration necessary to accommodate the complexities introduced by his later works.

Emphasizing our "real *specific prematurity of birth*," Lacan notes that the characteristically uncoordinated human neonate inhabits a body dispersed by the fragmentary play of partial drives.[43] The human form, he adds, "holds the child's interest in the first months of life, and even, in the case of a human face, from the tenth day."[44] The constitution of the *moi*, accordingly, is linked to the "first captation by the image" around the age of six months, which marks the shift whereby libido is displaced from the fragmentary forms of the *Nebenmensch* (face, voice, gaze, breast, etc.) and captivated/captured by the human form as a whole. One can recognize this shift by "the signs of triumphant jubilation and playful discovery that characterize, from the sixth month, the child's encounter with his image in the mirror."[45] Again: "This jubilant assumption of his specular image by the child at the *infans* stage, still sunk in his motor incapacity and nursling dependence, would seem to exhibit in an exemplary situation the symbolic matrix in which the *I* is precipitated in a primordial form, before it is objectified in the dialectic of identification with the other, and before language restores to it, in the universal, its function as subject."[46]

Condensed in this citation is a reference to the basic movement that constitutes the fraternal-complex: namely, from fragmentation, through the jubilant identification with the mirror image that precipitates the primordial form of the "I" as the narcissistic *moi,* to the alienation, anxiety, and aggressivity associated with the *moi*'s "captation" by the alter ego. This movement, which leads up to the *moi*'s subjectification via the Oedipus complex, is common to all three articulations, even though the different nuances discernible in the axial notions of the fraternal-complex produce dramatically divergent articulations of the *moi.* Before I discuss their differences, then, I shall trace out this common thread.[47]

Importantly, Lacan notes, reflected in a flutter of play activity, it is clear that the infant takes the mirror image to be hers. What is remarkable about this uniquely human "phenomenon of recognition"[48] is that the mirror image, reflecting the "total form of the body,"[49] is a visually apprehended spatial unity quite foreign to an infant's own bodily experience.[50] In more abstract terms, it represents the "whole" ego as a bounded unity where all is coherently tied up in a seemingly closed and self-sufficient unity. Through its fixed size and its symmetry, this image, according to Lacan, "symbolizes the mental permanence of the *I.*"[51] It is in spite of the marked discrepancy between mirror image and actual experience that infants take the image to be their own. Moreover, what is remarkable about such identification is the radical transformation whereby infants take themselves to be something other than their experienced being.[52]

Related to this observation, Lacan claims that psychoanalytic theory should start out "from the *function of méconnaissance* [misrecognition] that characterizes the ego [*moi*] in all its structures."[53] The infant's jubilant assumption of a spatial identity not actually experienced represents what he calls an "orthopedic" misrecognition. On the basis of the total form reflected in the mirror, the subject initially, in the equivalent of childhood megalomania, makes the mistake of assuming that the *moi* is identical to the reflected perfection. In his words: "The *mirror stage* is a drama whose internal thrust is precipitated from insufficiency to anticipation—and which manufactures for the subject, caught up in the lure of spatial identification, the succession of phantasies that extends from a fragmented body-image to a form of its totality that I shall call orthopaedic."[54]

But the joyous affirmation of this promise of totality is soon enough followed by alienating experiences of discord that open up a gap (*béance*) between the unity promised by the external mirror image and the continuing fragmentary character of the infant's lived bodily experience. The image that offers the promise of an orthopedic totality soon enough becomes "the armour of an alienating identity, which will mark with its rigid structure the subject's entire mental development."[55] The lacking-I, whose lived experience remains in flux, cannot match the identity assumed by its own alter ego, and it remains, therefore, displaced by it, anxious, and never quite at home with it. Breaking out of the circle of the *Nebenmensch*-complex and facing the external human fraternity, then, as Lacan puts it, "generates the inexhaustible quadrature of the ego's [*moi*] verifications."[56] As Lee explains, Lacan plays here on the associative link between the mathematical term "quadrature," which is to make a square out of a circle and a commonly used example of logical impossibility, to underscore the internal conflict between the lacking-I and the *moi* identity.[57]

What occurs in the mirror stage forms the early prototype for "the deflection of the specular *I* into the social *I*."[58] The early stages of the "dialectic of identification with the other," however, remain predominantly narcissistic, for the form of another human is taken to be a form of the self, an alter ego rather than an other. Noting the "phenomenon of infantile *transitivism*"—"the child who strikes another says that he has been struck; the child who sees another fall, cries"[59]—Lacan argues that it is not attributable to empathy, "the absence of which is made abundantly clear in early infancy," but to the infant's "captation by the *imago* of the human form."[60] This captation by the form of another human marks the end of the mirror stage and, as Lacan puts it, "inaugurates, by the identification with the *imago* of the counterpart and the drama of primordial jealousy . . . the dialectic that will henceforth link the *I* to socially elaborated situations."[61] Here, as Lee explains, "the identity of the young child is shaped in profound and enduring ways by her adopting the visual identity offered by other people (in particular, by mother, father, and siblings)."[62] At this point, the subject becomes obsessed with the enigma of the other's desire. Lacan, as Fink puts it,

> formulates the subject's primordial experience of jouissance as stemming from its *traumatic encounter with the Other's desire.* The subject—lacking in being—is thus seen to consist in a relation to, or a stance adopted with respect to, the Other's desire as fundamentally

thrilling and yet unnerving, fascinating and yet overwhelming or revolting. While a child wishes to be recognized by its parents as worthy of their desire, their desire is both mesmerizing and lethal. The subject's precarious existence is sustained by fantasies constructed to keep the subject at just the right distance from that dangerous desire, delicately balancing the attraction and the repulsion.[63]

Such fantasies of identity, both prosthetic and alienating, go hand in hand with aggressivity.[64] Here, one reaches a sort of "structural crossroads" between narcissism and aggressivity, for every narcissistically loved prosthesis is always a structure of *méconnaissance* and is therefore necessarily simultaneously an objectifying, alienating armor subject to aggressive hatred.[65] Aggressivity in various forms, as the intrinsic other side of narcissism, in Lacan's words, "gnaws away, undermines, disintegrates . . . castrates . . . leads to death."[66] Although, as he points out, real constraints temper such aggressivity: "Its effects are more far-reaching than any act of brutality."[67] He proposes a difference, then, between such intrinsic aggressivity and specific acts of aggression.

Aggressivity, as the dialectical negative of jubilant identification with the imago, grows out of the moment of alienation.[68] As Lacan notes, the discrepancy between ego and ideal ego, whereby the ideal ego becomes a restrictive imposition, is at the root of aggressivity "in any relation to the other, even in a relation involving the most Samaritan of aid."[69] Representing the desire to break out of the alienating misrecognized identity imposed by the alter ego, all of our phantasmagoric images of aggressivity resurrect the fragmented body of our initial experience. These are the ubiquitous culture-, gender-, and age-independent "images of castration, mutilation, dismemberment, dislocation, evisceration, devouring, bursting open of the body."[70] One may turn from child's play and literature (which is rife with head-chopping, belly-ripping, and child-devouring monsters) to the works of Hieronymus Bosch, which, Lacan notes, provides "an atlas of all the aggressive images that torment mankind."[71] Aggressivity, then, implies the satisfaction to be obtained from smashing up the imago. In Lacan's words:

To the *Urbild* of this formation, alienating as it is by virtue of its capacity to render extraneous [constitute "me" on its outside], corresponds a peculiar satisfaction deriving from the integration of an original organic disarray [fragmentation], a satisfaction that must be conceived in the dimension of a vital dehiscence that is constitutive of man, and which makes unthinkable the idea of an environment that is preformed for him, a "negative" libido that enables the Heraclitean notion of Discord, which the Ephesian believed to be prior to harmony, to shine once more.[72]

The Masculine Libidinal Style

Caught in the crossfire between loved prosthesis and hated alienating armor, one style of libidinal response is to deny the discrepancy. Here, what is reflected in the mirror, along with the reflecting eyes of the other alter egos, is indeed not "me" after all but a projection of the ideal figure that I ought to become. In such self-idealization, characteristic of the masculine libidinal style, I anticipate the "maturation of my power" in the seductive mirage of the alter ego.[73] Masculine misrecognition, then, manifests as denial. The subject's intrinsic lack or castration is tacitly denied insofar as it is reduced to a temporary (or temporal) state of privation that the subject strives to overcome. This is correlatively to deny that the *moi* is an Imaginary construct.

Lacan argues that the masculine libidinal style promotes a paranoid fear of persecution, characterized by fixations that have "something stereotypical about them that suspends the workings of the subject/object dialectic [i.e., reality testing]."[74] Reflecting what he calls the paranoiac structure of human knowledge, the masculine libidinal style "constitutes the subject and its objects with attributes of permanence, identity and substantiality." In short, the transcendental relation is reduced to a relation between "entities or 'things' that are very different from the *Gestalten* that experience enables us to isolate in the shifting field, stretched in accordance with the lines of animal desire."[75]

This formal fixation introduces "a certain discord between man's organization and his *Umwelt*."[76] According to Lacan, "the formation of the *I* is symbolized in dreams by a fortress, or a stadium—its inner arena and enclosure, surrounded by marshes and rubbish-tips, dividing it into two opposed fields of contest where the subject flounders in quest of the lofty, remote inner castle."[77] But it is this very fictionalizing gap, this distance from reality testing, that enables the paranoiac to extend his world and his power indefinitely—for now his objects are made to mean what he wants them to mean, and discrepancies, loose ends, anomalies, differences are silently ignored. Similarly, his words acquire a "symbolic polyphony" (they mean what he says they mean), which gives them their "potential as defensive armour."[78] He lives, however, in a permanent state of paranoid anxiety concerning the ever-present threat of encroachment from the outside that he has necessarily constituted along with his inside.

Accordingly, the subject dreams of and strives for the anticipated power over its currently experienced lack, but impossibly and catastrophically, of course, for only absolute power will suffice. No matter how successfully in the subject's "coming into being" the discord between the *moi* and actual reality is resolved, the resolution will never match the unity represented by the mirror image (for the totality it represents is a retrospectively constructed illusion). At best, the ego will approach the narcissistically loved ideal ego asymptotically.[79] As Lacan sums it up: "It is in this erotic relation, in which the human individual fixes upon himself an image that alienates him from himself, that are to be found the energy and the form on which this organization of the passions that he will call his ego is based."[80] Further, the *moi*, as Lacan puts it, "will crystallize in the subject's internal conflictual tension, which determines the awakening of his desire for the object of the other's desire: here the primordial coming together . . . is precipitated into aggressive competitiveness."[81]

The correlate of narcissism so determined is the kind of aggressivity that has to do with jealous protection of the subject's imaginary "lack of lack." According to Lacan, primordial jealousy, closely linked to "identification with the *imago* of the counterpart,"[82] manifests as the desire for the other's desire. Capitalizing on the multivocal ambiguity of this phrase, one may, first, take it to refer to the narcissistic desire to be the object of the other's desire, that is, to match the ego with the ideal ego reflected in the gaze of the other. As Freud noted, this desire precipitates an internalized aggressivity, manifest as the subject's self-chastisement for not living up to the ideal.

Second, directed outward, this desire for the other's desire may in turn be interpreted as a demand for recognition from all others of the subject's place at the center of the universe. In this residue of infantile megalomania, the subject invests its energy in jealous protection of what it owns and in ruthless pursuit of the power that has supposedly been promised. Jealousy, then, rests on the subject's assumption that it rightfully possesses its place at the center, which it jealously guards from potential intruders. Lacan cites St. Augustine: "I have seen with my own eyes and known very well an infant in the grip of jealousy: he could not yet speak, and already he observed his foster-brother, pale and with an envenomed stare."[83]

This fear of intrusion, third, precipitates the "desire for the object of the other's desire" and the subject's drive to "domesticate" the other, in so doing securing himself against what the other has, either by gaining power over what the other possesses or by rendering it worthless or innocuous. In the analytical situation, for example, masculine aggressivity is characterized by belligerent resistance to treatment. Such "resistance to analysis" takes the form of a deeply held resentment toward the analyst for having the power to offer help. As Lacan puts it: "What appears here as the proud revenge of suffering will show its true face . . . in the form of that resistance of *amour-propre* . . . which is often expressed thus: 'I can't bear the thought of being freed by anyone other than myself.'"[84] In Lacan's view: "Only saints are sufficiently detached from the deepest of the common passions to avoid the aggressive reactions to charity."[85] It is unsurprising, then, that masculine aggressivity manifests as a "fight to the death" that has multiple faces bound up with the assumption that the subject has something to lose. By contrast, finally, the meaning of the phrase may be extended to include the desire to possess (command, control, or neutralize) the other's very capacity for desire. This nuance, as I shall discuss presently, distinguishes jealousy from envy.

The Feminine Libidinal Style

Similarly caught between loved prosthesis and alienating armor, the feminine libidinal response is characterized by a refusal to be seduced by its love for the unity of the mirror image. Instead, lack or castration is not denied but acknowledged as originary. Here, what is reflected in the mirror and in the gaze of the alter ego is certainly not "me" at all, but the projection of an alienating and restrictive artifice that I ought to resist. The mirage in this case is not the figure of an anticipated fullness but is viewed as the restrictive and alienating armor of an artificial unity that is as impossible to achieve as it is an undesirable obstacle to restitution of the All. Feminine misrecognition, one may suggest, manifests as a wholesale acceptance of lack, and therefore, correlatively, relentless resistance to the seductive imago (a refusal of its status as a necessary fiction) for the sake of the All, again misconstrued, but this time as infinity rather than totality. The feminine counterpart to narcissism as "idealization," then, manifests as a drive to undo all ideals for the sake of returning to the oceanic state, the absolutely primary narcissism of the fluid, all-encompassing plenum or the great libidinal reservoir of partial drives and partial objects where nothing is left on the outside.

If the masculine libidinal style promotes paranoia, the feminine counterpart is maintained in the grip of a hysterical paralysis, whereby she can merely resist the armor of an alienating identity without commanding the means to reconfigure another identity. Indeed, held in the grip of this drive toward utter dissolution, if she has power enough, she uses it to configure a state of affairs that is guaranteed to maintain her distance from worldly relations. As Copjec puts it: "Distancing herself from her world, the hysteric eroticizes her solitude while acting as a puppeteer of an erotic coupling elsewhere."[86] The strictures that command a pure state of rebellion are as inflexible, rigid, and paralyzing as those that are associated with masculine paranoia.

The correlate of feminine narcissism is an aggressivity that shows itself in attempts to return to a state of fragmentation. First, such aggressivity manifests in the enjoyment of "self-shattering," or in the dissolution of the ideal ego in the name of a shifting collection of multiple, discrete, or atomistic selves, which amounts to the eradication of the subject. It also manifests in the subtle kind of aggressivity toward others that aims to break them down, both physically and mentally, not for the purpose of establishing hierarchical power over them but for the sake of rendering them equally powerless.

In this case, I tend to agree with those feminists who insist that Hegel's master/slave dialectic does not include a feminine moment. Feminine aggression shows itself, rather, in the nuance that, on Copjec's account, separates jealousy from envy.[87] As Copjec notes, "jealousy is grounded in the possession of a certain pleasure" that one fears losing, "whereas envy stems precisely from a lack of it." In other words, envy is rooted in the subject's recognition that it is not the other's sole object of desire, or that it has no place there at the center of the world, but remains constitutionally on the outside, and thus positioned only to envy the other his enjoyment of a privileged position there at the center. Yet, Copjec continues, "one would be wrong to assume that envy's lack can be filled by the possession of that pleasure it is pained to see the other enjoying. . . . All endeavors . . . to satisfy an envious man are fruitless. Why? Because what he wants and what he perceives as the other's enjoyment are not at all the same thing." The desire that motivates envy is directed neither toward robbing the other of some possession nor toward taking another's place at the center. The envious subject does not want to assume the fake, alienating identity reflected in the mirroring eyes of the alter ego; what it wants is jouissance, and what it envies is the jouissance the other seems to be experiencing. Sick at the sight of another's enjoyment, envy "wants nothing so much as to spoil the very capacity for enjoyment."[88]

The Feminine Paradox

While both masculine and feminine libidinal styles, caught between prosthesis and armor, remain tied up in the aporias associated respectively with paranoiac jealousy and hysterical envy, Lacan does not argue that there is any form of escape from the structures of either narcissism or aggressivity and maintains that, in principle, vacillation between prosthesis and armor is ineradicable. However, on a certain understanding of this "structural crossroads" in which the subject recognizes the aporetic structure of the mirror image, both paranoiac jealousy and hysterical envy lose their teeth.

In this case, what is reflected in the mirroring eyes of the alter egos is simultaneously both "me" and not "me," because the "wholeness" of the ego represented by the mirror image is construed neither as an ideal, prosthetic totality nor as the restrictive obstacle to self-infinitization. Instead, the subject recognizes the necessity of the prosthesis, for one cannot be anything without a sustaining narrative fiction of identity while at the same time accepting its status as a constraining armor that does not properly fit. Yet, because the subject remains wise to its necessity, it is not subject to hysterical dissolution. At the same time, because the subject is also wise to its fictional status, it is not tied up in paranoiac stagnation, and the subject remains free to open it up to self-sublimating reinvention. In a revised version of narcissism, then, the subject presses its own limits precisely because it loves what amounts to an ineradicable internal excess that cannot be bound by these limits. However, it presses these limits without, on the one hand, working toward a totalizing imaginary picture of what the final product should be, and, on the other, pretending to erase the limits altogether. There perpetually remains an "I" to reinvent the *moi*.

This is not to suggest that the process of unbinding and rebinding the *moi* is nonaggressive. There is always a degree of violence associated with binding together certain strands to form the narrative fiction of one's identity and leaving others out. This violation remains unavoidable because some erotic binding together is necessary for self-invention to be possible at all, but if there is only binding up, reinvention becomes impossible. At the same time, then, there is equal violence in opening up an invention for reinvention. Destructive, untying dissolution is necessary for invention to become possible again, but if there is only dissolution, invention becomes impossible. It is the fixation to one or the other side of the death drive that allows masculine paranoia or feminine hysteria to take hold of the subject. If there is aggressivity in the paradox of binding and unbinding, then, it is the least destructive kind of violence, because it puts the death drive on hold. The death drive is always to come, but only because the open-endedness of the necessary fiction means, paradoxically, that it has already come. In other words, a certain kind of immortality is already available here and now.

The Paternal-Complex: Law, Transgression, and the Sex/Civilization Antinomy

Lacan's treatment of the paternal-complex focuses on his version of the development of the superego (in the resolution of the Oedipus-complex). The intrinsically or structurally "castrated" other associated with the paternal-complex takes the form of the Symbolic Order, that is, a culture, discourse, or language game inscribed in the language of the parents. Lacan ties the castration of the Symbolic Order to an account of it as simultaneously decapitating and dissolving. It is decapitating in the sense that one is obliged to submit to the underlying rules of a pregiven discourse, inscribed in the language one learns to speak, in order to form a *moi* identity that is recognized in a community. As Lacan puts it: "I identify myself in language, but only by losing myself in it like an object."[89] Yet, while establishing a meaningful, discursively articulated identity (tying signifiers to signifieds) is necessary and possible, it remains simultaneously impossible, for in language as such, there is no necessary, internal limit to the sliding of the signifier over the signified. This is the sense in which language, for Lacan, is equally "dissolving."

In other words, tied to the general logic of language, which one can articulate in terms of the "plural logic of the aporia," the Symbolic Order as such (as a general term that stretches across its multiple actual manifestations as various language games or discourses) cannot form a whole. Instead, its logical moments of "limiting decapitation" and "limitlessness dissolution" are articulated according to the vel of alienation. On the one hand, any discourse under the label of "law" consists of a network of artificially fixed significations or repeatable stereotypes that constitute the discursive rules of the game. These are for the most part unconsciously absorbed and unthinkingly applied, that is, taken for granted. On the other hand, transgression of these stereotypes is always already inscribed in the discourse as a logical moment on account of the slippage intrinsic to language, whose limitation is precisely its lack of limits.[90]

Lacan, then, views the general logic of the Symbolic Order, implicated in the constitution of the *je*, as an aporetic articulation of the mutually incompatible logical moments of paranoiac law, its hysterical transgression, and the paradox of another transgression, which recognizes the excess internal to law that he calls *até*.[91] *Até* marks the paradox that law itself is inherently criminal in the sense that it necessarily involves the tyrannical violation of singularity in the name of the common.[92] He accordingly recasts the process of "captation" by the paternal imago, that is, entry into the Symbolic Order, or oedipalization, in terms of three logical possibilities in the formation of the *je*, which, in contrast to the "spoken" *moi*, describes the acting, speaking "I."

In this case, the economic, masculine libidinal style is associated with ideological interpellation through oedipalization. As Freud insists, every young person is obliged to leave the family circle, enter the "cultural mode of life," and negotiate the seemingly unavoidable rift between love and civilization. "On the one hand," he argues, "love comes into opposition to the interests of civilization; on the other, civilization threatens love with substantial restrictions."[93] The work of civilization, then, for Freud, requires substantial "instinctual sublimations." Moreover, he adds: "Since a man does not have unlimited quantities of psychical energy at his disposal, he has to accomplish his tasks by making an expedient distribution of his libido. What he employs for cultural aims he to a great extent withdraws from women and sexual life."[94] However, according to Lacan, if Freud doomed humanity to endemic discontent by arguing that sublimation (as desexualization of the libido in the name of cultural edification) deflects the drive from its aim, which is jouissance (satisfaction, happiness), he simultaneously "tells us repeatedly that sublimation is also satisfaction of the drive."[95] In other words: "Between these two terms—drive and satisfaction—there is set up an extreme antinomy that reminds us that the use of the function of the drive has for me no other purpose than to put in question what is meant by satisfaction."[96] Lacan takes up the task of resolving the antinomy in Freudian theory between sex and civilization by showing that it is derived from Freud's conservative side, which ties the entry into the Symbolic Order via oedipalization (in Freud's terminology, the introjection of culture or civilization, which is inscribed in the psyche via the superego) to the masculine illusion. It is only as a function of this link that narcissism together with sublimation implies that the subject strives hopelessly toward edification by matching the ego with the idealized superego imposed by a cultural tradition.

Lacan, by contrast, seeks a way out of this narrow, masculine articulation of oedipalization by revisiting (and revaluing) Freud's account of feminine oedipalization. Freud, struggling to force feminine oedipalization into a framework constructed on the masculine model, came to the conclusion that women fail to form a superego.[97] This, in turn, is interpreted as a matter of moral weakness; women cannot discipline their pathological, libidinal tendency to elevate love above law. Since women represent the interests of family and of sexual life, on Freud's account they "soon come into opposition to civilization and display their retarding and restraining influence."[98] Moreover, resentful when a man withdraws his libidinal attention to attend to the claims of civilization, she soon becomes hostile toward it. Freud admits that "feminists are not pleased to hear this,"[99] but Lacanians argue that they should be, for if Freud saw the inability to form a superego as a moral weakness, Lacan turns it into a source of ethical strength. As Silverman notes, Freud was right in a way he had not intended to be when, in his account of the castration complex in women, he argued that women do not automatically or properly develop a superego.[100]

Lacan achieves this reversal by indeed attaching the superego to convention, conscience, and guilt, but not to an ethical capacity. In fact, it can be demonstrated that the cruel superego demands a kind of ethical fanaticism that leads directly to multiple evils. Those who adopt a feminine position of suspicion vis-à-vis conventional masculine morality have a better chance of acting ethically, because they are not already fixated to the cruel demands of the superego. Having been excluded from the start, they are not first obliged to break off the bonds of a dominating ideology, and therefore (being closer to the Real understood as *différance*) they have already taken the first step along the long and difficult path to ethical action. In short, by retaining the traditional labels, descriptive of the situation for men and women in the predominant patriarchal symbolic order, which still associates masculinity with universality and femininity with particularity, Lacan offers a means of revising their value.

The Lacanian revisions have subjected Freud's version of the development of the superego to a complex elaboration, which shows that if the ego as a "whole" is interpreted as either an oceanic fluidity or a self-renewing object *a*, narcissistic self-love will set it against the restrictive superego. Here, a space opens up for explaining the possibility of resistance to the superego that does not fall into the trap of opposing sex and culture. According to the feminine illusion, admittedly, the opposing force becomes what Hegel calls the "eternal irony" of any community, for the opposing, aneconomic, feminine libidinal style is associated with hysterical transgression of all such ideological conditioning, due (mercifully) to the failure of oedipalization. Lacan, however, aims to avoid the extremism of this reactive, hysterical stance.

A reading of this complex, finally, in terms of the aporia of paradox is associated with the ethical ability to negotiate these aporias, engendering the capacity for a nondestructive critique of cultural laws and values because the critique takes the form of the inventive sublimation that constitutes for an individual an immortal place in the fabric of the community. Copjec explains this notion through Lefort's conception of immortality as a paradoxical infinity within time, by linking immortality with posterity, or, that is, with the act of inventive sublimation possible to the independent individual, whose singularity is recognized.[101] She cites Lefort as claiming that "the sense of immortality proves to be bound up with the conquest of a place *which cannot be taken*, which is invulnerable, because it is the place of someone . . . who, by accepting all that is most singular in his life, refuses to submit to the coordinates of space and time and who . . . for us . . . is not dead."[102] The social, she adds, "is composed, then not just of those things that will pass, but also of relations to empty places that will not." These singular, eternal places hold the world together in time.

Lacan's account of the paternal-complex may be viewed as part of a sustained critique of Freud's pessimism by showing that the lacking subject is not necessarily discontented. Our capacity for inventive sublimation, which recognizes the singularity of the object of the drive, of the narcissistically loved *moi*, and of an individual's place in the cultural fabric, enables one to see how the subject can avoid the fixations of masculine or feminine fanaticism and find both satisfaction and infinity within the world. The following chapters, which thematize ethical action and discursive power, are directed toward adding substance to this claim.

11

The Death Drive and Ethical Action

Introductory Remarks

In answer to the question of how Sophocles' *Antigone*, a relatively neglected Athenian tragedy, so captured the ethical imagination that it has become a regular reference point for ethical speculation, Copjec proposes that German idealism recharged the play by finding in it the paradigmatic universality/particularity problematic of modern ethics.[1] The abyssal complexity of Hegel's dialectic of the "ethical order," to which it is indexed, has generated such a rich tapestry of readings that this reference point is, indeed, most likely to be Hegel's Antigone. Lacan's interpretation of the play, then, is as much a matter of finding contemporary relevance in an ancient text as it is of responding to Hegel's reinvention of Antigone "as the paradigmatic figure of modern ethics."[2] Notably, agreement concerning Hegel's argument is far from assured, but to define a point of comparison with Lacan's treatment of ethical action, I shall very briefly outline Hegel's proposition that the ethical order is constituted by a dialectical opposition between the ethical principles of universality and particularity, which he calls "masculine" and "feminine," and for which Creon and Antigone stand as metonyms. The purpose of this starting point is to situate the Lacanian account of the ethical in relation to the structure of Hegel's dialectic, to which it is a critical response. This, in turn, allows one to establish an accord with the "plural logic of the aporia," which can be understood as the equivalent Derridean response to Hegel's dialectic.

Because I find it difficult, however, to empathize with Antigone's ethical obligation to bury her brother lest he wander the underworld as a wraith in perpetuity, I take Hegel's Antigone only as a point of departure, and, shifting focus to a contemporary instance of dramatic fiction that addresses more familiar ethical questions and dilemmas, I draw Alejandro Amenábar's film *The Sea Inside* into the discussion. In outline, Ramón Sampedro, having existed for twenty-eight years as a quadriplegic after a diving accident in his youth, expresses, and finally manages to act upon, an unyielding desire to end his life. In the form of characters whose intricate array of ethical stances are varied according to whether or not they support or dispute his argument for the right to an assisted suicide, and in the degree to which they are willing to act upon their convictions, the film poses the question of whether it ultimately narrates the story of criminal or ethical action. Amenábar's sympathies are clear enough, and the film might have been made expressly to stage a Lacanian challenge to the "conventional morality" that presides over Ramón's existence.[3] It therefore provides a clear illustration of a theory of ethical action that is by no means easy to grasp in its rather abstruse Derridean and Lacanian formulations.

Hegel's Antigone and Ethical Fanaticism

Hegel uses the context, characters, and events of the *Antigone* to exemplify and critique the "ethical fanaticism" that emerges as the dialectical opposite of pure reasoning in ethics. In other words, to begin with, he challenges two extremes as equally inadequate to concrete ethical decision making. He objects to the emptiness of pure reasoning, which places individuals outside the communal (discourses, institutions, politics) and requires them to make ethical judgments from this disinterested position of critical distance. Yet, through his account of the dialectical collapse of the ethical order, he also resists what one may call the fanaticism of its natural opposite, namely the turn to ethical substance. I shall take "fanaticism," along with Kant (ironically), to denote the kind of self-delusion that wills some vision of content beyond all the bounds of sensibility.[4] In this case, the construction of an ethical edifice rests on the mere dream that one may gain access to all there is to "see" on the basis of pregiven ethical principles. Further, fanaticism involves a "fixation" to this dream, a refusal to give it up no matter what the cost.

Hegel's diagnosis of the problematic turn to ethical substance is as follows: First, the condition under which two varieties of ethical fanaticism, represented by Creon and Antigone, become possible is an immature notion of community that defines the whole as a mere aggregation of parts, or community as an aggregate of family units/private associations. On this misunderstanding of community, whole and parts are "separately" realized on the basis of inherently conflicting ethical principles (namely universality and particularity), neither of which alone covers all of the ethical substance.

Second, because this immature notion of community already creates the structural conditions for conflict, ethical appropriation too becomes oppositional. Both Antigone and Creon understand their ethical agency as a passion: they believe themselves to be entirely "possessed by," or "given to," an ethical authority (in contemporary terms, an ideology), which opposes and supersedes whatever self-possession they may in principle be capable of by virtue of their own powers of active reasoning. The element of passion here, which was originally supposed to have tempered the arrogance of active reason, becomes a source of fanatical fixation because it takes shape as impassioned obedience to a single ethical authority (either human or Divine law), which is taken to cover "all there is" and therefore blinds itself to the other authority (and to their paradoxical interdependence).

For Hegel's Creon, accordingly, the authoritative whole that covers "all there is" takes shape as the positive system of human law, which is knowable in its entirety. For him human law is all encompassing; it fills all the possible space for ethical thinking, without gaps. However, as Hegel has demonstrated, his belief that his whole is identical with "the All" is an impossible fantasy, a delusion, upon which action would be disastrous. For Hegel's Antigone, by direct contrast, the whole of human law only becomes all encompassing by contingent artifice or decree. It completes itself only by externalizing what exceeds its dictates (the excess constituted by that which, in principle, cannot be made explicitly known) and by repressing this violation. It therefore will never be "the All," but merely a closed system, limited by an outside (a Divine law) it cannot encompass. It is in principle an impossible task to take account of this unspeakable outside, which is indicated in the notion of the "Divine" but converted into an oxymoron in the notion of a "Divine law." Hegel's Antigone, nevertheless, mistakenly believes that she must take account of the "Divine," and she therefore violates its absolute externality (or alterity) precisely in its translation into specific ethical action. Ethical fanaticism, then, is the insistence on the possibility of ethical action on the basis of either of these two impossibilities.

Hegel's underlying dialectical strategy is to show that whenever a binary opposition is set up, the two poles cannot be separated sharply, because they are interdependent. If one side is privileged as self-sufficient (as covering "all there is") and the other relegated to a derivative status, then the latter is violated, and this equally turns out to be a violation of the former. In this quintessentially modern conflict, the principles of universality and particularity stand in binary opposition, and accordingly, as Copjec puts it:

> What makes Antigone and Creon equally guilty, in Hegel's eyes, is the fact that in choosing one course of action they thereby lose something that is not merely expendable, but that sustains, or is the necessary condition of, the very thing they choose. Antigone and Creon act on behalf of the particular and the universal, respectively, but since there is no particular without the universal, and vice versa, each choice ends in a betrayal of that in the name of which it is made.[5]

To act for the whole (the community) at the cost of the part (the family) is to destroy the community too, because the family network forms the structure of the community. But to act for the part (the family) at the cost of the whole is to destroy the family too, because the family has no security or stability except as part of a whole. In short, there is no hope of acting to satisfy both authorities simultaneously, and the ethical act must become violent. The tragedy of the Ethical Order, then, is that the ethical deed is inherently a violation of the ethical substance. Hegel, however, views the collapse of the Ethical Order into self-contradiction as a necessary stage on the way to a more mature notion of community as speculative unity, which dissolves the condition for the possibility of fanaticism. For Hegel, the ethical aporia indicates a false opposition derived from misunderstanding the whole as a mere aggregation of parts, whereas the ultimately true notion of "the All" is the speculative unity of sameness and difference. Here, on analogy with a magnet, he envisages an organic unity in which macrocosm and microcosm mirror one another. (No matter where a magnet is cut, it will never be divided into positive and negative sides. Rather, all parts, no matter how small, mirror the polarity of the whole.) For Hegel, the collapse of the Ethical Order makes way for a higher-order synthesis leading to the speculative unity that would eradicate the aporia.

While rejecting Hegel's resolution, both Derrida and Lacan grant Hegel's insight concerning the aporetic relation between these binaries and accept his conclusion that ethics is impossible if either side of the opposition is hypostatized, for each ethical principle (universality or particularity) both denies and depends on the other. This claim may seem surprising on the face of it, for Lacan explicitly challenges Hegel's insistence that both Antigone and Creon are structurally guilty of equal but opposite crimes.[6] Hegel's interpretation, he insists, does not do justice to Antigone's act, which alone, and in contrast to the fixated action of a fanatical Creon, is truly ethical. This seems to imply that Lacan inconsistently makes a choice (already interdicted by his own arguments) for one side of the binary over the other. But there is a subtle line between what Lacan can be understood to be granting and challenging in Hegel's analysis of the Ethical Order, because, like Derrida, he is here dealing not with two but three options, which changes everything.

Thus, Lacan does not have to deny Hegel's point that both masculine and feminine approaches (set up as a binary opposition) lead to ethical fanaticism in order to argue that Antigone's act surpasses the binary opposition. In other words, in his view, she escapes the feminine variety of ethical fanaticism because she challenges the intrinsic authority claimed by "law" as such. In her act, implicitly guided by the notion of *até*, she exposes the criminal being of "law," that is, the notion that "law," which always covers over its inherent lack, inevitably bears the trace of a necessarily violent externalization and repression of that which exceeds it. For Lacan, in contrast with Hegel, the *Antigone* illustrates the difference between two kinds of acts: the fixated "mere actions" of those who insist on obedience to the law (whether human or Divine) and the persevering ethical action of those who are willing to transgress the law—not simply to destroy "law" as such, but to dismiss the absolute power claimed by any imposed law over their actions. Lacan's Antigone, then, resists the power claimed by Creon's law, not in abject obedience to a different kind of law, but in favor of her autonomous decision to cherish her love for her brother. In other words, Lacan disagrees with Hegel that Antigone is motivated by a hypostatized "law," or principle, of particularization, and insists instead that she is motivated to act by a different kind of passion, namely the power of *Eros*.[7]

This simply means that Lacan's Antigone is not the same person as Hegel's Antigone. Hegel would, in effect, call Antigone hysterical. Resisting the very possibility of there being desire between brother and sister, he sees her act as clearly motivated by blind, dutiful obedience to the dictates of Divine law. Lacan argues, by contrast, that it is precisely desire that lies between brother and sister in the *Antigone*, and he replaces the motivation of duty with the singularity of her autonomous love for Polynices. Whether there is sufficient textual evidence in the play to support either interpretation of her motives is not my concern here. It is hardly unknown for philosophers to bend literature (which is quintessentially multivocal) to fit the shape of a particular theory. Instead, what is philosophically important in Lacan's disagreement with Hegel concerning the status of Antigone's act is the addition of a third possibility that exceeds the binary. Lacan, then, is quite willing to concede Hegel's theoretical point that those who act in blind obedience to a principle of pure particularity may be called fanatical or hysterical. He just does not accept that this description fits Antigone. For him, Antigone, who acts out of singular, autonomous love for another, takes a different, inventive, and, in his view, genuinely ethical path that disrupts the "vel of alienation." It seems to me, then, that Lacan does not go beyond Derridean undecidability when he chooses Antigone over Creon; rather, in this choice, he chooses the aporia of paradox, and in so doing, chooses such undecidability.

The Lacanian/Derridean Challenge to Hegel's Resolution

For Hegel, the collapse of the Ethical Order is an inevitable moment that makes way for a higher speculative unity that ultimately eradicates the aporia. This resolution is rejected by Lacan and Derrida on the same basis, namely that the "truth" is not the whole, but *différance*.[8] Lacan insists that there is no substantiation for "a philosophy that culminates in Hegel's discourse—a plenitude of contrasts dialecticized in the idea of an historical progression" and asks instead whether "the formalization of mathematical logic, which is based only on writing" would not better "serve us in the analytic process."[9]

Derrida similarly argues that the dialectical process of mutual negation that promises speculative unity as its *telos* is artificially constituted by Hegel in violent attempts to force diversity into systematic binary oppositions. Speculative unity, then, itself becomes a form of fanaticism, for to construct a single system that pretends to cover it "All," Hegel has to suppress all manner of anomalies, loose ends, and indigestible fragments. In other words, the Ethical Order indeed collapses, but only in name of a more encompassing tyranny, for Hegel's system depends on eliminating precisely what both Derrida and Lacan aim to preserve, namely an irremediable excess, remainder, or supplement in any system.

Because the "introduction *into* Hegel" that Derrida names *Glas* ranges across Hegel's entire corpus, and Derrida's interpretation of the Ethical

Order forms just part of a monumental work of exegesis, one might imagine that he supports the contention that Hegel only makes sense when a part is read with the whole in mind, and one cannot achieve a productive reading of any developmental stage without describing Spirit's entire dialectical development.[10] But *Glas* is unreadable—except in fragments—and this is precisely its point. The "whole" text or corpus, for Derrida, is an inconceivable, impossible notion, and *Glas* represents a performative challenge to anyone's claim to "have the whole in mind," not least of all Hegel's.

Derrida's exegesis of Hegel's text, then, is an introduction into it of shattering fragments, not only from its various "outsides" (e.g., in its associative contiguity with the adjacent text, on pages divided into two columns) but also from within its "own" sinister columnar space. To take just one example, Derrida argues that Hegel's speculative unity is impossible because the dialectical process that promises it as its *telos* is artificially constituted by Hegel's violent attempts to force difference as "mere diversity" into difference as "proper opposition," but since something is necessarily violated in this move, the dialectic will be undone by the inevitable questions this violence engenders. Reading Hegel, then, Derrida looks for the moments when diversity is forced into opposition by a violent erasure of alternatives, without good enough reason. He sees the brother-sister relation, privileged by Hegel as the only ethical family-relation, as just such a moment.[11]

To detail the intricate arguments that underpin Hegel's privileged choice here would be to move far beyond the scope of this interjection; suffice it to remark that his dialectic requires a proper opposition of masculine and feminine equals to represent the paradoxical antagonism and interdependence that characterizes the relation between family and community, and he bends the family structure into a shape that suits his purpose. Accordingly, he selects without justification a particular (Western, Greek) model of family life and insists that the ethical bond that ties families together to form the underlying substructure of a community obtains only in a nondesiring relation of mutual recognition between brother and sister. He remains unaccountably silent about family members other than parents, children, and siblings, as well as the matter of the relation between sisters.[12] Again, from a singular event where brothers, originally committed to power sharing, rise against each other, Hegel generalizes the monstrosity of there being more than one brother in the family.[13] The implication in both cases is that there should only ever be one sister and brother in each family. Noting the violence of this structural imposition,

Derrida sets his questioning loose on the text, reminding Hegel's readers not to pass too quickly over these small, indigestible fragments.

Ironically, the dissatisfaction one experiences reading *Glas* emerges from a surfeit of satisfaction. Derrida's text is as abyssal as Hegel's, but for opposite reasons. Hegel tried to realize the systematized whole that encompasses all there is, without gaps, but the very impossibility of this aim generates an endless critical response. Derrida shatters the crystalline structure of Hegel's whole into fragments, themselves limitless, which never add up to a whole.[14] Again, the thinking never comes to an end, and the dissatisfaction in both cases is endemic. Facing the structural impossibility of taking it all in, however, Derrida agrees with those Lacanians who warn against becoming hysterical. Adumbrating the character of ethical action that takes shape in Lacan's account of the ethics of psychoanalysis, one may argue that for Derrida, one must not, above all, sacrifice the enjoyment of the text, snap the book shut, and entomb oneself on the outside of it. Instead, one can, with his blessing, love the fragment, the partial object, a fragment of this fragment, the one that attracts thought's desire and is sublimated in its limitless supply of compounded satisfactions.

On Derrida's account, Hegel's speculative unity is impossible because the dialectical process that promises it as its *telos* can only be artificially constituted by violent attempts to force diversity into binary opposition. How, then, does one proceed if one wishes, along with Hegel, to get beyond ethical fanaticism without resurrecting Kant's faith in the Categorical Imperative, but if, against Hegel, one sees speculative unity as itself a form of fanaticism? Both Derrida and Lacan insist that ethical action is a matter of finding a way to act ethically face to face with, even because of, the inevitable aporias that emerge from the very notion of "principality itself," be it the universal "force of law" imposed in the name of the whole or the universal law of transgression imposed in the name of the part.

Moreover, since ethical action apparently must, but cannot, be a matter of choosing one or the other side of this opposition, they agree that there must be something wrong with the binary setup. For both thinkers, what is wrong with the binary setup, then, is not the fact of the aporia, which is ineradicable, but the belief that it forces a choice between interdependent opposites. Both, then, accept the inevitability of the aporia but refuse to make the choice that destroys the possibility of ethical action. Each considers instead how ethical action nevertheless becomes possible in the negotiation of aporetic demands, that is, in the very attempt to do the impossible: to act with equal justice to both sides.

Derrida best articulates the call for ethical action not in a response to Hegel's Antigone but in "The Force of Law," which addresses the aporetics of ethical decision making. It might still seem surprising to claim that

Lacan articulates a parallel response by aligning ethical action with feminine sublimation, given how often it is said that Derrida, following Levinas, focuses on the other, while Lacan, following Freud, focuses on the subject. But if one has learned anything from either, it surely must be a healthy suspicion of one-sided formulations, for it should be clear that for both thinkers "subject" and "other" are never uncontaminated. Instead of seeking in vain for differences, I shall argue that their accounts of ethical action concur in that both oppose such action, in principle, to any acts that simply rely on "conventional morality." For both, the necessity for ethical action arises precisely when individuals are tied up in the aporia of paradox, where the obligation to act imposes itself in the absence of clear directives.

On the one hand, one is compelled to act for "the good" without, in principle, any nonsubjective means of knowing what "the good" is (for "the good" is a function of singular desire). As Lacan puts it in a discussion of Aristotelian ethics:

> Beside the major premise—one must always taste what is sweet—there is a particular concrete minor premise, i.e., this is sweet. And the principle of wrong action is to be found in the error of a particular judgment relative to the minor premise. Where is the error to be found? Precisely in the circumstance that the desire which is subjacent to the major premise causes the wrong judgment to be made concerning the reality of the supposed sweetness toward which the action is directed.[15]

To translate: Subjacent to the major premise that "one must always do what is good" is the implied qualification that relates "the good" to desire, namely, "if one desires the pleasure of happiness." The error of judgment concerning what "the good" is pertains to the relation between desire and "the good": if something gives me pleasure or happiness, it is good.

If acting on the basis of a subjective conflation of my desire with "the good" seems inimical to ethical action, acting consistently in accordance with pregiven conventions or rules, on the other hand, is equally problematic. Both Derrida and Lacan argue that an ethical act cannot be a matter of blindly applying preexisting rules to novel situations but must be a matter of making decisions about the validity of such rules, after which there is no return, for a decision that lives up to its name implies that any rule can be suspended or transgressed. Even if it is subsequently reconfirmed, having once been suspended in order to make reconfirmation possible, it can (indeed must) always be suspended again in the future. This power of distance taking, which underscores an individual's relative autonomy vis-à-vis any conventional morality, as Lacan's Antigone demonstrates, becomes the basis for ethical action. This is a point starkly illustrated in the film *The Sea Inside*, to which I have tied my discussion of Lacan's account of the ethics of psychoanalysis.

Conventional Morality as Represented in *The Sea Inside*

To be guided by the dictates of conventional morality is to be guided in ethical practice by those principles that the legal system strives to approximate as fully as possible in specific laws. The film focuses on one of these principles in particular, namely the sanctity of life. Notably, Ramón's own ethical position is ambiguous from the point of view of a conventional morality that inscribes this principle in its laws. As argued by one of the lawyers in the film (Marc): suicide may be inscribed in law as a criminal act, but those whose attempted suicides fail are not regularly prosecuted. Tacitly, then, while suicide may be frowned upon from an ethical or religious standpoint, law no longer stretches its reach so far as to make it a positively criminal act. Nevertheless, it will stretch to criminalize those who actively aid a suicide.

The conventional morality featured in the film allows for a straightforward assessment of the film's main protagonists in terms of their moral rectitude. The question of ethical action, as I shall discuss later, is trickier. Here, the most morally untainted character turns out to be a quadriplegic priest, Francisco de Galder, whose unwavering conviction concerning the rectitude of his insistence upon the sanctity of life under any circumstances (and he should know, after all) reflects the fundamental principle of conventional morality at issue here. Moreover, by at least ostensibly considered argumentation, he sets about actively promoting "the general good" by publicly and privately attempting to convince Ramón that one ought to respect the sanctity of life and perhaps show gratitude by holding oneself responsible for capitalizing on what one is given, as he demonstrably tries to do. From the point of view of conventional morality, de Galder's virtue, then, lies in the fact that he tries to talk Ramón out of a frame of mind from which issues his threat to transgress one of the "sacred cows" of conventional morality, had he the means. Further, his proactive attitude suggests that he would have done everything in his power to "save Ramón from himself," had he known at any point that a "crime" was about to be committed.

Like the priest, Ramón's brother (José) tries to talk him out of this transgressive frame of mind, albeit for altogether different reasons. There is no indication in the film that José has reflected in any depth on the impersonal, metaphysical question of the sanctity of life. Instead, he requires Ramón to live, and to desire life, for only this desire, he believes, can make sense of the enormous personal sacrifice that has been required of him for the sake of Ramón's care. It is out of passionate love and anger, rather than a reasoned appropriation of conventional morality, that he rails so bitterly against Ramón's desire to die, and refuses point blank to aid him. This motivation (while important for understanding his ethical position) is irrelevant to an assessment of his position on conventional morality's "scale of virtue," for, regardless of motive, his attempts to elicit from Ramón a desire for life, while fruitless, would nonetheless also be viewed as actively promoting "the general good." What taints him morally is simply that when Ramón has finally engineered the means to carry out his desire for death, José knows of his intentions but does nothing to stop him. At the crucial moment when he could have acted, he sits on the wall (metaphorically the fence), paralyzed by his ambivalence. His inaction, while not criminal, could be subject to moral censure.

Strictly speaking, Manuela's position on the scale of conventional morality slips behind that of her husband (José), because she does not even attempt to talk him out of his transgressive frame of mind. In fact, her stance is altogether more ambiguous than her husband's. She has a similar motivation for desiring Ramón's desire for life, since her own life is entirely invested in caring for him, and his loss would deprive her life of purpose. Yet, because she loves him without the anger that paralyzes her husband, she can express sympathy for his desire to die. Nevertheless, despite this sympathy, she does not encourage him to seek death, and one is tacitly made aware that she could not have brought herself to commit a crime by aiding him in his illegal quest for an aided suicide. Instead, she talks him into supporting a legal challenge to the principle that obstructs his desire (the insistence upon the absolute "sanctity of life" underpinning conventional morality), by encouraging him to testify in a court case. While his testimony is unlikely to help him personally, she convinces him to go ahead anyway by arguing that it could help others after him. In the end, the court case is lost, leaving conventional morality intact on the question of the sanctity of life. Again, while Manuela does not act illegally, what taints her morally is not only that she supports Ramón's defiance of conventional morality but also that she knows of his intention to commit suicide and does nothing to stop him.

Julia, the lawyer initially hired to fight Ramón's case for the right to an aided suicide, treads a fine borderline between moral and criminal action. She knows that Ramón is planning to commit suicide, and she promises not simply to aid him but indeed to join him. Ramón had specifically chosen her as a legal representative because she suffers from a degenerative condition characterized by periodic strokes that are progressively more debilitating. However, her promise is made in a state of fear and similarly broken, for she loses her nerve and backs out of the agreement at the last minute. Since Ramón requires help to commit suicide, this also effectively prevents them from committing the crime.

A case for criminal action could arguably be made against one of the members of the "die with dignity" association, Gené, who instigates the legal battle to modify the sanctity-of-life principle, on the basis that it derives from an archaic metaphysical worldview no longer at the center of the universe. Although the case is lost, she nevertheless plays a small but active part in helping Ramón commit suicide. However, Rosa, a young factory worker and occasional disc jockey who visits and befriends Ramón after seeing his televised plea for the legal right to an aided suicide, is easily placed at the bottom of this scale of virtue, because she plays the decisive role in aiding his suicide, and in so doing unambiguously opens herself to the possibility of criminal charges.

In sum, based on the conventional morality represented in the film, de Galder (the priest) is the only genuinely moral actor entirely uncontaminated by the crime. All of the other principal characters are implicated in one way or another and could face greater or lesser moral disapproval and even criminal charges. The most criminal of all is Rosa, who betrays her initial moral convictions concerning the sanctity of life to the extreme point of being willing to commit murder.

The film, however, encourages an intuitively felt objection to these arguments, for the portrayal of Rosa engages one's sympathies, while her binary counterpart in this schema, de Galder, comes across far less agreeably. Moreover, the film audience comes to know Rosa in her quirky singularity during the course of the narrative, while the priest remains a stereotypical and peripheral caricature. In the figure of Rosa's singularity, then, the film tacitly supports an ethical discourse that challenges the generalized stereotypes inscribed in this (and any other) conventional morality, and for which both Derrida and Lacan, among many others, offer philosophical grounds.

Lacan and the Ethics of Psychoanalysis

I cannot pretend to cover what Lacan has to say concerning the ethical. Instead, I shall tease out the broad implications of Lacan's insistence that ethical action is motivated by love rather than law.[16] One may begin by suggesting that the masculine libidinal style of "ideological paranoia" (associated with the death drive as an inertial drive to return to an immortal state of fullness) and the feminine libidinal style of "neurotic hysteria" (associated, by contrast, with an entropic desire for the dissolution of all tensional bonds, or, that is, for a state of immortal Nirvana) may be set up as a binary opposition, related according to the "vel of alienation" in a way that closely matches Hegel's articulation of the divide between a masculine and feminine fanaticism that splits the Ethical Order.[17]

For Lacan, ethical action is not possible within the bounds of the masculine libidinal style, which is represented metonymically in *The Sea Inside* by the priest, based on the outright rejection of castration, and underpins all systems of conventional morality, whatever principles are inscribed in their laws. For both Lacan and Derrida, as suggested, genuinely ethical action does not happen in the safe domesticity of law and order, of system and rule, happiness and balance, calculation and the equal distribution of goods, all of which privilege the species as a whole above the individual. Lacan, indeed, rejects the masculine ethic as in principle incompatible with genuinely ethical action and insists upon a necessary turn to the feminine characterized by the acceptance of castration or lack. But the turn to the feminine, as argued, can take two paths. One path leads in a pendulum swing directly to the other pole of the binary, namely, a hysterical fixation upon the transgression of universals, which is another version of fanaticism according to which individuals simply exclude themselves from any form of unity. Since, for Lacan, the masculine and feminine ethics are related in terms of the "vel of alienation," neither allows for genuinely ethical action. Notably, there is no clear representative of the purely feminine ethic in *The Sea Inside*. Lacan argues that both masculine and feminine fixation implicitly but mistakenly deny that the death drive is always aim inhibited (that is, sublimated). By aligning ethical action within the feminine ethic to a revised version of Freud's notion of sublimation, he traces a third path to genuinely ethical action. It is Rosa who takes this path, as I hope to show in more detail. Lacanian ethics enables one to construct an ethical scale that diverges dramatically from the one just discussed in that, *inter alia*, it reverses the ethical status of Rosa and the priest. Like Antigone and Creon, however, Rosa and the priest are not binary counterparts on Lacan's account of ethical action.

The Masculine Death Drive and the Ideological Paranoia of the Priest

Facing the possibility that being is "not-all," or that being is split such that there are only partial objects, the masculine libido is unwilling to apply this "truth" of "original castration" to itself.[18] Or, as Silverman puts it, "the identification of woman with lack functions to cover over the absent real and the foreclosed site of production—losses which are incompatible with the 'phallic function' in relation to which the male subject is defined."[19] Rather, on the basis of his discontented perception of a gap between the philosophical ideal of absolute knowledge, goodness, or happiness, and its "unsatisfied actual state" in living individuals, he retrospectively constructs an imaginary lost plenum that calls for restitution. Caught up in this attitude, he tries to force into being a whole (defined as any universal system within which all parts are contained and ordered) that is adequate to "the All" (*das Ding*). In ethical terms, as Lacan puts it, the masculine error of judgment is to "promote the good of all as the law without limits."[20] Thus deluded, masculine libido pretends to the throne of immortality.

The Sea Inside presents two versions of the masculine delusion of immortality. The older delusion, embodied by de Galder (the quadriplegic priest), still dreams the medieval religious dream of returning from a fallen state to the immortal "whole" (Absolute Goodness, Knowledge, Happiness, etc.) conceived of as an eternity beyond time. Hence the words he delivers to Ramón: "and since we live within eternity, life doesn't belong to us." It is no accident here that Amenábar constructs the scene of the discursive situation such that these words are whispered from priest to priest and repeated by rote before they are finally delivered to Ramón. By the simple device of an overly narrow staircase, Amenábar ensures that de Galder cannot meet Sampedro face to face and is obliged to conduct the "debate" via an envoi, Father Andrés, who carries the words of both quadriplegics up and down the stairs, repeating the main points along the way, to inscribe them in memory. This alienating technique underscores the stereotypical nature of a moralistic rhetoric that, in everyday life, is still regularly passed by rote from priest to parish without the intervention of thinking.

One might think that the Enlightenment injunction to surrender the religious dream has put paid to the thought of an "immortality" beyond these borrowed moments of worldly life. Although, in Copjec's words, "officially we moderns are committed to the notion of our own mortality, we nevertheless harbor the secret, inarticulable conviction that we are *not* mortal."[21] In other words, "immortality" as a notion has survived secularization well enough, but (at least in our masculine moments) we have refashioned it through a switch that makes of the lost plenum a temporally inscribed ideal to strive for. Masculine libido in a patriarchy is duped by a promised restitution of the Good, Knowledge, Happiness, etc., in an ideal of future fulfillment, which remains relentlessly attractive because he does not believe the truth of "originary castration."

Here, then, the anticipated immortal whole is no longer understood as belonging to an eternity beyond time. Rather, it progressively unfolds within the life process, and individuals participate in it as the mortal sparks that motor its movement. Further, given that "progress" is understood as an accumulation of acquisitions that endure beyond the reach of any mortal individual, the immortal whole is identified as the possession of the species.[22] In this case, individuals are exhorted to concentrate on the interests of the species, since this will, in turn, be the best guarantee of individual interests. Assuming, for example, that human evil, ignorance, and suffering are to be gradually eliminated, an individual's best bet, it is said, is to choose in favor of tireless and selfless work in pursuit of the immortal whole, so becoming a willing cog in the universal species-machine, which is putatively designed for the ultimate benefit of all humans.[23]

In this move, the egotistical jealousy of childhood megalomania is cajoled and bullied into submitting to a formalized fraternal equality. Recall that, for Freud, the guarantee of mutual fraternal recognition was the renunciation of singular desires and the adoption of some version of the "social contract." Here, however, as Copjec notes, "we end up depriving ourselves of our own pleasure, choosing instead, for the sake of a more pacific relation to the Other, to invest our pleasure in his (lost) cause."[24] Note, then, the vel of alienation: certainly, to choose against the species, and for the individual, is to choose against the individual's prospects for material goods and happiness and, therefore, against the individual. But at the same time, an individual's attempt to participate in immortality through submission to formalized universals is again a matter of self-annihilation.[25]

In such "annihilation" of the individual, a secular state and religious ideology join forces, for both in principle must promote the species over the individual, conformity above singularity, law above critical idiosyncrasy, equality over freedom, paranoiac knowledge over flexible invention, and in so doing, "ideally" strive to produce dependent individuals who are slaves to the prescribed laws of the state machinery.

A persistent motif throughout *The Sea Inside* is the "deafness" of those who claim to hold some position of institutional authority, backed by conventional morality, to Ramón's persistent request for official recognition of his singularity and respect for the dignity of his ethical autonomy. Taking the form of misrecognition, inflexibility, and the simple refusal to hear his voice, this structural inability to make room for singularity stretches across the religious "authority" claimed by de Galder, the secular authority claimed by the judiciary, and even the patriarchal authority claimed by José, Ramón's older brother and self-proclaimed "head of the household."

Notably, Amenábar's response to these authority claims is to highlight their irrationality by exposing some of their discursive contradictions. José, for example, insists that he wants what is best for Ramón but inflexibly refuses to entertain the idea that this might take the form of the freedom and power to make the choice for death. Further, the words of de Galder, "I hear you," are laden with heavy irony, since they punctuate the discursive exchange mentioned above, which highlights precisely a lack of communication. This irony is compounded by the content of the interchange where Ramón reflects upon certain contradictions in de Galder's arguments, for example, the very institution that is here so precious about the sanctity of life has a long, bloody history of murder, including burning people alive, in the name of its fundamental principles.

Secularization does not remove this contradiction. Ironically, fixated by the "just causes" represented by ideals of universal human rights, progress, and the sanctity of life, the conventional moralities supported by masculine libido, as much as outright tyrannies and fascisms, regularly demand "the torture and execution of those who oppose them."[26] In a secularized state, as Copjec notes, the finite bodies of particular individuals are conceived only "objectively" in terms of the pervasive risk of injury and death.[27] Preservation of the immortal whole as the succession of bodies requiring protection from injury or unnatural death demands a universal principle endorsing the sanctity of life, and, as she argues, citing Agamben, this means that "*life exposed to death (bare life or sacred life) is the originary political element.*"[28] In short, the pervasive risk of injury allows natural life to become the concern of the state, politics becomes biopolitics, and power sinks deep into the minutest aspects of individual life, presiding over every kind of vulnerability, since a universal principle sanctifies "bare life" above any life of a particular quality. Thus, Ramón is legally obliged to endure a suffering life patiently, for it is required as an endorsement of an abstract, universal principle that protects the sanctity of life.

Psychoanalysis explains how people become "captated" (against reason and often against intuitively held values) by the abstract ideals of a conventional morality, by casting the self-annihilating story of the desire for immortality in terms of the masculine oedipal drama in which a superego is inscribed in the psyche through identification with the lost parent figures.[29] The superego ideal in which the promotion of "the good of all as the law without limits" finds an ally is formed as that measure of "civilization" for which individuals ought to strive through "sublimation," here defined in the sense that predominates in Freud's texts, namely, as the replacement of crude bodily passions (such as sexual urges) for finer pleasures, for a nobility of soul the approximation of which is a measure of human progress. Yet the superego characteristically becomes harsher and more demanding the more "saintly" the subject becomes, for the superego, as argued earlier, is a substitute for an imaginary loss. As Copjec explains: "If the superego always demands more sacrifice, more work, this is because the ideal it sets in front of the subject is kept aloft by a loss that the subject is unable to put behind him."[30]

In an aggressive turn, then, the masculine death drive aims at an immortal abstraction forever beyond "mere" worldly objects, for which an individual pointlessly strives, in the process devaluing or negating what actually is. The superego, in Copjec's words, cruelly "fosters in the subject a distaste for mundane, compromised pleasures and maintains us in a state of dissatisfaction."[31] But, of course, the anticipated ideal for the sake of which a person must sacrifice the small satisfactions and tolerate the sufferings of the present is only the perpetual promise of restitution in the future. But because the ego can never measure up to the superego, it remains relentlessly and guiltily driven to close the gap between what is demanded and what is actually achieved. The only remedy for such endemic dissatisfaction, one may add, is the paranoiac delusion of a quadriplegic priest who "knows" that "life isn't just moving your arms and running around trying to kick a ball."

This statement becomes symptomatic of a delusion in its sheer mockery of the body, as if physicality could ever be reducible to activity as comparably inane and ridiculous as football. What de Galder cannot accommodate in his worldview is the singularity of individual differences, for some live more sensually than others. Ramón Sampedro has been a physical being: a sea adventurer who had traveled the world as a ship's mechanic. His being-in-the-world as a young man had the quality of an intense, voluptuous, sea-sharp sensuality. For him, rendered numb to the sea that had once given him life, his current condition is a limbo, a living death of relentless, yearning suffering. Yet, in his ridicule of bodily pleasure, de Galder attributes Ramón's suffering not to the unavailability of the Good but to some form of privation or moral defect, a failure of sublimation or a lack of love. "Ramón says he wants to die. But one must wonder. . . . Could Ramón actually be making some sort of plea to society, to all of us for attention? Maybe the people around him, his family can't provide him with the love and support he needs." Thus, as Copjec puts it: "By imputing evil to mortal defect or privation, as that which interfered with the full appearance of the Good, the various solutions to the problem of evil were designed to leave both the Good and God unscathed, and thus, ultimately, justified.[32]

De Galder falls silent in the end, not in the comfort zone of sufficiently generalized intellectual arguments, but in front of Manuela's admonishment for this unthinking remark. Given these considerations, one may reassess the ethical status of the priest in *The Sea Inside*. While he was given primary position on the scale of virtue represented by conventional morality, his captation by the masculine death drive renders his ethical stance dubious.

Feminine Transgression: Hysteria and Eternal Irony

The disturber of the masculine peace is not the force of the philosopher's *Eros* that desires something like Hegel's speculative unity of all with all. Rather, it is the inevitable persistence of traumatic interruptions from the constituted "outside" that will not let the ideological circle close. The repressed forces, the anomalies that have to be ironed out, rationalized away, and glossed over to keep the circle closed inevitably return as disruptive symptoms (slips, gaps, irrationalities, silences, inconsistencies). To avoid the masculine fanaticism that rigidly works to suppress these symptoms and to set out on the path to the ethical act, Lacan insists that one must begin by taking the feminine route, whose initiation rite is to accept that the ineradicability of such symptoms indicates the fact of original castration or lack. Recognizing that the Real is lacking, those who adopt a feminine libidinal style testify to the "truth" that a whole is impossible—that fullness, thought of as the systematic unity of all with all, is merely a retrospective illusion produced by the masculine Imaginary.[33] Feminine libido, then, recognizes the lack in any system of conventional morality. It knows that, in Lacan's words: "The good cannot reign over all without an excess emerging whose fatal consequences are revealed to us in tragedy."[34]

Like the masculine, feminine libido remains dissatisfied with the way things are, and it desires jouissance (ultimate satisfaction, or lack of desire).[35] Ultimate satisfaction also remains constitutionally unavailable, but in a different way. Masculine libido believes that jouissance lies in finally realizing the ideal whole, but its death drive toward the retrospective illusion of this "lost" ideal is inherently inhibited because it aims at a delusion, which, therefore, cannot ever be realized. Feminine libido, to the contrary, already knows that the world lacks any legitimate ideal that could ground, unify, and organize all of its parts. Feminine libido, in other words, remains open to Nietzsche's radical nihilism, whereby the world seems not inadequate to the ideal but intrinsically inauthentic, made up of an aggregation of particular façades with no underlying support. In a situation where nothing has intrinsic value, no particular object is the measure for any other.

Feminine libido, then, automatically indicts existing laws and standards as unfounded and takes on the negative task of breaking down ideals, systems, or wholes, with the aim of forcing the impossible Real to appear. Thus, the feminine death drive is characterized as a transgressive drive toward the complete dissolution of the constraining bonds, borders, restrictive barriers, and circumscriptions by which all symbolic objects are constituted according to an accredited inside and an excluded outside. In order to include all that there is without exception, the feminine death drive aims to dissolve all bonds, leaving only fragments or an endless aggregation of parts. However, to try to force the impossible Real to appear will bring about, on the other side of masculine fanaticism, another kind of terror, namely the will to utter destruction or the will to a chaotic, schizoid state where nothing stable can ever take hold.[36]

Those fixated to the feminine death drive compulsively and relentlessly resist any existing order. In other words, to become "hysterical" is to become fixated to a nonplace in the community and to define oneself, mimicking Hegel, as its "eternal irony." A hysteric fixes her desire on remaining on the outside of an unsatisfying reality and must sacrifice every possible worldly satisfaction for its sake, to the extent that if she produces relations in the world, it is only to secure her exclusion from them. Satisfaction, here, twists into the sacrifice of worldly satisfaction to the point that jouissance would entail her total exclusion from the world of the living.

To sum up so far, the masculine drive begins as the erotic attachment to a lost plenum but ends as the aggressive exclusion of an outside. The feminine drive begins as erotic, since it can exclude nothing. But since it entails the realization that no whole can form, it becomes thanatic (in its dissolving, destructive sense) as aggression toward the established wholes (and self-aggression as entombment on the outside). Žižek articulates the distinction in terms of a radical split between the masculine "jouissance of the drives" and the feminine "jouissance of the Other."[37] The former, he argues, is characterized by "the closed, ultimately solipsistic circuit of drives that find their satisfaction in idiotic mastubatory (auto-erotic) activity, in the perverse circulating around object *a* as the object of a drive."[38] The latter, by contrast, strives for access to jouissance outside of the solipsistic totality, or, that is, in the Other. A feminine hysteric, then, fixated on the sacrifice of her own "masturbatory jouissance" for the sake of the Other jouissance, finds that her enjoyment is entirely alienated or externalized in the Other, since it resides only in the effect she has on the other.[39] Her fixation on self-sacrifice, then, becomes just as fanatical as the perverse masculine fixation on the lost jouissance of an unattainable ideal. The masculine and feminine positions are related according to Derrida's aporia or Lacan's "vel of alienation," which implies the impossibility of acting ethically if one chooses either.

This suggests that the willingness to transgress established orders, which, notably, does not automatically amount to their outright rejection, is a necessary but insufficient condition for ethical action. Such willingness is the necessary condition for making an ethical decision concerning the dictates of an order or rule, for one must be able to assess it independently. Having "suspended" the rule in order to make a decision, one could well confirm its validity and decide to reinstate it. The point is only that the willingness to transgress allows for the reversal necessary for an ethical act, whereby blind acceptance of the rule does not dictate the decision, but the decision dictates the rule. This relation between transgression and decision suggests the way forward to genuinely ethical action. If the turn to the feminine, which Lacan has already prescribed, entails the acceptance that nothing has intrinsic value, this should not mistakenly be conflated with the belief that nothing, therefore, is of any value. Rather, for Lacan, one may surpass hysterical fanaticism through a transformation that one could call the moment of inventive sublimation.

Feminine Inventive Sublimation: Rosa

For Lacan, an ethical act escapes the "vel of alienation," the lose/lose of the mugger's choice, for it arises out of a different scene, where the choice is that of the revolutionary: "freedom or death." To be sure, to choose freedom on pain of death (to choose to die rather than relinquish freedom) is to lose life. But, on Lacan's account, the lose/lose circle of alienation does not close here, because in dying for the sake of freedom, one does not also lose the freedom. One might immediately object that to call a corpse "free" is patently absurd. This is the form of de Galder's objection to Ramón's argument in *The Sea Inside.* For him, there simply is no freedom to speak of, in the embodied, worldly state, without life as a precondition. This objection, however, rests on the reduction of worldly life and death to mere biological states. By contrast, the revolutionary's choice presupposes an understanding of life that, while worldly and embodied, includes something like the life of the spirit. To be alive in this case requires something more than a biological condition. It requires, that is, some state named by "freedom," which one could describe as ethical sovereignty, or the power invested in individuals to make their own decisions concerning their singular being-in-the-world. From the point of view of the revolutionary, there is no life without freedom. Even if one is still biologically alive, in the absence of such sovereignty, a person becomes dead in spirit: a living body animated by external command, an *automaton.*

Further, to choose freedom, even on pain of physical death, is to choose life in the sense of spiritual immortality. For, by insisting upon ethical sovereignty, I constitute for myself a singular, irreplaceable, and therefore eternal place in the weave that binds the world together. The revolutionary's choice, therefore, is aligned with a third conception of immortality: particular individuals who pass away in time relate not only to each other but also to these places in our cultural fabric, which persist over time and provide a weave that keeps the particulars together.[40] To sum up, one chooses the freedom of one's sovereign decisive power, which is also an affirmation of singularity, and one is willing to die for the power to make such a choice. But this does not carry a lose/lose outcome: freedom so defined is not lost but immortalized, and it remains what it is beyond physical death. Death in the name of freedom gains one the immortality of a Steve Biko or Ché Guevara.

Does this suggest that one has to be a revolutionary to act ethically? Bluntly, yes. Ethics, for Lacan, belongs neither to the domestic order of conventional morality nor to the chaotic disorder of hysterical transgression. Famous revolutionaries act on a grander scale than the minor revolutionaries of ethical life, but the structure of the act remains the same. In other words, for Lacan, the revolutionary's choice for freedom can certainly be converted into everyday terms, captured in the injunctions to "assume your desire" or not to "cede [give way on, or as to] your desire."[41] These by no means simple formulations inscribe incompatible injunctions. Subjects are exhorted, first, to recognize and elect their "true" desires and to persevere with them to a limit that does not exclude death. But, second, they are exhorted *not* to persevere in such desires as if they could ever truly represent an essentially traumatic being, but to persevere in *desire.* This, in an aporetic twist, means that, having committed oneself to persevere with a desire to a limit that does not exclude death, one must also paradoxically be willing to give it up to reinvention.

To make sense of this double injunction, it helps to recall that Lacan structures subjectivity as an articulation of incompatible resisters. On the one hand, in the register of the Imaginary, what is called the subject's "identity" consists in the narrative fiction built up for the ego or *moi*. The *moi*, represented metaphorically by an integrated mirror image—although it can also be described as a configuration shaped as a response to the other's desire (via unreflectively adopted discourses, ideologies, cultural demands)—functions for this reason as an agent of unity, conformity, and fixation (a prosthesis or armor) that, unchecked, is adopted without question or resisted without remedy. On the other hand, in the register of the Real, that which I "am" consists of an unconscious, traumatic, singularizing desire. Granting that a full or absolute uncovering of a traumatic kernel remains impossible, it is still possible to argue that some interpretations are more appropriate than others. Here, then, subjects are capable of self-knowledge to the extent that we can know our desires. Remaining oblivious to such desires, subjects remain beholden to their unconscious vicissitudes. If I fail to recognize my desire, in other words, I do not "have" it, but I allow it instead to "have" me. This translates Copjec's succinct formula for one of Lacan's rearticulations of Freud's famous aphorism *Wo es war, soll Ich werden*:[42] "There where it (my desire) was, there must (the ethical must) I (not, ego, but *je* or subject) become."

On a Lacanian account, then, the first step toward ethical action, having taken the feminine turn, which recognizes that all *moi* values are invented, is to "assume your desire." This implies, first, that the *je* must be capable of uncovering or recognizing something of the impossible desire of its Real being. The uncovering of singularizing desire in the register of the Real, however, must necessarily occur as a traumatic invasion of the habitual fabric of the subject's *moi* identity. To assume a singularizing desire, then, is to allow it its traumatizing effects. Or, put differently—for it is not often a matter of an explicit choice to open the *moi* to a desire—in the crisis of its invasion, to assume your desire is first of all to recognize it and, second, to gather the courage to face it. An exemplary case of this invasion of desire occurs in *Sophie's Choice*. As Alenka Zupančič argues in her reading of the film version, the extreme and terrible circumstances in which Sophie was forced to act revealed to her the devastating desire that allowed her to choose one of her children over the other. This was a desire she did not want and experienced as a crushing violation.[43]

Importantly, harsh as it may seem in relation to the example of Sophie's unbearable desire, Lacan's injunction to assume your desire is an injunction not only to acknowledge the shape of a traumatic desire when it finds you, even if you do not want it, but also to take it up, to decide how to invent its value and how to integrate it into the fabric of your *moi* identity. For the consequence of doing nothing, of passively undergoing its traumatic effects, or of repressing them, is spiritual death and ethical paralysis. In other words, facing the disconcerting self-knowledge represented by a singularizing desire, ethical action requires the courage to elect the desire in question; that is, the *je* is required to take it up or bring it into existence, rather than remain subject to its unconscious vicissitudes. It is important to emphasize here that one first brings desire into existence by articulating it in speech. As Lacan puts it: "That the subject should come to recognize and to name his desire; that is the efficacious action of analysis. But it isn't a question of recognizing something which would be entirely given. . . . In naming it the subject creates, brings forth, a new presence in the world."[44] However, he adds that desire and speech are in principle incompatible. In the words of Dylan Evans, "it is this incompatibility which explains the irreducibility of the unconscious. . . . Although the truth about desire is present to some degree in all speech, speech can never articulate the *whole* truth about desire; whenever speech attempts to articulate desire, there is always a leftover, a surplus, which exceeds speech."[45]

To assume your desire, then, is not necessarily to want the desire that characterizes you but to know both that it characterizes you and that you are always irreducible to it. It cannot be denied or disavowed, but one need not allow it to become a tyranny or fixation, since it is always already invented in its articulation through speech, and it can be reinvented. Taking up a desire amounts to a refusal to accept its potentially tyrannizing power and an insistence on retaining the freedom and ethical sovereignty of the *je*, which allows the subject to put this desire in its place. But, in this case, in acknowledging and taking up a traumatizing desire, in inventing its value, the *je* cannot but have woven around the traumatic event of its invasion an imaginary identification or defining fiction. In other words, to choose to acknowledge a "true" desire and to persevere in this choice by taking it up is to risk all over again the opposite tyranny of Imaginary fixation. Ethical action, then, necessarily finds itself caught up in an aporetic circle. There is no ethical action unless subjects find and assume true desires and persevere with them to the last. But in persevering to the last, their actions become not ethical but fanatical. Therefore, subjects cannot act ethically unless they are ready to give up such desires. But if they are ready to give up such desires, they cannot have persevered to the last and therefore cannot act ethically. Usually philosophy views such circular logic as the sign of an error. Lacan and Derrida, however, insist that this circularity represents the facticity of life, and we cannot pretend to dissolve such paradoxes without falling into the ideological trap of the Imaginary. All we can do is live through them: negotiating between committed perseverance and obsessive fixation, through persistent but careful reinvention of traumatic desires, taking into account the revisable contexts in which we find ourselves.

To conclude this discussion, one could say that Lacan's ethical injunction rests upon his rearticulation of "narcissism," which avoids the extremes of masculine paranoia and feminine hysteria. Recall that the death drive in its masculine aspect represents the fruitless striving for a lost plenum, whereas its feminine aspect represents a destructive Nirvana. Assuming that narcissism defines the ego's self-love, or, that is, its love of itself as a whole, then under the pressure of the masculine death drive, narcissism describes an impossible ego-love (except in self-deception) that depends on matching the ego with the unified ideal of wholeness given by the mirror image. On the other hand, under the pressure of the feminine death drive, narcissism implies a similarly impossible ego-love expressed as the pleasure taken in self-shattering in the name of matching the ego with the absolute All. In both cases, if one is honest, one remains endemically dissatisfied with the ego as one of the projected objects of the everyday world and therefore capable of heartless, aggressive, and guilty self-hatred.

What both extremisms neglect, however, is that the death drive is always aim inhibited.[46] It is stopped temporarily but continuously by the projected objects of desire (objects *a*), which provide an unending stream of partial satisfactions. This open-ended stream of partial satisfactions provides the key to a conception of "sublimation" that, for Lacan, replaces the notion predominant in Freud's texts and infuses it with ethical significance.[47] For the most part, driven by superego idealism, sublimation has been thought of in terms of the sublimation of desire: as the translation of crude sexual desire into the "higher" (more morally acceptable) pleasures associated with producing and contemplating cultural objects such as artworks. The notion of sublimation, however, may be developed in a different direction, suggesting instead that desire sublimates the object.[48] Here, the sublime immortality of everyday objects is to be found precisely in the fact that they do not extinguish desire once and for all. The basic idea here, to reiterate, is that the worldly object—any partial object—gains in value precisely because I love it just for what it is. In this case, it becomes more than what it is, for it becomes the object plus my desire for it, which is both satisfied by it and circulates endlessly around it. Thus, the inestimable value of an object is invented precisely through the restlessness/insatiability of desire. Because my love or interest adds a "supplement" that allows the object to exceed itself, I tend to reinvent its being as I go along. "Iterability" is Derrida's name for this paradoxical logic of excess, whereby I repeat the object as just what it is but always with the inestimable difference made by the "supplement" of my love/interest.

Such sublimation, then, allows one to counteract the devaluation of projected objects in the everyday world (including the *moi* as object), which derives from the masculine or feminine versions of discontent. It revalues such ordinary objects by discovering their immanent sublimity. Further, inventive sublimations, because they are never static, affect the weave of the worldly fabric in massive or minor ways, after which the weave cannot assume its old shape. If the *moi*, as much as another creature or object, is a thing in the world, the act of self-sublimation possible to the autonomous individual turns on the ability to open the *moi* to persistent solicitation by the knot of traumatic desire. In this case, the *moi* identity becomes an explicitly chosen inventive weave, or text, that interprets and reinterprets the ineradicable traumatic desire. The same immortalizing "iterability" applies to the invention of a *moi* identity, and narcissism here becomes not love of the ego as absolute being nor as absolute nonbeing in self-shattering, but as a being of lack (as a complex dynamic of being and nonbeing). This self-sublimation, or invention and persistent reinvention of the *moi* is, finally, the shape of the subject's ethical task.

In *The Sea Inside*, it is the character of Rosa, mimicking the situation of an analysand who undergoes a successful analysis, who offers the example of one who is confronted with the traumatic event of a desire that she neither recognizes at first nor wants. During the course of the narrative, she eventually comes to acknowledge and assume her desire, thus becoming for the first time capable of ethical action. (Rosa's narrative of ethical actualization is set in contrast to Julia's progressive ethical disability, for which her physical debilitation to the point of entirely losing her capacity to make any decision at all stands as an appallingly graphic metaphor, for she lacked the courage to uncover and assume her desire, allowing fear instead to dictate her choices.) Ramón plays the part of Rosa's analyst. Here again, Ramón's physical condition (his almost total paralysis) is metaphorically accurate, for Lacan is clear concerning the limits of psychoanalysis in the ethical domain: it can do no more than help analysands uncover their desires. The tasks of assuming the uncovered desire and of making related ethical decisions if it comes to that remain entirely the analysand's. Analysts cannot direct analysands in ethical matters without taking away precisely the freedom that will enable them to act ethically.

Rosa is introduced into the narrative in a sharp cut from the words of resignation issuing from Ramón's father: "As long as it's God's will, he'll have to go on living." One observes her from a distance, trimming meat on a factory line, stained to the elbows, and being subjected in her lunch break to some form of castigation by a superior. Reinforcing the impression of an existence that is impoverished, monotonous, degrading, and embattled on all fronts, she ends her day by selecting certain factory scraps and trudging home laden and alone to face an evening of domestic chores. During this time, the voiceover of a television program slowly begins to intrude. It is a documentary made by Ramón to further his plea for the right to an aided suicide. Gathering up her sleeping child from the couch in front of the television, his voice finally arrests Rosa's attention: "maybe they'll realize this is no excuse for a life." Rosa's stunned gaze, over the shoulder of her child, suggests that "the letter has reached its destination."

But her immediate response is to misrecognize it. She finds herself compelled to seek Ramón out personally, ostensibly to "do some good" by convincing him of the sacred value of life, no matter what. However, when Ramón finally draws from her an admission of why she paid him a visit, her words are telling, for they hardly sound a note of conviction: "That's why I came." "Why?" "Well, to make you want to live. To tell you that life . . ." "Life what?" "Isn't it worth it?" Ramón quickly disabuses her of this illusion. Without mincing words, he voices his assessment of the situation: "Let's talk about the real reason you're here. About how you're obviously just a frustrated woman who woke up this morning hoping to give her own life some meaning." In other words, what she misrecognizes as her altruistic desire to convince him of the sanctity of life is in fact an attempt to reaffirm her wavering convictions concerning this principle, which have suffered the traumatic shock of her "true" desire to end her own misery.

What he reflects back to her in the mirror of his angry words, then, is that her projection is merely a disguise born of her refusal to acknowledge that she is frustrated with her own life and that what she really desires for herself is a life that is, in her own estimation, worth loving. Yet, conditioned by the ostensibly unquestionable principle of the sanctity of life, she cannot acknowledge her own dissatisfaction, for inscribed in this principle is a moral injunction to accept patiently whatever life one is given regardless of the joys or suffering it might entail. Thus, were Rosa to acknowledge that she desires a life that is, in her own estimation, worth loving, she would concomitantly have to acknowledge that she cannot obey the moral injunction to value life regardless of its quality. There it is, then. Her true desire lies out in the open from the start, waiting for her to recognize it: namely the desire to end her own unsatisfactory existence. Notably, this assessment is retroactively confirmed much later in the film when she admits to Ramón that it is he who gives her the strength to live.

This recognition does not come easily, for it contradicts her deeply held commitment to the sanctity of life. In response to the crisis of Ramón's assessment, Rosa's first response is to refashion her desire. When she finds in him a man who treats her with compassion, honesty, interest, and patience, in contrast with the rough treatment she experiences from other men, she comes to desire precisely his desire. In other words, in what Freud describes as narcissistic desire, she desires him to desire her. As manifest in her competition with Manuela over his care, she wants to become the loved object that makes his life worth living. Again, this involves projecting the responsibility for her unacknowledged desire for a life worth living onto Ramón. In effect, she is asking him to desire life in order to underwrite the value of her life. Julia's second visit represents a crisis for Rosa's narcissistic desire. She is forced to face the truth that this desire cannot be satisfied; she will not be the love object that makes Ramón's life worth living, because his libidinal attention, including a vivid fantasy life, is directed exclusively toward Julia.

Concerning the fashioning of her desire, then, Rosa faces difficulties all along the way. Initially she perseveres with her desire for Ramón's desire. Her attentions become obsessive and excessive, to the desperate annoyance of Manuela. But ultimately she cannot force a recalcitrant reality to comply with her desire, for certain facts intrude too obviously to be ignored. Perseverance to the last in this context promises only suffering. Not only is she obliged to contend with Julia's claim to Ramón's libidinal affections but, far more seriously, she is forced to face Ramón's resistance. When she declares her love, Ramón's response is clear: "Rosa, you can't be asking me to stay alive for you. . . . It's too much to for me bear. . . . You call that love? Holding me against my will? The person who really loves me will be the one who helps me die. That's love, Rosa." Rosa's pained shake of the head indicates that she has not yet recognized her true desire, which, articulated in the terms of the revolutionary's choice, "freedom or death," is entirely isomorphic with Ramón's. Rosa could simply have given up on her pursuit of Ramón and directed her attentions to finding a substitute satisfaction for her narcissism. That this is something she is evidently unwilling to do, as we discover when she next appears, suggests that something new has happened.

Although the film audience is not made privy to Rosa's reflections, we can surmise from her subsequent action that another transformation has occurred in her desire. What she realizes in silence is that she loves Ramón, and the implications of this love have begun to dawn on her. Through this reversal of her narcissism through love and its power of sublimation, Ramón becomes more than what he was for her—namely the one whose desire she sought for her own purposes. She comes to understand her narcissism for what it was: a willingness to prolong his suffering because she needed his desire for life to endorse the value of her own. This line of thinking, however, poses a challenge to the moral principle (the sanctity of life) she has been unwilling to question throughout the narrative. By analogy, it reflects a generalized willingness to prolong an individual's suffering because humanity requires, without exception, individual endorsement of a general principle that guarantees the worth of human life as such, regardless of its quality. When Rosa lets go of this principle, she is finally able to acknowledge her true desire. Instead of remaining beholden to an externally imposed moral obligation to desire life no matter what, her true desire is to have a life that is, in her own estimation, worth living, and, conversely to resist a life, even to the point of death, that is not, in her estimation, worth living. At this point, she can at last empathize with Ramón.

When we next see Rosa, she is a transformed woman. She confesses to Ramón that she now understands what he has said to her: if you love me you will be willing to give me up, to help me die. Notably, she has "known" this all along, not only intellectually, due to the fact that Ramón has pointed it out to her often enough, but also unconsciously, because the letter reached its destination some time ago at the moment of revelation in front of the television set. Until this point, however, she has been swayed from this "truth" by a powerful resistance stemming from the dominating effect of the superego, in the form of an unexamined moral conviction adopted in conformity with convention rather than on the basis of independent deliberation. Helped along by the crisis of her frustrated narcissism, Rosa finally takes her distance from the dominating superego, assumes her true desire, and is thereby, for the first time, able to act ethically.

This capacity is immediately put to the test. To act upon her rearticulated desire means transgressing conventional morality and facing the terror of an ethical decision concerning the act that conventional morality judges to be criminal. She does not fail this test of perseverance. Yet, of course, this decisive act does not absolve her of a future responsibility to renegotiate the irresolvably aporetic circulation between perseverance and fixation that she will have to live through time and again.

Concluding Remarks

One could characterize Rosa's true desire for a life worth living, as represented in the narrative, as the desire to become an autonomous being capable of ethical action. In realizing this desire, she undergoes a transformation from narcissistic dependence on an external source to affirm life's worth for her to an autonomous readiness to offer the gift of love. This newfound power to make her own assessments of value enables her to suspend a previously unquestioned principle of conventional morality, subject it to critique, and ultimately to decide in favor of transgressing it. But this critical power, in turn, involves the correlative responsibility to invent a singular value for her life. In other words, Rosa (representing all of us) remains a perpetual beginner in the field of ethical action. With her newfound capacities, she only now faces the task of uncovering and assuming her desire, which is the correlate of inventing a singular value that will make her life worth living.

We see no more of her in the film and are left guessing concerning what singular value she does subsequently invent for her life. Nevertheless, whatever it is, she will unavoidably have to tread a tightrope. Her newly uncovered and assumed desire will have transgressed (suspended) and reinvented the conventional. But no sooner has it formed a pedestal for the construction of a new life, her very perseverance will put it at risk of becoming a fixated obsession. Thus, for her action to remain ethical, she may, at some point, have to give up this pedestal. To understand her desire as invented means that, as Derrida would say, she is obliged to keep reinventing it, which is to keep subjecting it to the risk of fixation. There is no getting beyond this eternal oscillation. In ethical terms, for example, one cannot simply abdicate the responsibility for making a decision in face of an aporia (the only situation in which a decision strictly speaking becomes necessary and therefore an ethical experience becomes possible), even if it means that one must invent a path, thereby reducing the aporia to something recognizable, namely a problem, and in that sense doing violence to the singularity of the situation and, in effect, ruining one's chance of calling the decision ethical. For Derrida, it is not such a bad thing for a person to recognize the impossibility of ever living up to the dream of genuine ethicality, as long as this "lack" is not given as grounds for abdication but for persistent "love" directed toward "the impossible."

In conclusion, one may pose a final question: did Rosa act for the sake of the good? Or: is there room in Derridean/Lacanian ethical discourse for an assessment of the singular invention of value in terms of good or evil? Clearly, it would go against the grain of an argument for the aporetic structure of the Real to suggest that Lacan's model allows for any absolute and final measure of the good. Instead, one may address this question along the following lines. If the invention of value is singular, it simultaneously does not "fall from the sky" but reconfigures the weave of conventional morality in massive or minor ways. Recall that an invention of singular value creates an immortal place in the fabric of human life that survives individual death and in relation to which others orient their own actions. In its realization through action, then, one automatically exposes a singular invention of value to the risk of publicity and to the intersubjective test of the good. At best, then, its status as good or evil is decided retrospectively (*nachträglich*) and periodically subjected to context-specific revisions in the public domain through intersubjective debate. This is, admittedly, hardly a satisfactory or stable measure of good or evil, but the alternatives (a rigidly law-governed conventional morality or utter moral relativism) risk the far greater terrors of ethical fanaticism. Rosa, then, will constantly have to negotiate the ethical status of her invented value; she, like all of us, will never once and for all *be* an ethical person.

12

The "Talking Cure"

Language and Psychoanalysis

Introductory Remarks

Lacan sees in Edgar Allan Poe's tale "The Purloined Letter" an uncannily perspicacious illustration of certain aspects of his psychoanalytic theory, which in most respects is so well adapted to his purposes that it might have been written expressly to suit them. He hints, however, that it is precisely insofar as Poe was not consciously expounding a psychoanalytic theory that he unconsciously and therefore all the more accurately arrived at certain psychoanalytic insights. I shall offer a brief synopsis of the tale below, with the caveat that Lacan scrutinizes many of the apparently extraneous (but psychoanalytically significant) details I shall have to pass over in the retelling.

In examining his interpretation of this story in his "Seminar on 'The Purloined Letter,'" I shall focus first on his demonstration of how Poe's tale, which involves an intentional and illuminating engagement with the necessary components of any tale, "a drama, its narration, and the conditions of that narration,"[1] illustrates the structural interrelations between the orders of the Real, Imaginary, and Symbolic. In his seminar, he capitalizes on both the literary metaphor and the ambiguity of the story's axial motif (namely, the "letter," which allows for the play of multiple metaphorical manipulations) to demonstrate that these orders can and must be understood in linguistic terms. This accords with his insistence on the fundamental importance of a linguistic theory in psychoanalysis and undergirds his call for psychoanalytic theory to situate Freud's fundamental concepts "in a field of language" and to order them "in relation to the function of speech." In his words: "I would assert that the technique cannot be understood, nor therefore correctly applied, if the concepts on which it is based are ignored. It is our task to demonstrate that these concepts take on their full meaning only when orientated in a field of language, only when ordered to the function of speech."[2] As many commentators have noted, then, Lacan's so-called return to Freud may be characterized as a reminder to analysts that psychoanalysis remains at bottom the "talking cure." Yet, because he revises the linguistic presuppositions that underpin Freud's basic concepts to take account of structuralist and more contemporary poststructuralist developments, his emphasis on the role of language in psychoanalysis simultaneously constitutes an important revision of Freudian theory.[3]

Accordingly, an important thread in the complex theoretical web he weaves around Poe's tale is that three unconsciously occupied subject positions, constitutive of the Symbolic Order, impose specific discursive points of view on individuals, which condition the conscious narratives by which they aim to recount the "drama" (or, synonymously, the "event").[4] I shall argue here that these three logical orders of signification that constitute the "conditions of the narration" can be described easily enough in the familiar terms of Derrida's "plural logic of the aporia." Having laid out Lacan's account of the structural interrelations between the Real, Imaginary, and Symbolic, as illustrated in Poe's tale, I shall turn to his analysis of the logic governing the displacement of an individual from position to position and the consequences of such shifts. Again, Poe's tale might have been written expressly for the purpose of examining three important interrelated points. (1) One may discern an initial progressive movement from a position of ideological blindness through transgressive insight to analytical insight. (2) In this movement, occasioned by the irruption of an event and the associated motivating force of one's desire for mastery, there is a kind of intersubjective relativity at work, which places/displaces individuals in relation to one another. (3) One may also discern a strange reverse logic of retrogressive slippage in this movement, or a kind of blindness associated with every form of insight, which again has to do with the force of one's desire for mastery.

Turning finally to the application of this theoretical edifice to the question of psychoanalytic intervention, it is clear that for Lacan its efficacy depends on the psychoanalyst's grasp that the fundamental question of mastery underpins both the principle of unconscious structuring and the logic of displacement in the intersubjective network. As I shall explain in more detail, the insight that he derives from Poe's tale is this: to the extent that one misrecognizes analytical mastery as being a matter of power over others, rather than the self-mastery that is the precondition for ethical action, one retrogresses to the subject position of blindness represented by the King. This is the form of Lacan's warning to all analysts (institutional or otherwise).

This warning concerning mastery and the questions it poses will guide the concluding remarks of this study. Clearly the risk of retrogression is ever present. Can one ever be vigilant enough as an analyst to prevent analytical mastery from devolving into ideological mastery? Perhaps one can, in principle, with ruthless and interminable self-analysis. More pointedly, does Lacan as analyst rise above this risk and withdraw from the retrogressive movement that drives the Symbolic circuit more successfully than his counterpart in the form of Poe's character C. Auguste Dupin? Derrida evidently does not think so. An assessment of this opinion will form the conclusion of this study.

Synopsis of Poe's "The Purloined Letter"

Poe's tale is constructed around three scenes, the second and third of which are in many respects repetitions of the first.[5] The entire tale is told by an unnamed gentleman, a friend of C. Auguste Dupin and admirer of his impressive expertise in solving enigmas,[6] who happened to be present at the time of a visit from the Prefect of Police. The Prefect wished to consult Dupin about a troubling affair in the royal household. The first scene then, narrated by the Prefect of Police, involves the intersubjective relations between a triad of figures: the King, Queen, and Minister. The Queen, initially alone in the royal *boudoir*, receives a letter. While its specific contents are never revealed, the reader is nevertheless informed that the King's knowledge of this letter would compromise her honor and safety. Taken by surprise upon his entry, she has no time to hide the document and, in a ploy that depends on the inattentiveness of the securely ensconced, places the letter, openly, albeit face down, on the table. At this point, the Minister enters, from whose "lynx eye" no detail escapes (the letter, the handwriting of the author, the King's oblivion, and the Queen's discomfort). Astutely assessing the situation, he contrives, under the Queen's fearfully silent gaze, to place one of his own letters, similar in appearance, next to the one exposed, and eventually to effect a switch. Having purloined the Queen's compromising letter in front of her eyes, the blackmailer's power he wields over her, which he soon begins to use for political purposes, lies not in the "employment of the letter" but in the threat of this that its possession poses. The Queen, unable to reclaim her letter openly, entrusts the task to the Prefect of Police. Aware that the nature of the intrigue compels the Minister to keep the letter very close at hand, he embarks on a minutely painstaking, ostensibly secret search of the Minister's premises by well-trained police agents, over many months. Moreover, the Minister has been waylaid on several occasions for a supposedly random body search, and undoubtedly expecting more of the same, clearly does not carry it on his person. The Prefect confesses to Dupin that despite the extreme urgency of the task and the very liberal reward offered for the recovery of the letter, all searching so far has been in vain. Not without first extracting a careful description of the letter, Dupin merely advises the Prefect to search again.

The second scene is narrated by Dupin about a month later, after another double visit from his friend (the narrator of our tale) and the despairing Prefect, whereupon, to the astonishment of both visitors, he produces a checkbook and offers the Prefect the Queen's letter in exchange for a very liberal check. The Prefect does not wait for the explanation that follows, from which one may discern another intersubjectively related triad of figures: namely, the Prefect, proxy for the Queen, who mirrors the King's state of unawareness; the Minister who faces precisely the Queen's predicament; and Dupin, now mimicking the Minister's "lynx-eye." Dupin grants that the police could not be faulted within the limits of their *modus operandi* but argues that the measures they used were entirely unsuitable for the case in question, which required a more flexible, "poetic" kind of reasoning. He enters into a lengthy assessment of the conditions that underpin the Prefect's instrumental ("mathematical") approach to the task of recovering the letter and, emphasizing that the Minister is both mathematician and poet, the Minister's "poetic" approach to hiding it.[7] He reveals that his own success in uncovering the Minister's ploy lay in his ability (like a boy playing the game of odds and evens) to mirror the Minister's intellectual style and thereby arrive at the correct conclusion that the Minister, wise to the skills and limitations of the rule-governed police mentality, must have risked placing the letter in full view as the best way of hiding it from them. Armed with dark glasses and the complaint of "weak eyes" to conceal his surveying glance, Dupin paid a visit to the Ministerial quarters, finding the Minister at home in a state of feigned boredom and lethargy. Simultaneously conducting an animated conversation with his host on a topic guaranteed to quicken his interest, Dupin, under the cover of his glasses carefully surveyed the apartment, his eyes finally coming to rest on his quarry, apparently carelessly thrust into a pasteboard card rack hanging just beneath the mantelpiece and conspicuously different from the letter purloined from the

Queen in every detail but size. Having committed these details to memory, Dupin took his leave of the Minister, contriving, however, to leave his snuffbox behind. Armed with a facsimile, he called for it the following day, having prearranged for a commotion to occur in the street below, so distracting the Minister sufficiently to allow him to make the switch. Soon thereafter he took his leave of the Minister, but not without leaving a trace.

When the Minister takes up the letter in response to the Queen's defiance of his blackmailer's demands, he will discover therein a citation (a line from Crébillon: "So baleful a plan, if unworthy of Atreus, is worthy of Thyestes") written in Dupin's hand, with which he is familiar. Although also acting as a partisan of the Queen, this parting gesture establishes Dupin's theft of the letter as an act of revenge for a past disservice at the hands of the Minister. It is this clue that provides Lacan with the material for detecting a third scene in the tale, involving another intersubjective triad of figures, again displaced one position along. This triad consists of the Minister, now mirroring the unawareness of the Prefect and the King; Dupin, who takes over the Queen's position from the Minister; and Lacan himself, whose position as interpreter matches the investigative position previously occupied by Dupin.

Real, Imaginary, and Symbolic in Lacan's "Seminar on 'The Purloined Letter'"

"The Drama" as Synonym for the "Impossible Real"

For Lacan, the "letter" in Poe's tale in the first instance stands for the "thing,"[8] "happening," or "drama," which occasions (in the form of the *tuché*) the tale in the first place. These notions can be taken as synonymous with the earlier examined notion of "event" or "trauma," all of which serve as markers for what Lacan has called "the impossible Real." The letter's equivocal status as "event" is brought out graphically in Poe's tale by the fact that his readers are never enlightened as to its specific contents[9] but are nonetheless left in no doubt that it bears no innocent greeting and represents instead a transgression of the established order, such that in simply receiving it the Queen's honor and safety are compromised. As Lacan notes: "Love letter or conspiratorial letter, letter of betrayal or letter of mission, letter of summons or letter of distress, we are assured of but one thing: the Queen must not bring it to the knowledge of her lord and master."[10]

In another synonymous term, Lacan also names the letter the "pure signifier"[11] that initiates (*tuché* again) a chain of signification, that is, a chain of attached signs, all of which aim, without the prospect of complete success, to explain or account for the signifier retroactively. Lacan insists that, as is the case with all "events," the "materiality" of this letter, or "pure signifier," is anomalous or odd. In his words, "if it is first of all on the materiality of the signifier [the event] that we have insisted, that materiality is *odd* [*singulière*] in many ways, the first of which is not to admit partition. Cut a letter in small pieces, and it remains the letter it is." Lacan is invoking here the impossible, immortal "wholeness," "oneness," or "singularity" belonging to an as yet undetermined "thing" or singular "it happens." This singularity of the unspeakable has no measure. In his words, "the signifier is a unit in its very uniqueness, being by nature symbol only of an absence."[12]

What kind of an absence? The "letter" as "pure signifier" or "event" symbolizes the absence of the kind of specifiable, measurable, determinable "content," the present central concept or set of conceptual relations that would supposedly preexist, initiate, anchor, and order its subsequent linguistic interpretation. Yet the absence of such an anchoring or transcendental signified (implied by the term "pure signifier") cannot be conflated with an absolute absence in the Real (this would open psychoanalysis to the charge of subjective idealism). One must therefore remain wary of formulations that insist too one-sidedly on the absence of content: certainly a particular content is never revealed, but we are left in no doubt at all that this is no innocent thank-you note from a beloved granddaughter. As Lacan points out, the event is also "not nothing"; it signifies that something importantly transgressive happened to initiate a chain of significations, all of which vainly attempt to reconstruct (in retrospect) what happened. This is why, as he notes, one cannot say of the letter that it is either present or absent: "we cannot say of the purloined letter that, like other objects, it must be *or* not be in a particular place but that unlike them it will be *and* not be where it is, wherever it goes."[13] In other words, whenever the letter reaches its destination, it will simultaneously be and not be there.[14]

The Narration as a Function of the Imaginary Order

In a move that makes deciphering his text quite tricky, Lacan insists in addition that the word "letter" also stands for the language by means of which the singular "letter" or epistle received by the Queen, the event, is thought, interpreted, constituted, spoken, or narrated. The word's double duty, one should grant, emphasizes that there are no uninterpreted events. Again, the interpretation of an event is anomalous. An event is constituted as such both by means of its interpreting recognition and due to the failure of such recognition, and this is always a matter of a linguistic narration that necessarily both gives it measure and fails to take its measure. The aporetic anomaly, then, lies in the unavoidable consequence that an event is simultaneously constituted and lost in its narration. As Lacan notes: "Language delivers its judgment to whomever knows how to hear it: through the usage of the article as partitive particle. It is there that spirit—if spirit be living meaning—appears, no less oddly, as more available for quantification than its letter." Again: "The narration, in fact, doubles the drama [event] with a commentary without which no *mise en scène* would be possible." Yet, he adds, "nothing of the drama could be grasped, neither seen nor heard, without, dare we say, the twilighting which the narration, in each scene, casts on the point of view that one of the actors had while performing it." There *is* no event without its narration from a particular point of view, but, as the word "twilighting" suggests,[15] it is precisely because narration must occur from a point of view that the event is both illuminated and obscured (framed and missed) by means of the narration. Something happens, but to establish what happened requires a retrospective, linguistic construction, a necessary fiction that is the product of the Imaginary Order, whose nature is such that the event is covered over the moment it is disclosed, or enclosed within certain boundaries, which means that what happened remains undisclosed and ever open to interpretation. So far, then, the relation between the Real and the Imaginary may be understood in terms of the relation between the so-called pure signifier (event) and the aporetic dis/order imposed upon it by the necessity of its narration from a particular point of view.

The Conditions of Narration as Determined by the Symbolic Order

Lacan argues further that the points of view that provide the "conditions of the narration" for the conscious speech that aims to narrate the event (or attach a signified to the "pure signifier") are generally unconscious. By making a distinction between the narration and the conditions of narration, he ties the analytic dialogue to the important structuralist distinction between *parole* (actual, conscious everyday speech or linguistic phenomena, such as gestures) and *langue* or *langage*, which, synonymous with the terms "discourse" or "language game," refers to the "unconscious infrastructure" behind conscious linguistic phenomena.[16] According to Lee, Lacan's Symbolic Order "is (at a first degree of approximation) the background system or 'language' that makes possible and meaningful the wide variety of human behaviors."[17] Following in the footsteps of Claude Lévi-Strauss—who argues that "forms of human behavior can be (indeed, must be) studied as analogous to utterances, these behaviors making sense only in relation to a background system of rules, which can be thought of as the language of such behaviors"[18]—Lacan's notion of the Symbolic Order as constituted by three constant subject positions incorporates the insight that a "social bond" or intersubjective linkage is essential to make particular speech acts possible or meaningful. In short, Lacan's notion of the symbolic presupposes the predominance of the symbol over significance or value in the mathematical sense where, for example, x and y can take on any value but are themselves related in certain ways according to certain structural laws that do not change whatever the value they can be taken to represent.

Each subject position imposes certain conditions on the narration, regardless of who narrates and what is narrated, and to the extent that characters occupy one or another of these subject positions, they manifest the power and weakness of the point of view it imposes. To the extent that a subject position is passively or unreflectively occupied by individuals and remains unconscious, their speech becomes what he describes as undirected, automatic, innocent, or "empty." "Empty speech" denotes what is said without thinking. On Lacan's definition of the repetition compulsion, to shift to a different subject position, as Poe's story illustrates, is unconsciously to fall under the spell of the narrative style imposed by that position; in other words, what is repeated in different characters is the unconscious subject position that conditions their narration.

At this point there is little to suggest that Lacan's theory avoids being a version of discursive determinism, which is based on the assumption that we are entirely spoken by discourse. To demonstrate how Lacan escapes this charge requires a brief explanatory detour. He accepts Saussure's well-known dictum that "language" or discourse is an articulated system of differences "*without positive terms*," where any term takes on meaning because of its relations with other terms. On a structuralist account, the system of differences that constitutes a discourse is indeed seen as thoroughly relational, but the relations are taken to be ordered and stabilized by some form of anchor (an ultimate or central "transcendental signified" or principle or set of rules or relations).

As already noted, Lacan's thinking both adopts and subverts structuralist principles. He grants that all discourses, from the more particularized and localized to the most general, are built upon presupposed, implicitly desired *points de capiton* that serve to orient the speech acts within them.

Here, he proposes the metaphor of a musical score: "There is in effect no signifying chain that does not have, as if attached to the punctuation of each of its units, a whole articulation of relevant contexts suspended 'vertically,' as it were, from that point."[19] The ultimate *point de capiton*, as Lee explains, may also be described as "the point of convergence which allows the retroactive and prospective situating of everything that happens in this discourse." Functioning as a "transcendental" signified, the *point de capiton* is taken to be the condition that underpins what is in play in the signifying chains of a subject's discourse.

The Lacanian subversion occurs with the insight that the *points de capiton*, for which the phallus is a general term, remain traumatic. In Lee's words: "The phallus is present beneath every signifier as the signifier that has been repressed, and as such every signifier is a metaphor substituting for the phallus."[20] Notably, however, and this is the twist, the phallus is a word that stands for the impossible "jouissance." The phallus, Lee adds, serves to signify "that fullness of being, that complete identity, the lack of which is the fact of our ineluctable want-of-being."[21] Thus the *points de capiton* are not actually present in the signifying chain at all. Rather, replaced in the chain by other signifiers serving as metaphorical substitutes (or symptomatic disguises) for them, they serve only to mark the assumption of an underlying meaningful coherence, which retains its orienting function only if left unexamined. For Lacan, then, to explicate the sense of any discourse is to bring to light the *points de capiton* that have been repressed by that discourse, that is, its unconsciously presupposed transcendental conditions of possibility (or, one should add, quasi-transcendental conditions of possibility/impossibility). Psychoanalysis, in his view, through careful attention to the analysand's discourse, seeks to uncover the "unsaid" within the signifying chain itself, which nevertheless constitutes the meaning of that discourse.[22]

What underpins speaking as such is a drive to regain the lost jouissance, which manifests in different ways. We speak as a demand to the other, not for something, but for an impossible recognition of our desires. But desire is metonymy; that is, a desire for something is a projection of the death drive toward jouissance.[23] In other words, desire itself can never quite be articulated; it is already an interpretation of the jouissance that slips away in the moment of truth. No matter what an individual speaker demands, it can only be articulated as an object that might satisfy need. The desire for recognition is "masked by and thus alienated in" one's demand for something.[24]

All attempts to articulate desire are in vain and see the subject slipping from one signifier to another. "Each of these signifiers is linked metonymically to the want-of-being, which the desirer hopes will be filled by the other's reply to his demand."[25] It is only the other's total recognition of the absolute power of my demand that will restore the lost jouissance (masculine death drive). Alternatively, it is only the other's recognition of the falsity of all discourse that will restore the lost jouissance (feminine death drive). Further, "to the extent that all of our speech is a metonymic attempt to cover over this fundamental want-of-being [the trauma], all human speech is figuratively linked to the phallus [designating lost jouissance] as the central *point de capiton* of our discourse."[26] This twist ensures that the background discourse makes individual speech acts both possible and impossible, both meaningful and incapable of full meaning. If my discourse is underpinned by the demand for recognition of me as a meaningful whole, it will turn out to be a restrictive prison (aporia of limit). If it is underpinned by the demand for freedom from such restriction for the sake of including all, it paradoxically puts me in the prison of exclusion (aporia of unlimitedness). If my discourse is underpinned by the acknowledgment of the part that functions as a whole, then I have to accept the aporetic nature of all experience (aporia of paradox), reflected in statements such as the following: In order to be just I have to apply the law, but in applying the law I cannot be just. In order to be ethical I have to make a decision, but in making a decision, I cannot be ethical. In order to invent myself, I have to establish an identity, but in establishing an identity, I have to submit to convention. In order to be ethical I have to persevere with my project to the limit, but if I am unwilling to give up my project, I cannot be ethical.

The phallus, then, contrary to structuralist principles, names an excess to the linguistic system, which produces paradox. It takes little ingenuity to propose that when humans try to say what happened, the different kinds of aporias in which we find our narration inescapably tied up are associated with points of view that may be described in the familiar terms of the "plural logic of the aporia." Or in other terms, the most general discursive "rule" or quasi-condition of discourse articulates the aporias of limit (universal), limitlessness (particular), and paradox (singular universal). This means that the position from which anyone speaks is autodeconstructing. In a patriarchy, as noted, the logical articulation of the Symbolic Order takes on the characteristic form of the masculine and feminine death drives and feminine sublimation. In his interpretation of Poe's tale, accordingly, Lacan demonstrates that it differentiates these three subject positions in terms of an interplay of blindness and insight that corresponds respectively with the masculine aporia of limit (metaphysics of presence), the feminine aporia of transgression (antimetaphysics), and the feminine aporia of paradox (quasi-transcendental thinking) that describes the position of the analyst.

Represented by the King in the first scene, the Prefect of Police as the Queen's proxy in the second, and the Minister in the third, the "masculine" point of view, which one could call the moment of blind faith in an established ideological order, involves "a glance that sees nothing."[27] Such "blindness" takes different forms, as should become clearer in due course, but they all boil down to some version of the metaphysics of presence. As represented by the King, who does not see the letter at all, the blindness of his position is the consequence of erroneously converting the anomaly of the Real into fully present terms. In other words, the King represents the kind of subject who interprets anything that happens only in terms of the grid of relations provided by some or other existing order and does not grasp that there is a nonevident background "language" or discourse that conditions any narrative. A narrative from the subject position represented by the King misses even the possibility of the enigmatic anomalies that occasion events. Thus, precisely because he misses the very form of the Queen's transgression, the King sees nothing amiss, which leaves him open to being duped by the transgressor who sees more than he.

The "feminine" glance (represented in the first scene by the Queen, in the second by the Minister, and in the third by Dupin) is, in Lacan's words, a "glance which sees that the first sees nothing and deludes itself as to the secrecy of what it hides."[28] This characterization condenses two important moments associated with the feminine subject position, namely its "progressive" moment of insight, which is also that of transgression, and its "retrogressive" moment of blindness (discussion of which I shall defer to the next section). Lacan ties the moment of insight to the irruption of an event.

An "event" by definition is a traumatic interruption of any established order, regardless of the kind of transgression or the particular order transgressed. For Lacan, then, "receiving the letter" can stand as a metaphor for acquiring a certain kind of insight into the "conditions of narration," which would amount to acknowledging the nonnatural, discursively constructed, fabricated, artificial, manmade nature of any system of Law. This is an insight that immediately places the one who acquires it on the outside of, or at a reflective distance from, not just the contingent order of this particular King but from established order as such.[29] To "see" the letter as an event, then, is automatically to occupy a transgressive position vis-à-vis any established order. (Notably, to recognize an event in a patriarchy is automatically to occupy a feminine subject position, which is by definition transgressive in relation to a masculine subject position.)

It is fitting, then, that the first to "receive" the letter in Poe's tale is the Queen. As Lacan notes, "the existence of the letter situates her in a symbolic chain foreign to the one which constitutes her faith. This incompatibility is proven by the fact that the possession of the letter is impossible to bring forward publicly as legitimate."[30] The Queen's insight illustrates what Lacan means when he remarks that the displacement—but one could also add the placement—of the characters that people Poe's tale "is determined by the place which a pure signifier—the purloined letter—comes to occupy in their trio."[31] In other words, a kind of intersubjective communication operates whereby a character's occupation of the transgressive subject position upon receiving the letter (which entails her or his recognition of the Real, the event, lack, or castration) in turn relationally constitutes others as blind subjects. Here, the Queen's recognition of the letter as an event, which by definition reconfigures the fabric of the world, immediately places the King and those who along with him do not recognize the event in the position of the blind or innocent who remain tied up in the net of existing relations.

The occupation of an analytical position, which is a more sophisticated way of receiving the letter, or recognizing the event, constitutes both the masculine and feminine positions as still tied up in the Imaginary.[32] The analytical glance sees that faith in the established order and its transgression represent two opposing logical moments or subject positions inscribed in the Symbolic Order.

If the King's blind masculine glance converts the anomalous Real into pure presence, the Queen's perceptive feminine glance involves an equal but opposite misrecognition of the Real, which converts it into a pure absence. She seems unable to envisage anything to replace what is for her, on receiving the letter, the shattered order of the King. From her point of view, there is only the artificial order and the "sign of contradiction and scandal constituted by the letter."[33] In this subject position, then, conditioned by the background discourse of hysterical resistance to all restricting boundaries, the Queen remains paralyzed.[34] Even if she had the power to modify or replace existing structures, from this subject position she is constitutionally unable to find any cause worth fighting for, since one is as much a fake as any other. Moreover, unwilling to risk her honor and her life in open subversion, her only option is to hide the transgressive insight and pretend to play the game by the King's rules. This, however, leaves her silenced, for she remains subject to an order she does not acknowledge as legitimate. Lacan notes that the double bind of her position is that her only recourse if she wishes to have her possession of the letter openly respected is to invoke her right to privacy. But this is the very right that is not granted to those who commit a felony, such as treason.[35] As he sums it up, "this sign is indeed that of woman, insofar as she invests her very being therein, founding it outside the law, which subsumes her nevertheless." Paralyzed within the King's order as its mere negativity, "she has but to remain immobile in its shadow." Yet, in hiding she leaves herself vulnerable to the analytical glance.[36]

According to Lacan, the "analytical" glance (represented by the Minister in the first scene, Dupin in the second, and Lacan himself in the third) is a glance of reflective distance and self-consciousness that "sees that the first two glances leave what should be hidden exposed to whomever would seize it."[37] In other words, wise to the anomalous Real and the conditions of narration, including its own, what this glance "sees" is that the first two are related according to the "fallacious complementarity" of the vel of alienation. What one finds in their relation is a lose/lose situation of equivalent blindness rather than a lose/win situation of blindness and insight. The analytical glance finds in this awareness the opportunity to rise above the paralyzing limitations of both naïve realism and its secret transgression and gain thereby the power of decisive action. In Poe's story, this analytical awareness is converted into the chance for larceny, and in a certain sense such action would always have to be "criminal."[38] One should note, however, that the opening allowed by the analytical gaze equally gives one the chance for ethical action, and the difference between these two kinds of action is crucial if one is to see in the tale an allegory for psychoanalysis. I shall return to this important point in due course.

As Lacan sums up so far, one can read Poe's tale in terms of "three moments, structuring three glances, borne by three subjects."[39] But there is more to the logic of the Symbolic Order than the constant structure of subject positions "incarnated each time by different characters" and the progressive logical movement toward insight from the discourse of the King, through that of the Queen, to that of the Analyst. As Lacan points out, one may detect in the shift of characters in the three triads a strangely retrogressive logic of displacement.

The Twist in the Tale: The Desire for Mastery and the Logic of Retrogression

The Retrogressive Slip from Transgressive Insight to Blindness

How does the Queen of the first triad slip in the second triad into the position of blindness characteristic of the King? Or: how does one slip into blindness having once received the letter? The Queen's new blindness cannot be precisely the same as the King's, because there is no return to innocence once transgression has occurred. It will be, instead, the self-delusion specific to one who has shaken off any naïve faith in the metaphysics of presence but unwittingly allows it in through the back door. In other words, if the masculine glance as represented by the King involves the kind of blindness associated with the naïve assumption that one *is* master of the situation, those who see the illegitimacy of this assumption can nevertheless retrogressively slip into an equivalent blindness associated with the assumption that one can in principle regain mastery of a situation in the wake of an event. In Poe's tale, metaphorically speaking, this "blindness" is represented by the Queen's assumption that, in order to restore her mastery over the situation, it is imperative, and therefore in principle possible, to re-find the letter. The implicit assumption here is that with the recovery of the document, all will return to how it was in the beginning, as if nothing has happened—as if one could reinstate the past as it was, making nothing of time and of the event. Yet because the letter, precisely because it is an event, irrevocably changes the fabric of the world, there is no "proper" return of the letter, even if the document is recovered. The Queen's delusion, which now mirrors the King's, is to have mistakenly conceived of the letter as synonymous with a physical object. Her misrecognition of the letter is graphically illustrated in Poe's tale by the irony that, in order to recover it, she resorts to the very mechanisms of law enforcement whose legitimacy it invalidates.

Further, the discrepancy between the letter and the document she seeks to recover is highlighted, fittingly, by the Prefect's misapplication of instrumental methods in his search for it. Bound by the blindness associated with faith in the metaphysics of presence, the Prefect of Police (representing the Queen's slip into the masculine position), knows that something is amiss, unlike the King, but immediately interprets the trouble along the lines of there being some known object that has gone missing from its proper place in the order. As Lacan puts it: "what is hidden is never but what is *missing from its place*, as the call slip puts it when speaking of a volume lost in a library."[40] He therefore searches for it on the assumption that it can in principle be re-found. Put in other terms, if the letter as "event" represents the Real in contrast with physical reality, "the detectives have so immutable a notion of the real that they fail to notice that their search tends to transform it into its object."[41]

Lacan associates masculine blindness with what he calls "the realist's imbecility," which has two sides.[42] On the one hand, as it pertains to the Prefect, such blindness represents his obliviousness to the possibility that, paradoxically, what is "seen" in the clear light of day, that is, everything that can be made present or established in terms of a certain order of presence, simultaneously exposes and hides "the truth." In Poe's story, this is demonstrated by the paradoxical situation of the letter, which is hidden out in the open by someone one step ahead of the Prefect. The Prefect, then, is duped by the Minister, not because he sees nothing amiss (like the King), but because, like the Queen, he does not grasp the paradoxical nature of the Real but rather relies on the "scientific methods" that will "help you not to think of truths you'd be better off leaving in the dark."[43] Hence Dupin's assessment of the Prefect: "A certain set of highly ingenious resources are, with the Prefect, a sort of Procrustean bed, to which he forcibly adapts his designs."[44]

The Retrogressive Slip from Analytical Insight to Blindness

How does an individual slip from the position of analyst to the position of blindness? Again, this cannot be a matter of returning to the ideological blindness represented by the King, nor can it be a matter of the contradictory belief that re-finding the letter will efface the happening of the event, or, that is, negate time. Rather, the blindness here is double: like the Queen, both the Minister and Dupin assume that a superior intellect (or the insight that is consequent upon receiving the letter) places a person one step ahead of an "adversary" and therefore in a position of mastery over the situation. Further, in the cases of the Minister and Dupin, this blindness is associated with the assumption that one has achieved mastery over the transgressed other upon "receiving" and holding the letter and not only successfully hiding it, like the Queen in relation to the King, but also in knowing just how to take advantage of it.

But there is another side to the "realist's imbecility," which Lacan describes as pertaining to those who do not "pause to observe that nothing, however deep in the bowels of the earth a hand may seek to ensconce it, will ever be hidden there, since another hand can always retrieve it."[45] This description applies straightforwardly to the masculine ploys of the common criminals who try to hide what is stolen in the most obscure cracks and crevices (and who will never by this means outwit the Prefect's mode of searching). But in a paradoxical twist, it applies equally to the feminine ploys of the Queen, the Minister, and Dupin, all of whom hide "the letter" out in the open, so outsmarting the King and the police but simultaneously leaving this ploy exposed to those with eyes enough to see it, who may at any point simply stretch out a hand to retrieve it. The assumption of mastery, then, involves a misrecognition of the situation, since it takes into account only the intellectual prowess of the transgressed. Implicitly, then, all assumptions of mastery are based only on one's assessment of the available evidence, the trouble being that this assessment is in principle never made with a full deck in hand, leaving the assessor permanently exposed to those of equal or greater analytical perspicacity. This means, in the end, that, like the King, the transgressor remains blind to the "tricks" of those who see more clearly.

For example, "in playing the part of the one who hides," Lacan notes that the Minister first slips from the analytical position that enabled him to purloin the letter in the first place to the feminine position previously occupied by the Queen.[46] Here we find that, in holding the letter, "a man man enough to defy to the point of scorn a lady's fearsome ire undergoes to the point of a metamorphosis the curse of the sign he has dispossessed her of."[47] So we find him "trapped in the typically imaginary situation" whereby he sees that he is not seen by the police: "The Minister acts as a man who realizes that the police's search is his own defense, since we are told he allows them total access by his absences."[48] But, lulled into the false sense of invincibility afforded by their blindness, he "fails to recognize that outside of that search he is no longer defended."[49] In short, he misconstrues the real situation, in which he is "seen not seeing" by someone who sees further than he: Dupin.[50] What, then, does Dupin grasp that the Minister misses? Precisely that in the game of odds and evens, a sharper intellect would expose his ploy.

If Dupin in this tale emerges as the mark of a supreme analytical intellect, are we to suppose that this character ought to stand as a model for the analyst (or the psychoanalytically realized subject) in psychoanalytical theory? And if the task of the psychoanalyst is to engender the power of the analyst in the analysand, does Dupin's method of detection provide a model for analytical interpretation? Clearly not, for it is not fortuitous that Lacan emphasizes the savageness of Dupin's attack on his adversary and alter ego in this tale, the other analyst and his mirror image, whom he labels "that *monstrum horrendum*, an unprincipled man of genius."[51] The implication here is that the aggression is a function of identification and that this act of aggression establishes that Dupin, as much as the Minister, deserves the label of *monstrum horrendum*.

Lacan's "analysis" of Dupin as a character is important because it details his view of the kind of insight that makes for an analyst and what kind of blindness threatens any analyst with the logic of retrogression. Dupin's insight is laid out in the contrast Lacan details between his narration of the second scene in Poe's tale and the Prefect's narration of the first. In constructing the work so that the scenes are narrated by characters occupying different subject positions, Poe offers a comparison between the masculine blindness of the Prefect and Dupin's analytical insight insofar as they make opposite use of the powers of speech. Between the two scenes, Lacan notes, "a transition is made here from the domain of exactitude to the register of truth." I shall return to the ambiguity of Lacan's notion of truth; suffice it to note here that at bottom he links "truth" to the notions of "event" or "trauma." As Lee notes: "In the Freudian Thing—the thing in question here being quite precisely truth, Lacan adopts a Heideggerian account of truth, understanding truth as essentially a state or process of disclosure." But a truth is a particular disclosure, "the effect of which is that reality is no longer the same for us as it was before."[52] Truth, by extension, is linked to the recognition of the consequent unavoidability of aporias in any narrative.

Accordingly, Lacan calls the first dialogue between the Prefect of Police and Dupin (and companion) "a play without words," suggesting that it is a play unaware of its aporetic literary character.[53] The Prefect of Police narrates without knowing the conditions of his narration. He simply tells it the way it "is." His narration, Lacan notes, takes on the character of a game "played as between a deaf man and one who hears." The real complexity of the event certainly emerges in the dialogue, but only for the analyst, here Dupin. Lacan has in mind, for example, the following early exchange between the Prefect and Dupin:[54] The Prefect begins by contradicting himself: "The fact is, the business is *very* simple indeed, and I make no doubt that we can manage it sufficiently well ourselves; but then I thought Dupin would like to hear the details of it, because it is so excessively *odd.*" This contradiction is at once underscored by Dupin ("Simple and odd"), forcing the Prefect to admit his perplexity openly: "Why, yes; and not exactly that, either. The fact is, we have all been a good deal puzzled because the affair *is* so simple, and yet baffles us altogether." Dupin then presses the point by proposing more than once that the truth might lie in paradox, but this is a notion the Prefect immediately and automatically dismisses, negates, scoffs at, and renders null ("Perhaps it is the very simplicity of the thing which puts you at fault"; "What nonsense you *do* talk"; "Perhaps the mystery is a little *too* plain"; "Oh, good heavens! Who ever heard of such an idea?"; "A little *too* self-evident"; "Ha! Ha! Ha!").[55] The automaticity of his response to a notion beyond the narrow framework of the position from which he speaks, reflected performatively in the repetition of the interchange (like a stuck record), signifies the unconscious repetition compulsion that characterizes his imaginary capture. As Lacan notes, it is "as though the highly significant commentary into which he who understands integrates it, could, because unperceived by him who does not understand, be considered null."[56]

Dupin's narration of the second scene stands in stark contrast to the Prefect's mode of speech, by virtue of its evident self-consciousness, as indicated by his lengthy analyses of both the *modus operandi* of the Police and of the Minister. He is clearly wise to the conditions of narration that underpin the masculine and feminine subject positions and is aware of how they relate. He is also, at least apparently, aware of the conditions of his own narration, for he describes in erudite detail his own *modus operandi*. This show of erudition and the easy cunning with which he uses the power of analytical reasoning (a combination of mathematical and poetical genius) to outwit and trick the Minister is all but guaranteed to install in the listener (the reader of the tale) the impression that Dupin is the true master of the situation and the hero of the tale. Moreover, this impression is confirmed, it would seem, by the fact that he does not try to hold the letter but exchanges it for a check, thus apparently allowing him to withdraw from the "symbolic circuit of the letter."[57]

If Dupin sees that he has tricked the minister by the power of his reasoning, and constitutes himself thereby as fully master of the situation, Lacan, however, expresses an early suspicion that there is "a certain dissonance . . . between, on the one hand, the admittedly penetrating though, in their generality, not always quite relevant remarks with which he introduces us to his method and, on the other, the manner in which he in fact intervenes."[58] As he puts it: "The profit Dupin so nimbly extracts from his exploit, if its purpose is to allow him to withdraw his stakes from the game, makes all the more paradoxical, even shocking, the partisan attack, the underhanded blow, he suddenly permits himself to launch against the Minister, whose insolent prestige, after all, would seem to have been sufficiently deflated by the trick Dupin has just played on him."[59]

If Dupin occupies the position of analyst by virtue of a certain intellectual knowledge of the conditions of narration, there is nevertheless something troubling about his action, which reminds Lacan of a definition he once gave of the modern hero: "whom ludicrous exploits exalt in circumstances of utter confusion." As indicated in a footnote, this is a reference to his insistence in "Function and Field" that the kind of psychoanalyst who did not take account of language "resembles the type of modern hero famous for his vain exploits in situations entirely beyond his control." In other words, for Lacan, like the analyst who does not take "proper" account of the conditions of narration (the function of language and its relation to the unconscious), Dupin does not really know what he is doing. Instead, in constituting himself as master analyst, Dupin remains blind to the function of the unconscious (or, that is, the function in the dialogue of his own desire), which, like an undertow, drives the logic of retrogression.

It is not simply that his act of revenge undermines the outward impression created that he "won the day" through the neutral power of reasoning. It is rather that it confirms what is already there to be found symptomatically in his discourse: namely that if winning was the point of employing his analytical prowess, then this prowess serves only his own drive for mastery. Lacan notes the eristic quality of the "enigmas, paradoxes, and even jests presented to us as an introduction to Dupin's method."[60] In other words, the games he uses as metaphors for his strategy suggest that it is aimed at winning rather than reaching the truth. The implication is that Dupin is as unconsciously invested as all of the other characters in acquiring power or mastery over the rest. His discourse on his *modus operandi*, ostensibly a mode of enlightening the reader concerning what it takes to be an analyst, forms a smokescreen of rational neutrality that veils his hunger for power. The solver of enigmas could equally turn out to be an impressive hoax, the august joker who has duped us all into believing that he alone has secured his withdrawal from the symbolic circuit. "What could be more convincing," Lacan asks, "than the gesture of laying one's cards face up on the table? So much so that we are momentarily persuaded that the magician has in fact demonstrated, as he promised, how his trick was performed, whereas he has only renewed it in still purer form."

Lacan thus claims to be more analytically aware than Dupin of the "conditions of his narration," for in the symptomatic irruptions just discussed, he can fathom the unconscious motivation (a desire for analytical mastery defined as power over others) that Dupin misses.[61] What Lacan, unlike Dupin, knows as an analyst has to do with the nature of genuine mastery. According to Lacan, in misrecognizing mastery as power over others, what Dupin does not see is that his analytical *modus operandi* engenders the radically destabilizing situation of odds and evens between adversaries of equal intellectual power.[62] If adversaries are equal, then there is only chance and no longer reason in the game. Dupin, for example, is certain of the Minister's downfall or disgrace when he tries to use the letter. "For eighteen months the Minister has had her in his power. She has now him in hers; since, being unaware that the letter is not in his possession, he will proceed with his exactations as if it was. Thus will he inevitably commit himself, at once, to his political destruction. His downfall, too, will not be more precipitate than awkward."[63] But Lacan notes that he has probably underestimated the Minister: "if he is truly the gambler we are told he is, he will consult his cards a final time before laying them down and upon reading his hand, will leave the table in time to avoid disgrace" and no doubt will begin to plot his revenge. In this case, the intellects are matched and the game devolves into a pessimistic no-win situation of perpetual power struggle. The warning to analysts (of every ilk) that Lacan extracts from Dupin's blindness, therefore, is that genuine mastery cannot be understood in terms of exercising power over others. Rather, what psychoanalysis in principle requires of an analyst, or aims at in any psychoanalytically realized subject, is a form of self-mastery, which is defined as the power of inventive self-renewal through the interminable labor of self-analysis.

Concluding Remarks: "Empty Speech"/"Full Speech" and the "Talking Cure"

Lacan's seminar on "The Purloined Letter" presents the theoretical underpinnings for Lacan's claim that psychoanalytic practice, among other things, should aim to bring analysts into being. Like Socrates, those who are already analysts should serve as self-effacing midwives at the birth of new analysts. Their task, in other words, is to intervene where the death drive in either of its manifestations becomes a disempowering aporia for individuals and to facilitate their progressive shift from the subject positions dominated by Imaginary fixations to the position of analyst. To make this shift requires not only the birth of self-consciousness, defined as a progressively achieved insight into the unconscious conditions of narration, but also a grasp of the intersubjective dynamics of the unconscious desire for mastery and the permanent risk this poses of blinding retrogression.

These requirements are not restricted to the analytic dialogue but apply generally to ordinary dialogue in any context, precisely because speaking is in principle structured in terms of call and response. As Lacan puts it in another text: "In analysis, a subject offers himself as being capable of being understood, and indeed *is* capable of being understood."[64] That is, a listener is inscribed in the very notion of speech: "there is no speech without a reply, even if it is met only with silence, provided that it has an auditor."[65] To speak at all is to place another in the position of "analyst" or, that is, constitute another individual intersubjectively as the Other whom I call upon to recognize my desire. Because of the responsibility consequently conferred on any auditor in her/his capacity as other, dialogue in general is a situation of risk and responsibility, for it is here that the subject comes into being. As Lacan puts it: "Henceforth the decisive function of my own reply appears, and this function is not, as has been said, simply to be received by the subject as acceptance or rejection of his discourse, but really to recognize him or to abolish him as subject. Such is the nature of the analyst's *responsibility* whenever he intervenes by means of speech."[66]

The risks and responsibilities are magnified in the analytic dialogue because the psychoanalyst is charged with the task of deliberately abolishing and recognizing the analysand as subject, making the analytical dialogue extremely vulnerable to the retrogressive undertow of the analyst's desire for power. Lacan's challenge to the analytic establishment, then, is to make good the claim inscribed in the name "psychoanalysis," instead of playing the modern hero (where the analysand may be helped despite the analyst), by taking seriously the function of language and its association with power. As he insists: "Whether it sees itself as an instrument of healing, of training, or of exploration in depth, psychoanalysis has only a single medium: the patient's speech. That this is self-evident is no excuse for our neglecting it."[67]

The movement of call and response, according to Lacan, lies at the heart of the function of language in analysis.[68] Further, in accordance with the structuralist division between *parole* (individual speech or narration) and *langue* (the conditions of the narration), he divides the analytic dialogue into two parts: "the first concerned with the 'here and now' of the analysand's free association and the second focused on the *Anamnesis* or recollection, which makes possible the symbolic interpretation of the analysand's discourse."[69]

Within the analytic dialogue, analysands begin by taking the risk of narrating their life stories by means of free association (of saying whatever comes to mind), and the analyst assumes the responsibility of offering an acute, interventionist response, where often enough the intervention takes the form of silence.[70] Initially, speaking about oneself is relatively easy, as Lee notes, for we have ample recourse to the superficial, media-propagated stereotypes by means of which "we can avoid a genuine 'speaking' about ourselves."[71] In Lacan's terms, the *moi* is a concatenation of unreflectively absorbed or passively received identifications (a caring doctor, an academic, an obsessive compulsive). However, precisely because the subject is split and the *je* is in principle in excess of any *moi* identifications, Lacan argues that frustration (sometimes coupled with aggression) is the inevitable ultimate consequence of free association.[72] When the *je* tries, in analysis, to gather the *moi* identifications into a coherent narrative, it finds gaps, discrepancies, and contradictions it is ordinarily entirely unaware of (I am a caring doctor, bound by the Hippocratic oath: I am a shareholder in a private hospital).[73]

Bearing in mind that analysands seek intervention precisely because of subjective troubles, the analytic dialogue is initially focused on abolishing the analysand as a *moi*. While analysands work to weave their narratives into an objectifying coherence, analysts initially work to counter the call for affirming recognition implicit in such self-objectification, in the hope of dismantling the illusion that identity is ever properly captured in any *moi* construction.[74] The first insight gained from free association, then, is that all self-identifications are essentially fictional, derived from the alienating misrecognitions of the mirror stage. This insight, in turn, dispossesses analysands of their overt desires, for they come to realize that these have been shaped by various pregiven symbolic systems. It is in this sense that a subject's speech is what Lacan calls "empty."

The art of the analyst, according to Lacan, is not simply a matter of dissolving paralyzing identifications. Psychoanalysts are also responsible for facilitating the analysand's reconstitution of a more satisfying narrative identity, that is, the reconstitution of a discourse that manifests the analysand's "truth."[75] Lacan's notion of truth, as mentioned, is notoriously paradoxical. In his words, the analysand's narrative "presents us with the birth of truth in speech, and thereby brings us up against the reality of what is neither true nor false."[76] Recalling his conception of truth as trauma ("the effect of which is that reality is no longer the same for us as it was before"), one could begin by suggesting that the birth of the analysand's truth occurs in the recognition of her desire. But this involves recognizing both what this desire is and that it lacks. In other words, insofar as the imaginary structures that analysands tend to imitate remain unconscious, their narrative continues to be lived merely as an unreflective, meaningless, unstructured, incomprehensible stream of consciousness. They grasp the truth of their narratives when they see how their actions have been structured by unconscious subject positions and come to grasp the articulation of those structures.[77] This should be a life-changing "event" whose truth is, in an important sense, still to come: it will be conferred retroactively.

Truth, then, in a second sense, is best captured in the oxymoron of a "necessary fiction." In other words, a narrative will be "true" insofar as subjects are ready not only to reject false desires but to recognize "true" desires and "assume" them, by taking responsibility for weaving them into a necessary fiction, which is, then, paradoxically, the "true" story. This activity of reconstitution invokes, as Lee points out, "Freud's notion of *Nachträglichkeit* or 'deferred action' (in French *après-coup*), the notion that the meaning and physical effectiveness of early experiences and memories can be and routinely are revised or even constituted for the first time in the light of later experiences."[78] For Lacan, in short, analysts are charged with the responsibility of facilitating the process whereby analysands come to recognize and assume their desires. "In order to free the subject's speech," according to Lacan, "we introduce him into the language of his desire, that is to say, into the *primary language* in which, beyond what he tells us of himself, he is already talking to us unknown to himself, and, in the first place, in the symbols of the symptom."[79] Again, in his words:

> The analytic experience allows us to feel the pressure of intention [the drives]. We read it in the symbolic meaning of symptoms, as soon as the subject throws off the defences by which he disconnects them from their relations with his daily life and his history, in the implicit finality of his behaviour and his rejections, in his unsuccessful acts, in the avowal of his privileged phantasies, and in the riddles of his dream life.
>
> We can measure it partly in the demanding tone that sometimes underlies his whole discourse, in his unfinished sentences, his hesitations, his inflexions and his slips of the tongue, in the inaccuracies of his descriptions of events, irregularities in his application of the analytic rule, late arrivals at sessions, calculated absences, and often in recriminations, reproaches, phantasmic fears, emotional reactions of anger, attempts at intimidation.[80]

Analysts, then, help analysands break down fixated desires by intervening at the point of such symptomatic interruptions in the otherwise meaningless flow, or empty speech, of free association. Lacan calls such analytical interventions "punctuation breaks." He notes that the absence of punctuation is a source of ambiguity in ancient manuscripts. Moreover, he adds, "the punctuation, once inserted, fixes the meaning; changing the punctuation renews or upsets it; and a faulty punctuation amounts to a change for the worse."[81] Just as a punctuation mark retroactively confers sense upon a relatively indeterminate or ambiguous concatenation of words, so careful analytical questions or gestures have the effect of conferring meaning on the analysand's discourse.[82] Through carefully chosen breaks in the associative discourse of their analysands, analysts highlight features of their imaginary *moi* identities, allowing them to grasp, for example, the gap between subject and predicate inherent in a statement of the form "I am . . . a caring doctor." The analyst's punctuating intervention, then, which has the effect of compelling analysands to clarify something ambiguous and construct a "symbolic interpretation" of it, brings into existence a signification that, as Lee puts it, "was only virtually present in the discourse."[83]

For Lacan, the further analytic task involves empowering analysands to construct their own punctuation marks: to take on the responsibility of becoming the *je* who narrates, punctuates, confers meaning, in short, actively constructs the necessary narrative fiction. Such active "interpretation," while a necessary step, however, is not sufficient to "transform the 'empty speech' of the analysand into the 'full speech' of the psychoanalytically realized subject."[84] Analysis cannot end at this point—for it is entirely contrary to the spirit of Lacanian psychoanalysis to imagine that its aim is to arrive at any objectifying discourse that simply helps analysands find out anew who they *are*. Instead, Lacan is persistently at pains to oppose the kind of analysis that leads an analysand to the point of saying "I *am* . . . ." In Lacan's words: "Psychoanalysis may accompany the patient to the ecstatic limit of the '*Thou art that*,' in which is revealed to him the cipher of his mortal destiny, but it is not in our mere power as practitioners to bring him to that point where the real journey begins."[85] I take him to mean that analysts can help analysands recognize their desires but, in the same sense that one cannot die for another, analysts cannot relieve analysands of the responsibility involved in assuming them and, thereby, stepping into the aporetic circle.

Truth, accordingly, in a third sense, for Lacan, is a matter of recognizing temporality and change—unlike the Queen, who desires to negate time. However, he agrees with Heidegger that understanding one's temporality does not imply an acknowledgment of human finitude in the sense that one is heading toward death one minute, day, year at a time.[86] Recognizing "truth" as temporality, then, is not reducible to the commonplace that we all die but is a matter of recognizing that any finite identity is a necessary fiction, that the "I" is always in excess of that fiction, which means that the fiction requires inventive iteration. To recognize temporality is to recognize that the "kernel of truth" is a traumatic event around which human subjects build their necessary fictions, which are impossible to do without but which remain always to some extent alienating. It is only if one becomes fixated with a particular fiction (and, in this sense, desire to subject time itself to paralysis) that disorders occur.

Accordingly, the final part of the analytical task is to engender a recognition in the analysand that the narrative constructed by the *je* to define the *moi* on the basis of events is a necessary fiction that remains permanently open ended. Just as all events are constituted retrospectively through their narration (*nachträglich*), so the deliberate punctuation mark retroactively confers meaning or "truth" on a narrative. But punctuation is intrinsically paradoxical: "Punctuation continually resolves ambiguities retroactively, only to generate others."[87] This understanding frees the *je* from the narration and opens it up for reinvention, allowing new strands to weave their way in and perhaps, again retroactively, to throw new light on the existing narrative. As Lacan puts it, "in psychological anamnesis, it is not a question of reality, but of truth, because the effect of full speech is to reorder past contingencies by conferring on them the sense of necessities to come, such as they are constituted by the little freedom [the artistic license] through which the subject makes them present."[88]

It is clear that for Lacan the "psychoanalytically realized subject" theorized in his "Seminar on 'The Purloined Letter,'" accords with his later conception of ethical being, defined as the ethical power of inventive sublimation, which marks the apotheosis of human being. The fully realized human subject is one who has achieved such ethical power, which, paradoxically, amounts to an awareness of the persistent responsibility to keep striving for "mortal immortality" as the appropriately human end. This should not be taken to mean that at any point psychoanalysis produces subjects who can finally claim to be fully realized or ethical. The psychoanalytically realized subject is, paradoxically, one who knows in what sense the task of becoming an analyst is interminable.

Conclusion

To Do Justice to Lacan

To review the course of this study, I have tried to demonstrate how the "plural logic of the aporia" emerges from out of the relative ruin of the transcendental tradition, for which Freud, among others, is fingered, and how it comes into its own in Derrida's thinking as a "repetition compulsion" that one could also call iterability. Turning to the family resemblance that joins Derrida to Lacan, I have described how this logic informs Derrida's reading of key Freudian texts. Turning to Lacan, I have tried to demonstrate that he rereads Freud's texts in terms of a "structural logic" that accords precisely with the "plural logic of the aporia." This makes of Lacan's return to Freud just as much an iteration of psychoanalysis, or an inventive repetition, as Derrida's. Thus, in response to Derrida's question: "Is there some psychoanalysis—X-ian, his, yours, mine—that can hold up or that is coming?" both thinkers produce the yes-and-no answer by which psychoanalysis becomes the traumatic event of psychoanalysis.[1] The brothers both kill and rescue father Freud by reinventing him. That an accord can quite easily be established between deconstruction and Lacanian psychoanalysis on the basis of a shared poststructural "logic" makes Derrida's stubborn resistance to Lacanian discourse all the more curious, and one could even say distressing, for those, and I count myself among them, who have above all placed faith in Derrida's perspicacity and admired deconstruction's power to open the wrapping without losing the present. While acknowledging the clear injustice of Derrida's criticism, and without wishing to make excuses for the inexcusable, I shall by way of conclusion follow Barbara Johnson's example in trying to salvage something of value from it.

First, what did Derrida say when Lacan's *Écrits* and deconstruction arrived on the scene simultaneously? "For the Love of Lacan" inscribes Derrida's retrospective reflections upon this beginning at the end of an era (speaking in honor of Lacan shortly after his death). At this "end-point," Derrida notes that he faced at the time what he calls a chiasmus.[2] Granting that Lacan's encounter with the philosophers was "so much more interesting than what was then going about in a dogmatic slumber under the name of psychoanalysis," Derrida, the deconstructive "philosopher," nevertheless found Lacan's "philosophizing reconstitution of psychoanalysis" too at home with the philosophers.[3] Moreover, he found that Lacan's "handling of philosophical reference . . . was in the best of cases elliptical and aphoristic, and in the worst, dogmatic." Further, he criticized Lacan's "frequent, decisive, self-confident, and sometimes incantatory" recourse to Heideggerian discourse, which is paradoxical, because Heidegger's texts are themselves in any case a call for deconstructive questions to be asked. The paradox is deepened, he insisted, if one notes that ever since Freud, psychoanalysis has moved to "deconstruct the privilege of presence."

Looking back, Derrida claims to have been provoked into this kind of "discussion" (which prompted his critical essay "Le Facteur de la Vérité") by Lacan's "Seminar on 'The Purloined Letter,'" which he describes as "a forceful, relatively coherent, and stabilized configuration of a discourse at the time of the collection and binding of *Écrits*."[4] Citing Lacan, who granted the seminar "the privilege of opening the sequence [the sequence of the *Écrits*] despite the diachrony," he insists upon the status of this seminar as a retroactively effective "punctuation mark," which is "thereby given the 'privilege' of figuring the synchronic configuration of the set and thus *binding* the whole together," and he claims this privilege as legitimation for his privileged interest in the seminar.[5] He reiterates that the "Seminar on 'The Purloined Letter,'" which was placed first in *Écrits* and intended to be the difficult way into Lacan's writings, binds together at least eight of the most deconstructible motifs of philosophy. One could list them quickly as the motifs of the proper and circular trajectory, truth as adequation or as unveiling, full speech and future anterior, privilege of the living in discourse and reduction of mechanical repetition and essential iterability, the transcendental position of the phallus, phonocentrism, the reduction of the parergonal effect, and the reduction of the effects of the double.[6]

Derrida argues that these eight motifs are tied together in a configuration that is indispensable as the support for Lacan's grounding affirmation, articulated in the last words of the seminar: "Thus it is that what the 'purloined letter,' nay, the 'letter in sufferance,' means is that a letter always arrives at its destination."[7] Further, as he sums up the earlier argument of "Le Facteur de la Vérité":

> Now this conclusion was possible only insofar as the letter (which for Lacan is not the signifier, but the place of the signifier) is not divided. Lacan says that it "does not suffer partition": "Cut a letter into small pieces," he says, "and it remains the letter it is." Consequently, what Lacan then calls the "materiality of the signifier," which he deduces from an indivisibility that is nowhere to be found, always seemed and still seems to me to correspond to an "idealization" of the letter, to an ideal identity of the letter.[8]

In Derrida's estimation here, Lacan's "surreptitious idealization," based on the indivisibility of the letter, is directly challenged by the work/play of *différance*, in view of which he insists that no letter ever has a proper place insofar as the "there" where it should "be" (or would otherwise have been) is always divided, and not only by a binary opposition but by various kinds of difference. Concerning "this letter, which Lacan says does not bear partition," Derrida notes: "By contesting this thesis, which I hold to be dogmatic and idealist, by giving the counter-demonstration that the letter is divisible, I was recalling in effect a principle of interminable analysis."[9] In other words, because of such trouble at the "origin" he accordingly insists upon the phenomenon of "*destinerrance*," which in his words "inflicts an internal drift on the destination of the letter, from which it may never return."[10] Such an internal drift ensures that the phrase " 'I fail to arrive' means at the same time 'I do not arrive' . . . *and* I fail or I do not arrive *because* I arrive."[11] Again: "Even in arriving (always to some 'subject'), the letter takes itself away *from the arrival at arrival.*"[12] That, in this sense, "the letter may always not arrive" is supposedly what one learns not from Lacanian psychoanalysis but from deconstruction.

To sum up, toward the end of the 1960s, Derrida insisted upon a rift between deconstructive philosophy and philosophical psychoanalysis: "it was possible to witness a theoretical binding of the Lacanian discourse that made the most strenuous, and powerfully spectacular use of all the motifs that were in my view deconstructible, undergoing deconstruction."[13] Would it be plausible to suggest that Derrida's criticism of Lacan's "Seminar on 'The Purloined Letter' " represents a precipitous early assessment that has since been revised in the approximately thirty years that intervened between "Le Facteur de la Vérité" and "For the Love of Lacan"? Not at all. In fact, Derrida has not moved an inch from his earlier stance. In his words: "So, since then? Since then, have we exited from this chiasmus? I do not believe we have."[14]

And yet, it is not at all difficult to undo the axial argument of Derrida's criticism by demonstrating that Lacan's insistence on the indivisibility of the letter is by no means a fundamental idealization (akin to one of Husserl's eidetic structures) that supports a covert metaphysics of presence. Given, as argued in the previous chapter, that the letter is another nickname for a transgressive "event," Lacan's insistence that it cannot be divided evokes no "thing-in-itself" but the Real in its unspeakable singularity, for an unspeakable "it happens," on his account, is only measured and divided up retroactively in its narration, and it is thereby in principle misrecognized. Lacan's point here is, simply enough, that however one may (and must) divide the traumatic "event" up into "units" of understanding, however one may interpret it or take its measure via the partitive article (the letter as "a") down to the smallest possible grid of analytical measurements, one will still have missed it, for it does not submit to such processes of analytical, interpretative division. Whatever we do by way of analysis it remains excessive, an event in its singular unspeakability. Or, in different terms, as Johnson argues, "by saying that the letter cannot be divided, Lacan does not mean that the phallus must remain intact, but that the phallus, the letter, and the signifier *are not substances*."[15] Moreover, Lacan repeatedly affirms that the Real is a matter of splitting rather than presence or absence. When Derrida insists upon the ineluctable divisibility of "the letter or the name,"[16] indicating thereby that what is "original/originary" is not a substance but the scission and division of *différance*, he is not, therefore, in fundamental disagreement with Lacan, for indivisibility and infinite divisibility turn out to be different ways of saying precisely the same thing about the Real.

In turn, a dissolution of the axial disagreement concerning the indivisibility or otherwise of the letter undoes Derrida's argument concerning the important motif of circular return or repetition. Derrida ties the motif of circular return to a snippet from Lacan's seminar, where, speaking of the purloined letter, he comments, "since it can be diverted, it must have a course *which is proper to it*."[17] This is listed as, in Derrida's words: "The motif of the proper and circular trajectory, of the reappropriating trajectory of the letter that returns to the circumscribable place of lack from which it had become detached, that letter about which Lacan says that 'since it can be diverted, it must have a course *which is its own* . . .' and a 'straight path,' obviously a circular straight path."[18]

Derrida's argument here matches his critique of Husserl for insisting that "there is" originally an ontological system of eidetic structures. On this account, any eidetic structure, for example (supposedly) the Oedipus complex, no matter where it finds itself, repeats itself as precisely the same. In other words, whatever the particular context, be it Victorian Vienna, consumerist California, or tribal Africa, one can be certain that the Oedipus complex will be at work there and can be re-found at work through anamnesic analysis. Similarly, in "The Seminar on 'The Purloined Letter,'" "the letter" represents an essential, fundamental, and determinate structure (in this case, the "circumscribable" structure of "lack"), which can be misrecognized or distorted as it passes through the defiles of linguistic misappropriation but which can always be "returned" to its proper place (i.e., understood properly) by perspicacious psychoanalytic theorizing. This allows us to think, as Derrida puts it, that "'a letter always arrives at its destination,' authentic, intact and undivided."[19] The "letter," on this account, stands as metaphor for the formalizable structure of the Symbolic Order (the structure of intersubjectivity that gathers around the axis of "lack"), which is repeated across every particular context and can be re-found by analysis of any intersubjective situation. Derrida argues that this repetition compulsion, defined as a "structural determinism," is, from Lacan's point of view, "the true subject" of Poe's tale, whereas according to Derrida, Poe's tale "makes of chance as writing what we shall be careful not to call 'the real subject' of the tale."[20]

As criticism of the kind of structural determinism that underpins institutional psychoanalysis, Derrida's argument might well hold water. Yet, if his critique of "what he calls psychoanalysis" might be entirely justified, as Johnson notes, "it does not quite apply to what Lacan's text is actually saying."[21] Why not? Because, as I have tried to demonstrate in the previous chapter, the formalizable intersubjective "structure," both *simple and odd* (indivisible and divisible), to be re-found in every situation associated with the incidence of "the letter" (the event and its narration), turns out to be a precise equivalent of the "plural logic of the aporia," which, notably, imposes itself upon Derrida's own texts "in a number of different contexts," with what he describes as a "formalizable regularity."[22] In other words, to return to the metaphor of "circular return," the so-called proper path of the letter, which is diverted through the misrecognizing misappropriation of paranoiac idealization or hysterical transgression, turns out to be the impasse of an "improper" paradox or aporia. The terrain, then, has shifted in this way from "circular return" as the repetition of the eidetic structures that belong to a metaphysics of presence to the iterable logic of quasi-transcendental thinking. Here, one might remind oneself of Lacan's words: "we cannot say of the purloined letter that, like other objects, it must be *or* not be in a particular place but that unlike them it will be *and* not be where it is, wherever it goes."[23] One must wonder how this could be anything but a statement of something precisely equivalent to Derrida's *destinerrance*.

Notably, because Derrida argues that the eight motifs listed above are tied together in a mutually supporting configuration, pulling the thread of the axial claims concerning indivisibility and circular return that they support must in turn unravel the entire configuration. Without going into detail, one might argue that Lacan's discourse concerning "truth" cannot be reduced to a matter of adequation or unveiling; that neither "lack" (absence) nor "the phallus" (fullness) is granted the status of a transcendental signified, but both give way to the quasi-transcendental function of the Real, which is neither the absence nor the fullness of being but a fundamental splitting akin to *différance*; that empty and full speech are not terms that tie Lacan's discourse to Heideggerian "jargon of authenticity" but serve as respective markers for the misrecognition and the acknowledgment of the "plural logic of the aporia"; and so on.

Along with Žižek, therefore, one may counter Derrida's oversimplifying reduction of Lacan's conclusion (that "a letter always arrives at its destination") to the quintessential circular motif of the metaphysics of presence, by arguing that his reproach ("a letter can also miss its destination") involves a misreading of Lacan's thesis that reduces it to precisely what Lacan calls into question.[24] Insisting upon taking Lacan at his word, Žižek argues instead that this proposition "is far from being univocal: it offers itself to a series of possible readings," all of which oppose its reduction to the terms of a metaphysics of presence. Brutally reducing Žižek's arguments to formulas, these readings claim that the letter always reaches its destination because (1) "its destination is wherever it arrives," (2) what goes around comes around: one gets out what one puts in, and (3) we all die.

While granting that the phrase by itself is ambiguous enough to sustain multiple Lacanian readings, however, Žižek's criticism of Derrida's reproach compounds one missed encounter with another. His multiple readings take Lacan's phrase out of the context of the "Seminar on 'The Purloined Letter,'" yet this is the only context within which Derrida's reproach functions. In other words, assuming that Derrida's reproach is transferable intact to new contexts, Žižek proposes to challenge it by proposing readings of the phrase to which Derrida would by no means raise objections. To avoid unnecessary and confusing antagonisms, then, it is important to restrict Derrida's reproach to the context of his critique of the "Seminar on 'The Purloined Letter.'" It seems clear enough that Lacan here ties his phrase to his claim that the poststructural logic of the Symbolic Order generates an unconscious repetition compulsion in those subject to it. Derrida's reproach functions only in this context, and only because he mistakenly construes Lacan's phrase to be part of an edifice that supports a metaphysics of presence, whereby something like a Husserlian eidetic structure repeats itself intact no matter what the context. In other words, Derrida's warning that "the letter can also not arrive" is a reminder (unnecessary as it turns out) to the metaphysician of presence that he mistakenly takes Lacan to be that the "logical structure" that underpins the repetition compulsion is a matter not of essence and presence but of *différance*.

Derrida's error of judgment, then, is not a blankly rigid resistance to the multivocality of a phrase (how could it be?) but a violent strategy of persistently flattening out ambiguity and paradox in the "Seminar on 'The Purloined Letter,'" framing its meaning as a univocal endorsement of the metaphysics of presence. As Johnson argues, Derrida's argument with the "Seminar on 'The Purloined Letter'" rests on a violent reading that "depends for its force upon the presupposition of unambiguousness in Lacan's text."[25] In the terms of this study, Derrida persistently refuses to see in this, and whatever of Lacan's texts he did open, any equivalent of the "plural logic of the aporia."

What is problematic and interesting for this is that Derrida's reading here does not match the spirit of inventive "iteration" with which he reads Freud's texts. His response is blunter than one is accustomed to, lacking in the overly fine nuance one has grown to expect from him. Is it plausible that Derrida intentionally "frames" Lacan simply as a consequence of personal acrimony or sibling rivalry? One would not like to think so. That Derrida, around thirty years later, did not move an inch from his earlier stance unfortunately belies Barbara Johnson's more charitable suggestion, namely, that because it seems so easy to counter the axial argument around which the entire edifice of Derrida's critique turns, his flatly inaccurate reading of Lacan's seminar might have been not a matter of oversight but of intentional framing: a parody rather than a mistake. In her words: "Derrida being the sharp-eyed reader that he is, his consistent forcing of Lacan's statements into systems and patterns from which they are actually trying to escape must correspond to some strategic necessity different from the attentiveness to the letter of the text which characterizes Derrida's way of reading Poe."[26]

Johnson's suggestion that Derrida might be less concerned here with what Lacan's text says than with its textual effect (with how it is likely to be read) finds some support from William Kerrigan and Joseph Smith, who comment on his growing interest in the performative dimension of a reading that would function by "allowing itself to become, in Derrida's words, 'an example of that of which it speaks or writes.'"[27] They add: "Derrida's interpretations often radicalize rather than diminish chance. Neither his examples nor his example illustrate in the conventional way. They question, make questionable, and often because they are questionable."[28] Granted that Derrida's criticism of Lacan's "Seminar on 'The Purloined Letter'" is entirely questionable, it becomes more productive (whatever his intentions might have been) to read the protocols for reading Lacan that derive from it as less about theoretical content than about rhetorical strategy. I wish, then, to take up Barbara Johnson's less likely but more inventive suggestion and consider what would happen if one treats Derrida's reading as a parody that mirrors what this text may potentially produce as an effect.[29]

Johnson's suggestion takes on its importance (plausibility aside) if one interprets Lacan's seminar as a response precisely to a question Freud posed in the form of a joke concerning the nature of truth: "Why are you lying to me?" one character shouts breathlessly. "Yes, why do you lie to me saying you're going to Cracow so I should believe you're going to Lemberg, when in reality you *are* going to Cracow?"[30] Freud's comment concerning the serious content of the joke is as follows: "Is it the truth if we describe the way things are without troubling to consider how our hearer will understand what we say?"[31] Part of the argument of Lacan's seminar is that one does not speak the truth in the domain of exactitude or in "free association," for here one is not aware of the conditions of the narration. Derrida turns this question onto Lacan: if Lacan insists that one cannot speak the truth unless one knows the conditions of the narration, then does he speak the truth if he does not explicitly mark and problematize the potential textual effects of the metaphysical baggage attached to the philosophical terms he imports into psychoanalytic discourse? Lacan refashions all of the terms he makes use of ("Truth," "Real," "full and empty speech," "Symbolic Order," "Immortality," "Ethics," and so on), but Derrida argues that he does not deal carefully enough with the metaphysical baggage that still produces its effects.

Derrida's concern would be this: Lacan was not careful enough in following his own psychoanalytic advice, namely to remain vigilant concerning the word and to pay careful attention to its "truth" defined in terms of its effects, rather than adequation. Because of an overly cavalier use of metaphysically loaded terms, one can press the ambiguities of his text into the service of a relatively coherent "metaphysical" reading that ties up a number of mutually reinforcing motifs, such as the one Derrida deliberately frames here. Although there might be warrant for not doing this in Lacan's text, there is nevertheless enough of a thoroughgoing metaphysical residue in his terminology to allow one very easily, but misleadingly, to tie it up into a systematic endorsement of a metaphysics of presence. On such a reading, Derrida's service to Lacanian scholarship would be to alert prospective readers to the textual effects of these intertwined motifs. As an aside, this insistence on taking an interest in the textual effect of the words one chooses rebounds as kind of ironic aftereffect, because it is precisely against the (albeit opposite) textual effect of his own words that Derrida is constantly forced to apply deconstructive counterarguments.

If, on the one hand, Derrida reduces Lacanian discourse to a covert metaphysics of presence, then, on the other hand, he converts it into a freeplay relativism. He persistently complains about an argumentative looseness and opacity that, in his view, enables any reader to make Lacan say anything, just as it pleases him or her. First, he claims, Lacan, always sensitive to theoretical movements (understandably enough) and even to a Derridean critique correspondingly readjusted, recast, or sometimes contradicted earlier claims. But he thinks that Lacan's discursive sensitivity to sea changes in philosophical spirit goes hand in hand with a rhetoric intimating that what has been changed in his discourse after the fact (a shift, for example, from speech to writing) was in fact always already there in his discourse from the beginning, as a necessity "to come." He argues that Lacan's ideas change, but he presents them as if the new had always already been inscribed in the earlier work (which can now be seen as merely propadeutic or preparatory). He does not acknowledge influence, and he does not mark changes. Thus, Derrida grumbles, there will always be ways of putting together textual evidence that will make his reading of the "Seminar on 'The Purloined Letter'" seem unjust. Second, since Lacan's discourse took the form of spoken discourse, which was recorded in various ways and edited with an active and heavy hand, who will ever know just who said what and when? Finally, this uncertainty of origin in the Lacanian text is compounded by an equal uncertainty of destination, whose stakes hang on interpretative decisions to be made by those faced with Lacan's allusive, elliptical, hyperbolic grotesqueries of style. All of this makes it impossible to tell for sure, or in the end, what Lacan would or would not have said. The question here becomes: is one speaking "the truth" if one pretends to describe things as they are, knowing full well that the ambiguity and equivocality of what is said makes it impossible for those who hear to assess it?

As a later-generation reader, of course, I am in no position to assess, or set much store by, this gripe, suffice it to suggest that the Lacanian equivalent of the "plural logic of the aporia" seems too thoroughgoing and fundamental to have been inserted as an afterthought. In any case, such uncertainty, for Derrida, is not the most serious problem. Rather, the problem would lie with a reading that still, in face of this, insists that "there is" a true Lacan to be re-found. Concerning analysis or interpretation of the Lacanian text, Derrida insists that Lacan *in general* does not exist for him. In contrast to what he sees as the tendency toward a circumscribing, protective "jealousy and mastery" in the relations between Lacan and his interpreters, he insists that (as a matter of principle) he has never pretended to enclose Lacan "himself" in his readings. Even if he aims to uncover and open up some or other relatively stable configuration to be found in a specific Lacanian text, he does so in a way that would not be a totalizing, homogenizing, critical (in Kant's sense of limiting), or objectifying metadiscourse *on* Lacan's texts. In any case, there have since been countless "countersignatures" that constantly put all of what he has to say back into play in what he calls "other scenes *en abyme*." Derrida insists that his own text, on a text on a purloined and wandering letter (his own letter), is set adrift, without the prospect of a necessary return (and all of this is a good thing). Lacan, he insists, knows this, but his readers (his analysts) must be wary of what unconscious motives in Lacan make him pretend not to know, that is, what in him, contrary to his own discourse, promotes the guru-supplicant relation. Here, in my view, one at last comes to what Derrida is "really" resisting in relation to Lacan.

As a self-proclaimed authentic interpreter of Freud in opposition to the more dominant, but for Lacan inappropriate, appropriation of Freudian insights by "ego psychologists," Lacan's "return to Freud" is hardly the substitution of one foundational discourse for another; it is a movement away from domestication by the ego psychologists who are economizing on Freud, in order again to face the complexity and difficulty of paradox. Yet, if Lacan's reading of Freud is a matter of the inventive repetition that is consonant with the spirit of what he says, Derrida accuses him of contradicting this overt discourse by maintaining all the problematic metaphors of master and disciple in relation to his own readers. Lacan, as "second generation master Analyst," in Derrida's estimation, performatively ties his discourse to all of the traditional motifs of disciplinary institutionalization he has elsewhere deconstructed. Despite all he has to say about the undertow of power, for example, he offers these insights as the truth bestowed on the supplicants by the Master who already knows all of it. Notably, a criticism of Lacan for a performance inconsistent with what he says tacitly already grants that the discourse itself cannot conform to the metaphysics of presence. Derrida's resistance to Lacan's power concerns less the content of what he is saying, then, than its performance and the effects of this performance on the reader. Hence the epigraph to "Le Facteur de la Vérité," which is a citation from Baudelaire: "They thank him for the great truths he has just proclaimed—for they have discovered (O verifier of that which cannot be verified!) that everything he has uttered is absolutely true;—although at first, the good people confess, they had had the suspicion that it might indeed be a simple fiction. Poe answers that, for his part, he never doubted it."[32]

This charge, however, is not confirmed in the work of many of Lacan's close readers, who treat his writings precisely as a gift, a stimulus to keep writing. Jacques-Alain Miller describes the situation well. Reading Lacan's *Seminar*, he remarks, "is not unlike the *lectio* of the Middle Ages," where "the lesson of a master was to be divided into three parts: *littera*, *sensus*, and *sententia*." The discipline of commentary focuses on the deeper levels of meaning (*sententiae*) that underlie what is explicit at the level of sense and grammar. Lacan, commenting on Freud's writing, makes maxims (*sententiae*). The question of interpreting Lacan, for Miller, centers on deciding what to do with these maxims, whose effect, he notes, is seemingly to present Lacan "as an author in the medieval sense of the word, that is, as the one who knows what he says." Yet, as Miller argues:

> Despite his *sententiae*, however, Lacan is not an author. His work is a teaching. We must take this into consideration; we must know that following his star requires that we do not synchronize and dogmatize this teaching, that we do not hide but rather stress its contradictions, its antinomies, its deadlocks, its difficulties. For a teaching on the analytic experience is like *work in progress* and implies a back-and-forth motion between text and experience.[33]

When it comes down to it, the conflict, due to which many Lacanians and Derrideans refuse to acknowledge each other even before texts are opened, is to a large extent about legitimation. In a border dispute with Lacan concerning the status of institutional and noninstitutional analysts/analysands, Derrida poses the problem of the right to psychoanalysis. Here, he notes that Lacan insists twice on Derrida's "real" status in this regard, whereas he of all people should have been suspicious of the limits or borders of these institutional sites. First, Lacan insists that Derrida is really an "institutional nonanalyst." According to Lacan, Derrida, who is not an (institutionally recognized) *analyst* and who is therefore, by implication, a philosopher only, "does not deal with people who are suffering," meaning by that "people who are in analysis." By implicitly suggesting that Derrida cannot rightfully speak of suffering or transference since he does not deal with people in analysis, Lacan is here, in effect, making institutionalized clinical treatment and the rules that organize the analytic situation into criteria of absolute competence for speaking about such things. In response, Derrida points out that one does not need the analytic situation to become the victim of suffering and transference, that is to say, "love." In short, these experiences are not restricted to the analytic situation, and institutionalized analytical training is not the only way to achieve competence to speak about or deal with them. Second, Lacan mistakenly suggested in a seminar that Derrida was in analysis, that is, was really an "institutional analysand." Again, Derrida counters that he has never been in analysis in the institutional sense of the analytic situation, but it matters little, since anyone can be both analyst and analysand in their own ways, without the institutional stamp.

To sum up, Lacan, as an institutionally recognized analyst, claims to offer *the* legitimate "return to Freud." Due to the insecurity of Freudian concepts, however, Derrida insists that something beyond psychoanalysis is already inscribed in its commencement. In other words, not even Freud has an inalienable "right to psychoanalysis," and this, accordingly, puts the idea of a "return" into question. Derrida has an interest in challenging Lacan's institutional grounds for legitimation, for they in principle deny that a Derridean reading of Freud can have a bearing on psychoanalytic practice, since Derrida operates not as an institutional analyst but in the interstice between literature and philosophy. Hence the border disputes between the "inside" of institutional psychoanalysis and its marginalia (for example, deconstructive philosophers deeply interested in psychoanalytic events). In spite of Lacan's ceaseless resistance to the psychoanalytic "master discourse" of ego psychology, Derrida insists upon the paradox of his insistence upon institutionalizing psychoanalysis. But one could just as easily argue here for an iterability, consonant with the spirit of his discourse, for the sake of which Lacan kept reinventing the institution.

Against the backdrop of these critical thrusts and counterthrusts, it seems fair to call Derrida's refusal to budge regarding his initial assessment of Lacanian discourse an injustice. Moreover, given the abundant evidence adduced here to the effect that their thinking is characterized by an isomorphic logic, their divergent intellectual temperaments and discursive styles notwithstanding, one might question Derrida's curious resistance to what seems clear enough to many other readers. To speculate about the source of such resistance does not really fall within the purview of this study. Rather, the philosophical question that directed the various investigations that compose its overall argument was simply whether Derrida's deconstructive philosophy and Lacan's philosophical psychoanalysis are as different as they are often made out to be. A recognition that they are not, moreover, promises both mutual clarification and generative cross-fertilization.

Both Derrida and Lacan recognize the power of psychoanalysis to address contemporary political and ethical issues, and both challenge traditional institutional psychoanalysis to step beyond its domesticating tendencies and address these issues in the radical way of which it is capable. Derrida argues in *Without Alibi* that the issues around war, sovereignty, and cruelty (i.e., the death drive) are as pertinent today, in the face of globalization, as they were on the eve of the Second World War, when Freud and Einstein corresponded. He argues that institutional psychoanalysis has failed to speak up here, in a domain where psychoanalysis specially, because of its concept of the death drive, has something to say.[34] On the other hand, it is precisely the Lacanian challenge to institutional psychoanalysis, with its emphasis on the death drive, that in principle opens up the way to rethink these issues (via, for example, notions of radical evil and sublimation), and there is plenty of evidence in practice that the Lacanian revisions have enabled thinkers to address relevant ethical and political questions.

Textual difficulties, differences of style that derive from and appeal to different temperaments, and unjust criticism and counter-criticism should not be allowed obscure the deep theoretical accord between Derrida and Lacan, evident in their shared aim to theorize the human condition as an ineradicable state of aporia, and to do justice to this rupture in their texts and practice. I am convinced that the "plural logic of the aporia" provides a tremendously helpful key for understanding the complexity of both Lacan's and Derrida's approach to the ancient and specially vexing phenomenon of errance that Plato, for example, raises in the *Timaeus*, namely, that despite our best efforts at resolving different kinds of theoretical, ethical, and political difficulties, such resolutions inevitably find themselves troubled in turn by further difficulties.

Notes

Introduction: "For the Love of Lacan"

1. Jacques Derrida, "For the Love of Lacan," in *Resistances of Psychoanalysis*, trans. Peggy Kamuf, Pascale-Anne Brault, and Michael Naas (Palo Alto, Calif.: Stanford University Press, 1998), 45–46.

2. This is a reference to the essay by Jean-Luc Nancy and Philippe Lacoue-Labarthe entitled *The Title of the Letter: A Reading of Lacan*, trans. François Raffoul and David Pettigrew (Albany, N.Y.: SUNY Press, 1992).

3. Derrida, "Love of Lacan," 51.

4. Jacques Lacan, "Aggressivity in Psychoanalysis," in *Écrits: A Selection*, trans. Alan Sheridan (London: Tavistock, 1977), 8.

5. John D. Caputo, ed., *Deconstruction in a Nutshell: A Conversation with Jacques Derrida* (New York: Fordham University Press, 1997), 41.

6. Jacques Derrida, *Of Grammatology*, trans. Gayatri Chakravorty Spivak (Baltimore, Md.: The Johns Hopkins University Press, 1976), 158.

7. For Hegel's attempt to bend Kant's critical philosophy into the shape of subjective idealism, see, for example, G. W. F. Hegel, "Critical Philosophy," in *The Logic of Hegel*, in *The Encyclopaedia of the Philosophical Sciences, Second Edition*, trans. William Wallace (Oxford: Oxford University Press, 1968). On Hegel's account, "Kant and his philosophy" amounts to a self-conceited, gravely defective, and barbarously formulated "subjective idealism" to which, he comments, "plain minds have not unreasonably taken exception" (85–94). Kant, he claims, "holds that both the form and the matter of knowledge are supplied by the Ego—or knowing subject—the form by our intellectual, the matter by our sentient ego" (90). He takes this to be a simple case of "the reduction of the facts of consciousness to a purely personal world, created by ourselves alone" (93). It

is time, he insists, to move beyond the "ugly look" (89) of Kantian philosophy to "the true statement of the case" (93), which amounts to his own "absolute idealism." For the Kantian rejoinder, which acknowledges that "existence cannot be constructed," see, for example, Immanuel Kant, *Critique of Pure Reason*, trans. Norman Kemp Smith (London: Macmillan, 1933), A160/B199, A179/B222. Again, Kant insists that "whether other perceptions than those belonging to our whole possible experience, and therefore a quite different field of matter, may exist, the understanding is not in a position to decide. *It can deal only with the synthesis of that which is given*" (A230–231/B283–284; my emphasis).

8. Jacques Derrida, "Autoimmunity: Real and Symbolic Suicides," in *Philosophy in a Time of Terror: Dialogues with Jürgen Habermas and Jacques Derrida*, ed. Giovanna Borradori (Chicago: University of Chicago Press, 2003), 87–88. Again, as Caputo puts it: "We are always inside/outside textuality, for textuality makes it possible to say everything we say about the individual, including that the individual is ineffable, which is the most striking thing we say about individuals. But textuality makes it impossible that we would ever reach a pure, unmediated, naked, pre-textual, un-textual, de-contextualized fact of the matter." John D. Caputo, *Against Ethics: Contributions to a Poetics of Obligation with Constant Reference to Deconstruction* (Bloomington: Indiana University Press, 1993), 78.

9. Jacques Derrida, "Structure, Sign, and Play in the Discourse of the Human Sciences," in *Writing and Difference*, trans. Alan Bass (Chicago: University of Chicago Press, 1978), 292–93.

10. Caputo makes this point in *Deconstruction in a Nutshell*, 40.

11. Marshall W. Alcorn Jr., "The Subject of Discourse: Reading Lacan Through (and Beyond) Poststructuralist Contexts," in *Lacanian Theory of Discourse: Subject, Structure, and Society*, ed. Mark Bracher et al. (New York: New York University Press, 1994), 28–29.

12. Kaja Silverman, *The Subject of Semiotics* (New York: Oxford University Press, 1983), 25.

13. Ibid., 34.

14. Ibid., 38.

15. Jacques Derrida, "*Différance*," in *Margins of Philosophy*, trans. Alan Bass (New York: Harvester, 1982), 18–19.

16. Kaja Silverman, *The Acoustic Mirror: The Female Voice in Psychoanalysis and Cinema* (Bloomington: Indiana University Press, 1988), 70.

17. Joan Copjec, *Read My Desire: Lacan Against the Historicists* (Cambridge, Mass.: MIT Press, 1994), 60.

18. Slavoj Žižek, "The Real of Sexual Difference," in *Reading Seminar XX: Lacan's Major Work on Love, Knowledge, and Feminine Sexuality*, ed. Suzanne Barnard and Bruce Fink (Albany, N.Y.: SUNY Press, 2002).

19. Jacques Derrida, *Positions*, trans. Alan Bass (Chicago: University of Chicago Press, 1981), 107–113.

20. Ibid., 107.

21. I shall argue for a theoretical accord whose lineaments can be traced to Lacan's earliest essays, and this suggests that Derrida's assessment is precipitate.

22. Barbara Johnson, "The Frame of Reference: Poe, Lacan, Derrida," in *The Purloined Poe: Lacan, Derrida, and Psychoanalytic Reading*, ed. John P. Muller and William J. Richardson (Baltimore, Md.: The Johns Hopkins University Press, 1988), 219.

23. Derrida, *Positions*, 108–110.

24. Derrida, "Love of Lacan," 56.

25. Geoffrey Bennington and Jacques Derrida, *Jacques Derrida* (Chicago: University of Chicago Press, 1993). *Jacques Derrida*, which consists of Bennington's "Derridabase" above the line and Derrida's "Circumfession" below, supposedly simulates a duel between reader and author for rights to the singular name "Jacques Derrida."

26. Derrida, "*Différance*," 10.

27. Jacques Lacan, *The Four Fundamental Concepts of Psycho-Analysis (Seminar XI)*, trans. Alan Sheridan (New York: W. W. Norton, 1981), 29–30.

28. Lacan, *On Feminine Sexuality, The Limits of Love and Knowledge, Encore, (Seminar XX)*, ed. Jacques-Alain Miller, trans. Bruce Fink (New York: W. W. Norton, 1998), 70.

29. Jacques Lacan, *Feminine Sexuality, S: XX*, 65–66.

30. John D. Caputo, *More Radical Hermeneutics: On Not Knowing Who We Are* (Bloomington: Indiana University Press, 2000), 139.

31. Ibid., 140.

32. Joan Copjec, *Imagine There's No Woman: Ethics and Sublimation* (Cambridge, Mass.: MIT Press, 2002), 93. Clearly the terms of this study require a distinction between something like "pseudo-transcendental" and "quasi-transcendental," for, on my understanding, "essence" and the "quasi-transcendental *a priori*" are not at all synonymous.

33. For a summary of Žižek's debate with Butler on this issue, See Žižek, "The Real of Sexual Difference," 71–73. For a fuller treatment of this and the broader issues, see Judith Butler, Ernesto Laclau, and Slavoj Žižek, *Contingency, Hegemony, Universality: Contemporary Dialogues on the Left* (New York: Verso, 2000).

34. Colette Soler, "What Does the Unconscious Know About Women?" in *Reading Seminar XX: Lacan's Major Work on Love, Knowledge, and Feminine Sexuality*, ed. Suzanne Barnard and Bruce Fink (Albany, N.Y.: SUNY Press, 2002), 101.

35. Dylan Evans, *An Introductory Dictionary of Lacanian Psychoanalysis* (London: Routledge, 1996), ix. Similar sentiments are expressed by Jonathan Scott Lee, *Jacques Lacan* (Amherst: University of Massachusetts Press, 1990), ix.

36. Derrida, *Positions*, 110.

37. Jacques Derrida, "Resistances," in *Resistances of Psychoanalysis*, trans. Peggy Kamuf, Pascale-Anne Brault, and Michael Naas (Palo Alto, Calif.: Stanford University Press, 1998), 29–30. The term is taken up and extensively elaborated by Rudolphe Gasché, *The Tain of the Mirror: Derrida and the Philosophy of Reflection* (Cambridge, Mass.: Harvard University Press, 1986), 142. Here,

Gasché articulates Derrida's quasi-transcendental logic in terms of infrastructures and argues that "the very concept of infrastructure, as the *formal rule* that each time regulates differently the play of the contradictions in question, is an intrinsic part of his original contribution to philosophy." One should note that Gasché uses the term "contradiction" in its broader Hegelian/Marxist sense rather than in the strict technical sense governed by the law of noncontradiction. For Hegel, a "contradiction" occurs in a system when two of its features together produce an unstable tension. He finds capitalism "contradictory," for example, because it requires precisely what it aims to eradicate: namely, a degree of unemployment. See Simon Blackburn, *The Oxford Dictionary of Philosophy* (Oxford: Oxford University Press, 1994), 81. I prefer to avoid this wider use of the term "contradiction," since it conflates distinct discursive forms, only one of which I believe (*aporia* or dilemma) accords with what I shall try to articulate in the name of Derrida's thinking.

38. He has in mind here "concepts" such as justice, gift, event, decision, responsibility, forgiveness, ethics, politics, hospitality, analysis, iterability, etc.

39. Derrida, "Resistances," 29–30.

40. Jacques Derrida, *Aporias*, trans. Thomas Dutoit (Palo Alto, Calif.: Stanford University Press, 1993), 20–21.

41. Ibid., 13, 20.

42. William Angus Sinclair, *The Traditional Formal Logic: A Short Account for Students* (London: Methuen, 1966), 83.

43. Blackburn, *Oxford Dictionary of Philosophy*, 105.

44. Lee, *Jacques Lacan*, 134.

45. Paul Verhaeghe, "Lacan's Answer to the Classical Mind/Body Deadlock," in *Reading Seminar XX: Lacan's Major Work on Love, Knowledge, and Feminine Sexuality*, ed. Suzanne Barnard and Bruce Fink (Albany, N.Y.: SUNY Press, 2002), 114.

46. Copjec, *Imagine*, 1–5.

47. Lacan, *Four Fundamental Concepts, S: XI*, 210–212.

48. Copjec, *Imagine*, 17.

49. Ibid., 18.

50. These formulas are lifted from Alejandro Amenábar's film *The Sea Inside*, which I shall discuss in chapter 11.

51. Bruce Fink, *The Lacanian Subject: Between Language and* Jouissance (Princeton, N.J.: Princeton University Press, 1995), xiv.

52. Copjec, *Imagine*, 10.

53. John D. Caputo, *Radical Hermeneutics: Repetition, Deconstruction, and the Hermeneutic Project* (Bloomington: Indiana University Press, 1987), 6–7.

54. Lee, *Jacques Lacan*, 134.

55. Bruce Fink, "Knowledge and Jouissance," in *Reading Seminar XX: Lacan's Major Work on Love, Knowledge, and Feminine Sexuality*, ed. Suzanne Barnard and Bruce Fink (Albany, N.Y.: SUNY Press, 2002), 33.

56. Lee, *Jacques Lacan*, 135: He cites the "untranslatable and virtually unintelligible" title of the 1976–1977 seminar *L'insu que sait de l'une-bévue, s'aile à*

mourre, in which, through a long series of associations, he finds embedded "Freud's German term for the unconscious" and "the central psychoanalytic notions" of love, death, and chance.

57. Derrida, *Positions*, 110–111.

58. Fink, *The Lacanian Subject*, xvi.

Part 1: From Transcendentals to Quasi-Transcendentals

1. One excellent way to trace the shift to quasi-transcendental thinking, then, would be to follow Caputo in *Radical Hermeneutics* and trace the outlines of Derrida's early deconstructive critiques of first Husserl and then Heidegger.

2. Martin Heidegger, *Contributions to Philosophy (From Enowning)*, trans. P. Emad and K. Maly (Bloomington: Indiana University Press, 1999), 81. See also Jacques Derrida, "Autoimmunity," 90, where Derrida makes much of this paradoxical articulation: "to the extent that the thought of *Ereignis* in Heidegger would be turned not only toward the *appropriation* of the proper (*eigen*) but toward a certain *expropriation* that Heidegger himself names (*Enteignis*). The undergoing of the event, that which in the undergoing or in the ordeal *at once opens itself up to and resists experience*, is, it seems to me, a certain *unappropriability* of what comes or happens. The event is what comes and, in coming, comes to surprise me, to surprise and to suspend comprehension."

3. Alan D. Schrift, *Nietzsche and the Question of Interpretation: Between Hermeneutics and Deconstruction* (London: Routledge, 1990), 126.

4. Ibid., 123.

5. Freud, "New Introductory Lectures on Psycho-Analysis," in *The Standard Edition of the Complete Psychological Works of Sigmund Freud Vol. XXII*, ed. and trans. James Strachey (London: Hogarth Press, 1968), 92 (hereafter *SE*). "The deeper we penetrate into the study of mental processes the more we recognize their abundance and complexity. A number of simple formulas which to begin with seemed to meet our needs have later turned out to be inadequate. We do not tire of altering and improving them."

6. Freud models the psyche first in terms of permeable neurons (sensation), impermeable neurons (memory and facilitation or synthetic processing), and consciousness neurons (awareness and perception). His second model describes the psyche in terms of three impersonal systems: the unconscious (primary process), the preconscious (secondary process), and conscious perception. His third model describes the psyche in terms of three psychical agencies: the id, ego, and superego. See Freud, "New Introductory Lectures," *SE: XXII*, 69–73.

Chapter 1: The "Ruin" of the Transcendental Tradition

1. Blackburn, *Oxford Dictionary of Philosophy*, 269–70.

2. Notably, in *The Order of Things*, Foucault remarks that Kant's "transcendental turn," poised at "the threshold of our modernity," marks an *episteme* (paradigm) from which thinking has not emerged. Michel Foucault, *The Order of Things: An Archaeology of the Human Sciences* (New York: Vintage, 1994), 242.

3. This assessment is evident *inter alia* in both prefaces to Kant's *Critique of Pure Reason*.

4. Kant, *Critique of Pure Reason*, A407/B433. This is an alternative expression of the "principle of reason."

5. Ibid., A654–58/B682–86.

6. One may use the terms "objective world" and "phenomenal reality" synonymously. I prefer the term "phenomenal reality" here because "objective world" still often carries the connotations of externality.

7. Caputo, *Radical Hermeneutics*, 39.

8. For Kant and Husserl, the dividing line between conscious and unconscious processing falls quite neatly between unconscious image thinking and conscious conceptualization (to which linguistic articulation is appended). In the later thinkers, things become more complex. For Heidegger, what is prethematic or preconceptual is not prelinguistic. Instead, he speaks of an implicit (unconscious) and an explicit (conscious) dimension to both thinking and speaking. For Nietzsche, what remains unconscious is only "the great stupidity [that] we are . . . our spiritual *fatum* . . . what is *unteachable* very 'deep down.'" All processing, then, is a matter of converting this "unspeakable" into conscious discourse. It is with Freud, finally, that the notion of the unconscious is developed in its full enigmatic complexity. See Friedrich Nietzsche, *Beyond Good and Evil: Prelude to a Philosophy of the Future*, trans. Walter Kaufmann (New York: Vintage, 1966), 162, §231.

9. See Edmund Husserl, *Cartesian Meditations: An Introduction to Phenomenology*, trans. D. Cairns (The Hague: Martinus Nijhoff, 1960), 79, where Husserl confirms this point: "In early infancy . . . the field of perception that gives beforehand does not as yet contain anything that in a mere look might be explicated as a physical thing" and it is rightly said that "in infancy we had to learn to see physical things." See also Freud, "Civilization," *SE: XXI*, 66–68.

10. Notably, then, rather than being the qualities of independently existing external objects, "space" and, more fundamentally, "time" become a priori forms of intuition (or, that is, the twelve specific determinations of time form the rules according to which productive imagination operates).

11. Again, Husserl confirms this in *Cartesian Meditations*, 78: "Anything built by activity necessarily presupposes, as the lowest level, a passivity that gives something beforehand; and, when we trace anything built actively, we run into constitution by passive generation."

12. Husserl, *Cartesian Meditations*, 78.

13. Ibid., 78–79.

14. Kant, *Critique of Pure Reason*, A108–9.

15. Werner Pluhar makes this argument in his illuminating translator's introduction to Kant's Third Critique. See Immanuel Kant, *Critique of Judgment*, trans. Werner S. Pluhar (Indianapolis, Ind.: Hackett, 1987).

16. Caputo, *Radical Hermeneutics*, 4. See also 44 for a more extensive account of Husserl's thesis concerning the annihilability of the world.

17. Husserl, *Cartesian Meditations*, 81.
18. Caputo, *Radical Hermeneutics*, 41–42.
19. Ibid., 47.
20. Ibid., 38.
21. Ibid., 38.
22. Ibid., 4.
23. Ibid., 55.
24. Husserl, *Cartesian Meditations*, 11–16.
25. Caputo, *Radical Hermeneutics*, 54.
26. Ibid., 54.
27. Ibid., 57.
28. Derrida shows, however, that his description of transcendental life cannot do without recourse to the work of signs, and this, despite Husserl's efforts to the contrary, opens the way to granting the constitutive value of nonpresence in the production of presence, and, therefore, to the delimitation of the metaphysics of presence. Jacques Derrida, "Speech and Phenomena," in *Speech and Phenomena and Other Essays on Husserl's Theory of Signs*, trans. D. Allison (Evanston, Ill.: Northwestern University Press, 1973), 65–66.
29. For a fuller treatment of this, see Jacques Derrida, "Introduction to '*The Origin of Geometry*,'" in *Edmund Husserl's Origin of Geometry: An Introduction*, trans. John P, Leavey Jr., ed. David B. Allison (Stony Brook, N.Y.: Nicolas Hays, 1978).
30. Caputo, *Radical Hermeneutics*, 56.
31. I shall not here open the Pandora's box of the question concerning animal being.
32. Martin Heidegger, *Being and Time*, trans. J. Macquarrie and E. Robinson (Oxford: Basil Blackwell, 1962), 174. For *Dasein*, as he puts it: "The expression 'thrownness' is meant to suggest the *facticity of its being delivered over*."
33. Ibid., 95.
34. Ibid., 184.
35. Caputo, *Radical Hermeneutics*, 63.
36. Heidegger, *Being and Time*, 183.
37. Ibid., 188–95.
38. Ibid., 32, 182.
39. Ibid., 190. "This intuitive understanding may be described in terms of three fore-structures; namely 'fore-having,' 'fore-sight,' and 'fore-conception.'" See ibid., 191–92.
40. Ibid., 191–92.
41. Ibid., 190–91.
42. Ibid., 203–4.
43. Ibid., 204.
44. Ibid., 200.
45. Ibid., 207–8.
46. Ibid., 199.

47. Ibid., 196–97.
48. Ibid., 199.
49. Ibid., 200.
50. Ibid., 177.
51. Ibid., 211–14.
52. Ibid., 202–13.
53. Ibid., 195.
54. Ibid., 207.
55. Ibid., 195.
56. Caputo, *Radical Hermeneutics*, 63.
57. Ibid., 72.
58. Ibid., 67.
59. Ibid., 72.
60. Nietzsche, *Beyond Good and Evil*, 162, §231.
61. Friedrich Nietzsche, "On the Pathos of Truth," in *Philosophy and Truth: Selections from Nietzsche's Notebooks of the Early 1870s*, ed. and trans. Daniel Breazeale (Amherst, N.Y.: Humanity Books, 1999), 65.
62. Ferdinand de Saussure, *Course in General Linguistics*, ed. Charles Bally and Albert Sechehaye with the collaboration of Albert Riedlinger, trans. Roy Harris (LaSalle, Ill.: Open Court, 1983), 75.
63. Nietzsche, *Beyond Good and Evil*, 3 (preface), 90, §154.
64. Ibid., 35, §24.
65. Ibid., 46–47, §54.
66. Ibid., 43, §31.
67. Ibid., 31, §23.
68. Ibid., 203, §259.
69. Notably, this account draws to some extent from Derrida's essay "Psyche: Inventions of the Other," in *Reading de Man Reading*, ed. Lindsay Waters and Wlad Godzich, trans. Catherine Porter (Minneapolis: University of Minnesota Press, 1989), where he implicitly makes much of this dynamic of the "will to power" in his analysis of the "event" and its correlates "invention," "convention," and "adventure." The metaphorics of "forgetting" and the "forgetting of forgetting" are drawn from Heidegger's *Contributions to Philosophy*, 81.
70. Bert Olivier, "Nietzsche en die 20ste-Eeuse Denke," in *Wysgerige Perspektiewe op die 20ste Eeu*, ed. Daniel Strauss (Bloemfontein: Tekskor, 1994), 56–71.
71. Nietzsche, *Beyond Good and Evil*, 49, §39.
72. Ibid., 10, §2.
73. Jacques Derrida, *Spurs: Nietzsche's Styles*, trans. Barbara Harlow (Chicago: University of Chicago Press, 1979), 91–92.
74. Schrift, *Nietzsche*, 126–27.
75. This is an allusion to the first moment in Nietzsche's "History of an Error," in which he claims that the oldest form of the idea may be inscribed in the proposition "I, Plato, *am* the truth." Friedrich Nietzsche, *Twilight of the Idols*, in *Twilight of the Idols and the Anti-Christ*, trans. R.J. Hollingdale (Middlesex: Penguin, 1968), 40.

76. Nietzsche, cited in Schrift, *Nietzsche*, 127.
77. Ibid., 127.
78. Ibid., 129.
79. Ibid., 127.
80. Nietzsche, "Pathos of Truth," 61–66.
81. Ibid., 61.
82. Ibid., 61–62.
83. Shrift, *Nietzsche*, 128.
84. Nietzsche, "Pathos of Truth," 63.
85. Ibid., 63–64.
86. Ibid., 64.
87. Ibid., 65.
88. Ibid., 65.
89. Ibid., 66.
90. Copjec, *Imagine*, 2. This conjunction between "deconstruction" and "dispersion," which promotes a one-sided and therefore inaccurate view of deconstruction, is quite common. See also, for example, Fink, *The Lacanian Subject*, xi: "Unlike most poststructuralists, who seek to deconstruct and dispel the very notion of the human subject, Lacan the psychoanalyst finds the concept of subjectivity indispensable."
91. For a fuller discussion of a viable form of nominalism in Derrida's thinking, see Caputo, *Against Ethics*, 72–79.

Chapter 2: Freud and the Transcendental Relation

1. Freud, "New Introductory Lectures," *SE: XXII*, 58–59.
2. Freud never tires of reiterating the vagueness of this border. See for example, Freud, "On Narcissism: An Introduction," *SE: XIV*, 73–74. "Narcissism in this sense would not be a perversion, but the libidinal complement to the egoism of the instinct of self-preservation, a measure of which may justifiably be attributed to every living creature."
3. Freud, "Civilization and its Discontents," *SE: XXI*, 65–66.
4. Freud, "New Introductory Lectures," *SE: XXII*, 58–59.
5. Ibid., 70.
6. For a succinct account, see Richard Wollheim, *Freud*, 2nd ed. (London: Fontana Press, 1991), 158–60.
7. Freud, "Civilization," *SE: XXI*, 66.
8. Husserl's rejection of the notion of an unconscious on the grounds that it is "an absurdity to speak of a content of which we are 'unconscious,' one of which we are conscious only later (*nachträglich*) . . . retention of a content of which we are not conscious is impossible," does not do justice to the complexity of Freud's understanding of the unconscious. Cited in Derrida, "Speech and Phenomena," 63.
9. Within the phenomenological tradition, the critique of Husserlian phenomenology stemming from Heidegger accords with Freud's insight here that we never constitute a world in passive genesis as neutral perceivers.

10. Wollheim, *Freud*, 53.

11. Notably, the *Standard Edition* translation of Freud's "*Trieb*" as "instinct" is misleading because it suggests an a priori, biological necessity, whereas, as Lacan points out, what Freud describes under this name is a complex, articulated phenomenon that must be understood as an impulse thoroughly mediated by convention. See Lacan, *Four Fundamental Concepts*, *S: XI*, 162–64; 175–77. Following common practice, I shall here substitute the term "drive" for what is translated as instinct. I should also point out that Freud's development of his libido theory is marked by multiple revisions that he was not especially consistent in applying. He therefore left a legacy of discrepancies in a field of inquiry already marked by openly expressed hesitations and reversals, the vicissitudes of which I shall not try to trace here.

12. Freud, "Beyond the Pleasure Principle," *SE: XVIII*, 52–54; Freud, "The Ego and the Id," *SE: XIX*, 40–41.

13. Freud, "The Ego and the Id," *SE: XIX*, 40.

14. Ibid., 40–41.

15. Ibid., 42–47.

16. This central notion will be elaborated on further in due course.

17. Much of this discussion derives from Copjec's discussion in *Imagine*, 50–67. I will return to it more than once.

18. See Freud, "On Narcissism," *SE: XIV*, 77. "A unity comparable to the ego cannot exist in the individual from the start; the ego has to be developed." Again, "young children are amoral and possess no internal inhibitions against their striving for pleasure" (Freud, "New Introductory Lectures," *SE: XXII*, 62). See also Freud, "Negation," *SE: XIX*, 237.

19. Freud, "The Ego and the Id," *SE: XIX*, 25. Freud describes the ego as, before its own diversification into superego, "that part of the id which has been modified by the direct influence of the external world." I shall discuss this mechanism in more detail presently. On a terminological note, Freud does not consistently distinguish between the terms "ego-ideal," "ideal ego," and "superego," although the terms are also not synonymous, and a clear distinction is warranted. Lacan, to begin with, emphasizes such a distinction between the "ideal ego" and the "superego," which I have found to be sufficient for my purposes here. I shall, therefore, not follow him into the further complexities of developing a more nuanced difference between "ideal ego" and "ego-ideal." For more on these distinctions, see Evans, *Introductory Dictionary*, 52.

20. In other words, within the organism there is a general quantity of libido, "whose production, increase or diminution, distribution and displacement should afford us possibilities of explaining psychosexual phenomena observed." Freud, "Three Essays on the Theory of Sexuality," *SE: VII*, 217.

21. Freud, "New Introductory Lectures," *SE: XXII*, 105: "but what we have in mind here is rather the id, the whole person." See James Strachey, "The Great Reservoir of Libido," appendix B of "The Ego and the Id," *SE: XIX*, 63–66.

22. Here Freud argues, "at the very beginning, all the libido is accumulated in the id, while the ego is still in the process of formation or is still feeble. The

id sends part of this libido out into erotic object-cathexes, whereupon, the ego, now grown stronger, tries to get hold of this object-libido and to force itself on the id as a love object. The narcissism of the ego is thus a secondary one, which has been withdrawn from objects" (Freud, "The Ego and the Id," *SE: XIX*, 46).

23. See Freud, "An Outline of Psycho-Analysis," *SE: XXIII*, 150: "It is hard to say anything of the behaviour of the libido in the id and in the super-ego. All that we know about it relates to the ego, in which at first the whole available quota of libido is stored up. We call this state absolute, primary *narcissism*. It lasts till the ego begins to cathect the ideas of objects with libido, to transform narcissistic libido into object-libido. Throughout the whole of life the ego remains the great reservoir from which libidinal cathexes are sent out to objects and into which they are once more withdrawn, just as an amoeba behaves with its pseudopodia."

24. Lacan, *Four Fundamental Concepts*, *S: XI*, 197–98.

25. See Freud, "Civilization," *SE: XXI*, 67.

26. Freud, "Negation," *SE: XIX*, 237.

27. Notably, in Husserl's passive genesis, other people would be treated simply as initially neutral objects in my world among others. For Freud, by contrast, there is reciprocity in the relation—a looking back, which ensures that significant others have a crucial, primary role to play in the constitution of the transcendental relation. Freud's views are reflected in Levinas' claim that what appears first on the other side of the transcendental relation is not a neutral "ready-made" object to be looked at, but a "face." Freud, however, reflects on the ambivalent love and aggressivity directed toward the soliciting other. As he notes, the command of neighborly love is precisely a command because such love is so far from natural inclination. He argues that this ambivalence goes back to the experience of the *Nebenmensch* (the first significant other, usually the mother) as both the source of all pleasure and as a dangerous threat against which protection is needed. See Freud, "Civilization" *SE: XXI*, 109–11.

28. Freud calls this "the primary function," as distinguishable from what he later calls "the primary process."

29. Freud, "Three Essays," *SE: VII*, 182; Freud, "On Narcissism," *SE: XIV*, 87–88.

30. Freud, "Introductory Lectures," *SE: XVI*, 314; Freud, "Three Essays," *SE: VII*, 181–82.

31. Freud, "Three Essays," *SE: VII*, 181–82.

32. Freud, "New Introductory Lectures," *SE: XXII*, 87.

33. Freud, "Civilization," *SE: XXI*, 66–67.

34. Ibid., 67.

35. Freud, "Three Essays," *SE: VII*, 222.

36. Wollheim, *Freud*, xxxix.

37. Notably, both Derrida and Lacan point to the difficulties involved in this paradoxical notion of the "first" impression or "original" repetition. I shall discuss this in greater detail in the chapters to follow.

38. Jacques Lacan, *The Ethics of Psychoanalysis (Seminar VII)*, trans. Dennis Porter (New York: W. W. Norton, 1992), 39.

39. Wollheim, *Freud*, 166–67.

40. Ibid., 123.

41. Freud, "The Ego and the Id," *SE: XIX*, 47.

42. Wollheim, *Freud*, 56.

43. Freud, "The Ego and the Id," *SE: XIX*, 45.

44. Freud, "New Introductory Lectures," *SE: XXII*, 74: "Contrary impulses exist side by side, without canceling each other out or diminishing each other: at the most they may converge to form compromises under the dominating economic pressure towards the discharge of energy."

45. Wollheim, *Freud*, 55, 107.

46. Lacan will later challenge this designation, arguing that it is based on an overly traditional understanding of language that associates "word production" with logic and reasoning.

47. Freud, "Beyond," *SE: XVIII*, 34.

48. Freud, "New Introductory Lectures," *SE: XXII*, 74.

49. Ibid.

50. Freud, "Beyond," *SE: XVIII*, 28. See also Freud, "New Introductory Lectures," *SE: XXII*, 74: "The relation to time, which is so hard to describe, is also introduced into the ego by the perceptual system; it can scarcely be doubted that the mode of operation of that system is what provides the origin of the idea of time."

51. Freud, "New Introductory Lectures," *SE: XXII*, 75.

52. Ibid., 76.

53. Ibid., 77.

54. Ibid., 75.

55. Freud, "The Ego and the Id," *SE: XIX*, 45.

56. Freud, "New Introductory Lectures," *SE: XXII*, 76.

57. Freud, "Negation," *SE: XIX*, 237–38.

58. The experience of pain complicates, but does not change, the logic. The ego represses what causes excessive pain and does not allow it to become a conscious presentation at all, and therefore does not grant it reality status. Yet, as Freud points out, analysts can detect the paradoxical unconscious granting of reality status in the very act of negation.

59. Freud, "New Introductory Lectures," *SE: XXII*, 74: "what distinguishes the ego from the id quite especially is a tendency to synthesis in its contents, to a combination and unification in its mental processes which are totally lacking in the id." See also Freud, "The Ego and the Id," *SE: XIX*, 45: a "tendency to unity . . . is particularly characteristic of the ego."

60. Wollheim, *Freud*, 61.

61. Freud, "New Introductory Lectures," *SE: XXII*, 76.

62. Caputo, *Radical Hermeneutics*, 4.

63. Wollheim, *Freud*, 169–70.

64. Ibid.
65. Freud, "The Ego and the Id," *SE: XIX*, 20.
66. Ibid., 23.
67. Saussure, *Course*, 65–67.
68. Ibid., 67.
69. Copjec, *Imagine*, 53.
70. Freud, "On Narcissism," *SE: XIV*, 87.
71. I will discuss the Oedipus complex and its associated difficulties, for example concerning gender, in the chapters to follow.
72. Freud, "New Introductory Lectures," *SE: XXII*, 124.
73. Ibid., 87.
74. Ibid., 64.
75. These remarks already reflect my decision to adopt a traditional line of interpretation as a basis for comparison with the Lacanian revisions. Copjec, by contrast, supports a far less traditional account than that proposed here, based on Freud's revisions of his libido theory in and after his essay "On Narcissism," which, in her view, already opens a space (in the separation between sublimation/narcissism in relation to the ideal ego and idealization in relation to the superego) for a narcissistic pleasure in "self-shattering" rather than ego-unity. See, Copjec, *Imagine*, 53–64. It is hard to stretch "On Narcissism" so far as to find this moment of "self-shattering." However, I can see that the "auto-deconstructing" discrepancy that Lacan detects at the "origin" of the ego (related to the vacillation between totality and infinity in the conception of the whole) must affect all of the related notions, and I do not dispute the warrant for the Lacanian revision in which the moment of self-shattering certainly becomes explicit in his aporetic account of the constitution of the *moi*. I shall return to this revision in chapter 10.
76. Freud, "New Introductory Lectures," *SE: XXII*, 63.
77. Ibid.
78. Ibid. Notably, Freud adds, "identification and object-choice are to a large extent independent of each other; it is however possible to identify oneself with someone whom, for instance, one has taken as a sexual object, and to alter one's own ego on his model."
79. Freud, "On Narcissism," *SE: XIV*, 94. As Freud puts it, "sublimation is a process that concerns object-libido and consists in the instinct's directing itself towards an aim other than, and remote from, that of sexual satisfaction; in this process, the accent falls upon deflection from sexuality. Idealization is a process that concerns the *object*; by it that object, without any alternation in its nature, is aggrandized and exalted in the subject's mind." One can, for example, idealize a person or institution on the basis of fear, without granting to the ideal any degree of libidinal cathexis.
80. Ibid., 76–77.
81. Ibid., 94.
82. Ibid., 74–75.

83. Ibid., 93–94.
84. Freud, "The Ego and the Id," *SE: XIX*, 45–46.
85. Ibid., 45.
86. Ibid., 48–49.
87. Freud, "New Introductory Lectures," *SE: XXII*, 64.
88. Freud, "On Narcissism," *SE: XIV*, 94.
89. Ibid., 100.
90. Freud, "New Introductory Lectures," *SE: XXII*, 67.
91. Ibid.
92. Freud, "On Narcissism," *SE: XIV*, 93–94: "This ideal ego is now the target of the self-love which was enjoyed in childhood by the actual ego."
93. Ibid., 91. Freud also here names a feminine narcissism (I love someone who was once part of me, namely my child).
94. Freud, "New Introductory Lectures," *SE: XXII*, 62: "the super-ego takes the place of the parental agency and observes, directs and threatens the ego."
95. Freud, "New Introductory Lectures," *SE: XXII*, 64–65: The super-ego "is also the vehicle of the ego-ideal [ideal ego] by which the ego measures itself, which it emulates, and whose demand for ever greater perfection it strives to fulfil."
96. Freud, "Three Essays," *SE: VII*, 207.
97. Bruce Fink, "Knowledge and Jouissance," 28. As we shall see, it is the fantasy of sexual complementarity that Lacan aims to eliminate from psychoanalytic theory and practice.
98. Freud, "On Narcissism," *SE: XIV*, 89.
99. Ibid., 74–75.
100. Ibid., 93.
101. Ibid., 88.
102. Freud, "Three Essays," *SE: VII*, 178.
103. Freud, "On Narcissism," *SE: XIV*, 149. See also Freud, "Three Essays," *SE: VII*, 182.
104. Freud, "New Introductory Lectures," *SE: XXII*, 89–90.
105. Ibid., 90.
106. Ibid., 90. See also Freud, "Three Essays," *SE: VII*, 182.
107. Lacan, *Ethics*, *S: VII*, 44–45: "it is obvious that the things of the human world are things in a universe structured by words, that language, symbolic processes, dominate and govern all." Derrida, too, argues that the conflict between economic (secondary) and aneconomic (primary) modes of processing happens within the broader domain of signifying practice indicated by the term archiwriting (a substitute for *différance*).
108. Saussure, *Course*, 67–73.
109. Ibid., 70.
110. Ibid., 74.
111. Lacan, *Ethics*, *S: VII*, 46.
112. Freud, "New Introductory Lectures," *SE: XXII*, 80.

Chapter 3: Derrida: *Différance* and the "Plural Logic of the Aporia"

1. Derrida, "*Différance*," 14–15.
2. Ibid., 6.
3. But also the chances, one should add.
4. Richard Rorty, "Derrida and the Philosophical Tradition," in *Truth and Progress: Philosophical Papers, Volume 3* (Cambridge: Cambridge University Press, 1998), 328.
5. Richard Rorty, "Philosophy as a Kind of Writing: An Essay on Derrida," in *Consequences of Pragmatism (Essays: 1972–1980)* (Minneapolis: University of Minnesota Press, 1982), 103.
6. Rorty, "Derrida and the Philosophical Tradition," 331.
7. Christopher Norris argues that Rorty politely "passes over those aspects of Derrida's work that do not fit in with his own argumentative purposes." See Christopher Norris, "Philosophy as Not Just a 'Kind of Writing': Derrida and the Claim of Reason," in *Redrawing the Lines: Analytic Philosophy, Deconstruction, and Literary Theory*, ed. Reed Way Dasenbrock (Minneapolis: University of Minnesota Press, 1989), 192.
8. Rorty, "Philosophy as a Kind of Writing," 92–93.
9. Rorty, "Derrida and the Philosophical Tradition," 332.
10. Rorty, "Philosophy as a Kind of Writing," 90–93. See also Rorty's *Philosophy and the Mirror of Nature* (Princeton, N.J.: Princeton University Press, 1979), 3–13.
11. Rorty, "Philosophy as a Kind of Writing," 96. Notably, such nominalism derives from a one-sided appropriation of Saussure's diacritical model of signification, which ignores Saussure's complex articulation of two fundamental principles, namely arbitrariness and linearity. I will address this shortly.
12. Ibid.
13. See Derrida, *Of Grammatology*, 62. Speaking of Husserl's transcendental phenomenology, for example, Derrida insists that "*a thought of the trace can no more break with a transcendental phenomenology than be reduced to it.* Here as elsewhere, to pose the problem in terms of choice, to oblige or to believe oneself obliged to answer it by a *yes* or *no*, to conceive of appurtenance as an allegiance or nonappurtenance as plain speaking, is to confuse very different levels, paths, and styles. In the deconstructive thinking of the arche, one does not make a choice." This resistance to either/or choice is reiterated in many texts. See also Derrida, "*Différance*," 19; "Structure, Sign, and Play," 292–93; "Form and Meaning: A Note on the Phenomenology of Language," in *Speech and Phenomena: And Other Essays on Husserl's Theory of Signs*, trans. David B. Allison (Evanston, Ill.: Northwestern University Press, 1973), 128; Jacques Derrida, "Force of Law: The 'Mystical Foundation of Authority,'" in *Deconstruction and the Possibility of Justice*, ed. Drucilla Cornell, Michel Rosenfeld, and David Gray Carlson (New York: Routledge, 1992), 4.
14. Rorty, "Philosophy as a Kind of Writing," 100. For a sustained criticism, see Richard Rorty, "Deconstruction and Circumvention," in *Critical Inquiry* 11 (1984): 1–23.

15. Rorty, "Derrida and the Philosophical Tradition," 331.

16. Rorty, "Philosophy as a Kind of Writing," 99–103.

17. Ibid., 103.

18. Rorty cites from Allison's translation: Jacques Derrida, "Differance," in *Speech and Phenomena: And Other Essays on Husserl's Theory of Signs,* translated by David B. Allison (Evanston, Ill.: Northwestern University Press, 1973), 159. In the Bass translation, marked as Derrida, *"Différance,"* which I have referred to otherwise, this citation appears on page 26.

19. Derrida, "Love of Lacan," 48.

20. Derrida, "*Différance*," 7–9.

21. See Derrida, "*Différance*," 9.

22. Derrida makes constant reference to such a chain of "substitutions" for *différance*. The scare quotes function as a reminder of his insistence that one can never substitute perfectly, that is, without loss or gain. See, for example, Derrida, "Structure, Sign, and Play," 280; "Resistances," 26.

23. Derrida, "Resistances," 31.

24. Derrida, *Aporias*, 13–21. Here he draws up an extensive index of the quasi-concepts deriving from what he calls "the places of aporia" in which his thinking has been "regularly tied up."

25. Derrida, "Differance" in *Speech and Phenomena*, 159–60.

26. Richard Rorty, "Remarks on Deconstruction and Pragmatism," in *Deconstruction and Pragmatism*, ed. Chantal Mouffe (London: Routledge, 1996), 16.

27. Concepts can easily be determined in the absence of those that are merely different; for example, the concept "animal" does not depend for its existence on the concept "tree." But concepts that form binary oppositions depend on each other for their existence; there is no concept of "dark" without "light," for example.

28. Rorty, "Remarks on Deconstruction and Pragmatism," 73.

29. Saussure, *Course*, 117–18.

30. This example, to which I shall return repeatedly, is derived from Derrida's treatment of the aporetic articulation of justice and law in Derrida's "Force of Law." See also Caputo, *Deconstruction in a Nutshell*, 136–39, for a lucid discussion of, as Caputo puts it, "three aporias, three examples of a single aporia that distributes itself across three domains, which might also be described as three axioms of Derrida's 'inventionalism.'"

31. Caputo, *Deconstruction in a Nutshell*, 136.

32. Žižek, "The Real of Sexual Difference," 65.

33. Lacan, *Feminine Sexuality, S: XX*, 65–66.

34. Žižek, "The Real of Sexual Difference," 65.

35. Ibid.

36. Thus—and the irony may be intentional—Žižek charges Derridean discourse with precisely the shortcoming that characterizes the admittedly unjust criticism that Derrida directs toward the Lacanian. Although it remains to be asked why Derrida would criticize Lacanian discourse for precisely the hypostatization of Lack that he supposedly embraces.

37. Žižek, "The Real of Sexual Difference," 65.

38. Ibid. Notably, one should not be too distracted here by the way that Žižek converts the "messianic promise" into hardly synonymous terms such as "authentic spirit" and, later in the text, "essential core," for he is not in fact surreptitiously converting the messianic promise into a positively determined Ideal. Rather, consistent with his interpretation of the Absolute Other as Absolute Absence, he in fact makes a different although equally problematic equation, namely between Absolute Absence and Derrida's notion of "the impossible."

39. Ibid., 66.

40. Ibid.

41. Ibid.

42. Ibid., 68.

43. Derrida, "Violence and Metaphysics," in *Writing and Difference*, 123–33.

44. Ibid., 82–83.

45. Ibid., 133.

46. Ibid., 84–85.

47. Ibid., 126–28.

48. Ibid., 127.

49. Ibid., 129–30.

50. Ibid., 82–83.

51. Ibid., 84.

52. Žižek, "The Real of Sexual Difference," 66.

53. Ibid., 67. My italics.

54. Ibid.

55. Ibid.

56. Ibid.

57. Ibid.

58. Ibid., 68.

59. Jacques Derrida, "A Word of Welcome," in *Adieu to Immanuel Levinas*, trans. Pascale-Anne Brault and Michael Naas (Palo Alto, Calif.: Stanford University Press, 1999), 98–99.

60. Ibid., 99.

61. Žižek, "The Real of Sexual Difference," 69.

62. Ibid.

63. Ibid., 68–69.

64. Ibid., 69.

65. Ibid., 70.

66. Ibid. The allusion here is not to the term "specter" but "spectrum."

67. Ibid.

68. Ibid.

69. Ibid., 71.

70. Caputo, *Deconstruction in a Nutshell*, 138. As I hope to demonstrate in chapter 8, this claim echoes Lacan's stance concerning the ethics of psychoanalysis.

71. These comments allude to the quasi-transcendental contamination of the terms "invention" and "convention" that Derrida analyses in "Psyche: Inventions of the Other."

72. Derrida, "Violence and Metaphysics," 82–83.

73. Derrida, "Force of Law," 28–29.

74. Derrida, "*Différance*," 7.

75. Jacques Derrida, "From Restricted to General Economy: A Hegelianism Without Reserve," in *Writing and Difference*, trans. Alan Bass (Chicago: University of Chicago Press, 1978).

76. Jacques Derrida, *Archive Fever: A Freudian Impression*, trans. Eric Prenowitz (Chicago: University of Chicago Press, 1996), 9–10.

77. Derrida, *Aporias*, 20.

78. See Caputo, *Deconstruction in a Nutshell*, 140. Caputo here confirms Derrida's insistence upon the necessary moment of calculation.

79. Derrida, "*Différance*," 18–19.

80. Derrida, "*Différance*," 8.

81. In Lacanian terms, this describes the relationship between deferred "jouissance" and the "death drive."

82. Derrida, "Restricted to General Economy," 255–56. See also, Derrida, "*Différance*," 19–20.

83. Derrida, "*Différance*," 8–9.

84. For Derrida, the difference between these two articulations of the relation occurred "when language invaded the universal problematic," hence the insertion of "sign" between "structure" and "play" in the title of his essay. See "Structure, Sign, and Play," 279–80.

85. Derrida, *Of Grammatology*, 20.

86. Derrida addresses this dream of presence in many texts: See, for example, "Structure, Sign, and Play," 279; *Of Grammatology*, 12.

87. See Derrida, "Psyche: Inventions of the Other," 54–55.

88. For example, the relative atomic mass of any element is measured by a calculation that compares the mass of a single atom to an elected constant, namely one-twelfth of the mass of a carbon-12 atom. Relative atomic mass now provides a basis for comparing the atoms of substances as diverse as oxygen and iron.

89. Žižek, "The Real of Sexual Difference," 57–58. Lacan goes on to add, however, that the "*point de capiton*" is also ultimately unspecifiable. In Žižek's words: "Suffice it to recall how a community functions: the master signifier that guarantees the community's consistency is a signifier whose signified is an enigma for the members themselves—nobody really knows what it means, but each of them some how presupposes that others know it, that it has to mean 'the real thing,' and so they use it all the time."

90. Derrida, *Aporias*, 11–12.

91. Ibid., 20.

92. Ibid.

93. Derrida, "*Différance*," 8–9.
94. Saussure, *Course*, 75.
95. Derrida, "*Différance*," 19.
96. Derrida, *Aporias*, 20.
97. For a detailed explication of the relation between law as "the possible" and Justice as "the impossible," see Derrida, "Force of Law," 16–17.
98. Derrida, "Force of Law," 17.
99. Ibid., 4.
100. Derrida, *Aporias*, 16.
101. For Kant's lengthy discussion of this, see his *Critique of Pure Reason*, A497–568/B525–596.
102. Besides the already cited section entitled "Critical Philosophy," in *The Encyclopaedia Logic*, Hegel's most direct criticism appears in the sections pertaining to critical philosophy in the following texts: G. W. F. Hegel, "Kantian Philosophy," in *Faith and Knowledge*, trans. Walter Cerf and H. S. Harris (Albany, N.Y.: SUNY Press, 1977), 67–96; and "Kant," in *Lectures on the History of Philosophy, Volume III*, trans. E. H. Haldane and F. H. Simson (London: Routledge & Kegan Paul, 1955), 423–78.
103. Gasché, *Tain of the Mirror*, 93–100.
104. See G. W. F. Hegel, *Phenomenology of Spirit*, trans. A. V. Miller (Oxford: Oxford University Press, 1977). This is evident in the preface as a whole, but is addressed specifically on 10–11.
105. Jacques Derrida, *Glas*, trans. John P. Leavey Jr. and Richard Rand (Lincoln: University of Nebraska Press, 1986). I will address this criticism in a little more detail in chapter 8.
106. Martin Heidegger, *The Principle of Reason*, trans. Reginald Lilly (Bloomington: Indiana University Press, 1991).
107. His criticism of Heidegger stems from other concerns, for example, from the way Heidegger sells this insight short in his blind moments of mythologizing nationalism. See John D. Caputo, *Demythologizing Heidegger* (Bloomington: Indiana University Press, 1993), 3–5, 39, 55–56. Here, Caputo, following a Derridean path, aims to "demythologize" the dangerous spell cast by Heideggerian mythmaking by exposing and disrupting with a "myth of Justice" Heidegger's invidious fabrication of a "myth of Being," whose grim historical outcome is well documented. Heidegger's myth, as a dual "being-historical" and "being-beautiful," emerges in his early texts and is revised in step with two "turnings" that mark three phases, extending from a new questioning of Being in the earlier texts, through the *Kampf*, responsibility, *Volk*, and destiny of Heidegger's "political" phase, to the poetics of *Gelassenheit* in the later Heidegger. In spite of its bitter associations and heedless of calls for renunciation, Caputo argues, Heidegger never did disengage from the myth that represented an essential Greek-German connection.
108. Derrida, "Structure, Sign, and Play," 280.
109. Ibid., 279.
110. Ibid.

111. That is, "*eidos, arche, telos, energeia, ousia* (essence, existence, substance, subject), *aletheia*, transcendentality, consciousness, God, man, and so forth," Derrida, "Structure, Sign, and Play," 279–80.

112. Rorty, notably, flatly will not swallow this quasi-transcendental complexity. Consistent nominalists, he argues, "would not say that widely used words stand for *incoherent* concepts, for there can be no better proof of a concept's coherence than the fact that (in Wittgenstein's words) 'this language game is *played*.'" Further, they would argue that "certain concepts were awkward, of limited utility, and replaceable, but not that they were incoherent or unintelligible." Rorty, "Derrida and the Philosophical Tradition," 330. For Derrida, to the contrary, successful practice is by no means the guarantee of a concept's coherence (an efficient legal system, for example, cannot make of "justice" a coherent concept). Instead, language games have to be played with unavoidably incoherent notions, which cannot be replaced with more viable alternatives.

113. Derrida, *Aporias*, 20.

114. Ibid.

115. Derrida, "Resistances," 36.

116. Ibid., 30.

117. Derrida analyses the gift in *Given Time: 1. Counterfeit Money*, trans. Peggy Kamuf (Chicago: University of Chicago Press, 1994). See also Caputo, *Deconstruction in a Nutshell*, 140–48, for an accessible discussion of Derrida's notion of the gift and its relation to justice.

118. Derrida, *Given Time*, 11–12.

119. Ibid., 12.

120. Ibid., 12–16.

121. Caputo, *Deconstruction in a Nutshell*, 141.

122. Derrida, *Given Time*, 30.

123. Derrida, "Restricted to General Economy," 252.

Part 2: Derrida Reading Freud: The Paradoxes of Archivization

1. Derrida, "Love of Lacan," 41.

2. Derrida, *Archive Fever*, 83–95.

3. Ibid., 2. Classically the *archons* presided over the archives. In Derrida's words: "The citizens who thus held and signified political power were considered to possess the right to make or to represent the law. On account of their publicly recognized authority, it is at their home . . . that official documents are filed. The archons are first of all the documents' guardians. They do not only ensure the physical security of what is deposited and of the substrate. They are also accorded the hermeneutic right and competence. They have the power to interpret the archives. . . . It is thus, in this *domiciliation*, in this house arrest, that archives take place."

4. Ibid., 15.

5. Ibid., 2.

6. Ibid., 15.

7. Ibid., 2.
8. Ibid., 91.
9. Ibid., 7.
10. Ibid., 90.
11. Ibid., 91.
12. Jacques Derrida, "Freud and the Scene of Writing," in *Writing and Difference*, trans. Alan Bass (Chicago: University of Chicago Press, 1978), 197–198.
13. Derrida, *Archive Fever*, 29.
14. Ibid., 91.
15. Ibid., 89–90.
16. Ibid., 84.
17. Ibid., 90.
18. Ibid., 7.
19. Ibid., 94.
20. Ibid.
21. Ibid., 90.

Chapter 4: The Im-Possibility of the Psyche

1. Derrida, *Archive Fever*, 91–94.
2. Ibid.
3. Derrida, "Freud and the Scene of Writing," 218.
4. Derrida, *Archive Fever*, 91–92.
5. Derrida, "Freud and the Scene of Writing," 205.
6. Derrida, *Archive Fever*, 92.
7. Ibid.
8. As I shall explain shortly, Derrida takes Freud's claim that the secondary system (which encompasses both primary and secondary processing in contrast with the reflex arc) is the vehicle of memory "and so probably of psychical processes in general" to indicate that, for Freud, memory is not one of the properties of the psyche but its "very essence." See, Derrida, "Freud and the Scene of Writing," 201.
9. Derrida, *Archive Fever*, 92–93. This is the side of Freudian discourse taken up in "ego-psychology."
10. See Freud, "Project For a Scientific Psychology." *SE: I*; Freud, "The Interpretation of Dreams," *SE: IV & V*; Freud, "A Note Upon the 'Mystic Writing-Pad,'" *SE: XIX*, 227–32.
11. Derrida, "Freud and the Scene of Writing," 206.
12. Ibid., 200.
13. Ibid.
14. Ibid., 221.
15. Elaine N. Marieb, *Human Anatomy and Physiology* (Redwood City, Calif.: Benjamin/Cummings, 1989), 347–55. I shall merely note here (without support, which would lead me too far from my main purposes) that access to this apparently small difference would already have obliged Freud to modify his understanding of the psychical apparatus substantially, for chemical propagation is

incompatible with Freud's notion of "cathexis," that is, the accumulation of excitation in the neurons.

16. Derrida, "Freud and the Scene of Writing," 200.

17. Freud, "Project," *SE: I*, 299. See also Derrida, "Freud and the Scene of Writing," 200.

18. Freud, "Project," *SE: I*, 296–97.

19. As noted in chapter 1, the primary and secondary functions should not be confused with the primary and secondary processes. Both processes are aspects of secondary functioning, although their means and aims are different.

20. Freud, "Project," *SE: I*, 298.

21. Ibid., 299–300.

22. Ibid., 300.

23. Marieb, *Human Anatomy*, 337.

24. *Bahnung* as noted is a problematic term that is variously translated: "facilitation" and "breaching" are here taken as synonyms.

25. Freud, "Project," *SE: I*, 300–301.

26. Ibid.

27. Ibid., 319. I take the terms "cathexis" and "cathect" to be synonymous with the terms "energization" and "energize."

28. Derrida, "Freud and the Scene of Writing," 201.

29. Freud, "Project," *SE: I*, 308.

30. Ibid.

31. Ibid., 340.

32. Ibid., 308.

33. Ibid., 309–10.

34. This is outlined in a letter to Fliess, appended to Freud's "Project," *SE: I*, 388–89.

35. In contemporary models, qualitative differentiation is understood in the complex terms of topography (location), structure, and frequency. Different sensory qualities are minutely encoded in the location and structure of the neural network. In my fingertips, for example, there are receptors uniquely dedicated to different kinds of sensation (of heat, light, chemicals, and pain), with their own neural paths, which are either activated or not, depending on circumstances. See Marieb, *Human Anatomy*, 344. Differences in intensity (but not differences in kind as Freud thought) are encoded in terms of frequency. See Marieb, *Human Anatomy*, 355. This confirms the difficulty of Freud's division of conscious perception and memory along the lines of a quantity/quality separation.

36. Freud, "The Unconscious." *SE: XIV*, 174–75.

37. Derrida, "Freud and the Scene of Writing," 201–2.

38. Ibid., 202.

39. Ibid.

40. Ibid., 202–3.

41. Ibid., 206.

42. The neurological is placed in suspension. See Freud, "Interpretation of Dreams," *SE: IV*, 41–42: "Even when investigation shows that the primary exciting cause of a phenomenon is psychical, deeper research will one day trace the path further and discover an organic basis for the mental event."
43. Letter 52 (1896), reproduced in Freud, "Extracts," *SE: I*, 233–35.
44. Freud, "Interpretation of Dreams," *SE: IV & V*, 48–49.
45. Ibid., 608.
46. Freud, "Beyond," *SE: XVIII*, 13.
47. Derrida, "Freud and the Scene of Writing," 205.
48. Ibid., 206.
49. Freud, "Interpretation of Dreams," *SE: IV & V*, 29–30.
50. Ibid., 96.
51. Ibid., 97–99.
52. Derrida, "Freud and the Scene of Writing," 207.
53. Ibid., 209.
54. Freud, "Interpretation of Dreams," *SE: IV & V*, 277–79.
55. Ibid., 293–94.
56. Hence Lacan's characterization of it as metonymic. In contrast, he associates dream displacement with metaphor.
57. Freud, "Interpretation of Dreams," *SE: IV & V*, 305–08.
58. Ibid., 339.
59. Ibid., 312–13.
60. Ibid., 344.
61. Ibid., 488–89.
62. Ibid., 312.
63. Ibid., 341.
64. Derrida, "Freud and the Scene of Writing," 209.
65. Freud, "Interpretation of Dreams," *SE: IV & V*, 311–13.
66. Ibid., 277.
67. Derrida, "Freud and the Scene of Writing," 209.
68. Ibid., 209–10.
69. Freud, "Interpretation of Dreams," *SE: IV & V*, 350–53.
70. Derrida, "Freud and the Scene of Writing," 211–12.
71. Ibid., 212.
72. Ibid.
73. Freud, "Interpretation of Dreams," *SE: IV & V*, 49.
74. Derrida, "Freud and the Scene of Writing," 218–19.
75. Ibid., 213.
76. Freud, "Interpretation of Dreams," *SE: IV & V*, 536–40; 610–11.
77. Derrida, "Freud and the Scene of Writing," 212–13.
78. Ibid., 212.
79. Ibid., 215.
80. Freud, "Interpretation of Dreams," *SE: IV & V*, 610–11; Derrida, "Freud and the Scene of Writing," 215.

81. Freud, "Interpretation of Dreams," *SE: IV & V*, 537; Derrida, "Freud and the Scene of Writing," 216.

82. Derrida, "Freud and the Scene of Writing," 217.

83. Ibid., 221.

84. Ibid.

85. Ibid.

86. Ibid., 221–22.

87. All citations to follow from Derrida's discussion of these two senses refer to "Freud and the Scene of Writing," 228.

88. Derrida, "Freud and the Scene of Writing," 222.

89. Freud, "Note," *SE: XIX*, 228–29.

90. Derrida, "Freud and the Scene of Writing," 224.

91. Ibid., 225.

92. Ibid.

93. Ibid.

94. Ibid., 226–27.

95. Ibid., 226.

96. Ibid., 227.

97. Ibid.

98. Ibid., 227–28.

99. Ibid., 204. To reiterate, to trouble this distinction is not to collapse it altogether.

100. Derrida, *Archive Fever*, 8.

101. Ibid., 15.

102. Ibid., 16–17.

103. Leonard Shlain, *The Alphabet Versus the Goddess: The Conflict Between Word and Image* (New York: Penguin Arkana, 1998), 1–7.

104. Derrida, *Archive Fever*, 14.

105. This, however, cannot be said of the Lacanian revisions.

106. Derrida, *Archive Fever*, 17.

107. Ibid., 15.

108. Derrida, "Freud and the Scene of Writing," 228.

Chapter 5: The Death Drive and the Im-Possibility of Psychoanalysis

1. Derrida, *Archive Fever*, 12.

2. This turn of phrase might seem contrary to the Lacanian claim that the death drive is one of the "fundamental concepts" of psychoanalysis, but I think the apparent discrepancy here is merely semantic. Derrida questions the possibility of unified "concepts" in psychoanalysis, rather than quasi-transcendentals, because he finds that every psychoanalytic notion is split up by an aporetic complexity. Moreover, this complexity does not take the form of an ordered plurality of motifs where the fundamental principle, finally, would be the principle that orders the plurality of meanings. Rather, it takes the form of an aporetic articulation of incompatible motifs between which there is no rational basis for

choice. He sees the death drive as one of many such notions. The death drive is similarly complex and aporctic for Lacan, as I aim to demonstrate in part 4, for the "object" that gives it its character (or that toward which it aims) cannot be unified into a concept but remains divided across three versions of "the All," which one could name, for short, "totality," "infinity," and a specifically Lacanian sense of paradoxical "sublimity."

3. Derrida, *Archive Fever*, 94–95. Although "psyche" was taken in the previous chapter to designate a system other than that of consciousness, it is often used to describe the mental apparatus as a whole. The entanglements of the psychical systems just discussed legitimate this wider use of the term.

4. Derrida, "Resistances," 1–25.

5. Freud, "Beyond," *SE: XVIII*, 7–64. Derrida, "Love of Lacan," 41.

6. Freud, "Beyond," *SE: XVIII*, 7–9.

7. Ibid., 10–11.

8. Ibid., 12–14.

9. Freud, "Interpretation of Dreams," *SE: V*, 550.

10. Freud, "Beyond," *SE: XVIII*, 14–17.

11. Ibid., 18–19.

12. Ibid., 19–21.

13. Freud notes that "the motives of the resistance, and indeed the resistances themselves, are unconscious at first during the treatment," which suggests that the ego has both conscious and unconscious aspects.

14. Freud, "Beyond," *SE: XVIII*, 21–22.

15. Ibid., 22–23.

16. Ibid., 24–29.

17. That is, the protective shield represented by the celluloid outer covering of the Mystic Pad.

18. Freud, "Beyond," *SE: XVIII*, 29: "This is the origin of *projection*, which is destined to play such a large part in the causation of pathological processes."

19. Ibid., 29–31.

20. Ibid., 31–33.

21. Ibid., 32.

22. Ibid., 34–36.

23. Ibid., 36.

24. Ibid., 37.

25. Ibid., 37–41.

26. Ibid., 38.

27. Ibid., 39.

28. Ibid., 39–41.

29. Ibid., 44–49.

30. Ibid., 49.

31. Ibid., 49–50.

32. Ibid., 41–43. Development is not, therefore, as some have suggested, governed by an instinct toward perfection.

33. Ibid., 40–41.
34. Ibid., 50–56.
35. Ibid., 60–61.
36. Ibid., 50.
37. Ibid., 53.
38. Ibid., 53–54.
39. Ibid., 54.
40. Ibid., 54–55.
41. Ibid., 55. For Freud, instinctual life (condensed in the germ cells) produces tensions that disturb and resist the inertial tendency of somatic processes. In his words, "the life process of the individual leads for internal reasons to an abolition of chemical tensions, that is to say, death, whereas the union with the living substance of a different individual increases those tensions, introducing what may be described as fresh 'vital differences' which must then be lived off."
42. Ibid., 57–58. Freud reconstructs this myth briefly as follows: "'The original human nature was not like the present, but different. In the first place, the sexes were originally three in number, not two as they are now; there was man, woman, and the union of the two. . . .' Everything about these primaeval men was double: they had four hands and four feet, two faces, two privy parts, and so on. Eventually Zeus decided to cut these men in two, 'like a sorb-apple which is halved for pickling.' After the division had been made, 'the two parts of man, each desiring his other half, came together, and threw their arms about one another, eager to grow into one.'"
43. Ibid., 61.
44. Ibid., 59.
45. Ibid., 60.
46. Ibid., 6–63.
47. Derrida, *Archive Fever*, 94–95. Derrida's metaphors here pertain to his reading of Freud's "Delusions and Dreams in Jensen's '*Gradiva*,'" *SE: IX*.
48. Freud, "Constructions in Analysis," *SE: XXIII*, 266–69.
49. This "space" of synthetic processing, as "spacing" (and timing), is not a "space," but it is not for this reason nothing.
50. See Caputo, *Deconstruction in a Nutshell*, 84–88.
51. Cf. Lacan, *Ethics, S: VII*, 31. I shall address Lacan's argument in more detail in chapter 7.
52. Freud, "Beyond," *SE: XVIII*, 27.
53. Copjec, *Imagine*, 33.
54. I shall address Lacan's arguments in more detail in part 3.
55. See Lacan, *Ethics, S: VII*, 139. Lacan, notably, coins the neologism extimacy (*extimité*) to capture such paradoxical interweaving of inside and outside represented by this enigmatic barrier. See also Jacques-Alain Miller, "*Extimité*," in *Lacanian Theory of Discourse: Subject, Structure, and Society*, ed. Bracher et al. (New York: New York University Press, 1994), 76. Miller, importantly, notes that one of the consequences of the receptive/protective trouble at the interface

between organism and environment is that what is supposed to be the most intimate (the deepest kernel of truth) turns out to be "not a point of transparency but rather a point of opacity," that is, a knot that cannot be untied.

56. These measures, as mentioned in the previous chapter, are (1) condensation and displacement in the primary process and (2) secondary revision, which involves considerations of representability and censorship.

57. Freud, "Civilization," *SE: XXI*, 93.

58. Freud, "The Psychotherapy of Hysteria," *SE: II*, 269.

59. Ibid., 288–90.

60. Ibid., 285.

61. Ibid., 290.

62. Freud, "Interpretation of Dreams," *SE: V*, 577: "it is a prominent feature of unconscious processes that they are indestructible. In the unconscious nothing can be brought to an end, nothing is past or forgotten." See also Freud, "Civilization," *SE: XXI*, 69: "in mental life nothing which has once been formed can perish . . . everything is somehow preserved and . . . in suitable circumstances (when, for instance, regression goes back far enough) it can once more be brought to light."

63. Derrida, *Archive Fever*, 98–99.

64. Ibid., 97–98.

65. Freud, "Analysis Terminable and Interminable," *SE: XXIII*, 237.

66. Freud, "Civilization," *SE: XXI*, 81.

67. Freud, "Creative Writers and Day-Dreaming," *SE: IX*, 146.

68. Freud, "Civilization," *SE: XXI*, 81.

69. Ibid., 84–85.

70. Derrida, *Archive Fever*, 101.

71. Derrida, "Resistances," 19–20.

72. At this point, the "reality status" of the trauma matters little; it is enough to suppose that one is here dealing with something decisive in an analysand's personal narrative, be it a wish, event, delusion, etc.

73. Derrida, "Resistances," 21.

74. Ibid., 5–6.

75. Freud, "Interpretation of Dreams," *SE: IV*, 111.

76. Derrida, "Resistances," 6: "Freud is in the process of analyzing his own dream, a dream that he himself will end up by presenting, in conclusion, as a defense in the form of kettle logic, to wit: (1) the kettle I'm returning to you is intact; (2) what is more, the holes were already in it when I borrowed it, and (3) besides, you never lent me a kettle."

77. Ibid., 3–4.

78. Ibid., 5.

79. Ibid., 7.

80. This indictment is not directed specifically at the institutionalized analyst, but it pertains to the role of analyst, which could, indeed should, also be occupied by the analysand in self-analysis.

81. Freud, "Psychotherapy of Hysteria," *SE: II*, 268–69; Freud, "Introductory Lectures," *SE: XV*, 292. Derrida, "Resistances," 16–17.

82. Freud, "Psychotherapy of Hysteria," *SE: II*, 268, 270, 272.

83. Derrida, "Resistances," 17. Freud, "Psychotherapy of Hysteria," *SE: II*, 282.

84. Derrida, "Resistances," 6.

85. Freud, "Interpretation of Dreams," *SE: IV*, 108. See also Freud, "Introductory Lectures," *SE: XVI*, 280–81: "The doctor's knowledge is not the same as the patient's and cannot produce the same effects. If the doctor transfers his knowledge to the patient as a piece of information . . . it does not have the result of removing the symptoms, but it has another one—of setting the analysis in motion, of which the first signs are often expressions of denial." See also, Freud, "Beyond," *SE: XVIII*, 18–19.

86. Derrida, "Resistances," 5.

87. Ibid., 6.

88. This division between rational analytic solution (the part of the analyst) and nonrational resistance to it (the part of the analysand) may play out in single individuals if, for example, they fail to live in accordance with values held dear at an intellectual level.

89. Freud, "Introductory Lectures," *SE: XVI*, 290–91.

90. Freud, "Interpretation of Dreams," *SE: IV*, 108. See also, Derrida, "Resistances," 7.

91. Derrida, "Resistances," 17–18.

92. Ibid., 17–18.

93. Ibid., 7–8.

94. Freud, "Interpretation of Dreams," *SE: IV*, 110–11. Cited in Derrida, "Resistances," 9.

95. Derrida, "Resistances," 9.

96. Freud, "Interpretation of Dreams," *SE: IV*, 108. Cf. Derrida, "Resistances," 7.

97. Derrida, "Resistances," 10.

98. Ibid., 13.

99. Ibid., 10.

100. Ibid., 13–14.

101. Freud, "Interpretation of Dreams," *SE: V*, 525. Cited in Derrida, "Resistances," 14.

102. Derrida, "Resistances," 10–11.

103. Ibid., 11.

104. Ibid., 15.

105. Ibid.

106. Ibid., 23.

107. Ibid.

108. Ibid.

109. Freud, "Moses and Monotheism," *SE: XXIII*, 75–76.

110. Derrida, "Resistances," 22–23. Here Derrida notes: "The principle of a series also transcends it and, withdrawn from the meaning that it confers, it comes to deprive of meaning the very thing to which it gives meaning."

111. Ibid., 23.

112. Ibid., 24.

113. Ibid.

114. Freud, "Psychotherapy of Hysteria," *SE: II*, 282 (my italics). Derrida, "Resistances," 18.

115. Derrida, "Resistances," 24.

116. Ibid., 18–19.

117. Ibid., 19–20.

118. Ibid., 20.

119. Ibid., 16.

120. Ibid.

121. Ibid., 21.

Chapter 6: Institutional Psychoanalysis and the Paradoxes of Archivization

1. Freud, "Moses," *SE: XXIII*, 109.

2. Derrida, *Archive Fever*, 95.

3. Derrida's extended example in *Archive Fever* is Freud's outright rejection (sans guilt) of the religious tradition within which he was brought up.

4. Freud, "Totem and Taboo," *SE: XIII*, 141.

5. Interestingly, because totem identity rather than biology determines a bloodline and because the mother's totem is passed on to the children, sexual intercourse between mothers and sons would automatically be seen as incestuous—but not between fathers and daughters. To prohibit father-daughter incest, more complex systems of prohibition become necessary. See Freud, "Totem," *SE: XIII*, 6–17.

6. Freud, "Totem," *SE: XIII*, 141–42.

7. Freud, "Introductory Lectures," *SE: XV*, 335.

8. Freud, "Totem," *SE: XIII*, 141–43.

9. See ibid., 142: "Cannibal savages as they were, it goes without saying that they devoured their victim as well as killing him."

10. Ibid., 142, n. 1.

11. Ibid., 143, n. 1.

12. Ibid., 144, 147–48.

13. Ibid., 144.

14. Ibid., 145.

15. Ibid., 143.

16. Ibid., 144. But this is a weak point in Freud's construction, for there seems to be no reason why the brothers could not in principle simply have agreed to share the women.

17. Freud, "Moses," *SE: XXIII*, 119.

18. Freud, "Totem," *SE: XIII*, 143. Freud "Moses," *SE: XXIII*, 121.

19. Freud, "Moses," *SE: XXIII*, 121.
20. Freud, "Totem," *SE: XIII*, 145.
21. Freud, "Moses," *SE: XXIII*, 134–35.
22. Freud notes that primitives tended to kill the deity if the crops failed.
23. Freud, "Totem," *SE: XIII*, 142.
24. Ibid., 145.
25. Freud, "Introductory Lectures," *SE: XV*, 332: "In a study of the beginnings of human religion and morality . . . I put forward a suggestion that mankind as a whole may have acquired its sense of guilt, the ultimate source of religion and morality, at the beginning of its history, in connection with the Oedipus complex." See also Freud, "Outline," *SE: XXIII*, 187.
26. Or, at least, the degree of success in resolving the Oedipus complex places individuals on a continuum between the extremes of neurosis and health.
27. Freud, "Introductory Lectures," *SE: XV*, 331.
28. Freud, "Outline," *SE: XXIII*, 187–88.
29. Schafer is cited in Stephen A. Mitchell and Margaret J. Black, *Freud and Beyond: A History of Modern Psychoanalytic Thought* (New York: Basic Books, 1995), 16.
30. Freud, "Outline," *SE: XXIII*, 189.
31. Freud, "Introductory Lectures," *SE: XV*, 369.
32. Freud, "Outline," *SE: XXIII*, 189–90. Freud, "Introductory Lectures," *SE: XV*, 317–18.
33. Freud, "The Dissolution of the Oedipus Complex," *SE: XIX*, 176.
34. Freud, "Outline," *SE: XXIII*, 190.
35. Freud, "New Introductory Lectures," *SE: XXII*, 129.
36. Freud, "Outline," *SE: XXIII*, 191.
37. Freud, "Introductory Lectures," *SE: XV*, 311.
38. Notably, Freud argues that a feature of the primitive, narcissistic psychic life of the child is a belief in the omnipotence of thought, whereby imagined and actual deeds are not clearly distinguished. See Freud, "Totem," *SE: XIII*, 5–6.
39. Freud, "Introductory Lectures," *SE: XV*, 337.
40. As noted, Freud does not tire of reiterating that the normal and the pathological form a continuum.
41. Freud, "Introductory Lectures," *SE: XV*, 258–59.
42. Ibid., 260.
43. Ibid., 264.
44. Ibid., 259–60.
45. Ibid., 273.
46. Ibid., 352–59, 374–75.
47. Freud, "Introductory Lectures," *SE: XV*, 301; *Outline*, 186; *Introductory Lectures*, 298–99.
48. Freud, "Outline," *SE: XXIII*, 186.
49. Freud, "Introductory Lectures," *SE: XV*, 309.
50. Freud, "Totem," *SE: XIII*, 26.

51. Freud, "Moses," *SE: XXIII*, 58.

52. Freud, "Outline," *SE: XXIII*, 173–74.

53. Freud, "Outline," *SE: XXIII*, 173.

54. Freud, "Totem," *SE: XIII*, 143. See also Freud, "Introductory Lectures," 335: "Mother-incest was one of the crimes of Oedipus, parricide was the other. It may be remarked in passing that they are also the two great crimes proscribed by totemism, the first socio-religious institution of mankind."

55. From the boy's point of view, it seems, the sisters are disregarded as non-starters in the competitive rivalry for the mother. Of course, one must wonder about single-sex families, but this is all the more reason to view Freud's articulation of the Oedipus complex as a metaphor.

56. Freud, "Outline," *SE: XXIII*, 193.

57. Ibid. One can only smile at how jaw-droppingly little Freud understood concerning the "dark continent" of feminine pleasures.

58. Ibid.

59. Ibid., 194.

60. Jacques Derrida, "Ulysses Gramophone: Hear Say Yes in Joyce," in *A Derrida Reader: Between the Blinds*, ed. Peggy Kamuf, 571–98 (New York: Harvester Wheatsheaf, 1991).

61. The "event of signature" encompasses multiple acts of signification, but I shall focus on the act of "signing" (as inventing or making meaning, as giving out, or putting together "texts" in the broadest sense possible) and to the act of "countersigning" (as interpreting, or reading given texts, as making sense of them).

62. Derrida, "Ulysses," 590.

63. Derrida, "Psyche," 25, 32, 47.

64. Ibid., 41, 46.

65. Ibid., 29.

66. Ibid., 46.

67. Ibid., 26, 28–29. Here, Derrida notes, one could consider "the convergence of several modes of coming or of venue, the enigmatic collusion of *invenire* and *inventio*, of event, of advent, of future or time-to-come (in French, *avenir*), of adventure, and of convention."

68. Freud insisted on this, for example, concerning his "discovery" of the unconscious.

69. Derrida, "Ulysses," 573, 576–77.

70. Derrida, "Psyche," 28.

71. Ibid.

72. Ibid., 48.

73. Ibid., 56–57.

74. Ibid., 46.

75. Ibid., 57.

76. Ibid., 46.

77. Derrida, "Ulysses," 576–77.

78. Derrida, "Psyche," 27–28.
79. Derrida, "Ulysses," 586–89.
80. Lacan, *Ethics*, *S: VII*, 37.

Part 3: Interweaving

1. This logic, to reiterate, articulates three related aporias: the economic aporia of limit, the aneconomic aporia of limitlessness, and the aporia that describes their paradoxical articulation.

2. Lacan, *Ethics*, *S: VII*, 58. Lacan, *Four Fundamental Concepts*, *S: XI*, 50–51, 165, 175, 179.

3. Derrida, "Love of Lacan," 48–53. Derrida is careful to limit his criticism to an isolated Lacanian text and does not pretend to have captured "Lacan" himself, which he believes to be an impossible notion. However, he makes no later amendments to his claims but suggests to the contrary that further reading has only confirmed his critique. I shall return to this in the conclusion.

4. Sheridan, in Lacan, *Écrits: A Selection*, trans. Alan Sheridan (London: Tavistock, 1977), ix.

5. I will return to these notions of "punctuation" and "*Nachträglichkeit*" in the final chapter.

6. This is the kind of "truth" that the later Heidegger elaborates on in *The Principle of Reason*.

7. Sheridan, in Lacan, *Écrits*, x.

8. Sheridan, in Lacan, *Écrits*, x. See also Lacan, *Four Fundamental Concepts*, *S: XI*, 167.

9. Lacan, *Four Fundamental Concepts*, *S: XI*, 53–64.

10. Caputo, *Radical Hermeneutics*, 14–15.

11. Sheridan, in Lacan, *Écrits*, x.

12. Lee, *Jacques Lacan*, 136.

13. Copjec, *Imagine*, 1–9.

14. Lacan, "Feminine Sexuality," *S: XX*, 12. See also 45, 47, 59, 113–14, 120, 126, 144.

15. Fink, "Knowledge and Jouissance," 29.

16. Lacan, "Feminine Sexuality," *S: XX*, 6.

17. Evans, *Introductory Dictionary*, 181.

18. Žižek, "The Real of Sexual Difference," 62. See also, Fink, "Knowledge and Jouissance," 40–43.

19. In *Points*, notably, Derrida speaks of difference *as* sexual difference. See Jacques Derrida, "Choreographies" (correspondence with and trans. by Christie V. McDonald), in *Points . . . Interviews, 1974–1994*, ed. Elisabeth Weber, trans. Peggy Kamuf et al., 89–108 (Stanford, Calif.: Stanford University Press, 1995), 100.

20. Fink, "Knowledge and Jouissance," 36.

21. Ibid., 43.

22. Derrida, *Spurs*.

Chapter 7: The Lacanian Real

1. Copjec, *Imagine*, 104. The interjection in brackets is mine. Its aim is to generalize a snippet taken from Copjec's discussion of racial origins.

2. Lacan, *Four Fundamental Concepts*, *S: XI*, 53–64.

3. See Lacan, *Ethics*, *S: VII*, 30: "Idealism consists in affirming that we are the ones who give shape to reality, and that there is no point in looking any further. It is a comfortable position. Freud's position, or that of any sensible man for that matter, is something very different." See also Lee, *Jacques Lacan*, 23, where Lee describes this difference succinctly: psychoanalysis "offers a vision of knowledge as caught up in an ever-changing dialectic between the data derived from a subject's experience and that subject's complexly mediated identity that shapes the very nature of data."

4. Lacan, *Four Fundamental Concepts*, *S: XI*, 53.

5. Ibid.

6. Ibid., 53–54.

7. Ibid., 55.

8. Lacan, *Ethics, S: VII*, 31.

9. Lacan, "Aggressivity," *E*, 22.

10. Lacan, *Ethics, S: VII*, 31, 44–47.

11. Freud, "The Unconscious," *SE: XIV*, 167.

12. Lacan, *Ethics, S: VII*, 47.

13. Ibid., 31.

14. Lacan, *Four Fundamental Concepts*, *S: XI*, 54.

15. John Forrester, *The Seductions of Psychoanalysis: Freud, Lacan, and Derrida* (Cambridge: Cambridge University Press, 1990), 95–96.

16. Ibid., 95.

17. Lacan, *Four Fundamental Concepts*, *S: XI*, 54.

18. Ibid., 55.

19. Jacques Derrida, "Autoimmunity," 86.

20. Ibid., 90.

21. Lacan, *Four Fundamental Concepts*, *S: XI*, 55.

22. Ibid., 55–56.

23. Derrida, "Autoimmunity," 90–91.

24. Ibid., 86–87.

25. Lacan, *Four Fundamental Concepts*, *S: XI*, 55.

26. Ibid., 56.

27. Ibid.

28. Ibid., 57.

29. Ibid., 57–59.

30. Ibid., 58–59.

31. Ibid., 58.

32. Ibid., 59. See Jacques Derrida, "Circumfession," in *Jacques Derrida*, trans. Geoffrey Bennington (Chicago: The University of Chicago Press, 1993), 6, 13. Here, in a similar vein, Derrida asks whether a reader such as Bennington, even

if he could draw the entire inside outside and subject it to minute analysis, would then know "what blood will have been for me."

33. Lacan, *Four Fundamental Concepts*, *S: XI*, 59.
34. Derrida, *Archive Fever*, 101.
35. Lacan, *Four Fundamental Concepts*, *S: XI*, 60.
36. Ibid., 59.
37. Ibid., 60–61.
38. See Caputo, *Radical Hermeneutics*, 20. I shall address the ethics of psychoanalysis in more detail in chapter 11.
39. Søren Kierkegaard, *Repetition: An Essay in Experimental Psychology*, trans. Walter Lowrie (New York: Harper & Row, 1964).
40. Lacan, *Four Fundamental Concepts*, *S: XI*, 61.
41. This is addressed in greater detail in chapter 8.
42. Kierkegaard, *Repetition*, 35–36.
43. Ibid., 36–37. One should note here that Kierkegaard carefully sets up a thoroughgoing contrast between the two men, for each, in his view, represents a preliminary misunderstood notion of repetition, which the concept "repetition" passes through on the way to attaining itself.
44. Ibid., 39.
45. Ibid., 40.
46. Ibid.
47. Ibid., 41.
48. Ibid., 44.
49. Ibid., 42.
50. Lacan, *Four Fundamental Concepts*, *S: XI*, 61.
51. Caputo, *Radical Hermeneutics*, 14.
52. Kierkegaard, *Repetition*, 52.
53. Lacan, *Four Fundamental Concepts*, *S: XI*, 61.
54. Freud, "Beyond," *SE: XVIII*, 35.
55. Lacan, *Four Fundamental Concepts*, *S: XI*, 61.
56. Kierkegaard, *Repetition*, 45–47.
57. Ibid., 48.
58. Ibid., 82.
59. Ibid., 77.
60. Lacan, *Four Fundamental Concepts*, *S: XI*, 61–62.
61. Cited in Caputo, *Radical Hermeneutics*, 21.
62. Kierkegaard, *Repetition*, 14.
63. Ibid.
64. Ibid., 15.
65. See for confirmation Lacan, *Four Fundamental Concepts*, *S: XI*, 167: "By snatching at its object, the drive learns in a sense that this is precisely not the way it will be satisfied."
66. Copjec, *Read My Desire*, 61.
67. Ibid., 14.

68. Lacan, *Four Fundamental Concepts*, *S: XI*, 63–64.
69. Copjcc, *Imaginc*, 3.
70. Ibid.
71. Ibid., 2.
72. Ibid., 3–4.
73. Ibid., 93.
74. Ibid., 116.
75. Ibid., 4.
76. Ibid., 92.
77. Ibid., 93.
78. Ibid., 116.
79. Ibid., 92.
80. Notably, when Derrida insists on the motif of infinite divisibility in relation to trauma, it is a reference to the endlessness of its "naming." If Lacan insists on the motif of indivisibility, it is a reference to the undeconstructible trauma as that which cannot be erased. The suggestion that this is not a point of disagreement but accord between Lacan and Derrida becomes important when one considers that the question of the divisibility or indivisibility of "the letter" (which, as I aim to demonstrate in chapter 12, functions precisely as a traumatic, transgressive "event") forms the axis around which Derrida's criticism of Lacan's "Seminar on 'The Purloined Letter'" turns.
81. Copjec, *Imagine*, 96.
82. Ibid., 93.
83. See ibid., 42–43. Copjec explains this compounding "inventive sublimation" as analogous to the way in which love sublimates the beloved.
84. Ibid., 96–97.

Chapter 8: Sexual Difference

1. Derrida, "Choreographies," 98.
2. Žižek, "Holding the Place," 309–10.
3. Judith Butler, cited in Žižek, "Holding the Place," 309.
4. Ibid., 308.
5. Ibid., 309.
6. Žižek, "Holding the Place," 308.
7. Žižek, "The Real of Sexual Difference," 73.
8. Ibid., 71.
9. Ibid., 73.
10. Ibid., 61.
11. Ibid., 72.
12. Jacques Derrida, "Geschlecht: Sexual Difference, Ontological Difference," in *A Derrida Reader: Between the Blinds*, ed. Peggy Kamuf, 380–402 (New York: Harvester Wheatsheaf, 1991).
13. Derrida emphasizes this in "Geschlecht II: Heidegger's Hand," trans. John P. Leavey Jr., in *Deconstruction and Philosophy*, ed. John Sallis (Chicago: Chicago University Press, 1987), 161.

14. Derrida, "Geschlecht," 381.

15. Ibid., 382. Including even, Derrida notes, "the analyses of being-in-the-world as being-with-others, or of care either in its self or as *Fürsorge.*"

16. Ibid., 383. Including the structures of "*In-der-Welt-sein als Mit- und Selbst-sein, Räumlichkeit, Befindlichkeit, Rede, Sprache, Geworfenheit, Sorge, Zeitlichkeit, Sein zum Tode.*"

17. Ibid., 380.

18. Ibid., 381. For an elaboration of this argument, see Derrida "Choreographies," 101. I shall return to this later in the exposition.

19. Ibid., 382.

20. Ibid., 383–84. Derrida here cites the course given at the University of Marburg an der Lahn in the summer semester of 1928, entitled *Metaphysische Anfangsgründe der Logik im Ausgang von Leibniz, Gesamt-Ausgabe*, volume 26, and in particular §10, which deals with *"the problem of transcendence and the problem of SEIN UND ZEIT.*"

21. This juxtaposition is echoed in a second place of deafening silence in the Heideggerian text, to which he turns in the second moment of his reading.

22. Derrida, "Geschlecht," 384.

23. Ibid., 385.

24. Ibid., 384.

25. Ibid., 384–85.

26. Ibid., 384.

27. Ibid., 385.

28. Ibid., 386

29. Ibid., 385. Yet, as Derrida points out, if one reads further in Heidegger's works, this easy interpretation quite soon begins to unravel, and it is entirely undone by the time that "*Geschlecht*" has accumulated its "polysemic richness: sex, genre, family, stock, race, lineage, generation" and the Heideggerian text has unsettled itself as a consequence of the aporias engendered by this complexity. This remark adumbrates the broader concerns of the seminar to which this was an introduction. These are elaborated to some extent in the essay that follows on from this one, namely "Geschlecht II."

30. Ibid., 384–85.

31. Ibid., 388.

32. Ibid., 386–87.

33. Ibid., 388. This does not make libido homogeneous—it remains differentiated according to three libidinal styles. I will take this up in the next section.

34. Ibid.

35. Both Derrida and Lacan adapt and generalize this Hegelian insight according to the logic of the "mugger's choice" associated with all binaries.

36. Derrida, "Choreographies," 100–101.

37. Derrida, "Geschlecht," 388.

38. Assuming the Derridean deconstructive modification to come, the equivalent of Heidegger's ontological difference in Lacanian discourse may quite easily

be found in the difference Lacan proposes between phenomenal reality and the traumatic Real. In other words, for him, as for Derrida, "sexuality" and all of the other "universals" that constellate around the term *Geschlecht* remain traumatic, empty signifiers.

39. Derrida, "Geschlecht," 388.

40. Ibid., 388–89.

41. Ibid., 389. Libido must take an embodied form that is either male or female, but libido itself exceeds determination in terms of sexual difference.

42. Ibid.

43. Lacan, *Feminine Sexuality, S: XX*, 84–88.

44. This was discussed in chapter 5.

45. Lacan, *Feminine Sexuality, S: XX*, 6.

46. Fink, "Knowledge and Jouissance," 40. See also, Lacan, *Feminine Sexuality, S: XX*, 9: "Jouissance, qua sexual, is phallic." Again, "when one loves, it has nothing to do with sex" (25), and "the Other presents itself to the subject only in an *a*-sexual form. Everything that has been the prop, substitute-prop, or substitute for the Other in the form of the object of desire is *a*-sexual" (127).

47. Paul Verhaeghe, "Lacan's Answer," 111–12.

48. Suzanne Barnard, "Tongues of Angels: Feminine Structure and Other Jouissance," in *Reading Seminar XX: Lacan's Major Work on Love, Knowledge, and Feminine Sexuality*, ed. Suzanne Barnard and Bruce Fink (Albany, N.Y.: SUNY Press, 2002), 176.

49. Lacan, *Feminine Sexuality, S: XX*, 11.

50. Derrida, "Geschlecht," 389–90.

51. Ibid., 390.

52. Ibid.

53. Ibid., 390–91.

54. Ibid., 391.

55. Ibid., 391–92.

56. Ibid., 392.

57. Ibid., 393.

58. Ibid. The "supplementary turn" that Derrida has in mind here concerns what befalls the positive, economic motif of possibility when it is found that the negative, aneconomic motif of fatality, entropy, or the death drive cannot be altogether reduced out of the picture.

59. Ibid.

60. Ibid., 394.

61. Ibid., 395.

62. Ibid., 396.

63. Ibid.

64. Ibid., 396–97.

65. Ibid., 397.

66. Žižek, "The Real of Sexual Difference," 61–64.

67. Ibid., 61.

68. Ibid., 61–62. As hinted at by the names Žižek gives these two subgroups, this analogy may be extended to a political space divided into Left and Right, each with different perceptions of, as Žižek puts it, "the very disposition of the political space—a leftist as the field that is inherently split by some fundamental antagonism, a rightist as the organic unity of a Community disturbed only by foreign intruders."

69. Ibid., 62.

70. Ibid.

71. Ibid., 63–64.

72. Ibid., 62.

73. Ibid., 62–63.

74. Ibid., 63.

75. Derrida, "Geschlecht," 398.

76. Ibid.

77. Ibid.

78. Ibid., 398–99.

79. Ibid., 399.

80. Ibid.

81. Ibid., 400.

82. Ibid.

83. Ibid., 401.

84. Ibid.

85. Ibid.

Chapter 9: Feminine Sexuality

1. Derrida, "Geschlecht," 401.

2. Žižek, "The Real of Sexual Difference," 57.

3. Lee, *Jacques Lacan*, 61. According to Lee, the term *point de capiton* refers to the "'anchoring points' or 'buttons' that keep upholstery attached to the framework of a piece of furniture."

4. Jacques Lacan, "The Signification of the Phallus," in *Écrits: A Selection*, trans. Alan Sheridan (New York: W. W. Norton, 1977), 285.

5. Žižek, "The Real of Sexual Difference," 58.

6. Ibid., 57–58.

7. Ibid., 58.

8. Ibid.

9. In an unholy mix of gender stereotyping, Nietzsche, for example, mocks philosophy for styling itself as quintessentially masculine, while in truth, he argues, philosophers are really merely women, since they belong in the ranks of the castrating castrated.

10. Nietzsche, *Beyond Good and Evil*, 31; §23.

11. Derrida, *Spurs*, 101. The interjection of Lacan's notorious remark is mine.

12. Ibid., 95–101. Notably, again resisting the kind of reading that reduces "Derrida's operation" to its aneconomic moment, Derrida insists: "to use parody

or the simulacrum as a weapon in the service of truth or castration would be in fact to reconstitute religion, as a Nietzsche cult, for example, in the interest of a priesthood of parody interpreters" (100).

13. Ibid., 95.

14. Ibid., 97, 101. Notably, these propositions, respectively, match the economic/paranoiac, aneconomic/hysterical, and paradoxical libidinal styles that constitute the matrix of the Lacanian account of the transcendental relation, to be discussed in the next chapter.

15. Derrida, *Spurs*, 87. Nietzsche, *Twilight of the Idols*, 40.

16. Nietzsche, *Beyond Good and Evil*, 53; §43.

17. Derrida, "Ulysses," 577–81. Notably, the sign of inventive "signature" is inscribed in the word "countersignature," rendering it aporetic.

18. Nietzsche, *Beyond Good and Evil*, 53; §43.

19. Ibid., 51; §40.

20. Lacan, "Signification of the Phallus," 285.

21. Derrida, *Spurs*, 87.

22. Ibid., 89.

23. Nietzsche, *Beyond Good and Evil*, 16; §9.

24. Ibid., 12; §5.

25. Ibid., 13; §6.

26. Ibid., 13–14; §6.

27. See especially ibid., 162–70; §§232–39.

28. Nietzsche, *Gay Science*, 125; §64.

29. Nietzsche, *Beyond Good and Evil*, 1 (preface).

30. Ibid., 130; §208.

31. Derrida, *Spurs*, 89.

32. Nietzsche, *Beyond Good and Evil*, 163; §232.

33. Derrida, *Spurs*, 53, 61, 97.

34. Nietzsche, *Beyond Good and Evil*, 89–90; §148.

35. Ibid., 16; §9.

36. Ibid., 35–37; §25.

37. Derrida, *Spurs*, 89.

38. Nietzsche, *Beyond Good and Evil*, 21; §13.

39. Ibid., 27; §20.

40. Ibid., 36; §25.

41. Ibid., 134–35; §210.

42. Nietzsche, *Twilight of the Idols*, 43; cited in Derrida, *Spurs*, 93.

43. Nietzsche, *Beyond Good and Evil*, 12; §4.

44. Nietzsche, *Gay Science*, 123–24; §60. Derrida, *Spurs*, 47–49.

45. Derrida, *Spurs*, 49.

46. Ibid.

47. Ibid.

48. Ibid., 51.

49. *Gay Science*, 271–72; §339. Cited in Derrida, *Spurs*, 51–53.

50. Derrida, *Spurs*, 53.
51. Ibid.
52. Ibid., 55.
53. Ibid., 65.
54. Nietzsche, *Beyond Good and Evil*, 162; §231.
55. Ibid., 36; §25.
56. Ibid., 12; §5.
57. I say the feminine, without wishing to invoke any kind of "feminism," because I agree with Derrida that insofar as it becomes ideological, feminism is a repetition of the masculine gesture. Derrida, *Spurs*, 65.
58. Derrida, *Spurs*, 61.

Part 4: Lacan and the "Plural Logic of the Aporia"

1. Fink, *The Lacanian Subject*, xv–xvi.
2. Lee, *Jacques Lacan*, 13–15.
3. Ibid., 21.
4. Ibid., 13–14, 20.
5. Ibid., 20.
6. Copjec, *Imagine*, 50.
7. Žižek, "The Real of Sexual Difference," 70.
8. Copjec, *Imagine*, 37.
9. Ibid., 5–9, 16, 100.
10. Lacan, *Feminine Sexuality*, *S: XX*, 71–72. The terms masculine and feminine are metaphors: Concerning the masculine style or phallic function, Lacan remarks: "One ultimately situates oneself there by choice—women are free to situate themselves there if it gives them pleasure to do so. Everyone knows there are phallic women, and that the phallic function doesn't stop men from being homosexuals." Similarly, any speaking being, he insists, can situate itself under the banner "women."
11. I shall discuss the example of Antigone in a later chapter.
12. Fink, *The Lacanian Subject*, xii.
13. Ibid., xii–xiii.
14. Ibid., xiii.
15. Lee, *Jacques Lacan*, 64.
16. Lacan's "Seminar on 'The Purloined Letter'" and the critical essay by Barbara Johnson, "The Frame of Reference," appear together in *The Purloined Poe: Lacan, Derrida, and Psychoanalytic Reading*, ed. John P. Muller and William J. Richardson (Baltimore, Md.: The Johns Hopkins University Press, 1988). Derrida's reading of Lacan's "Seminar on 'The Purloined Letter'" may be found in Jacques Derrida, "Le Facteur de la Vérité," in *The Post Card: From Socrates to Freud and Beyond*, trans. Alan Bass (Chicago: The University of Chicago Press, 1987). The protocols for reading Lacan that stem from this reading are listed in Derrida, "Love of Lacan," 53–69.

Chapter 10: The Transcendental Relation in Lacanian Psychoanalysis

1. Freud, "Civilization," *SE: XXI*, 68.

2. Copjec, *Imagine*, 33.

3. Ibid., 50: As Copjec puts it: "The mouth is no longer simply that which ingests or spews out, but also and significantly that which kisses and sensuously sucks."

4. Lacan, *Four Fundamental Concepts, S: XI*, 197–98.

5. Freud, "Beyond," *SE: XVIII*, 26.

6. Lacan, *Four Fundamental Concepts, S: XI*, 199.

7. Ibid., 177. Lacan underscores the paradoxical nature of the drives, citing a well-known Heraclitean fragment: "*To the bow (Biós) . . . is given the name of life* (*Bíos*, the accent being this time on the first syllable) *and its work is death*."

8. Ibid., 205.

9. Freud, "Beyond," *SE: XVIII*, 40–41, 55.

10. Lacan, *Four Fundamental Concepts, S: XI*, 205.

11. This is assuming that we moderns, having given up on the idea of immortality as an atemporal eternity, must find a sense of immortality that takes account of time. See Copjec, *Imagine*, 20–21.

12. See Copjec, *Imagine*, 23.

13. Ibid., 51.

14. Ibid., 34.

15. Lacan, *Four Fundamental Concepts, S: XI*, 64. The fear of castration, or of permanent loss, precipitated by the gap opened up in the object of the drives, as Lacan remarks, "is like a thread that perforates all the stages of development. It orientates the relations that are anterior to its actual appearance—weaning, toilet training, etc. It crystallizes each of these moments in a dialectic that has at its center a bad encounter."

16. Ibid., 176.

17. Evans, *Introductory Dictionary*, 124.

18. Fink, *The Lacanian Subject*, xiii.

19. Lacan, *Ethics, S: VII*, 52: According to Lacan, one imagines that *das Ding* "will be there when in the end all conditions have been fulfilled." Again: "The world of our experience, the Freudian world, assumes that it is the object, *das Ding*, as the absolute Other of the subject, that one is supposed to find again."

20. Ibid.: "It is, of course, clear that what is supposed to be found cannot be found again. It is in its nature that the object as such is lost. It will never be found again. Something is there while one waits for something better, or worse, but which one wants." Further: "It is to be found at the most as something missed. One doesn't find it, but only its pleasurable associations."

21. Ibid., 52–53.

22. Notably, Lacan offers here the articulated "structural" logic of these relations and not a psychological account of what would make a particular infant gravitate toward a particular libidinal style.

23. Freud, "Project," *SE: I*, 331. Cited in Copjec, *Imagine*, 34. The ensuing discussion draws primarily from a reading of Copjec's account of what she calls the Kantian analogy.

24. Copjec, *Imagine*, 35.

25. Cited in Lee, *Jacques Lacan*, 14.

26. Lacan, *Ethics*, *S: VII*, 58.

27. Copjec, *Imagine*, 35.

28. Freud, "On Narcissism," *SE: XIV*, 96. Notably, according to Freud, paranoiacs construct speculative systems.

29. Copjec, *Imagine*, 35.

30. Copjec, *Imagine*, 35–37. Lacan, *Four Fundamental Concepts*, *S: XI*, 106.

31. Copjec, *Imagine*, 53.

32. Ibid., 54.

33. Lacan, *Four Fundamental Concepts*, *S: XI*, 180.

34. Ibid., 167.

35. See Kaja Silverman, *The Threshold of the Visible World* (New York: Routledge, 1996), 75: "to elevate an object to the status of the Thing is to constitute it as an *objet a.*"

36. Copjec, *Imagine*, 51–53.

37. Slavoj Žižek, "Why Does a *Letter* Always Arrive at its Destination?" in *Enjoy Your Symptom: Jacques Lacan in Hollywood and Out* (New York: Routledge, 1992), 15: "the subject pursues his everyday life within its closed horizon of meaning, safe in his distance with respect to the world of objects, assured of their meaning (or their insignificance), when, all of a sudden, the psychoanalyst pinpoints some tiny detail of no significance whatsoever to the subject, a stain in which the subject 'sees nothing'—a small, compulsive gesture or tic, a slip of the tongue or something of that order—and says: 'you see, this detail is a knot which condenses all you had to forget so that you can swim in your everyday certainty, it enframes the very frame which confers meaning on your life, it structures the horizon within which things make sense to you; if we unknot it, you will lose the ground from under your very feet!' "

38. Copjec, *Imagine*, 34.

39. Ibid.

40. Lacan, "Aggressivity," *E*, 18. According to Dylan Evans, the term "captation" is a neologism not coined by Lacan but adopted by him "to refer to the imaginary effects of the specular image," which has an ambiguous power. "On the one hand, it has the sense of 'captivation,' thus expressing the fascinating, seductive power of the image. On the other hand, the term also conveys the idea of 'capture,' which evokes the more sinister power of the image to imprison the subject in a disabling fiction." Dylan Evans, *Introductory Dictionary*, 20.

41. If Freud associated such narcissistic imitation and identification primarily with the dissolution of the Oedipus complex and the constitution of an ideal ego under the threat of castration, Lacan insists that narcissistic imitation and identification occur much earlier, in the *infans*, or preverbal, stage of development.

42. Lacan, "Aggressivity," *E*, 22.

43. Lacan, "The Mirror Stage," *E*, 4.

44. Lacan, "Aggressivity," *E*, 18.

45. Ibid., 18.

46. Lacan, "The Mirror Stage," *E*, 2.

47. I have here used as a guide the broad outline offered by Lee, *Jacques Lacan*, 19–20.

48. Lacan, "Aggressivity," *E*, 18. According to Lacan, it is not noticeable in chimps, for example, who are at this age ahead of humans in instrumental intelligence.

49. Lacan, "The Mirror Stage," *E*, 2.

50. Lacan, "Aggressivity," *E*, 18. As Lacan notes, an infant is capable of recognizing a mirror image as its own before it is able to control and integrate its bodily movements.

51. Lacan, "The Mirror Stage," *E*, 2.

52. Lee, *Jacques Lacan*, 18.

53. Lacan, "The Mirror Stage," *E*, 6.

54. Ibid., 2. Lee, *Jacques Lacan*, 19: "Orthopaedic" suggests "a totality that makes the child proper or correct in its form."

55. Lacan, "The Mirror Stage," *E*, 4.

56. Ibid.

57. Lee, *Jacques Lacan*, 19.

58. Lacan, "The Mirror Stage," *E*, 5.

59. Lacan, "Aggressivity," *E*, 18.

60. Ibid., 19.

61. Lacan, "The Mirror Stage," *E*, 5.

62. Lee, *Jacques Lacan*, 20.

63. Fink, *The Lacanian Subject*, xii.

64. Lacan, "Aggressivity," *E*, 16. Notably, Lacan takes pains to stress that narcissism and aggressivity are correlative: "Aggressivity is the correlative tendency of a mode of identification that we call narcissistic, and which determines the formal structure of man's ego and of the register of entities characteristic of his world."

65. Ibid., 21.

66. Ibid., 10.

67. Ibid., 11.

68. Lee, *Jacques Lacan*, 25.

69. Lacan, "The Mirror Stage," *E*, 6.

70. Lacan, "Aggressivity," *E*, 11.

71. Ibid.

72. Ibid., 21.

73. Lacan, "The Mirror Stage," *E*, 2.

74. Lacan, "Aggressivity," *E*, 16–17. Lacan lists these as "rising in stages from a motivation based on the register of a highly primitive organicism (poison), to

a magical one (evil spells), a telepathic one (influence), a lesional one (physical intrusion), an abusive one (distortion of intention), a dispossessive one (appropriation of secrets), a profanatory one (violation of intimacy), a juridical one (prejudice), a persecutive one (spying and intimidation), one involving prestige (defamation and attacks on one's honour), and revenge (damage and exploitation)."

75. Ibid., 17.

76. Ibid.

77. Lacan, "The Mirror Stage," *E*, 5.

78. Lacan, "Aggressivity," *E*, 17.

79. Lacan, "The Mirror Stage," *E*, 2.

80. Lacan, "Aggressivity," *E*, 18.

81. Ibid.

82. Lacan, "The Mirror Stage," *E*, 5.

83. Lacan, "Aggressivity," *E*, 20.

84. Ibid., 13.

85. Ibid.

86. Copjec, *Imagine*, 121.

87. Copjec, *Imagine*, 159–161. I have lifted Copjec's distinction between jealousy and envy from a text that deals with the distinction between feminine sublimation on the one hand and masculine idealization on the other and which therefore places both jealousy and envy on the same (masculine) side of the equation. Although I have complexified my account to include the aneconomic feminine moment of "anti-idealization," I do not think that it clashes with Copjec's, for, taken in contrast with feminine sublimation, both masculine idealism and the feminine counterpart (intrinsically tied together by the vel of alienation) fall on the same side of the equation.

88. Ibid., 160.

89. Lacan, "The Function and Field of Speech and Language in Psychoanalysis," *E*, 86.

90. Joan Copjec, "Sex and the Euthanasia of Reason," in *Supposing the Subject*, ed. Joan Copjec (London: Verso, 1994), 19–20.

91. Lacan, *Ethics*, *S: VII*, 263–70.

92. Cf. Derrida's account of the paradoxical relation between law and justice as outlined in "Force of Law." Three related aporias are outlined in chapter 3.

93. Freud, "Civilization," *SE: XXI*, 103.

94. Ibid., 103–4.

95. Lacan, *Four Fundamental Concepts*, *S: XI*, 165.

96. Ibid., 166.

97. Freud, "New Introductory Lectures," *SE: XXII*, 129: If in boys the castration complex dissolves the Oedipus complex, in girls it prepares the way for entry into it. Penis envy for her leads her to reject the mother and transfer her libidinal desires to her father. She has no motive for surmounting the Oedipus complex, since the fear of castration is lacking. For this reason, she remains in it for an

indeterminate length of time, demolishes it late and, even so, incompletely. "In these circumstances the formation of the super-ego must suffer; it cannot attain the strength and independence which give it its cultural significance."

98. Freud, "Civilization," *SE: XXI*, 104.

99. Freud, "New Introductory Lectures," *SE: XXII*, 129.

100. See Silverman, *Subject of Semiotics*, 144–45.

101. Recall that Lacan emphasizes such singularity by replacing death as merely the demise of the body with the paradoxical libidinal notion of the death drive.

102. Copjec, *Imagine*, 23.

Chapter 11: The Death Drive and Ethical Action

1. Copjec, *Imagine*, 14.

2. Ibid.

3. The film tends to support the contention that a person who believes that "life that costs freedom isn't life" ought to have the right to choose death.

4. Kant, *Critique of Judgment*, 135/Ak 275. The irony is that, on this definition, Hegel, having criticized fanaticism in the ethical domain, turns out to be the ultimate fanatic. It is, moreover, Kant, for whom Hegel reserves his most vociferous criticism, who initiates the tradition of thinking that enables one to resist Hegel's ultimate fanaticism.

5. Copjec, *Imagine*, 17.

6. Lacan, *Ethics, S: VII*, 254. Copjec, *Imagine*, 15.

7. Lacan, *Ethics, S: VII*, 254.

8. Recall that Lacan, like Derrida, argues that the Real is not a unity, an ordered plurality, or an atomistic freeplay, but the paradoxical split in being, prefigured by Freud, for which he offers various nicknames that match Derrida's *différance*.

9. Lacan, *Feminine Sexuality, S: XX*, 93.

10. Derrida, *Glas*, 4.

11. Ibid.

12. Ibid., 147–49.

13. Ibid., 175.

14. One is reminded of the number series: not only can one more always be added, but between each number lies an infinity of fractions.

15. Lacan, *Ethics, S: VII*, 29–30.

16. For more detailed treatment of what is schematized here, one may refer particularly to the first and fourth chapters of Copjec's *Imagine*. The first (12–47) deals with the *Antigone* specifically, in terms of Eros and sublimation. The fourth (108–131) has more to say concerning masculine and feminine approaches to the problem of "the All."

17. The following discussion of these masculine and feminine positions draws from various parts of Copjec's *Imagine*. See particularly her discussions of immortality (19–25), feminine sublimation (38–40), superego idealism (45–47), the Real in Lacan (95–97), the masculine and feminine problems of the All (6–9, 115–118), and evil (134–150).

18. Copjec, *Imagine*, 4–6.
19. Silverman, *Acoustic Mirror*, 2.
20. Lacan, *Ethics*, *S: VII*, 259.
21. Copjec, *Imagine*, 20.
22. Ibid., 21, 24.
23. Ibid., 22–24.
24. Ibid., 173–74.
25. Ibid., 44–45.
26. Ibid., 137.
27. Ibid., 25.
28. Ibid., 27.
29. Freud, "New Introductory Lectures," *SE: XXII*, 63–67.
30. Copjec, *Imagine*, 46.
31. Ibid.
32. Ibid., 138.
33. Ibid., 46–47, 115–17.
34. Lacan, *Ethics*, *S: VII*, 259.
35. Copjec, *Imagine*, 117–18.
36. Alenka Zupančič, *Ethics of the Real: Kant, Lacan* (New York: Verso, 2000), 236.
37. Žižek, "The Real of Sexual Difference," 59.
38. Ibid.
39. Ibid., 59–60.
40. Copjec, *Imagine*, 22–23.
41. Lacan, *Ethics*, *S: VII*, 311. The ambiguity of these formulations is repeated in the following question posed by Lacan: "Have you acted in conformity with your desire?"
42. Freud, "New Introductory Lectures," *SE: XXII*, 80.
43. Zupančič, *Ethics of the Real*, 217.
44. Lacan *S: II*, 228–29, cited in Evans, *Introductory Dictionary*, 36.
45. Evans, *Introductory Dictionary*, 36.
46. Copjec, *Imagine*, 38–40, 42–45.
47. Ibid., 42–43.
48. Notably, this mirrors Kierkegaard's comments concerning the self-reflective activity that makes of the ego both what it is and more than what it is.

Chapter 12: The "Talking Cure": Language and Psychoanalysis

1. Lacan, "Purloined Letter Seminar," 29. Edgar Allan Poe's tale "The Purloined Letter," appears in Thomas Ollive Mabbott, "Text of 'The Purloined Letter,' with Notes," in *The Purloined Poe, Lacan, Derrida, and Psychoanalytic Reading*, ed. John P. Muller and William J. Richardson (Baltimore, Md.: The Johns Hopkins University Press, 1988).
2. Lacan, "Function and Field," *E*, 39.
3. See, for example, Lee, *Jacques Lacan*, 34.

4. It is quite easy to see in Lacan's seminar on "The Purloined Letter" an important precursor to Lacan's seminar on the Four Discourses. I will not attempt any detailed comparison, suffice it to suggest that one can find the equivalent of the Master's discourse in the "masculine" subject position as represented by the King. The discourse of Knowledge finds its equivalent again in the masculine subject position, but this time as represented by the Prefect of Police. The Hysteric's discourse finds its match in the feminine subject position, represented most obviously by the Queen, and the Analyst's discourse matches the feminine-analytical subject position represented here, albeit improperly in both cases, by the Minister and Dupin. See Mark Bracher, "On the Psychological and Social Functions of Language," in *Lacanian Theory of Discourse: Subject, Structure, and Society*, ed. Mark Bracher et al. (New York: New York University Press, 1994).

5. Here I go along with Muller and Richardson, who argue that Lacan's interpretation of Poe's story demonstrates that there is a third scene through which the reader/analyst (in this case Lacan) is drawn into the tale. See John P. Muller and William J. Richardson, "Lacan's Seminar on 'The Purloined Letter': Overview," in Muller and Richardson, eds., *The Purloined Poe*, 61–62.

6. Lacan, "Purloined Letter Seminar," 33. But perhaps as much, in the end, for his production of them, for as Lacan hints, one should not miss the homophony between Dupin and dupe, making of C. Auguste Dupin an impressive gamer, player, or trickster.

7. Lacan, "Purloined Letter Seminar," 38. As Lacan points out, in associating mathematical and instrumental or technical reasoning and in contrasting this kind of reasoning with poetical thinking, Dupin operates with a reductive and inaccurate conception of mathematics, which Lacan considers to be far closer to poetical thinking.

8. The scare quotes are there as a reminder that this "thing" will function not as a physical object but rather as *das Ding* or object "a."

9. See Johnson, "Frame of Reference," 216. Johnson points out here that the only exception to direct quotation made by the narrator of the tale occurs as a most telling reversal of convention, precisely where one would expect the letter's message to be revealed. At the moment when, responding to Dupin's request, the Prefect reads out aloud a minutely accurate description of the letter's internal and external appearance, the narrator shifts from direct quotation to paraphrase. As Johnson notes, "whereas it is generally supposed that the function of paraphrase is to strip off the form of a speech in order to give us only its contents, here the use of paraphrase does the very opposite: it withholds the contents of the Prefect's remarks, giving us only their form."

10. Lacan, "Purloined Letter Seminar," 41–42.

11. This turn of phrase is somewhat unfortunate because of the accumulated metaphysical baggage associated with the dream of purity and also, perhaps, because the notion of a "pure" signifier makes no sense if signifier and signified always already imply one another and belong together, like, as Saussure puts it, either side of a sheet of paper. Nevertheless, the notion of "event" that Lacan is

trying to point to with these words is clearly enough not a matter of the metaphysics of presence.

12. Lacan, "Purloined Letter Seminar," 39.

13. Ibid.

14. I shall return to this important point in the conclusion of this study.

15. The word (neither still light nor yet dark) picks up on a thoroughgoing Heideggerian thread in Lacan's analysis that associates "truth" with the paradoxical covering/uncovering or veiling movement of *aletheia*.

16. Lee, *Jacques Lacan*, 35–37.

17. Ibid., 38.

18. Ibid., 37. This is in turn a response to Saussure's call for the development of " 'semiology' as a '*science that studies the life of signs within a society.*' "

19. Lacan, "The Agency of the Letter in the Unconscious: Or Reason Since Freud," *E*, 154.

20. Lee, *Jacques Lacan*, 66–67.

21. Ibid., 67.

22. Ibid., 61–62.

23. Ibid., 59.

24. Ibid., 60.

25. Ibid., 59.

26. Ibid., 67.

27. Lacan, "Purloined Letter Seminar," 32.

28. Ibid.

29. One may acquire this insight quite intuitively without its theorization, which would amount to making the "transcendental" and "linguistic" turns (shorthand for an awareness not only of the constituted nature of reality but also of the linguistic dimension in the process of constitution). The glance of the Queen represents this insight, which is a precondition for, but not a guarantee of, the movement beyond it to the poststructural thinking attributed by Lacan to the subject position of analyst. One may know that all systems, institutions, etc. are artificially constituted, but it takes a Kant, or later a Lacan or a Derrida, to explain why.

30. Lacan, "Purloined Letter Seminar," 42.

31. Ibid., 32.

32. Ibid., 31.

33. Ibid., 45.

34. Ibid., 34.

35. Ibid., 42.

36. Ibid., 45.

37. Ibid., 32.

38. Ibid.

39. Ibid.

40. Ibid., 40.

41. Ibid., 39.

42. Ibid., 50.

43. Ibid. See also Lacan, "Function and Field," *E*, 45. Here Lacan gives the basis of his critique of a certain kind of psychology: "The analyst is vouchsafed no other reality of the analysand than that of his speech (and the language behind it). To search for a reality lying behind or beyond the analysand's speech is for the analyst to give in to the temptation of misrecognizing for the analysand's *moi* the analyst's own imaginary projections." Again, Lacan, "Function and Field," *E*, 44: "nothing could be more misleading for the analyst than to seek to guide himself by some supposed 'contact' experienced with the reality of the subject."

44. Poe, "The Purloined Letter," 15.

45. Lacan, "Purloined Letter Seminar," 40.

46. Ibid., 44.

47. Ibid., 45.

48. Ibid., 44.

49. Ibid.

50. Ibid.

51. Poe, "The Purloined Letter," 23.

52. Lee, *Jacques Lacan*, 80.

53. Lacan, "Purloined Letter Seminar," 34.

54. Poe, "The Purloined Letter," 7.

55. Ibid.

56. Lacan, "Purloined Letter Seminar," 34.

57. Ibid., 49.

58. Ibid., 33.

59. Ibid., 49.

60. Ibid., 36.

61. Ibid., 42: Lacan suggests, further, that Poe allows Dupin to let slip key words that uncover the conditions of his narration (*ambitus*, *religio*, and *homines honesti*), none of which are what they seem on the face of it. See also note 17 to Poe's "The Purloined Letter," in *The Purloined Poe*, 25.

62. Johnson, "Frame of Reference," 220.

63. Poe, "The Purloined Letter," 23.

64. Lacan, "Aggressivity," *E*, 9.

65. Lacan, "Function and Field," *E*, 40.

66. Ibid., 87.

67. Ibid., 40.

68. Ibid.

69. Ibid., 41–56.

70. Lee, *Jacques Lacan*, 39–40.

71. Ibid., 69.

72. Lacan, "Function and Field," *E*, 41.

73. This contradiction is starkly illustrated in relation to medical care in South Africa, where no person, no matter how urgently in need of medical attention, will be admitted to a "private hospital" without *first* producing verification

of medical aid membership or, alternatively, handing over an obscene sum of money. One should bear in mind here that the alternative (admission to a state hospital) is widely regarded as the equivalent of signing one's own death certificate.

74. Lee, *Jacques Lacan*, 78–79.
75. Ibid., 79.
76. Lacan, "Function and Field," *E*, 47–48.
77. Lee, *Jacques Lacan*, 44.
78. Ibid., 43.
79. Lacan, "Function and Field," *E*, 81.
80. Lacan, "Aggressivity," *E*, 10.
81. Lacan, "Function and Field," *E*, 98–99.
82. Ibid., 44.
83. Lee, *Jacques Lacan*, 89.
84. Lacan, "Function and Field," *E*, 46.
85. Lacan, "The Mirror Stage," *E*, 7.
86. Lee, *Jacques Lacan*, 91–92.
87. Ibid., 89.
88. Lacan, "Function and Field," *E*, 47–48.

Conclusion: To Do Justice to Lacan

1. Derrida, "Resistances," 69.
2. Derrida, "Love of Lacan," 55.
3. Ibid., 54.
4. Ibid., 48–49.
5. Ibid., 49.
6. Ibid., 57–59.
7. Ibid., 59.
8. Ibid., 59–60.
9. Derrida, "Resistances," 33.
10. Derrida, "Love of Lacan," 42–43.
11. Ibid., 42.
12. Ibid., 65.
13. Ibid., 54.
14. Ibid., 56.
15. Johnson, "Frame of Reference," 242.
16. Derrida, "Love of Lacan," 44.
17. Lacan, "Purloined Letter Seminar," 43.
18. Derrida, "Love of Lacan," 57.
19. Derrida, "Le Facteur," 493.
20. Cited in Joseph H. Smith and William Kerrigan, "Introduction," in *Taking Chances: Derrida, Psychoanalysis, and Literature*, eds. Joseph H. Smith and William Kerrigan (Baltimore, Md.: The Johns Hopkins University Press, 1984), xiv.

21. Johnson, "Frame of Reference," 227.
22. Derrida, *Aporias,* 13.
23. Lacan, "Purloined Letter Seminar," 39.
24. Žižek, *Enjoy your Symptom,* 9–10.
25. Johnson, "Frame of Reference," 226.
26. Ibid., 227.
27. Smith and Kerrigan, in *Taking Chances,* xi.
28. Ibid., xiv.
29. Johnson, "Frame of Reference," 227.
30. Cited in Lacan, "Purloined Letter Seminar," 36.
31. See Muller and Richardson's notes to Lacan's seminar, in *The Purloined Poe,* 89.
32. Derrida, "Le Facteur," 413.
33. Miller, *Extimité,* 74.
34. Jacques Derrida, "Psychoanalysis Searches the States of Its Soul: The Impossible Beyond of a Sovereign Cruelty," in *Without Alibi,* ed. and trans. Peggy Kamuf (Palo Alto, Calif.: Stanford University Press, 2002), 250–52.

Bibliography

Alcorn, Marshall W. Jr. "The Subject of Discourse: Reading Lacan Through (and Beyond) Poststructuralist Contexts." In *Lacanian Theory of Discourse: Subject, Structure, and Society*, edited by Mark Bracher et al., 19–45. New York: New York University Press, 1994.

Barnard, Suzanne. "Tongues of Angels: Feminine Structure and Other Jouissance." In *Reading Seminar XX: Lacan's Major Work on Love, Knowledge, and Feminine Sexuality*, edited by Suzanne Barnard and Bruce Fink, 171–85. Albany: SUNY Press, 2002.

Bennington, Geoffrey, and Jacques Derrida. *Jacques Derrida*. Chicago: The University of Chicago Press, 1993.

Blackburn, Simon. *The Oxford Dictionary of Philosophy*. Oxford: Oxford University Press, 1994.

Bracher, Mark. "On the Psychological and Social Functions of Language." In *Lacanian Theory of Discourse: Subject, Structure, and Society*, edited by M. Bracher et al., 107–28. New York: New York University Press, 1994.

Bracher, Mark, Marshall W. Alcorn Jr., Ronald J. Corthell, and Françoise Massardier-Kenney, eds. *Lacanian Theory of Discourse: Subject, Structure, and Society*. New York: New York University Press, 1994.

Butler, Judith, Ernesto Laclau, and Slavoj Žižek. *Contingency, Hegemony, Universality: Contemporary Dialogues on the Left*. New York: Verso, 2000.

Caputo, John D. *Against Ethics: Contributions to a Poetics of Obligation with Constant Reference to Deconstruction.* Bloomington: Indiana University Press, 1993.

———, ed. *Deconstruction in a Nutshell: A Conversation with Jacques Derrida.* New York: Fordham University Press, 1997.

———. *Demythologizing Heidegger.* Bloomington: Indiana University Press, 1993.

———. *More Radical Hermeneutics: On Not Knowing Who We Are.* Bloomington: Indiana University Press, 2000.

———. *Radical Hermeneutics: Repetition, Deconstruction, and the Hermeneutic Project.* Bloomington: Indiana University Press, 1987.

Copjec, Joan. *Imagine There's No Woman: Ethics and Sublimation.* Cambridge, Mass.: The MIT Press, 2002.

———. *Read My Desire: Lacan Against the Historicists.* Cambridge, Mass.: The MIT Press, 1994.

———. "Sex and the Euthanasia of Reason." In *Supposing the Subject,* edited by Joan Copjec, 16–44. London: Verso, 1994.

Derrida, Jacques. *Aporias.* Translated by Thomas Dutoit. Stanford, Calif.: Stanford University Press, 1993.

———. *Archive Fever: A Freudian Impression.* Translated by Eric Prenowitz. Chicago: The University of Chicago Press, 1996.

———. "Autoimmunity: Real and Symbolic Suicides: A Dialogue with Jacques Derrida." In *Philosophy in a Time of Terror: Dialogues with Jürgen Habermas and Jacques Derrida,* edited by Giovanna Borradori, 85–136. Chicago: University of Chicago Press, 2003.

———. "Choreographies." In *Points . . . Interviews, 1974–1994,* edited by Elisabeth Weber, translated by Peggy Kamuf et al., 89–108. Stanford, Calif.: Stanford University Press, 1995.

———. "Circumfession." In *Jacques Derrida,* translated by Geoffrey Bennington, 3–315. Chicago: The University of Chicago Press, 1993.

———. "*Différance.*" In *Margins of Philosophy,* translated by Alan Bass, 1–27. New York: Harvester, 1982.

———. "For the Love of Lacan." In *Resistances of Psychoanalysis,* translated by Peggy Kamuf, Pascale-Anne Brault, and Michael Naas, 39–69. Stanford, Calif.: Stanford University Press, 1998.

———. "Force of Law: The 'Mystical Foundation of Authority.'" In *Deconstruction and the Possibility of Justice,* edited by Drucilla Cornell, Michel Rosenfeld, and David Gray Carlson, 3–67. New York: Routledge, 1992.

———. "Form and Meaning: A Note on the Phenomenology of Language." In *Speech and Phenomena: And Other Essays on Husserl's Theory of Signs*, translated by David B. Allison, 107–128. Evanston, Ill.: Northwestern University Press, 1973.

———. "Freud and the Scene of Writing." In *Writing and Difference*, translated by Alan Bass, 196–231. Chicago: The University of Chicago Press, 1978.

———. "From Restricted to General Economy: A Hegelianism Without Reserve." In *Writing and Difference*, translated by Alan Bass, 251–277. Chicago: The University of Chicago Press, 1978.

———. "*Geschlecht*: Sexual Difference, Ontological Difference." In *A Derrida Reader: Between the Blinds*, edited by Peggy Kamuf, 380–402. New York: Harvester Wheatsheaf, 1991.

———. "*Geschlecht* II: Heidegger's Hand." In *Deconstruction and Philosophy*, edited by John Sallis, 161–96. Chicago: The University of Chicago Press, 1987.

———. "Introduction to '*The Origin of Geometry*.'" In *Edmund Husserl's Origin of Geometry: An Introduction*, edited by David B. Allison, translated by John P. Leavey Jr., 23–153. Stony Brook, N.Y.: Nicolas Hays, 1978.

———. "Le Facteur de la Vérité." In *The Post Card: From Socrates to Freud and Beyond*, translated by Alan Bass, 413–496. Chicago: The University of Chicago Press, 1987.

———. *Given Time: 1. Counterfeit Money*. Translated by Peggy Kamuf. Chicago: The University of Chicago Press, 1994.

———. *Glas*. Translated by John P. Leavey Jr. and Richard Rand. Lincoln: University of Nebraska Press, 1986.

———. *Of Grammatology*. Translated by Gayatri Chakravorty Spivak. Baltimore, Md.: The Johns Hopkins University Press, 1976.

———. *Positions*. Translated by Alan Bass. Chicago: The University of Chicago Press, 1981.

———. "Psyche: Inventions of the Other." In *Reading de Man Reading*, edited by Lindsay Waters and Wlad Godzich, translated by Catherine Porter, 25–65. Minneapolis: University of Minnesota Press, 1989.

———. "Psychoanalysis Searches the States of Its Soul: The Impossible Beyond of a Sovereign Cruelty." In *Without Alibi*, edited and translated by Peggy Kamuf, 238–80. Stanford, Calif.: Stanford University Press, 2002.

———. "Resistances." In *Resistances of Psychoanalysis*, translated by Peggy Kamuf, Pascale-Anne Brault, and Michael Naas, 1–38. Stanford, Calif.: Stanford University Press, 1998.

———. "Speech and Phenomena." In *Speech and Phenomena: And Other Essays on Husserl's Theory of Signs*, translated by David B. Allison, 1–104. Evanston, Ill.: Northwestern University Press, 1973.

———. *Spurs: Nietzsche's Styles*. Translated by Barbara Harlow. Chicago: University of Chicago Press, 1978.

———. "Structure, Sign, and Play in the Discourse of the Human Sciences." In *Writing and Difference*, translated by Alan Bass, 278–93. Chicago: The University of Chicago Press, 1978.

———. "Ulysses Gramophone: Hear Say Yes in Joyce." In *A Derrida Reader: Between the Blinds*, edited by Peggy Kamuf, 571–598. New York: Harvester Wheatsheaf, 1991.

———. "A Word of Welcome." In *Adieu to Immanuel Levinas*, translated by Pascale-Anne Brault and Michael Naas, 15–152. Stanford, Calif.: Stanford University Press, 1999.

Evans, Dylan. *An Introductory Dictionary of Lacanian Psychoanalysis*. London: Routledge, 1996.

Fink, Bruce. "Knowledge and Jouissance." In *Reading Seminar XX: Lacan's Major Work on Love, Knowledge, and Feminine Sexuality*, edited by Suzanne Barnard and Bruce Fink, 21–45. Albany: SUNY Press, 2002.

———. *The Lacanian Subject: Between Language and* Jouissance. Princeton, N.J.: Princeton University Press, 1995.

Forrester, John. *The Seductions of Psychoanalysis: Freud, Lacan, and Derrida*. Cambridge: Cambridge University Press, 1990.

Foucault, Michel. *The Order of Things: An Archaeology of the Human Sciences*. New York: Vintage, 1994.

Freud, Sigmund. "Analysis Terminable and Interminable." In *The Standard Edition of the Complete Psychological Works of Sigmund Freud*, edited and translated by James Strachey, 23:216–53. London: The Hogarth Press, 1968.

———. "Beyond the Pleasure Principle." In *The Standard Edition of the Complete Psychological Works of Sigmund Freud*, edited and translated by James Strachey, 18:7–64. London: The Hogarth Press, 1968.

———. "Civilization and Its Discontents." In *The Standard Edition of the Complete Psychological Works of Sigmund Freud*, edited and translated by James Strachey, 11:64–145. London: The Hogarth Press, 1968.

———. "Constructions in Analysis." In *The Standard Edition of the Complete Psychological Works of Sigmund Freud*, edited and translated by James Strachey, 23:257–69. London: The Hogarth Press, 1968.

———. "Creative Writers and Day-Dreaming." In *The Standard Edition of the Complete Psychological Works of Sigmund Freud*, edited and translated by James Strachey, 9:143–53. London: The Hogarth Press, 1968.

———. "Delusions and Dreams in Jensen's '*Gradiva*.'" In *The Standard Edition of the Complete Psychological Works of Sigmund Freud*, edited

and translated by James Strachey, vol. 9. London: The Hogarth Press, 1968.
———. "The Dissolution of the Oedipus Complex." In *The Standard Edition of the Complete Psychological Works of Sigmund Freud*, edited and translated by James Strachey, 19:173–79. London: The Hogarth Press, 1968.
———. "The Ego and the Id." In *The Standard Edition of the Complete Psychological Works of Sigmund Freud*, edited and translated by James Strachey, 19:12–66. London: The Hogarth Press, 1968.
———. "The Interpretation of Dreams." In *The Standard Edition of the Complete Psychological Works of Sigmund Freud*, edited and translated by James Strachey, vols. 4–5. London: The Hogarth Press, 1968.
———. "Introductory Lectures on Psycho-Analysis (Part III)." In *The Standard Edition of the Complete Psychological Works of Sigmund Freud*, edited and translated by James Strachey, 16:243–463. London: The Hogarth Press, 1968.
———. "Moses and Monotheism." In *The Standard Edition of the Complete Psychological Works of Sigmund Freud*, edited and translated by James Strachey, 23:7–137. London: The Hogarth Press, 1968.
———. "Negation." In *The Standard Edition of the Complete Psychological Works of Sigmund Freud*, edited and translated by James Strachey, 19:235–239. London: The Hogarth Press, 1968.
———. "New Introductory Lectures on Psycho-Analysis." In *The Standard Edition of the Complete Psychological Works of Sigmund Freud*, edited and translated by James Strachey, 22:5–182. London: The Hogarth Press, 1968.
———. "A Note Upon the 'Mystic Writing-Pad.'" In *The Standard Edition of the Complete Psychological Works of Sigmund Freud*, edited and translated by James Strachey, 19:227–32. London: The Hogarth Press, 1968.
———. "On Narcissism: An Introduction." In *The Standard Edition of the Complete Psychological Works of Sigmund Freud*, edited and translated by James Strachey, 14:73–102. London: The Hogarth Press, 1968.
———. "An Outline of Psycho-Analysis." In *The Standard Edition of the Complete Psychological Works of Sigmund Freud*, edited and translated by James Strachey, 23:144–207. London: The Hogarth Press, 1968.
———. "Project For a Scientific Psychology." In *The Standard Edition of the Complete Psychological Works of Sigmund Freud*, edited and translated by James Strachey, vol. 1. London: The Hogarth Press, 1968.

———. "The Psychotherapy of Hysteria." In *The Standard Edition of the Complete Psychological Works of Sigmund Freud*, edited and translated by James Strachey, 2:253–305. London: The Hogarth Press, 1968.

———. *The Standard Edition of the Complete Psychological Works of Sigmund Freud*. 24 vols. Edited and translated by James Strachey. London: The Hogarth Press, 1968.

———. "Three Essays on the Theory of Sexuality." In *The Standard Edition of the Complete Psychological Works of Sigmund Freud*, edited and translated by James Strachey, 7:130–243. London: The Hogarth Press, 1968.

———. "Totem and Taboo." In *The Standard Edition of the Complete Psychological Works of Sigmund Freud*, edited and translated by James Strachey, 13:1–161. London: The Hogarth Press, 1968.

———. "The Unconscious." In *The Standard Edition of the Complete Psychological Works of Sigmund Freud*, edited and translated by James Strachey, 14:166–215. London: The Hogarth Press, 1968.

Gasché, Rudolphe. *The Tain of the Mirror: Derrida and the Philosophy of Reflection*. Cambridge, Mass.: Harvard University Press, 1986.

Hegel, G. W. F. "Critical Philosophy." In *The Logic of Hegel, in The Encyclopaedia of the Philosophical Sciences*, 2nd ed., translated by William Wallace, 82–120. Oxford: Oxford University Press, 1968.

———. "Kant." In *Lectures on the History of Philosophy*, translated by E. H. Haldane and F. H. Simson, 3:423–78. London: Routledge & Kegan Paul, 1955.

———. "Kantian Philosophy." In *Faith and Knowledge*, translated by Walter Cerf and H. S. Harris, 67–96. Albany: State University of New York Press, 1977.

———. *The Phenomenology of Spirit*. Translated by A. V. Miller. Oxford: Oxford University Press, 1977.

Heidegger, Martin. *Being and Time*. Translated by J. Macquarrie and E. Robinson. Oxford: Basil Blackwell, 1962.

———. *Contributions to Philosophy (From Enowning)*. Translated by P. Emad and K. Maly. Bloomington: Indiana University Press, 1999.

———. *The Principle of Reason*. Translated by Reginald Lilly. Bloomington: Indiana University Press, 1991.

Husserl, Edmund. *Cartesian Meditations: An Introduction to Phenomenology*. Translated by D. Cairns. The Hague: Martinus Nijhoff, 1960.

Johnson, Barbara. "The Frame of Reference." In *The Purloined Poe: Lacan, Derrida, and Psychoanalytic Reading*, edited by John P. Muller and William J. Richardson, 213–251. Baltimore, Md.: The Johns Hopkins University Press, 1988.

Kant, Immanuel. *Critique of Judgment*. Translated by Werner S. Pluhar. Indianapolis, Ind.: Hackett, 1987.
———. *Critique of Pure Reason*. Translated by Norman Kemp Smith. London: Macmillan, 1933.
Kierkegaard, Søren. *Repetition: An Essay in Experimental Psychology*. Translated by Walter Lowrie. New York: Harper & Row, 1964.
Lacan, Jacques. "The Agency of the Letter in the Unconscious: Or Reason Since Freud." In *Écrits: A Selection*, translated by Alan Sheridan, 146–178. London: Tavistock, 1977.
———. "Aggressivity in Psychoanalysis." In *Écrits: A Selection*, translated by Alan Sheridan, 8–29. London: Tavistock, 1977.
———. *The Ethics of Psychoanalysis: 1959–1960, The Seminar of Jacques Lacan, Book VII*. Edited by Jacques-Alain Miller. Translated by Dennis Porter. New York: W. W. Norton, 1992.
———. *Four Fundamental Concepts of Psychoanalysis*. Edited by Jacques-Alain Miller. Translated by Alan Sheridan. New York: W. W. Norton, 1981.
———. "The Function and Field of Speech and Language in Psychoanalysis." In *Écrits: A Selection*, translated by Alan Sheridan, 30–113. London: Tavistock, 1977.
———. "The Mirror Stage." In *Écrits: A Selection*, translated by Alan Sheridan, 1–7. London: Tavistock, 1977.
———. *On Feminine Sexuality, The Limits of Love and Knowledge: 1972–1973, Encore, The Seminar of Jacques Lacan, Book XX*. Edited by Jacques-Alain Miller. Translated by Bruce Fink. New York: W. W. Norton, 1998.
———. "Seminar on "The Purloined Letter."" In *The Purloined Poe: Lacan, Derrida, and Psychoanalytic Reading*, edited by John P. Muller and William J. Richardson, translated by Jeffrey Mehlman, 28–54. Baltimore, Md.: The Johns Hopkins University Press, 1988.
———. "The Signification of the Phallus." In *Écrits: A Selection*, translated by Alan Sheridan, 281–291. New York: W. W. Norton, 1977.
Lee, Jonathan Scott. *Jacques Lacan*. Amherst: University of Massachusetts Press, 1990.
Marieb, Elaine N. *Human Anatomy and Physiology*. Redwood City, Calif.: Benjamin/Cummings, 1989.
Miller, Jacques-Alain. "*Extimité*." In *Lacanian Theory of Discourse: Subject, Structure, and Society*, edited by M. Bracher et al., 74–87. New York: New York University Press, 1994.
Mitchell, Stephen A., and Margaret J. Black. *Freud and Beyond: A History of Modern Psychoanalytic Thought*. New York: Basic Books, 1995.

Muller, John P., and William J. Richardson. "Lacan's Seminar on 'The Purloined Letter': Overview." In *The Purloined Poe, Lacan, Derrida, and Psychoanalytic Reading*, edited by John P. Muller and William J. Richardson, 55–76. Baltimore, Md.: The Johns Hopkins University Press, 1988.

———, eds. *The Purloined Poe: Lacan, Derrida, and Psychoanalytic Reading*. Baltimore, Md.: The Johns Hopkins University Press, 1988.

Nancy, Jean-Luc, and Philippe Lacoue-Labarthe. *The Title of the Letter: A Reading of Lacan*. Translated by François Raffoul and David Pettigrew. Albany: State University of New York Press, 1992.

Nietzsche, Friedrich. *Beyond Good and Evil: Prelude to a Philosophy of the Future*. Translated by Walter Kaufmann. New York: Vintage Books, 1966.

———. *Twilight of the Idols and the Anti-Christ*. Translated by R. J. Hollingdale. Middlesex: Penguin, 1968.

———. *The Gay Science*. Translated by Walter Kaufmann. New York: Random House, 1974.

———. "On the Pathos of Truth." In *Philosophy and Truth: Selections from Nietzsche's Notebooks of the Early 1870s*, edited and translated by Daniel Breazeale. Amherst, N.Y.: Humanity Books, 1999.

Norris, Christopher. "Philosophy as Not Just a 'Kind of Writing': Derrida and the Claim of Reason." In *Redrawing the Lines: Analytic Philosophy, Deconstruction, and Literary Theory*, edited by Reed Way Dasenbrock, 189–203. Minneapolis: University of Minnesota Press, 1989.

Olivier, Bert. "Nietzsche en die 20ste-Eeuse Denke." In *Wysgerige Perspektiewe op die 20ste Eeu*, edited by Daniel Strauss, 56–71. Bloemfontein: Tekskor, 1994.

Poe, Edgar Allan. "The Purloined Letter." In *The Purloined Poe, Lacan, Derrida, and Psychoanalytic Reading*, edited by John P. Muller and William J. Richardson, 6–23. Baltimore, Md.: The Johns Hopkins University Press, 1988.

Rorty, Richard. "Deconstruction and Circumvention." *Critical Inquiry* 11 (1984): 1–23.

———. "Derrida and the Philosophical Tradition." In *Truth and Progress: Philosophical Papers, Volume 3*, 327–350. Cambridge: Cambridge University Press, 1998.

———. *Philosophy and the Mirror of Nature*. Princeton, N.J.: Princeton University Press, 1979.

———. "Philosophy as a Kind of Writing: An Essay on Derrida." In *Consequences of Pragmatism (Essays: 1972–1980)*, 90–109. Minneapolis: University of Minnesota Press, 1982.

———. "Remarks on Deconstruction and Pragmatism." In *Deconstruction and Pragmatism*, edited by Chantal Mouffe, 13–18. London: Routledge, 1996.

Saussure, Ferdinand de. *Course in General Linguistics.* Edited by Charles Bally and Albert Sechehaye with the collaboration of Albert Riedlinger. Translated by Roy Harris. LaSalle, Ill.: Open Court, 1983.

Schrift, Alan D. *Nietzsche and the Question of Interpretation: Between Hermeneutics and Deconstruction.* London: Routledge, 1990.

Shlain, Leonard. *The Alphabet Versus the Goddess: The Conflict Between Word and Image.* New York: Penguin Arkana, 1998.

Silverman, Kaja. *The Acoustic Mirror: The Female Voice in Psychoanalysis and Cinema.* Bloomington: Indiana University Press, 1988.

———. *The Subject of Semiotics.* New York: Oxford University Press, 1983.

———. *The Threshold of the Visible World.* New York: Routledge, 1996.

Sinclair, William Angus. *The Traditional Formal Logic: A Short Account for Students.* London: Methuen, 1966.

Smith, Joseph H., and William Kerrigan. Introduction to *Taking Chances: Derrida, Psychoanalysis, and Literature*, edited by Joseph H. Smith and William Kerrigan, vii–xvi. Baltimore, Md.: The Johns Hopkins University Press, 1984.

Soler, Colette. "What Does the Unconscious Know About Women?" In *Reading Seminar XX: Lacan's Major Work on Love, Knowledge, and Feminine Sexuality*, edited by Suzanne Barnard and Bruce Fink, 99–108. Albany: SUNY Press, 2002.

Verhaeghe, Paul. "Lacan's Answer to the Classical Mind/Body Deadlock." In *Reading Seminar XX: Lacan's Major Work on Love, Knowledge, and Feminine Sexuality*, edited by Suzanne Barnard and Bruce Fink, 109–139. Albany: SUNY Press, 2002.

Wollheim, Richard. *Freud.* 2nd ed. London: Fontana Press, 1991.

Žižek, Slavoj. "Holding the Place." In *Contingency, Hegemony, Universality: Contemporary Dialogues on the Left*, by Judith Butler, Ernesto Laclau, and Slavoj Žižek, 308–329. New York: Verso, 2000.

———. "The Real of Sexual Difference." In *Reading Seminar XX: Lacan's Major Work on Love, Knowledge, and Feminine Sexuality*, edited by Suzanne Barnard and Bruce Fink, 57–75. Albany: SUNY Press, 2002.

———. "Why Does a *Letter* Always Arrive at Its Destination?" In *Enjoy Your Symptom: Jacques Lacan in Hollywood and Out*, 1–28. New York: Routledge, 1992.

Zupančič, Alenka. *Ethics of the Real: Kant, Lacan.* New York: Verso, 2000.

Index